Language, Culture, and Communication

The Meaning of Messages

Fourth Edition

S0-ABB-099

Nancy Bonvillain

241-258
262-269
272-285

Prentice
Hall

Upper Saddle River, New Jersey 07458

Library of Congress Cataloging-in-Publication Data

Bonvillain, Nancy.
    Language, culture, and communication : the meaning of messages / Nancy Bonvillain.—
4th ed.

        p. cm.
    Includes bibliographical references and index.
    ISBN 0-13-097953-8
        1. Language and culture.   2. Communication.   3. Linguistics.   I. Title.

P35 .B6 2003
306.44—dc21

2002074889

Publisher: *Nancy Roberts*
Managing Editor (Editorial): *Sharon Chambliss*
Editorial Assistant: *Lee Peterson*
Executive Managing Editor (Production): *Ann Marie McCarthy*
Production Liaison: *Fran Russello*
Editorial/Production Supervision: *Kim Gueterman*
Prepress and Manufacturing Buyer: *Ben Smith*
Cover Director: *Jayne Conte*
Cover Designer: *Bruce Kenselaar*
Director, Image Resource Center: *Melinda Reo*
Manager, Rights and Permissions: *Zina Arabia*
Interior Image Specialist: *Beth Boyd-Brenzel*
Cover Image Specialist: *Karen Sanatar*
Cover Image Credit: *Jose Ortega/Stock Illustration Source*
Image Permission Coordinator: *Joanne Dippel*
Copyeditor: *Donna Mulder*
Marketing Manager: *Amy Speckman*

This book was set in 11/12 Garamond by ElectraGraphics, Inc.
and was printed and bound by Courier Companies Inc.
The cover was printed by Phoenix Color Corp.

 © 2003, 2000, 1997, and 1993, by Pearson Education, Inc.
Upper Saddle River, New Jersey 07458

Printed in the United States of America
10   9   8   7   6   5   4   3   2

ISBN   0-13-097953-8

Pearson Education LTD., *London*
Pearson Education Australia PTY, Limited, *Sydney*
Pearson Education Singapore, Pte. Ltd.
Pearson Education North Asia Ltd., *Hong Kong*
Pearson Education Canada, Ltd., *Toronto*
Pearson Educación de Mexico, S.A. de C.V.
Pearson Education—Japan, *Tokyo*
Pearson Education Malaysia, Pte. Ltd.
Pearson Education, *Upper Saddle River, New Jersey*

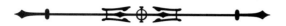

Contents

Preface

This book presents a discussion of the multifaceted meanings and uses of language. It emphasizes the ways that language encapsulates speakers' meanings and intentions. It includes data from cultures and languages throughout the world in order to document both similarities and differences in human language.

Following an introduction (Chapter 1) and a presentation of structural features of language (Chapter 2), cultural meanings of words and metaphors are analyzed in Chapter 3. The next two chapters (Chapters 4 and 5) describe situational and interactive aspects of communication. Chapter 6 focuses on speakers' class and race as significant determinants of speech style. Chapters 7 and 8 discuss the role of gender. The next two chapters (Chapters 9 and 10) describe the processes of language acquisition. Chapter 11 focuses on language use, loyalty, and conflict in multilingual nations; Chapter 12 discusses multilinguism in communicative interaction. The book concludes with a chapter devoted to analyzing inequalities of power in institutional encounters (Chapter 13).

I wish to express my thanks to Prentice Hall's reviewers for their useful critique of the manuscript: Hoyt Alverson, Dartmouth College; Joseph Errington, Yale University; and Joel Sherzer, University of Texas. I also wish to thank my publisher, Nancy Roberts, for suggesting and encouraging this book. I also thank Kim Gueterman, project manager, for expertly guiding the book's production; Sharon Chambliss, Managing Editor of Anthropology and Sociology; and Alexandra Shandell for preparing the index.

Nancy Bonvillain

1

Introduction

Language is an integral part of human behavior. It is the primary means of inter-action between people. Speakers use language to convey their thoughts, feelings, intentions, and desires to others. Language links interlocutors in a dynamic, reflex-ive process. We learn about people through what they say and how they say it; we learn about ourselves through the ways that other people react to what we say; and we learn about our relationships with others through the give-and-take of com-municative interactions.

Language is enriched by the uses that people make of it. These uses, and the meanings transmitted, are situational, social, and cultural. *Situational* meanings are conveyed through forms of language that occur or are excluded in various contexts. For example, in formal encounters, speakers pronounce sounds clearly, avoid slang or profanity, and employ elaborate grammatical constructions. *Social* meanings are signaled by linguistic alternatives chosen by different groups of people within a community. For example, women and men may pronounce sounds differently; workers in particular occupations employ special terminology or jargon; members of diverse social classes typically use more or less complex sentence patterns. Finally, *cultural* meanings are expressed both in the symbolic senses of words and by the ways that interlocutors evaluate communicative behavior.

When situational, social, and cultural factors are considered, the apparent variation in speaking actually becomes quite systematic. Consistent patterns of speech emerge in given situations, and consistent cultural norms are used to inter-pret communicative behavior.

Speaking is an action through which meaning is contextually created. Its complex functions are best studied ethnographically. An *ethnography of communi-cation* (Hymes 1974) includes analysis of speech, situational contexts, and cultural norms used in evaluating talk. An ethnographic perspective that emphasizes the

1

vital links between language and culture is important in the fields of linguistics, anthropology, and sociology. It enables linguists to appreciate the range of social and cultural meanings conveyed by words and grammatical constructions. It enables anthropologists and sociologists to appreciate the contribution that communication makes to all human activity. In order for social scientists to understand how people organize their lives, carry out work, practice religions, and the like, they need to be aware of how people talk to each other. Studying behavior within one's own or another culture is limited if it ignores a critical aspect of behavior—namely, speech—just as studying language is limited if it ignores the cultural contexts in which language is produced.

In subsequent chapters of this book, we will explore the many interconnections among language, culture, and communicative meaning. We will stress interactional, situational, and social functions of language as they take place and are actively created within cultural contexts. The notion of cultural models will be relevant to much of the ensuing discussion. A *cultural model* is a construction of reality that is created, shared, and transmitted by members of a group. It may not be explicitly stated by participants but it is, nevertheless, used to guide and evaluate behavior. For example, people in all cultures construct models expressing their views of the dimensions of the physical universe, the structure and functioning of their society, and proper ways for people to live and to treat each other. Because cultural models are shared and accepted, they are assumed by members to be natural, logical, necessary, and legitimate. As they become a background for behavior, they are not recognized as culturally constructed but, rather, are considered the natural order of life. According to Naomi Quinn and Dorothy Holland, "Largely tacit and unexamined, [cultural] models embed a view of 'what is' and 'what it means' that seems wholly natural—a matter of course. Alternative views are not even recognized, let alone considered" (1987:11). As we shall see, language and language use express, reinforce, and thus perpetuate underlying cultural models.

Although people within a given culture share many assumptions about the world, they are not a completely homogeneous group. People are differentiated on the basis of gender, age, and status in all societies. In addition, distinctions of class, race, and ethnicity are used to segment populations in most modern nations. All these factors contribute to diversity in communicative behavior and to disparities in evaluations given to the behavior of different groups of people. Interrelationships between social differentiation and communication are relevant to many topics pursued in subsequent chapters and will be discussed accordingly.

Talk takes place within a *speech community* consisting of people who, although heterogeneous, are united in numerous ways. Several researchers have taken pains to define such a community. Leonard Bloomfield described it as "a group of people who interact by means of speech" (1933:42). Bloomfield recognized that in addition to speaking the same language, these people also agree about what is considered "proper" or "improper" uses of language (ibid.:155). Dell Hymes stressed the fact that members of a speech community are unified by norms about uses of language: "A speech community is defined as a community sharing knowledge of rules for the conduct and interpretation of speech. Such sharing comprises knowledge of at least one form of speech, and knowledge also of its patterns of use" (1974:51). And "a person who is a member of a speech community knows not only a language but also what to say . . . sharing of grammatical knowledge of a form of speech is not sufficient. There may be persons whose English I could grammatically identify, but whose messages escape me. I may be ignorant of what counts as a coherent sequence, request, statement requiring an answer, situation requiring a greeting, requisite or forbidden topic" (ibid.:123, 49).

In discussing speech communities, William Labov emphasized the social and evaluative norms shared by members: "A speech community cannot be conceived as a group of speakers who all use the same forms; it is best defined as a group who share the same norms in regard to language . . . who share a set of social attitudes toward language" (1972:158, 248). In Labov's view, norms are revealed by the ways that members of a community evaluate their own and others' speech.

Although the notion of speech community is useful in delineating a group of speakers, it is an abstraction in the sense that individuals do not interact with all other members. In order to focus on people who actually do interact, Lesley Milroy and James Milroy developed the concept of *speech network* (Milroy and Milroy 1978; Milroy 1980). People in a speech network have contact with each other on a regular basis, although the frequency of their interactions and the strength of their association vary. Thus, people in "dense networks" have daily, or at least frequent, contact. They are likely to be linked by more than one type of bond—that is, they may be related, live in the same neighborhood, and work together. In addition, all of their associates also know each other. People in "weak networks" have less regular contact and do not know all of each other's associates.

Dense networks exert pressure on members to conform because values are shared and individuals' behavior can be readily known. Because linguistic usage is one type of behavior that is monitored and regulated within dense networks, members tend to maintain speech norms with little variation (Milroy and Milroy 1992:13). In contrast, members of weak networks do not share values as consistently. And weak networks do not have mechanisms that can apply social sanction against nonconformists on an individual basis, although the society as a whole does exert pressures for conformity through the transmission of cultural models on both conscious and nonconscious levels.

The concept of speech network is useful because it focuses on actual speakers and explains the mechanisms of control that lead to establishing and maintaining group norms in small-scale, daily interactions. Speech is constantly, although nonconsciously, evaluated. Speakers, therefore, are always vulnerable to the judgments of their peers.

Throughout this book, we frequently return to issues of language use and evaluation of talk within speech communities and networks as they reveal social and cultural beliefs about how society is structured and the ways that people are expected to act and interact.

Studies in language, culture, and communication are based on two different but compatible methodologies. One, an ethnographic or *ethnolinguistic* approach, employs anthropological techniques of gathering data from observations of people's daily lives and of attempting to understand behavior from the participants' point of view. Ethnolinguists try to extract communicative rules by observing the behaviors that do or do not occur in various contexts and the reactions of members of a community to each other's actions. They attempt to understand what one needs to know in order to function appropriately in a given culture—how to make requests, issue commands, and express opinions, for example.

Studying language use within speech communities from an ethnolinguistic approach includes analysis of contexts, norms of appropriateness, and knowledge of language and its uses. Analyses of these facets of communicative behavior reveal underlying cultural models and demonstrate the cognitive and conceptual bonds that unify people within their culture.

Ethnolinguists also use elicitation techniques for obtaining linguistic data. They work with individual native speakers in order to collect material dealing with specific categories of vocabulary or types of grammatical constructions.

The second approach to studying communicative behavior is *sociolinguistic*. This method is concerned with discovering patterns of linguistic variation. Variation in language use is derived from differences in speech situations and from social distinctions within a community that are reflected in communicative performance. Although some speech differences are idiosyncratic, it is possible to study intracommunity variables by recording and analyzing actual speech behavior of members of distinct sectors of a population.

A basic assumption in sociolinguistics is that two complementary processes operate in the dynamic connection between language and social factors. From one viewpoint, social differentiation among people is correlated with differences in their speech and, from the other, divergence in the way language is used is a gauge of social segmentation. Factors such as gender, age, class, region, race, ethnicity, and occupation frequently account for linguistic differences. Interrelationships between societal factors and language use are extremely complex for several reasons. For one, sociolinguistic behavior is "inherently variable"; that is, each speaker makes use of the full range of options available in the community, such as alternatives of pronunciation, vocabulary, and sentence construction. However, options chosen in a particular instance of speech cannot be predicted. Sociolinguistic "rules," therefore, are actually statements of probability rather than rules that can predict any single speech occurrence. Both individual and societal patterning are based on behavior exhibited over time and in diverse situations.

Also, individuals are not isolates of sociological factors. A person is not simply female or male, child or adult, employer or worker. Rather, each person embodies an aggregate of factors, as, for example, a female adult worker. Choices in speech style are motivated by many aspects of one's identity. Sociolinguistic studies consider the ways that specific attributes influence a speaker's selection in any given situation.

A third complication in sociolinguistic analysis is that of context itself. Components of speech contexts, such as setting, participants, topics, and goals, all influence speech. In some cultures, the styles of speech used in different contexts are sharply distinguished, whereas in others linguistic styles are less differentiated. Even within a culture, some people are more sensitive than others to contextual cues and adjust their speech accordingly. Sensitivity to context may be related to such social factors as gender or class, or it may be related to an individual's participation in many different types of situations.

Because sociolinguistic patterns are discoverable on the basis of frequencies of usage, research methodologies emphasize interviews, experimental and situational observations, and quantitative analysis. Sociolinguists ideally collect large samples of ongoing communicative behavior and then try to isolate determining factors that result in linguistic variation.

We will review many studies of linguistic behavior that are based on one or both of the methodological and analytic approaches. Each reveals a different aspect of the communicative process. Taken together, they allow us to understand the full range of interactional, social, and cultural meanings conveyed by talk. In Chapter 2 structural properties of language and nonverbal behavior are presented, and then analyses of cultural and social meanings, contexts, and uses of language. In Chapters 3 and 4 we focus on connections between language and cultural models. Rules of conversation and linguistic means for expressing politeness are discussed in Chapter 5. The next three chapters present analyses of linguistic variation and societal segmentation: In Chapter 6 we discuss factors of class and race; in Chapters 7 and 8 gender differences in language and speech are considered with data from numerous societies throughout the world. Topics in acquisition of linguistic and communicative skills are treated in Chapters 9 and 10. Chapters 11 and 12 present reviews of language and its functions in multilingual communities. Finally, in Chapter 13 we discuss the ways that talk is managed in several institutional settings. The diversity of topics dealt with in this book is an indication of the breadth of the field of language, culture, and communication and a demonstration of the importance of language in human behavior.

REFERENCES

BLOOMFIELD, LEONARD. 1933. *Language.* New York: Holt, Rinehart & Winston.

HYMES, DELL. 1974. *Foundations of Sociolinguistics.* Philadelphia: University of Pennsylvania Press.

LABOV, WILLIAM. 1972. *Sociolinguistic Patterns.* Philadelphia: University of Pennsylvania Press.

MILROY, LESLEY. 1980. *Language and Social Networks.* Oxford: Blackwell.

MILROY, LESLEY, AND JAMES MILROY. 1978. Belfast: Change and variation in an urban vernacular. In *Sociolinguistic Patterns in British English,* ed. P. Trudgill. London: Edward Arnold, pp. 19–36.

MILROY, LESLEY, AND JAMES MILROY. 1992. Social network and social class:

Toward an integrated sociolinguistic model. *Language and Society* 21: 1–26.

QUINN, NAOMI, AND DOROTHY HOLLAND. 1987. Culture and cognition. In *Cultural Models of Language and Thought,* ed. D. Holland and N. Quinn. New York: Cambridge University Press, pp. 3–40.

2

The Form
of the Message

Language is a communicative system consisting of formal units that are integrated through processes of combination. Components of sound, structure, and meaning are obviously interrelated and expressed simultaneously, but they can be separated for analytic purposes. In this chapter we present descriptions of formal properties of language and introduce relevant concepts and terminology in the field of linguistics. We then discuss some aspects of nonverbal communication as they contribute to transmission of speakers' messages.

Structural linguistic topics are presented here as background for the following two chapters, which directly explore relationships among language, communication, and culture. Although the focus of this book is on cultural, social, and interactional functions of communication, it is important to understand what it is that people do when they speak.

PHONOLOGY: THE SOUNDS OF LANGUAGE

Phonology is the study of sound systems in language. It includes *phonetics,* the description of sounds occurring in a language, and *phonemics,* the analysis of the use of these sounds to differentiate meanings of words.

Phonetics

The first task of phonology is to describe how sounds are produced, or *articulated.* Human language is made possible by manipulation of the vocal apparatus, consisting of lungs, pharynx, larynx, glottis, vocal cords, nose, mouth, tongue, teeth, and lips (Figure 2.1).

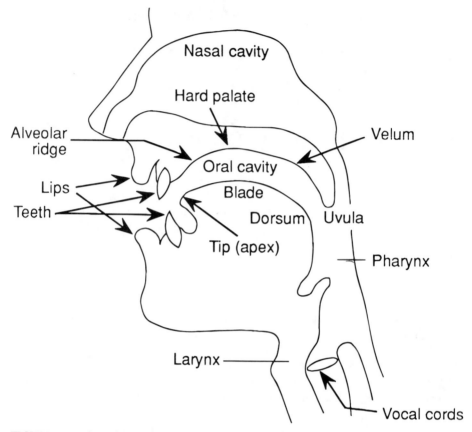

FIGURE 2.1. The Vocal Apparatus.   (Adapted from Wardhaugh 1977:33)

Components of the vocal apparatus can be modified by speakers to produce sounds of different qualities. This ability is essential, for speakers must make distinctions among numerous sounds so that meanings of words can be differentiated. Several kinds of contrasts serve to distinguish sounds, and we discuss them in subsequent sections. (Note that examples given to illustrate linguistic structure are obtained from a number of sources, including Bonvillain 1973; Bonvillain n.d.; Cowan and Rakusan 1987; Finegan and Besnier 1989; Gleason 1955; Ladefoged 1982; and O'Grady et al. 1989.)

I. Sounds are either voiced or voiceless, depending on activity of the vocal cords, a pair of small muscular bands in the throat. If vocal cords are close together when air passes through, the cords vibrate and produce *voiced* sounds; if they are apart and stationary, resulting sounds are *voiceless*. Voiced/voiceless contrasts can be illustrated by *minimal pairs,* two words composed of sounds that are identical except for one feature of significant difference. The following list contains some voiced/voiceless consonant pairs in English (examples written in standard orthography):

Voiceless	Voiced
p : p̲it	b : b̲it
ta̲p	ta̲b
t : t̲en	d : d̲en
bi̲t	bi̲d
f : f̲an	v : v̲an
grie̲f	grie̲v̲e
s : s̲ap	z : z̲ap
hi̲s̲	hi̲s̲

All vowels in English are voiced. However, voiceless vowels occur in many other languages, including Japanese, Totonac (Mexico), and Chatino (Mexico). In Totonac, voiceless vowels always occur at the ends of words (voicelessness is indicated by a small circle [V̥] beneath a vowel):

/kuku̥/	"uncle"
/miki̥/	"snow"
/snapapḁ/	"white"

In both Chatino and Japanese, vowels are voiceless when they occur between two voiceless consonants. The following are some examples from Chatino (superscript numbers indicate tones: 2 = mid, 3 = high):

/kḁta^3/	"you will bathe"
/ki̥su^3/	"avocado"
/ti̥hi^2/	"hard"

II. Sounds are either *oral* or *nasal*—the former produced by raising the velum to the back of the throat and expelling air only through the mouth (oral cavity), the latter by relaxing the velum and allowing air to pass through the nose. For instance, *m* and *n* are nasal consonants. All languages have some nasal consonants, and many have nasal vowels as well. The latter group includes French, Portuguese, Hindi (India), Tibetan, Yoruba (Nigeria), and Navajo (native North America).

III. In addition to binary characteristics relevant for all sounds (voiced/voiceless, oral/nasal), each sound is produced by manipulating parts of the vocal apparatus. Figure 2.2, which illustrates most consonants found in human language, classifies sounds according to two dimensions: place of articulation and manner of articulation. *Place of articulation* refers to where the sound is formed ("articulated") in the mouth; for example, *bilabial* sounds are formed by the two lips, and *apicoalveolar* sounds are made with the tip of the tongue (apico = apex) and the alveolar ridge. The second dimension, *manner of articulation,* refers to the degree of interference or modification made of the airstream as it passes through the oral cavity; for example, *stops* are produced by momentary complete blockage of air, and *fricatives* *the way in which you change the air flow* (handwritten)

different points in mouth where tongue can touch (handwritten)

Place of Articulation

Manner of Articulation

Manner of Articulation		Bilabial	Labiodental	Apicodental	Apicoalveolar	Retroflex	Alveopalatal	Palatal	Dorsovelar	Uvular	Pharyngeal	Glottal
Stops												
Plain	vl.	p			t	ṭ	tʸ	ḳ	k	q		?
	vd.	b			d	ḍ	dʸ	g̣	g	G		
Aspirated	vl.	pʰ			tʰ				kʰ			
	vd.	bʰ			dʰ				gʰ			
Glottalized	vl.	p'			t'				k'			
Labialized	vl.	pʷ			tʷ				kʷ			
	vd.	bʷ			dʷ				gʷ			
Nasals	vl.	m̥			n̥		ñ̥		ŋ̥			
	vd.	m			n	ṇ	ñ		ŋ	N		
Affricates	vl.				c		č	ç				
	vd.						ǰ					
Fricatives	vl.	Φ	f	θ	s	ṣ	š		x		ħ	h
	vd.	β	v	ð	z		ž		ɣ		ʕ	
Liquids Laterals					l	ḷ	ł					
Central					r	r						
Flaps					ř							
Trills					r̄					R		
Glides								y	w			

FIGURE 2.2. Classification of Consonants.

by narrowing the vocal channel and thus creating turbulence or friction in the airstream. Each difference in place and/or manner of articulation results in a difference in sound quality. Symbols in the chart in Figure 2.2 are written in phonetic transcription adapted from the International Phonetic Alphabet, a system of standardized notation applicable to all languages. (For a detailed discussion of phonetic notational systems, see Pullum and Ladusaw 1986.) In some cases symbols in the chart correspond to English letters, but in others they do not. Note also, vd. = voiced, vl. = voiceless.

Vowels are produced with relatively greater openness of the vocal tract and relatively less interference with the airstream than is characteristic of consonants. Differences in vocalic quality are made by movement of the tongue and rounding or unrounding of the lips, resulting in changes in resonance. Additionally, voicing/unvoicing or oral/nasal contrasts are significant in many, but not all, languages. Figure 2.3 illustrates the physical manipulations involved in vowel production. Tongue positions are depicted for three English vowels: [iy], as in the word "beet," [a] as in "pot," and [uw] as in "boot."

Common vocalic segments, represented by phonetic symbols, are classified in

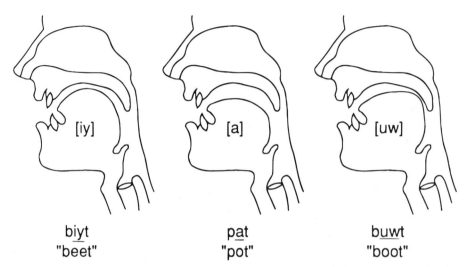

biyt
"beet"
p<u>a</u>t
"pot"
bu<u>w</u>t
"boot"

FIGURE 2.3. Tongue Positions for Three English Vowels. (Adapted from O'Grady et al. 1989:28)

Figure 2.4. Dimensions of vowel production are position in the mouth from front to back and height from high to low. Lip-rounding (rd.) or unrounding (unrd.) is also significant.

Each language selects its phonetic inventory from among the possible human sounds. No language contains all sounds because requiring speakers to make too many or too fine articulatory distinctions is not feasible. Languages vary in the number of their sounds, ranging from as few as 8 consonants in Hawaiian to as many as 96 in !Kung (spoken in Namibia). Some languages have only three vowels, although about half of all languages contain five vowels, and others, such as English and French, have more than a dozen. Following are representative English words illustrating some of the symbols in the consonant (Figure 2.2) and vowel (Figure 2.4) charts.

1. *Oral stops* (complete closure or blockage of airstream):

   Bilabial: p : pɪn (pin)
              b : bɪn (bin)

		Front		Central		Back	
		Unrd.	Rd.	Unrd.	Rd.	Unrd.	Rd.
High	Upper	i	ü	ɨ		ɰ	u
	Lower	ɪ	ʊ	ɨ			ʊ
Mid	Upper	e	ö	ə			o
	Lower	ɛ	æ	ʌ			ɔ
Low		æ		a		ɑ	

FIGURE 2.4. Classification of Vowels.

Apicoalveolar:	t :	tɛn	(ten)
	d :	dɛn	(den)
Dorsovelar:	k :	kat	(cot)
	g :	gat	(got)

2.   *Nasals* (velum is lowered to allow air to pass through the nose):

Bilabial:	m :	mʌt	(mutt)
Apicoalveolar:	n :	nʌt	(nut)
Dorsovelar:	ŋ :	hʌŋ	(hung)

3.   *Affricates* (complete closure followed by narrow opening for air to pass through):

Palatal:	č :	čɪn	(chin)
	ǰ :	ǰɪn	(gin)

4.   *Fricatives* (narrowing and partial obstruction of vocal passage resulting in turbulence or friction):

Labiodental:	f :	fæn	(fan)
	v :	væn	(van)
Interdental:	θ :	θay	(thigh)
	ð :	ðay	(thy)
Apicoalveolar:	s :	sæp	(sap)
	z :	zæp	(zap)
Palatal:	š :	šap	(shop)
	ž :	ruwž	(rouge)
Glottal:	h :	hɛd	(head)

5.   *Liquids* (relatively less obstruction of airstream resulting in modification of air but no turbulence):

Lateral:	l :	lɛd	(led)
Central:	r :	rɛd	(red)

6.   *Glides or semivowels* (little obstruction; intermediate between consonants and vowels):

Palatal:	y :	yɛt	(yet)
Velar:	w :	wɛt	(wet)

7.   *Vowels:* In English, some vowels are *monothongs,* produced in one place in the mouth; others are *dipthongs* or *glides,* involving movement of the sound from one position to another. Dipthongs are noted by a *y* or *w* following the vocalic symbol:

Front (all unrounded):

iy :	biyt	(beet)
ɪ :	bɪt	(bit)

ey :   beyt   (bait)
ε :   bεt   (bet)
æ :   bæt   (bat)

Central (all unrounded):

ʌ :   bʌt   (but)
ay :   bayt   (bite)
aw :   bawt   (bout)

Back (all rounded):

uw :   buwt   (boot)
ʊ :   bʊk   (book)
ow :   bowt   (boat)
oy :   boy   (boy)
ɔ :   bɔt   (bought)

Phonemic Analysis

Every language organizes its phonetic inventory into a system of phonemes. A *phoneme* is a minimal unit of sound that functions to differentiate the meanings of words. It may have only one phonetic representation or it may contain two or more sounds, called *allophones,* that occur in predictable linguistic environments based on rules of allophonic patterning. For example, in English, the voiceless stops /p/, /t/, and /k/ each has two allophones: One is *aspirated,* produced with a strong release of air; the other is *unaspirated.* Allophones for English voiceless stops are produced with aspiration when they occur at the beginning of a syllable, whereas they are unaspirated following /s/ in the same syllable. Aspirated and unaspirated allophones are illustrated in the following words:

/p/	aspirated:	[pʰɪn]	(pin)
	unaspirated:	[spɪn]	(spin)
/t/	aspirated:	[tʰʌn]	(tun)
	unaspirated:	[stʌn]	(stun)
/k/	aspirated:	[kʰɪn]	(kin)
	unaspirated:	[skɪn]	(skin)

Native speakers of English are likely unaware of the fact that the *p*'s, *t*'s, and *k*'s in the words above have slightly different articulations. Speakers learn to make nonconscious allophonic distinctions in early stages of language acquisition. Because the rules are applied consistently thereafter, without exception, they become automatic patterns not requiring conscious thought.

Liquids and glides in English also have allophones that occur in accordance with conditioning rules. Voiceless counterparts of /l, r, w, y/ occur following voiceless stops /p, t, k/. In all other environments, liquids and glides are voiced. Compare the following contrasts (voicelessness is indicated by a small circle [C̥] beneath a consonant):

/r/	voiceless:	[tr̥ɪp]	(trip)
	voiced	[drɪp]	(drip)
/l/	voiceless:	[pl̥ayt]	(plight)
	voiced	[blayt]	(blight)
/w/	voiceless:	[tw̥ɪn]	(twin)
	voiced	[dwɪndl]	(dwindle)
/y/	voiceless:	[ky̥uwt]	(cute)
	voiced	[argyuw]	(argue)

Specific allophonic patterns are not universal but, instead, operate within each language according to its own rules. In some languages, the difference between aspirated and unaspirated stops is not allophonic, as in English, but phonemic. *Phonemic* contrasts signal differences in meanings of words. The following words in Korean constitute minimal pairs for plain /k/ and aspirated /kʰ/ and have separate meanings:

| /keda/ | "fold" |
| /kʰeda/ | "dig out" |

Similarly, Chinese contrasts /p/ and /pʰ/ (note that high pitch is indicated by a rule [V̄] above a vowel):

| /pā/ | "trumpet" | /pī/ | "compare" |
| /pʰā/ | "strip" | /pʰī/ | "indigestion" |

Finally, aspirated /tʰ/ and unaspirated /t/ are separate phonemes in Hindi (a language of India):

| /táli/ | "key" | /tórṇa/ | "pluck" |
| /tʰáli/ | "dish" | /tʰōra/ | "little" |

Some sounds that are separate phonemes in English are allophones in other languages. As we have seen, English distinguishes between voiceless and voiced stops, p/b, t/d, k/g; but in the Mohawk language (spoken in New York State and Ontario and Quebec, Canada), these sounds are allophones rather than phonemes. They occur in predictable environments. In Mohawk, voiceless stops are produced at the ends of words or preceding other consonants (except glides), whereas voiced stops occur preceding vowels or glides:

/t/ →	[t]/	at ends of words:	[salá:dat̠]	"pick it up!"
		preceding a consonant:	[ohyót̠saʔ]	"chin"
	[d]/	preceding a vowel:	[odáhsaʔ]	"tail"
/k/ →	[k]/	at ends of words:	[wisk̠]	"five"
		preceding a consonant:	[jik̠s]	"fly"
	[g]/	preceding a vowel:	[gá:lis]	"stocking"
		preceding a glide:	[á:gwɛks]	"eagle"
			[g̠yóhdu]	"nine"

As evidence of the automatic, nonconscious nature of allophones, when Mohawk speakers use English they frequently follow Mohawk allophonic patterns so that, for example, the English word "chicken" /čıkın/ is pronounced [čıgın]. This pronunciation is consistent with Mohawk rules requiring voiced stops preceding vowels. In fact, a "foreign accent" in any language consists, in part, of the application of native allophonic rules when speaking foreign languages.

Prosodic Features

In addition to consonants and vowels, sound systems make use of *prosodic,* or *suprasegmental,* features to alter and, therefore, contrast the sounds or rhythms of speech. Three prosodic features that often affect meaning are stress, pitch, and length.

Stress. The term *stress* or *accent* refers to the degree of emphasis placed on the syllables of words. In multisyllabic words, stress is not evenly distributed on all syllables. Rather, different syllables receive different degrees of stress. In some languages, stress rules are automatic. For example, in Czech, Finnish, and Hungarian, every word is accented on the first syllable; in French and Mayan (Mexico), words are accented on the final syllable; and in Polish, Swahili (Africa), and Samoan (Polynesia), the penultimate (next to last) syllable is always stressed. Stress placement in other languages is unpredictable, and, therefore, changes in stress can serve to differentiate meanings or functions of words. Note the following contrasts in some English words where the difference in stress signals the difference between a noun and a verb: nouns are stressed on the first syllable; verbs are stressed on the second syllable. (Note that slight differences in vowels when unstressed are not marked here.)

	Noun	*Verb*
present	prézɛnt	prɛzént
object	ábjɛkt	abjékt
construct	kánstrʌkt	kanstrʌ́kt
implant	ímplænt	ımplǽnt
retest	ríytɛst	riytést

Pitch. *Pitch* or *tone* refers to the voice pitch accompanying a syllable's production. Variation in pitch results from changes in relative tension of the vocal cords. Pitch generally occurs with vowels, although some consonants (e.g., /l, r, m, n/) can function as syllable nuclei and carry tone. Many languages use pitch to distinguish meanings of words—for example, Asian languages, such as Chinese and Thai; African languages, including Yoruba, Zulu, and Luganda; Native American languages, such as Navajo (Southwest) and Sarcee (western Canada); and the European Latvian.

The following sets of Chinese words have separate meanings, each signaled by patterns of pitch:

high level:	mā	"mother"	fū	"skin"
high rising:	má	"hemp"	fú	"fortune"

| low falling/rising: | mǎ | "horse" | fǔ | "axe" |
| falling: | mà | "scold" | fù | "woman" |

In some languages, changes in tone function to signal different grammatical meanings. Compare verbs from Bini, a language spoken in Nigeria:

low pitch:	ìmà	"I show" (timeless)
high/low:	ímà	"I am showing" (continuous)
low/high:	ìmá	"I showed" (past)

Pitch is a feature of all languages on units of clauses and/or sentences. It is one of the components of intonation. In English, declarative statements and questions are characterized by contrastive pitch contours. Level or falling pitch appears at the ends of statements, whereas rising pitch terminates questions:

Statement: They came in.

Question: They came in?

Length. *Length* refers to continuation of a sound during its production. Some languages use length to differentiate meanings of words. Short and long vowel contrasts occur in Danish, Czech, Finnish, Arabic, Japanese, Korean, Cree (Canada), Yap (Pacific), and others. Here are some examples from Korean (long vowels are indicated by V: following a vowel):

/il/	"day"	/i:l/	"work"
/seda/	"to count"	/se:da/	"strong"
/pam/	"night"	/pa:m/	"chestnut"

Contrastive length for consonants is less common than for vowels, but it is found in several languages, including Turkish, Finnish, Hungarian, Luganda (Africa), and Arabic. In Luganda, the word /kúlà/ "grow up" contains a short /k/, whereas /kkúlà/ "treasure" has a long /k/. In Classical Arabic, a long consonant in a verb signals the grammatical meaning of causative (making or causing something to happen), as in the following words:

/ʕada/	"he passed"
/ʕadda/	"he made to pass"
/ðakara/	"he remembered"
/ðakkara/	"he reminded" (caused to remember)
/ʕaðaba/	"he abstained"
/ʕaððaba/	"he restrained" (caused to abstain)

Although not all languages use length to distinguish meanings, changes in the duration of sounds can serve as markers of emphasis or exaggeration. Lengthening a vowel in English can indicate exaggeration, as in

"He is bi-i-i-i-ig!"

This utterance implies greater size than would be conveyed by simply saying "he is big" (Lakoff and Johnson 1980:127–128).

MORPHOLOGICAL: THE STRUCTURE OF WORDS

Morphological Analysis

Morphology is the analysis of word structure. Words are composed of units of sound and meaning called *morphemes*. A word may contain one morpheme—{kæt} "cat"—or it may contain two or more morphemes:

cat-s   /kæt-s/
sing-ing   /sɪŋ- ɪŋ/
good-ness   /gʊd-nɛs/
un-happi-ly   /ʌn-hæpɪ-liy/

Morphemes can be added to words in cycles, producing longer and more complex sequences:

act
active   (act-ive)
inactive   (in-act-ive)
inactivity   (in-act-iv-ity)

Some morphemes, called *roots* or *stems,* represent basic lexical or referential meanings of words (e.g., cat, sing, good, happy). They refer to or name objects, events, qualities, ideas, and the like. Other morphemes, called *affixes,* are attached to roots or stems (e.g., un-, -s, -ing, -ness, -ly). They express grammatical or relational meanings, such as number, tense, aspect, person, gender, or case. Affixes are of three varieties: *Prefixes* precede stems (*un-*happy), *suffixes* follow stems (happi-*ness*), and *infixes* appear within the stem itself.

The infix is absent from English but occurs elsewhere. Infixes are especially productive in Malayo-Polynesian languages, spoken in parts of Asia and the Pacific. Note the following words from Tagalog (a language of the Philippines):

1.   stem: {-basa-}   "read"

     with infix {-um-}:   /bumása akó naŋ libró/
                          read   I   the book
                          "I read the book" (completed)
     with infix {-in-}:   /binása aŋ   libró/
                          was read the book
                          "the book was read"

2.   stem: {- kaʔɪn-}   "eat"

     with infix {-um-}:   /kumáʔɪn   akó/
                          ate   I
                          "I ate (it)"
     with infix {-in-}:   /kináʔɪn   aŋ   mansánas/
                          was eaten   the   apple
                          "the apple was eaten"

In Bontoc, another Philippine language, an infix {-um-} denotes change from a noun or adjective into a verb of becoming:

/fikas/	"strong"	/fumikas/	"he is becoming strong"
/bato/	"stone"	/bumato/	"he is becoming stone"
/fusul/	"enemy"	/fumusul/	"he is becoming an enemy"

Morphemes may occur in one constant form, or they may have two or more shapes, called *allomorphs*. Allomorphs of each morpheme have the same meaning but vary in phonological form. They occur in predictable conditioned environments. The English plural suffix {-s} has three allomorphs, accounted for by these rules:

{-s} →	/-iz/	following sibilants (/s, z, š, ž, č, ǰ/)
	/-s/	following voiceless consonants (except sibilants)
	/-z/	following voiced consonants (except sibilants); following all vowels

Application of this set of rules is illustrated in these examples:

klæs / klæsiz	(class / classes)
kæt / kæts	(cat / cats)
tʌb / tʌbz	(tub / tubs)
biy / biyz	(bee / bees)

The fit between form and meaning in construction of words is not always consistent. Irregularities or exceptions to morphological patterns sometimes occur. For instance, although the rules given above for English plural marking account for the overwhelming majority of nouns, unpredictable exceptions exist. Some plurals are signaled by vowel changes in stems:

maws / mays	(mouse / mice)
fʊt / fiyt	(foot / feet)
wʊ́mɪn / wímɪn	(woman / women)

Three nouns take a restricted, nonproductive suffix, {-ɪn} (spelled "en"): child/children, ox/oxen, and the somewhat archaic brother/brethren. Additionally, a set of words having foreign sources retains the original plural markers—for example, datum/data (from Latin), phenomenon/phenomena (from Greek), cherub/cherubim (from Hebrew). A final class of nouns does not change at all, and, therefore, singular or plural meaning must be inferred entirely from context: deer, sheep, caribou.

Irregular forms must be learned for each individual case. Because it is much easier to learn a standard rule and apply it systematically than to memorize specific exceptions, languages limit the proliferation of irregularities. Preference for consistency accounts for children's tendency to overgeneralize morphological rules when acquiring language, as in mouse/mouses and foot/foots.

Morphological Typologies

Languages differ in their methods of creating words out of morphemes. Three types of languages will first be defined and then examples will be given.

Languages are often described as either isolating, agglutinating, or synthetic. *Isolating* languages (such as English or Chinese) allow comparatively few morphemes per word and have relatively simple methods of combining morphemes within words. *Agglutinating* languages have words containing many morphemes that are combined according to highly regular rules. *Synthetic* (or polysynthetic) languages also have words containing many morphemes, but their rules for combining morphemes may be quite complex. The form of morphemes is often altered considerably when morphemes are combined within words. A few examples from isolating, agglutinating, and polysynthetic languages are given below.

Mandarin Chinese (an Isolating Language). In Mandarin Chinese, most words consist of only one morpheme. Lexical meanings are expressed by using separate words. Grammatical meanings are conveyed either by separate words, by the order of words within sentences, or simply by context.

1a. wǒ gāng yào gěi nǐ nà yì bēi chá
    I   just want for you bring one cup tea
    "I am about to bring you a cup of tea."

1b. xià yǔ
    down rain
    "It was/is/will be raining."

Turkish (an Agglutinating Language). Turkish permits a large number of morphemes to combine within a word. These morphemes express many different kinds of lexical and grammatical meanings. In order to translate a single Turkish word into English, many words and possibly rather complex sentences are required. (Note abbreviations used in examples: INF = infinitive; CAUS = causative; PAS = passive; NEG = negative.)

2a. stem: öl- "die"
    öl-mɛk "to die" (stem + INF)
    öl-dür-mɛk "to kill" (stem + CAUS + INF)
    öl-dür-mɛ-mɛk "to not kill" (stem + CAUS + NEG + INF)
    öl-dür-ül-mɛk "to be killed" (stem + CAUS + PAS + INF)
    öl-dür-ül-mɛ-mɛk "to not be killed" (stem + CAUS + PAS + NEG + INF)

2b. öldürɛ bilɛ mɛsɛydim
    "I wish I hadn't been able to kill"
    öl - dür-ɛbil -ɛmɛ -sɛy - d - im
    die-cause-able-not-wish-past-I

2c. stem: yɨkan- "wash oneself"

yɨkan-mak "to wash oneself" (stem + INF)
yɨkan-dɨr-mak "to make X wash oneself" (stem + CAUS + INF)
yɨkan-dɨr-ɨl-mak "to be made to wash oneself"
(stem + CAUS + PAS + INF)
yɨkan-dɨr-ɨl-ma-mak "to not be made to wash oneself"
(stem + CAUS + PAS + NEG + INF)

2d. yɨkandɨ ɪɪ lmamɨštɨ mmɨ

"Had I not been made to wash myself?"
yɨkan - dɨr - ɨl -ma -mɨš-t -ɨm- mɨ
wash oneself-cause-passive-not-had-past- I-question

Mohawk (a Polysynthetic Language). Mohawk combines many morphemes within a word. As in agglutinating languages such as Turkish, morphemes in Mohawk may express different kinds of lexical and grammatical meanings. However, rules for morpheme combination are not as regular as they are in agglutinating languages. When morphemes co-occur, they often undergo changes in their sounds. Also, a single morpheme may express multiple grammatical concepts so that the fit between form and function is more complex than in isolating or agglutinating languages.

Mohawk verbs can contain a large number of morphemes expressing various grammatical meanings. Prefixes denote person, number, negation, mood, location or direction, simultaneity of action, and so on. Several suffixes indicate different verbal aspects. A few illustrative examples follow. (Note that $\bar{v}$ indicates a nasal vowel.)

3a. tehatkahtúnyūs
"he looks all around"
te - h- at -kaht- ū - nyū - s
two-he-self-look-in state of-all around-doing

3b. tʌ̃ǰitewatekháhši²
"we all will part, separate"
t - ʌ̃ - ǰi - tew -ate - khah - si -²
two-will-again-we all-self-border-undo-once

3c. shikoya²tisakūhákye²s
"since I search for you all over"
shi-ko- ya²t-isak - ū - hakye - ²s
since-I:you-body-search for-in state of-all the time-doing

3d. yakonʌ̃yohlūkwʌ̃hákye²
"she's gathering up stones as she's coming along"
yako-nʌ̃y-ohlūkw - ʌ̃ - hakye - ²
she- stone-gather up-in state of-all the time-in state of

Inuktitut (a Polysynthetic Language of Arctic Canada). The following word in Inuktitut illustrates complexities of morpheme meaning and structure possible in polysynthetic languages:

4a. qasuirrsarvigssarsingitluinarnarpuq
      "someone did not find a completely suitable resting place"
      qasu-irr-sar-vig-ssar-si-ngit-luinar-nar-puq

qasu	-irr	-sar	-vig	-ssar
tired	-not	-cause to be	-place	-for suitable
-si	-ngit	-luinar	-nar	-puq
-find	-not	-completely	-someone	-3rd sg. (he/she)

Grammatical Concepts

As mentioned, morphemes express lexical or grammatical meaning. Grammatical meaning includes concepts applying to nouns, verbs, modifiers, and so on. Some common concepts for nouns are case, number, and gender. *Case* refers to grammatical relationships between nouns (e.g., subject or object) or between nouns and verbs within larger constructional units such as clauses and sentences. Some languages, called *inflecting,* mark case with affixes. For instance, Russian nouns have inflectional suffixes to indicate cases. The paradigm below presents the inflection of a masculine noun {zavod-} "factory, plant." Feminine and neuter nouns select different sets of suffixes.

{zavod-} "house"

Case	Singular	Plural
Nominative	zavod	zavod-i
Genitive	zavod-a	zavod-ov
Accusative	zavod	zavod-i
Dative	zavod-u	zavod-am
Locative	zavod-ɛ	zavod-ax
Instrumental	zavod-om	zavod-ami

Uses of these cases are illustrated in the following simple sentences:

Nominative:	zavód	bolšóy	
(subject)	factory	big	
	"the factory is big"		
Genitive:	éto	kríša	zavód-a
(possessive)	this	roof	factory+genitive
	"this is the roof of the factory"		
Accusative:	aní	vídyeli	zavód
(direct	they	saw	factory (accusative)
object)	"they saw the factory"		
Dative:	aná	pisála	iván-u

(indirect object)	she wrote Ivan+dative
	"she wrote to Ivan"
Locative:	na zavód-ɛ poryádok
	in factory+locative order
	"there is order is in the factory"
Instrumental:	ya pišú karandaš-óm
	I write pencil+instrumental
	"I write with a pencil"

Different languages may express grammatical concepts in different ways. For instance, the notion of *number* has a variety of manifestations. Some languages do not indicate singular/nonsingular differences; number is signaled solely by separate enumerators and/or by context. Sentences out of context, therefore, can be ambiguous. The noun in the following sentence, in Nancowry, a language spoken on the Nicobar Islands of India, can refer to one or many "pig(s)":

sák	nɔ́t	ʔin	ciʔʌy
spear	pig	the	we

"We speared the pig(s)."

In Indonesian, number is not overtly marked for subjects or objects. Whether nouns are definite (refer to a specific entity) or indefinite is likewise not marked. Therefore, nouns in sentences can have multiple possible senses:

harimau	makan	kambing
(the, a) tiger(s)	eat (ate, will eat)	(the, a) goat(s)

If context does not supply enough information to disambiguate meanings, separate specifying words can be added.

Other languages, such as English, make distinctions between singular and plural (two or more):

one cat
two or more cat<u>s</u>

And still other languages have markers for singular, dual (two), and plural (three or more), for example, Inuktitut (Arctic Canada):

/iglu/	"a house"
/iglu<u>k</u>/	"two houses"
/iglu<u>t</u>/	"three or more houses"

and Mohawk:

ǎhska kanúhsa?	"one house"
tégeni <u>te</u>kanúhsa<u>ke</u>ʔ	"two houses"
(dual + house + enumerator)	
áhsʌ̃ <u>ni</u>kanúhsa<u>ke</u>ʔ	"three houses"
(plural + house + enumerator)	

Many languages organize their nouns into separate classes that are overtly marked and differentiated. A common type of classification system is called *gender,* usually dividing nouns into masculine and feminine or masculine, feminine, and neuter. European languages of the Romance, Slavic, and Germanic families (except English) have systems of this type. In Romance languages, gender is signaled by the form of definite articles that precede nouns, for example, French "*le* mur" (masculine) "the wall" and "*la* table" (feminine) "the table." Slavic languages indicate gender by forms of case endings that are suffixed to nouns, for example, Russian /dom/ "house" (masculine), /kriša/ "roof" (feminine), /okno/ "window" (neuter).

Some languages categorize nouns on the basis of complex kinds of meanings. For instance, Navajo noun classes are determined by shape and texture of objects. Navajo transitive verbs have different forms, depending on the class of noun that occurs as their direct objects according to the following characteristics, exemplified by the verb "to handle" (Young and Morgan 1987:251–263; note that nasal vowels are marked by a curve [Y] beneath the vowel):

Class	Examples	"handle"
solid, roundish	nut, car, newborn baby	/níʔą́/
slender, flexible	chain, feather, flower	/nílá/
slender, stiff	corn, fork, tree trunk	/nítą́/
flat, flexible	blanket, dollar bill, pillow	/nítsooz/
mushy, viscous	mashed potatoes, mud, molasses	/nítłééʔ/
noncompact	cornsilk, shredded cabbage, moss	/nítjool/
in open vessel	broth, dirt in a shovel, stew	/níká/
load, quantity	bundle, firewood, wool fleece	/níyį́/

Swati, a Bantu language of Africa, has more than a dozen noun classes based on various meanings, each class noted by a distinctive prefix on a noun. Some of these are given below:

Class	Prefix	Example	
persons	um(u)	um-fana	"boy"
body parts, fruit	li	li-dvolo	"knee"
instruments	s(i)	si-tja	"plate"
animals	in	in-ja	"dog"
abstract properties	bu	bu-bi	"evil"
locations	pha	pha-ndle	"outside"

Grammatical concepts relevant to verbs include *tense* (time of an event's occurrence), *aspect* (manner in which an event occurs), and *mode* (likelihood of an event's occurrence or speaker's attitude toward such an occurrence). Additionally, many languages mark such categories as person, number, gender, and/or case relations by affixes within verbs. Examples from Mohawk illustrate some possibilities of mode and aspect (note: {-k-} "I"; {-yʌtho-} "plant"):

1.   Modes (prefixes):
   a. Definite (definite present or past occurrence):
      {waʔ-}
      <u>waʔ</u>kyÁthoʔ   "I planted (it)"
   b. Indefinite (probable or desired occurrence): {a-}
      wakū́ʔ wéskwaniʔ   neʔ   <u>a</u>kyÁthoʔ
      I like   that   I plant
      "I like to plant"
   c. Future (definite occurrence in future): {ʌ̃-}
      ʌ̃<u>ky</u>Áthoʔ   "I will plant"

2.   Aspects (suffixes):
   a. Punctual   (single event):   {-ʔ}
      waʔkyÁtho<u>ʔ</u>   "I planted (it)"
   b. Serial   (repeated events):   {-s}
      kyÁtho<u>s</u>   "I'm planting, I'm a planter"
   c. Perfective   (states):   {-ū̃}
      kayÁth<u>ū̃</u>   "it is planted"

SYNTAX: THE STRUCTURE OF SENTENCES

Most talk consists of multiword units, not single words spoken in isolation. Every language has rules of *syntax* that describe possibilities of co-occurrences and orders of constituents. Syntactic patterns are often used to express case relations between words. Note the following contrastive sentences in English:

> The dog chased the cat.
> The cat chased the dog.

Subject and direct object are indicated by relative sequence of words. Subjects precede verbs, direct objects follow verbs. The words themselves do not undergo internal changes.

In the next two sentences, direct and indirect objects are also strictly ordered. Direct objects precede indirect ones when the preposition "to" is used; otherwise, indirect objects come first:

> I sent a letter to Ruth.
> I sent Ruth a letter.

A language like English, which signals case by word order, is fundamentally different from an inflecting language like Russian. In Russian, word order does not affect underlying case relations because, as we have seen, cases are marked by affixes attached to nouns. The following Russian sentences express the same referential meaning, translated as "the cat is chasing the dog" (*košk-a* = cat + nominative; *sobak-u* = dog + accusative; *presleduet* = is chasing):

Koška presleduet sobaku.
Sobaku presleduet koška.
Presleduet koška sobaku.
Presleduet sobaku koška.
Koška sobaku presleduet.
Sobaku koška presleduet.

Although changes in word order in inflecting languages do not alter the fundamental meaning of sentences, they signal other kinds of meanings or uses. They may mark focus or emphasis, relations between topics and comments, or stylistic preferences. In the set of Russian sentences, the first example best answers the question, "What is the cat chasing?" whereas the second is a response to "What is chasing the dog?" Each of the other sentences also has its contextual usage.

Isolating languages, such as Chinese, rely heavily on word order to convey grammatical meaning. In the following two sentences, word order alone expresses the difference between definite and indefinite nouns:

1a. huǒ   che   lái   le
     train   arrive   new-situation
     "The train has arrived."

1b. lái   huǒ   che   le
     arrive   train   new-situation
     "A train has arrived."

The next two sentences exemplify word orders that distinguish between active and passive meanings in Chinese:

2a. Zhū   laǒshī   pīyè   lè   wǒdė   kaǒshì
     Zhu   professor   mark   PAST   my   test
     "Professor Zhu marked my test."

2b. wǒdė   kaǒshì   beì   Zhū   laǒshī   pīyè   lè
     my   test   by   Zhu   professor   mark   PAST
     "My test was marked by Professor Zhu."

Most languages organize the three basic units of subject, object, and verb in one of three patterns. Unmarked sequences (simple, common constructions) are:

Verb + Subject + Object (VSO)
Subject + Verb + Object (SVO)
Subject + Object + Verb (SOV)

The contrasting feature is essentially that of the relative placement of verbs either initially, medially, or finally. Subjects occur prior to objects. Only a few of the world's languages have unmarked word orders that place objects before subjects. Because subjects precede objects in the vast majority of languages, this pattern probably reflects human cognition. People perceive subjects as more salient than objects because they have the potential of agency, that is, an ability to initiate, control, direct, or affect actions and events. Objects are not doers but receivers of actions and are, therefore, less cognitively prominent. Significantly, cognitive prominence is reflected in linguistic structure.

Since Noam Chomsky revolutionized the field of linguistics with his publications in 1957 (*Syntactic Structures*) and 1965 (*Aspects of the Theory of Syntax*), linguists have attempted to describe and explain syntactic systems in terms of universal rather than language-specific patterns. A fundamental principle in linguistics is that words do not occur in sentences as random or isolated units but, rather, co-occur with others and form larger units called *phrases*. An important component of grammar is a set of "phrase structure" rules that describes the possible units internal to sentences. The most basic phrase structure rule states that a sentence (S) is composed of a Noun Phrase (NP) and a Verb Phrase (VP), shown by the notation:

S ⟶NP   VP

Noun Phrases consist minimally of a Noun but may also contain Determiners (DET; e.g., the, a, this, some), Adjectival Phrases (ADJ), and/or Prepositional Phrases (PP). Verb Phrases must contain a Verb and may have Noun Phrases, Adverbial Phrases (ADV), and Prepositional Phrases as well. Sentences may also contain Auxiliaries (Aux; e.g., forms of be, have, do, can, will). As an example, the simple sentence "the dog chased the cat" can be described by the following rules:

```
S    ⟶NP      VP
NP   ⟶Det     Noun
VP   ⟶Verb    NP
NP   ⟶Det     Noun
[Det ⟶the
Noun⟶dog, cat
Verb ⟶chase(d)]
```

Linguists also represent sentences by tree diagrams (or phrase markers) to depict constituents of phrases and their syntactic relations. The tree diagram for "the dog chased the cat" is

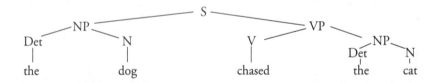

More complex sentences are represented by more elaborate tree diagrams, but they are all based on similar principles of grouping and relating constituents. Following is a tree diagram for the sentence "the good student will read a book in the library":

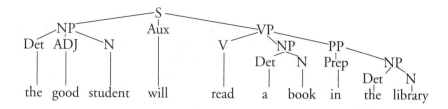

The purpose of a grammar is to describe linguistic facts so as to be able to produce, or *generate,* rules accounting for all possible sentences in a particular language. A *generative grammar* should also block or constrain generation of impermissible constructions.

Chomsky introduced the distinction between *surface structure*—the surface appearance of sentences as they appear in actual speech—and *deep structure*—the underlying order of words as they are generated by basic phrase structure rules. Deep structure is transformed into surface structure by *transformations* that act on underlying components and, by stages, result in actual speech. The deep and surface structures of a sentence may be similar, as in the simple sentence illustrated earlier, "The dog chased the cat." However, many sentences require changes or transformations of the underlying order of components. For example, "Did the dog chase the cat?" is a question requiring several transformations. It begins with the string "INTERROGATIVE + the dog chase the cat." The interrogative transformation introduces an auxiliary "do," which is then shifted to initial position. The auxiliary also attracts tense markers applicable to verbs, for example, "do" + Past "did."

Additionally, transformational rules can account for nonoccurrence of segments in surface structure by *deletion,* eliminating redundancies that might otherwise be generated. When sentences are combined through conjunction ("and"), redundant sequences are deleted:

The cats played in the yard and the dogs played in the yard.
The cats and dogs played in the yard.

Transformational grammar provides insights that enable linguists to decipher the origin of ambiguity in sentences. Consider one of Chomsky's well-known examples:

Flying planes can be dangerous.

This sentence is an ambiguous surface realization of two different deep structures, expressible as

1.   To fly planes can be dangerous.
2.   Planes—planes fly—can be dangerous.

The latter sentence exemplifies a process of *embedding,* common in English and many, but not all, languages. One sentence, "planes fly," is first embedded within the matrix "planes can be dangerous." It is then transformed into an adjective, "flying," eliminating the redundant "planes." Finally, "flying" is moved to its proper adjectival position preceding the head noun "planes." By these transformations, the deep structure "Planes—planes fly—can be dangerous" becomes the surface sentence "Flying planes can be dangerous." In the first underlying sentence, "To fly planes can be dangerous," the infinitive "to fly" is turned into a gerund, "flying," that remains in initial position preceding its direct object.

This example demonstrates the steps by which two different deep structures can eventually have the same surface appearance. Different transformational rules were applied, coincidentally achieving identical end results.

SEMANTICS: THE ANALYSIS OF MEANING

The function of language is to express the speaker's meaning. Although meaning is global in the sense that it is thought and experienced as a simultaneous whole, it must be encoded through language in segmented linear form. Morphemes have semantic content (meaning) and combine with one another to produce further meaning. And words are, in turn, combined in larger, multiword constructions, yielding additional meaning.

Semantic analysis, or the study of meaning, is complex because meaning includes many kinds of input. Words have referential senses, labeling persons, objects, events in the world, or in thought and imagination. Words also have cultural meanings, reflecting attitudes, values, or shared symbols (e.g., apple pie). Words and sentence constructions can have situational relevance, some used in formal contexts and others in informal situations (e.g., Please pass the salt/Gimme the salt). Words or constructions can be associated with different kinds of encounters; their selection, therefore, conveys interactional meaning (e.g., Dr. Jones/sweetheart). Finally, utterances can have affective meaning, indicating attitudes of speakers (e.g., John told me about his accomplishments/John boasted about his accomplishments). Here we will touch only briefly on some notions in semantic analysis; subsequent chapters will deal at length with issues of cultural, situational, and interactional meaning.

Influenced by advances in generative grammar, linguists attempt to discover universal principles in semantics. One approach is to specify meanings of words in terms of underlying semantic components. Once components are identified, linguists can determine the types of features that co-occur or are blocked from co-occurring. For instance, Chomsky's famous example of an unacceptable sentence, "Colorless green ideas sleep furiously," is rejected because of semantic inconsistencies even though it is grammatically well formed; that is, adjectives, noun, verb, and adverb are all placed in correct sequence. The problem with the sentence is that its semantic components cannot co-occur: "ideas" do not "sleep"; "ideas" are not "green"; something that is "green" cannot be "colorless." Syntactic rules alone do not provide adequate constraints; rather, restrictions are based on semantic rules, identifiable as co-occurrences of certain kinds of features with one another. Semantic features need not be overtly marked, but they are, nonetheless, significant attributes of words.

Nouns may contain the following *semantic features* (among others):

count/mass
specific/generic
potent/nonpotent
animate/inanimate
masculine/feminine
human/nonhuman

The presence of particular components can be discovered for any given noun. For example:

COW : count, potent, animate, feminine, nonhuman

Semantic features may be expressed through various linguistic forms. Some languages overtly mark features of animate/inanimate, mass/count, definite/indefinite, and so on, whereas others do not. In English, animate or inanimate nouns are not differentiated in their structure but are distinguished by their ability to occur as subjects of certain verbs. For example, only animate nouns can be subjects of "breathe, eat, sleep." The feature of count or mass is indicated by whether a noun can be enumerated or counted: "two cats" but not "two waters." And definite/indefinite distinctions are signaled by articles—for example, definite: "*the* cat came home"; indefinite: "*a* cat ran by the house."

Nouns in sentences fulfill several types of *semantic roles*. Common roles in transitive sentences include the following:

agent: performer of an action
patient: entity affected by an action
source: starting point of an action
goal: end point of an action

These roles can be identified in the sentence "Amy sent a letter from Paris to her friend in Iowa."

agent: Amy
patient: a letter
source: Paris
goal: her friend in Iowa

Other semantic roles occur as well:

experiencer (entity experiencing some action or state): *Ruth* likes classical music.
instrument (entity used to carry out an action): Ruth cut the cake with *a knife.*

The following sentences demonstrate that the surface grammatical subjects of verbs can fulfill a variety of semantic roles (Finegan and Besnier 1989:203):

agent: *The janitor* opened the door.
patient: *The door* opened easily.
instrument: *His first record* greatly expanded his audience.
cause: *Bad weather* ruined the corn crop.
experiencer: *Serge* heard his father whispering.
benefactive: *The young artist* won the prize.
locative: *Arizona* attracts asthmatics.
temporal: *The next day* found us on the road to Alice Springs.

Verbs can be semantically characterized as actions, processes, or states. Each type selects a particular semantic relation with accompanying nouns. Consider the following sentences (adapted from Chafe 1970:98):

action: Jane ran.
process: The wood dried.
action/process: Jane dried the wood.
state: The wood is dry.

Action verbs take *agent* nouns as grammatical subjects. In the first sentence, "Jane" acted as agent; she did something (she ran). By contrast, *process* verbs take *patient* subjects. In the second sentence, "the wood" did not do anything; rather, something happened to it. *Action/process* verbs (transitives), exemplified by the third sentence, require an agent subject who does something and a patient as object that has something done to it. Finally, *states,* as in the last example, select patient subjects. They depict inherent conditions or states of being. These distinctions among verbs reflect the importance of differentiating between surface grammatical subjects/objects and underlying semantic roles of agent/patient.

MANUAL LANGUAGE

The term *manual language* refers to a system of communication that employs hand movements to convey meanings. This complex system forms the basis of American Sign Language (ASL), used by deaf people in the United States. ASL, and sign languages developed and used by people in other countries, are complete languages consisting of rules of phonology, morphology, and syntax. Several features of ASL are briefly described in this section.

Formation of Signs

ASL signs are composed of formally distinct features that co-occur in various combinations. Composition of signs, then, is analogous to phonological structure of oral languages. ASL employs four basic kinds of articulatory parameters in the production or articulation of signs. These include (1) hand configuration: how the hands are shaped; (2) place of articulation: where a sign is formed in relation to a

signer's body; (3) movement of hands in space; and (4) orientation of hands in relation to the body.

Hand Configuration. ASL contains 41 different hand shapes (Friedman
1977:16 –17). The most commonly used configurations are illustrated in Figure
2.5. Six of these are called "neutral" shapes: A, B, 5, G, C, and O. Of all hand configurations, these six shapes occur most frequently in ASL words. These neutral
shapes are employed in sign languages used in other countries as well. Friedman
suggests that their frequency of occurrence in words and their universality are due

/ B /	/ A /	/ G /	/ C /	/ 5 /	/ V /
/ B /	/ A /	/ G /	/ C /	/ 5 /	/ V /
flat hand	fist hand	index hand	cupped hand	spread hand	V hand

/ O /	/ F /	/ X /	/ H /	/ L /	/ Y /
/ O /	/ F /	/ X /	/ H /	/ L /	/ Y /
O hand	pinching hand	hook hand	index-mid hand	L hand	Y hand

/ 8 /	/ K /	/ I /	/ R /	/ W /	/ 3 /	/ E /
/ 8 /	/ K /	/ I /	/ R /	/ W /	/ 3 /	/ E /
mid-finger hand	chopstick hand	pinkie hand	crossed-finger hand	American-3 hand	European-3 hand	nail-buff hand

FIGURE 2.5. Hand Shapes in American Sign Language. (Klima and Bellugi, *The Signs of
Language*, 1979:46. Harvard University Press, Copyright © 1979 by the President and Fellows of
Harvard College)

to the fact that they are the "least complex shapes the hand can assume (in terms of muscular arrangement)" (ibid.:18).

Place of Articulation. Signs are formed, or articulated, in "signing space" consisting of the area in front of a signer's body extending from the top of the head to the waist and from side to side to the extent of arm's reach with elbow bent. The most frequently used space in ASL is located on or near a signer's face and head. Because ASL depends on visual channels for transmitting messages, it makes sense to produce signs in proximity to the face or head. In addition, Friedman suggests that this area is chosen for articulation because there are more distinct "landmarks" on the face than elsewhere on the body (ibid.:40). Such landmarks include forehead, eyes, nose, mouth, and cheeks.

Signs are formed with one or both hands. According to Klima and Bellugi, approximately 40 percent of ASL signs are made with only one hand, 35 percent with both hands moving actively, and 25 percent with one hand acting on the other as a base (1979:42). In order to produce signs, hands may assume different spatial relations to one another. For example, "establish" is formed with one hand above the other; "with" is made with one hand beside the other; "follow" is made with one hand behind the other; and "assistant" is formed with one hand below the other (ibid.:44).

Movement of Hands. Hand movements in ASL are complex, involving use of various dimensions of physical space and of changes in hand position. Direction of movement is a significant articulatory factor. Possibilities include movement along a vertical axis: upward, downward, up and down; and movement along a horizontal-depth axis: rightward, leftward, side to side.

Another distinctive feature is manner of movement of hands—that is, whether the hand moves in a straight, circular, or twisting path. Manner of hand movement also includes bending at the wrist or knuckles, wiggling the fingers, and opening or closing the hand.

Orientation. The fourth articulatory parameter in ASL is the orientation of palms of hands in relation to a signer's body. Hands may be oriented with palms up or down, facing left or right, or directed toward or away from a signer. Orientation of hands may involve contact between parts of the hand and other parts of a signer's body. Points of contact on the hand include fingertips, thumb tip, palm, side of hand, and back of hand.

Figure 2.6 illustrates signs that contrast on the basis of hand configuration, place of articulation, or movement of hands. These signs are, thus, analogous to "minimal pairs" of oral languages.

ASL Vocabulary and Grammar

The vocabulary of ASL consists of thousands of distinct signs. Most signs are completely arbitrary in the sense that their form has no inherent physical relationship to their meaning. Arbitrariness of form and meaning is, therefore, a linguistic trait

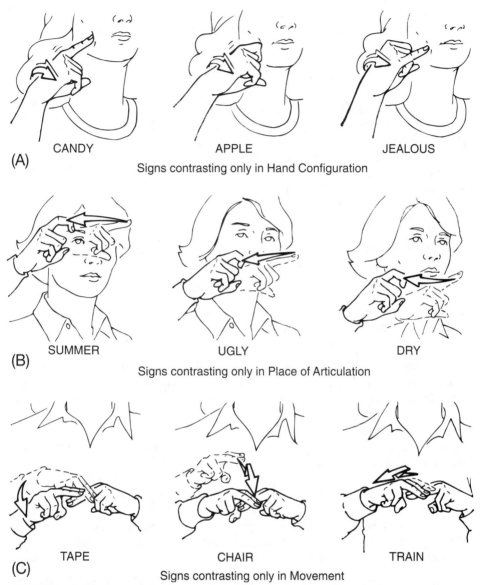

FIGURE 2.6. Some Contrastive Signs in ASL. (Klima and Bellugi, *The Signs of Language*, 1979:42. Harvard University Press, Copyright © 1979 by the President and Fellows of Harvard College)

shared by both oral and manual language. However, some ASL signs do have an "iconic" relationship to concepts that they express. That is, they convey meaning through direct physical depiction. For instance, reference to signer or addressee (i.e., "I," "you") is conveyed with the hand in a neutral shape pointed toward the signer's body ("I") or toward the addressee ("you"). Spatial relations of hands can also have iconic functions. Examples cited earlier demonstrate such a process; for example, "with" is signed with one hand beside the other, and "follow" is made with one hand behind the other.

Although a number of ASL signs do have some physical correspondence to their meanings, it is important to note that even these signs are conventionalized, stylized representations. Similar to words in oral language, they are "socially constituted" symbols (McNeill 1987:244).

Words in ASL may contain a single sign or a combination of signs. Principles of word structure and word formation are, thus, similar in both ASL and oral language. Morphological rules apply in both systems. Just as morphemes can be combined in oral languages, manual morphemes can be combined within ASL words. Nouns, verbs, adjectives, and adverbs are often formed through compounding (Klima and Bellugi 1979:205):

Compound Sign	*Meaning of Compound*
sick + spread	epidemic
face + new	stranger
eat + noon	lunch
sleep + sunrise	to oversleep
think + alike	to agree
wrong + happen	accidentally or by chance
sure + work	seriously

Grammatical meanings are conveyed in ASL through modifications of signs. For instance, in order to represent meanings of "intensification" of an activity (translated as "very"; e.g., "very fast," "very slow"), a sign is produced with a short, rapid movement as contrasted with its neutral articulation.

The grammatical concept of tense is depicted in ASL as a vertical spatial plane running along the side of a signer's body. If a sign is made in this space immediately in front of a signer's body, present tense is conveyed; if a sign is made further in front, a verb has a future tense meaning; and if a sign is made in the side vertical area behind a signer's body, a verb is interpreted with reference to past tense (Friedman 1977:51–52).

Signs can be modified in their production in order to transmit aspectual meanings of verbs. Among the many aspects depicted in ASL are the following (ibid.:249, 257, 293 – 294):

1. *Continuative* (continuation of action or state)—"My brother's leg has pained him for a long time."

2. *Incessant* (frequent occurrence and duration of a trait or quality)—"My sister gets sick incessantly; it never stops."

3. *Predispositional* (tendency to have a trait or quality)—"That's his way; he is characteristically quiet."

4. *Allocative* (allocation or distribution of objects)—"He gave something to each of them."

In addition to articulatory and morphological rules, ASL contains syntactic rules as well. Most sentences follow Subject-Verb-Object (SVO) order, similar to the basic word order of oral English.

In sum, structural and functional characteristics of ASL demonstrate both its complexity and its adherence to standardized rules of lexical and grammatical formation. It is, therefore, a distinct, elaborate, and meaningful linguistic system, used by a population in the United States estimated to number from 250,000 to 500,000 (Woodward 1991).

NONVERBAL COMMUNICATION

Nonverbal Actions

People convey meaning not only through spoken language but also through gestures, facial expressions, body posture, and use of space. These aspects of communication are not merely embellishments to talk but are critical components of participants' messages. Nonverbal communication makes use of both kinesic and proxemic acts. The term *kinesics* refers to gesture, facial expression, eye contact, and body posture. *Proxemics* includes uses of touch and definitions of personal space.

Research in nonverbal behavior reveals both universal and culture-specific patterns. Because human bodies are constructed on a species-wide model, it follows that possible behavioral repertories are determined by the same fundamental constraints throughout the world. However, just as each language employs only some of the possible sounds that the human vocal apparatus can produce, each system of nonverbal communication selects only some possible human gestures, facial expressions, and so on. And nonverbal actions that "look the same" in different systems may have very different meanings because the meanings are culturally constructed and assigned. The meanings of gestures, expressions, and body postures do not flow from the actions themselves any more than the meanings of words flow from the particular sounds with which they are made.

Researchers in nonverbal communication generally emphasize one of two modes of interpretation. Although these interpretations are sometimes framed as opposites, they need not be incompatible. One school stresses biological/behaviorist features of nonverbal communication. Jolly (1972) states that certain gestures, body postures, and facial movements may have universal (or at least widespread) significance. In fact, some may be of primate origin. According to Jolly, humans and other primates appear to employ similar signals of enjoyment, distress, threat, and submissiveness. For example, observe the human and nonhuman primate expressions in the photographs in Figure 2.7 (Jolly 1972:156–165).

Some kinesic acts may have widespread functions. The eight photographs in Figure 2.8 illustrate the "eyebrow flash," which Eibl-Eibesfeldt describes as a "universal expressive pattern used during greeting at a distance" (1972:304ff). Each

FIGURE 2.7a. Human tense-mouth face. Heads of
state are dominant males, often photographed
making gestures of confident threat.   (AP/Wide
World Photos)

set contains two pictures, one of a person with lowered eyebrows at the start of
greeting and the second of the same person with maximally raised eyebrows. Ethnic groups in the photos are (a) French and (b) Balinese (Eibl-Eibesfeldt
1972:304ff).

Although biological/behaviorist interpretations of nonverbal actions are still
common, more recently anthropologists studying nonverbal communication have
argued that little, if any, actions are universal in their meaning. Instead, they stress
the fact that all human behavior is culturally constructed and, therefore, all meaning is culturally assigned (Farnell 1995).

FIGURE 2.7b. The red uakari open-mouth threat.
(Copyright © 1999 Zoological Society of San Diego,
San Diego, California, U.S.A. All rights reserved.)

FIGURE 2.7c. The human smile is a greeting gesture, but it more often grades into our laughter and play face rather than into a fear grin or a grimace. Tony Jacklin after winning the 1969 British Open Championship. (Photo of Ed Lacey/Associated Sports Photography)

Some researchers have attempted to develop a system for notating gestures, expressions, and movements that could be used for comparative analyses of kinesic behavior in diverse cultures. Ray Birdwhistell's "kinesograms" (1970) are symbols specifying each possible expression, gesture, and change of position. Although planned as comparable to the International Phonetic Alphabet in its worldwide relevance, problems in its application arise because nonverbal communication is essentially fluid. Whereas sounds are segmentable into discrete units that can be represented by a single symbol (e.g., /p/, /o/), kinesic behavior is continual and multilayered. It is, therefore, difficult to decide where one segment ends and another begins. As an alternative, some researchers use notational systems based on Labanotation, a system originally introduced in the 1930s by Laban for recording dance movements (Farnell 1995).

Whatever the origin of nonverbal actions, all behaviors are learned as part of socialization within one's group. As Sheila Ramsey stated, "According to culturally prescribed codes, we use eye movement and contact to manage conversations and to regulate interactions; we follow rigid rules governing intra and inter personal touch, our bodies synchronously join in the rhythm of others in a group, and

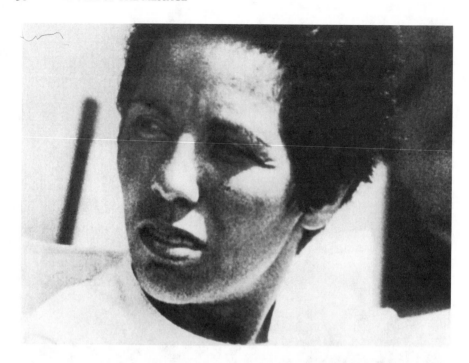

FIGURE 2.8a. French "eyebrow flash."   (Both Photos by Hans Hass / Prof. Dr. Irenaus Eibl-Eibesfeldt / From I. Eibl-Eibesfeldt, Human Ethology; New York: Aldine de Gruyter, 1989.)

FIGURE 2.8b. Balinese "eyebrow flash."   (Both photos: Prof. Dr. Irenaus Eibl-Eibesfeldt /
From I. Eibl-Eibesfeldt, Human Ethology; New York: Aldine de Gruyter, 1989.)

gestures modulate our speech. We must internalize all of this in order to become and remain fully functioning and socially appropriate members of any culture" (1979:111).

Some nonverbal actions have the status of "emblems." These are gestures that are understood by participants to express a specific meaning, often substituting for spoken words. Emblems in Euro-American societies include head-nods to signal assent or shrugging the shoulders to convey uncertainty. Because emblems function within a particular interpretive system, similar actions may have different meanings in different cultures.

Cultural diversity in interpreting nonverbal behaviors can lead to misunderstandings between people of different ethnic backgrounds. Two sources of problems are possible. One is that an emblem or signal used by one participant is absent from the repertory of the other and, therefore, no meaning is conveyed. The other problem is more serious: Similar behaviors exist for both participants, but their meanings differ. When someone is confronted with an unfamiliar act, the person knows that she or he cannot properly decode the message intended by the sender, but when a nonverbal act is familiar in its form, an addressee decodes the message according to her or his own norms without realizing that the intended meaning is different. "Misled by the familiarity of the gesture, the decoder will most likely be unaware of this discrepancy, and consequently act according to [his/her] erroneous interpretation. . . . While a strange gesture will cause discommunication, the false decoding of familiar gestures will produce miscommunication, i.e. misunderstanding" (Schneller 1988:155–156).

Misunderstanding between people of diverse ethnicities has been documented in Israel, a multicultural country (Schneller 1988). Even though most Israelis speak a common language (Hebrew), their diverse origins can lead to misinterpretation of nonverbal messages. In experimental situations, Israeli college students from 14 cultural backgrounds viewed videotaped gestures made by recent immigrants from Ethiopia. Of the 26 Ethiopian emblems demonstrated, 85 percent were recognized by the students. However, only 23 percent of the recognized gestures were correctly decoded; 7 percent were given "approximate" decodings; and 70 percent were misinterpreted (ibid.:158). Misunderstanding, then, is much more common than nonunderstanding.

Additional research by Raphael Schneller demonstrated that decoding of gestures commonly used by native-born Israelis also was problematic. In this experiment, Israelis from five different cultural backgrounds were shown videotapes of other Israelis and were asked to attribute meanings to gestures. Of the nine emblems shown, 85 percent were recognized, although many were incorrectly decoded. Some emblems had high rates of correct decoding, but others had extremely low rates. Frequencies of misunderstanding varied, but some gestures were incorrectly interpreted by as much as 70 percent of respondents (ibid.:160–161).

These studies demonstrate the lack of congruence between participants' intended and received messages. When speech accompanies gestures, understanding is, of course, much more likely. Problems can still arise, though, because discrepancies between the perceived meanings of verbal and nonverbal behaviors result in confusion. And because nonverbal decoding usually occurs nonconsciously, people are unaware of the source of their confusion, potentially deepening their sense of discomfort with co-participants.

Although different meanings attributed to nonverbal behaviors by members of different groups can contribute to tense encounters, the discrepancies can also be a source of cultural humor. For example, the Western Apache of Arizona have developed joking routines that play, in part, on the intrusive, domineering communicative styles of Anglos (Basso 1979:48–55). In the routines, Apaches imitate numerous behaviors that Anglos typically perform but which Apaches consider offensive. These include making direct eye contact with or staring at interlocutors and touching another person while talking to them, stereotyped by the friendly backslap or hug.

Within a given society, patterns of nonverbal behavior often function to signal differences in status. Gestures, eye movements, smiles and other facial expressions, touching, and defining personal space are used in displays of status. In many cultures, a constellation of nonverbal behaviors appears to be consistent with high status or power. Dominant people tend to use broad gestures, look or even stare at others, maintain "serious," unsmiling faces, and inhabit wide areas of personal space. Conversely, in encounters between unequals, subordinates tend to use restricted, small gestures, avert their eyes when looked at, smile frequently, and allow their space to be encroached on even to the point of being touched. Whereas high-status people use expansive gestures and attempt to enlarge the appearance of their bodies, low-status individuals act to limit their body images by lowering their heads and keeping their legs together and their arms close to their bodies.

In some cultures, specific gestures can be used as general markers of politeness. Patterns of bowing in Japan and other Asian societies are intricate signs of respect and deference. Reciprocal bowing (both participants bow to the same degree) signals equality and mutual respect. Nonreciprocal bowing occurs when a subordinate person bows deeply to a high-status person who acknowledges the bow with a head-nod (Morsbach 1988:190–191).

Nonverbal behaviors reflecting gender inequalities have been well documented in Western societies, including the United States. The constellation of acts mentioned above associated with dominant people tends to be employed by men, whereas women tend to use nonverbal markers of subordination or deference. Women typically smile, avert their eyes when looked at, condense their bodies and gestures, avoid encroaching on others' space, and allow intrusions into their own space (Hall 1984; Henley 1977). Nancy Henley reported numerous studies demonstrating that in mixed-sex interactions, men touched women twice as often as women touched men, men initiated eye contact twice as often with women as women did with men, and women returned smiles of men nearly all the time, whereas men returned only two-thirds of the smiles given by women (1977:115, 164, 176).

The Meaning of Silence

Silence is an act of nonverbal communication that transmits many kinds of meaning dependent on cultural norms of interpretation. Our tendency to describe silence as an absence of speech reveals a particular cultural bias, implying that something is missing, but silence is a "something" with purpose and significance. Silent behavior occurs in all societies, although its message varies both between and within different groups. It conveys meaning, as does all communication, partly from the situational and interactional contexts of its use. Emphasizing the "use" of silence also focuses on the fact that silence does not simply exist but is actively created by participants.

In American society, silence is required of individuals or groups engaged in several types of encounters. Most tend to have a ceremonial or formalized character where participants have established roles and behave in predictable ways. Audiences at ceremonies, governmental or legal proceedings, and theatrical events generally are constrained from speech or are limited to making brief, formulaic responses.

Silence or paucity of speech also underscores status differences between individuals in various kinds of role relationships, including employer/employee, teacher/student, and adult/child. In encounters between unequals, disproportionate use of talk or silence reveals underlying social hierarchies. Individuals of higher status tend to talk more, whereas those of lower rank are expected to be silent or less talkative.

In American society, interpersonal silence is not well tolerated, especially between people who are not intimates. Greater familiarity leads to greater ability to refrain from speech. In the opinion of Ishii and Bruneau, "One function of speech is to avoid silence" (1988:313). This assessment offers a possible explanation of Western behaviors such as formulaic greetings, so-called "small talk," and frequent question-and-answer sequences occurring in much daily conversation.

Because talk is preferred in interpersonal encounters, silence is often given negative interpretations. Feelings of hostility, disdain, disinterest, or anger are often attributed to silent participants. Despite these attitudes, silence is sometimes perceived as a mark of an individual's contemplative thought, respect for others, or desire to avoid conflict. Contrasting interpretations may be motivated by context or by social or personality attributes of participants.

In other cultures, as expected, the situational and interactional functions of silence are varied, although some cross-cultural similarities do pertain. Among the latter are status-related patterns in which people of lower status in unequal encounters tend to be more silent than those of higher rank.

Cultural variations, though, abound in terms of contexts where silence is expected. Among the Western Apache, silence is the norm in situations of ambiguity or uncertainty, such as encounters between strangers, initial courtship, times of mourning, greeting people who have been away for an extended period, and reactions to displays of anger (Basso 1972:71–79). These circumstances have a common theme: An individual is interacting with someone who is unpredictable either because he or she is unknown, not known well, has been absent for some time, or is in a distressed psychic state. When interacting with such people, one must take care to silently observe them in order to pick up clues and anticipate their likely behavior.

Among the Igbo of Nigeria, talk and social gregariousness are highly valued, so that silence stands out as unusual behavior. It is mandated in ritual or ritualized situations. For example, four days after a death in a household, villagers show sympathy by entering the house, standing in silence in front of bereaved family members, sitting silently for a period, and again presenting themselves to mourners before departing (Nwoye 1985:186). Silence is the norm in other ritual endeavors, including sacrifices and consulting with ancestor spirits (ibid.:186–187). In these contexts, silence marks the occasion's solemnity and signals the detachment of participants from normal routines.

Silence is also employed by Igbos as a means of social control. Wrongdoers are punished by group silence. All villagers refuse to speak to the guilty party and his or her family (ibid.:188). In the traditional life of communal interdependence, wrongdoers quickly correct their behavior. Finally, Igbo silence can be used to demonstrate hostilities between people, especially by withholding greetings. Because greetings are signals of sociability, silence eloquently speaks of disharmony. Therefore, Igbos' refusal to greet or speak to each other is a clear manifestation of animosity or evil intentions. In Gregory Nwoye's words, "The Igbo expression of the English equivalent of 'not to be on speaking terms' is much more sinister than its English equivalent" (ibid.:190).

It is important, of course, to be wary of overgeneralizing or stereotyping any society. Not all members are equally silent or loquacious or adhere to interpretive norms to the same degree. Discrepancies always exist between ideals and actual practice.

SUMMARY

In this chapter, we have explored various means by which co-participants produce messages. This is the essence of communication: transmission of meaning from one individual to another. To accomplish this purpose, people employ verbal and nonverbal techniques.

Linguists have developed numerous descriptive and explanatory tools to analyze the structure of language. Talk is achieved through the interdependent components of sounds, words, sentences, and meanings. Although every language is unique, some universals can be specified, including the human range of phonetic inventories, recurring types of morphological and syntactic constructions, and underlying semantic relationships.

Nonverbal communication also consists of unique and common behaviors. Although some actions may occur in many societies, they are always given culturally specific interpretations. Silence is also a universal activity, but its display and contextual meaning are affected by cultural rules.

REFERENCES

BASSO, KEITH. 1972. To give up on words: Silence in Western Apache culture. In *Language in Social Context*, ed. P. Giglioli. Harmondsworth, England: Penguin, pp. 67–86.

BASSO, KEITH. 1979. *Portraits of "The Whiteman."* New York: Cambridge University Press.

BIRDWHISTELL, RAY. 1970. *Kinesics and Context.* Philadelphia: University of Pennsylvania Press.

BONVILLAIN, NANCY. 1973. *A Grammar of Akwesasne Mohawk.* Mercury Series No. 8. Ottawa: National Museum of Canada.

BONVILLAIN, NANCY. n.d. Fieldnotes for Mohawk, Russian, Tagalog, Turkish.

CHAFE, WALLACE. 1970. *Meaning and the Structure of Language.* Chicago: University of Chicago Press.

CHOMSKY, NOAM. 1957. *Syntactic Structures.* The Hague: Mouton.

CHOMSKY, NOAM. 1965. *Aspects of the Theory of Syntax.* Cambridge, MA: MIT Press.

COWAN, WILLIAM, AND JAKOMIRA RAKUSAN. 1987. *Source Book for Linguistics,* 2nd rev. ed. Philadelphia: John Benjamins.

EIBL-EIBESFELDT, I. 1972. Similarities and differences between cultures in expressive movements. In *Nonverbal Communication,* ed. R. Hinde. New York: Cambridge University Press, pp. 297–312.

FARNELL, BRENDA. 1995. Movement and gesture. In *Encyclopedia of Cultural Anthropology,* ed. D. Levinson and M. Ember. New Haven, CT: Human Relations Area Files.

FINEGAN, EDWARD, AND NIKO BESNIER. 1989. *Language: Its Structure and Use.* New York: Harcourt Brace Jovanovich.

FRIEDMAN, LYNN. 1977. Formational properties of American Sign Language. In *On the Other Hand: New Perspectives on American Sign Language,* ed. L. Friedman. New York: Academic Press, pp. 13–56.

GLEASON, HENRY. 1955. *Workbook in Descriptive Linguistics.* New York: Holt, Rinehart & Winston.

HALL, JUDITH. 1984. *Nonverbal Sex Differences: Communication Accuracy and Expressive Style.* Baltimore: Johns Hopkins University Press.

HENLEY, NANCY. 1977. *Body Politics: Power, Sex and Nonverbal Communication.* Englewood Cliffs, NJ: Prentice Hall.

ISHII, SATOSHI, AND TOM BRUNEAU. 1988. Silence and silences in cross-cultural perspective: Japan and the United States. In *Intercultural Communication,* ed. L. Samovar and R. Porter. Belmont, CA: Wadsworth, pp. 310–315.

JOLLY, ALISON. 1972. *The Evolution of Primate Behavior.* New York: Macmillan.

KLIMA, EDWARD, AND URSULA BELLUGI. 1979. *The Signs of Language.* Cambridge, MA: Harvard University Press.

LADEFOGED, PETER. 1982. *A Course in Phonetics,* 2nd ed. New York: Harcourt Brace Jovanovich.

LAKOFF, GEORGE, AND MARK JOHNSON. 1980. *Metaphors We Live By.* Chicago: University of Chicago Press.

MCNEILL, DAVID. 1987. *Psycholinguistics.* New York: Harper & Row.

MORSBACH, HELMUT. 1988. Nonverbal communication and hierarchical relationships: The case of bowing in Japan. In *Cross-cultural Perspectives in Nonverbal Communication,* ed. F. Poyatos. Lewiston, NY: CJ Hogrefe, pp. 189 –199.

NWOYE, GREGORY. 1985. Eloquent silence among the Igbo of Nigeria. In *Perspectives on Silence,* ed. D. Tannen and M. Saville-Troike. Norwood, NJ: Ablex, pp. 185– 191.

O'GRADY, WILLIAM, MICHAEL DOBROVOLSKY, AND MARK ARONOFF. 1989. *Contemporary Linguistics: An Introduction.* New York: St. Martin's Press.

PULLUM, GEOFFREY, AND WILLIAM LADUSAW. 1986. *Phonetic Symbol Guide.* Chicago: University of Chicago Press.

RAMSEY, SHEILA. 1979. Nonverbal behavior: An intercultural perspective. In *Handbook of Intercultural Communication,* ed. M. Asante, E. Newmark, and C. Blake. Beverly Hills, CA: Sage, pp. 105 –143.

SCHNELLER, RAPHAEL. 1988. The Israeli experience of cross-cultural misunderstanding: Insights and lessons. In *Cross-cultural Perspectives in Nonverbal Communication,* ed. F. Poyatos. Lewiston, NY: CJ Hogrefe, pp. 153–171.

WARDHAUGH, RONALD. 1977. *Introduction to Linguistics.* New York: McGraw-Hill.

WOODWARD, JAMES. 1991. Personal communication. Gallaudet University, Washington, DC.

YOUNG, ROBERT, AND WILLIAM MORGAN. 1987. *The Navajo Language,* rev. ed. Albuquerque: University of New Mexico Press.

3

Language
and Cultural Meaning

Compare the different ways that speakers of English and Navajo express their intentions and actions (note that Navajo utterances have been translated into English):

ENGLISH SPEAKER: I must go there.

NAVAJO SPEAKER: It is only good that I shall go there.

ENGLISH SPEAKER: I make the horse run.

NAVAJO SPEAKER: The horse is running for me.

In their use of language, speakers of English and Navajo express different views of events and experiences. By framing their intentions or activities with contrasting words and grammatical forms, they show in these examples that they have different attitudes about people's rights and obligations. English speakers encode the rights of people to control other beings (people or animals) or to be controlled or compelled themselves. In contrast, Navajo speakers give all beings the ability to decide for themselves, without compulsion or control from others.

The words used by speakers of English and Navajo express and reflect attitudes about the world that come from their own cultures. Although the attitudes indicated by these examples are specific, the process of encoding values, ideas, and emotions in language is universal. Such culturally shared attitudes, or *cultural models*, are based on people's ideas about the world they live in. Cultural models are expressed in several ways, but language is key to their transmission. Cultural models may be stated overtly, as in proverbs such as "don't cry over spilt milk" or "the early bird catches the worm," that either direct one's actions and attitudes or provide explanations for one's circumstances. Beliefs about the world may also be conveyed through accepted myths and legends, whether religious or secular, for example, the depiction of events in the Garden of Eden or the story of George Washington and the cherry tree. Such accounts guide human thought and action by providing moral lessons for individual behavior. More frequently, however, cultural models are covertly expressed throughout daily communicative interaction. The words we use have many layers of meaning, including concrete reference to objects and events and metaphoric or symbolic significance. Taken together, cultural meanings and models form a unique worldview, providing both an understanding of the world as it is thought to be and a blueprint for the way one ought to behave. Reality is not absolute or abstract; it is lived in within familiar contexts of social behavior and cultural meanings.

In this chapter we examine some linguistic means used to express models of the physical and social universe, including ideas about the shape and content of the environment, the kinds of forces affecting humans, and the ways people are expected to interact. We also explore the role of language in helping to construct and reinforce these models. All of these issues are addressed in the field of linguistic anthropology. Studies examine the *lexicon*, or vocabulary, of a language in order to discover direct and indirect meanings of words. Issues raised include the degree of specialization in various areas of meaning, the extent to which the words available in a language influence people's perceptions of their world, and the ways that words encode and transmit cultural, emotional, and symbolic meanings and values.

Researchers also seek to understand whether grammatical categories and structure affect speakers' worldviews. These studies raise questions concerning how the grammatical requirements of a language influence, direct, and reflect people's thought.

FOUNDATIONS OF LINGUISTIC ANTHROPOLOGY

The two most influential figures in the development of linguistic anthropology were Edward Sapir (1884–1939) and Benjamin Whorf (1897–1941). Both men studied the languages and cultures of several Native American peoples. Among Sapir's many interests and contributions to the field were his discussions of the importance of analyzing vocabulary in order to uncover the "physical and social environment" in which people live. According to Sapir, "The complete vocabulary of a language may indeed be looked upon as a complex inventory of all the ideas, interests and occupations that take up the attention of the community" (1949a:90–91). Sapir argued that all human experience is, to some extent, mediated through culture and language. Objects or forces in the physical environment become labeled in language only if they have cultural significance—that is, if they "take up the attention of the community." And once a language provides a word for an object or activity, that object or event becomes culturally significant. The relationship of vocabulary and cultural value is multidirectional. Speakers give names (words) to important entities and events in their physical and social worlds, and, once named, those entities and events become culturally and individually noticed and experienced. Through this interdependent process, unique cultural models are created and reinforced. As Sapir noted, "The worlds in which different societies live are distinct worlds, not merely the same world with different labels attached" (1949b:162).

Sapir's statement applies most concretely to geographic features, which can either be named in minute detail or glossed over with general terms. People name details when their survival depends directly on their environment. For example, in the language of Paiute people living in semidesert areas of Arizona, Utah, and Nevada, among the geographic terms translated by Sapir are the following: "divide, ledge, sand flat, semicircular valley, circular valley or hollow, spot of level ground in mountains surrounded by ridges, plain valley surrounded by mountains, plain, desert, knoll, plateau, canyon without water, canyon with creek, wash or gutter, gulch, slope of mountain or canyon wall receiving sunlight, shaded slope of mountain or canyon wall, rolling country intersected by several small hill-ridges" (1949a:91). The English language is able to express these numerous topographical features in a descriptive way, as shown by Sapir's translations, but it lacks separate words unique to each. The Paiute language labels each feature with a separate name and thereby gives it distinctive value. A motivating force behind the strategies of both English and Paiute is the relative interest and importance that speakers attribute to environmental conditions. Vocabularies in different languages can, therefore, be compared and conclusions can be drawn about cultural attitudes from the degree of specialization within sectors of vocabulary.

One caution, though, is worth noting concerning relationships between cultural interest and elaboration of vocabulary. Because cultures often change more rapidly than do languages, a "linguistic lag" can account for the fact that words or contrasts may reflect previous rather than current cultural interests. In time, as linguistic change catches up with cultural change, such words are likely to shift in meaning or to disappear.

Benjamin Whorf, who had been a student of Sapir, investigated whether grammatical structures provide frameworks for orienting speakers' thoughts and behaviors. He believed that the influence of language can be seen both through vocabulary and through more complex grammatical relations. For example, while Whorf was working for a fire insurance company, he noticed that fires were often caused by a person's inappropriate behavior motivated by labels given to objects. He found that workmen occasionally threw matches and cigarette stubs into "empty" gasoline drums even though the drums contained combustible vapors and invisible traces of gasoline. Whorf concluded that the men's behavior resulted from their misinterpretation of the word "empty," which usually refers to "null and void, negative, inert" (1956b:135).

Whorf also wrote extensive analyses of the language spoken by Hopi people in Arizona, focusing on its distinctive underlying grammatical categories. One important issue raised through this research is the role that grammar plays in influencing the kinds of relations that speakers perceive in their world. In Hopi, there are three words translated as "that" in English. Each Hopi word signals a different relationship between clauses in a sentence (Whorf 1956a:85). Compare the following:

1. I see that it is red.
2. I see that it is new.
3a. I hear that it is red.
3b. I hear that it is new.

In the first sentence, a speaker makes deductions based on direct sensory (in this case, visual) awareness. In the second sentence, a speaker makes inferences about "newness" based on evaluations of data (possibly including that "it" is shiny, clean, etc.). In sentences 3a and 3b, a speaker repeats or reports a fact provided by someone else, not directly experienced by the speaker herself. Comparing Hopi forms with English, we can conclude that because Hopis must choose among the various words, they are directed by grammatical requirements of their language to notice underlying causes of their knowledge of things (through direct senses, through inference, or through reported facts), whereas speakers of English need not pay attention to such differences. This does not mean that English speakers cannot become aware of different sources of knowledge; it simply means that they are not habitually led to making such distinctions.

In a comparison of Hopi and a language like English (which Whorf categorized as Standard Average European, SAE, to emphasize that European languages share basic grammatical characteristics), Whorf concluded that Hopi and English have different ways of conceptualizing time, number, and duration (1956b). He felt that these concepts are fundamental in creating a culture's metaphysics or view of the universe. According to Whorf, the Hopi language emphasizes continuity, cyclicity, and intensity in events, whereas SAE emphasizes the boundedness and objectification of entities. For example, English uses nouns to refer to phases in a cycle of time, such as "summer" or "morning." Hopi, though, treats phases as continuing events (or "eventings"). Words like "morning" are translated into Hopi as kinds of adverbs such as "while morning-phase is occurring" (ibid.:142–143). Contrasting the verb systems of English and Hopi, Whorf noted that English tenses divide time into three distinct units of past, present, and future, whereas Hopi verbs do not indicate the time of an event as such but, rather, focus on the manner or duration of an event. Whorf concluded that "concepts of 'time' and 'matter' are not given in substantially the same form by experience to all [people] but depend upon the nature of the language or languages through the use of which they have been developed" (ibid.:158).

The Sapir-Whorf Hypothesis

The opinions of Sapir and Whorf on relationships among language, thought, and behavior have come to be known as the *Sapir-Whorf hypothesis*. One summation of this theory, sometimes referred to as the "weak version," is that some elements of *language determines how you look at what you see around you*

language, for example, in vocabulary or grammatical systems, influence speakers' perceptions and can affect their attitudes and behavior. The "strong version" suggests that language is ultimately directive in this process. The difference between the two versions seems to be the degree of control that language exerts. The "strong" position is clearly unprovable. In fact, both Sapir and Whorf wavered in their statements on the issue of causal or directional relationship between language and thought. To quote Sapir,

> Human beings do not live in the objective world alone, nor alone in the world of social activity as ordinarily understood, but are very much at the mercy of the particular language which has become the medium of expression for their society. The fact of the matter is that the "real world" is to a large extent unconsciously built up on the language habits of the group. (1949b:162)

However, in the very next paragraph, Sapir stated that "we see and hear and otherwise experience very largely as we do because the language habits of our community predispose certain choices of interpretation" (ibid.). There is a difference between being "at the mercy" of one's language and being predisposed to "choices of interpretation," the latter implying options of thought.

In answer to one of Whorf's own questions as to whether there are "traceable affinities between (a) cultural and behavioral norms and (b) large-scale linguistic patterns," Whorf answered that "there are connections but not correlations or diagnostic correspondences" (1956b:159). Discussing the historical development of the "network of language, culture and behavior," Whorf asked, "Which was first: the language patterns or the cultural norms?" And he answered: "In the main they have grown up together, constantly influencing each other. But in this partnership the nature of the language is the factor that limits free plasticity and rigidifies channels of development in the more autocratic way" (ibid.:156).

Sapir also discussed historical processes and asserted that "culture and language may be conceived of as in a constant state of interaction and definite association for a considerable lapse of time. This state of correlation, however, cannot continue indefinitely." Because cultures change more rapidly than do languages, "the forms of language will in course of time cease to symbolize those of culture" (1949b:102).

A review of the writings of Sapir and Whorf indicates that neither thought of the relationships among language, culture, and human thinking as rigid and mechanistic but, rather, as coexisting in fluid and dynamic interactions.

A Contemporary Comment

Working in an entirely different tradition, but overlapping historically with Sapir and Whorf, the Soviet linguist V. N. Volosinov expressed quite similar views about relationships of language, thought, and experience. Like the American researchers, Volosinov believed that language and speakers' perceptions of experience are intertwined. He stated:

There are two elements in expression: that inner something which is *expressible,* and its *outward objectification* for others (or possibly for oneself). . . . By becoming external, by expressing itself outwardly, the inner element does undergo alteration. After all, it must gain control of outer material that possesses a validity of its own apart from the inner element. In this process of gaining control, of mastering outer material and making it over into a compliant medium of expression, the experiential, expressible element itself undergoes alteration and is forced to make a certain compromise. . . .

There is no such thing as experience outside of embodiment in signs. . . . It is not experience that organizes expression, but the other way around—*expression organizes experience.* Expression is what first gives experience its form and specificity of direction [emphasis in original]. (1973:84, 85)

Volosinov believed that an individual's thought is guided by possibilities offered by his or her language:

It is a matter not so much of expression accommodating itself to our inner world but rather of our inner world accommodating itself to the potentialities of our expression, its possible routes and directions. (ibid.:91)

Finally, Volosinov stressed the social nature of inner personal experience: "The structure of experience is just as social as is the structure of its outward objectification. The degree to which an experience is perceptible, distinct and formulated is directly proportional to the degree to which it is socially oriented" (ibid.:87).

There are no indications that the American and Soviet scholars knew of each other's work, but their contemporaneous intellectual interests and conclusions were compatible.

LEXICAL AND CULTURAL CATEGORIES

Building on the pioneering foundations of the first half of the twentieth century, modern researchers have broadened the exploration of topics in language and culture. Some study taxonomic systems in vocabulary and raise questions about possible universality of linguistic and cognitive processes. Other research investigates how cultural values and symbols are encoded in words or expressions and are then used by speakers to transmit emotional, attitudinal, and symbolic meanings.

Domains

Studies of categories and taxonomies in vocabulary often focus on analyses of semantic domains. A *semantic domain* is an aggregate of words, all sharing a core meaning, related to a specific topic—for example, kinship terms, body-part words, colors. Words within a domain are united by similarities and contrasts. The words share certain features of meaning because they refer to the same type of object, person, or event, but each word contrasts with all others in the set and labels a distinctive entity. By discovering systematic principles of similarity and contrast in a given domain, we can make inferences about how speakers experience their world. The number of distinctions made within a domain reflects the degree of cultural interest, as shown, for instance, by comparing the English and Paiute topographical terms given earlier from Sapir's research.

Cultural focus can also be seen in distinctions made by English terms for animals. For certain animals, we note age and sex, whereas for others we ignore such factors. For instance, within the species of "horse," we have separate words for female and male adults (mare and stallion), for babies (foal), and for female and male preadults (filly and colt). Age and sex of cattle are similarly distinguished: cow, bull, calf, heifer, and bullock. Also, we have numerous words for different breeds of these animals. In contrast, we treat other animals in much more generalized ways, using only one term for all individuals—for example, chipmunk, otter, moose. These differences in linguistic treatment obviously parallel, and are based on, our cultural interest in various kinds of animals because of our economy, eating habits, or other needs.

Cultural interest is not static but, rather, changes over time as new items and practices are introduced. When innovations are adopted, words are required to label these new entities and activities. Speakers can either create new words or extend the semantic range of existing words to include new items. In some cases, innovations replace indigenous objects, resulting in changes in meanings or functions of native words. For instance, shifts have occurred in meanings of the word *čih* (now meaning "sheep") in a dialect of Tzeltal, spoken by native people in Mexico (Witkowski and Brown 1983:571). When sheep were introduced to the Tzeltal people by the Spanish in the sixteenth century, Tzeltal speakers applied their indigenous word for "deer," *čih*, to this new animal, adding a descriptor, "cotton," *tunim*, so that "sheep" were called *tunim čih* ("cotton deer"). Over the centuries, sheep have been incorporated into the Tzeltal economy while at the same time, deer have become of peripheral interest. Now the word *čih* is used exclusively for "sheep," whereas "deer" is labeled as *teʔtikil čih*, literally "wild sheep." In this process, special marking for "sheep" has disappeared, emerging instead on "deer" in the modifier "wild."

In many languages of native North and South America, replacement of indigenous items and changes in cultural importance are reflected in marking older entities with attributes such as "native," "real," or other descriptive terms. When new items are introduced, speakers associate them with already existing entities and name them with indigenous words. Then, when older entities become eclipsed in importance by innovations, shifts occur in meanings so that the new item is the neutral term and the indigenous one receives modification. These processes can be seen in the following examples (ibid.:572–575):

1.   Huastec (Mexico):
     precontact: *bičim*   "deer"

contemporary: *bičim*   "horse"

 tenek bičim   "deer"   (lit. native horse)

2.   Biloxi (southeast United States):
kcixka   "pig"
kcixka yoka   "opossum"   (lit. swamp pig)

3.   Kiowa (U.S. Plains):
tsēī   "horse"
tsēī hiH   "dog"   (lit. real horse)

4.   Karok (California):
xuská· mhar   "gun"
ʔarara xuská· mhar   "bow"   (lit. Indian gun)

5.   Comanche (U.S. Plains):
kahnı   "house"
nïmïkahnı   "teepee"   (lit. Indian house)

Lexical Components

In some domains of vocabulary, cross-cultural comparisons uncover basic differences in the ways that people perceive their universe. For example, study of kinship terms (words used to name relatives) can reveal people's perceptions of their social relations. Americans generally use the following words for relatives: grandmother, grandfather, mother, father, aunt, uncle, sister, brother, cousin, daughter, son, niece, nephew, granddaughter, grandson. By analyzing the kinds of contrasts made with these words, we can discover systematic components of meaning that are used to name relatives. First, we distinguish between generations: grandmother/mother/ daughter/granddaughter. Second, we note the sex of relatives: mother/father; sister/brother. Third, we distinguish between direct or lineal relatives and collateral relatives: mother/aunt; son/nephew. These three sets of contrasts—that is, generation, sex of relative, and lineality—define the features of our kin that we consider meaningful. Another interesting aspect of English terminology is the reciprocity between alternate generations. The same combining form /grand-/ is used when skipping up one generation or downward: grandparent/grandchild.

The procedure used to determine significant contrasts is called *componential analysis,* developed by Ward Goodenough in studies of American kinship (1956, 1965). Words in a domain are viewed as being composed of isolable "components" of meaning that co-occur in different combinations, for example, younger generation + female + lineal → daughter. Comparisons of distinctive components used in any system of terms allow linguists and anthropologists to understand better the *ethnosemantics,* or indigenous systems of meaning, of a culture and its members.

Underlying principles or components in the English system are not necessarily used in all languages. Other languages and, therefore, their speakers employ different sets of contrasts. In languages of Iroquoian peoples, indigenous inhabitants of present-day New York State and Ontario and Quebec, Canada, the following kinds of relatives are named (examples are from Seneca, one of the Iroquoian languages; Lounsbury 1964):

grandmother (and her sisters):   *?akso:t*
grandfather (and his brothers):   *hakso:t*
mother and mother's sister: *no?yēh*
father and father's brother: *ha?nih*
mother's brother: *hakhno?sēh*
father's sister: *ake:hak*
older sister: *ahsti?*
younger sister: *khe?kē:?*
older brother: *hahtsi?*
younger brother: *he?kē:?*
cousin: *akya:?se:?*
daughter: *khe:awak*
son: *he:awak*
niece: *khehsō?neh*   (female speaker);   *kheyē:wō:tē?*   (male speaker)
nephew: *hehsō?neh*   (female speaker);   *heyē:wō:tē?*   (male speaker)
granddaugther: *kheya:te?*
grandson: *heya:te?*

This system is organized around several key principles, some similar to English terminology and others that differ. Both systems use notions of generation and sex of relative. However, Iroquoian speakers have separate terms for older and younger siblings (older sister/younger sister and older brother/younger brother). A major contrasting feature between the two languages is their treatment of lineal and collateral relatives. In English, sisters of one's mother and father are lumped together with one term, "aunt," as are brothers of one's mother and father, "uncle." In the Iroquoian system, one's mother's sisters are called by the same word as one's own mother, whereas one's father's sister is named separately. Similarly, father's brother is called "father," whereas mother's brother is distinguished. This principle of associating mother and father with their same-sex sibling is carried logically through succeeding generations and results in merging some relatives who we would call "cousin" into categories of sister/brother:

mother's sister's daughter = sister
mother's sister's son = brother
father's brother's daughter = sister
father's brother's son = brother

The logic here is based on the fact that a child of one's mother or father is one's sibling; therefore, a child of anyone called "mother" or "father" is called "sister" or "brother."

Differences in kinship terminologies are not merely linguistic but, rather, reflect societal attitudes toward one's relatives. Individuals called by each kin term are understood by speakers to stand in particular social relationships and to have certain rights and obligations vis-à-vis speakers. The meanings of words, then, reflect one's social universe.

Lexical Classifications

Research in vocabularies reveals that in some domains, distinctions are clear and unequivocal, whereas in others, components and categories are more complex. In a domain such as kinship, people are easily differentiated from one another; for example, a person is either female or male, either younger or older than the speaker. But in other domains, items cannot be classified absolutely. In addition, speakers may disagree about whether to include or exclude particular items in any given category. And they need to know which aspects of an entity are critical in determining the category to which the entity belongs.

In order to classify words, speakers need to know defining characteristics of each class. For example, in the United States, many people include a "whale" in the category of "fish," because whales live in the ocean and locomote by swimming, even though they are biologically mammals, giving birth to live young. The "mistake" of classifying a whale as a fish reveals that definitional criteria of category membership do not all have equal weight. Certain traits are considered by speakers to be more important than others. The most obvious facts about whales are that they look like fish, swim in the ocean, and never come ashore (unlike seals and walrus, which do come ashore). Because whales share some key diagnostic criteria of the "fish" category, they can be thought of as "fishlike."

Category membership, then, is not always absolute but frequently involves questions of degree or "fuzziness." Fuzzy sets or categories are based on the idea that "instead of just being in the set or not, an individual is in the set to a certain degree" (Lakoff 1972:185). Fuzzy category membership is often signaled linguistically in English by use of *hedges,* "words whose meaning implicitly involves fuzziness," such as "sort of, loosely speaking, somewhat, essentially" (ibid.:195–196). In the case of whales, one can say:

a.   Strictly speaking, a whale is a mammal.
b.   Loosely speaking, a whale is a fish.

In (a), a speaker focuses on primary diagnostic criteria of biological traits, whereas in (b), the speaker ignores these and instead focuses on secondary criteria of habitat and behavior. Both (a) and (b) are true statements, although

c.   Strictly speaking, a whale is a fish.
d.   Loosely speaking, a whale is a mammal.

are false.

Inherent fuzziness of hedges can also be shown by the falseness of either

e.   Strictly speaking, a robin is a bird.
f.   Loosely speaking, a robin is a bird.

Because a robin is unquestionably a bird, the sort of hedge that implies uncertainty cannot be used because the entity is a typical example of its category.

Criteria used for classification are different in different languages. For example, some languages organize noun categories on the basis of gender (masculine/feminine/neuter) or animate/inanimate distinctions. Others employ semantic criteria of form or use (Swahili, Swati) or shape and texture (Navajo; see Chapter 2). However, labels used by linguists to refer to noun classes may be misleading because they may reflect Western thinking about attributes of referents rather than accurately capture indigenous worldviews. This point has been discussed by Mo Kaa (1976) in an analysis of Algonkian languages (spoken in eastern and central North America).

Linguists usually claim that Algonkian languages (Ojibwa, Cree, Blackfoot, Cheyenne) base noun classes on a distinction between animates and inanimates. Leonard Bloomfield's influential grammar of Algonkian noted the following members of the "animate" category: "all persons, animals, spirits, and large trees, and some other objects, such as tobacco, maize, apple, raspberry, calf of leg, stomach, spittle, feather, bird's tail, horn, kettle, pipe for smoking, snowshoe" (1946:94). Although this list may seem haphazard from a Euro-American sense of "animate" (to be "alive"), Kaa suggested that the problem is not with Algonkian inconsistencies but with the failure of Western terminology to express native meanings adequately.

Kaa offered an alternative statement of Algonkian "animate" that may be less concise but more attuned to the Algonkian people's perspective: "Animate" entities are "more spiritually relevant and personalized beings, things, and phenomena" (ibid.:92). This definition embodies several important aspects of Algonkian worldview. First, it states criteria in relative rather than absolute terms, thus avoiding Western tendencies to think in polarities. Second, because the definition is relative, it recognizes that noun classifications are sensitive to contextual and individual variation, accounting for the fact that some nouns are categorized differently by different speakers. Third, it emphasizes the similarity among "beings, things, and phenomena" rather than their oppositions.

A conversation between an Ojibwa speaker and A. Irving Hallowell corroborated Kaa's description of Algonkian "animates." Hallowell was interested in discovering Ojibwa concepts of "personhood," understanding that "this category of being is by no means limited to *human* beings" (emphasis in original) (1960:22). Hallowell noted that "stones" are classed grammatically as "animates," so he asked an Ojibwa speaker: "Are *all* the stones we see about us here alive?" "No! But *some* are" was the reply (ibid.:26). In Ojibwa worldview, stones have potential for motion and can occasionally take on other animate attributes. They are most apt to do so in religious contexts, especially related to rituals associated with *Midewiwin,* an Ojibwa ceremonial and curing society. Stones, therefore, can have agency and perform actions or, to quote Kaa again, they are "spiritually relevant and personalized."

Ethnoscience

The term *ethnoscience* refers to systems of classification that people construct to organize knowledge of their universe. The term *ethnoscience* is derived from the Greek word *ethnos,* meaning "people" or "a division of people." Such systems are based on taxonomic hierarchies in which some entities are ordered hierarchically (e.g., a "spaniel" is a kind of "dog") and other entities are contrasted taxonomically (e.g., "dog" and "cat").

Studies of ethnoscientific domains in different cultures demonstrate the variety of underlying assumptions that can be used to group entities. For example, the Papago, a native people living in Arizona, divide the category of life forms into two large classes: "living things" and "plants." Living things (*háʔicu dóakam*) include (Mathiot 1962:346):

> people (*hémajkam*)
> birds (*ʔúʔuvhig*)
> animals (*háʔicu dóakam*)

Of interest in this subdivision is the fact that the label for "animal" is the same as that for "living thing." Applying an ethnolinguistic interpretation, we might assume that, for Papagos, animals are the most general exemplar of living things, whereas people and birds are distinctive.

The class of birds is divided by Papago speakers into two groups (each with its distinctive morphological marker) based on habit of flight. One group includes birds that rarely fly (quail, chicken, roadrunner) and the second group includes birds that often fly (eagle, hawk, crow, dove) (ibid.:344). The class of birds, then, is subdivided according to relative rather than absolute criteria. The fact that some birds are more likely than others to fly is considered important by Papago speakers and is directly expressed in their language. Such a dichotomy raises questions about graded categories: At what point do the classes become differentiated? Although Mathiot did not discuss this problem, one can assume that disagreement might arise among Papago speakers when classifying some birds whose habits of flying are in an intermediate range. A tangential anecdote that may reflect this quandary was given by Mathiot, who reported that a Papago man told her that he had quit his job sorting oranges because it was difficult for him to decide between good and bad oranges (ibid.:349).

The other major category in the Papago science of life forms is that of plants (*háʔicu mo vúušan*: "things that grow"). This category contains five classes (ibid.: 346):

1. trees (*háʔicu ʔúʔus*: "stick things")
2. cacti (*hóʔi*: "stickers")
3. cultivated seasonals (*háʔicu ʔéʔes*: "things planted from seeds")

4.   wild seasonals (*héjal   vúušñim*: "growing by itself")
5.   unlabeled   (wild perennials that are neither cacti nor trees and bushes)

The Papagos' system of plant science highlights their interests in environment and economy. The class of cacti is singled out, no doubt because of the preponderance of cacti in the Papagos' semidesert terrain. Seasonal plants are distinguished on the basis of their origins. Cultivated seasonals are "planted from seeds," whereas wild seasonals "grow by themselves." Finally, the category including "wild perennials which are neither cacti nor trees and bushes" is a miscellaneous class of entities that, one can assume, is of least interest to Papagos inasmuch as they do not even bother to name it.

Universal Processes: Color Terms

Rather than emphasizing linguistic and cultural differences in systems of categorization, many linguists are discovering universal principles of classification. Much attention has been given to the domain of color terminology. In a groundbreaking and influential study, *Basic Color Terms* (1969), Brent Berlin and Paul Kay presented a theory of universal color categories and their sequential development. In their study, Berlin and Kay collected color-term data from 98 languages by asking speakers to sort 329 color chips into categories that could not be subsumed within any other class. This testing procedure resulted in terms such as "red" but not "scarlet" or "maroon" because the latter two are recognized as "kinds of" red. On the basis of consultants' responses, Berlin and Kay postulated 11 basic color terms: white, black, red, green, yellow, blue, brown, purple, pink, and gray. Not all languages contain all 11 terms. By examining the content of various color systems, Berlin and Kay proposed the following evolutionary sequence, which starts on the left and incrementally incorporates colors to the right.

white	→ red →	green	→ blue →	brown	→ purple
black		yellow			pink	
					orange	
					gray	

Note that no language distinguishes less than two colors. A one-color system would actually be impossible because a classification scheme by definition must contain at least two members; that is, two items must be seen to contrast with each other. Berlin and Kay's sequence provides that if a language contains only two color terms, they are always "white" and "black." Additional terms are added in the order of development presented with examples in the following table:

Kay (1975) later revised the original sequence somewhat in order to account for the fact that certain languages—for example, Japanese, Inuktitut (Arctic Canada), Aguaruna (Peru)—encode a color of "green-blue" that may occur before labeling "yellow." Kay called this color category "GRUE" and placed it either preceding or following "yellow" in development. He noted that the category "GRUE" never splits separately into both "green" and "blue" before the naming of "yellow."

Number of Terms	Color Terms	Language
Two	white, black	Jale (New Guinea), Ngombe (Africa)
Three	white, black, red	Arawak (Caribbean), Swahili (southern Africa)
Four	white, black, red, yellow	Ibo (Nigeria), Tongan (Polynesia)
Five	white, black, red, yellow, green	Tarascan (Mexico), !Kung (southern Africa)
Six	white, black, red, yellow, green, blue	Tamil (India), Mandarin (China)
Seven	white, black, red, yellow, green, blue, brown	Nez Percé (Montana), Javanese
Eight–eleven	white, black, red, yellow, green, blue, brown, purple and/or pink and/or orange and/or gray	English, Zuni (New Mexico), Dinka (Sudan), Tagalog (Philippines), etc.

SOURCE: Compiled from Berlin and Kay 1969:152–156.

The revised sequence, then, is:

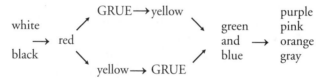

A few languages seem to necessitate further minor modifications. For example, Russian does not have a word for a single color "blue" but, rather, distinguishes "dark blue" and "light blue." However, Berlin and Kay's sequence has essentially been substantiated.

Focal Meaning and Prototypes

Berlin and Kay's work in color systems has proven to be of great significance because it raised important questions concerning universal cognitive and linguistic processes. It also uncovered complexities in the organization of classes and in understanding how speakers make discriminations. These discoveries are not limited to color terms but have wider applicability in language.

The concept of focal meaning within classes has become relevant in ethnolinguistic studies. The *focal meaning* of a word is its central sense within the whole range of meanings that it has. A word's focal meaning refers to the "best example" or "most typical example" of possible meanings that it encompasses. For instance, in color terminology, each word covers a graded range of different hues along a continuum, rather than a discrete and absolute quality; but each word also has a central meaning, a "best example." Speakers in a community agree on the focal meaning of a word, although they may well disagree about including or excluding peripheral cases in given categories. So, if asked to pick out the "best example" of "red," speakers agree on a color sometimes called "scarlet" or, colloquially, "fire-engine red." In their study, Berlin and Kay found that focal meanings of basic color terms were substantially similar in all languages, suggesting a universal color system based on physical stimuli (Kay and McDaniel 1978).

The concept of prototypes can also be generally applied in semantic analyses. A *prototype* is an idealized, internalized conceptualization of an object, quality, or activity. Real-life objects and activities are measured against these internalized concepts and are named according to how well they approximate the ideal. As Charles Fillmore stated, a prototype approach to semantics "seeks to represent the meaning of a linguistic expression, not through a statement of the necessary and sufficient conditions for membership in a category . . . but rather through the analysis of instances (or near instances) of the category in terms of approximations to the prototype" (1982:32). For example, a category such as "bird" "is identified in terms of a fixed set of conditions, but the best examples are those that are close to an idealization of that category" (ibid.:33). Therefore, although a robin, penguin, and ostrich are all kinds of birds, speakers (in our culture) agree that "robin" is closest to the prototype or idealization or, as Fillmore said, "is somehow 'birdier' than the other two" (ibid.).

In classifying concrete objects, speakers may disagree about whether to place items in given categories because they disagree about whether the items approximate enough prototypical characteristics. For instance, "prototypical" or "best example" of "chair" in North American culture is an object with four legs, a seat, back, and two armrests. Although speakers generally include an object fitting such a description in the category "chair," they may disagree about whether to include objects lacking one or another defining property.

People categorize objects based on their use as well as on physical properties. In an experimental study, William Labov showed subjects drawings of cups and cuplike containers and asked them to provide names for these objects, such as cup, mug, bowl, dish, pitcher (1973:353–355). People were then asked to imagine the same series of objects containing coffee, mashed potatoes, or flowers. Respondents were most likely to label borderline or peripheral (i.e., untypical) objects as "cups" if they contained coffee and least likely to do so if they held flowers. Labov concluded that "language is essentially a categorical device" and that in order to understand it, processes of categorization must be studied "at work" (ibid.:368).

People and activities can also be evaluated with reference to prototypical constructs. In these cases, of course, speakers depend on cultural models consisting of expectations for and evaluations of behavior. A social category of this type, illustrated by the word "bachelor," "is defined in terms of a set of conditions, but the best examples are those which are situated in a standard or prototype background setting" (Fillmore 1982:34). Although "bachelor" can be defined as an unmarried adult male, not all unmarried men would be appropriately called bachelors; a man living in a stable, conjugal relationship, a boy abandoned in a jungle and grown to maturity alone, a brain-damaged boy grown to adulthood in a coma, or the pope are examples (Quinn and Holland 1987:23). The point here is that categories like these cannot be defined abstractly but, rather, are appropriately understood only in the context of culturally shared expectations. This is what Fillmore termed a *background setting*.

Prototypes can also be used as guides in evaluating one's own or another's behavior. Because all communication occurs in cultural contexts, speakers' understanding of what is happening is often measured against prototypical constructs. Speech events, that is, instances of communicative interaction, form a domain that encompasses many kinds of genres, including conference, argument, negotiation, debate, lecture, confession, and apology. Participants evaluate ongoing behavior and form conclusions about what kind of interaction is taking place. Consensus among participants may or may not exist, depending on their perceptions of how the encounter conforms to a prototype model. Lack of consensus can also result when participants are motivated to define encounters in particular ways given their own goals and purposes—for example, people can disagree about whether they're having an argument.

These examples illustrate the importance of situating our understanding of the meaning of words and their usage in the context of culture.

CULTURAL PRESUPPOSITION

The vocabulary of a language is not merely an inventory of arbitrary labels referring to objects, entities, or events. Words also convey many kinds of cultural meanings that add to, transform, or manipulate basic senses of words. Research into these areas of meaning and usage includes investigation of cultural presuppositions, associational or extensional meanings, and uses of words to carry symbolic or ideological content.

The concept of *cultural presupposition* refers to the fact that participants in speech interactions come to encounters with an array of knowledge and understandings (models) of their culture as expressed and transmitted through language. The relevance of some of this shared knowledge is fairly obvious. For instance, if a speaker mentions the World Series, he or she assumes that listeners understand that reference is to baseball, that teams compete throughout a season, and that winners of league competitions play each other for the championship. For conversation to run smoothly, much of what speakers say depends on their accurate assessment of hearers' knowledge. These presuppositions are collected by people during their lifetime of involvement in and learning through their experiences, that is, their enculturation. Because all human experiences are cultural, a tremendous amount of accumulated but unstated knowledge is continuously carried with us.

Other kinds of cultural presuppositions are more complex, and their incorporation into meanings of words is more subtle. For example, as shown in the four sentences that opened this chapter, English and Navajo express different concepts presupposing people's (and other animate beings') rights to individual autonomy

(Young 1978). English has many terms expressing various types of coercion: cause, force, oblige, make, compel, order, command, constrain, must, have to, ought to. In contrast, the Navajo language, spoken in New Mexico and Arizona, does not contain verbs of this sort. Rather than saying "I *must* go there" or "I *have to* go there," a Navajo speaker says *ákǫ́ǫ́ deesháałgo t'éiyá yáʔ át'ééh* "it is only good that I shall go there." This construction "lacks the force of compelling necessity" (ibid.:168). Whereas English readily expresses the idea that a person has a right to impose her or his will on another animate being, Navajo again does not express direct compulsion, as seen in the contrasting sentences in English (I *make* the horse run) and Navajo (*łį́į́ shá yilghoł* "the horse is running for me"). The Navajo sentence "implies an action on the part of the horse that is essentially voluntary, . . . lacking the important overtone of coercive authority" (ibid.).

In order to use and interpret words appropriately, speakers make assumptions about each other's intentions, desires, or goals. For example, "joking" and "insulting" speech share certain important features; a speaker may "joke" or "insult" an addressee by pointing out the latter's mistakes, weaknesses, or inappropriate behavior. The difference between jokes and insults lies primarily in the speaker's perceived intent that she or he must make clear through choice of word, tone of voice, and/or facial expression. Interpretations of intent rely on cultural and social norms as well, because appropriate topics or targets of joking are determined by culture. In some societies people never joke with or tease their parents, whereas in other societies such behavior could be acceptable in certain contexts but not in others.

Cultural norms of communicative behavior also involve presuppositions. In our society, when two acquaintances meet, they may use such greetings as "Hi! How are you?" or "What's happening?" If a speaker uses the greeting "How are you," does he actually want a substantive answer to this question? In casual encounters between acquaintances, a response that reveals personal problems or serious illness would be considered highly inappropriate. In order for a participant to behave in an acceptable manner, he has to know the social purposes of particular words or utterances. In this example, speakers must know that an utterance that has been expressed in interrogative form is actually not intended as a question, that is, a request for information. Rather, it is a routinized request for a routinized response.

Words can also be used to convey symbolic meanings expressing cultural values and shared assumptions. For example, describing a group of people as "terrorists" expresses a strongly negative judgment against them. The power of language is not only that values attached to words reveal attitudes of speakers but also that words are used to create compatible attitudes in hearers. Labeling someone as a "terrorist" is, in part, an attempt to influence hearers' opinions about this person because "terrorism" is an act that is socially condemned. In contrast, describing a person as a "freedom fighter" attempts to create a positive response.

Advertisers of products in our society (and presumably in many others as well) make use of an interrelated constellation of words and symbols that rely on and reinforce underlying cultural presuppositions. Advertisements often describe products as "new," "bigger," and "improved." These seemingly innocuous words reveal central themes of change and progress. An unstated assumption links concepts of newness and bigness with advances over both items previously produced by the same company and those of competitors.

These are concepts implicit in commodity production, marketing, and consumerism. They are also interconnected with philosophical ideas of evolution. Life-forms are dynamic and ever-changing and lead naturally to better ("improved") versions. Change is conceived of as competitive based on analogies with biological processes—that is, organisms compete for econiches, resulting in "survival of the fittest." These ideas of change are so commonplace in our society that we take them to be natural, inherent in entities and processes themselves rather than understand that they are cultural constructs. Because change is "naturally" an advance, innovations are assumed to be desirable improvements. Advertisements that stress the diversity of products within a competitive environment have not created this imagery but, rather, exploit it. Repetitive exposure to such use of language reinforces overt and covert cultural messages implied and presupposed by the words.

All language use has a manipulative aspect to it in the sense that speakers employ words in order to have an effect on hearers, such as to convey information, ask questions, or issue commands. But the words chosen are often not neutral in their connotations. They have associated senses that presuppose culturally shared symbolic meanings. Cultural symbols are transmitted through language and obtain their strength because speakers/hearers nonconsciously accept their indirectly expressed assumptions. The power of language to convey social messages is recognized, for instance, by many American women who object to being called "girl" or by African-American men who object to being called "boy."

Because of the covert symbolic aspect of language, it is difficult to understand the full range of meanings expressed by speakers in another culture. In order to gain insights into a people's worldview or system of values, it is necessary to ascertain the cultural symbols embedded in their words. This is one reason why translation from one language into another is never completely accurate. Words in isolation can be translated, but the full sense of those words in context cannot be easily or succinctly conveyed.

EXTENDED AND TRANSFERRED MEANING

Metaphor and Metonymy

Cultural meanings are additionally expressed through complex processes of semantic extension and transfer. One such process is that of *metaphor*. Metaphors are based on unstated comparisons between entities or events that share certain features. The comparisons implicitly highlight similarities while ignoring contrasts. According to George Lakoff and Mark Johnson, "[T]he essence of metaphor is understanding and experiencing one kind of thing in terms of another" (1980:5). Analysis of recurring metaphors in a language reveals underlying concepts that help construct the reality or worldview of speakers. In a statement consistent with writings of Sapir and Whorf, Lakoff and Johnson explain that "[c]ultural assumptions, values and attitudes are not a conceptual overlay that we may or may not place upon experience as we choose. It would be more correct to say that all experience is cultural . . . we experience our 'world' in such a way that our culture is already present in the very experience itself" (ibid.:57). They also argue that analyses of metaphor provide insights into cultural constructions of reality because "our ordinary conceptual system, in terms of which we both think and act, is fundamentally metaphorical in nature" (ibid.:3).

An example from their work that illustrates a frequent construct in English is the pervasive theme "Time is money" (ibid.:7–9). This concept is embedded in these statements:

> You don't use your time *profitably.*
> How do you *spend* your time these days?
> This gadget will *save* you hours.

These expressions are based on metaphors that treat intangible entities or qualities as though they were concrete objects. In our conceptual model, we conceive of "time" as a particular kind of object or commodity. "Time in our culture is a valuable commodity. It is a limited resource that we use to accomplish our goals. . . . Thus we understand and experience time as the kind of thing that can be spent, wasted, budgeted, invested wisely or poorly, saved or squandered" (ibid.:8).

Another recurring metaphorical construct discussed by Lakoff and Johnson is the orientational opposition between "up" and "down." Activities or states viewed positively are expressed as "up"; those evaluated negatively are expressed as "down" (ibid.:15–17). The following list presents some of these comparisons:

	Up	*Down*
Emotions:	You're in *high* spirits.	He's feeling *low* today.
Consciousness:	Wake *up!*	She *sank* into a coma.
Health:	He's in *top* shape.	Her health is *declining.*
Control:	I'm *on top* of the situation.	He *fell* from power.
Status:	She'll *rise* to the *top.*	He's at the *bottom* of society.
Virtuousness:	He's *high*-minded.	I wouldn't *stoop* to that.

The English language characteristically employs lineal metaphors to describe many different kinds of events. Common expressions include trace a relationship, follow a line of thought, set a course of action, follow the direction of an argument, bridge a gap in conversation. Certain ways of talking indicate that lineal order is positively valued in our society: line up support for one's cause, set the record straight, keep someone in line, straighten up! Additionally, contrasting expressions reveal cultural attitudes; "keeping to the straight and narrow" is virtuous, whereas "wandering from the path" is suspect. Similarly, in conversation, "getting straight to the point" is desirable in our society, but "talking around an issue" or "beating around the bush" indicates deception.

Another type of metaphoric construction common in English is the use of container images when depicting nonphysical entities or processes. This pattern is consistent with tendencies in English to make objects out of intangibles. Once a nonconcrete entity is transformed into an object, it can be contained, entered, left, held, or the like. Use of locative prepositions (prepositions that denote location, direction, or movement in regard to an object) often signals this type of metaphor:

> He's *out of* his mind.
> They're *in* love.
> I feel *under* the weather.

In these expressions, subjects are depicted "as if" they were in some physical relation to a defined and contained space, for example, to be *in* love. Here, "love," an internal emotion, is transformed into a tangible object and then treated as if it were an objectified and tangible place on the model of actual physical space, such as "they're in the house."

Every language has characteristic conceptual metaphors that structure not only the language itself but also particular views of reality that speakers share and unconsciously assume. For example, in the Navajo language, the categorization of motion is a major focus of the verb system. Dozens of verbs denote specific aspects of movement and/or of objects affected by motion. Most importantly, many kinds of events are described with verbs having the theme of movement as their focal meaning. That is, Navajo uses metaphors of motion in "understanding and experiencing" the world. The following list of verbs with their Navajo meanings demonstrates this pervasive metaphor (Hoijer 1951:116–117):

one dresses:	one moves into clothing (*ʔé:h-há:h*)
one lives:	one moves about here and there (*ná-há:h*)
one is young:	one moves about newly (*ʔánį:-nà-há*)
to sing:	to move words out of an enclosed space (*ha-di-ʔà:h*)
to greet someone with a message:	to move a round solid object to meet someone (*o-dá:h-ʔà:h*)

A special type of metaphor occurring in many languages is *personification*— the process of attributing animate or human qualities to nonliving entities or events. Here are some examples from English:

> High prices are *eating up* my paycheck.
> Anxiety is *killing* him.
> The window *looks out* over the mountains.

These sentences are semantically inconsistent or anomalous in a literal sense, but they are transformed into culturally acceptable expressions through metaphor. In the last sentence, an inanimate object, window, is interpreted "as if" it were capable of an action, looking, which is inherently possible only for animate beings. In the other expressions, intangible processes are likewise treated as though they were concrete animate beings and therefore able to eat or kill.

Metonymy, another type of semantic transfer, is the substitution of one entity by another based on their shared occurrence in context rather than similarity of their attributes. It is a process of replacing one entity with another, not because one is treated "as if" it were another (metaphor), but because one is taken to "stand for" the other on the basis of some contextual relationship. Metonymic transfers highlight one aspect of an entity by decomposing the totality of the object or person and singling out one of its attributes. Associations between two entities may be of various kinds, including substitution of part of an object to represent the whole, producer for the object produced, or object used or owned by someone for the user/owner. Some examples from English are the following:

> This business needs some new blood.
> > (part for whole: blood for person)
> She likes to read Thomas Hardy.
> > (producer for product: author for books written by him)
> The '54 Chevy lives around the corner.
> > (object for owner: car for owner of car)

In these sentences, one object stands for another with which it is contextually related, so that the phrase "the '54 Chevy" substitutes for the person who owns it. Use of metonymy may stress a speaker's particular interest in an entity; for example, the most important aspect of the speaker's neighbor is that she owns a '54 Chevy. Whereas metaphor adds to the meaning of words by increasing their semantic range through comparisons with other entities, metonymy narrows the semantic focus by highlighting only one aspect of an entity and ignoring its other attributes.

Metaphors of Kinship

In an analysis of extended and transferred meanings, each association of linguistic form and cultural content necessitates its own culturally based interpretation. However, certain domains tend to be extended metaphorically and/or metonymically in many languages. Kinship terminology is one such domain. *Kin terms* are frequently used to refer metaphorically to nonrelatives. In our society, in some families children call close friends of their parents by kin terms, usually "aunt" or "uncle." For these families, it is considered impolite for a child to call an adult by first name. But calling one's parents' close friend by title + last name, such as "Ms. Smith" or "Mr. Jones," appears highly formal and distant. The compromise of extending kin terms, such as "Aunt Susan" or "Uncle John," expresses informality and intimacy of a relationship without being rude. An adult is spoken about (or spoken to) "as if" she or he were a relative. For some speakers, the kin terms "brother" and "sister" are used in political, social, or religious contexts. Sisters and brothers are equals, share experiences of life, and owe each other reciprocal respect and support.

Another example of metaphoric extension of kin terms comes from the Navajo language. The morpheme for "mother" {-ma} is used to refer to the following entities: mother, the earth, agricultural fields, corn, sheep, and Changing Woman (a major Navajo deity) (Witherspoon 1975:15–16). These meanings are connected by a constellation of symbols of motherhood. In Navajo culture, the primary social and emotional bond is that between mother and child. Mother and child are linked through birth and nurturance. A mother gives life to her child and then continually safeguards that life with physical and emotional support.

The metaphor of motherhood is extended to the earth and agricultural fields because they share an essential attribute of mothers; they are fertile and bring forth life, in the form of plants and foods. By giving birth to plants and foods, the earth and fields nurture and sustain human beings. Metaphoric reference to corn and sheep is based on their economic importance to Navajos. Corn is their most important crop and the basis of traditional subsistence. Sheep are of great cultural significance, both as source of income and as measurement of personal wealth. For all these reasons, then, corn and sheep sustain Navajo people "as if" they were mothers. Finally, metaphoric use of "mother" to refer to the deity Changing Woman combines fertility and nurturing themes of motherhood. In Navajo myths, Changing Woman came into being at a time of chaos when people were not able to reproduce. The first puberty rite was conducted for her so that she could menstruate and become fertile. Afterward, she created the original Navajo clans from pieces of her skin. And she gave corn to the people, thus contributing to their daily sustenance. This myth expresses complex meanings linking Changing Woman's being, her fertility, and her actions to the birth and survival of Navajo people. She is, therefore, a quintessential metaphor of motherhood.

Kinship terms (as well as other words) can be affected by multiple processes of semantic transfer, demonstrating the richness of language's creative possibilities. Meanings of the word *amma* (mother) in Kannada, a Dravidian language spoken by some 26 million people in India, are interconnected by complex processes of extension and transfer (Bean 1975). *Amma* has the focal meaning of "mother" but is extended through metaphor to refer to any adult woman and to goddesses. *Amma* is also used as a metonym in reference to smallpox. In order to appreciate the consistency of these meanings of *amma,* we need to understand the cultural implications of adulthood and the belief systems of Hindus.

According to Susan Bean, the word *amma* is extended to any adult woman, especially in polite speech, because in rural Indian society all adult women are assumed to be married and, therefore, assumed to be mothers (ibid.:320–321). All women, therefore, are addressed "as if" they were mothers. The metaphor of "mother" is also extended to Hindu goddesses, who are either benevolent and nurturing or fierce and dangerous (ibid.:323–324). Benevolent goddesses are "like" one's mother and dangerous goddesses are spoken of "as if" they were mother in order to appease and placate them so that by treating them respectfully they will respond with kindness (like a mother). Finally, the word *amma* can be used in a metonymic transfer to refer to smallpox. The metonym results from a believed association between certain goddesses and smallpox (ibid.:324). Because the deities can cause and cure smallpox, they have become linguistically linked to the disease. The word *amma,* which was first extended through metaphor to "goddess," is then substituted through metonymy for "smallpox."

Metaphors of the Body

Another underlying metaphor found commonly in languages is the use of body-part terms to describe actions or states or to label inanimate objects. The latter process can entail personification, as in "leg of a table" or "arm of a chair." These items of furniture are depicted "as if" their physical structure were analogous to a human body. In English, we also use body-part imagery in more complex verbal expressions, such as

> Let's get to the *heart* of the matter.
> She's willing to *face* her problem.
> She *shoulders* many responsibilities.
> The criminal *fingered* his accomplice.
> *Head* for the hills!

Widespread use of corporeal metaphors probably results from the fact that human beings give central importance to their own bodies. We extend the imagery of body to inanimate objects and to descriptions of activities. It is a process of observing and experiencing the world through human eyes and, by analogy, with human form.

Many languages use body-part terms to describe activities or noncorporeal entities. In Zapotec, a language spoken in Oaxaca, Mexico, the human body provides the prototypical model for describing parts of any animate being or inanimate object (MacLaury 1989). The bodies of all animals are named from the perspective of human anatomy. For example, the front legs of a four-legged animal are called "hand" and the hind legs are called "foot." An animal is described "as if" it were a person walking on all fours (ibid.:121). In addition, human body-part names are extended metaphorically to describe inanimate objects by the following analogies:

> top = head   (*gɨk*)
> front = belly   (*làʔáyn*)
> upper front = face   (*lò*)
> lower front = foot   (*yeʔe*)
> back = back   (*tīč*)
> side = side   (*koʔo*)
> underneath = bottom, buttocks   (*gɨ̂t*)

entrance, opening = mouth, lips   (*roʔo*)
inside = stomach   (*laʔayn*)

Note: The pitch markings on vowels follow these conventions: (′) extra high; (ˋ) high; (ˉ) low; (unmarked) extra low; (ˆ) extra high-high.

Figures 3.1 to 3.4 illustrate Zapotec human body-part terms and their analogous meanings related to various animate and inanimate entities. Figure 3.1 shows the words for human body parts, and Figure 3.2 their application to an animal.

Body-part terms are applied to containers in Figure 3.3. The top of a box is called "head," front is "face," back is "back," inside is "stomach," and bottom is "foot."

Figure 3.4 shows body-part terms applied to a jar or round container. Lid is "head," inside is "stomach," rim is "mouth/lips," outside front surface is "belly," and bottom is either "foot" or "buttocks."

In Zapotec, the words for "stomach" (*laʔayn*) and "face" (*lō*) are further extended and used to refer to inside/outside surfaces of any object. For example, in the sentence "He grabbed a club and kept banging (*the outside of*) the bell," Zapotec speakers say "*face* bell" and in "The children are playing *in* the hammock," they say "*stomach* hammock" (ibid.:142–143). Here are two further examples (C = completive aspect; H = habitual-continuative aspect):

g-aʔa	*yag*	*r-kʷ eʔe-n*	*lō*	*gib*
C-grab	wood	H-beat-he	*face*	metal

He grabbed a club and kept banging (*the outside of*) the bell.

leʔe	*taʔa*	*ndoʔo*	*r-git*	*laʔayn*	*gišto*
subject	plural	child	H-play	*stomach*	hammock

The children are playing *in* the hammock.

Nearby indigenous languages belonging to the Mixtecan family also extend body-part terms, endowing them with many complex meanings (Hollenbach 1995). As in the semantic processes demonstrated in Zapotec, the words for "face" and "foot" are used for analogous parts of inanimate objects and for the space that "projects out from that part," or what Hollenbach calls "projecting space" (1995:171). Examples of "projecting space" for "face" include "the *front surface* of the house," "the *area in front* of the house"; examples for "foot" include "the *base* of the tree," "the *space near the foot* of the tree." In addition, words for "face" and "foot" are extended into temporal domains. That is, the spatial use of "face" to refer to "place (where)" has become the temporal "time (when)" and the spatial use of "foot" to refer to "bottom of" has become the temporal "beginning of" (ibid.:172). The Mixtecan words are further extended metaphorically so that "face" can mean "if," while "foot" can mean "basis for," "about," and "because." Hollenbach suggests that "the mechanism by which these extensions take place involves metaphorical mapping from one conceptual domain to another" (ibid.). Examples translated from various Mixtecan languages include

[handwritten note: Metanomy - Substituting "He for hamburger"]

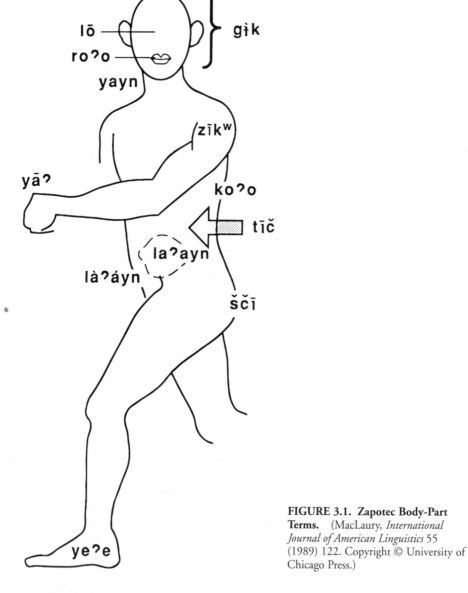

FIGURE 3.1. Zapotec Body-Part Terms. (MacLaury, *International Journal of American Linguistics* 55 (1989) 122. Copyright © University of Chicago Press.)

"face": the *top surface* of the table; the *right side* of the fabric; the *cutting edge* of the knife; the *area in front of* the house; God's *presence* (the *space within the view* of God); you won't answer at the *time when* I speak; I'll go see *if* I can't get a rabbit; he threw it *into* the fire; he borrowed the chair *from* John; you're bigger *than* I am; he gave advice *to* Peter;

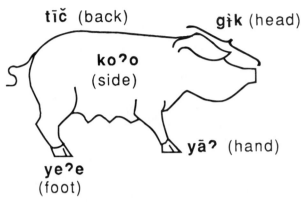

FIGURE 3.2. Zapotec Terms Applied to Animals. (MacLaury, *International Journal of American Linguistics* 55 (1989) 123. Copyright © University of Chicago Press.)

"foot": the *foundation* of the house; the *base* of the tree; the *beginning* of the week; there is more *basis* for using cassettes than books; we will work *for the benefit of* our children; we are talking *about* our town; he received money *in exchange for* corn; they cheated me *because* I was naïve.

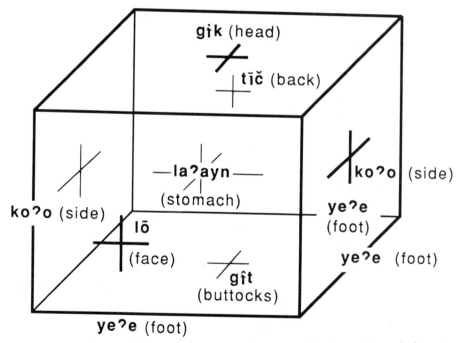

FIGURE 3.3. Zapotec Terms Applied to Boxes. (MacLaury, *International Journal of American Linguistics* 55 (1989) 124. Copyright © University of Chicago Press.)

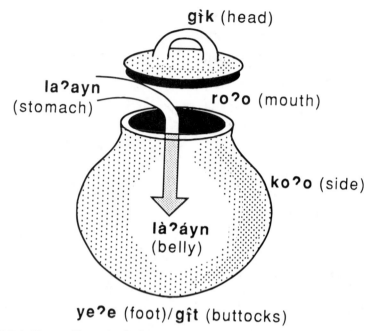

gɨk (head)

laʔayn
(stomach)

roʔo (mouth)

koʔo (side)

làʔáyn
(belly)

yeʔe (foot)/**gɨ̂t** (buttocks)

FIGURE 3.4. Zapotec Terms Applied to Jars. (MacLaury, *International Journal of American Linguistics* 55 (1989) 125. Copyright © University of Chicago Press.)

The Mohawk language frequently uses the noun morpheme for "body," {-*yaʔt*-}, in verbs with metaphoric meaning. Some examples are the following (Bonvillain 1989:346–347):

> I had a nightmare: it pressed, squeezed my body.
> *ũ-k-yaʔt-ò:lalak-eʔ*
> DEF-I-body-press, squeeze-ASP

> He judged it, weighed it: he cut the body in half.
> *waʔ-t-ha-yaʔt-ò:leht-eʔ*
> DEF-two-he-body-cut in half-ASP

> She's grown up now: her body is completed, her body is full.
> *ye-yaʔt-aná:nʌ̃-ʔ*
> she-body-full, complete-ASP
> (DEF = definite mode; ASP = aspect marker.)

Other metaphoric constructions in Mohawk employ specific body-part terms, such as (Bonvillain 1990):

> I'll kill him: I'll break his brains.
> *ʌ̃-hi-nũʔwal-yà:k-hũ*
> future-I:him-brains-break-ASP

You're crazy: Your brain is stirred, mixed.
te-se-nũʔ wal-awʌ́:lye-ʔ
two-you-brains-stir, mix-ASP

I choked her: I broke her breath in two pieces.
waʔ-khe-hṹl-yaʔk-eʔ
DEF-I:her-breath-break in two-ASP

I take her advice: I stand up my inner ear to her.
khey-at-ahṹhsa-t-eʔ
I:her-self-inner ear-stand up-ASP

Human senses frequently provide the basis for metaphoric constructs. In English, the visual sense is particularly prone to such uses, as in "I see what you mean" or "that was an insightful remark"; or in a nice combination of visual, lineal, and bodily metaphors: "I can see where this argument is heading." The term *worldview* also derives from this same underlying sensory concept.

SUMMARY

Cultural models provide frameworks for understanding the physical and social worlds we live in. These models are implicitly and explicitly transmitted through language. Therefore, linguistic analyses, particularly of words and expressions, reveal underlying assumptions, interests, and values.

Several different kinds of ethnolinguistic evidence contribute to an understanding of associations between language and cultural meaning. First, degrees of specialization and principles of classification within semantic domains indicate cultural interest and discrimination. Second, focal meanings of words and prototypes of categories demonstrate the ways that people make sense of the multitude of objects and events in their world. And third, the symbolic content of language, expressed in words and in metaphoric extensions, transmits and reinforces complex social and cultural messages.

REFERENCES

BEAN, SUSAN. 1975. Referential and indexical meanings of *amma* in Kannada: Mother, woman, goddess, pox and help! *Journal of Anthropological Research* 31:313–330.

BERLIN, BRENT, AND PAUL KAY. 1969. *Basic Color Terms: Their Universality and Evolution.* Berkeley: University of California Press.

BLOOMFIELD, LEONARD. 1946. Algonquian. In *Linguistic Structures of Native America,* ed. H. Hoijer. Publications in Anthropology No. 6. New York: Viking Fund, pp. 85–129.

BONVILLAIN, NANCY. 1989. Body, mind and idea: Semantics of noun incorporation in Akwesasne Mohawk.

International Journal of American Linguistics 55:341–358.

BONVILLAIN, NANCY. 1990. Noun incorporation and metaphor: Semantic process in Akwesasne Mohawk. *Anthropological Linguistics* 32:173–194.

FILLMORE, CHARLES. 1982. Towards a descriptive framework for spatial deixis. In *Speech, Place and Action,* ed. R. J. Jarvella and W. Klein. New York: Wiley, pp. 31–59.

GOODENOUGH, WARD. 1956. Componential analysis and the study of meaning. *Language* 32:195–216.

GOODENOUGH, WARD. 1965. Yankee kinship terminology: A problem in componential analysis. In *Formal Semantic Analysis,* ed. E. Hammel. *American Anthropologist* 67:259–287.

HALLOWELL, A. IRVING. 1960. Ojibwa ontology, behavior and world view. In *Culture in History: Essays in Honor of Paul Radin,* ed. S. Diamond. New York: Columbia University Press, pp. 19–52.

HOIJER, HARRY. 1951. Cultural implications of some Navaho linguistic categories. *Language* 27:111–120.

HOLLENBACH, BARBARA. 1995. Semantic and syntactic extensions of body-part terms in Mixtecan. *International Journal of American Linguistics* 61, no. 2:168–190.

KAA, MO. 1976. The logic of non-European linguistic categories. In *Universalism versus Relativism in Language and Thought: Proceedings of a Colloquium on the Sapir-Whorf Hypothesis,* ed. R. Pinxten. The Hague: Mouton, pp. 85–96.

KAY, PAUL. 1975. Synchronic variability and diachronic change in basic color terms. *Language in Society* 4:257–270.

KAY, PAUL, AND CHAD MCDANIEL. 1978. The linguistic significance of the meanings of basic color terms. *Language* 54:610–646.

LABOV, WILLIAM. 1973. The boundaries of words and their meanings. In *New Ways of Analyzing Variation in English,* ed. C. Bailey and R. Shuy. Washington, DC: Georgetown University Press, pp. 340–373.

LAKOFF, GEORGE. 1972. Hedges: A study in meaning criteria and the logic of fuzzy concepts. *Papers from the 8th Regional Meeting of the Chicago Linguistic Society.* Chicago: Chicago Linguistic Society, pp. 183–228.

LAKOFF, GEORGE, AND MARK JOHNSON. 1980. *Metaphors We Live By.* Chicago: University of Chicago Press.

LOUNSBURY, FLOYD. 1964. The structural analysis of kinship semantics. In *Proceedings of the IXth International Congress of Linguists,* ed. H. Lunt. The Hague: Mouton, pp. 1073–1093.

MACLAURY, ROBERT. 1989. Zapotec body-part locatives: Prototypes and metaphoric extensions. *International Journal of American Linguistics* 55:119–154.

MATHIOT, MADELEINE. 1962. Noun classes and folk taxonomy in Papago. *American Anthropologist* 64:340–350.

QUINN, NAOMI, AND DOROTHY HOLLAND. 1987. Culture and cognition. In *Cultural Models of Language and Thought,* ed. D. Holland and N. Quinn. New York: Cambridge University Press, pp. 3–40.

SAPIR, EDWARD. 1949a (1912). Language and environment. In *Selected Writings of Edward Sapir,* ed. D. Mandelbaum. Berkeley: University of California Press, pp. 89–103.

SAPIR, EDWARD. 1949b (1929). The status of linguistics as a science. In *Selected*

Writings of Edward Sapir, ed. D. Mandelbaum. Berkeley: University of California Press, pp. 160–166.

VOLOSINOV, V. N. 1973 (1929). *Marxism and the Philosophy of Language.* Cambridge, MA: Harvard University Press.

WHORF, BENJAMIN. 1956a (1941). A linguistic consideration of thinking in primitive communities. In *Language, Thought and Reality,* ed. J. B. Carroll. Cambridge, MA: MIT Press, pp. 65–86.

WHORF, BENJAMIN. 1956b (1941). The relation of habitual thought and behavior to language. In *Language, Thought and Reality,* ed. J. B. Carroll. Cambridge, MA: MIT Press, pp. 134–159.

WITHERSPOON, GARY. 1975. *Navajo Kinship and Marriage.* Chicago: University of Chicago Press.

WITKOWSKI, STANLEY, AND CECIL BROWN. 1983. Marking-reversals and cultural importance. *Language* 59:569–582.

YOUNG, ROBERT. 1978. English as a second language for Navajos. In *A Pluralistic Nation,* ed. M. Lourie and N. Conklin. Rowley, MA: Newbury House, pp. 162–172.

4

Contextual Components:
Outline of an Ethnography
of Communication

"Would you be so kind as to pass the salt?"
"Gimme the salt!"

These sentences demonstrate a basic fact about language use: Alternative means can be used to achieve the same goal (in this case, obtaining salt). These sentences might be employed by different speakers and/or by the same speaker in different contexts. Variation in ways of speaking stems both from segmentation of the speech community into groups based on class, gender, race, and the like, and from differences in the contexts of speech events. In this chapter we explore language use as it is influenced by the context of speech events (we will analyze factors of community segmentation in subsequent chapters). We examine various features of setting, participants, topics, and goals as they influence how people speak in any given encounter. We end the chapter with a discussion of some types of speech acts.

ETHNOGRAPHY OF COMMUNICATION

Speech behavior should be analyzed in its widest cultural and social context in order to discover culturally relevant features of variation. An *ethnography of communication* (Hymes 1974) includes descriptions of all explicit and implicit norms for communication, detailing aspects of verbal, nonverbal, and social parameters of interaction. To quote Dell Hymes: "The starting point is the ethnographic analysis of the communicative conduct of a community" (1974:9). Hymes lists several components of communication requiring description: (1) participants, minimally speaker and addressee; (2) code used by interlocutors; (3) channel (e.g., speaking, writing, nonverbal signals); (4) setting or context; (5) form or genre (e.g., conversation, folktale, chant, debate); (6) topics and attitudes (ibid.:10).

In analyzing communicative events, primary consideration should be given to functions of speech. We need to recognize that there are many ways to achieve similar purposes, as in the two ways of requesting salt noted at the beginning of this chapter. We also need to recognize that any linguistic form may serve different functions. For example, the utterance "How are you?" can be a legitimate question if spoken by a close friend, or it may be a simple routine greeting.

All cultures provide rules for appropriate communicative interaction, defining behaviors that *should* occur, that *may* occur, and that *should not* occur in given contexts. These rules are learned through both formal and informal processes of socialization that begin in childhood. Children may be overtly instructed about how to act and what to say (or not say) in particular places or to particular people—for example, "Say 'thank you' to the nice lady" or "Don't shout in the bus!" But children learn most rules of appropriate communicative behavior from their own observations of family, peers, and even strangers in public places. Interactional norms are specific to each society and convey cultural messages of shared values and expectations. We use these guidelines to shape our own behavior and to evaluate actions of others.

An ethnographic approach to analyzing communication stresses the cultural specificity of rules of communication and the totality of factors needing description. The most important aspects are settings, participants, topics, and goals. Each of these components can be studied separately, but it should be remembered that a speech event is an integrated occurrence and all of its components are interdependent. Relative primacy of any one factor depends on speakers' assessment of the entire situation and their judgment of likely outcomes. Certain behaviors tend to co-occur in given contexts and lead to an overall sense of consistency or coherence. For instance, speech actions in contexts designated as formal often take place in specified settings, among expected participants, and concern relatively fixed topics. A brief sketch of court proceedings in the United States provides a good example of the interconnectedness of factors.

1. *Setting:* Trials or hearings are communicative events that occur in particular settings, namely, courtrooms. The courtroom itself has a structural design separating seating areas for various categories of participants and orienting them in relation to one another.

2. *Participants:* Participants include judges, lawyers, defendants and plaintiffs, witnesses, jurors, spectators, and court officials. Each participant's behavior is conditioned by his or her role. The judge is singled out by her or his seating position in the front, usually on a raised platform, of the courtroom and by special attire. The judge clearly controls communicative behavior of the other participants, each of whom has certain obligations to speak or not to speak. In fact, failure to speak when so directed and failure to be silent otherwise are legally punishable offenses ("contempt of court"). Only judges, lawyers, and witnesses may speak publicly. Other participants (jurors, spectators, officers) must remain silent. Specific discourse patterns are expected

of each type of participant. Lawyers may make introductory and concluding statements or ask questions. Witnesses answer questions. Judges have greater latitude in the kinds of speech appropriate for them; they can make statements, ask questions, issue commands, and make rulings.

3. *Topics:* Topics of discussion are rigidly defined. The communicative event is about "something," and all speech behavior must be relevant to that issue. Rights of participants to introduce or change topics are narrowly limited, and permission must be asked of the judge (and granted) in order to incorporate extraneous speech. In lawyers' questioning of witnesses, it must be clear that questions are relevant to the central issue or are a logical development from it. Similarly, witnesses' answers must be germane to the topic. Judges have some flexibility in topic choice, but they, too, are limited by the overall focus.

4. *Goals:* Goals of participants vary according to their role in the proceeding. Speakers choose words, tone of voice, facial expression, gesture, and so on, to accomplish their purpose. For example, the judge must appear impartial, lawyers speak and act aggressively, defendants portray themselves as innocent, witnesses appear honest and reliable, and jurors remain silent but convey interest in the speech and behavior of others.

Although communicative events taking place in informal interactions are not as highly structured as are court proceedings, they, too, are constrained by cultural norms of roles, rights to speak, and ways of speaking. However, rules governing informal behavior are rarely objectified by participants and are not consciously stated or even recognized. We usually assume that behavior in these contexts is "natural," although it is in fact conditioned by our culture just as much as activities in formal settings.

The notion of an "ethnography of communication" is relevant also to analyzing informal communicative behavior. Underlying and unstated rules become evident by observing variation in actions and speaking styles. Reactions by individuals to ongoing behavior, showing either approval or disapproval, likewise indicate cultural norms. We generally become most aware of informal communicative norms when they are violated, that is, when someone speaks inappropriately. Then we can evaluate the "mistake" against our culturally shared models of appropriate behavior. Needless to say, all people make errors in communication, although, on the whole, they act in accordance with their society's expectations. Speakers' errors often come from misjudging the relative importance of given components within speech events—that is, misjudging the weight of settings, participants, topics, and goals in framing one's speech style, choice of words, and nonverbal cues.

SETTINGS

Settings of communicative events provide arenas for action, both in a physical and a social sense. They help define events as particular kinds of occasions, invoking certain behaviors and restricting others. Settings for communication can be classified along a continuum of formality or informality. Although people in all societies make distinctions about relative formality/informality, the array of settings in each category differs across cultures.

After reviewing descriptions of formal events in many cultures, Judith Irvine suggested that the following four *aspects of formality* are universal: increased structuring, consistency of co-occurrence choices, emphasis on positional identities of participants, and emergence of a central situational focus (1979:776–779). Increased structuring of formal events is reflected in rules of etiquette that influence participants' attire and demeanor as well as their speech. Markers of formality may include features of pronunciation, intonation, facial expression, grammar, and vocabulary, with tendencies to use more prestigeful or "correct" speech and to appear "serious." Rights of participants to speak may be curtailed or directed into certain kinds of exchanges and turn-takings. Our example of courtroom proceedings demonstrates these principles of event structuring.

Participants in formal events tend to make stylistic choices that are highly consistent with the overall theme of "seriousness" appropriate to the occasion. People rarely make jokes, tease, or use expletives in highly formal situations, although they may be free to do so at other times.

Irvine's third aspect of formality refers to the social identities of participants. All people have multiple roles or identities: parent, friend, teacher, president of an organization. Formal situations define people by their "positional and public" rather than "personal" identities (ibid.:778). By invoking public roles, social distance rather than intimacy is stressed. An emphasis on positional identities is often reflected linguistically in forms of address. For instance, a married couple working together as doctors in a shared office are unlikely to address or refer to each other by first name in the presence of patients but instead use socially distancing forms such as Dr. Smith. They would be unlikely in this context to call each other "Honey" or to use any other term of endearment normally appropriate in their private interactions.

Finally, formal situations tend to focus on specific issues and happenings. This aspect of events typically is reflected in constraints on topic choice and in restrictions on speakers' rights to change or introduce elements. For example, during religious ceremonies in our culture, speech is limited by participants' roles. Ceremonies are centered on particular rites, and most speech is highly predetermined, with few, if any, opportunities for shifts of focus. Even when delivering sermons or other individualized speech, speakers must keep within narrow guidelines of topic and topic relevance.

Norms for communicative behavior in informal settings are much more diffuse and flexible, although participants always assess speech and nonverbal actions according to cultural models of appropriateness. Structuring of informal situations is relatively loose. Speakers are able to select stylistic features of pronunciation, grammar, and vocabulary based on their individual habits and preferences rather than on dictates of the situation. Conversational patterns likewise are usually adaptable and spontaneous, given general cultural constraints. Topics also shift frequently within encounters and are dependent upon interlocutors' interests.

PARTICIPANTS

As we turn now to analyses of additional components of communicative events, the guidelines of ethnography remind us of the interrelatedness of factors and of the diversity of cultural norms of behavior. Participants, topics, and goals are constrained by settings and overall contexts, but not in a linear manner. Rather, people choose ways of speaking after evaluating an entire communicative and social situation.

Participants in speech events include speakers, addressees, and audience. Individuals usually change roles during a given event. In two-party conversations, each person is alternatively speaker or addressee as they exchange speaking turns. Only in the most formal occasions, such as religious ceremonies, public speeches, or lectures, does one person monopolize all (or nearly all) of the rights to speak. Even in these events, audiences have a communicative role to play by making appropriate responses to the speech of officiators.

People make choices about language use based on characteristics of other participants in a speech event. Such choices include many aspects of linguistic and nonverbal behavior:

1. *Pronunciation:* distinctiveness of articulation
2. *Prosodic features of intonation:* velocity (speed of speaking), volume (loudness/softness)
3. *Syntax:* complexity or simplicity of word order, phrase construction, and so on
4. *Choice of words*
5. *Nonverbal cues:* facial expression, eye contact, touch, physical distancing

Speakers determine, usually nonconsciously, which communicative features are most appropriate given the person(s) to whom they are speaking. So, if someone is a victim of a fender-bender episode, words chosen to describe the incident and the perpetrator will likely be different in recounting the event to one's friends or grandparents. Adult speech directed toward children typically consists of short, common words and simple sentence construction. And speaking to students in a lecture hall requires increases in loudness and decreases in speed as compared to normal forms of speech.

In addition to these linguistic features, choice of topic also depends on the speaker's awareness of cultural and individual expectations. Certain topics will be selected for discussion with some people but not when conversing with others. In our society, it is considered highly inappropriate to talk about one's personal problems to a stranger or even to a casual acquaintance. Indeed, such topic selection would likely be evaluated as a symptom of a psychological disorder.

Finally, norms of conversational interaction are patterned in recognition of other participants in speech events. Such dynamics as turn-taking, topic development, and signals of listenership are attuned to specific relationships between interlocutors. For instance, employers speaking with employees are more likely to take longer turns, to control topics, and to exert power through interruption than are workers when speaking to their employers.

Terms of Address

One of the most sensitive features of language in reflecting speakers' assessment of co-participants is the term of address chosen in a speech event. Terms of address include several linguistic types, all of which name, refer to, or address hearers. They may be personal names, titles, kinship terms, or personal pronouns that can be used separately or concomitantly.

In American English, the most frequently used address forms are First Name (FN) and Title + Last Name (TLN). There are three possible exchanges of these forms in two-party interactions: reciprocal FN (each participant calls the other by FN), reciprocal TLN, or nonreciprocal FN-TLN (one member uses TLN but receives FN, the other uses FN and receives TLN). Speakers select among the options, depending on the perceived relationship between themselves and their addressee. Speakers evaluate socially meaningful characteristics of individuals and then make judgments about their own status relative to that of the addressee. In general, reciprocal forms of address (mutual exchange of either FN or TLN) occur between status equals, and nonreciprocal forms are typical of unequal relationships. Reciprocal FN tends to indicate intimacy or casualness, that is, lack of social distance. Reciprocal TLN marks formality or politeness. Many societal factors influence speakers' decisions, including age, gender, class, and ethnicity.

In a complex multiethnic and class society such as the United States, it is impossible to make generalizations that realistically apply to all people. However, in a well-known study of American address forms based on analysis of dialogue in American plays written from the 1930s through 1958 and of observations in business organizations located in Boston, Massachusetts, Roger Brown and Marguerite Ford (1961) found that reciprocal FN is the most common address form used by status equals. Reciprocal TLN is used between adults who have only recently become acquainted. Speakers shift from TLN to FN fairly quickly, especially if both speaker and addressee are young and/or of the same gender. In a historical note, characters in earlier American plays written between 1830 and 1911 allowed more time to elapse before switching to mutual FN than did those in modern plays (ibid.:377). Although plays are art forms and not actual life, they are reliable reflectors of social practice, and the difference portrayed in earlier and later works is undoubtedly an accurate indicator of changing social norms.

Use of nonreciprocal TLN-FN requires a complex assessment by speakers of their position vis-à-vis addressees. Brown and Ford found that occupational status and relative age were the most significant factors in choice of form. Occupation was especially critical, whether as an ongoing relationship (e.g., in an employer–employee dyad) or as a situational contact (e.g., waiter/customer). Status superiors use FN to subordinates but receive TLN in return. For instance, an employer calls workers John, Jane, and so on, but is addressed as Ms. Jones. Or a customer is addressed as Mr. Smith by an auto mechanic, who is called by his first name in turn.

Combining evidence from reciprocal and nonreciprocal usage, Brown and Ford concluded that the underlying meaning of FN is both "intimacy and condescension," whereas TLN marks "distance and deference" (ibid.:380). The specific social meaning of FN or TLN varies, depending on who is being addressed. FN indicates intimacy if spoken by a friend or relative but shows condescension if used by a superior to a subordinate in nonreciprocal exchanges.

As mentioned, other social factors can add complexity to the meanings of address forms. A study of address among Navajo women who relocated from the Navajo Nation in the Southwest to Los Angeles found different patterns of usage, depending on the ethnicity of addressee (Fiske 1978). The women typically used TLN when conversing with Anglos, even of the same age as themselves, whereas they usually used FN to age equals. When talking to other Native Americans (but not to members of other "minority" ethnic or racial groups such as blacks, Hispanics, and Asians), TLN is used if the addressee is older than the speaker. This pattern parallels traditional Navajo extensions of kinship terms meaning "grandmother" and "grandfather" to unrelated elders (ibid.:81–82). Navajos' use of TLN, therefore, can have multiple meanings. First, it reflects recognition of the social and political powers of Anglos. Second, it indicates respect and deference when used for elder Native Americans, an attitude not accorded to members of other ethnic groups. Thus, in one context, to Anglos, TLN marks social distance, but in another, to elder Native Americans, it marks social solidarity.

American address is additionally complicated by possibilities of multiple usages to the same person, especially to intimates. We have several patterns of FN forms: full FN (Thomas), shortened FN (Tom), diminutive (Tommy). Nicknames and abbreviated or otherwise changed forms of LN are also possible. Many factors influence speakers' choices, especially age, gender, and personal relationship. Children are usually addressed by shortened and/or diminutive names both by other children and by adults. Boys, especially, tend to "outgrow" diminutives when they reach later adolescence and make new acquaintances. Their relatives and childhood friends, however, typically continue to use them in address or reference. Many names for girls already contain the English diminutive /-y/ on the proper name itself (Amy, Nancy). Other girls' names undergo shortening and diminution in one step (Catherine/Cathy). In any case, diminutives for female names tend to continue as address forms much longer than for male names, indeed, often throughout life. Although address patterns directed toward the genders may differ, when used mutually between adults, diminutives signal intimacy and affection.

Pronouns

In most European languages (other than English), complexity of address is demonstrated in pronominal systems. Languages in the Romance, Slavic, and Germanic families have two pronouns for addressee (called "second-person pronouns") in contrast to modern English, which has only one, "you." European pronouns distinguish both number of hearers and relationship between participants. When talking to more than a single individual, a speaker must use the plural pronoun, referred to as the V form (from the French word *vous,* which has equivalents in all the other languages). When talking to one person, speakers choose either the grammatically singular, referred to as the T form (from French *tu*), or the V form.

Choice of form is a sensitive indicator of personal relationships and societal values. According to Roger Brown and Alfred Gilman (1960), two semantic components operate in selecting pronouns: power and solidarity. When pronouns are exchanged reciprocally, solidarity between participants is stressed, whereas nonreciprocal usage reflects an unequal power relationship. That is, a superior uses T and receives V, whereas a subordinate uses V and receives T (ibid.:256–259). (Recall that the American naming address system was shown to function in parallel patterning.) Differences in power stem from various factors, including class, occupational hierarchies, age, and gender. For example, adults address children with T but receive V; employers address workers with T, receiving V.

Brown and Gilman show that class distinctions affected the reciprocal use of V or T in former times. Members of upper classes exchanged V, and lower-class speakers addressed each other with T. Evidently this difference among equals within classes was based on emphasizing mutual solidarity. Because upper-class speakers were accustomed to receiving V from subordinates, they exchanged it among themselves. Likewise, lower-class speakers were regularly addressed with T.

Modern European pronominal systems have all shifted away from nonreciprocal usage. Brown and Gilman assert that "the reciprocal solidarity semantic has grown with social mobility and an equalitarian ideology. . . . The development of open societies with an equalitarian ideology acted against the non-reciprocal power semantic and in favor of solidarity. The larger social changes created a distaste for the face-to-face expression of differential power" (ibid.:264, 267). The result has been an increased preference for mutual exchange of T. The T pronoun has been chosen rather than V because the latter was formerly used by upper-class speakers among themselves and was the form given to them in nonreciprocal power relations. Therefore, V is associated symbolically with elite privilege, inconsistent with currently prevailing notions of equality (ibid.:265).

Changes in social and linguistic norms for addressing interlocutors do not occur instantaneously; rather, they proceed through periods of transition and instability. Speakers are often uncertain and feel awkward when trying to adapt to new patterns, especially if they were socialized under previous conditions. For example, Christina Paulston's study (1976) of the shift in pronominal usage in Sweden from nonreciprocal forms to reciprocal T found that individuals may have personal difficulties adjusting to changing norms even while approving them. It is worth quoting one of Paulston's Swedish informants at length because she reveals the dilemma experienced by perceptive people in the midst of social change. The woman, who was 40 years old at the time, reported:

> And myself, I have also changed my attitude to using *du* [the T form in Swedish]—
> I react with pleased gratitude if I am addressed with *du* by strangers and sex makes
> no difference. I know that others in my age group can easily feel depressed about this,
> feel that it is below their dignity to be *duad* by the landlord. I think they seem so
> small and afraid in their attitude. I am so proud to have changed. I try also myself
> to say *du* to everyone but meet certain difficulties and feel at times uncertainty. The
> uncertainty comes when I am struck dumb by respect before a high imposing title
> and I forsake my good resolutions. I want very much to say *du* to everyone and make
> no distinction and I get into conflict when I all the same make a difference on the
> basis of social position. (p. 372)

Patterns of pronominal address in France, as well as attitudes of speakers toward pronominal usage, also reveal the linguistic, social, and personal complexities that arise in social systems undergoing change. Although people in France report that usage has shifted toward a generalized use of *tu,* observation of actual speech shows considerable ambiguity and variation. Although the reciprocal use of *tu* has increased in the last 20 or 30 years, reciprocal *vous* as well as nonreciprocal uses also persist. Many French speakers view the generalized use of *tu* as a sign of social progress, greater social equality, and the decline of barriers of hierarchical relationships, but others decry the loss of politeness and decency reflected in the use of *vous.* For example, a woman in her early fifties commented,

> I think we're going to a generalized use of *tu.* It's part of a general movement toward
> less ceremonial and more relaxed relations. I believe it's essentially a form of progress.
> The use of *tu* gives you a certain liberty that you don't have with *vous,* certain free-
> dom to exchange things with others. (Morford 1997:11)

But as *tu* has become commonplace in interactions between people of different ages, genders, and statuses, some people believe that there has been a decline in the ability of the language to signal real intimacy. As one man, a senior executive in a large company, commented,

> At work, everyone calls each other *tu.* There is a negation of certain barriers, a refusal
> of authority. . . . This use of *tu* does not at all indicate true familiarity. And it doesn't
> really help people have better relations with others. I think there is more apparent
> proximity but fewer real relations, less true exchange and sharing of things, fewer
> relations that can admit the existence of conflict. (ibid.)

Some speakers prefer reciprocal exchange of *vous* as a sign of respect, politeness, and social distance appropriate for speakers who do not know each other well. An initial exchange of *vous* also makes possible the affective significance of a switch to *tu* later in a relationship, signaling familiarity, affection, and intimacy. A middle-aged housewife who, along with her husband, hosts monthly discussion groups for students from their Catholic parish reported that she regularly greets the students with *tu:* "I do it intentionally. It's nicer, and it encourages them to say things that they would not say elsewhere" (ibid.:21). But others note that in some job situations it is strategically advantageous to use reciprocal *vous* because *tu* implies too much camaraderie that might make it difficult for status superiors to exert authority:

> Using *vous* keeps relations distant. It helps avoid confusion. It allows you to maintain a form of distance that is sometimes useful for both people. Saying *tu* in such a case makes for a mix of hierarchical and friendly relations. (ibid.:23)

Such a mix may lead to confusion, lack of efficiency in the workplace, and resentment when the affective meanings conveyed by *tu* are violated in the practical running of a workplace. These examples demonstrate that selection of a term of address is not a simple matter of making a choice between two options. Instead, language choice results from complex social and emotional processes of evaluating one's goals and relationships.

Patterns of address in the People's Republic of China have been transformed since the revolution of 1949, affecting pronominal usage and employment of various titles. The Chinese language marks second-person singular (addressee) by either *ni* or *nin* (Fang and Heng 1983:502–503). Prior to the revolution, these pronouns were selected in similar fashion to the European *tu/vous*. The Chinese T pronoun, *ni,* expressed notions of familiarity and intimacy. It was employed reciprocally between friends, colleagues, and generational equals within the family, such as spouses and siblings. However, *ni* expressed differences in status when used nonreciprocally by employers or customers to clerks, workers, servants, and also to soldiers. The Chinese V pronoun, *nin,* marked the high status of addressees and was used in speaking to officials, landlords, and wealthy individuals. It was also employed to kin of ascending generations, such as parents and grandparents. Finally, *nin* was exchanged reciprocally between strangers as a marker of politeness and distance.

According to Fang and Heng, *nin* has been eliminated from colloquial speech altogether in modern China (ibid.:503). Evidently, the power semantic of inequality expressed by *nin* has led to its demise. In contrast, because *ni* encodes familiarity and solidarity, it has won out as the linguistic reflection of an altered social ideology.

In addition to pronouns, Chinese speakers employ several titles and other forms of address. The most popular appellation is *tóngzhì* "comrade," which began as a marker of respect among revolutionary cadre and then was quickly adopted by the entire population after 1949 (ibid.:496). It is used singly as a greeting or in combination with other address forms. For example:

Full name + *tóngzhì: Mao Zedong tóngzhì* "Comrade Mao Zedong"

Title (or profession) + *tóngzhì: shòupiàoyuán tóngzhì* "Comrade Conductor" (e.g., bus or train conductor)

Tóngzhì has undergone a further broadening of its meaning range so that it currently means "person" (ibid.:497):

Tā shì ge lǎo tóngzhì "He's an old man/cadre."
Tāmen duō shì niánqīng tóngzhì "They're all young people."
Tóngzhìmen dài wǒ hěn hào "Everyone/All treated me very well."

The Chinese system of address includes many words that mark status and rank. Although the egalitarian ideology prevailing in China after 1949 led at first to the elimination of titles (Secretary X, Bureau Chief X, etc.), Fang and Heng report a recent renewal of their use. They suggest that "the gap between those of higher social status and those of lower social status has become wider, and the kind of comradely relationship that was established during the Revolution Period of the 1930s has been weakened" (ibid.:498). The government responded by formally advocating use of *tóngzhì* in reciprocal exchange between all people, instructing officials to encourage the practice. Such efforts have had uneven successes.

In China, then, pronominal usage has shifted to reciprocal *ni* because it is recognized as a signal of egalitarian social relations. However, according to Blum (1997), Chinese speakers often avoid the use of pronouns altogether because of the very neutrality of the terms. People continue to favor linguistic markers of social distinctions, particularly to signal a hierarchical relationship between junior and senior. Furthermore, reemergence of titles in addressing officials seems to have resulted from pressure from those elites who wish to have their status and power socially marked. In both cases, choice of address terms both expresses cultural models of people's rights and achieves specific goals in relation to officials who have power to grant requests.

Kinship Terms

Speakers can signal social meanings of intimacy, solidarity, or deference toward co-participants by extending kinship terms as address forms to nonkin. We saw examples in Chapter 3 of American children's use of "Aunt" and "Uncle" to friends of their parents as markers of intimacy, and the extension of sibling terms with a sol-idarity semantic among members of political or religious groups. Many other cultures make much more productive use of kin terminology to demonstrate and manipulate status and attitudinal relations. Speakers can fictively apply kin terms to addressees in order to accomplish acts of either flattering and honoring or insult-ing and denigrating. For example, when Turkish villagers use the term *dayi* ("mother's brother") to address a man of one's own generation, they convey the social meaning of "increased age-status relative to speaker" (Casson 1981:241). In a society where seniority connotes power, this practice indicates respect and dis-tance. In contrast, when a speaker uses the kin term *aga* ("father's sister's son") to a man of his or her own generation and with whom he or she normally shares mutually egalitarian status, an attitude of "decreased solidarity in relation to speaker" is expressed (ibid.). The term, therefore, signals avoidance and denigration of the relationship between speaker and addressee.

Data on kin-term usage in China demonstrate subtleties in the negotiation of status and relations between co-participants. Speakers use kinship terms when addressing people senior to themselves, either within their own generation or in ascending generations. The most respectful term for addressing a man is *bóbö,* "elder paternal uncle," that is, father's brother, older than father (Hong 1985:207). This word incorporates deferential meanings associated with relative seniority (older than father) and patrilineal descent. Its use implies a combination of the exalted status of the addressee, worthy of extreme respect, and the concomitant humbling of the speaker. By using this kin term to a nonrelative, the speaker signals his attitude toward the addressee. In modern China, recipients of respectful address do not always accept such appellations because traditional ideals of the power of seniors are being eroded by an emphasis on solidarity. In the following dialogue of parents introducing their school-age child to a male friend of their own generation, co-participants nicely negotiate the propriety of address (ibid.:207–208). (Note that literal translations and tone markers are added, supplied by Amy Cheng.)

PARENT: Jiào   Wáng   bóbö.
            call   Wang   elder uncle
            "Say Hello to *bobo* Wang."

WANG: Zĕmme kéyĭ?   Bù găndāng,   bù găndāng.
            how can it be possible?   not easy   not easy
            "Oh, no, you do me too much honor."
            Jiào   shūshū   jiù xíng lè.
            call   younger uncle   it's fine
            "Just call me younger uncle."

According to Beverly Hong, most speakers currently prefer the term *shūshū,* father's younger brother, because it is not so heavily weighted with honor but, rather, implies respect between equals (ibid.:208).

In a contrasting, revealing gender status, the kin term used for female non-relatives is *ayi,* "mother's younger sister," unless the addressee is actually much older than the speaker (ibid.:208–209). This kin term does not connote as much social respect as the term used for men. Note also that *ayi* labels a relative on the mother's side, automatically conveying less prestige than the father's kin.

Whatever the term chosen, it is mandatory for the junior relative to address his or her senior by a kin term reflecting respect and implying social hierarchy. This linguistic practice is consistent with cultural models or prototypes of the valued relationship between "benevolent older kin who take care of the younger ones, who reciprocate with affection [and] later in life with care. Invocation of the kinship term calls up images of the prototype for speaker and hearer" (Blum 1997:372).

Honorifics

Honorifics are linguistic markers that signal respect toward an addressee. Honorific meanings can be expressed by a variety of linguistic forms, including nouns, pronouns, and verbs. Languages may also contain different levels of speaking to reflect degrees of respect. The Nahuatl language, spoken in Mexico, has four distinct levels of direct address, marked by prefixes and suffixes in pronouns, personal names, titles, and yes/no responses to questions (Hill and Hill 1978:124–125). The four distinctions are:

I.   Intimacy or subordination
II. Neutrality or distance
III. Honor
IV. *Compadrazgo* relationship

Level I is used among intimates of similar age and status to signify closeness and solidarity. It is also employed by adults to children as a signal of the latter's subordination. Level II prefixes can be employed as neutral forms with strangers unless they are very young (Level I would be used) or very old (Level III would occur). Level II forms are not necessarily respectful but, rather, recognize social distance or "strangerness" (ibid.:130). However, they can convey respect if the speaker knows the addressee well; for example, they are used by younger speakers to their elder relatives. When occurring outside the personal address system, Level II prefixes on verbs in Nahuatl have the meaning of physical motion away from the speaker (ibid.:125). In a sense, Level II markers in address are metaphors of physical distance transferred to social relationships. Level III forms are used to address men and women of advanced age or exceptionally high status, such as village priests or officials. Level IV forms are restricted, occurring only between people in a *compadrazgo* relation, that is, parents and godparents or co-godparents of the same child.

In using this complex system, Nahuatl speakers obviously have to make fine judgments about their relationships with co-participants.

In other languages, honorifics can signal the relative status of participants directly by marking the high status of an addressee or indirectly by lowering the speaker's status in relation to the addressee. The Japanese language contains both types of honorifics, as well as a third class expressing respect to the addressee by deferential marking of an entire utterance. In order to use the honorific system appropriately, Japanese speakers must be aware of relationships between themselves, their interlocutors, and the persons, entities, and activities spoken about.

One set of honorific affixes denotes the high status of addressees or referents. For example, in the following two sentences, the first given in plain form, the second marked with respect, several honorifics are used, including a noun suffix -*san*, a noun prefix *o-*, and a verb suffix -*are-*. (Note that honorifics are underlined in the examples; Yamanashi 1974:760–762):

1.   yamada ga   musuko to   syokuzi o   tanosinda.
        yamada   son   dinner   enjoyed
        "Yamada enjoyed dinner with his son."

2.   yamada-<u>san</u> ga   musuko-<u>san</u> to   <u>o</u>-syokuzi o   tanosim-<u>are</u>-ta.
        yamada-HON   son-HON   HON-dinner   enjoyed-HON
        "Yamada enjoyed dinner with his son."

In the second sentence, the target of honor is Yamada, and, therefore, other people associated with him (his son) and entities and activities involving him (enjoying dinner) are all marked for respect.

The following sentence illustrates the fact that honorifics are used selectively, depending on relationships between the honored target and other referents. *Musuko* "son" refers to the speaker's son and is rendered without an affix because it is Yamada who is honored.

3.   yamada-<u>san</u> ga   musuko to   <u>o</u>-syokuzi o   tanosim-<u>are</u>-ta.
        yamada-HON   son   HON-dinner   enjoyed-HON
        "Yamada enjoyed dinner with (speaker's) son."

A second set of affixes indirectly honors someone by humiliating the speaker or those associated with him or her. In the next example, "son," *gusoku,* contains a marker of humility because it refers to the speaker's son:

4.   yamada-<u>san</u> ga   gusoku to   <u>o</u>-syokuzi o   tanosim-<u>are</u>-ta.
        yamada-HON   HUMIL-son   HON-dinner   enjoyed-HON
        "Yamada enjoyed dinner with (speaker's) son."

A third method of honorific marking includes the addition of the affixes *-masi-* and *-mas* to words within a sentence to "indicate speaker's polite attitude toward [his/her] interlocutor" (ibid.:762). These affixes can be added to any type of utterance, but they are particularly effective in issuing requests that are thereby mitigated, signaling deference to the addressee. Compare the following contrastive pair, first a direct command and second a mitigated request (ibid.:763):

5.   mado o akete kure.
        "Open the window!"

6.   mado o akete kure-<u>masu</u> (ka)?
        "Will you open the window?"

Appropriateness of honorific usage may depend on the semantic content of statements. The utterance "His son helped Yamada" can be marked to honor Yamada (yamada-*san*) and also his son (musuko-*san*), but in the sentence "His son murdered Yamada," "son" would not be honored because of the nature of the act reported (ibid.:766).

All the diverse systems discussed here, including American names, European and Chinese pronouns, Turkish and Chinese kin terms, and Nahuatl and Japanese honorifics, demonstrate the complexities of the interdependence of language and social knowledge. In order to speak appropriately, members of each culture must evaluate various characteristics of co-participants before deciding on proper linguistic form. People may want to show intimacy or respect, but they need to know how to do so without making errors that insult addressees or exaggerate expressions of sentiment.

TOPICS AND GOALS

In addition to setting and participants, another component of speech events that is sensitive to overall context is the topic of conversation or discussion. People choose topics based on combinations of personal interest and sensitivity to preferences of co-participants, all within boundaries set by cultural norms. Violation of accepted rules for topic selection can result in mild social disapproval or in feelings of embarrassment, anger, or distress by addressees. Formal contexts such as ceremonies, lectures, or governmental proceedings tend to predetermine a specific range of topics. Informal interactions are less constraining, but cultural values are relevant to choice of topic, too. For instance, in our society, discussion of bodily functions during meals is generally countered with such admonitions as "Don't talk about it at the dinner table!" or "I don't want to hear about that while I'm eating."

A speaker's compliance with the wishes of others or the speaker's persistence in pursuing a topic of her or his own preference reveals issues concerning a speaker's goals in conversation. People have both individual and communal goals. They seek to express personal interests and engage co-participants in ego-centered topics, but, as social beings, they want to minimize potential conflict with others, to appear agreeable, cooperative, and polite. The latter goal is achieved, in part, by acting in accordance with culturally approved ways of speaking.

Goals of speakers can be expressed by a variety of linguistic forms, sensitive to contextual evaluation. Recall the two sentences that began this chapter: "Would you be so kind as to pass the salt?" and "Gimme the salt!" In both cases the speaker wants to obtain salt but uses alternative ways of conveying this intent. It is easy to imagine contexts in which a speaker would choose each option, the first perhaps at a formal holiday dinner and the second at a casual picnic on the beach. The sentences are characterized by use of different words, one containing polite, mitigating words such as "be so kind" and "pass" and the other containing the colloquial "gimme." Also note that the two expressions are of different linguistic types: The first is an interrogative (question), whereas the second is an imperative (command). The form and force of the sentences differ, but their underlying intent is the same, namely, to get the hearer to perform a specific act for the speaker's benefit. Imperatives express this directly; interrogatives do so indirectly.

The linguistic form of an utterance does not have an automatic correlation with particular goals, but, rather, its interpretation is necessarily contextual. Interrogatives are generally either "requests for information" or "requests for confirmation." In the first instance, speakers ask questions when they want hearers to provide information known to the latter but unknown by the former. In the second, speakers ask hearers to confirm or deny propositions (yes/no questions). The question "Would you be so kind as to pass the salt?" is framed as a "request for confirmation," but clearly the speaker does not want a yes/no response. It is evident that both this sentence and the imperative "Gimme the salt!" are "requests for action." Speakers choose linguistic form dependent on personal stylistic preferences and assessment of settings and co-participants.

Alternative ways of phrasing the same goal can also covertly involve different assumptions about individuals' rights, obligations, and accepted norms of interaction. Rules of politeness often lead speakers to express judgments of other people's actions indirectly. Rather than telling someone who is late for an appointment "I always have to wait for you" or "I'm angry at you for making me wait," we can say, "I was beginning to worry that something happened to you."

Adults frequently convey implicit messages in their attempts to control a child's behavior. The following list offers possible ways of phrasing caregivers' admonitions (adapted from Halliday 1973:65):

1. That's very naughty of you.
2. I'll smack you if you do that again.
3. I don't like you to do that.
4. That thing doesn't belong to you.
5. You're making me very unhappy by doing that.
6. That's not allowed.

The basic goal underlying all of these sentences is essentially the same: to convince a child not to continue or repeat a particular act. But each sentence carries a somewhat different, although mutually compatible, social message:

1. Behavior disapproved on moral grounds
2. Threat of punishment
3. Emotional appeal
4. Action violates notions of private ownership
5. Emotional blackmail
6. Behavior violates external rules

Just as the same goal can be expressed by a variety of linguistic forms, the same linguistic form can express diverse intents, depending on contextual components of setting, participants, and topics. For instance, the sentence "I love you like my brother" conveys solidarity and emotional closeness when said by a man to his friend but conveys limitations on a relationship if spoken by a woman to a man. And it can mean something entirely different if the addressee knows that the speaker actually hates his or her brother (and the speaker knows that the addressee knows this) (see Bach and Harnish 1979:5).

Variation in linguistic form and variation in interpretation of linguistic messages do not occur randomly. They are ethnographically situated, resulting from speakers' and hearers' judgments about implications of alternative ways of communicating in given contexts.

SPEECH ACTS

The term *speech act* refers to the fact that through speaking, a person accomplishes goals. Speakers choose ways of expressing themselves based on their intentions, on what they want hearers to believe, accept, or do. Several linguists and philosophers have proposed typologies that classify differences among speech acts. John Austin's distinction among utterances in terms of their purpose and effect has become a widely used framework (1962:94–101):

1. A *locutionary act* is an act of "saying something." It contains the speaker's verbalized message.

2. An *illocutionary act* indicates the speaker's purpose in saying something, specifying in what way she or he is using the locution. Some illocutionary acts are asking or answering questions; giving information, assurance, or warnings; making an identification; announcing an intention; making a criticism.

3. A *perlocutionary act* produces sequential effects on the feelings, thoughts, or actions of hearers.

The following demonstrates the distinct nature of each type of act (ibid.:101):

Locutionary act:	He said to me, "You can't do that."
Illocutionary act:	He protested against my doing that.
Perlocutionary act:	He pulled me up, checked me.
	He stopped me, brought me to my senses.
	He annoyed me.

Speech act theorists have given attention to delineating illocutionary acts. Prominent among these is John Searle, whose classification and definitions are the following (1976:10–13):

1. *Representatives:* Commit the speaker (in varying degrees) to something's being the case, to the truth of the expressed proposition; for example, state, conclude, represent, deduce.

2. *Directives:* Attempts (of varying degrees) by the speaker to get the hearer to do something; for example, command, offer, invite, ask, order, request, beg, permit, dare, challenge.

3. *Commissives:* Commit the speaker (again in varying degrees) to some future course of action; for example, promise, pledge, threaten.

4. *Expressives:* Express the psychological state of the speaker toward a particular state of affairs; for example, thank, congratulate, apologize, condole, deplore, welcome.

5. *Declarations:* Bring about the correspondence between the propositional content and reality; for example, appoint, nominate, sentence, pronounce, fire, resign.

Speakers can ask questions, make predictions, issue commands, express wishes, and state hypothetical conditional intentions, as illustrated in the following utterances (Searle 1965:225):

1. Will John leave the room?
2. John will leave the room.
3. John, leave the room!
4. Would that John left the room.
5. If John will leave the room, I will leave also.

Underlying the notion of illocutionary acts are certain conditions, most importantly that interlocutors share beliefs about speakers' sincerity in expressing their intents. Participants also accept basic notions that they cooperate with each other and that they expect cooperation from one another. Because it is impossible to fully know what is in someone else's mind, interlocutors have to share assumptions about how linguistic form relates to inner thoughts. They have to base their interpretations of speech on the same or at least very similar presuppositions about the range of intentions and the way the speaker expresses these goals linguistically.

Although Searle and others writing on speech acts imply that their taxonomies and underlying presuppositions reflect universal themes, this claim is open for cross-cultural empirical investigation. Michelle Rosaldo, for instance, contended that Western theorists' emphasis on speakers' internal states as a criterion for speech act distinctions is itself a culture-bound notion, stemming from Western philosophical biases that view "language as a 'resource' that can represent the world (and that the individual can then 'use' as a tool to argue, promise, criticize or lie)" (1982:210). Rosaldo's research among the Ilongot, a tribal people of the Philippines, led her to formulate their appreciation of language in quite different terms. For Ilongots, "words are not made to 'represent' objective truth, because all truth is relative to the relationships and experiences of those who claim to 'know.' We may . . . think that meaning grows from what the individual 'intends' to say. For Ilongots, it is relations, not intentions, that come first" (ibid.).

Speech act theorists such as Searle stress the importance of sincerity conditions, that is, assumptions about speakers' beliefs in the truth of their assertions, certainty of their promises, necessity of their commands, and the like. However rational these conditions may appear to Westerners, they may not be of equal concern to other peoples. Rosaldo asserted that "Ilongots lack 'our' interest in considerations like sincerity and truth; their lives lead them to concentrate, instead, on social bonds and interactive meanings. For the Ilongots, verbal actions [should] be divided into those which roughly correspond to social situations wherein norms of 'sameness' and autonomy prevail, and those belonging to relationships defined by continuity and hierarchy" (ibid.:222).

Rosaldo classified Ilongot speech acts into two groups: declaratives and direc-tives. *Declaratives* include acts of assertion and comment through which speakers express their beliefs, opinions, and feelings. *Directives* include acts of commanding and requesting that lead to subsequent actions of hearers, most typically in the form of compliance with the directive (i.e., carrying out a command or acceding to a request) (ibid.). Ilongots emphasize directives because these speech acts call forth cooperative bonds between people, and such cooperation is the foundation of their social system. In addition, Ilongots' beliefs about people's rights and obli-gations, which are based on gender and age inequalities, affect usage of directives; that is, men are more likely to command women, elders are more likely to com-mand juniors.

These facts clearly lead to the conclusion that cultural knowledge and assumptions play a critical role in co-participants' response to each other's mes-sages. The ability to speak and comprehend a particular language is a necessary but not sufficient condition for mutual understanding. People also need to share the same set of norms about the kinds of goals expressed in speaking, norms that are learned through socialization in one's culture. The required competence consists of presupposed models of behavior and beliefs and knowledge of the way these are interconnected and manifested verbally.

NARRATIVES

Narratives are stories or framed segments of ongoing discourse that relate or report events in chronological sequence. There are many kinds of narratives: historical narratives that recount events in the history of a community or a people; mythic narratives that recount happenings in primordial times or in a realm other than our own; and personal narratives that relate events in the speaker's life (or in the lives of persons whom the speaker is describing). For our purposes, we will be analyz-ing the third category, that is, personal narratives.

One of the foremost researchers in the field of narrative analysis, William Labov, noted that "narratives are privileged forms of discourse that play a central role in almost every conversation" (1997:396). That is, in most conversational interactions, people talk about their experiences, past events that have meaning in their lives. Although storytelling may not be the focus of all conversations, narra-tives are frequently included to exemplify or dramatize a person's feelings, thoughts, and opinions. Labov defined a personal narrative as "a report of a sequence of events that have entered into the biography of the speaker by a sequence of clauses that correspond to the order of the original event" (ibid.:398). This definition captures several important features. Narratives are told in chrono-logical order, with beginnings, middles, and ends that follow the sequence of the experienced events. In addition, a personal narrative recounts events that are mean-ingful to the speaker's life and that are "emotionally and socially evaluated and so transformed from raw experience" (ibid.:199). A narrative is not an exhaustive recounting of every element of the reported experiences but is the outcome of the narrator's editing. Speakers select certain events, highlight some features and episodes, and trim or eliminate others to make a story that is coherent, dramatic, and convincing. Personal narratives must be "reportable." Since narratives tend to occupy more conversational space (i.e., they are longer) than other contributions, the narrative must be of interest to the audience; it must be reportable. Narratives must also have a point. Speakers may assert causality, praise, or blame, or comment on the competence or incompetence of people in the story. Narratives must also be credible; that is, a narrator asserts that the events recounted have actually taken place. Credibility, thus, distinguishes personal narratives from jokes, tall tales, or fantasies.

A fundamental issue in narrative analysis is the attempt to understand "how experience is translated from the narrator to the audience" (ibid.:411). Personal narratives, unlike literary accounts, relate events seen exclusively through the eyes of the narrator. The chronological sequencing of events contributes to the transfer of experience as the audience becomes aware of the events "as if" they were participants. Finally, successful narratives describe experience in objective terms, avoiding the subjectivity of the narrator's emotions. According to Labov, "those narratives that have the greatest impact on audiences—that seize the attention of listeners and allow them to share the experience of the narrator—are those that use the most objective means of expression" (ibid.:412). Events reported objectively are taken as more credible than events reported subjectively or through the emotional filter of the speaker. In contrast, when narrators add "subjective reports of emotion to the description of an objective event, listeners become aware of that event as if it were the narrator's experience and not their own" (ibid.:413).

The following is a brief but highly dramatic personal narrative, told by Harold Shambaugh about events that occurred to him while he was in South America (ibid.:398).

a. Oh I w's settin' at a table drinkin'
b. And—this Norwegian sailor came over
c. an' kep' givin' me a bunch o' junk about I was sittin' with his woman
d. An' everybody sittin' at the table with me were my shipmates.
e. So I jus' turn aroun'
f. an' shoved 'im,
g. an' told 'im, I said, "Go away.
h. I don't even wanna fool with ya"
i. An' nex' thing I know I'm layin' on the floor, blood all over me,
j. An' a guy told me, says, "Don't move your head.
k. Your throat's cut."

Shambaugh's story satisfies the criteria of personal narrative in every respect. Events are recounted in chronological order with a bare minimum of detail, honing in on the critical features of context, setting, significant characters, and directly relevant actions: the arrival of the Norwegian sailor, Shambaugh's responses (physical and verbal), and the result of the Norwegian's actions. Indeed, these actions are not themselves described but left to the imagination of the listener; only their violent consequences are stated. Notice, too, the use of direct quotation: Shambaugh quotes himself making what he presumably thought was an appropriate response to the Norwegian's accusations but that evidently provoked the latter to retaliate; and Shambaugh quotes a companion who reported the dramatic conclusion of events. Although the narrative recounts an occurrence of undoubtedly intense emotion for Shambaugh, it is told in objective, dispassionate language. This is clearly a reportable event, conveyed credibly and succinctly by a skilled narrator.

Since the 1970s, linguistic anthropologists have developed analytic techniques aimed at uncovering the structures of oral narratives. Dell Hymes is one of the important innovators in this field. A number of his foundation essays, drawn together in *In Vain I Tried to Tell You* (1981), examine oral texts from the perspective of ethnopoetics to discover the structural organization underlying their form. According to Hymes, oral narratives are usually structured in terms of lines and groups of lines, together forming units that constitute sets. Hymes proposes that commonly occurring patterns include sets of two and four or three and five. Moreover, sets of three reflect a natural sequence of "onset, ongoing, outcome" of action (1985:409). In sets of five, the middle is often a pivot that concludes the first set of three and begins the second set of three. Hymes suggests that the patterning of sets of two and four and of three and five may be universal, although he does not speculate as to the origin of this "natural" organization: "This argument obviously only indicates a possibility, it is not a proof. The likely universality of internal organization of spoken narrative in terms of lines (verses) points to a grounding in human nature" (1997:485).

In different texts, different structural features may signal the beginnings of lines and verses. These may include intonation contours (obviously not analyzable in printed texts) or grammatical features, sentence particles, repeated words, or changes in turns at talk. A text's underlying structure can be ascertained on the basis of "the general principle of poetic organization called equivalence":

> Equivalence may involve any feature of language. Features that count to constitute lines are well known: stress, tonal accent, syllable, initial consonant (alliteration), and such forms of equivalence commonly called metrical. Lines of whatever length may also be treated as equivalent in terms of the various forms of rhyme, tone group or intonation contour, initial particles, recurrent syntactic pattern, consistency of contrast of grammatical feature, such as tense or aspect. (1996:166)

Narrative form is built on series of units, marked and linked by equivalence, that combine and build through sequencing or "succession": "Succession is not a matter simply of linear sequence, of counting. Successive units give shape to action" through development and creation of "an implicit rhythm" that leads to an ending (1994:332).

When the same narrative is recounted or performed on different occasions, the length of the text as well as specific details may vary considerably in response to differences in contexts of performance and differences in the intent of the narrator, but the underlying structure remains constant. For example, Hymes (1985) compared two tellings of a narrative called "Salmon's Myth" in Kachlamet Chinook (recorded from speaker Charles Cultee in 1891 and 1894 by anthropologist Franz Boas) and found that in both versions lines were organized into sets of three and five. In a close analysis of the two versions, Hymes noted similarities of structure and sequencing of acts, reflecting a "stability of tradition" but differences in detail and variations of order within acts, reflecting selective performances. The second version "shows fuller command of the content of the tradition," stimulated by Boas's visit three years earlier that "activated memory of the story" (ibid.:422).

Hymes has also applied the techniques of ethnopoetic analysis to the personal narratives of ordinary people in a study of three short accounts collected from urban African American children by William Labov (1972:367) and Sarah Michaels (1981:33). Despite the surface simplicity of vocabulary, syntax, and plot development in these stories, Hymes finds that they, too, are built on a framework of lines and groups of lines organized in sets of three and five.

As an outgrowth of his work in ethnopoetic analysis, Hymes has championed the rethinking of procedures for presenting the oral literatures of nonliterate peoples in print form. Rather than previous renditions in which myths and folklore were printed in prose paragraphs, Hymes advocates their presentation by line, segmented according to principles of equivalence that reveal their patterning and structure. The same procedures can profitably be applied to everyday narratives of personal experience, as demonstrated by the following printing of an account given by a young African-American boy (Labov 1972:367–368; Hymes 1996: 173–174):

A (a) When I was in fourth grade—
no, it was in third grade—
this boy he stole my glove.
(b) He took my glove
and said that his father found it downtown on the ground.
[And you fight him?]
B (a) I told him
that it was impossible for him to find downtown
cause all those people were walking by
and just his father was the only one
that found it?
(b) So he got all mad.
C (a) So then I fought him.
(b) I knocked him all out in the street.
D (a) So he say he give.
(b) And I kept on hitting him.
E (a) Then he started crying
and he ran home to his father.
(b) And the father told him
that he ain't find no glove.

Here we see displayed a structure based on sets of three and five. The first three sets (ABC) lead to the outcome of the fight, whereas the second section of three sets (CDE) leads to the outcome of the glove. The third set (C) functions as the pivot, ending the first grouping of three and beginning the second grouping of three.

Another approach to analyzing oral narrative has been pioneered by Dennis Tedlock (1972, 1983) working primarily with the oral literatures of the Zunis, an indigenous nation in New Mexico. Tedlock segments Zuni narrative on the basis of structuring by pause units. Noting that "past translations of Zuni narratives have suffered from neglect of 'oral' or 'paralinguistic' features such as voice quality (tone of voice), loudness, and pausing" (1983:45), Tedlock renders Zuni narratives with transcription conventions that note changes in volume (louder, softer) and notations of raspiness, tightness, and breaks in voice production. The following is an excerpt from "The Boy and the Deer," narrated by Andrew Peynetsa (ibid.:46).

SO' NAHCHI.
The little baby came out.
   "Where is the little baby crying?" they said.
He was nursed, the little boy was nursed by the deer.
   "I will go to Kachina Village, for he is without clothing, naked."
When she got back to her children they were all sleeping.
   "HE SAW A HERD OF DEER.
BUT A LITTLE BOY WAS AMONG THEM."
   "PERHAPS WE WILL CATCH HIM."
THEN THIS DEER MOTHER TOLD HIM EVERYTHING.
   "THAT IS WHAT SHE DID TO YOU, SHE JUST DROPPED YOU."
The boy became
Very unhappy.
AND ALL THE PEOPLE WHO HAD COME KILLED THE DEER,
   KILLED THE DEER, KILLED THE DEER
   And his uncle dismounting,
Caught him.
   "THAT IS WHAT YOU DID AND YOU ARE MY REAL MOTHER."
He put the quiver on and went out.
There he died.
THIS WAS LIVED LONG AGO. LEE———SEMONIKYA.

Notation of prosodic, tonal, and rhythmic patterns that include shifts in volume, changes in voice quality, and pausing to determine line properly reflects the dramatic and aesthetic elements of performance. These narratives do not describe emotional states but "evoke them" (ibid.:51) by dramatic shifts of pause and voice. Of course, structural linguistic elements of repetition and parallelisms occur in Zuni narratives as found elsewhere. Although Tedlock's presentation provides dramatic markers of performance qualities, it is obviously only possible to render materials in this manner if there are voice recordings or the analyzer is present at the narration.

Both Hymes's and Tedlock's approaches add to our understanding of the underlying structure of narratives and the features that give life to their performance. Because all narratives are text, they have structural and grammatical features, and because they are performed they also have elements of voice that contribute to their dramatic quality. The importance to an audience of both types of features is indicated in Paul Kroskrity's report of members of the Arizona Tewa community's discussion of criteria used to evaluate skilled narrators (1985: 195–196). According to Tewa members, the following characteristics are significant contributors to the effectiveness of a narrative performance:

1. use of storytelling conventions (story words)
2. use of archaic words both in the dialogue of characters and in the narrative itself
3. use of facial expression in the dramatic imitation of characters
4. use of prosodic linguistic effects by the narrator, especially in vocal characterization
5. use of song
6. "carrying it hither," that is, situating narratives for the present audience

Arizona Tewa listeners actively participate in narrative performances by making individual or group responses, often an interjection (*uh* meaning "yes") at significant pauses within the narration. Such pauses occur at "line demarcations occupied by *ba* (a syntactic particle) in the narrative portion of the text" (ibid.:196). Narrators and audience, thus, co-construct an oral performance.

Examination of multiple tellings of the same story by the same speaker may reveal intriguing consistencies as well as significant variations. In a comparison of five tellings of a Wasco Coyote story by the same bilingual speaker (the earliest in 1972 and the latest in 1986), Robert Moore (1993) provides a "longitudinal, historical perspective on a traditional performance genre [that] enables one to see how alive the tradition really is" (ibid.:236). Three versions of the story were told in the indigenous language, Wasco Chinookan, one account was given in English, and one in a mixture of English and Chinookan. The versions were told in different social settings, some spontaneously produced and others elicited by researchers Robert Moore in the 1980s (four versions) and Michael Silverstein in 1972 (one account). Remaining constant in all five versions were instances of quoted speech, that is, direct quotations in the voices of Coyote, Raccoon, and other mythic figures. All tellings contained the same five episodes in the same order, but the length of episodes varied and details of events were sometimes elaborated or simplified. Of special significance, even in the accounts that were in English or in a mixture of English and Chinookan, all speech quoted from mythic characters was given in the indigenous language and was identical in all five versions (ibid.:214). In the native culture, "directly quoted character speech is absolutely central to the constitution of myth-recital as a recognizable performance genre, and its enduring centrality suggests analogies to theater and related performing arts" (ibid.:236).

In the study of narrative, attention is often directed toward the analysis of quoted or reported speech. Quoting or reporting the speech of another may serve different functions in different contexts. We saw previously how one narrator, Harold Shambaugh, effectively employed reported speech to highlight dramatic turning points in his story. In other contexts, quoting an absent speaker may absolve the narrator from responsibility for the reported speech. Such a use of language may function strategically in arguments, allowing the narrator to slip into the background of ongoing talk, citing the words of others to substantiate the narrator's own claims or to evade blame and responsibility. But the use of reported speech may not achieve the goal of evading responsibility unless the narrator is seen to be entitled to quote the original source. Indeed, arguments between people may be triggered by the unentitled quotation of previous speech of nonpresent participants. In a study of inner-city junior high school students, Amy Shuman found that disputes sometimes arose over "challenges to entitlement" in the use of reported speech (1992:136). Reported speech might be challenged on the grounds of accuracy or sincerity, but it might also be challenged on the grounds of entitlement, that is, that the narrator is not entitled to repeat privileged speech: "The offense of using reported speech can focus on a lack of correspondence between original and reported remarks (a problem with accuracy), or on an unauthorized use of those remarks (a problem of entitlement)" (ibid.:148). A listener can challenge the reporter's accuracy and can also challenge the competence of the narrator and his or her relationship to the original text. In adolescent dispute narratives studied by Shuman, talking and quoting others were both ways to fight and to avoid fighting: "The girls talked about fights more than they fought. If a girl could shift the focus from an initial offense to some other offense, usually talking behind someone's back, she could successfully divert antagonisms away from herself" (ibid.:149).

Narratives are enmeshed in larger conversational sequences and interchanges, but they also contribute to the construction of the interaction itself. As Shuman observed,

> The relationship between the storytelling situation and the events described is especially complicated in the narratives of everyday life since the storytelling can be part of the ongoing experience. Stories about everyday experiences do not replicate experiences, they construct them. The clarity of an account, the accuracy of the portrayals, and the presentation events in chronological order are conventions for concealing as well as for revealing information. (ibid.)

In a study of speaking styles on the Polynesian atoll of Nukulaelae, Niko Besnier has shown that people frequently used quoted speech in everyday discourse, in part because it is considered inappropriate to speculate about other people's thoughts and emotions. Furthermore, a speaker can quote the words of others even when not a witness to the original speech. Indeed, children are taught the skills of accurate reporting from their early years when they are prompted to repeat messages exactly as originally uttered (1992:165). Believing that speech and action are of equal importance and that speakers and actors are equally responsible for their behavior, people on Nukulaelae believe that a speaker who quotes another

CONTEXTUAL COMPONENTS: OUTLINE OF AN ETHNOGRAPHY OF COMMUNICATION

must repeat the exact words and the identical prosodic features (voice quality, volume, intensity, pitch) of the source. The reproduction of prosodic features, in fact, is critical because different prosodic cues are associated with different emotional states. However, speakers may misrepresent the quoted source by changing prosodic features if the speaker wishes to present the person negatively (e.g., in gossip). Although this practice violates the norm of accuracy, because prosodic features are less consciously focused on by an audience, the speaker is usually able to evade direct responsibility for the shifts that they have made. Nukulaelae speakers, thus, employ indirect, covert means to characterize the emotions of others while, at the same time, quoting their words accurately. As Besnier concludes, "While adhering to the cultural norm dictating that speech be reported faithfully, Nukulaelae islanders can also superpose affect in a covert off-record manner, in a manner that is also most likely to escape scrutiny" (ibid.:177).

In some cultures, narratives function in complex ways to invoke specific cultural and interactional meanings. Keith Basso's work among Western Apaches (1990) reveals the extraordinary depth of meaning conveyed by the telling of "historical tales." Such tales recount events that happened "long ago," typically (but not always) before 1872 when Apaches were forced to settle on reservations (Basso 1990:115). On the surface, historical tales inform listeners of significant past events that occurred at specific, named places, but the telling of the stories functions interactionally to "alarm and criticize social delinquents (or, as the Apache say, to "shoot" them), thereby impressing such individuals with the undesirability of improper behavior and alerting them to the punitive consequences of further misconduct" (ibid.).

Characteristics of Western Apache historical tales conform to a specific set of stylistic devices, especially an opening and closing line containing the place-name where the events occurred. Apache place-names are highly detailed and evocative, describing salient characteristics of the physical environment that allow hearers to visualize the named place and imagine that they are there. Examples include the following: "water flows down on top of a regular succession of flat rocks," "water flows inward underneath a cottonwood tree," and "white rocks lie above in a compact cluster" (ibid.:109). When historical stories are told, they are aimed (to use the Apache hunting metaphor) at a particular hearer who comes to understand that the message in the story is directed at them. They appreciate the wisdom of their ancestors in relating the moral of the story to their own behavior. For example, consider the following tale (ibid.:119–120):

> It happened at "men stand above here and there." Long ago, a man killed a cow off the reservation. The cow belonged to a Whiteman. The man was arrested by a policeman living at Cibecue at "men stand above here and there." The policeman was an Apache. The policeman took the man to the head army officer at Fort Apache. There, at Fort Apache, the head army officer questioned him. "What do you want?" he said. The policeman said, "I need cartridges and food." The policeman said nothing about the man who had killed the Whiteman's cow. That night some people spoke to the policeman. "It is best to report on him," they said to him. The next day

the policeman returned to the head army officer. "Now what do you want?" he said. The policeman said, "Yesterday I was going to say HELLO and GOODBYE but I forgot to do it." Again he said nothing about the man he arrested. Someone was working with words on his mind. The policeman returned with the man to Cibecue. He released him at "men stand above here and there." It happened at "men stand above here and there."

This story impresses upon Apache listeners the moral obligation to be loyal to their own people, not betray them or act "too much like a Whiteman" (ibid.:120). When the Apache policeman in the story was about to accuse his fellow Apache of theft, someone used witchcraft on him so that he forgot what he wanted to say and instead acted in a way that was "absurd and laughable" (ibid.).

Basso reports the way in which this particular story was used to criticize the behavior of a 17-year-old Apache woman who attended a girls' puberty ritual with her hair rolled up in pink curlers in violation of the norm prescribing that women wear their hair loose when attending such ceremonies. Two weeks after the rite, at a gathering of friends and relatives at the camp of the young woman's maternal grandmother, the grandmother recounted the historical tale of events at "men stand above here and there" and the humiliation of the Apache policeman who acted like a Whiteman. The young woman stood up after the story was told and quietly walked away. About two years later when Basso happened to be driving near "men stand above here and there" in the company of the young woman, she observed "I know that place. It stalks me everyday" (ibid.:123). Her comment exemplifies an analysis offered by one of Basso's Apache consultants, Nick Thompson:

> This is what we know about our stories. They go to work on your mind and make you think about your life. Maybe you've not been acting right. Maybe you've been stingy. Maybe you've been chasing after women. Maybe you've been trying to act like a Whiteman. People don't *like* it. So someone goes hunting for you—maybe your grandmother, your grandfather, your uncle.
>
> So someone stalks you and tells a story about what happened long ago. It doesn't matter if other people are around—you're going to know he's aiming that story at you. All of a sudden it *hits* you! It's like an arrow, they say. No one says anything to you, only that story is all, but now you know that people have been watching you and talking about you. They don't like how you've been acting. So you have to think about your life. (ibid.:124–125)

ROUTINES

Several kinds of speech acts—greetings, partings, apologies, thanks, compliments—are frequently expressed by highly predictable and stereotyped linguistic routines. They combine verbal material and social messages in patterns expressive of cultural values and sensitive to interactional context. Their appropriate use requires that speakers know rules dictating both linguistic form and situational relevance. They are, therefore, good examples of the need to understand communication in ethnographic perspective, as every culture has its own norms for displaying and interpreting routine behavior.

Although each type of routine has unique characteristics, they share several key features. First and foremost is their similarity of function in social interaction. To one degree or another, they all create, reaffirm, and/or negotiate social solidarity. Their primary goal is social rather than referential. Second, routines typically occur as sequences of exchanges between participants, minimally consisting of an utterance by the first speaker followed by a return or acknowledgment by the second speaker.

1a.   Hello.
1b.   Hello.

2a.   Thank you.
2b.   You're welcome.

3a.   I'm sorry.
3b.   Don't worry, it's nothing.

4a.   That's a nice sweater.
4b.   Thanks.

A third common trait of routines is that they are formulaic in structure. Each category (greetings, compliments, etc.) consists of instances of patterned forms used by most speakers on most occasions. The expectable and redundant linguistic form of these speech acts is what, in fact, makes them routines.

We will review some research dealing with greetings and apologies, focusing on their structure and the purposes for which they are employed. Analyses of such behavior are principally based on data from two sources: One is elicited, constructing test frames or situations and asking subjects to project their behavior; the other is ethnographic, observing actual speech and collecting large samples of occurrences with attention to situational and interactional parameters. The latter approach is especially useful in revealing recurring forms and functions of routines.

Greetings

Greetings function to begin communicative interactions or to acknowledge the presence of others. In Erving Goffman's words, they "mark the transition to a condition of increased access" (1971:107). Speakers also use greetings to manipulate particular outcomes with addressees. Although their basic structure is stereotyped within each culture, optional elaborations or innovations are possible. Speakers can use more or less formal constructions, pronunciations, and/or prosodic features to create diverse introductions to encournters. Different kinds of greetings are offered, depending on situational context, status relationships between interlocutors, and personal goals.

Alessandro Duranti has postulated six recurring features that can be used as criteria for identifying greetings cross-culturally (1997:67). These include:

1.   near-boundary occurrence (greetings occur at the beginning of a social encounter)

2.   establishment of a shared perceptual field (people engaged in greeting recognize each other's presence in the same conceptual field)

3.   adjacency-pair format (greetings are typically part of one or more sets of adjacency pairs, i.e., two-part sequences in which the first pair is uttered by one party and the second is a reply by another)

4.   relative predictability of form and content

5.   implicit establishment of spatio-temporal unit of interaction (greetings occur only once in an interaction)

6.   identification of the interlocutor as a distinct being worth recognizing.

Greetings in American society are usually variants of "Hello" or "How are you?" Some, such as these, can be employed at any time of day, whereas others are temporally restricted (e.g., "Good morning"). Typical responses to greetings include identical returns or minor modifications, such as "Hello"/"Hi," or formulaic acknowledgments, "Good morning"/"The same to you." In some languages, responses produce an effect of linguistic balance. The following exchange is common in Arabic (Ferguson 1976:143):

1a.   *assalāmu ʕalaykum*   "Peace be on you."
1b.   *waʕalaykumu ssalām*   "And on you be peace."

Another frequent pattern of response is what Ferguson called "the principle of 'the same or more so,' " exemplified by Arabic rejoinders to *marhaba* "hello," which are *marhaba, marhabten, mit marhaba,* or *marahib,* meaning "hello, two hellos, a hundred hellos, hellos" (ibid.).

An additional type of Anglo-American greeting takes the stereotyped form of "phatic communion" or "small talk" (Laver 1981:301). Initial remarks often fall into three categories, depending on their orientation (ibid.:301–302):

2a.   *Neutral:* factors common to both speaker and addressee:
       "Nice day," "Frost tonight," "About time the trains were cleaned."
2b.   *Self-oriented:* factors personal to speaker:
       "Hot work, this," "I do like a breath of fresh air."
2c.   *Other-oriented:* factors specific to addressee:
       "That looks like hard work," "Do you come here often?"

Anglo-American greetings are used to create impressions, whether real or false, of social equality and camaraderie. Patterns of response also demonstrate this function. Identical or modified returns and acknowledgments are linguistic metaphors for desired social balance.

In contrast, greeting exchanges in some cultures are manipulated in order to affirm status inequalities between participants. This is so among the Wolof, a stratified Muslim society in Senegal. Wolof etiquette dictates that co-presence requires talk, and that talk must be formally initiated (Irvine 1974:168). Social status is immediately relevant because "ideally, one greets 'up': it should be the lower-ranking party who greets the higher" (ibid.:169).

Wolof greeting behaviors reflect an underlying cultural assumption that social relationships are inherently unequal. This cultural model is repeatedly enacted by Wolof speakers as they engage in obligatory linguistic routines. Wolof greetings express status relations by a constellation of verbal and nonverbal behaviors. Prior to speaking, an initiator moves toward the addressee. Movement and activity are conceived in Wolof culture as traits of low-status people, whereas high-status people remain stationary and passive. And, as mentioned, people of lower rank speak first, commencing the exchange. Because moving and speaking are necessary components of greetings, it is impossible to avoid displays of social inequality, succinctly expressed in a Wolof proverb, "When two persons greet each other, one has shame, the other has glory" (ibid.:175).

People can use various strategies to lower or elevate their status vis-à-vis interlocutors. A person may engage in self-lowering in order to deflect social consequences of high status; namely, high-ranked people are obligated to grant financial or material requests of low-ranked individuals. Self-lowering can be accomplished by initiating greetings and/or by showing deference through a proliferation of questions about the addressee and his or her family (ibid.:175–176).

Strategies of self-elevation include attempts to avoid initiating exchanges. Such reluctance can be problematic if both parties have the same intention because eventually someone must begin. Another possibility is to refrain from asking elaborate questions but, instead, to proceed quickly into topics of conversation (ibid.: 178–179).

Apologies

Apologies are verbalized social acts. Their purpose is to maintain or reestablish rapport between participants. They are occasioned by actions that are perceived to have negative effects on addressees and for which speakers take responsibility. In apologizing, a speaker "splits [him-/herself] into two parts, the part that is guilty of an offense and the part that dissociates itself from the delict and affirms a belief in the offended rule" (Goffman 1971:143). As linguistic routines, apologies are expressed by predictable forms within each speech community. Naturally, what counts as a deed or intent necessitating an apology is entirely dependent on cultural models of offensive or regrettable behavior. An act of apologizing is verbal recognition of some social breach either past, present, or future:

1a. I'm sorry I broke your dish.
1b. I'm sorry to be bothering you now.

1c.   I'm sorry that I'll have to inconvenience you tomorrow, but I'll be late pick-
      ing you up.

Apologies are middle segments of three-part sequences. The first part, which
may be verbal or behavioral, constitutes the "object of regret" (Coulmas 1981:75).
Following an apology, the last segment consists of the addressee's response. In
Western societies, such turns typically are acknowledgments, often in a form
intended to downgrade the offense, as in the following:

2a.   I'm sorry.
2b.   Don't worry about it.
      It was nothing.
      Forget it. Etc.

Responses to apologies may, however, fully acknowledge the weightiness of an
offense:

3a.   I'm sorry.
3b.   OK, but don't do it again.
      I hope this is the last time it happens.
      You always say that. Etc.

The two types of replies clearly have different contextual uses and speaker intents.
Those in the second group are polite and mitigating, whereas those in the third are
potentially aggravating and confrontational.
      Apologies are routinized in the sense that they are expressed with stereotyped
formats. The following strategies were attested in research conducted by Janet
Holmes in New Zealand, given with examples from her data (1990:167):

1.   *An explicit expression of apology:*
     a.   Offer apology: "I apologize"
     b.   Express regret: "I'm afraid"; "I'm sorry"
     c.   Request forgiveness: "excuse me"; "forgive me"

2.   *An explanation or account, an excuse or justification:*
     "I wasn't expecting it to be you"; "we're both new to this"

3.   *An acknowledgment of responsibility:*
     a.   Accept blame: "it was my fault"
     b.   Express self-deficiency: "I was confused"; "I wasn't thinking"; "I
           didn't see you"
     c.   Recognize hearer as entitled to an apology: "you're right"; "you deserve
           an apology"
     d.   Express lack of intent: "I didn't mean to"
     e.   Offer repair/redress: "we'll replace it for you"; "I'll bring you another"
4.   *A promise of forebearance:*
     "I promise it won't happen again"

In Holmes's study of 183 apologies collected ethnographically through observation of spontaneous occurrences, 162 (88.3 percent) employed strategies of "explicit expression of apology" (strategy 1). Apologies were overwhelmingly based on recurring syntactic and semantic components (ibid.:172). The most common, accounting for approximately 80 percent of the data, were variants with "sorry," as in "I'm sorry," "I'm so (very) sorry," "I'm (so, very) sorry to/if/for," "I'm (so, very) sorry about that/it." Other patterns included "excuse me," "pardon me," and "I would like to apologize."

As already mentioned, apologies are motivated by offenses, obviously contingent on behavioral norms specific to each culture. The most typical offenses found by Holmes's New Zealand research (presumably applicable to other Western societies) were instances of inconvenience, infringements on space, talk, time, or possessions, and social gaffes (ibid.:177). More serious breaches triggered more elaborate apologies.

Social relationships between participants influence the occurrence and form of apologies. In Holmes's data, most occurred between equals (probably because people more often interact with status equals). Of the remaining cases, lower-status individuals were twice as likely to apologize to those of higher rank than the reverse. And low-status participants tended to use more explicit and complex strategies (ibid.:188–189). However, instances of elaborate apology are frequent between intimates (relatives, close friends) as well, possibly because serious offenses, which often trigger elaborate forms, are more likely to occur in these contexts than in formal or public situations.

Comparison with other cultures reveals some similarities and differences in apology routines. For example, Japanese social norms require apologies in more contexts than would be expected in Western societies. According to Florian Coulmas, citing Sugiyama Lebra, Japanese people are highly conscious of their effects on others and concerned with not infringing on others' rights and needs. They strive to avoid embarrassment either to themselves or their interlocutors (1981:82–83). Not only are apologies frequently issued for offenses, they are also "used to line other speech acts such as greetings, offers, thanks with an apologetic undertone" (ibid.). In fact, a common utterance, *sumimasen* (literally: "this is not the end" or "it is not finished"), can be translated as either "I'm sorry" or "thank you" and is used to express apology or gratitude. And in contexts such as upon leaving someone's home where a Westerner might say, "Thank you for a wonderful evening," a Japanese guest often says *o-jama itashimashita* "I have intruded on you" (literally: disturbance have done to you). As in Western societies, Japanese speakers typically respond to apologies with polite downgraders, for example, *iie, iie, do itashimashite* "no, no, don't mention it" (ibid.).

Japanese interactional norms require explicit recognition of people's effects on each other in the form of apology for actual or implicated intrusions, disturbances, and infringements. Apologies are perceived as polite, considerate, and deferential according to Japanese models of social rights. The most common apologies in Japanese are

1.   *sumimasen*   "This is not the end; it is not finished."
2.   *shitsurei shimasu*   "I was very rude."

These occur in either intimate or casual contexts when the offense is relatively slight. Serious breaches and/or formal situations invoke more elaborate apologies (ibid.:88–89):

3.   *o-yurushi kudasai*   "I beg your pardon." (in the literal meaning)
4.   *o-wabi itashimasu*   "I offer my apologies."
5.   *mōshiwake arimasen*   "There is no excuse; this is unpardonable."
6.   *sore-wa kyoshuku desu*   "I feel ashamed."
7.   *o-kindodoku-sama degozaimashita*   "This must have been poison to your soul."

SUMMARY

We have used the framework of an ethnography of communication to analyze components of communicative events, emphasizing interrelationships among settings, participants, topics, and goals. Language is used by speakers in conformity with culturally shared expectations. Ethnographic-linguistic analysis includes discussion of both behavior and its evaluation. People not only speak in ways considered appropriate in their culture, but they also assess the speech of others by these same norms.

Choices of linguistic form, whether of sounds, grammar, or words, are made, usually nonconsciously, after weighing co-occurrences of significant components. Settings of relative formality or informality provide the background for participants' interactions and help determine topic selection and methods of phrasing personal intents. Speakers can signal their relations with co-participants by manipulating various aspects of language, revealed especially in their choice of words and in forms of address. Finally, speakers' goals can be expressed through speech acts directly or indirectly after considering cultural rules of propriety and the likelihood of specific outcomes. Some speech acts, such as greetings and apologies, are expressed as stereotyped, formulaic social and linguistic routines.

REFERENCES

AUSTIN, JOHN. 1962. *How to Do Things with Words.* Cambridge, MA: Harvard University Press.

BACH, KENT, AND ROBERT HARNISH. 1979. *Linguistic Communication and Speech Acts.* Cambridge, MA: MIT Press.

BASSO, KEITH. 1990. *Western Apache Language and Culture.* Tucson: University of Arizona Press.

BESNIER, NIKO. 1992. "Reported Speech and Affect on Nukulaelae Atoll." In *Responsibility and Evidence in Oral*

Discourse, ed. J. Hill and J. Irvine. New York: Cambridge University Press, pp. 161–181.

BLUM, SUSAN. 1997. Naming practices and the power of words in China. *Language in Society* 26, no. 3:357–380.

BROWN, ROGER, AND MARGUERITE FORD. 1961. Address in American English. *Journal of Abnormal and Social Psychology* 62:375–385.

BROWN, ROGER, AND ALFRED GILMAN. 1960. The pronouns of power and solidarity. In *Style in Language,* ed. T. Sebeok. Cambridge, MA: MIT Press, pp. 253–276.

CASSON, RONALD. 1981. The semantics of kin term usage: Transferred and indirect metaphorical meanings. In *Language, Culture and Cognition,* ed. R. Casson. New York: Macmillan, pp. 230–244.

COULMAS, FLORIAN. 1981. "Poison to your soul": Thanks and apologies contrastively viewed. In *Conversational Routine,* ed. F. Coulmas. The Hague: Mouton, pp. 69–91.

DURANTI, ALESSANDRO. 1997. Universal and culture-specific properties of greetings. *Journal of Linguistic Anthropology* 7, no. 1:63–97.

FANG, HANQUAN, AND J. H. HENG. 1983. Social changes and changing address norms in China. *Language in Society* 12:495–507.

FERGUSON, CHARLES. 1976. The structure and use of politeness formulas. *Language in Society* 5:137–151.

FISKE, SHIRLEY. 1978. Rules of address: Navajo women in Los Angeles. *Journal of Anthropological Research* 34, no. 1:72–91.

GOFFMAN, ERVING. 1971. *Relations in Public.* New York: Basic Books.

Halliday, M. A. K. 1973. *Explorations in the Functions of Language.* Hawthorne, NY: Elsevier North-Holland.

HILL, JANE, AND KENNETH HILL. 1978. Honorific usage in modern Nahuatl. *Language* 54:123–155.

HOLMES, JANET. 1990. Apologies in New Zealand English. *Language in Society* 19:155–200.

HONG, BEVERLY. 1985. Politeness in Chinese: Impersonal pronouns and personal greeting. *Anthropological Linguistics* 27:204–213.

HYMES, DELL. 1974. *Foundations in Sociolinguistics: An Ethnographic Approach.* Philadelphia: University of Pennsylvania Press.

HYMES, DELL. 1981. *"In Vain I Tried to Tell You": Essays in Native American Ethno-Poetics.* Philadelphia: University of Pennsylvania Press.

HYMES, DELL. 1985. Language, memory, and selective performance: Cultee's "Salmon's Myth" as twice told to Boas. *Journal of American Folklore* 98, no. 390:391–434.

HYMES, DELL. 1994. Ethnopoetics, oral-formulaic theory, and editing texts. *Oral Tradition* 9, no. 2:330–370.

HYMES, DELL. 1996. *Ethnography, Linguistic, Narrative Inequality: Toward an Understanding of Voice.* London: Taylor & Francis.

HYMES, DELL. 1997. When is oral narrative poetry? Generative form and its pragmatic conditions. *Pragmatics* 8, no. 4:475–500.

IRVINE, JUDITH. 1974. Strategies of status manipulation in the Wolof greeting. In *Explorations in the Ethnography of Speaking,* ed. R. Bauman and J. Sherzer. New York: Cambridge University Press, pp. 167–191.

IRVINE, JUDITH. 1979. Formality and informality in communicative events. *American Anthropologist* 81:773–790.

KROSKRITY, PAUL. 1985. Growing with stories: Line, verse, and genre in an

Arizona Tewa text. *Journal of Anthropological Research,* 183–199.

LABOV, WILLIAM. 1972. *Language in the Inner City.* Philadelphia: University of Pennsylvania Press.

LABOV, WILLIAM. 1997. Some further steps in narrative analysis. *Journal of Narrative and Life History* 7, 395–415.

LAVER, JOHN. 1981. Linguistic routines and politeness in greeting and parting. In *Conversational Routine,* ed. F. Coulmas. The Hague: Mouton, pp. 289–304.

MICHAELS, SARAH. 1981. Sharing Time: Children's Narrative Styles and Differential Access to Literacy. *Language in Society* 10:423–442.

MOORE, ROBERT. 1993. Performance form and the voices of characters in five versions of the Wasco Coyote Cycle. In *Reflexive Language,* ed. J. A. Lucy. New York: Cambridge University Press, pp. 213–240.

MORFORD, JANET. 1997. Social indexicality in French pronominal address. *Journal of Linguistic Anthropology* 7, no. 1:3–37.

PAULSTON, CHRISTINA. 1976. Pronouns of address in Swedish: Social class semantics and a changing system. *Language in Society* 5:359–386.

ROSALDO, MICHELLE. 1982. The things we do with words: Ilongot speech acts and speech act theory in philosophy. *Language in Society* 11:203–237.

SEARLE, JOHN. 1965. What is a speech act? In *Philosophy in America,* ed. M. Black. Ithaca, NY: Allen & Unwin and Cornell University Press, pp. 221–239.

SEARLE, JOHN. 1976. A classification of illocutionary acts. *Language in Society* 5:1–23.

SHUMAN, AMY. 1992. "Get outa my face": Entitlement and authoritative discourse. In *Responsibility and Evidence in Oral Discourse,* ed. J. Hill and J. Irvine. New York: Cambridge University Press, pp. 135–160.

TEDLOCK, DENNIS. 1972. *Finding the Center: Narrative Poetry of the Zuni Indians.* Lincoln: University of Nebraska Press.

TEDLOCK, DENNIS. 1983. *The Spoken Word and the Work of Interpretation.* Philadelphia: University of Pennsylvania Press.

YAMANASHI, MASA-AKI. 1974. On minding your p's and q's in Japanese: A case study from honorifics. *Papers from the Tenth Regional Meeting of the Chicago Linguistic Society.* Chicago: Chicago Linguistic Society, pp. 760–771.

5

Communicative Interactions

A: "What is she, small?"

B: "Yes, yes, she's small, smallish, um, not really small but certainly not very big."

Talk is the primary means by which people interact and satisfy personal and social goals. In the dialogue above, speaker B responds to A's question by performing an intricate series of linguistic moves that accomplish the personal goal of stating an opinion while also accomplishing the social goal of avoiding conflict by being conciliatory and agreeable. If B had not wanted to be polite and avoid conflict, she could have said, "No, she's not small, she's big." But such a statement, by baldly contradicting the implied assumption in A's question (namely, that "she's small"), would have been a challenge to A's competence and, therefore, to A's social being. In all situations, speakers have options of ways to express themselves. Their choices reveal underlying cultural models of behavior, rights, and obligations. In this chapter we will deal with issues of conversational interaction, beginning by examining the structural properties of conversation, proceeding to an analysis of how people accomplish goals through talk, and ending with a discussion of rules of politeness.

STRUCTURAL PROPERTIES OF CONVERSATION

Conversation is based on principles of turn-taking that can be structurally defined but that are also influenced by context. The basic structure of turns, their alternation and allocation, are context-free, but the ways that turns are used by speakers, their length and content, are sensitive to situation, allowing greater or lesser opportunities for co-participants.

Harvey Sacks et al. suggested the following mechanisms for turn-taking in American practice (1974:700–701):

- Speaker change recurs, or, at least, occurs.
- Overwhelmingly, one party talks at a time.
- Occurrences of more than one speaker at a time are common, but brief.
- Transitions from one turn to a next with no gap and no overlap or with slight gap or slight overlap make up the vast majority of transitions.
- Turn-allocation techniques are used; a current speaker may select next speaker or parties may self-select.

• Additional aspects of turn-taking, such as order of turns (in multiparty encounters), size of turn, and length of conversation, vary. However, even these features are not totally random but, rather, are sensitive to social constraints based on relative status of participants. Generally, in encounters between unequals, higher-status members assume more rights to turns and to longer turns than do those of lower status.

Conversing includes exchanges of turns, based on certain rules. In two-party interactions, turns alternate automatically between the participants so that each person has the same number of turns. The next speaker normally begins his turn at the completion of a *turn-constructional unit* (ibid.:702). Such units are composed of at least a single word but may contain multiple clauses, phrases, and/or sentences. Some examples from Sacks et al. (ibid.:702–703) are illustrative. (The asterisks indicate the relevant turns.)

Single-Word Turns

DESK:	What is your last name Loraine?
*CALLER:	Dinnis.
*DESK:	What?
*CALLER:	Dinnis.

Single-Phrase Turns

A:	Oh I have the—I have one class in the evening.
*B:	On Mondays?
A:	Y-uh Wednesdays.
B:	Uh—Wednesday.
A:	En it's like a Mickey Mouse course.

Single-Clause Turns

A:	Uh you been down here before havenche.
B:	Yeh.
*A:	Where the sidewalk is?

B: Yeah.

*A: Whur it ends?

B: Goes all a' way up there?

A: Yeah.

In multiparty conversations, turns do not rotate in a fixed sequence but are, instead, variable in their distribution. Turns are allocated in two ways: current speaker selection and self-selection. In the first, the current speaker may select the next speaker directly by asking questions, making requests, or issuing invitations and offers. These are examples of *adjacency pairs,* utterances that are linked automatically to particular kinds of responses (Schegloff and Sacks 1973:295). Adjacency pairs occur as sequences of interaction: question/answer (What time is it?/Four o'clock), request/grant or refusal (May I come in?/Yes), invitation or offer/acceptance or decline (Come for dinner tonight/Sorry, I'm busy).

Linguistic constructions called tag questions are particularly effective mechanisms for ending a turn. *Tag questions* are utterances beginning with a declarative proposition to which a question, or "tag," is added (e.g., "It's hot in here, isn't it?"). They function as "exit techniques" (Sacks et al. 1974:718) because the addressee is obliged to respond by confirming or denying the tag.

When the current speaker completes his turn without choosing the next speaker, each participant may self-select, principally by starting first. Sacks et al. noted that self-selectors often "begin with a beginning," typically using such words as "well," "but," "and," or "so." These *turn-entry devices* signal a person's desire to speak next (ibid.:719).

Because conversing is a human activity, it is subject to errors, such as simultaneous talk in the form of overlaps or interruptions. In these cases *repair mechanisms* are used to correct errors so that one party in simultaneous talk stops and allows the other to complete her turn. Although in theory a participant can either terminate or continue, in practice social norms based on status affect actual outcomes. In accordance with societal rights to speak, higher-status people tend to interrupt or complete their turns when interrupted, whereas lower-status individuals are apt to be successfully interrupted.

Throughout conversation, while speakers talk, listeners have supportive work to do in order to signal their interest, or *active listenership.* Listener responses, or *backchannel cues* (Yngve 1970:574), include such words and vocalizations as "yeah," "right," "uh-huh," and "hmm." These devices are referentially meaningless, but they have great interactional import by indicating one's attention to and ratification of the speaker's talk. They must be well timed to clauses and phrases within the speaker's turn. Too many vocalizations by listeners can be perceived as interruptive, and too few discourage the speaker by implying a lack of interest.

Although conversation is structured in all societies and is everywhere based on principles of turn-taking, rules that dictate the timing, length, and allocation of turns differ in accordance with cultural norms. For instance, Native Cree people living in western Canada follow rules for conversational interaction that are quite distinct from those of American-Canadian practice. Whether speaking English or their indigenous language, Cree speakers allow longer pauses within and between turns (Darnell 1985:67). The "no gap" or "slight gap" pattern observed by Sacks et al. for most Americans is not followed. Cree speakers employ pauses in their own turns in order to consider what they will say next. They wait at the end of the previous speaker's turn before beginning their contribution, to show respect for the co-participant. For Cree conversationalists, "Anything serious enough to be worth responding to requires a pause to register and evaluate the words, before speaking in answer" (ibid.).

Cree people actively indicate their attentiveness by using backchannel cues at pauses during interlocutors' turns. The most frequent signal is *ehe* "yes," which is an "acknowledgement of what is said, not an agreement with it" (ibid.). A stronger response, *tapwe* "truly," is reserved for the endings of developed argumentation.

Informal conversation may appear to be loosely structured, but close examination reveals that people follow organizational rules in exchanging turns and in negotiating and achieving the overall format of encounters. Conversations have beginnings and endings that frame the activity of talk. In our society, conversations typically begin with some sort of greeting and end with some sort of closing. Greetings and closings are examples of adjacency pairs and are exchanged sequentially. As we saw in Chapter 4, greetings often consist of routinized formulas having no true semantic content but functioning to mark a person's availability for talk. An initial greeting by one party, "Hello," must be acknowledged by the other through a return, "Hi, how're you doin'?" Both participants signal by their response that they understand and agree to a jointly negotiated behavior, indicating their willingness to engage in talk.

After an initial greeting exchange, participants propose and ratify topics of conversation. Here, too, each party is, in theory, in equal position to introduce topics, but, in practice, people of higher status assume more rights to select topics.

Termination of encounters is usually achieved in our culture through a gradual process at the end of some topic unit. Various techniques for "closing down a topic" are used, including words of agreement, such as "okay," "alright," or "fine," and other vocalizations, such as "well" or "so" (Schegloff and Sacks 1973:306). Proverbial or conventional expressions of "morals or lessons" commonly occur as initiators of closings, as in the following example (ibid.:307):

DORRINNE:	Uh-you know, it's just like bringin' the—blood up.
THERESA:	Yeah, well, things uh always work out for the best.
DORRINNE:	Oh certainly. Alright Tess.
THERESA:	Uh huh.
THERESA:	Okay.
DORRINNE:	G'bye.
THERESA:	Goodnight.

Another type of closing is the return to a prior topic, highlighting and repeating a main theme. This pattern frequently occurs in telephone conversations where a caller begins with a specific reason for calling and ends by mentioning the same issue. In telephone talk, either party can begin closings by referring to activities immediately prior to the call: "Well, I'll let you get back to your book" or "I gotta go finish making dinner" or simply "I gotta go."

As is the case for all social practices, different cultural norms lead to diverse rules for framing interactions. In contrast to American-Canadian custom, Cree speakers do not employ formal greetings or leave-takings because they interpret such markers as "giving the impression that the relationship is restricted to that occasion" (Darnell 1985:69). Cree speakers choose to emphasize the continuity of social bonds by avoiding indicators of closure.

Conversations are internally cohesive because of their formal structure and because of techniques that speakers use to relate current talk to previous interactions. One of the subtle linguistic devices speakers frequently use to achieve cohesion is repetition. Speakers can repeat entire utterances intact, make partial repeats with variation, and paraphrase previous utterances (Tannen 1987). Repetitions of whatever type involving words, phrases, and sentences bind constructional units to each other, performing an essential cohesive role (Halliday and Hasan 1976:282).

Repetition serves multiple communicative purposes, allowing speakers to stall while formulating their talk, providing redundancy to hearers as an aid in comprehension, and connecting turns of talk. It has varied interactional purposes as well, such as controlling the floor, demonstrating active listenership, ratifying the previous speaker's talk, showing or appreciating humor, and emphasizing one's own or another's contribution (Tannen 1987:583–584). According to Deborah Tannen, repetition in conversation is both a linguistic and an interpersonal device to make experience coherent: "Perceiving meaning through the coherence of discourse, as well as perceiving oneself as coherent in the interaction constituted by the discourse, creates an emotional experience of connectedness; this permits not only participation in the interaction, but also understanding of meaning" (ibid.:584). Additionally, use of repetition within discourse expresses the "eternal tension between fixity and novelty that constitutes creativity. It sends a metamessage of rapport between the communicators, who thereby experience that they share communicative conventions and inhabit the same world of discourse" (ibid.:585).

Some of Tannen's examples of repetition in naturally occurring conversation follow (ibid.:589–591):

1. *Repetition to signal participation and familiarity:*
   [S is serving wine, L declines, and her refusal is immediately repeated by N and S, speaking almost in unison]

L: I don't drink wine.

N: She doesn't drink wine.

S: Libby (L) doesn't drink wine.

2. *Repetition for humorous effect:*
   [D had requested permission to tape an ongoing encounter]

P: Just to see if we say anything interesting?

D: No. Just to see how you say nothing interesting.

P: Oh. Well I—I hardly ever say nothing interesting.

3. *Repetition for expansion or "scaffolding" of talk:*

D: Do you read?

P: Do I read?

D: Do you read things just for fun?

P: Yeah. Right now I'm reading "Norma Jean the Termite Queen."

Cohesion in discourse can also be accomplished through punning; that is, speakers can tie talk to either their own or previous speaker's talk by conscious or unconscious use of puns. Nondeliberate punning in conversation is often not consciously noticed by either speaker or hearer, but its occurrence provides evidence of a linguistic binding mechanism. Puns often occur at the ends of utterances or topic episodes, providing a framing that comments on previous talk. They also function interactively and creatively to pull together participants' talk and their meanings. Some examples from actual conversations follow:

1. Nutritionist talking about intestinal ailments:
   Well, there are nutritional supplements you can take to rectify the problem.

2. Talking about nuclear energy plants:
   The issue of nuclear explosions is a real hot topic now.

3. Sportscaster talking about a baseball pitcher who played in a game even though he had a broken toe:
   He admitted it was bothering him; he made no bones about it.

Finally, the following example comes from Harvey Sacks (1973:136–137):

4. In discussion of Ken's 12-year-old sister:

KEN: She came in there the other night with scotch tape an' every inch of the room. You couldn't—the roof I think she's got done in Beatle pictures and she lays in bed at night—

ROGER: She's doing that cause all her friends are (//) the Beatles.

LOUISE: Well, they need some kinda idol you know, something to look up to.

CONVERSATIONAL POSTULATES

When people converse, they have certain assumptions about the situation and co-participants based on cultural models of interaction, of the fit between behavior and context, and of people's rights and obligations. Cultural norms also dictate what can be said and what should not be said in particular situations, as well as the ways to say what can be said. If interlocutors belong to the same culture, none of these assumptions need be stated or even consciously recognized; they are learned through socialization and presupposed in daily life.

According to H. P. Grice, a "cooperative principle" is presumed to operate in most social encounters (1975:45). Participants have common aims to make "mutually dependent contributions" to conversation. Grice described the *cooperative principle* as "making your conversational contribution such as is required, at the state at which it occurs, by the accepted purpose or direction of the talk exchange in which you are engaged" (ibid.). This statement, although seemingly plausible, glosses over many crucial qualifications. For instance, notions expressed by phrases such as "is required" and "accepted purpose or direction" are influenced both by cultural expectations and by individual motives. What is the "accepted purpose" of a given interaction? Who defines or controls the "direction of the talk exchange"? Do co-participants always share a common aim, or do they merely appear to do so? Or is the "common aim" that of appearing to share a common aim? In analyzing actual speech, attention to intricacies of cooperation reveals a great deal of complexity.

Grice further developed a number of "maxims" that he believed account for and direct communicative interaction (ibid.:45–46):

1. *Quantity: Be informative.*
   a. Make your contribution as informative as required (for the current purposes of the exchange).
   b. Do not make your contribution more informative than required.
2. *Quality: Be truthful.*
   a. Do not say that which you believe to be false.
   b. Do not say that for which you lack adequate evidence.
3. *Relation: Be relevant.*
4. *Manner: Be perspicuous.*
   a. Avoid obscurity of expression.
   b. Avoid ambiguity.
   c. Be brief.
   d. Be orderly.

The first maxim, "be informative," implies a minimum and maximum on quantity, giving as much but no more information than is needed. The second maxim, "be truthful," refers to the speaker's sincerity and obligation not to mislead the hearer. The maxim to "be relevant" means that discourse or conversation should be coherent. Speakers' utterances should be topically, situationally, and interpersonally relevant. Last, the maxims of manner, "be brief" and "be orderly," refer to the use of linguistic form that clearly and succinctly expresses one's ideas, goals, and so on.

All of these maxims, of course, are ideals that are relative in their realization. Contextual, social, and cultural constraints limit the degree to which they are appropriately fulfilled. It may be necessary to violate the maxim "be truthful" in order not to insult or betray another individual. Similarly, a speaker may not "be informative" if she wishes to avoid conveying hurtful or upsetting messages. Finally, speakers may choose not to "be brief" but, rather, may use elaborate mitigating linguistic forms in order to blunt the force of their speech.

Grice recognized that conversational maxims are often ignored, evaded, or flouted in actual practice. Indeed, he noted, but did not elaborate, the possibility of additional maxims of an "aesthetic, social or moral" nature, such as "be polite" (ibid.:47).

Speakers can use certain linguistic devices as prefaces to statements to signal or acknowledge their violations of presupposed maxims. The following examples illustrate such functions of *but* in English (Baker 1975:40–41):

1. *Quantity:* Don't give too much or too little information.
   a. You probably have enough examples by now, but—
   b. This is just a minor point, but—
2. *Quality:* Don't say things you don't believe or don't have adequate evidence for.
   a. This may just be my own intuition, but—
   b. I'm probably totally wrong on this, but—
3. *Relevance:* Stick to the topic.
   a. I don't want to get too far off the topic, but—
   b. I'm not sure if this is relevant, but—
4. *Manner:* Avoid ambiguity and obscurity; be brief and orderly.
   a. I don't know if this makes any sense, but—
   b. It's difficult to state this clearly, but—

Cultural expectations and rules of etiquette affect the way that conversational maxims are fulfilled. For instance, the need to "be truthful" raises the question "How truthful?"; "be brief" leads to the query "How brief?" Even the maxim "be informative" is open for cultural interpretation, as Elinor Ochs Keenan (1976) showed in a study of conversation among the Malagasy of Madagascar. The Malagasy treat information as a valuable commodity and do not share it readily. Keenan attributes this attitude to the fact that, given the public nature of activities in small villages, most of what transpires is seen or quickly known by all. Therefore, "information that is not already available . . . is highly sought after. If one manages to gain access to 'new' information, one is reluctant to reveal it. As long as it is known that one has that information and others do not, one has some prestige over them" (1976:70).

Also, Malagasy speakers hesitate to fully answer questions or make explicit claims because "they do not want to be responsible for the information communicated" (ibid.). The Malagasy blame a person whose statements result in any unpleasantness. Finally, Malagasy villagers are reluctant to make claims about future activities because they would feel shamed if events do not occur as predicted. An example of complicated avoidance of the maxim to "be informative" was a woman's response to Keenan's inquiry about when the woman's brother would return home: "If you don't come after five, you won't find him" (ibid.:71).

Interpersonal relationships existing between Malagasy co-participants also affect whether speakers give information to hearers. The Malagasy classify people into three categories: *havana,* close kin and neighbors; *havan-davitra,* distant kin; and *vahiny,* strangers (ibid.:77). People regularly exchange information with *havana* because they are trusted, but the Malagasy do not give information to distant kin or strangers because they are not trusted. Finally, women generally are more informative than are men because men cultivate an air of caution and polite detachment in their speech, whereas women are more direct and confrontational (ibid.:77–78).

DIRECTIVES

Speakers are expected to respect the rights of others and to be sincere, that is, mean what they say (although they may not always say what they mean). These norms are displayed, for example, in patterns for issuing *directives,* utterances intended to result in an action by the hearer. In order for *directives,* or *requests for action,* to be heard as legitimate, they must satisfy certain sincerity, or felicity, conditions (Gordon and Lakoff 1971:64):

1. Speaker wants hearer to do act.
2. Speaker assumes hearer is able to do act.
3. Speaker assumes hearer is willing to do act.
4. Speaker assumes hearer would not do act in the absence of the request.

Linguistic forms of directives can be tailored to focus on each of these assumptions (ibid.):

1. I want you to take out the garbage.
2. Can you take out the garbage?
3. Would you be willing to take out the garbage?
4. Will you take out the garbage?

Note that none of these requests is expressed as an overt imperative; they are either assertions or questions. However, they are intended as directives and are appropriately understood as such. Hearers are expected to react to speakers' underlying intentions, not necessarily to the surface linguistic form of utterances.

Gordon and Lakoff pointed out that speech acts must be reasonable (ibid.:67). Each kind of speech act—stating, directing, requesting, promising—has its particular basis in reasonableness. Assertions are reasonable inasmuch as the beliefs expressed are reasonable; directives are reasonable if all the sincerity conditions apply.

Speech acts can be challenged if they diverge from the principles of sincerity or reasonableness. Hearers can make challenges by questioning underlying assumptions or by denying assumed conditions. The following utterances are challenges to directives:

1. Why do you want me to close the window? It's hot in here.
2. My arm hurts, so I can't close the window.
3. Why do you think I'd be willing to close the window?
4. You don't have to tell me to do it. I was just going to close the window anyway.

The rights and obligations of participants may be shared equally by all or be monopolized by certain individuals based on status differences. Higher-status speakers are less often challenged when making statements, regardless of the accuracy of their remarks, or when issuing directives, regardless of the inconvenience of complying.

Directives are particularly sensitive to contexts of speaking and to specific social characteristics of the issuer and addressee. Their complexity stems from the fact that a speaker should phrase requests so as to have the greatest likelihood of positive result, namely, compliance; but because a social relationship of some sort exists between interlocutors (even if it is one of "stranger"), speakers must be sensitive to addressees' feelings. An issuer of directives needs to navigate between two extremes of clarity: He must make his request clear enough so that the addressee comprehends the directive intent, yet he must also pay attention to the addressee's needs not to be imposed on by a blunt presumption of the speaker's power.

In English, and presumably in all languages, many linguistic alternatives exist for issuing directives. They are generally classified into six types:

1. *Need statement* (speaker asserts her need or want):
   "I need some salt."

2. *Imperative* (speaker commands an action of hearer):
   "Give me the salt!"

3. *Embedded imperative* (command is embedded in another linguistic frame):
   "Could you give me some salt?"

4. *Permission directive* (speaker asks permission, implying action of hearer):
   "May I have the salt?"

5. *Question directive* (speaker asks a question, indirectly implying action of hearer):
   "Do you have any salt?"

6. *Hints* (speaker makes assertion, hinting a request):
   "The salt's not here."

Directives in each of these categories can be expressed with greater or lesser mitigation. For instance, markers of politeness, principally "please" in English, can be added: "May I please have the salt?" Other elaborate linguistic frames are employed in certain contexts: "Would you be so kind as to give me the salt?" In our culture, politeness and mitigation are generally used by speakers who are subordinate to addressees or who, for reasons either of context or personality, wish to soften the force of a directive. In situations socially marked as "formal," blunt demonstrations of authority, even by high-status speakers, are considered inappropriate. In contrast, some speakers select especially bald imperative forms to emphasize their rights to command addressees. Adult speech to children often includes threats or warnings: "Clean up your room, or I'll spank you."

Because many directives are not imperative in form, it is necessary that hearers interpret them appropriately. Hearers need to understand speakers' intent. Comprehension of speakers' intentions is based on knowledge of context, of what kinds of goals people express in language, and of the linguistic alternatives that potentially express those intents. For example, the interrogative "Do you have any salt?" uttered during a meal, is normally interpreted as a directive because a "request for information" about addressee's possession of salt seems irrelevant. Interpreting this interrogative form as a "request for information" is excluded on the grounds of an absence of legitimacy. A yes/no reply by addressee, then, would usually be intended as a joke. Otherwise, if an addressee responds to the surface linguistic form rather than the underlying intent of a directive, he can be interpreted as making a challenge.

Speakers select among linguistic alternatives for issuing directives based on context and on relationships with addressees. A speaker can mitigate statements of need and many types of imperatives either by deleting the command verb or by supplying additional linguistic frames that soften the speaker's message. The following examples of directives are obtained from actual conversations recorded by Susan Ervin-Tripp (1976:29–45):

1. *Need statements:*
    a. (Physician to technician) "I'll need a routine culture and a specimen."
    b. (Head of office to subordinate) "I want you to check the requirement for stairs."

2. *Imperatives:*
    a. Deleted imperative:
        (Customer to waitress) "Coffee, black."
    b. You + imperative:
        (Passenger to driver) "You should turn right here, then you go straight."
    c. Attention-getters:
        (A child is yelling in the vicinity of a group of adults talking; father to child) "Please!"
    d. Post-posed tags:
        (Professor to colleague) "Carry some of these, will you?"
    e. Rising intonation:
        (Student to another) "Give me a copy?"

The next two categories of directives are indirect in their surface representation, having been converted into the form of questions. Their underlying purpose, however, is still obvious.

3. *Embedded imperatives:*
   a. (Hospital nurse to aide) "Would you hand me Mr. Adams's chart, please?"
   b. (Nurse to nurse) "Julie, how about bringing me back a Coke when you go to dinner?"
   c. (To stranger in theater) "Can you move your coat over there?"
4. *Permission directives:*
   a. (Brother to sister) "Can I have my records back?"
   b. (Salesman to clerk) "May I have change for a dollar?"

The final two categories, question directives and hints, provide options for hearers because they can be interpreted as assertions, requests for information, or requests for confirmation rather than as directives. Speakers frequently use negative tag questions if they assume that noncompliance is at least as likely as compliance.

5. *Question directives:*
   a. (Office worker to another) "Are we out of coffee?" (Give me some coffee.)
   b. (Hospital patient to orderly) "Do you feel a draft?" (Give me a blanket.)
   c. (Motorist to gas station attendant) "You don't happen to have any change for the phone, do you?"
6. *Hints:*
   a. (Child to adult) "I'm hungry."
   b. (Daughter to mother) "Mother, you know I don't have a robe."
      "I know."
      "Well, we're having a slumber party tomorrow night."
   c. (Student to roommate) "There's a big can of tomato sauce." (Use it up.)

Because utterances often have multiple possible interpretations, reactions to linguistic form can be manipulated for various effects, including humor:

(Son to mother) "I need a ten-speed bicycle."
"I'm sure you do."

Linguistic strategies for formulating directives can be classified on the basis of both the orientation of requests and the kinds of linguistic devices employed. Orientation refers to which element of the request matrix is stressed: speaker, addressee, or action to be performed (data from Blum-Kulka and Olshtain 1984:203):

1. *Hearer-oriented:* Could *you* tidy up the kitchen soon?
2. *Speaker-oriented:* Do you think *I* could borrow your notes from yesterday's class?
3. *Speaker- and hearer-oriented:* So, could *we* please clean up?
4. *Impersonal:* So it might not be a bad idea to *get it cleaned up.*

Directives can be mitigated through various types of linguistic devices (ibid.: 203–205):

1. *Syntactic downgraders or mitigation:*
    a. Interrogative: Could you do the cleaning up?
    b. Negation: Look, excuse me. I wonder if you *wouldn't mind* dropping me home?
    c. Past tense: I *wanted* to ask for a postponement.
    d. Embedded "if" clause: I would appreciate it *if* you left me alone.
2. *Pragmatic mitigation:*
    a. Consultative devices (indirectly asking for addressee's cooperation): *Do you think* I could borrow your lecture notes from yesterday?
    b. Understaters (minimizing request): Could you tidy up *a bit* before I start?
    c. Hedges (avoiding commitment): It would really help if *you did something* about the kitchen.
    d. Downtoner (signaling possibility of noncompliance): Will you *perhaps* be able to drive me?

Children learn styles of formulating directives as part of socialization and acquisition of communicative norms. Comparison of directives used by Hungarian and Norwegian children demonstrated differences between the two cultures and also between younger (4 to 5 years old) and older (9 to 10 years old) children in each group (Hollos and Beeman 1978). In general, Hungarian children employed direct commands and requests, making a distinction between familiars (friends, family, neighbors) and strangers in selecting linguistic alternatives. For example, a bald imperative *adjal* "give!" is used to familiars, whereas polite, but still direct, forms such as *tessek szives lenni adni* "please to be kind to give" is used to strangers (ibid.:347). When initial requests were denied, Hungarian children resorted to intensified demands, repetition of requests, and forms of begging.

Norwegian children, in contrast, generally favored indirect means both to initiate and repeat requests. They used need statements, *jeg er sa torst* "I have so thirst"; interrogatives, *kann du hjelpe meg* "can you help me?"; and hints, *kann du finne litt saft* "can you find a little juice?" (ibid.:349). Norwegian children also distinguished between familiars and strangers, and in interactions with the latter, often attempted to enlist an adult's aid in obtaining their goals. When requests were denied, these children either gave up or repeated their requests in even more indirect styles.

As one would expect, older children employed a wider range of syntactic and lexical formulations. Their ability to use more complex grammatical structures is based on their advanced language acquisition. For example, a 5-year-old Norwegian child commanded his father: *Far, kom hit* "Father, come here!" whereas a 9-year-old asked: *Far, kann du komme?* "Father, can you come?" When these children intensified their requests, the younger said *Nei, kom na* "No, come now!"; the older asked *kann du ikke komme?* "Can you not come?" (ibid.:353).

DIRECTIVES AND RESPONSES IN CONTEXT

Analysis of the form of directives and of addressees' responses often reveals that speakers use indirect means in order to soften the force of their speech and to avoid responsibility for underlying implications. In a discussion of directives, William Labov and David Fanshel formulated the *rule of requests* (1977:78), which is based on assumptions similar to Gordon and Lakoff's *felicity conditions:*

Rule of Requests

If A addresses to B an imperative specifying an action X at a time T, and B believes that A believes that

1a. X should be done (for a purpose) (*need for action*).
1b. B would not do X in the absence of the request (*need for request*).
2. B has the *ability* to do X (with an instrument Z).
3. B has the *obligation* to do X or is willing to do it.
4. A has the *right* to tell B to do X, then A is heard as making a valid request for action.

This rule is predicated on mutually recognized needs, abilities, obligations, and rights. Such preconditions are usually not stated directly but exist as part of the participants' interactional competence. According to Labov and Fanshel, explicit reference to needs of speakers, abilities of addressees, or existential conditions (e.g., "This place is really dusty") is often perceived as mitigating the force of requests, whereas statement of speaker's rights or hearer's obligations is typically aggravating (ibid.:83). However, Labov and Fanshel's generalization should be tempered with the provision that context, relationship between interlocutors, and prosodic cues affect the mitigating or aggravating force of any utterance. For example, appeals to existential conditions, "Have you dusted yet?" or abilities, "Do you have enough time to dust the room?" that Labov and Fanshel consider mitigating can be intended and interpreted as sarcastic and, therefore, aggravating.

Just as speakers choose means for making requests, addressees select among alternative means of responding. If an addressee intends to comply with a request, a direct response is usually given. In contrast, noncompliant moves are often accomplished indirectly. Given the social nature of conversation and requirements that participants be cooperative, refusals of directives typically contain an "accounting" (ibid.:88) related to underlying validity conditions. An addressee can question the need for an action, her ability to perform the act, her obligation to comply, and/or the right of speaker to make the request. Most refusals, then, are indirect and call for additional justification by the requester, who can reinstate the directive by responding to the addressee's accounting.

Bald repetitions of directives are perceived in our culture as aggravated assertions of authority. Labov and Fanshel analyzed such responses as challenges to the competence of the addressee. They suggested that most challenges are in practice mitigated so as to avoid overt confrontation: "Though a challenge to competence is always present when a request is repeated, the more the surface structure is varied, the less strongly is this challenge felt" (ibid.:95). Challenges are often expressed as surface interrogatives. Because, like all questions, challenges are examples of adjacency pairs, they require a response from the addressee in the form of either a defense or an admission. Admissions of the validity of a challenge have interpersonal consequences not only for the moment of a particular episode but also for the future because they form part of the presupposed background of subsequent speech events.

The following examples, from Labov and Fanshel's analysis of a therapy session, demonstrate interactional complexities of conversation and the need to attend to personal histories of co-participants in order to develop a full understanding of what is meant by talk. The patient, Rhoda (age 19), begins an account of a telephone call to her mother, who was visiting Rhoda's married sister, with the following surface question (ibid.:155):

> And so-when-I called her t'day, I said, "Well, when do you plan to come home?"

Although this utterance takes interrogative form, Rhoda intends it as a directive, a request for action, namely, that her mother return home. Rhoda's question (implied request) satisfies preconditions for validity based on the rule of requests (ibid.:159):

1. Her mother should come home to help do the housework and does not seem to be doing so without being asked.
2. Her mother has the ability to come home.
3. Her mother has an obligation to come home, because she is the head of the household.
4. Rhoda has the right to tell her mother to come home.

Because Rhoda's underlying intent differs from the linguistic form she chooses, her question can be expanded to reflect its actual meaning (ibid.:160):

> *Rhoda:* When I called my mother today, I actually said "Well, in regard to the subject which we both know is important and is worrying me, when are you leaving my sister's house where any obligations you have already have been fulfilled and returning home where your primary obligations are being neglected as you should do as head of our household?"

Finally, Rhoda has accomplished an act of requesting in the context of a specific interaction with her mother. Labov and Fanshel explicated the interpersonal communicative work as follows:

> Rhoda requests information on the time that her mother intends to come home and thereby requests indirectly that her mother come home, thereby challenging her mother indirectly for not performing

her role as head of the household properly, simultaneously admitting her own limitations.

And how does Rhoda's mother respond to the indirect requests and implications? She also employs covert means to challenge Rhoda's question:

So she said, "Oh, why?"

This utterance cannot possibly be intended as a simple question. Labov and Fanshel offered the following expansion (ibid.:166):

So my mother said to me: "Oh, I'm surprised; why are you asking me when I plan to come home, and do you have a right to ask that? There's more to this than meets the eye: Isn't it that you can't take care of the household by yourself and I shouldn't have gone away in the first place, as I've told you before."

The interactional implications are

Mother asks Rhoda for further information which she already has, thereby putting off R's requests for action and for help and asserts indirectly that she knows that the answer to her own question is that R is asking for help because she cannot perform the obligations of household, thereby challenging R's status as an adult member of the household.

POLITENESS

Theories of Politeness

When people converse, they generally adhere to cultural norms, showing that they are "competent" speakers. Robin Lakoff suggested two underlying *rules of pragmatic competence* (1973:296):

1. Be clear.
2. Be polite.

Ideally, speakers try to fulfill both of these requirements. However, if the rules conflict, Lakoff claimed that politeness supersedes because "it is considered more important in a conversation to avoid offense than to achieve clarity . . . since in most informal conversations, actual communication of important ideas is secondary to reaffirming and strengthening relationships" (ibid.:297–298).

Lakoff's postulates for politeness are (ibid.:298):

1. Don't impose.
2. Give options.
3. Make A feel good—be friendly.

These rules are deceptively concise, but they are actually complex because languages provide multiple forms for expressing them. For example, passive constructions, such as "Dinner is served," are more polite than direct questions, "Would you like to eat?" (ibid.:299). The first sentence, in compliance with Rule 1, avoids intruding into the addressee's wants or needs and is, therefore, interpersonally distancing.

Speakers comply with Rule 2 (Give options) by using hedges and mitigated expressions that allow hearers to form and hold their own opinions. By not forcefully asserting propositions, hedges and mitigation blunt potential confrontations. Speakers can provide hearers with options to respond either affirmatively or negatively, as in "I guess it's time to leave" or "It's time to leave, isn't it?" (ibid.:300).

Rule 3 (Make A feel good—be friendly) is the most variable in terms of cultural meanings. It implies, as do all of Lakoff's rules, that co-participants share similar models and norms for behavior and that they evaluate speech according to the same presupposed notions.

In a widely acclaimed attempt to discover universal principles of politeness, Penelope Brown and Stephen Levinson (1987) compared linguistic data principally from English, Tzeltal (a native language of Mexico), and Tamil (spoken in India). They suggested that everywhere polite behavior is based on assumptions of cooperation because all social groups need to minimize conflict among co-members. In Brown and Levinson's terms, politeness is concerned with *face,* defined as an "individual's self-esteem" or the "public self-image that every member wants to claim for [him- or herself]" (1987:2, 161). The notion of face entails different kinds of desires, or *face-wants,* that all people have and that all people know others to have. These wants are of two basic types (ibid.:13):

1. *Positive face-wants:* desire (in some respects) to be approved of
2. *Negative face-wants:* desire to be unimpeded in one's actions

Although these wants are presumably universal, they are "subject to cultural specifications of many sorts—what kinds of acts threaten face, what sorts of persons have special rights to face-protection, and what kinds of personal styles (in terms of things like graciousness, ease of social relations, etc.) are especially appreciated" (ibid.:13).

Brown and Levinson distinguish strategies of polite behavior by differentiating face-wants (ibid.:2, 70):

1. *Positive politeness:* oriented to the positive image which hearer claims; speaker recognizes hearer's desire to have her or his positive face-wants respected. Positive politeness strategies express solidarity, friendliness, in-group reciprocity.

2. *Negative politeness:* oriented to H's desire not to be imposed upon; S recognizes H's rights to autonomy. Negative politeness strategies express S's restraint and avoidance of imposing on H.

3. *Off-record politeness:* indirect strategies which avoid making any explicit or unequivocal imposition on H.

Speakers choose among these modes and within each they select specific linguistic variants, depending on relationships to addressees within the overriding context of cultural assumptions about rights of co-participants, potential offensiveness of intended messages, and appropriateness of each behavior in any given event. Cultures vary, too, in the emphasis given to interactional qualities—for example, being tactful, modest, agreeable, generous, sympathetic. Finally, people in different social categories may be expected to display any of these qualities to a greater or lesser extent; for example, lower-status people may need to show modesty or tact when speaking to higher-status people.

According to Brown and Levinson, politeness strategies develop to deal with *face-threatening acts* or FTAs (ibid.:60), acts that intrinsically infringe on H's face-wants. For instance, requests by necessity impose on H's negative face (desire to be unimpeded). Requests and other FTAs can be done "bald on-record," that is, directly. However, most FTAs are accomplished with "redressive action," through some expression of positive or negative politeness. Figure 5.1 represents Brown and Levinson's schema of strategies and risks (ibid.:60).

The more threatening an act is, the more polite and indirect are the means used to accomplish it. Requests that involve minimal cost to H are made through positive politeness strategies, stressing solidarity between S and H. Requests involving greater imposition on H are made through negative politeness strategies that are more formal and distancing. The most imposing requests are expressed through indirection and hints (ibid.:59).

FTAs vary in terms of the kind of threat involved (ibid.:65–68). Some threaten H's negative face by imposing on H (requests, orders, dares, offers, expressions of anger). Other FTAs threaten H's positive face (desire to be respected) by indicating S's lack of concern for H's self-image (criticism, accusations, insults, contradictions, boasts). Finally, some FTAs are threatening to S rather than to H by either offending S's need not to be imposed upon (thanking, accepting offers,

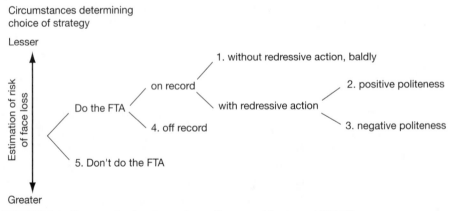

FIGURE 5.1. Communication Strategies.   (Brown and Levinson 1987:60)

making unwilling promises) or by offending S's need for positive self-image (apologies, confessions, admissions of responsibility).

Speakers select linguistic mechanisms for accomplishing FTAs dependent on three types of social factors having varying weight in any given encounter (ibid.:74):

1. *Social distance:* a symmetric relation between S and H
2. *Power:* an asymmetric relation between S and H
3. *Ranking:* an assessment of the degree of imposition entailed by the FTA

Cultural norms obviously affect the interpretation of these factors. Degree of social distance depends on cultural notions of familiarity or formality involved in any given relationship; relative power of S and H is contingent on social segmentation and the assignment of greater or lesser rights and obligations to members of distinct groups; and relative ranking of FTAs is only appropriate in the context of cultural assumptions about the risks and costs of given behaviors.

Speakers begin by wishing to accommodate H's face-wants to some degree in order to gain cooperation or compliance from H and to demonstrate S's own cooperativeness. Then S decides to what extent she or he should use politeness strategies to minimize the intended FTA, given the encounter's social and personal context and S's need to accomplish the FTA. Speakers consider these factors as they select linguistic means for expressing FTAs. As shown in Brown and Levinson's diagram (Figure 5.1), four types of strategies are possible: bald on-record, positive politeness, negative politeness, and off-record (indirect). Following is a compilation of various linguistic devices employed in English, Tzeltal, and Tamil to realize different strategies (ibid.:94ff):

1. Bald on-record (no effort to minimize threats to H's face):
   a. In emergencies:
      Help!
      eRu! eRu! periya paampu! (Tamil: Get up! Get up! There's a big snake!)
   b. In task-oriented activities:
      Give me the nails.
   c. In unequal power relationships:
      Bring me the wine, Jeeves.
   d. In joking or teasing:
      ʔokʼan. ʔilinan. (Tzeltal: Cry. Get angry.)
   e. In alerting H to something in his or her interest:
      Your headlights are on!
   f. In granting H's request:
      yakuk. laʔ čuka tey ʔa. (Tzeltal: OK. Come tie it there.)
   g. In greetings, leave-takings; formulaic offers:
      hič ʼan tal. laʔ weʔan. (Tzeltal: Pull [your chair] up. Come eat.)
2. Positive politeness (recognize H's desire to be respected):
   a. Claim common ground (indicate that S and H belong to same group, have similar needs, etc.):

1) Attend to H:
   You must be hungry, it's a long time since breakfast. How about some lunch?

2) Exaggerate approval, sympathy, etc.:
   viiTu payankaramaa kaTTirukkiraar. (Tamil: He built the house terrifyingly [i.e., lavishly].)

3) Use in-group identity markers:
   Help me with this bag here, will you pal?
   ç'usa kala ti²nail kançil. (Tzeltal: Shut my little door, my girl.)

4) Avoid disagreement:
   A: What is she, small?
   B: Yes, yes, she's small, smallish, um, not really small but certainly not very big.

5) Assume agreement:
   So when are you coming to see us?
   hk'opon hbakik ç 'in. (Tzeltal: We'll be talking together then.)

6) Hedge opinions:
   You really should sort of try harder.
   memel niwan. (Tzeltal: True maybe.)

7) Switch personal focus:
   en paNam elaam poocc alla. (Tamil: All my money's gone, hasn't it?)

8) Presuppose H's wants:
   ma ya² we wah me²? (Tzeltal: Won't you eat, Mother?)

9) Joke:
   OK if I tackle those cookies now?

b.   Convey cooperation between S and H:

1) Presuppose H's feelings:
   I know you can't bear parties, but this one will really be good—do come!

2) Be optimistic:
   I'll just help myself to a cookie then—thanks!
   onka vaNTi kuTukkiriinka, illeyaa? (Tamil: You'll lend me your bike, right?)

3) Include both S and H:
   Let's have a cookie, then.
   hk'antik²a²wala²aç 'am ²a. (Tzeltal: We [inclusive] want your little salt.)

4) Give (or ask for) reasons:
   bistuk ma ša² wak'betik bel hmahantik ²ä²son?
   (Tzeltal: Why don't you lend us your record player?)

3. Negative politeness (recognize H's desire not to be imposed upon):
   a.   Be conventionally indirect:

I'm looking for a comb.
inta paattiratt-le neriya koncam teeva paTutu.
(Tamil: This plate needs much more a little.)

b.   Don't presume or assume:
ya mel ˀ aˀ woˀ tan mak. (Tzeltal: You are sad, I guess.)
muTincaa, koncam paNam kuTunka. (Tamil: If you can, give some money.)

c.   Don't coerce H:
   1)   Be pessimistic, uncertain:
      Could you do it?
      onka-kiTTee sikaraTT irukkumaa? (Tamil: Will there be a cigarette on you?)
   2)   Minimize the imposition:
      I just want to ask you if I can borrow a little bit of paper.
      ya khˀan ala pēsuk. (Tzeltal: I want a little peso's worth, as it were.)

d.   Communicate a desire not to impose on H:
   1)   Apologize:
      a)   Admit imposition:
          I'd like to ask you a big favor.
          lom bolobon meˀ tik, ma ba hkˀoponat. (Tzeltal: I'm very stupid, Mother, I didn't greet you.)
      b)   Indicate reluctance:
          I don't want to bother you, but . . .
      c)   Give overwhelming reasons:
          I can think of nobody else who could . . .
      d)   Beg forgiveness:
          mannikkaNum. (Tamil: You should/must forgive me.)
   2)   Impersonalize:
      (onkalukku) aavasiyum. (Tamil: [To you] it is necessary that . . .)
      ma stak (yaˀ) pas mene. (Tzeltal: It is not possible [you] do that.)
   3)   Use passives:
      That letter must be typed immediately.
      ceyyaTTum. (Tamil: Let it be done.)
   4)   Use indefinites:
      One shouldn't do things like that.
      ˀay bal macˀa ˀay skˀu ya hmahan? (Tzeltal: Is there someone who would have a blouse I could borrow?)
   5)   Pluralize pronouns:
      We regret to inform you . . .
      vaanka, namma viiTTlee caappiTalaam. (Tamil: Come, let's eat at our house!)
   6)   Use distance:
      I was wondering whether you could do me a little favor.

7) State general rules:
   Latecomers cannot be seated until the next interval.
8) Nominalize:
   An urgent request is made for your cooperation.
   nii pooratu. (Tamil: You're going, that is, you should go.)

4. Off-record (indirect strategies):
   a. Give hints:
      It's cold in here.
      etoo paNam vaankinaa, paraville-ille? (Tamil: If some money is received, it wouldn't matter, would it?)
   b. Understate:
      It's not half bad.
      puersa k'ešlal ȼ'in mak. (Tzeltal: She's really embarrassed then maybe.)
   c. Overstate:
      I tried to call a hundred times, but there was never any answer.
   d. Be ironic:
      John's a real genius.
      yuʔ ma ʔihk'al čahpuk lah ta yalel ʔa ȼ 'i. (Tzeltal: Because it's not really bad-as-it-were then [i.e., it's really bad]!)
   e. Use rhetorical questions:
      What can I say? [i.e., Nothing, it's so bad.]
      ancu mailukku varra muTiyaataa? (Tamil: Can't you come five miles [to see us]? [i.e., Why haven't you come to visit?])
   f. Be vague or ambiguous:
      Perhaps someone did something naughty.

This survey of politeness strategies demonstrates both forms and functions of linguistic alternatives. Certain features of linguistic structure can readily accommodate speakers' needs to mitigate or redress FTAs, the essence of politeness. Grammatical mechanisms such as embedded interrogatives, passives, and impersonal nominalizations have differing forms and frequencies of use in diverse languages. And formulaic expressions and terms of address are part of the repertory of all languages, although their proliferation and usage vary cross-culturally.

Among the Akan of Ghana, the use of proverbs in conversation functions as a strategy to mitigate FTAs engendered by giving advice and admonitions, thereby protecting the face of both speaker and addressee (Obeng 1996). For example, in the following excerpt, a mother advises her adult son to send money home to contribute to the support of his aged parents by reminding him of his familial responsibility:

Mpaninfo   na   ekaa   se   se   obi   hwe
elders   FOC   said   that if   someone looks-after

wo   ma   wo   se   fifi   a,   ese se   wo   nso
you   for   your teeth develop if   must   you   also

```
wo   hwe   no   na   ne   se   tutu.
wo   look-after  him  FOC  his  teeth  uproot

Wonim   wo   papa   yadee   yi.   Seesi   ntumi
you-know  your  father  illness  this  now  he-cannot

nye   adwuma;   asetena   aye   den.
NEG-do work   life   has-become hard
```
(*Note:* FOC = focus; NEG = negative) (Obeng 1996:532.)

"It is the elders who said, <u>If someone looks after you when you're teething, you should also look after him when he loses his teeth</u>. You're aware of your father's illness. Now he's incapable of working. Life is hard these days." Here the mother begins a potential FTA by quoting a proverb handed down by "the elders" in order to soften the implied request for her son's financial assistance.

However, when examining politeness strategies, we should remember that linguistic forms can be manipulated in speech encounters in contradictory ways. Consider the following episode in which a nurse tries to convince an elderly hospitalized patient to take her medicine (data from Coupland et al. 1988:259):

NURSE: Edith. Hallo, my darling. Try and drink that for me. Drink that down for me.

EDITH: I've got to go to school.

N: Well drink that down first and then you can go to school.

E: (( ))

N: Down the hatch with it. And the rest. Straight down. Go on straight down, Edith. It's nice. Drink it straight down then. I've had mine you drink that up.

E: Oh, I don't want it.

N: Yes, drink it down you must. Doctor's orders.

E: Take it.

N: Doctor's orders. Come on, drink it down. Drink it down for me. Drink it now.

E: (( ))

N: No, drink it now. Come on then, drink it down. Quick, look, Mary is drinking hers. You drink yours straight down. You must quick. If you don't drink it you'll be very poorly.

(Nurse tries to force medicine)

E: Ow! Ow! Ow!

N: Come on. Drink it down.

SECOND NURSE: I'd leave her then if she don't want it that bad. I don't think she wants it.

In this encounter, the nurse employed many supposedly mitigating politeness strategies: addressing patient with familiar name and term of endearment (Edith, my darling); incurring a debt (drink that for me); using metaphor and humor (down the hatch with it); being optimistic (it's nice); including speaker and hearer in activity (I've had mine); impersonalizing (doctor's orders); exaggerating benefit to hearer (if you don't drink it you'll be very poorly). Nearly all of the nurse's turns contain at least one of these devices. But they hardly render the interaction any less intrusive or less coercive. Indeed, the proliferation of endearing, optimistic, inclusive formulations has the opposite effect. Rather than belittling the imposition on hearer, they belittle and demean the hearer herself.

Politeness in Japanese

Situational and cross-cultural studies supplement and illustrate theories about politeness and its linguistic and social meanings. The Japanese language provides a rich body of data for the investigation of politeness. Politeness is demonstrated in Japanese through *honorification*—the use of respect markers with nouns, verbs, and modifiers to show deference toward addressees or referents. Nouns representing worthy people or objects can be marked in several ways. First, Japanese contains some contrasting expressions for persons (Ide 1982:359):

1a. *ano hito* "that person" (plain)
1b. *ano kato* "that person" (honored)

Second, names and kin terms can co-occur with polite respect markers:

2a. Last name/first name/kin term + *san* (honored)
    Hanako-san; otoo-san "father"
2b. LN/FN/kin term + *sama* (exalted respect)
    Hanako-sama; otoo-sama "father"
2c. (LN) + *sensei* (literally: teacher)
    Satoo-sensei
2d. (LN) + *senpai* (literally: senior colleague)
    Satoo-senpai

Although *sensei* means "teacher," it can be used politely for any high-status professional, such as a doctor, politician, writer, and so on. *Senpai* "senior colleague" is also extended to any respected member of one's group.

Finally, nouns referring to objects can co-occur with the polite prefixes *o-* and *go-*. They are attached to objects associated with honored people. (*Note:* Examples are from Ide 1982:360–365; HON = honorific; TOP = sentential topic; NOM = nominative; DAT = dative; ACC = accusative.)

3a. teacher's book (possession)
    sensei   *no*   *go-hon*
    teacher   HON-book

3b. teacher's work (produced by teacher)
sensei   no   go-sakuhin
teacher   HON-work

Honorification of verbs and modifiers is more complex. Three different politeness devices are used to mark grammatical subjects, objects, or addressees. A fourth type humbles the speaker rather than (or in addition to) honoring the addressee or referent.

To show respect toward grammatical subjects, speakers combine prefix *o-* or *go-* and the ending *ni naru* with infinitives of verbs describing the respected subject's action. (*Note:* In the first example, contrasting plain and polite sentences are given; in subsequent examples, only polite forms are indicated.)

4a. Taro (plain) walked   to the station.
Taroo wa   eki   made   arui -ta
      TOP station to   walk PAST
4b. Professor Sato (honored)   walked to the station.
Satoo-sensei wa eki   made   o-aruki ni nat-   ta
      TOP station to   HON-walk-HON-PAST
Some verbs are marked for politeness with the suffix *(r)are:*

5.   Professor Sato (honored) wrote a book.
Satoo-sensei   ga   hon   o   kak-are-ta.
              NOM book ACC write-HON-PAST

The suffix *(r)are* is a homophone of the regular passive suffix in Japanese, confirming one of Brown and Levinson's postulates of universal linguistic practice, that is, use of passives as a politeness strategy.

Adjectives that describe the respected subject are marked with the *o-* or *go-* prefix:

6.   Professor Sato (honored) is busy.
Satoo-sensei wa   o-isogasii
              TOP   HON-busy

Adverbs, too, can be politely marked in association with the actions of an honored person:

7.   Professor Sato (honored) returned early.
Satoo-sensei wa   o-hayaku   o-kaeri   ni nat-ta
              TOP   HON-early HON-return-HON-PAST

In order to indicate respect toward grammatical objects, speakers combine the prefix *o-*, *go-*, or *hai-* and the ending *suru* with verbal infinitives:

8.   I asked Professor Sato (honored) the reason.
Watasi wa Satoo-sensei ni sono wake o o-tazune si-ta
I   TOP   DAT its reason   HON-ask-HON-PAST

To show respect toward addressees, verbs co-occur with the ending *masu*. In addition, the polite pronoun *anata* is employed:

9.   Are you (honored) coming?
     Anata wa   irassyai masu   ka
     you   TOP come (HON) HON QUESTION

Finally, respect toward referents and addressees can be demonstrated indirectly by humbling the speaker:

10a. I will go (plain).
     Watasi ga iku
     I   go
10b. I will go (humble).
     Watasi ga mairu.
     I   go (humble)

Humbling prefixes are sometimes attached to nouns labeling referents associated with the speaker:

11. *tuma*   "wife"   *gu-sai*   "my (stupid) wife"
     musuko "son".   *gu-soku* "my (stupid) son"
     mise   "shop"   *syoo-ten* "my (small) shop"
     bun   "sentence" *setu-bun* "my (bad) sentences"

These usages are not intended to insult wife, son, shop, and so on, but, rather, to indicate the speaker's modesty, thereby raising the status of the addressee (note, however, that there is no equivalent meaning "my (stupid) husband").

According to Sachiko Ide, Japanese social rules of politeness influence speakers' selection of various linguistic devices. The overriding rule of politeness is to "be polite in a formal setting" (1982:371). Formality is based on relationships among participants (lacking familiarity or solidarity), situational occasion (e.g., ceremonies, public meetings), and topic of talk (seriousness).

In addition to the general rule of formality, three other rules apply in Japanese social etiquette (ibid.:366–368):

1.   Be polite to a person of higher social position.
2.   Be polite to a person with power.
3.   Be polite to an older person.

Social position is an important aspect of one's identity, and it influences the linguistic treatment one receives. However, it is secondary to the operation of Rule 2, which takes precedence. Power is a characteristic of specific encounters and varies with the type of interaction. For example, professionals such as doctors have power over their patients or teachers over their students. In these cases, power and social position coincide, but in others they may not (a police officer issuing a traffic ticket to a doctor has power even though he has lower social status). People who control money have power in interactions (customers to merchants, employers to employees). Finally, a person making a request will be polite to an addressee, reflecting the latter's power to satisfy or deny requests (ibid.:367–368).

Ide reported that some individuals of high social status and power violate expected norms of politeness by using reciprocally polite speech to their subordinates. She suggested that "this may be caused by the egalitarian consciousness of upper-class guilt by which one denies Rule 1. . . . This trend is strongly observed in the behavior of women in higher positions [resulting from] a clash of the high professional position and the low status of women in general" (ibid.:367). Women typically use more polite speech than do men, characterized by a high frequency of honorifics, formal stylistic markers, and softening devices such as hedges and questions.

Experimental studies with Japanese men and women reveal additional factors contributing to women's more polite speech. When asked to rate numerous sentences containing a range of politeness markers, men and women ranked all sentences in the same relative order, but men rated each sentence as more polite than did women. Therefore, because women perceive each specific structure to be less polite, they must use a more strongly deferential utterance to express the same degree of politeness (Ide et al. 1986:30). Additionally, when women and men were directed to ask questions of a range of addressees (relatives, friends, superiors, strangers), women generally chose more polite stylistic alternatives than did men. The only exceptions to this pattern were that women spoke less politely to their children and neighbors. Ide et al. contended that notions of sociability and solidarity affect these cases (ibid.:34). Mothers have closer emotional bonds with their children than do fathers; and women establish more solidarity networks in private domains with their children and in their neighborhoods. Therefore, men's use of polite forms in these contexts may indicate social distance rather than deference. In most other situations (e.g., employment and public interactions), women are socially less secure and linguistically more deferential and polite than are men.

Interactions between spouses also indicate women's deferential behavior, as women consistently direct more polite speech to their husbands. And research by Tsunao Ogino found that husbands used their least polite styles when speaking to their wives, although wives employed moderately polite and formal speech to husbands (1986:43, 47).

SUMMARY

People interact primarily through talk, most often in informal conversation. Conversation is structured, framed by openings and closings, and internally characterized by rules of turn-taking and turn allocation. Although these properties can be defined abstractly, analysis of ongoing talk demonstrates situational and interactional complexities that influence how the structure of conversation is actualized.

Co-participants are expected to adhere to cultural norms or postulates of conversational behavior. Specification and strength of these postulates vary across cultures. They vary across speech events as well, depending on the relationships, rights, and purposes of interlocutors. These bases of variation are especially revealed in issuing directives. Because speakers want directives to produce responses or actions by addressees, they are sensitive to rights and obligations of co-participants. Directives can be issued in many linguistic forms. Speakers need to take care in their selection of form in order both to make clear their intent and to avoid an affront to addressees. Finally, culturally sanctioned rules of politeness affect the form and content of speech and provide participants with shared expectations to guide and evaluate behavior.

REFERENCES

BAKER, CHARLOTTE. 1975. This is just a first approximation, but. . . . In *Papers from the Eleventh Regional Meeting of the Chicago Linguistic Society.* Chicago: Chicago Linguistic Society, pp. 37–47.

BLUM-KULKA, SHOSHANA, AND ELITE OLSHTAIN. 1984. Requests and apologies: A cross-cultural study of speech act realization patterns. *Applied Linguistics* 5:196–213.

BROWN, PENELOPE, AND STEPHEN LEVINSON. 1987. *Politeness: Some Universals in Language Usage.* New York: Cambridge University Press.

COUPLAND, NIKOLAS, KAREN GRAINGER, AND JUSTINE COUPLAND. 1988. Politeness in context: Intergenerational issues. *Language in Society* 17: 253–262.

DARNELL, REGNA. 1985. The language of power in Cree interethnic communication. In *Language of Inequality,* ed. N. Wolfson and J. Manes. The Hague: Mouton, pp. 61–72.

ERVIN-TRIPP, SUSAN. 1976. "Is Sybill there?" The structure of some American English directives. *Language in Society* 5:25–66.

GORDON, DAVID, AND GEORGE LAKOFF. 1971. Conversational postulates. In *Papers from the Seventh Regional*

Meeting of the Chicago Linguistic Society. Chicago: Chicago Linguistic Society, pp. 63–84.

GRICE, H. P. 1975. Logic and conversation. In *Syntax and Semantics,* Vol. 3, *Speech Acts,* ed. P. Cole and J. Morgan. New York: Academic Press, pp. 41–58.

HALLIDAY, M. A. K., AND RUQAIYA HASAN. 1976. *Cohesion in English.* London: Longman.

HOLLOS, MARIDA, AND WILLIAM BEEMAN. 1978. The development of directives among Norwegian and Hungarian children: An example of communicative style in culture. *Language in Society* 7:345–355.

IDE, SACHIKO. 1982. Japanese sociolinguistics: Politeness and women's language. *Lingua* 57:357–385.

IDE, SACHIKO, ET AL. 1986. Sex difference and politeness in Japanese. *International Journal of the Sociology of Language* 58:25–36.

KEENAN, ELINOR OCHS. 1976. The universality of conversational postulates. *Language in Society* 5:67–80.

LABOV, WILLIAM, AND DAVID FANSHEL. 1977. *Therapeutic Discourse.* New York: Academic Press.

LAKOFF, ROBIN. 1973. The logic of politeness; or, minding your p's and q's. In

Papers from the Ninth Regional Meeting of the Chicago Linguistic Society. Chicago: Chicago Linguistic Society, pp. 292–305.

OBENG, SAMUEL GYASI. 1996. The proverb as a mitigating and politeness strategy in Akan discourse. *Anthropological Linguistics* 38:521–549.

OGINO, TSUNAO. 1986. Quantification of politeness based on the usage patterns of honorific expressions. *International Journal of the Sociology of Language* 58:37–58.

SACKS, HARVEY. 1973. On some puns with some intimations. In *Sociolinguistics: Current Trends and Prospects, Twenty-third Annual Round Table Meeting on Linguistics and Language Studies,* ed. R. Shuy. Washington, DC: Georgetown University Press, pp. 135–144.

SACKS, HARVEY, E. SCHEGLOFF, AND G. JEFFERSON. 1974. A simplest systematics for the organization of turn-taking for conversation. *Language* 50:696–735.

SCHEGLOFF, EMMANUEL, AND H. SACKS. 1973. Opening up closings. *Semiotica* 8:289–327.

TANNEN, DEBORAH. 1987. Repetition and variation as spontaneous formulaicity in conversation. *Language* 63:574–605.

YNGVE, V. H. 1970. On getting a word in edgewise. In *Papers from the Sixth Regional Meeting of the Chicago Linguistic Society.* Chicago: Chicago Linguistic Society, pp. 567–578.

6

Societal Segmentation and Linguistic Variation: Class and Race

What do these three speakers reveal about themselves?

"Where's toity-toid street?"
"We has a little fire, keeps us warm."
"It's just not convenient cause the office be closed on weekends."

In these sentences, the speakers use language that differs from the "standard" forms of English spoken in the United States and Great Britain. But their pronunciations, words, and grammatical constructions are not random or idiosyncratic. They conform to a definite set of rules that obtain within their speech communities or speech networks. Many, if not most, of the people these speakers converse with also use the sounds and words that they employ. Such use of speech signals people's membership in a particular community or network. The first example, "Where's toity-toid street?" is typical, stereotypical in fact, of a lower-class regional dialect spoken in New York City. The speaker replaces the fricative sound (written as "th") with the stop /t/ and replaces the vocalic segment (written "ir" in thirty-third) with the dipthong /oy/. The second example comes from a lower-class British speaker. Here the speaker replaces the standard plural form of "have" with the singular "has." The third speaker uses an invariant, unconjugated form of the verb "be," common in the dialect of American English known as African American Vernacular English, or AAVE. Speakers of AAVE use invariant "be" to mark verbs that report activities or states that are habitual.

As these three examples show, members of different speech communities use styles of speaking that are distinctive, consistent, and rule-governed. These styles may differ from forms of speech generally held to be "standard" in their choices of pronunciation, words, or grammar, but they are, nonetheless, "correct" and follow the rules accepted and used by speakers in their neighborhoods and networks.

Within speech communities, people are differentiated on the basis of many social factors, including gender, age, class, race, ethnicity, and occupation. In this chapter we focus on the interconnections between speech and the factors of social stratification and race, as these bases of segmentation are significant in many societies throughout the world. Social distinctions influence both the production of speech and its evaluation by community members.

SOCIAL STRATIFICATION

Social stratification is the hierarchical structuring of groups within a society, reflecting inequalities among sectors of a population. Inequality may be based on many factors, including income, occupation, education, and access to social, economic, and/or political power. These factors are in practice not distinct but, rather, interact in complex ways to produce and reproduce societal segmentation. Theories about origins and processes of stratification are controversial in sociology and anthropology and will not be explored here, but the concept itself has generally been adopted into sociolinguistic research as useful for understanding one of the parameters of linguistic variation. Speakers of socially ordered groups exhibit differences in frequency of use of certain sounds, words, and grammatical features. Of equal importance is the fact that members of all groups within a society are aware, either consciously or unconsciously, of speech styles characteristic of various social strata, and they use this knowledge in assessing their own and other people's speech.

CASTE

Social stratification can be stable and absolute, as in systems of caste, or potentially fluid and fluctuating, as in class systems. *Caste* is a term associated with a social hierarchy in which people are separated according to criteria of birth and are usually unable to change their group membership. It is a system that prevails in India, determining many aspects of a person's behavior. Residence, occupation, and marriage choices are all linked to caste groupings; members of particular castes live in certain areas of Indian villages, have specified occupations, and generally marry within their own group. In many cases, ritual activities and even styles of clothing further demarcate the castes. Language, too, is a marker of the pervasive social hierarchy.

Speech samples from Khalapur, a North Indian village of some 5,000 inhabitants that is divided into 31 castes, indicate that the population varies in the pronunciation of several sounds (Gumperz 1971). Higher castes—the Brahmins (ritually the purest) and Rajputs (or warrior-rulers)—use the sound system of the standard local dialect of Khari Boli, a subdialect of Hindi, India's official language. Lower castes, or "untouchables," in the village—chamars (landless laborers), leatherworkers, and sweepers—employ variants of some of the standard forms. The following list summarizes contrasting patterns of pronunciation observed in Khalapur (adapted from Gumperz 1971:32–33):

A. Dipthongs /aɪ/, /uɪ/, /oɪ/ before consonants contrast with single vowels /a/, /u/, /o/:

	Standard	Sweepers	
1.	baɪl	bal	ear of corn
2.	jhuɪl	jhul	cattle blanket
3.	khoɪr	khor	cattle trough

B. /u/ before a stressed vowel in next syllable contrasts with /ʌ/:

	Standard	Sweepers	
1.	nulána	nʌlána	(to) weed
2.	dutʌ́i	dʌtʌ́i	blanket
3.	mundassa	mʌṇḍássa	head cloth

C. Oral vowels contrast with nasal vowels:

	Standard	All Untouchables	
1.	ik	ĩk	sugar cane
2.	jua	jũa	joke
3.	khat	khãt	cot

Interviews with residents of Khalapur revealed that they were well aware of caste styles of speech. Members of higher castes often characterized nonstandard forms as "ignorant" or "backward." Lower castes were sensitive to the same norms. In one instance, when questioned about a chamar variant, two chamar men "evidenced a great deal of emotion on hearing the form. They did not answer the question, but entered into long explanations to the effect that chamars have hitherto been denied educational opportunities by the higher castes" (ibid.:32). These reactions indicate people's knowledge that speech differs and that certain pronunciations and their speakers are stigmatized.

Fundamentally it is not language in the abstract that is evaluated negatively or positively but language as it is used by specific segments of a population. Criticizing linguistic variants is actually a mask for the social denigration of speakers. We shall see this dynamic demonstrated again and again in the ways that members of a community judge their own and others' speech.

CLASS

In societies like the United States, social stratification takes the form of *classes* that are structured in terms of economic, political, and social relations. Most sociolinguistic studies assign consultants to classes based on arbitrary indices compiled from various attributes, including occupation, income, and education. This procedure is problematic in that it accepts and applies automatically a superficial definition of class. Unlike castes, which are named and overtly recognized groupings, the concept of class seems fuzzy, at least as it is applied by sociolinguists. In sociolinguistic research, class and class membership are generally assumed rather than investigated. Despite these real difficulties, social and economic differences among members of a community are reflected in many aspects of lifestyle, educational and occupational opportunities, and political power. These differences, perhaps summarized under the notion of class, have interdependent impacts on linguistic performance as well. Language use both reflects and reinforces class differences. Analysis of class styles is further complicated by the inherent variability of patterning. Most speakers use upper-class and lower-class features, but it is the frequency of usage that identifies speakers.

In the following review of research, we examine studies of class and language that draw on data from several countries and highlight different aspects of social and linguistic interconnections. An important caution should be noted regarding the methodologies used in some of the studies. Sociolinguistic research is usually based on one of two approaches. In one, researchers gather samples of speech from as many speakers as possible, numbering in the hundreds or even thousands. William Labov's study of New York City speech demonstrates the validity of research based on speech samples from large numbers of people. The second approach uses a small number of consultants who are assumed to be typical speakers of their class. Their speech is then taken to be representative of the features prevalent in their class style. The research by Jacqueline Lindenfeld on French and Jan van de Broeck on Netherlandic are examples of this type of study. Their results are intriguing and certainly consistent with findings in general on class-based speech styles, but the methodology does raise questions about whether the consultants used are in fact representative inasmuch as their representativeness is assumed rather than proved.

Class and Network

Before discussing research on class and language, we should examine an additional theoretical issue, the distinction and interplay between class and network analysis. The distinction between class and network is useful in sharpening the focus on two different kinds of societal organizations. As stated by Lesley Milroy and James Milroy, "Social class is a concept designed to elucidate large-scale social, political, and economic structures and processes, whereas social network relates to the community and interpersonal level of social organization" (1992:2). According to Milroy and Milroy, two very different types of relationships exist on the levels of class and of network. Systems of class are based on "conflict, division, and inequality," whereas networks are held together through "consensus" (ibid.:3). Linguistic variation, of pronunciations and grammatical forms, occurs between classes, whereas linguistic conformity tends to obtain within social networks. Close-knit networks where members share geographic location, family ties, and workplaces exert the strongest pressures for maintaining group norms.

In the opinion of Milroy and Milroy, close-knit networks are more typical of lower-class communities, whereas weak social networks, characterized by greater geographic mobility, looser kinship ties, and relationships with a wider range of people, predominate among the middle classes. Because of the strength of interpersonal bonds and community pressure in close-knit networks, members may maintain distinctive forms of speech that may actually be severely stigmatized by the society as a whole. Indeed, within such groups, "the persistence over centuries of stigmatized linguistic forms and low-status vernaculars in the face of powerful national policies of diffusing and imposing standard languages is remarkable" (ibid.:6).

Much of the research discussed in the following sections is based on analysis of class, although the data can be interpreted through appeal to the concept of social network as well. These two approaches are, in fact, complementary because they refer to the two levels of organization and integration: the societal level of class and the interpersonal level of network.

New York City

Studies of linguistic diversity by William Labov, beginning with *The Social Stratification of English in New York City* (1966), have become classics in the field. In his analysis of the speech of employees in three New York City department stores, Labov focused on the phonological variable known as *postvocalic /-r/*, the pronunciation of /-r/ following a vowel—for example, ca_r, ca_rd. The presence of /-r/ in this context is a marker of standard American English; its absence is generally stigmatized. Labov obtained data through rapid, anonymous observations by asking store employees the question "Excuse me, where are the women's shoes?" knowing the answer to be "fourth floor." Emphatic speech (in which speakers pay more attention to pronunciation) was then elicited by repeating the question. These elicitation frames tested occurrences of /-r/ in both words (fou_rth floo_r) and provided comparable data from all consultants.

Labov found that workers differed in their use of /-r/ and that this differentiation was linked to their employment in stores of ranked relative prestige, that is, Saks Fifth Avenue, Macy's, and S. Klein. He found that rates of /-r/ pronunciation among employees paralleled the stratification of the stores: highest in Saks, somewhat less in Macy's, and much lower in S. Klein. Ranking of the stores resulted from differences in the quality and cost of merchandise, attracting a clientele from specific social classes. Labov concluded that workers identified with the prestige of their employer and customers and that this identification was reflected in language use. The following tables present Labov's findings.

When employees were separated according to gender and race, some changes in frequencies of /-r/ were noted, but the overall patterning was confirmed.

Overall Distribution of /-r/

	Saks	Macy's	S. Klein
All /-r/	30%	20%	4%
Some /-r/	32	31	17
No /-r/	38	49	79
Number of subjects	68	125	71

SOURCE: Labov 1966:73.

Distribution of /-r/ for African-American Employees

	Saks	Macy's	S. Klein
All /-r/	50%	12%	0%
Some /-r/	0	35	6
No /-r/	50	53	94
Number	2	17	18

SOURCE: Labov 1966:77.

Distribution of /-r/ by Gender

	Women	Men
All /-r/	30%	22%
Some /-r/	17	22
No /-r/	54	57
Number	194	70

SOURCE: Labov 1966:89, n. 10.

Distribution of /-r/ for Native-Born White Women

	Saks	Macy's	S. Klein
All /-r/	34%	31%	26%
Some /-r/	33	28	4
No /-r/	33	41	70
Number	49	65	27

SOURCE: Labov 1966:79.

In a more complex survey among residents of New York's Lower East Side, Labov studied speech behavior of a large sample of speakers from different classes. Class membership was established on the basis of three equally weighted factors: occupation of main earner, education of respondents, and family income. Ten socioeconomic levels were delineated, grouped into four strata: lower class, working class, lower middle class, and upper middle class (Labov 1972b:112–113). Labov incorporated the variable of contextual style by recording pronunciations of certain sounds in five contrasting situations in interviews with speakers (adapted from Labov 1966:92–98):

A.   Casual speech (observed with members of the family)
B.   Careful speech (recorded during interview questioning)

C.   Reading style (subjects were asked to read stories)
D.   Word lists (subjects read lists of isolated, random words)
E.   Minimal pairs (subjects read pairs of minimally differentiated words, for example, dock/dark, sauce/source)

Through this procedure, linguists can observe whether respondents change their pronunciation in different contexts. The advantage of focusing on sounds is that speakers are generally not consciously aware of their pronunciation and, therefore, are unlikely to be able to control it. Linguists assume that as speakers become more attentive, they unconsciously select variants that they perceive to be closer to standard or prestige norms. The graph in Figure 6.1 for postvocalic /-r/ indicates that this assumption is valid for speakers of all social classes.

A number of important conclusions can be drawn from the data. First, members of disparate social classes use different amounts of /-r/ in their speech, demonstrating that the variable is a significant marker of social stratification. Second, members of all classes increase their use of /-r/ as context focused more attention

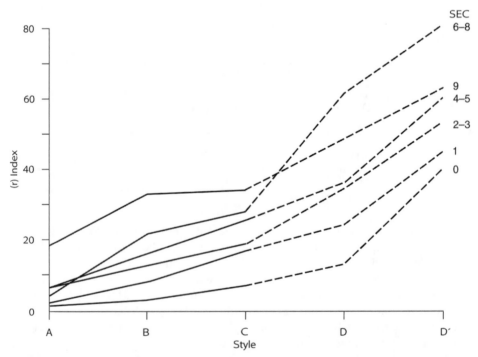

FIGURE 6.1. Class Stratification for /-r/.   (Labov 1972b:114)
Class stratification of a linguistic variable in process of change: (r) in *guard, car, beer, beard, board,* and so on. SEC (socioeconomic class) scale: 0–1, lower class; 2–4, working class; 5–6, 7–8, lower middle class; 9, upper middle class. A, casual speech; B, careful speech; C, reading style; D, word lists; D′, minimal pairs.

on pronunciation, indicating that they are aware of the same general norm giving value to /-r/ pronouncing. And third, in speech in the most careful contexts, members of the second highest class (LMC) use more /-r/ than do members of the highest group (UMC). According to Labov, such *"crossover" patterning* demonstrates that LMC speakers are most sensitive about negative evaluations of their own speech and most desirous of achieving prestige norms (1972b:117).

Social class differences are not only exhibited in people's speech but also in their judgment of the speech of others. "The correlate of regular stratification of a sociolinguistic variable in behavior is uniform agreement in subjective reactions towards that variable" (ibid.:249). Speakers' assessment of /-r/ was measured by asking them to rate tape-recorded speech on a scale of occupational suitability, judging whether the speech would be acceptable for a television personality, executive secretary, receptionist, switchboard operator, salesperson, or factory worker (Labov 1966:411). Following are scores for sensitivity to postvocalic /-r/ (Labov 1972b:131):

Lower class	50%
Working class	53
Lower middle class	86
Upper middle class	75

These subjective reactions show that just as members of the LMC are most attentive in their own use of /-r/, they are also most sensitive to its occurrence in the speech of others, once again outdoing members of the highest group. Labov referred to LMC patterns as evidence of "linguistic insecurity" (ibid.:133). However, it is the societal circumstances of these people that motivate their reactions. In other words, linguistic insecurity is a reflection of social insecurity stemming from disadvantages due to education, income, occupation, and the like, that members of this class experience. Perhaps they exhibit crossover behavior more than people of even lower groups because they are closest to the highest stratum and attempt to model their speech more directly on prestige norms.

When additional sounds were studied, Labov found similar patterns of class stratification in use and evaluation. Vowels /oh/ (as in off, caught, chocolate) and /eh/ (as in pass, dance) fluctuate from standard American English pronunciation to stereotyped and stigmatized New York City dialect. Figures 6.2 and 6.3 present data for three class groupings across contextual styles.

Responses for subjective reactions to these features in tape-recorded speech reveal the following percentages of negative judgments of nonstandard forms (Labov 1972b:130):

Negative Response to Nonstandard /oh/

LC	24%
WC	61
LMC	79
UMC	59

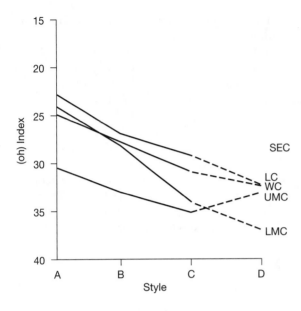

FIGURE 6.2. Class Stratification for /oh/. (Labov 1972b:129) Class stratification for (oh). SEC = socioeconomic class scale. A, casual speech; B, careful speech; C, reading style; D, word lists.

Negative Response to Nonstandard /eh/

LC	63%
WC	81
LMC	86
UMC	67

Crossover behavior exhibited by the LMC for the variables /-r/, /oh/, and /eh/ shows a consistent pattern in their own speech and their reactions to others. These three variables are undergoing change in New York City dialects. The prestige value of pronouncing postvocalic /-r/ spread to this area after World War II,

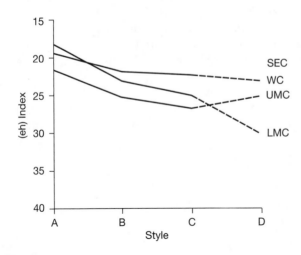

FIGURE 6.3. Class Stratification for /eh/. (Labov 1972b:127) Class stratification for (eh). SEC = socioeconomic class scale. A, casual speech; B, careful speech; C, reading style; D, word lists.

undoubtedly accelerated by use of the American standard /-r/ in the mass media. Vowel variants of /oh/ and /eh/ are also unstable and changing.

When speech behavior and judgments of these three variables are compared with two stable pronunciations, significant contrasting patterns emerge. The relevant stable features are the pronunciation of /th/ and /dh/ in such words as "thing" and "this," respectively. In standard English, these sounds occur as fricatives /θ/ and /ð/, with corresponding stigmatized use of stops /t/ and /d/, for example, "tirty" (thirty), "dese" (these). Labov found a complete, sharp stratification for all classes. All speakers decrease their use of stigmatized /t/ as context invokes more attentive speech. And for each style, each class is ranked consistently in relation to the other classes; the higher the class, the greater is the use of the standard fricative. The same pattern occurs for voiced /dh/. Figure 6.4 shows stylistic and class differentiation for /th/.

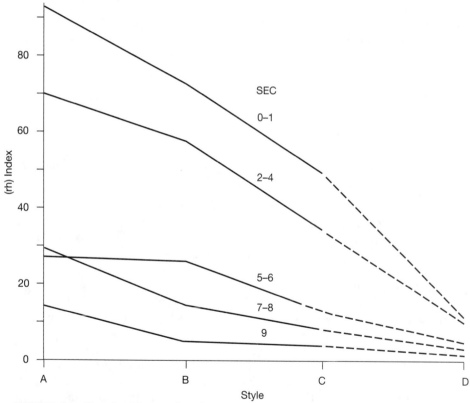

FIGURE 6.4. Class Stratification for /th/. (Labov 1972b:113)
Class stratification of a linguistic variable with stable social significance: (th) in *thing, through,* and so on. SEC (socioeconomic class) scale: 0–1, lower class; 2–4, working class; 5–6, 7–8, lower middle class; 9, upper middle class. A, casual speech; B, careful speech; C, reading style; D, word lists.

Subjective reaction tests for stable markers /th/ and /dh/ reveal a contrast to those for the three changing features /-r/, /oh/, and /eh/. Negative judgments to nonstandard /t/ were (Labov 1972b:131)

Lower class	58%
Working class	76
Lower middle class	81
Upper middle class	92

In subjective judgments, class stratification is sharp; negative reactions increase as class ranking increases. Crossover behavior of LMC speakers only occurs for phonological markers in the process of change. Thus it can be used as a reliable and consistent indicator of linguistic change, responding to overall social and linguistic stratification.

Norwich, England

Interconnections between social stratification and language have also been researched in Great Britain. In Peter Trudgill's study of class styles among speakers in Norwich, England, the following phonological features were measured (Trudgill 1974a):

1. /ng/: frequency of replacement of /-ng/ by /-n/ in words such as walk<u>ing</u>, runn<u>ing</u> walk<u>in</u>, runn<u>in</u>

2. /t/: frequency of replacement of /t/ by glottal stop /ʔ/ in words such as bu<u>tt</u>er, be<u>t</u> buʔer, beʔ

3. /h/: frequency of dropping /h/ in words such as <u>h</u>ammer, <u>h</u>at 'ammer, 'at

Consultants were assigned class membership on the basis of six factors: occupation, income, education, housing, locality, and father's occupation.

Trudgill found that members of social classes are stratified by their use of the three variables in parallel patterning. For all features, higher-class speakers use less nonstandard forms, meaning, of course, that they use more standard pronunciations. The reverse pattern is demonstrated by members of lower classes, whose speech is characterized by stigmatized pronunciations. Although all five class groupings are differentiated, Trudgill's research reveals a marked distinction between middle-class and working-class usage. Speech patterns among all middle-class speakers are more similar to each other, as are speech patterns among members of working-class categories.

The following table summarizes data for all classes, distinguished as middle middle class (MMC), lower middle class (LMC), upper working class (UWC), middle working class (MWC), and lower working class (LWC). Percentages reflect use of stigmatized variants: /n/ rather than /ng/, /ʔ/ rather than /t/, and loss of /h/ (Trudgill 1974b:47).

As the data show, distinctions among the three phonological variables occurred. Frequencies for nonstandard loss of /h/ at beginnings of words are much

	ng	*t*	*h*
MMC	31%	41%	6%
LMC	42	62	14
UWC	87	89	40
MWC	95	92	59
LWC	100	94	61

less for all classes than are rates for the other nonstandard forms, /n/ and /ʔ/, indicating that loss of /h/ carries greater stigma.

In addition, class differences were correlated with use or nonuse of the morphological marker on present-tense verbs for third-person singular, written as "-s," for example, she/he/it moves. The following list displays rates of omission of the suffix (Trudgill 1974b:44).

Percentage of Verbs
Without /-s/

MMC	0%
LMC	2
UWC	70
MWC	87
LWC	97

Although class stratification for the suffix follows the same trend as that for sounds, several significant differences occur. First, distinction between middle-class and working-class aggregates is especially sharp, from 0 to 2 percent for the former and from 70 to 97 percent for the latter. Second, behavior of the highest and lowest groups is almost reversed: MMC speakers always use standard /-s/, but LWC speakers use it only 3 percent of the time. These values can be compared to findings on pronunciations where differences between MMC and LWC speakers are not as extreme. Although LWC speech contains more nonstandard pronunciations, MMC speakers also use nonstandard variants; for example, they use nonstandard /-n/ at a rate of 31 percent.

Paris and Rouen, France

Class differences are reflected in the use of syntactic alternatives as well as in phonological or morphological features. Jacqueline Lindenfeld's (1969) research in Paris and Rouen demonstrated correlations among syntactic complexity, degree of formality of speech events, and speakers' class membership. Twelve subjects were selected and grouped into high (Class I) and low (Class II) strata based on education, occupation, and income, although the latter factor was given less weight. Class I occupations included lawyer, teacher, psychologist, and bank manager. Some Class II occupations were factory worker, practical nurse, and nursery school assistant. All members of Class I had at least three years of college education, whereas no Class II members had gone beyond junior high school.

Speech samples were obtained from subjects in an experimental situation designed to elicit formal and informal speech. Lindenfeld asked each respondent to role-play, first speaking to a large audience about his or her occupation and, second, to a family member or friend about his or her summer vacation. This methodology is problematic in its reliance on the speaker's out-of-context performance, although Lindenfeld claims that the linguistic differences among speakers are reliable.

The analysis focused on syntactic structure and the degree of complexity used by speakers where syntactic options are available. Three syntactic features were investigated: subordination, relativization, and nominalization. Contrasting examples, demonstrating alternatives of use or nonuse of these features, are presented below (ibid.:894):

1. Subordination
    a. No subordination:
        On a fini de déjeuner. On peut sortir. "We are finished with lunch. We can go out."
    b. Subordination:
        Puisqu'on a fini de diner, on peut sortir. "Since we are finished eating supper, we can go out."
2. Relativization
    a. No relativization:
        On est allées à Delos. On a vu toutes sortes de choses. "We went to Delos. We saw all kinds of things."
    b. Relativization:
        Nous sommes passés par Amsterdam, où nous avons fait un tour du musée. "We went through Amsterdam, where we visited the museum."
3. Nominalization
    a. No nominalization:
        Elle était toute triste. Jean était parti. "She was very sad. John had gone."
    b. Nominalization:
        J'étais content qu'il soit parti. "I was glad that he was away."

In addition to recording occurrences of these grammatical features, Lindenfeld noted sentence length, measured in number of words. She hypothesized that syntactic complexity and sentence length would increase along with factors of higher class and greater situational and topical formality. Indeed, results of the study confirmed all but one of the hypotheses. Nominalization, relativization, and sentence length were significant indicators of class and context. Although Class I and II speakers produced sentences of roughly equal complexity in their informal style, marked differences occurred in formal speech. Class I speakers employed higher rates of nominalization and relativization in formal contexts than in their informal speech, whereas members of Class II showed no difference between their

The Correlation of Linguistic Variation, Sociological Variation, and Contextual Variation

	Formal Context		Informal Context	
	Class I	*Class II*	*Class I*	*Class II*
Subordination	7	7	7	7
Relativization	11	7	8	8
Nominalization	13	8	9	7
Sentence length (number of words)	23	17	14	13

Figures represent averages for six subjects on the basis of 400-word samples.

formal and informal styles. Numerical results are presented in the table above (ibid.:894).

Thus, it is the differences in formal speech that distinguish members of Classes I and II. The former use greater syntactic complexity in formal contexts, whereas the latter employ the same kinds of sentence constructions in all contexts. Although sentence length is greater on average in formal situations for all speakers, the increase is sharper for members of Class I than of Class II (from 14 to 23 words for Class I and 13 to 17 words for Class II).

Members of distinct classes, then, exhibit differences in sensitivity to social context, at least as measured by their use of optional syntactic formations. This contrast is probably due, in part, to educational levels attained, inasmuch as people who have advanced educations are more familiar with and more comfortable using complex grammatical constructions.

Maaseik, Belgium

Relationships between social stratification and degrees of syntactic complexity in speech have also been found among speakers in Maaseik, a small town in Belgium (van de Broeck 1977). Jef van de Broeck selected eight male subjects and assigned them to middle-class or working-class groups on the basis of occupation, income, and education. Speech was recorded in a formal interview between the subject and a stranger and in an informal discussion with a friend in order to study the influence of both social stratification and context on linguistic performance (ibid.:152–153). Relevant features of syntactic complexity in Netherlandic (Dutch) were identified (note that sentence equivalents are given here in English) (ibid.:155–157):

1. Average length of main clause plus any attached or embedded clauses.

2. Subordination—for example: "I was glad that John had seen Mary."

3. Multiple embedding—for example: "After he had spoken to his father, whom he had not seen for a long time, John went to his mother's place, where he ate the best meal he had had in years."

4. Passives.

5. Passives without agents—for example: "My car was stolen" (compared to "they (someone) stole my car").

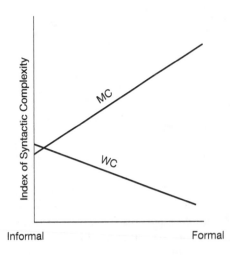

FIGURE 6.5. Class, Context, and Syntactic Complexity. (van de Broeck 1977:165) Reproduced by permission of Cambridge University Press.

Indices for each type of complexity were developed and measured. The same correlations among class, context, and syntax emerged for all features. Although middle-class and working-class speakers showed no significant differences in sentence complexity in informal situations, there was a marked distinction between the classes in formal contexts. In these situations, MC speakers used a high degree of complex constructions, consistent with Lindenfeld's findings for French. When speech was analyzed within each class, a striking contrast emerged in class behavior in the two contexts. MC formal syntax was always much more complex than MC informal speech, but WC formal syntax was actually somewhat less complex than WC informal style. Van de Broeck represented this finding by a diagram (see Figure 6.5) indicating directions of shifts from informal to formal speech for the two classes.

MC and WC speech move in different directions in formal situations, the former toward greater complexity and the latter toward greater syntactic simplicity. Such behavior requires an explanation that focuses on interconnections between class and context. Van de Broeck suggested that two attitudinal factors are operative. One is the desire of MC speakers to distinguish their style from that of the WC in formal situations, that is, in situations where all people feel "on display." They use linguistic mechanisms as an "act of conspicuous ostentation, a marker of social distance" (ibid.:169). The second factor concerns WC speakers, who also feel "on display" in formal circumstances but who recognize their relative powerlessness in those situations. They respond to their social subordination by moving away from prestigeful speech, possibly because they want to actively reject MC norms or because they are unsure of their linguistic abilities and prefer to use simpler speech rather than make mistakes (ibid.:170–171). Van de Broeck concluded: "The MC behaves linguistically 'with an eye on' the WC, not independent of them. And partly because the MC displays their handling of complex syntax, the WC refrains from trying to achieve the same norms. They react in the opposite way by under-performing, by appearing to a certain extent less verbally skilled than they actually are" (ibid.:171).

Reading, England

Speakers can manipulate their use of language in order to emphasize or de-emphasize their class identity in different speech situations. In a working-class neighborhood of Reading, England, Jenny Cheshire studied the relationship between language use and class identity among adolescents. Cheshire first developed a notion of "vernacular" culture in Reading and then rated teenagers' adherence to this culture in terms of their behavior—for example, fighting, swearing, participation in minor criminal activities, negative attitudes toward school, expectations of future blue-collar jobs, and choice of clothing and hairstyle (1982:155). Boys were divided into four groups based on their adherence to these norms; girls were divided into two groups, differentiated by similar factors.

Next, Cheshire examined the adolescents' speech, focusing on frequency of usage of nine nonstandard features of the Reading dialect of English (ibid.: 153–154):

1. present tense with non-third-person singular subjects:
    "We *goes* shopping on Saturdays."
2. *has* with non-third-person singular subjects:
    "We *has* a little fire, keeps us warm."
3. *was* with plural subjects (and singular *you*):
    "You *was* outside."
4. multiple negation:
    "I'm *not* going *nowhere*."
5. negative past tense *never*, used for standard *didn't*:
    "I *never* done it, it was him."
6. *what* used for standard *who, whom, which, that*:
    "There's a knob *what* you turn."
    "Are you the boy *what's* just come?"
7. auxiliary *do* with third-person singular subjects:
    "How much *do* he want for it?"
8. past tense *come*:
    "I *come* down here yesterday."
9. *ain't* used for negative present tense of *be* and *have*:
    "I *ain't* going."
    "I *ain't* got any."

Several of these features were shown to be reliable indicators of vernacular identity. The following table presents data from the speech of boys. The data are divided into three linguistic categories. Forms in Category A were consistently

Adherence to Vernacular Culture and Frequency of Nonstandard Forms

	Group 1	2	3	4
A: nonstandard -s	77.36	54.03	36.57	21.21
nonstandard has	66.67	50.00	41.65	(33.33)
nonstandard was	90.32	89.74	83.33	75.00
negative concord	100.00	85.71	83.33	71.43
B: nonstandard never	64.71	41.67	45.45	37.50
nonstandard what	92.31	7.69	33.33	0.00
C: nonstandard do	58.33	37.50	83.33	—
nonstandard come	100.00	100.00	100.00	(100.00)
ain't = aux. have	78.26	64.52	80.00	(100.00)
ain't = aux. be	58.82	72.22	80.00	(100.00)
ain't = copula	100.00	76.19	56.52	75.00

Figures in parentheses indicate that the number of occurrences of a variable is low (below 5) and that the indices may not be reliable.

correlated with identity; those in Category B were less consistent but still functioned as indicators of vernacular culture; and forms in Category C had no relevance to class identity (ibid.:156). (Note that in the table Group 1 consists of boys with strongest adherence to vernacular culture; Group 4 boys are weakest in this measure. Also note that a rate of 100.00 represents total use of the targeted feature.)

Category A features are clearly differentiated among the groups of boys, revealing a progression from highest frequencies in speech of boys identified most strongly with vernacular culture to lowest among boys with least vernacular identification. Category B features are also stratified. They appear most in speech of boys in Group 1 and least in speech of Group 4 boys; Groups 2 and 3 are intermediate but not in stable order. In contrast to Category A and B, Category C forms do not appear to be patterned in any consistent fashion and are, therefore, not diagnostic for identity but, rather, are general indicators of working-class Reading English.

The next table documents usage of nonstandard features by the two groups of girls, characterized as "good" (attending school, not swearing or stealing) and "other" (stronger adherence to vernacular norms). As in the speech of boys, frequency for use of nonstandard linguistic variables by girls is distinguished accord-

Use of Nonstandard Features by "Good" Girls and "Other" Girls

	"Good" Girls	"Other" Girls
nonstandard -s	25.84	57.27
nonstandard was	63.64	80.95
negative concord	12.50	58.70
nonstandard come	30.77	90.63
ain't = copula	14.29	67.12
nonstandard never	45.45	41.07
nonstandard what	33.33	5.56
nonstandard has	36.36	35.85

Stylistic Variation in Frequency of Nonstandard Forms

		Vernacular Style	*School Style*
A:	nonstandard -*s*	57.03	31.49
	nonstandard *has*	46.43	35.71
	nonstandard *was*	91.67	88.57
	negative concord	90.70	66.67
B:	nonstandard *never*	49.21	15.38
	nonstandard *what*	50.00	54.55
C:	nonstandard *do*	—	—
	nonstandard *come*	100.00	100.00
	ain't = aux. *have*	93.02	100.00
	ain't = copula	74.47	77.78

ing to speakers' cultural orientation. For most features, "good" girls use nonstandard forms much less often than girls identified with vernacular culture. Only one variable, nonstandard *what,* appears more often in speech of "good" girls (ibid.:163).

The context of speech was an important factor influencing adolescents' speaking styles. When boys were observed in informal playground settings, their speech contained many more Category A features (features identified with vernacular culture) than when their speech was recorded in school. In contrast, Category C features (features not indicative of identity) did not fluctuate in different contexts. The data in the table above show that boys associated with vernacular culture emphasized or downplayed their identity, depending on social context (ibid.:158).

Class-Based Codes

Use of different linguistic styles, or codes, may affect the ways that speakers participate in society. Basil Bernstein (1971b) made the point that class-based styles of speaking lead to differences in styles of thinking and how one experiences the world. He described two kinds of linguistic codes that he associated with different social classes. According to Bernstein, middle-class speech is characterized by use of an "elaborated" code that expresses "universalistic" meanings by use of nouns, adjectives, and verbs having explicit referents. In contrast, working-class style tends to employ a "restricted" code, expressing "particularistic" meanings by use of words that are more context-bound (1971b:175). (Bernstein's choice of terms is unfortunate because the words "elaborated" and "restricted" have value-laden connotations.)

Bernstein supported his thesis with examples of speech of middle- and working-class children. The following excerpts are illustrative. They are composites of speech of 5-year-old children who were asked to describe actions in a series of four photographs. Although the excerpts illustrate Bernstein's hypothesis, it is important to remember that they are not the children's verbatim speech (ibid.:178).

1. *Middle-class sample:* Three boys are playing football and one boy kicks the ball and it goes through the window the ball breaks the window and the boys are looking at it and a man comes out and shouts at them because they've

broken the window so they run away and then that lady looks out of her window and she tells the boys off.

2. *Working-class sample:* They're playing football and he kicks it and it goes through there it breaks the window and they're looking at it and he comes out and shouts at them because they've broken it so they run away and then she looks out and she tells them off.

A major difference between the two styles is that working-class children employ words with inexplicit references and pronouns lacking stated antecedents (e.g., "he kicks it and it goes through there"). Their language use, therefore, presupposes shared knowledge and experience with their interlocutors. In contrast, middle-class speakers make their meanings explicit, not relying as much on presuppositions (e.g., "one boy kicks the ball and it goes through the window").

Bernstein contended that use of explicit references in elaborated codes can allow speakers to think about meanings and relationships separate from their immediate context, potentially permitting them to "enter into a reflexive relationship to the social order." In contrast, restricted codes are limited in their ability to express abstract meanings, leading speakers to understand their experience primarily in relation to a specific context. Significantly, "one of the effects of the class system is to limit access to elaborated codes" (ibid.:176).

According to Bernstein, because members of different social classes use different modes of expression, they develop different patterns of thought and, thus, understand their world in different ways. In terms echoing Sapir and Whorf (who Bernstein credits with influencing the development of his ideas), Bernstein (1971a: 43) stated:

> Language is one of the most important means of initiating, synthesizing, and *reinforcing* ways of thinking, feeling and behaviour which are functionally related to the social group. It does not, of itself, prevent the expression of specific ideas or confine the individual to a given level of conceptualization, but certain ideas and generalizations are facilitated rather than others (emphasis in original).

Through their use of elaborated or restricted codes, members of stratified social classes orient and express their experiences and thoughts in different forms, thus affecting the ways that they participate in society. In addition, lack of familiarity and competence in middle-class ("elaborated") styles renders working-class speakers uncomfortable with members of higher classes (see also van de Broeck 1977). Finally, working-class speakers' discomfort with elaborated codes makes it difficult for them to read and write using formal styles of language.

All the studies of language and class demonstrate that separation of people into different social strata is powerfully reflected in linguistic variation. Speakers' sensitivity to context, their awareness of their own behavior and that of others, and their reactions both in subjective judgments and in modifications of speech all converge to mark one's place in a hierarchical system.

Speech styles associated with members of upper classes obtain and retain prestige because of the status of their speakers. People with lower status often exhibit speech patterns (e.g., crossover behavior) reflective of their linguistic (and social) insecurity. Their awareness of negative judgments toward their speech, judgments that they also hold, makes them attempt to use prestige norms of upper-class speakers. Class membership not only affects life circumstances but also influences the construction of personal identities. In the process, personal identities become socialized. Finally, language use is a recognized and recognizable reflection of one's social identity.

RACE

African American English in the United States

In the United States, and elsewhere, race has an impact on language use. Many (but not all) African Americans in the United States speak a variety of English known as African American Vernacular English (AAVE). Some speakers use this dialect in all of their communication; others use it only in certain contexts, as among family and friends, speaking standard English in other situations, as in school or at work. They may also switch from one style to the other during any speech event, depending on topic, attitude, and co-participants.

Studies of AAVE have documented both its linguistic and social features. We will begin with an examination of structural differences between AAVE and standard English. We then discuss the complex ways that use and evaluation of AAVE reflect and interconnect with societal attitudes and speakers' identities.

AAVE is a dialect that, like all dialects, has phonological and grammatical rules. Most of these rules are identical to those of the standard language, but there are some regularly occurring patterns in AAVE that, taken as a whole, distinguish it from other varieties. There has been much debate in linguistics about the origins of AAVE, principally whether it is derived from regional southern speech or from Creole languages of African slaves, incorporating syntactic and semantic traits of African languages. The current consensus among linguists is that both historical sources have contributed to the development of AAVE. Some features are derived from speech of rural white southerners whose language reflects the dialect of their Scots-Irish ancestors. Other features, particularly several grammatical aspects in the verb system, have their origins in earlier Creoles. Labov summarized the basic position as follows (1982:192; note that Labov's "Black English Vernacular" is the older term for "African American Vernacular English"):

1.   Black English Vernacular is a subsystem of English with a distinct set of phonological and syntactic rules that are now aligned in many ways with the rules of other dialects.

2.   It incorporates many features of southern phonology, morphology, and syntax; blacks in turn have exerted influence on the dialects of the South where they have lived.

3.   It shows evidence of derivation from an earlier Creole that was closer to the present-day Creoles of the Caribbean.

4.   It has a highly developed aspect system, quite different from other dialects of English, which shows a continuing development of its semantic structure.

In discussing linguistic features of AAVE, it should be remembered that speakers employ different styles, depending on relative formality or informality of situations, and on other social factors, including relationships with co-participants and topics of conversation.

The Structure of African American Vernacular English (AAVE)

Major phonological and morphological characteristics of AAVE are listed and exemplified first, followed by a discussion of AAVE's unique aspectual system. The unique grammatical features of AAVE are characteristic of the dialect spoken by many African Americans throughout the United States. Although it may have originated geographically among speakers in the South, AAVE is now a national, not a regional, dialect.

1. Reduction of Word-Final Consonant Clusters. In all dialects of English, when two (or more) consonants occur at the end of a word and the next word in an utterance begins with a consonant, speakers in normal, colloquial style reduce the cluster in the first word by eliminating the final consonant; for example, *last night* becomes *las' night.* Speakers of AAVE exhibit the same pattern but also modify word-final clusters at the ends of utterances or when the next word begins with a vowel, for example, *She came in las'.*

Reduction of clusters, though, is not always a simple phonological process. In English, some final consonants have an important role in marking morphological changes. In addition to their status as phonemes, the sounds /t/ and /d/ can occur at ends of verbs to denote past tense, as in "I liked (/laykt/) the movie" or "they solved (/salvd/) the problem." When the final consonant has a grammatical function, it is less likely to be deleted. John Baugh (1983) collected large samples of adult speech in Los Angeles and computed probability values for the likelihood of occurrences of phonological and morphological features in what he calls "Black street speech." Based on a scale from 0.000 (for full manifestation in all contexts) to 1.000 (for deletions of variables), the probability value for omission of /t/ and /d/ is .683 when the sounds have no grammatical function but only .353 when they mark past tense (ibid.:98). This clearly proves that speakers are well aware of the importance of the grammatical roles of sounds and are responsive to the meanings of words.

Similar patterning occurs for omission or retention of word-final /-s/. This phoneme can represent three different grammatical morphemes: plural (two cats), possessive (the cat's dish broke), and third-person singular (she likes it). Speakers of AAVE are most likely to retain /s/ at the ends of words when it marks plurality of nouns. In fact, for this meaning, /s/ is rarely deleted. It is, however, often omitted when it represents the possessive and especially when it denotes third-person singular. Baugh's probability values for loss of /s/ with these three meanings are plural, .173; possessive, .611; and third-person singular, .753 (ibid.:95).

Studies among African Americans in Detroit revealed gender differences in reducing final consonant clusters (Wolfram 1969). Men tended to delete final consonants in clusters more often than did women, with percentages of 57.8 and 43.7, respectively.

2. Variation of /r/. Another phonological feature of AAVE is the variation of postvocalic /-r/. Its occurrence in this dialect is similar to patterning in other variable dialects, as noted, for instance, in Labov's New York City research. African Americans tend to delete postvocalic /-r/ at higher rates than white speakers do in all contextual styles. In addition, /r/ is sometimes omitted between vowels as well, especially when a preceding vowel is stressed—for example, Carol → Ca'ol, interested → inte'ested (Labov 1972a:14).

3. Contraction and Deletion of the Copula. The English copula (the verb "to be") can be contracted in present tense in colloquial speech, as in "she is smart" → "she's smart." This rule describes the normal process in most dialects. A further development takes place in AAVE: deletion of present-tense forms entirely, as in "she smart." But AAVE does not omit the copula in all linguistic contexts. Deletion of the copula in AAVE is related to its contraction in standard English; that is, "wherever SE can contract, AAVE can delete *is* and *are,* and vice versa" (Labov 1972a:73). In SE, the copula cannot be contracted in "exposed position," particularly at ends of sentences. For example, it must occur in "Here I *am*" or "that's the kind of person he *is.*" Forms like "Here I'm" or "that's the kind of person he's" are not possible. Similarly, AAVE retains the full copula in these environments.

Deletion of the copula in AAVE also depends on the kind of grammatical form that follows. Some possibilities (examples from Labov 1972a:67–68) are the following:

1. *Noun phrase:* She the first one started us off.
2. *Predicate adjective:* He fast in everything he do.
3. *Locative:* We on tape.
4. *Negation:* They not caught.
5. *Progressive* (verb): He always coming over to my house to eat.
6. *Future* ("gonna" or "gon"): He gon' try to get up.

According to Baugh's probability values, speakers are most likely to omit the copula preceding "gonna" or a progressive verb (values of .691 and .662, respectively) and most likely to be retained preceding locatives and noun phrases (.294 and .315, respectively) (1983:101).

Studies in Detroit demonstrated gender and class differences in the pattern of this grammatical feature. Women tended to retain the copula with greater frequency than did men. And men and women who were members of higher classes tended to retain the copula. Walt Wolfram's data (1969), separated for gender and class, are presented in the following table.

Percentage of Copula Deletion

Class	Men	Women
Upper middle	6.4%	3.1%
Lower middle	16.4	5.3
Upper working	45.3	28.7
Lower working	66.3	47.5

For all phonological and morphological features—consonant reduction, variation of /r/, and deletion of the copula—AAVE seems to be advancing rules of the standard language: Standard English (SE) allows reduction of final consonant clusters before a next consonant, AAVE allows reduction of all final clusters; several regional dialects omit /r/ following vowels, AAVE omits /r/ between vowels as well; SE contracts the copula in certain environments, AAVE deletes the copula in these same contexts. Rules in AAVE, therefore, are sensitive to phonological and morphological traits of standard English but manifest innovative expansions.

Some speakers of AAVE exhibit behavior referred to as hypercorrection. *Hypercorrection* is a process of extending linguistic rules in an overly generalized and regularized fashion. For example, Baugh quoted a teenager who said, "They act like they think I really likes going to school" (1983:65). This speaker attaches the suffix /-s/ to a first-person verb even though it normally occurs only on third-person forms. Another hypercorrection in some AAVE speech is overgeneralization by analogy of the past-tense suffix /-d/, written "-ed," resulting in: look → lookted (/lʊktɪd/), love → loveded (/lʌvdɪd/).

Baugh suggested that hypercorrection occurs more frequently in formal contexts when speakers are particularly aware that their speech is stigmatized (ibid.). *Hypercorrection* is a response to social pressures and to people's sensitivity to the fact that their colloquial style is criticized by the "general" population. Speakers of AAVE know that they sometimes delete /-s/ and /-d/ on verbs and so they include them in linguistic environments where they do not belong. In attempting to correct their speech, speakers actually outdo standard norms by overextending grammatical rules. This kind of reaction is similar to pronunciations by lower-middle-class speakers in Labov's New York City research who exhibited crossover rates of standard speech in formal contexts. In both cases, people respond through their use of language to social perceptions of them, knowing that they are judged negatively and hoping to make a better impression by changing the way they speak. But, as we have already seen, negative evaluations of a linguistic style are actually metaphors for the powerlessness of its speakers.

The unique character of AAVE is demonstrated especially by its development of complex aspectual systems in verbs. *Grammatical aspects* indicate the manner or duration of an event's occurrence. For example, the progressive denotes action throughout a time period: "I was read*ing* all morning." AAVE contains many more kinds of aspect marking than are available in standard English. These properties of

AAVE may have originated in Creoles derived from African languages, although Anglo-Irish influences are also possible (Labov 1982:140; Baugh 1983:73). Whatever the historical antecedents, AAVE continually expands on aspectual meanings using contemporary forms. (Examples in the following discussion are taken from Baugh 1983:70–87, with the exception of #6, which is taken from Labov 1972a:188.)

1. Invariant *be:* Use of *be* generally marks habitual and/or durative aspect. The habitual refers to events that occur and are expected to recur and the durative denotes an action over time.
    a. It's just not convenient . . . y'know . . . cause the office *be* closed on weekends.
    b. She say, "Why you *be* runnin in the street so much?"
    c. But the teachers don't *be* knowing the problems like the parents do. Invariant *be* sometimes has only a durative meaning.
    d. . . . and we *be* tired from the heat, but he just made everybody keep on working.
        Finally, invariant *be* can occur in diverse syntactic environments.
    e. Preceding progressive verbs: He *be* hiding when he knows she's mad.
    f. Preceding locatives: They don't *be* on the streets no more.
    g. Preceding noun phrases: Leo *be* the one to tell it like it is.
    h. Preceding adjectives: It's not right to act like you *be* stupid in school.
2. Perfective *done:* Perfective aspect denotes an action that is completed.
    a. The teacher *done* lost her keys.
    b. We *done* told him bout these pipes already.
        Done also has meanings comparable to standard *already* and the emphatic *really.*
    c. It don't make no difference, cause they *done* used all the good ones by now.
    d. Well, we useta get into trouble and if Pop'd catch us, he say, "Boy— you *done* done it now."
3. Future perfective *be done:* This form is used for an event that will occur and be completed in the future. Its form is *be done* + past-tense verbs.
    a. We *be done* washed all the cars by the time Jojo gets back with the cigarettes.
    b. I'll *be done* bought my own radio waitin on him to buy me one.
4. Stressed *been:* Stress (or accent) on the word *been* marks an event that began in the past. In some cases, it marks completion of an event in the past, whereas in others, the action or state continues into the present.
    a. We *been* lived here.
    b. I *been* had that job.
5. Aspectual *steady: Steady* functions as an intensified continuative, emphasizing consistent and persistent continuation of an event. It usually occurs with progressive verbs and always takes an animate subject.

    a.   He all the time be *steady* complainin bout somethin.

    b.   Them fools be *steady* hustlin everybody they see.

           Verbs with *steady* are action or process verbs, not states. Therefore, sentences like the following are not possible.

    *c.   They be *steady* knowing the truth.

    *d.   He be *steady* resembling his mother.

6.   Multiple negation: Speakers of many English dialects use multiple negation in colloquial speech. AAVE is characterized by a proliferation of negation to mark emphasis and stylistic effect.

    a.   They didn't never do nothing to nobody.

    b.   He ain't not never gon say it to his face.

    c.   They can't do nothing if they don't never try.

           AAVE allows for the inversion of standard word order of noun + auxiliary + verb auxiliary + noun + verb with negation.

    d.   Didn't nobody see it, didn't nobody hear it!

Settings and Contexts

As with speakers of all languages, speakers of AAVE are sensitive to situational requirements and adapt their linguistic performance to context. As Baugh points out in his analysis of street speech, people employ stylistic alternatives, depending on the degree of familiarity and solidarity with co-participants in speech events. "All people are more comfortable when they are interacting with others who share common norms, and linguistic performance is one of the most important criteria for establishing rapport" (1983:33). Features of AAVE occur with greatest frequency in informal contexts when speakers share life experiences, expectations, and values. In contrast, speakers use standard English in situations of formality and social distance. In a mathematical measure of sensitivity to context, Baugh's probability values for phonological variables in different speech events reveal that speakers' deletion of the suffix /-s/ (described above) has the probability value of .615 (out of 1.000) in the most informal situations, whereas its value is .378 in the most formal contexts (ibid.:95). Other linguistic features showed similar situational variation.

Speakers are often acutely aware of their status in relation to co-participants and adjust their behavior accordingly. Research among adolescent boys in Harlem (Labov 1972a) revealed that when boys were interviewed in a somewhat formal manner, they typically gave minimal responses, answering in few words and in a hesitant and pause-filled fashion. But when the children felt relaxed, they were very talkative and exhibited a great deal of verbal creativity. In the first instance, "[t]he child is in an asymmetrical situation where anything he says can literally be held against him. He has learned a number of devices to avoid saying anything in this situation and he works very hard to achieve this end" (Labov 1972a:206). In the second instance, when people are socially at ease, they willingly express their individuality, knowledge, and opinions in a free and easy style. Evidence from other research on speech contexts and language use supports these same conclusions. Recall, for example, van de Broeck's work in Belgium showing that lower-class speakers used simpler syntactic constructions in formal situations than in informal ones, where they felt more comfortable.

A number of studies have demonstrated the significant use of African American Vernacular English as a device to display solidarity between speaker and addressee. In particular, code switching from standard speech to the vernacular was seen to emphasize community membership and create affective and supportive bonds. When Linda Nelson (1990) analyzed life-history narratives from African-American women in New York City, southern New Jersey, and Philadelphia, she noticed that the women began speaking in standard English but often switched to the vernacular at key points in the interviews. In some cases, switches were made to highlight incidents or feelings expressed, and others were triggered by Nelson's responses and/or her own use of vernacular features. Nelson later "translated" the women's utterances from AAVE into standard speech and asked the women whether they perceived a difference in meaning. Responses usually focused on the affective meanings transmitted by the vernacular but not by the standard forms. For example, when talking about the poverty experienced by her family in her childhood, one woman said, "Girl, you better get that 5-cent pack of Kool-Aid!" And when Nelson asked about the difference between her statement and a standard equivalent ("We really had to just go and get those 5-cent packs of Kool-Aid!"), the woman replied, "Your way [the standard English] simply focuses on words. The words [meaning hers] talking about a 5-cent pack of Kool-Aid are just being used to label a whole range of things. We had to improvise on a lot of things that weren't always available to us" (1990:150). Speaking about the influence of her elders, the woman said, "I always had an ear to what older folks talkin bout." When Nelson asked her to compare her statement with "I always listened to what the older people were talking about," she responded:

> I tried to convey a sense which meant I would sit and listen but also more, I would try to be in their presence, more than just eavesdropping. I'm trying to communicate a shoebox full when you only give them [the words] a matchbox. I'm trying to relate the spiritual meaning. (ibid.:151)

The speaker also conveyed her camaraderie with Nelson and her desire to display that relationship: "I am comfortable with you. I have to slip into my home tongue to get the message across" (ibid.).

The use of AAVE as a means of establishing rapport and solidarity was also demonstrated in a study of teacher–student interactions in a community college (Foster 1995). During classroom interactions, the teacher framed some of class time as "performance" by switching into vernacular language and style. "In performances, there is a shift away from mainstream language to language and behavior that is more Black. The resulting talk is more participatory, with students contributing spontaneously" (1995:337). Shifts included changes in rhythm, grammar, intonational patterns, and use of "images, symbolism and gestures" characteristic of

African-American styles. The teacher's talk incorporated features of a "Black sermonic tradition" (ibid.:140). In interviews with the teachers, Michele Foster found that the women switched within discourse from standard to vernacular speech, sometimes to highlight emotional aspects of their narratives, sometimes to set off episodes or reported speech within the narrative, and sometimes to display solidarity with the researcher. The significance of the latter function was revealed especially by contrasts when Foster interviewed male teachers. The men exhibited many fewer instances of code switching, suggesting that "gender plays some part in facilitating or inhibiting codeswitching behavior" (ibid.:346).

Studies such as those of Nelson and Foster have helped extend knowledge of the use of AAVE by including research among women. Nearly all studies conducting during the 1960s and 1970s focused on language used by boys and men. As John Rickford observed, "Research on discourse and verbal genres has highlighted male-centered activities and male sexual exploits. As a consequence, African American women are either erased from the urban landscape because of their purported linguistic conservatism or portrayed as willing interlocutors and audiences for the plethora of street hustler raps and misogynistic boasting reported by researchers" (1997:171). Nelson and Foster, therefore, have contributed insights into the creative rather than passive use of the vernacular by women in both private and public interactions.

Social issues related to the use of AAVE have arisen, particularly in contexts of school and educational practices. Children who speak AAVE are faced with multiple conflicts stemming from numerous factors, including teachers' negative judgments of a child's speech, children's desire to succeed in school, and their sometimes incompatible desire to be accepted by their own peers. And, overall, children have to resolve these conflicts in environments that they perceive to be hostile, not only to their behavior but also to themselves as persons. Because of the distinct grammatical rules of AAVE that differ from standard English, teachers are often not able to comprehend fully what the children say, or they may misinterpret a child's speech. Additionally, negative attitudes of teachers toward nonstandard language lead them to reject children who use this style.

Some of these issues were raised in a case brought to federal court in Michigan in 1977. The case arose because of parents' concerns about their children's poor school performance and their feeling that such performance did not reflect the children's ability but, rather, a lack of cultural and linguistic understanding between teachers and students. The plaintiffs argued that the local school in Ann Arbor had not taken any remedial action to address children's educational problems. After hearing testimony from many linguists about the origins and structure of AAVE, Judge Joiner handed down a historic decision in 1979, finding for the plaintiffs and ordering the Ann Arbor school board to institute procedures to correct teachers' misconceptions about AAVE and to help students better learn the standard language. Judge Joiner found that "the language barrier that did exist was in the form of unconscious negative attitudes formed by teachers towards children who spoke AAVE, and the reactions of children to those attitudes" (cited in Labov 1982:193). The school board began instructing teachers about the characteristics of AAVE and developing ways to help children learn the standard dialect.

In school settings, children having difficulty or refusing to use standard English are sometimes perceived as hostile and can even be labeled as learning disabled or mentally handicapped. Children's linguistic problems, though, should be seen as resulting from their awareness of teachers' negative judgments and their ensuing rejection of teachers' demands. Additionally, the effects of peer pressure can be considerable. Other children often ridicule and reject students who speak standard English and perform well in school. Because most children want to be accepted by their peers, combined with their perception that they will never get teachers' approval, they frequently rebel against standard norms. Labov's research found a close correlation between peer-group acceptance and reading failures among Harlem boys. An inverse relation was found between a boy's status in street groups and his reading abilities; the more prestige he had among his peers, the lower were his reading scores (1972a:247). Difficulties in reading clearly affect attainment of other educational skills and can result in lifelong underachievement with concomitant economic impact.

Attitudes of parents toward their children's speech are also factors affecting children's performance. Parental attitudes are often complex; parents want their children to be able to speak standard English while also recognizing the social and cultural validity of the vernacular. In a study of language preferences of parents in Oakland and East Palo Alto, California, Mary Hoover (1978) documented parental attitudes toward their children's speech styles in different social contexts. Hoover distinguished between "Black Standard English" and the "Black vernacular." The former is characterized by standard syntax but contains some phonological features common among African-American speakers, including simplification of consonant clusters, high rates of r-lessness, and weakening of final consonants, although if word-final consonants function as morphological markers (possessive or third-person /-s/, past tense /-ed/, future /-l/), they are retained. Additionally, standard AAVE has distinctive intonational patterns and some specialized vocabulary (Hoover 1978:69). Speakers of the vernacular employ linguistic features outlined in earlier sections of this chapter.

Parents of diverse income levels and social groupings were questioned about the acceptability of their children's use of either of the two styles in both formal and informal speech in home, community, and school. Hoover also noted parents' preferences in various channels of listening, speaking, reading, and writing. Hoover's study indicated that parents' attitudes were not rigid but were sensitive to setting, context, and channel. Parents recognized the value of both vernacular and standard speech, approving of the former's use in home and community for speaking and listening but not for reading or writing. Most parents rejected the use of vernacular speech in school, preferring that their children be educated in the standard. The following table summarizes Hoover's findings (1978:78).

Sociolinguistic Rules for Vernacular Black English

	Home		Community		School	
Channel	Informal	Formal	Informal	Formal	Informal	Formal
Listening	+	+	+	+	-	-
Speaking	+	+	+	=	-	-
Reading	NA	-	NA	-	=	-
Writing	-	-	-	-	=	-

+ Accepted.
- Rejected.
= Close to acceptance.

Positive evaluation of AAVE was correlated with other positive attitudes toward distinctive African-American culture, political involvement, and self-pride. People in higher income brackets more readily accepted AAVE in informal home and community contexts in combination with their overall greater positive evaluations of African-American culture (ibid.:83). Hoover explained this finding in terms of parents' control of the standard in their own speech: People who themselves easily use standard speech do not object to the vernacular in certain contexts, whereas parents who have difficulty with standard English tend to want their children to learn this style (ibid.:81). These parents "reveal an acute awareness of an economic system in which one of the indices to discrimination can be speech" (ibid.:82).

Once again, when people know that they are judged by linguistic performance, they try to modify their behavior and that of their children. But it is the larger social context that constructs both positive and negative attitudes and that stigmatizes certain sectors of a population indirectly by criticizing their speech. In situations of inequality, unequal burdens are placed on members of groups lacking power, who then are expected to adjust to norms imposed by the dominant society. Many African-American speakers are caught in this dilemma, compounded by conflicting attitudes toward AAVE and standard English. According to Geneva Smitherman, writing about social values of speech styles, "Both linguistic forms have been demanded for Black survival—Black language for use in the Black community where 'talkin proper' is negatively equated with 'talkin white,' white language for use in attempts to get admitted to the White American mainstream" (1984:108).

Although teaching literacy is a primary goal of the educational system, teacher–student interactions can significantly mold the way in which literacy learning takes place and the covert lessons children learn about what literacy involves. In a study of third-grade classrooms in a working-class African-American neighborhood in Chicago, James Collins (1996) found that teachers approached the task of literacy in different ways for children judged to be at different levels of skill. Collins observed classrooms in which children were separated into work groups based on high or low reading levels, each group working separately with the teacher at different times. The teacher exerted greater control over the behavior and interactions of children in the low-skill group than in the high-skill group. For example, although disruptive behavior occurred about equally in both groups, the teacher tended to ignore disruptions in the high-skill group, continuing to proceed with the lesson, whereas disruptions in the low-skill group led to interruptions in the flow of lessons. Children who called out of turn in the low-skill group were more likely to be reprimanded, whereas such behavior by children in the high-skill group was either ignored or treated as an appropriate comment or response. Children's responses were also dealt with differently. When high-skill children offered answers, the teacher responded positively, either embedding the child's answer in the teacher's comment or in the teacher's next question, but the answers of low-skill children were not taken up and incorporated into the teacher's next utterance.

Of special importance was Collins's surprising observation that although both groups of children were strong users of African American Vernacular English, the speech of children in the low-skill group was corrected twice as often as that of the high-skill group. Although the suppression of "nonstandard" dialects and of African American Vernacular English in particular is a pervasive feature of American prescriptive conventions, Collins's study demonstrates that dialect suppression is not uniform but arises in specific contexts: "Despite its historical durability, we must avoid viewing prescriptivism simply as some abstract cultural-linguistic authoritarianism, immanent in American culture. It is authoritarianism, but viewing it abstractly obscures its nature and dynamic" (1996:211).

Although the children in both groups learned to read, their strategies and orientations were directed toward different goals. As Collins notes, "'Poor readers' acquire early and maintain consistently a view of reading as fluent pronunciation of text. Conversely, 'good readers' acquire early and maintain consistently a view of reading as an interpretive process, a learning from text" (ibid.:223). These different strategies and goals cohere with a system of hierarchical distinctions based on class and race that characterizes societies like our own.

Research among African Americans in an inner-city neighborhood in Detroit showed that even within a small community differences exist in the rates of speakers' use of vernacular pronunciations and grammatical forms. Walter Edwards (1992) found that such differences were correlated with the strength of speakers' involvement with their neighborhood and their emotional attachment to their community. Edwards based his work on methods developed in Jenny Cheshire's study of adolescents in Reading, England (see the section on class in this chapter), as well as on network theory. Edwards first constructed an index to measure people's cultural identification. The Vernacular Culture Index was compiled from responses to ten questions, including whether most of a respondent's relatives and friends live in the neighborhood, whether most of their daily interactions are with neighborhood residents, whether they hope to remain in the neighborhood, and whether they think their neighborhood is a good place to raise children.

Edwards collected samples of speech from 33 male and 33 female consultants and noted the occurrence of four features of AAVE pronunciation (three vowel pronunciations and the presence or absence of /r/) and one grammatical trait (absence of copula in the present tense). As might be expected, he found that a person's use of AAVE speech was strongly correlated with his or her score on the Vernacular Culture Index. That is, the stronger a person's identification with the neighborhood and the person's involvement in a network of residents, the more likely he or she was to use more AAVE features (ibid.:107). This finding applied equally to men and women, as Edwards found no significant difference in rates of AAVE usage by gender.

However, age was an important factor. Groups of older speakers (age 40–59 and 60 plus) used more AAVE features than groups of younger speakers (18–25, 26–39) (ibid.:102). According to Edwards, the vernacular dialect and standard English are converging for younger speakers, leading to a merging of speech styles and a lack of distinctive AAVE traits. If this conclusion is correct, the Detroit community is markedly different from a community in Philadelphia studied by Labov and Harris (1986) that indicated increased separation of AAVE and SE. In addition, Edwards found that of the two younger groups, the age group of 26- to 39-year-olds used the most SE pronunciations and the least AAVE forms. Edwards applied network theory to explain this pattern, concluding that these speakers "are most geographically mobile and come into contact more often with speakers of SE," whereas members of the youngest group "interact more with their parents and elders" (ibid.:104).

The requirements of available jobs may be an additional factor motivating people to conform linguistically. In a study of African-American communities in Georgetown County, along the South Carolina coast, Patricia Nichols (1983) found relationships among employment, gender, age, and linguistic style. At one end of the speech continuum is a variety influenced by Gullah, a Creole derived from English and African languages, still spoken by residents of islands off the Carolina and Georgia coasts. The two other linguistic codes are an African-American vernacular and regional standard English.

Older women used the most creolized, nonstandard forms, whereas younger women showed greatest use of standard English. Although differences in style exist among men, they do not seem to be significantly affected by age. Gender distinctions are especially sharp between younger women and men, women using standard speech and men speaking the vernacular. Nichols interpreted these findings as related to differential employment opportunities for gender and age groups. Male jobs, concentrated in farm and construction work, have remained relatively constant over time. Neither of these occupations requires standard language skills, particularly as men usually work in local communities with friends and family. Jobs available to women, in contrast, have changed considerably. Older women most often worked as domestics in households and hotels and as farm laborers, jobs similarly involving few interactions with standard English. Women have recently obtained an increasing number of white-collar jobs in sales, nursing, and teaching. Because these jobs clearly require knowledge and use of standard English, young women continue their education in order to acquire linguistic and other job-related skills (Nichols 1983:61–63).

The research conducted by Hoover, Edwards, and Nichols demonstrates that speech communities are not homogeneous but, rather, that use of linguistic styles is affected by conditions of life and that people's choices are dependent on their economic and social participation in the community.

The Ebonics Controversy

In December 1996, the Oakland, California, school board passed a resolution to implement new methods and goals of teaching reading and language skills in its district. The directive unleashed a firestorm of controversy that actually distorted the thrust of the resolution, in part because of ambiguous wording in the resolution itself and in part because of underlying assumptions and prejudices in the nation as a whole. The Oakland school board's action was prompted by the poor performance of African-American children on reading and language arts tests. Because the children's poor performance was judged to derive from differences between the vernacular language that they used at home and in the community and the standard speech demanded in the school setting, the board resolved to implement a program of instruction that would inform and train teachers in the legitimacy of African American Vernacular English and that would enable speakers of the vernacular to acquire standard English. It is worth quoting the resolution because much of the ensuing controversy was sparked by a misreading of its stated goals:

> The Superintendent shall devise and implement the best possible academic program for imparting instruction to African-American students in their primary language for the combined purposes of maintaining the legitimacy and richness of such language . . . and to facilitate their acquisition and mastery of English language skills. (quoted in *The Black Scholar* 1997:4)

While there is considerable variability in research findings concerning standard and alternative approaches to reading instruction (Rickford 1997:180–181; McWhorter 1997b:2–3), the approach to teaching language skills advocated by the Oakland school board is consistent with some research demonstrating children's reading improvement when instruction and testing are carried out in their "primary language." For example, when test items in the Boehm Test of Basic Concepts were "translated" from standard into vernacular language, children in kindergarten and first and second grades scored significantly higher (Williams 1997:212).

In addition, in the 1970s, researchers developed a "Bridge" reading program. The program began with reading material written only in the vernacular, then presented texts that were written 50 percent in AAVE and 50 percent in standard English, and finally switched completely to the standard. Reading selections were followed by comprehension exercises and language arts drills. To motivate the students, stories were introduced by a recording made by a young man:

> What's happenin', brothers and sisters? I want to tell you about this here program called "Bridge," a cross-cultural reading program. Now I *know* what you thinkin'.

This is just another one of them jive reading programs, and that I won't be needin' no readin' program. But dig it. This here reading program is really kinda different. It was done by a brother and two sisters, soul folk, you know. . . . (quoted in Rickford 1997:179)

To evaluate the effectiveness of the Bridge approach, children in grades 7 through 12 were tested after four months and compared to a group who had not been exposed to the program. Reading scores of the Bridge children increased an average of 6.2 months, whereas those in the standard school programs increased only by 1.6 months. The Bridge children not only surpassed children in standard programs but also did better than the norm (four months' gain for four months of instruction) (Rickford 1997:179). Unfortunately, the Bridge readers were discontinued by their publisher because of criticism by educators and the media and not because they had been ineffective.

Despite evidence of the potential usefulness of a variety of alternative teaching methods, the intent of the Oakland school board was distorted by focus on the resolution's initial claim that what the board called "Ebonics" is derived from "Niger-Congo African languages" and is "genetically based and not a dialect of English." The claim that Ebonics is a separate language rather than the more accepted linguistic view that it is a dialect of English cannot be substantiated by linguistic data. And although AAVE certainly shares syntactic, semantic, and stylistic features with some African languages, its historical origins are much more complex than suggested by its roots in "Niger-Congo African languages." Finally, the statement that Ebonics is "genetically based" is at the least odd.

Although the board later modified or retracted these claims, its initial wording was unfortunate because it merely gave fuel to people opposed to the more important intent, that is, the desire to develop special educational programs to serve the needs of African-American children. Furthermore, the board's statement that teachers should recognize the legitimacy of AAVE as a rule-governed and valid form of language was distorted by opponents to mean that children would be taught to read, write, and speak AAVE and not be taught to communicate in standard English. Even some influential African Americans such as Jesse Jackson and Maya Angelou voiced opposition to the Oakland resolution, probably because they had not read the full text but had only heard media reports that took some of the board's statements out of context. Their quick reactions were unfortunate because they only helped to engender even less reasoned responses by people who never in the past showed any sympathy for African-American children. In response to the barrage of criticism in the media, the Linguistics Society of America voted unanimously to support the Oakland school board's resolution, but the society's voice was not widely reported nationally.

The important issue is not whether one agrees or disagrees with the Oakland text but, rather, what is to be done to teach reading and language skills to children whose "home" language differs from the standard. Some argue that the Oakland board's dual-language approach is the best answer; others believe that immersion in standard English is preferable. These divergent opinions were expressed by researchers and public figures in special journal issues of both *The Black Scholar* (1997) and *The Journal of Black Psychology* (1997).

However, in the midst of the controversy, it is well to remember the significance of social context and the multiple kinds of meanings conveyed not just by a language but by *choice* of language (or dialect). The lack of interest or even resistance of some African-American children to acquiring standard English must be seen in the historical and social contexts in which African Americans find themselves. Their educational difficulties are not due to the standard's incomprehensibility because of its divergence from their "home" dialect. As John McWhorter points out, children in countries such as Switzerland, Germany, and Scotland easily learn a standard dialect of their language when they enter school (1997a:12–13). But African-American children are confronted not merely with some relatively limited linguistic differences. They are also confronted with social attitudes that typically stigmatize their own style of speech, denigrating not only their language but their selves as well. Therefore, educational programs that respect their "home" speech and encourage their community-based verbal skills may facilitate their acquisition of the standard. As Geneva Smitherman and Sylvia Cunningham conclude:

> Many of our students resort to not-learning as a means of resistance. . . . We need to help them move beyond the resistance that keeps them stifled and saddled in the same place. We are advocating that educators provide Black youths with the history of Black and Standard English and encourage them to critically examine these two linguistic forms and the social and political situations that created them. Merging this knowledge with the pride and confidence that comes from a healthy sense of self and peoplehood, Black youths can move forward knowing the differences between languages and the value of language and culture, never having to surrender one language (Black English) for another (Standard English). (1997:230–231)

Afro-Caribbean Speakers in Great Britain

Migration of Caribbean peoples to Great Britain increased during the 1940s and 1950s as a result of postwar economic growth in Britain and a decline in economic and social conditions in the Caribbean. Also, in 1952, the U.S. Congress passed the Walters-McCarran Act, which established a quota system for immigration, thus forcing a majority of people wanting to leave the West Indies to settle in Great Britain rather than in the United States. At the same time, several British employer organizations, including London Transport, National Health Service, and British Hotels and Restaurants Association, actively recruited West Indian workers (Wong 1986:111–112). However, in 1961 and 1962, the British government enacted two Commonwealth Immigration Acts that severely restricted immigration from the Caribbean. Therefore, most young Afro-Caribbean Britons today are native-born (Sebba 1986:150). In the 1970s, estimates put the number of West Indians in Britain at 543,000, slightly more than 1 percent of the total population (Edwards 1988:35–36).

The speech repertory of young Afro-Caribbean Britons is complex. People of Caribbean ancestry living in London use at least two, often three, varieties of English. Most speakers employ a dialect of London English that Mark Sebba (1986) identifies as Afro-Caribbean London English. It is similar to the Cockney dialect. In addition, many Afro-Caribbean Londoners, especially young men, speak London Jamaican, a form of English heavily influenced by the Jamaican Creole of their parents. Finally, older residents who were born in Jamaica usually speak the Jamaican English or Creole of their native country (Sebba 1986:151).

Afro-Caribbean London English diverges from white London English in a number of sound, grammatical features and vocabulary (ibid.:151–154):

1. *Pronunciation:* Afro-Caribbean London English replaces the interdental voiceless fricative /θ/ with labiodental /f/, as in <u>th</u>ing → /fɪŋ/ or <u>th</u>rough → /fruː/. Although this replacement occurs in Cockney English as spoken by whites as well, its use is increasing in the Afro-Caribbean community and decreasing among whites.

2. *Prosodic features:* Afro-Caribbean English contains several prosodic features that differ slightly from white speech. These include qualities of "pitch, rhythm, volume, vowel length, nasality, aspiration, breathiness [which] add up to a 'Black accent'" (ibid.:152).

3. *Vocabulary:* A few words are used distinctively in Afro-Caribbean English. For example: *hug up* "hug, cuddle," *picky-picky* "peppercorn hair," *duppy* "ghost," *facety* "impertinent."

4. *Grammar:* Afro-Caribbean English contains a syntactic particle *se* or sɛɪ (pronounced "say") that occurs following a verb of knowing, believing, or perceiving. It is related to a similar form in Jamaican Creole and has obviously been borrowed into Afro-Caribbean London speech from this source. *Se* functions as an equivalent to the standard English "that," but is restricted in its use, occurring only after a limited category of "psychic state" verbs, as in the following examples (ibid.:154):

    a. If we lose, we lose, we know *se* we tried. (female, aged 16)
    b. A all white jury found out *se* 'e was guilty. (male, aged 15)
    c. Sometimes fings 'appen, right [pause] and you know *se* really an' truly it ain't gonna work out. (female, aged 20)
    d. I feel *se* they're 'olding it over there you know. (female, aged 15)

Another Afro-Caribbean London dialect, London Jamaican, contains several sounds that differ from both white London English and Afro-Caribbean London English. These distinctive traits are derived from Jamaican Creole (Sebba 1986: 162):

a.	ay [ɛɪ]	→	ie [ʌ]	*niem*	"name"
b.	ow [aw]	→	ou [ow]	*soun*	"sound"
c.	th [θ]	→	t [t]	*tiif*	"thief"

d.	th [ð]	→	d [d]	*di*	"the"
e.	u [ʌ]	→	o [ɔ]	*mekop*	"makeup"
f.	[ɔ:]	→	[a:]	*kaal*	"call"
g.	[æ]	→	[ɐ]	*man*	"man"

In a study of an Afro-Caribbean British community in West Midlands, Viv Edwards described numerous grammatical characteristics in the dialect she identified as "patois." Patois is spoken by teenagers and young adults of Jamaican ancestry living in Dudley, West Midlands (1986:97). The relevant traits are:

a.   Third-person singular present-tense verbs:
     John *swim* fast. Kevin *eat* a lot.

b.   Plurals:
     six *car*

c.   Simple past tense:
     Winston *see* di boy. Beverly *walk* away.

d.   First-person singular pronoun:
     Mi feel happy.

e.   Third-person singular pronouns:
     Im put *im* coat away.

f.   Third-person plural pronouns:
     Dem see di baby. Look at *dem* hat.

g.   Negatives:
     Di boy *no* see it.   (The boy doesn't see it.)

h.   Adjectival verbs:
     Di man *happy.*   (The man is happy.)

i.   Continuatives:
     John *a come.*   (John is coming.)

j.   Focus:
     A John do it.   (*John* did it/it was John who did it.)

k.   Questions:
     Mary *a go* home?   (Is Mary going home?)
     Harvey *see* di man?   (Did Harvey see the man?)

l.   Infinitives:
     John aks *fi* see it.   (John asked to see it.)

m.   Other pronouns:
     Unu want it.   (You [plural] want it.)

n.   Psychic state transitive verbs:
     Tony tell me *seh* im no know.   (Tony told me he didn't know.)

o.   '-dem' plurals:
     Give me *di* book-*dem.*

p.   Locating verb:
Mary *deh* a yaad.   (Mary is at home.)

q.   Equating verb:
Patrick *a* di winner.   (Patrick is the winner.)

r.   Past markers:
Roy *did* ready in di morning.   (Roy was getting ready in the morning.)

Speakers of Afro-Caribbean dialects in Great Britain vary their linguistic usage, as do speakers of all languages and dialects, on the basis of attitudes and contexts. Edwards found that a speaker's use of patois was correlated positively with her or his integration into the Afro-Caribbean community and her or his "critical attitudes towards mainstream white society" (1988:38). Allegiance to the Afro-Caribbean community was assessed by residence, participation in local churches, and socializing primarily with other Afro-Caribbean Britons. Attitudes toward white society were determined by responses to questions about school and the speaker's perceptions of white racism, particularly on the part of teachers and the police.

Speakers of Jamaican descent in Dudley used several dialects ranging from patois to the regional West Midlands standard. People chose their speech style based, in part, on who they were talking to. They used fewer patois features in talk to whites and other blacks who were not members of their own community. Use of patois, therefore, is a marker of racial and ethnic identity. It functions simultaneously to solidify in-group membership and to exclude outsiders.

Switching between styles is a common practice of Afro-Caribbean British speakers. Note the following excerpts of switching within and between turns (Sebba 1986:164–165):

B: and then I just laughed
and then 'e—'e just pulled me for a dance
I didn't mind dancing wiv 'im
'cause *mi nuo se, mi n' av notin ina* my mind
but to dance, and then we star'ed to talk and all
the rest of it and that's it. *ful stap*

I: *dem tomp im an kil im*

F: (fhm)

I: an' as I said righ', *im iz a*—he he's a baxer innit

F: yeah

I: *an i kan tek lik, i kan tek gud lik*

J: you 'ave a nice day then

C: 'course. 'e bough? me—*im bai mi dis kiipa* [keeper?] *ring guol chien*

Speakers are well aware of the varieties of language used in their community and of the frequency of switching styles. The following comments were made by a young woman in Dudley describing her friend's speech patterns (Edwards 1988:48–49). (Note dialectal variants: *ay,* corresponding to "isn't," *day* to "didn't," and *bay* to "be.")

> With Melanie right, you have to say she speaks *tri different sort of language when she want to. Cos she speak half Patois, half English and when im ready im will come out wid,* "I day and I bay and I ay this and I ay that. I day have it and I day know where it is." . . . And then she goes, *"Lord God, I so hot."* Now she'll be sitting there right and she'll go, "It's hot, isn't it?"

There is much debate in Great Britain, as in the United States, concerning the use of Afro-Caribbean vernacular speech in educational contexts. Within the range of positions are those advocating exclusive use of standard English in schools in order to provide speakers with linguistic means for upward mobility to those supporting use of Black English in school, recognizing the importance of language to speakers' identity (Richmond 1986:124).

Underlying this controversy are assumptions about the intelligence and worthiness of children based on (mis-)perceptions about their speech. John Richmond pointed out that many teachers, although wanting to help children overcome what they see as barriers to advancement, unwittingly transmit negative messages about the children's own code. He also noted that the lower-class status of most Afro-Caribbean Britons contributes to teachers' biased perceptions of these children (ibid.:129).

Richmond proposed a combination of approaches, stressing the value of acquiring competence in standard English, balanced with recognition of personal and creative roles of the vernacular. He contends that students should be taught to write and speak in standard style, appreciating its usefulness in formal, public contexts, and also be permitted and encouraged to use the vernacular in activities such as narrative writing, poetry, and drama (ibid.:130–131). This approach is a reasonable compromise as it respects children's identity and their use of a linguistic code that marks that identity and yet recognizes social realities of the need for standard English in some contexts.

SUMMARY

Linguistic variation is systematically interconnected with societal segmentation. Language is an important marker of a person's identity, and language use is one way for speakers to display their personal and social identities. Differentiation of sectors within a population can be based on various factors, including class and race. Group membership is often signaled by sharing linguistic styles and attitudes toward language use. Separation of social groups, in contrast, can be marked by differences in forms and functions of language. Similarities in linguistic performance not only reflect social solidarity but also contribute to maintaining solidarity, just as linguistic divergence transmits and reinforces segmentation.

Social stratification is basic to the structuring of many modern societies. Speakers employ varieties of language as markers of their place within a hierarchical order. Status relations, stemming from nonlinguistic factors, are expressed through linguistic use and are further reflected in evaluations of the speech behavior of different sectors of society. For people belonging to subordinate groups, sensitivity to negative judgments about their speaking styles is often manifested in both negative self-appraisals and reluctance to display verbal abilities in situations where they are most aware of their relatively low status. But attitudes, either favorable or unfavorable, toward linguistic styles associated with particular groups are actually messages about existing social relations.

Racial differences in the United States and Great Britain are also reflected in linguistic and stylistic devices employed by some (but not all) people of African ancestry that diverge from standard English. African American Vernacular English in the United States and Afro-Caribbean English in Great Britain have some unique features, although they share most linguistic rules with the standard spoken in their country. Attitudes toward vernacular speech are complex, both on the part of the speakers themselves and in the rest of society. Controversies in both countries focus primarily on proposals to incorporate vernacular speech in schools.

REFERENCES

BAUGH, JOHN. 1983. *Black Street Speech.* Austin: University of Texas Press.

BERNSTEIN, BASIL. 1971a. A public language: Some sociolinguistic implications of a linguistic form. In *Class, Codes and Control,* Vol. I, ed. B. Bernstein. London: Routledge and Kegan Paul, pp. 42–59.

BERNSTEIN, BASIL. 1971b. Social class, language and socialization. In *Class, Codes and Control,* Vol. I, ed. B. Bernstein. London: Routledge and Kegan Paul, pp. 170–189.

The Black Scholar. 1997. The Black Scholar Reader's Forum: Ebonics. 27, no. 1:2–37, no. 2:2–14.

CHESHIRE, JENNY. 1982. Linguistic variation and social function. In *Sociolinguistic Variation in Speech Communities,* ed. S. Romaine. London: Edward Arnold, pp. 153–166.

COLLINS, JAMES. 1996. Socialization to text: Structure and contradiction in schooled literacy. In *Natural Histories of Discourse,* ed. M. Silverstein and G. Urban. Chicago: University of Chicago Press, pp. 203–227.

EDWARDS, VIV. 1986. *Language in a Black Community.* Avon, England: Clevedon.

EDWARDS, VIV. 1988. The speech of British black women in Dudley, West Midlands. In *Women in Their Speech Communities,* ed. J. Coates and D. Cameron. London: Longman, pp. 33–50.

EDWARDS, WALTER. 1992. Sociolinguistic behavior in a Detroit inner-city black neighborhood. *Language in Society* 21:93–115.

FOSTER, MICHELE. 1995. "Are you with me?": Power and solidarity in the discourse of African American women. In *Gender Articulated: Language and the Socially Constructed Self,* ed. K. Hall and M. Bucholtz. New York: Routledge, pp. 329–350.

GUMPERZ, JOHN. 1971 (1958). Dialect dif-

7

Language and Gender: English and English Speakers

What clues do the following sentences contain that tell us whether the speakers are men or women?

"You're driving rather fast, aren't you?"
"Well, I guess it's approximately four feet high."

Both sentences are more typical of the speech of women than of men. The most significant stylistic feature is their use of mitigation to blunt a direct statement. In the first sentence, the speaker employs two devices to minimize the force of her criticism of the addressee's behavior. She uses a *hedge word,* "rather," to qualify the following word "fast." And she uses a linguistic device called a *tag question* ("aren't you?") that has the effect of questioning the declaration "you're driving rather fast." By asking a question rather than making an assertion, the speaker asks the addressee to confirm or deny the proposition contained in the statement. That is, the speaker lets the addressee decide whether she or he is driving fast.

In the second sentence, the speaker employs a series of hedges: " *Well,* I *guess* it's *approximately* four feet high." These words have the effect of creating uncertainty about the speaker's claims, uncertainty that she herself expresses about her own knowledge. Use of such devices blunts the intended statement, undermines the speaker's competence, and anticipates the possibility that she may be contradicted by the addressee.

The styles of speech illustrated here are more typical of women than of men because women and men are socialized to express themselves in different ways in accordance with cultural norms that teach and reinforce differentiated gender roles. Gender itself is a social construct. It is through concepts of gender that society transforms female and male human beings into social women and men, assigning them roles and giving them cultural value. Social norms construct and reinforce attitudes about women's and men's proper work roles, their participation in family and community life, modes of dress and demeanor, and their appropriate styles of communicative behavior. In this chapter we review research concerning the ways that men and women speak and interact. We begin with data from English-speaking societies. In the following chapter we add to our understanding of language and gender by examining several studies that document gender differences in other societies.

The interrelationship of language and gender can be approached from several perspectives. Sociolinguistic analyses inform us about women's and men's styles of speaking, including differences in pronunciation, use of prosodic cues (intonation, velocity, volume), grammatical forms, and choices of vocabulary. Speech performance can also be examined in order to discover gender differences in conversational interaction such as modes of topic introduction, topic control, and supportive or nonsupportive mechanisms used by speakers and listeners. Linguistic and semantic analyses inform us about categories in a language itself and the ways that cultural attitudes toward people are both expressed and reinforced in grammar and vocabulary.

It is probably a universal fact that in all cultures there are differences in how men and women communicate because in all cultures the genders are socially distinguished. As we have seen from studies of class and race, wherever societal distinctions are made among community members, linguistic and stylistic variations arise to reflect and reinforce existing segmentation. It is important to stress that although the obvious sexual female/male dichotomy is used in social differentiation of gender, it does not absolutely determine the roles and values given to women and men. If it did, behavior and evaluations of the two genders would be identical in all societies. This clearly is not the case. Cross-cultural differences in roles performed and rewards given to the genders are well documented. And societal roles and attitudes are subject to change as part of social processes resulting from economic and ideological transformations.

In English, and in many other languages, speech styles of women and men vary in the frequencies with which they employ particular sounds, grammatical features, or words. No patterns are exclusive to either gender; rather, different styles are culturally associated with each. These associations have become stereotypes in many cases so that members of the culture believe that certain communicative behavior is typical of women and other behavior typical of men. Stereotypes are sometimes based on people's actual behavior, but stereotypes also serve to reinforce conformity with prescribed norms. And reactions to people's behavior based on stereotyped assumptions can be complex because overt approval or criticism may actually carry conflicting messages. We will see that this is often the case in evaluations of gender-linked speech.

Before examining data revealing gender-related tendencies in language use, it is critical to caution against overstating differences between women and men. Numerous reviews of studies of linguistic behavior conclude that men's and women's speech are far more similar and overlapping than different. Stereotypes about people's behavior are often believed to be true without systematic evidence to support them. As Nancy Henley and Cheris Kramarae (1991) point out, Western societies tend to exaggerate linguistic, social, and psychological differences between women and men. It could be argued that such exaggerations construct and reconstruct divisions between the genders that help support a system of hierarchy favoring men and devaluing women. Linguistic behavior exhibited by women and men should be seen within the social context that gives it meaning and interpretation. Gender itself is not immutable or static but is a "holistic and dynamic concept" that affects language use (Uchida 1992:564). By examining linguistic behavior, we can "see how we, in the social context, are *doing* gender through the use of language" (ibid.).

It is also necessary to caution that while research findings may point to differences between women's and men's speech, the data are suggestive of tendencies and frequencies of use but not of prediction about any individual's speech in all or any context.

All women do not employ typical female styles, nor do all men employ male styles. In addition to individual variation, the context of communicative interactions is also significant. Contextual factors of formality/informality, speaker goals, and relationship between interlocutors influence the alternatives that people employ. Features of identity such as age, class, status, and race also help determine a speaker's choices. We need to be careful not to overgeneralize and therefore stereotype speakers when discussing gender differences. With these cautions in mind, we will review and evaluate some of the research concerning women's and men's speech.

PRONUNCIATION

Phonological Variants

Except for some regional variations, speakers of English make use of the same inventory of sounds. However, there are differences in the frequencies with which men and women use particular sounds. Several important studies have been carried out to investigate such gender distinctions. In researching children's speech in a small New England town, John Fischer (1958) found gender-related patterns in pronunciation of "*-ing*," the progressive suffix on verbs. Relevant variants are -ɪŋ ("-ing") and -ɪn ("-in"), as in rʌnɪŋ (running) or rʌmɪn (runnin). In Fischer's study, 12 boys and 12 girls were selected and divided into two groups, ages 3 to 6 and 7 to 10. They were observed and interviewed in several situational contexts, including a formal TAT (verbal Thematic Apperception Test) asking children to make up stories based on a starting sentence given by the tester; a formal questionnaire for older children; and an informal session concerning topics of everyday activities.

Gender and context were the most significant factors in frequencies of usage of -ɪŋ/-ɪn. The following table presents findings based on speech elicited in the TAT interviews (adapted from Fischer 1958:48).

	Prefer -ɪŋ	*Prefer* -ɪ*n*
Boys	5	7
Girls	10	2

Of the 12 boys, 5 used -ɪŋ more frequently than -ɪ*n*, whereas 7 used -ɪ*n* more often. For girls, the discrepancy is much more marked, only 2 of them using -ɪ*n* and 10 preferring -ɪŋ. Fischer concluded that "in this community, *-ing* is regarded as symbolizing female speakers and *-in* as symbolizing males" (ibid.:49).

A number of issues can be addressed from this study, with some answers suggested by other parts of Fischer's data. First, we see that gender is a factor in the choice of variant. No significant differences were reported between the two age groups, indicating that children learn this gender-appropriate behavior very early. But given that there is a gender-related preference, what motivates the specific choice of -ɪŋ for girls and -ɪ*n* for boys? One clue comes from a precise count of variants in the speech of a 10-year-old boy in three observational contexts. The following table displays the number of times this boy used the two variants (ibid.:50).

	-ɪŋ	-ɪ*n*
TAT	38	1
Formal interview	33	35
Informal interview	24	41

These figures demonstrate a strong correlation between -ɪŋ and formal situations and -ɪ*n* and informal situations. The variant -ɪŋ, then, carries social meaning of contextual formality as well as "symbolizing female speakers."

Another clue concerning cultural meanings of the variants is provided by a comparison of speech of two boys in TAT interviews. One boy was described by Fischer as a "model" boy, based on his good performance in school, his popularity with peers, and his "considerate" personality. In TAT tests, he used -ɪŋ 38 times and -ɪ*n* only once. The second boy was described as "typical" (an interesting choice of words) because he was strong, dominating, and mischievous. In TAT tests, this boy used -ɪŋ 10 times but -ɪ*n* with slightly greater frequency at 12 (ibid.:49). From these data, it appears that -ɪ*n* may be associated with compliance and politeness.

Taken together, the data suggest a link between speech variants favored by females and an interrelated constellation of cultural meanings, including formality, politeness, and compliance. Gender-specific speech, then, is one aspect of a unified cultural model of behaviors deemed appropriate for females and males.

A similar association of -ɪŋ/-ɪ*n* and gender was found among adult speakers in Norwich, England (Trudgill 1972). In discussing the data, we should keep in mind two other factors that produce linguistic variation, class and contextual style. Recall that class segmentation in Trudgill's Norwich study (see Chapter 6) was reflected in differences in occurrences of -ɪŋ/-ɪ*n*. Higher-class speakers tended to use standard -ɪŋ, whereas lower-class speakers used -ɪ*n*. In addition, for all phonological variables, speech context was an important influence on stylistic choices. In formal contexts, speakers regularly shifted to standard pronunciations. The Norwich data reveal that within class and context, women employed standard features at greater frequencies than did men. Women exhibited marked "style shifting," significantly increasing their use of -ıŋ as contexts became more formal.

The following table presents Trudgill's findings (ibid.:182). (Scores represent an index for -ıŋ in which 100 reflects consistent use of nonstandard -ı*n*, and 000 reflects consistent use of standard -ı*n;* note the abbreviations for class: MMC = middle middle class, LMC = lower middle class, UWC = upper working class, MWC = middle working class, LWC = lower working class; the following abbreviations are used for contexts: WLS = word-list style, RPS = reading passage style, FS = formal style, and CS = casual style.)

-ıŋ Index, by Gender, Class, and Style

Class	Gender	Styles			
		WLS	*RPS*	*FS*	*CS*
MMC	M	000	000	004	031
	F	000	000	000	000
LMC	M	000	020	027	017
	F	000	000	003	067
UWC	M	000	018	081	095
	F	016	013	068	077
MWC	M	024	043	091	097
	F	020	046	081	088
LWC	M	060	100	100	100
	F	017	054	097	100

Higher scores = less use of standard -ıŋ.

Gender differences in Norwich were particularly significant for highest and lowest social groups. In the MMC, women used standard pronunciation all the time, whereas men had an index of 31 in casual speech. In the next group, the LMC, women continued to use -ıŋ in all contexts except casual speech. At the lower end of the class hierarchy, men used nonstandard -ı*n* in all contexts except the most careful style ("word lists"), whereas women in the lowest group began to shift to standard -ıŋ in "formal style."

These data agree with the results of other studies that show women's greater use of standard pronunciations and quicker and more marked style shifting to the standard in increasingly formal speech contexts. The phonological variable of postvocalic /-r/ (we saw in Chapter 6 that it is sensitive to class distinctions and stylistic variation) has been analyzed in several American dialects in relation to gender differences. For example, William Labov's study (1966) of New York City speech demonstrated women's greater use of prestige /-r/.

Gender is also related to the use of postvocalic /-r/ among white speakers in North Carolina (Levine and Crockett 1967). In their study, Levine and Crockett presented subjects with two kinds of lists to be read aloud. One list was made up of sentences containing words with the targeted /-r/ feature. The second was composed of words to be spoken in isolation. The following table compares "R scores" (use of /-r/) for different contexts and also shows net increases for the more careful context of word-list readings (ibid.:95). Men's and women's sentence readings do not differ, but it is the "net increase" to isolated words that is most significant, showing that women have greater sensitivity to prestige norms, as evidenced by their increased use of the prestige variable in a context where more attention is given to speech.

	Sentences	Words	Net Increase
Men	52.3	57.4	5.1
Women	52.9	61.1	8.2

Another study demonstrated that African-American speakers follow the same patterns as do whites. Investigations of African American Vernacular English in Detroit indicated that gender had an impact on pronunciations, again given class and contextual parameters (Wolfram 1969). In this speech community, women used more of the prestige postvocalic /-r/ than did men.

Percentage of Postvocalic /-r/

	UMC	LMC	UWC	LWC
Men	66.7	52.5	20.0	25.0
Women	90.0	70.0	44.2	31.7

Male and female speakers in Detroit varied their use of other sounds as well, including omission of standard labiodental /θ/at ends of words (e.g., tooth) or between vowels (e.g., nothing) or its replacement with either a bilabial fricative /f/ or an alveolar stop /t/. Frequencies of such patterns are exhibited in the following table (ibid.).

Percentage of /θ/ Deletion or Replacement

	UMC	LMC	UWC	LWC
Men	14.6	21.9	70.1	72.3
Women	9.6	12.3	47.5	70.2

All these studies support the contention that pronunciations act, in part, as sociolinguistic markers of gender. Whether the research has been conducted among children, among speakers of American or British regional dialects, or among African Americans or whites, the conclusions are identical: Females use standard and prestige pronunciations at higher rates than do males of similar age and social or racial groups. And in studies that take account of context, females demonstrate quicker and sharper stylistic shifting toward prestige norms in increasingly formal styles. Again, we need to think about why this is so. One explanation is that women are more conscious of prestige norms and strive to use them because they are judged by their social self-presentation and are socialized to behave in ways considered polite and refined. Aware of strong social sanction if they do not conform, women use linguistic style as one manifestation of their "proper" behavior. Labov's notion of "linguistic insecurity," characteristic of members of the lower middle class, can be applied to women as well. Just as LMC speakers' linguistic patterns reflect their position in a system of class hierarchy in which they are stigmatized, women's "linguistic insecurity," manifested by careful speech, reflects their "social insecurity" in a hierarchical system of gender in which they are culturally relegated to second place.

Trudgill developed another explanation of gender differences that is compatible with the one just offered. He introduced the concept of "covert prestige" to account for the fact that men use less standard pronunciations and less style shifting toward the standard than do women. Although standard language is given overt social prestige, shown by comments about one's own or another's speech, a competing norm gives "covert prestige" to male behavior that rejects the standard. In other words, men and women are acting in accordance with different norms. An important indication of this is found in self-reports about one's own speech. Trudgill's subjects were given self-evaluation tests, asking them to specify which of two sounds they used, each set paired for standard and nonstandard features. Women tended to claim greater use of standard pronunciations, whereas men tended to claim greater use of the nonstandard than actually occurred in their speech. These patterns recurred for a number of consonants and vowels.

The following tables display relevant data (Trudgill 1972). The first table presents data for the segment *-yu,* as in the word "tune" (tyun/tun); the second concerns *-er,* as in "ear" or "here"; and the third shows values for the vowel *-o-,* as in "road" or "nose." (Note that Trudgill's term *overreport* refers to claims of standard use; *underreport* refers to claims of nonstandard use.)

Percentage of Informants Over- and Underreporting (yu)

	Total	Men	Women
Overreport	13	0	29
Underreport	7	6	7
Accurate	80	94	64

Percentage of Informants Over- and Underreporting (er)

	Total	Men	Women
Overreport	43	22	68
Underreport	33	50	14
Accurate	23	28	18

Percentage of Informants Over- and Underreporting (o)

	Total	Men	Women
Overreport	18	12	25
Underreport	36	54	18
Accurate	45	34	57

Trudgill's terms *overreport* and *underreport* are not semantically neutral and are actually somewhat misleading. Both women and men are overreporting or underreporting, depending on which norm is taken as the perspective. In fact, what is happening is that both are overreporting but they are overreporting use of different forms. In the case of women it is the standard, and for men the nonstandard. Whereas women claim to produce pronunciations having "overt prestige," men model their behavior purposely, although nonconsciously, toward nonstandard forms having "covert prestige."

Trudgill also noted an interesting link between masculinity and working-class behavior. In male self-reports, the nonstandard pronunciations that men often claim to use are stereotypical traits of working-class speech. In a significant finding, no differences were shown in men's self-reports when separated for class, so that middle-class men were just as likely to claim nonstandard speech as were working-class men (ibid.).

This observation raises additional questions about sociocultural models of gender. Perhaps an explanation lies in the complexities of gender dichotomization. Given that women are socialized to behave with propriety and politeness (reflected by "middle-class" speech), and given a system of gender stratification in which men are privileged and in which men who act like women are strongly criticized, men consciously or unconsciously strive toward speech norms that reject styles associated with women. Because women model their behavior on "middle-class" styles, men covertly prefer "working-class" speech.

Elizabeth Gordon (1997) approaches the question of women's use of standard speech from the opposite direction. Rather than explaining women's speech as reflecting a desire to model their behavior on middle-class norms for positive reasons, Gordon suggests that they may do so in order to avoid inferences associated with lower-class speakers. Whereas men may value stereotypical images of masculinity that are linked to the lower class, women avoid the stereotypical images of "immorality" or "sexual promiscuity" associated with members of the lower class (ibid.:48). Women are particularly vulnerable to condemnation for even the hint of sexual promiscuity because of the existing double standard that either overlooks or rewards men's sexual behavior but criticizes that of women. In this social context, "style-shifting to a more prestigious speech variety conveys the information that the female speaker is not lower class, and is consequently a 'respectable' person" (ibid.:50).

Finally, Penelope Eckert (1998) notes that many of the jobs available to women require the use of standard language. Since white-collar workers, such as secretaries, receptionists, flight attendants, and other "front-end" workers, represent their organizations to the public, they must employ standard or prestige speech in order to make a good impression. And women's work as elementary and high school teachers especially encourages knowledge and use of standard language. The relationship between language style and employment in white-collar and service occupations has also been demonstrated in Patricia Nichols's study of dialect and style shifting among African-American women in coastal Georgia (see Chapter 6).

Intonation

Intonation is a crucial feature influencing how people sound. *Intonation* is a complex combination of rhythm, volume, and pitch overlaying entire utterances. It is heard by listeners as relative changes in these prosodic features rather than as absolute qualities. Some intriguing research has investigated differences in female/male intonational patterns and has discovered cues people use in evaluating the speech of others. In general, women use more dynamic intonational contours than do men. They employ a wider range of pitches within their repertory and a more rapid and marked shift in volume and velocity. In studies of judgments by subjects asked to listen to tape-recorded speech and evaluate the "femininity" or "masculinity" of speakers, speech that varied more in overall rhythmic and pitch patterns was identified as "feminine," whereas speech within narrower limits was identified as "masculine" (Bennet and Weinberg 1979; Terango 1966).

In a review of research on gender differences in English intonation, Sally McConnell-Ginet noted that dynamic patterns are interpreted as indicating emotionality and natural impulses, whereas use of narrow intonational ranges is taken as evidence of control and restraint (1983:76–77). It is important to remember that this is primarily a cultural interpretation (although intonational changes may result from internal emotional states that have respiratory and muscular effects). By employing more monotonic styles, men are perceived as being in control of their emotions, as opposed to women, who are seen as more expressive. "Masculine speech melodies can be heard as metaphors for control and feminine speech melodies as uncontrolled" (ibid.:82). But women and men are not viewed simply as different; instead, women's behavior is negatively evaluated in relation to male (or "neutral") norms. "The problem is that the culture does not simply categorize [women] as emotionally expressive but also views [women] as unstable and unpredictable" (ibid.:77).

Intonational patterns may also serve social functions. McConnell-Ginet suggested that women's frequent changes in pitch and volume "may serve the important function of attracting and holding the listener's attention. Women may need this device more than men because of their relative powerlessness and their frequent contact with young children who are not yet socialized to attend reliably to verbal signals" (ibid.:83).

Studies of intonational patterns suggest that women and men employ sentence contours in distinctive ways in some linguistic or interactional contexts. For instance, women may raise pitch levels at the end of declarative sentences, whereas men use a steady or lowering pitch. Because rising pitch is a regular indicator of a question, some linguists, such as Robin Lakoff (1975:17), believe that when women use rising pitches, they are interpreted as hesitant, uncertain, and lacking assertiveness. Other linguists, including McConnell-Ginet (1983) and Pamela Fishman (1983), agree that rising pitch is heard as a question and suggest that women use this style in order to secure a response from hearers.

GRAMMATICAL VARIANTS

Although research on gender differences in pronunciation is consistent in demonstrating similar trends, studies of gender-related grammatical alternatives are often problematic. One reason is that many discussions of the subject are anecdotal or introspective. Also, results of experimental or observational studies sometimes present contradictory findings. Both of these issues deserve further clarification. Regarding the first problem, claims are made about characteristics of women's and men's speech without any testing or controlled observations. Examples to support hypotheses are constructed and presented not as data but as illustrations. A major difficulty encountered in this technique is the perplexing question of whether the claimed gender-based styles are actual or stereotypical. That is, do they reflect how women and men actually speak, or do they reflect cultural stereotypes of how people are thought to speak? Because people's perceptions of men's and women's speech are influenced by underlying cultural models, we need to be wary of statements about differences without careful analyses of the data presented.

This leads to the second problem of inconsistent results. Some research demonstrates clear distinctions, whereas other work does not. Part of the problem may be the small samples selected in research projects. Another problem is more difficult to address: The speaker's gender is only one of many factors that influence choice of grammatical forms. Additional factors include addressee, context, and speaker's intentions and goals. It is difficult to tease out all of the contributing influences on a speaker's use of language. With these cautions in mind, we now turn to an examination of some of the relevant research and debates dealing with gender and grammar.

Gender differences have been found in usage of nonstandard grammatical constructions by adolescent girls and boys in a working-class district of Reading, England (Cheshire 1982:153–154). In Chapter 6 we discussed Cheshire's data as they related to adolescents' adherence to working-class "vernacular culture." Here, we consider this research as it reveals gender differences among speakers. The following linguistic features were targeted:

1. Present-tense -s with nonsingular subjects:
   "We go*es* shopping on Saturdays."
2. *Has* with first- and second-person subjects:
   "We *has* a little fire keeps us warm."

3.   *Was* with plural subjects and singular "you":
    "You *was* outside."

4.   Multiple negation:
    "I'm *not* going *nowhere.*"

5.   Past-tense *never,* replacing standard "didn't":
    "I *never* done it, it was him."

6.   *What,* replacing "who, whom, which, that":
    "Are you the boy *what's* just come?"

7.   Auxiliary *do* with third-person singular subjects:
    "How much *do* he want for it?"

8.   Past-tense *come:*
    "I *come* down here yesterday."

9.   *Ain't* used for negative auxiliary "have":
    "I *ain't* got any."

10. *Ain't* used for negative auxiliary "be":
    "I *ain't* going to help."

11. *Ain't* used for negative copula:
    "It's her proper name, *ain't* it?"

In the Reading community, boys consistently employed nonstandard grammatical constructions more often than did girls (only the feature *do* was an exception). This finding is not surprising but, rather, is consistent with other research showing that females use more standard and prestige features than males, who prefer nonstandard forms. The following table presents scores for use of nonstandard forms (ibid.:163). (Note that a score of 100.00 reflects consistent use of the nonstandard.)

Gender Differences in Nonstandard Features

	Frequency Scores	
	Boys	*Girls*
Nonstandard *-s*	53.16	52.04
Nonstandard *has*	54.76	51.61
Multiple negation	88.15	73.58
Nonstandard *never*	46.84	40.00
Nonstandard *what*	36.36	14.58
Nonstandard *do*	57.69	78.95
Nonstandard *come*	100.00	75.33
Ain't = aux. "have"	92.00	64.58
Ain't = aux. "be"	74.19	42.11
Ain't = copula	85.83	61.18

In an influential book on gender differences, Robin Lakoff (1975) pointed out, from anecdotal evidence, that a number of grammatical patterns appear in women's speech more frequently than in men's. Of the syntactic constructions she discussed, the one receiving the most subsequent attention is the tag question. *Tag questions* are sentences in which a speaker makes a declarative statement and adds on a "tag" in the form of a question about the assertion, as in

> Jane came home, didn't she?
> It's cold in here, isn't it?

Lakoff stated that women use tag questions because they are reluctant to make direct assertions. They "can avoid committing [themselves] and thereby avoid coming into conflict with the addressee" (1975:16–17). Although such deferential style can be favorably evaluated, it can also be perceived as indicating uncertainty and a lack of definite opinions. These contrasting evaluations are examples of the positive/negative judgments often given to women's behavior.

Some studies of actual behavior demonstrate no clear gender preferences for use of tag questions (e.g., Dubois and Crouch 1975). Others indicate the critical effect of context and goals on linguistic usage. Tag questions may serve a variety of social functions. For instance, *modal* tags (Holmes 1984:53) are used to request information from the addressee or request that the addressee confirm a statement about which the speaker is unsure. Janet Holmes calls these tags "speaker-oriented" because they function to supplement the speaker's knowledge, as in

> She's coming around noon, isn't she?

A second type, called *affective* tags, are "addressee-oriented," indicating the speaker's interest in or concern for the addressee. One class of affective tags functions as "softeners" to mitigate the force of a command or criticism:

> Open the oven door for me, could you?
> You're driving rather fast, aren't you?

Another class of affective tags are "facilitative" and indicate the speaker's desire to engage the addressee in continuing conversation (ibid.:55):

> Still working hard at your office, are you?
> The hen's brown, isn't it?

These tags are essentially mechanisms to establish speaker turns. They "facilitate" conversation by inviting the addressee to build on a topic offered by the current speaker.

Holmes discovered a significant difference in the functional role of tags in women's and men's speech. Men more often use tags for speaker-oriented goals, to obtain or confirm information for themselves, whereas women more often use tags for addressee-oriented goals, particularly as strategies to engage addressees in talk. (Recall a similar possible function of women's use of rising or questioning intonational contours.) Note the following relevant statistical data (ibid.:54):

Type of Meaning	*Number of Tag Questions*	
	Women	*Men*
Modal	18 (35%)	24 (61%)
Affective		
Facilitative	30 (59%)	10 (25%)
Softening	3 (6%)	5 (13%)
Total	51	39

By taking account of interactional meaning, Holmes's research demonstrates the inadequacy of simply tabulating occurrences of form without attending to function in discourse.

Another study of tags pointed out their use in asymmetric status interactions (Cameron et al. 1988). Deborah Cameron and coworkers recorded television and radio talk-show and classroom programs and noted differences between "powerful" (e.g., medical expert, teacher, program host) and "powerless" (e.g., client, student, program guest) roles. Sampling included a balance between women and men in each asymmetric role. Although they found that women used more tags than men did, the numbers were not significant (61 and 55, respectively). However, role "power" seemed to influence the kind of tag employed. Using Holmes's terminology for classifying tags, Cameron et al. found that "powerful" participants employed "affective" tags, whereas "powerless" speakers preferred "modal" tags. The following table presents their results (ibid.:89).

Tag Questions in Unequal Encounters

Type of Tag	*Women*		*Men*	
	Powerful	*Powerless*	*Powerful*	*Powerless*
Modal	3 (5%)	9 (15%)	10 (18%)	16 (29%)
Affective				
Facilitative	43 (70%)	0	25 (45%)	0
Softeners	6 (10%)	0	4 (7%)	0
Total	Women: 61		Men: 55	

Although status asymmetry is an operative factor in the use of tags, gender is also significant. Cameron et al. do not discuss gender differences in the asymmetric roles, but an examination of their data shows support for Holmes's findings that powerful men were more likely than powerful women to employ modal tags (18 percent versus 5 percent) and, contrastingly, powerful women were more likely than powerful men to use affective tags (80 percent versus 52 percent).

CHOICES OF VOCABULARY

Numerous researchers have discussed differences in choice of vocabulary used by women and men, observing that certain words or categories of words appear with greater frequency in the speech of one or the other. Some domains of vocabulary are more elaborated by each gender. For instance, women use and recognize more specific terms denoting colors such as "magenta" or "turquoise." For other categories, men and women are expected to know the meanings of words within domains reflecting culturally stereotyped areas of their assumed expertise, as, for example, cooking and other domestic skills for women, sports and machinery for men.

One well-studied category of words with relevance to gender differences is that of profanity. It has often been claimed that, given class and context, men use curse words with greater frequency and greater profane force than do women while women tend to employ milder expletives. Although both genders use less profanity in cross-sex interactions, many women refrain from its use even in casual conversations with other women who are not their familiars (Bailey and Timm 1976; Jay 1980). However, it is unclear whether these claims are actually substantiated or whether they reflect cultural stereotypes and assumptions. In a study of South African teenagers, Vivian DeKlerk (1992) found no significant differences in the number of or semantic force of the words used by boys and girls to describe males and females. Age was a more important indicator of knowledge and behavior than was gender. Susan Hughes (1997) also criticized the accepted notion of men's greater use of profanity. She contends that "vernacular" speech of lower-class women, including the use of profanity, functions as a linguistic mechanism that reflects and reinforces solidarity and "bonding" between women.

Another area of vocabulary differences is that of modifiers (adjectives and adverbs). Ever since the Danish linguist Otto Jespersen's chapter "The Woman" appeared in his *Language* (1922), observers have pointed to women's tendency to use intensifiers such as "very," "so," or "extremely" and what some have called "empty" adjectives, as "wonderful" or "lovely." Jespersen interpreted these usages as an example of women's tendency to exaggerate and as a sign of linguistic and cognitive superficiality (1922:347). This explanation clearly reveals underlying cultural biases that interpret women's behavior in negative terms. In fact, adjectives such as "lovely" are not empty or devoid of meaning. They express personal affective judgments. Women are free to use intensifiers and modifiers because society allows them to display emotion. Men are expected to control their feelings and, therefore, to refrain from using words that have marked emotional expressiveness.

One last area of vocabulary differences is the noted tendency for women to use more *hedge words* in discourse—that is, words or expressions that covertly comment on assertions in one's statements; for example:

> *Perhaps* we *could try* fixing it.
> I've been *sort of wondering whether* I should go.
> *Well,* I guess it's *approximately* four feet high.

These constructions function to signal a speaker's uncertainty about the validity of her statement. In doing so, they create an impression of indecisiveness and lack of clarity. Use of hedge words reflects social inhibitions. Because females are socialized to defer to others and avoid conflict, they choose to state opinions interspersed with hedges to minimize confrontation with an addressee who may hold a different view. And making assertions in a tentative style allows speakers to modify or retract statements if they are challenged. But, once again, women who conform to sociolinguistic etiquette by avoiding a display of self-assertion are then often criticized for imprecision and uncertainty.

Hedges can also function to "express the speaker's attitude to the addressee, i.e. to signal affective meaning" (Holmes 1984:48); for example:

Well, I *think* George is a *bit, er, perhaps* foolish.

This statement was made by a woman commenting on the behavior of her friend's husband. By hedging the assertion that "George is foolish," the speaker demonstrated concern for the addressee by not making a blunt criticism.

Using hedges as part of a politeness strategy is invoked not only by gender but also by status and context. Note the following excerpt from an interviewer's questioning of the prime minister of New Zealand (quoted in Holmes 1984:49):

I *had the feeling* that with all the talk about the future that *perhaps* some of the Ministers were not talking *quite so strongly* in an election year context and I *wondered whether perhaps* you were surprised that. . . .

In order to test the relative weight of gender, status, and context on stylistic choice, Faye Crosby and Linda Nyquist (1977) examined speech produced in three different situations: laboratory experiments involving college students discussing a given topic, information-booth question/answer exchanges, and police-station interactions between personnel and clients. They measured usage of what they called the "female register" (ibid.:314), based on Lakoff 's characterization of women's speech. As they point out, the female register can be used by either women or men. "The distinguishing feature of the female register is not that it is used exclusively by women but rather that it embodies the female role in our society. The female register is both expressive (e.g., polite rather than direct and informative) and nonassertive. Both of these attributes are central aspects of the stereotyped feminine role in our culture" (ibid.).

Traits measured by Crosby and Nyquist included hedges ("kind of," "stuff like that," "I don't know"), expressive adjectives ("charming," "cute," "weird"), tag questions, intensifiers ("so"), and politeness formulas ("please," "thank you"). They discovered that in college experiments and police-station interactions, women more often produced speech conforming to the female register. In police-station observations, status also proved important, because clients of either gender used the female register more than police personnel did. Consistent results in information-booth exchanges were not found except that male-to-male speech tended to show least use of the targeted traits (ibid.:316–319). This context is highly artificial. Interpersonal contact is extremely brief, routinized, and impersonal. It is, therefore, not unexpected that speakers do not use affective styles in such situations.

In sum, although both men and women sometimes employ linguistic styles characterized by indecisive, imprecise, or mitigated speech, these traits are perceived to be more typical of women. They are, in actuality, more likely to be used by women (given contextual similarities) and also by people of either gender in subordinate roles. Subordinates (and women in general) are expected to behave politely and show deference to higher-status people. Females learn deferential styles as part of their socialization and employ them in most interactions. Through these processes linking style, gender, and status, cultural models of personal and gender images are reinforced and justified. And men have greater control over the assignment of social value to gender-linked behavior. Men's stereotyped behavior is taken to be the norm or neutral form, whereas women's behavior is judged to be deviant or deficient.

GENDER-RELATED CONVERSATIONAL STYLES

Differences between the genders are demonstrated in conversational style as well as in linguistic structures. Much of the research investigating women's and men's conversation reveals alternatives in speaker turns, topic introduction and control, and mechanisms of signaling active listenership.

In the study of gender-related styles, two different explanatory perspectives have emerged. One contends that men's and women's behavior stems from their socialization into contrasting "cultures," beginning in childhood and continuing into adulthood. It is claimed that girls and boys tend to play and interact in same-sex groups and develop different communicative skills based on different individual and social goals. The other approach analyzes linguistic behavior within a social context of male power and dominance. Men use communicative strategies that assert their control and prerogatives, whereas women employ strategies that are deferential, conciliatory, and sensitive to the other's "face"—to use Penelope Brown and Stephen Levinson's (1987) term.

Among the prominent proponents of the "cultural differences" theories are Daniel Maltz and Ruth Borker (1982) and Deborah Tannen (1986, 1990). Maltz and Borker place gender differences within the framework of research concerning "cross-ethnic miscommunication" (ibid.:196). To them, cross-sex conversation is sometimes problematic because of "cultural differences between men and women in their conceptions of friendly conversation, their rules for engaging in it, and, their rules for interpreting it" (ibid.:200). Maltz and Borker note the major reported conversational tendencies of women and men: women's tendencies to ask questions, encourage responses from interlocutors, make "positive minimal responses," and allow interruptions into their speaking turns; and men's tendencies to interrupt, challenge, and/or ignore the speech of interlocutors, introduce and control topics, and make direct assertions of fact and opinion. These modes of adult speech are the outcomes of childhood training in same-sex groups where girls learn "to create and maintain relationships of closeness and equality, to criticize others in acceptable ways, and interpret accurately the speech of others," and boys learn "to assert positions of dominance, to attract and maintain an audience, and to assert [themselves] when other speakers have the floor" (ibid.:205, 207). As a result, when women and men converse "as friends and equals" (ibid.:212), they misinterpret each other's cues.

Maltz and Borker criticize explanations based on gender-linked social power, stating that such explanations "do not provide a means of explaining why these specific features appear as opposed to any number of others. . . . They do not really tell us why and how these specific interactional phenomena are linked to the general fact that men dominate within our social system" (ibid.:199). In fact, though, theories based on situating speech in the social context of gender hierarchy do indeed explain why "these specific features" appear and how they are linked to male dominance. Stylistic strategies associated with men are (as Maltz and Borker themselves note) those of asserting control and dominance (interrupting another's turn, insisting on introducing and developing topics while ignoring those introduced by others, failing to encourage another's talk), whereas women's strategies are indicative of relative powerlessness (encouraging another's talk through questions and positive responses, mitigating criticism, deferring to others' interruptions and attempts at control).

The "cultural differences" approach has also been championed in the academic and popular writings of Tannen (1986, 1990). Tannen states the claim even more strongly than do Maltz and Borker: "Boys and girls grow up in different worlds . . . And as adults they travel in different worlds, reinforcing patterns established in childhood" (1986). Boys and girls "talk differently" because "[f]rom the time they're born, they're treated differently."

Although Tannen acknowledges that girls and boys are "treated differently," she never attempts to understand why. Instead, she focuses on the "misunderstandings" between men and women because of their "incongruent expectations" and differences in how they "view the role of talk in relationships." Going one step farther than Maltz and Borker, Tannen states that male-female conversations are not similar *to* but actually *are* instances of "cross-cultural communication" (1990:47). Just as people from different cultural backgrounds misinterpret the stylistic intents and meanings of each other's speech, Tannen cautions her readers that "not seeing style differences for what they are, people draw conclusions about personality or intentions. . . . Understanding the other's ways of talking is a giant leap across the communication gap" (ibid.:298).

However, Tannen herself has been accused of "not seeing style differences for what they are." For example, by "regard[ing] socialization as the main influence shaping identified patterns of adult linguistic behaviour," Tannen fails to address "both what the triggers for such behaviour patterns in the first place are and what ensures [their] continuation from child to adulthood" (Davis 1996:75). And as Uchida (1992) points out, "the sexual division of labor in conversation is not a mere result of cultural differences." Instead, it reflects "a hierarchy, a power structure in the society [that] affects our everyday interaction" (ibid.:559–560). In addition to the differences in communicative strategies that result in women working harder to maintain conversation than do men, the negative consequences of "miscommunication" are borne more by women. Men's behavior (being in control, assertive, rational) is given public approval, whereas women's behavior (being deferential, unassertive, emotional) is devalued or trivialized. Again quoting Uchida:

> An analysis of miscommunication must take into consideration who gets what they want, who is punished, who is forgiven, and in what ways—both on the individual level and on the societal level—after the miscommunication. . . . The approach that dismisses this aspect has the danger of being used to legitimize blatantly misogynist behavior on the ground that it is a case of innocent miscommunication caused by cultural differences. (ibid.:562)

Finally, Senta Troemel-Ploetz discounts Tannen's premise that women and men do not understand each other:

> On the contrary, they understand each other quite well. They know who is allowed to use dominant speech acts, like commands, orders, explanations, contradiction, criticism, evaluations, definitions, attacks, challenges, accusations, reproaches; and who has to apologize, defend, ask for favors, beg, request permission, justify herself, agree, support, adjust, accommodate, and accept someone else's definition of the situation. (1998:447)

In conversation, men and women reproduce their social rights by the way that they present themselves and interact. Men are typically able to get their interactional needs fulfilled more often than women do. Communication differences between men and women are, therefore, not simply differences of style that can be resolved by attempting to understand each other. By taking linguistic interaction out of the social context that produces it, the meaning of the interaction is lost. And any fundamental remedy is made impossible. As Troemel-Ploetz notes, by avoiding the social and political implications of conversation and by "selling the status-quo, [Tannen's] by-intention apolitical book becomes a highly political act" (ibid.:450).

Rather than explaining men's and women's behavior as derived from separate cultures, other researchers emphasize the context of power and dominance that permits men to assert control while it teaches women to support and defer to the goals of others. Henley and Kramarae draw similarities between the social relations of the genders and those of unequal ethnic, racial, and class groups and note similarities in conversation interaction and interpretation:

> Hierarchies determine whose version will prevail; whose speech style will be seen as normal; who will be required to learn the communication style, and interpret the meaning, of the other; and who will be required to imitate the other's style in order to fit into the society. (1991:19–20)

It is typically men's speech style that is considered "normal" and that of women as deviant or in need of explanation. Women bear more of the burden of interpreting men's interactive style. And in order to be considered serious and competent, women must use speaking styles generally associated with men. As Henley and Kramarae point out, "Females, not males, [must] learn to read the silence, lack of emotional expression, or brutality of the other sex as not only other than, but more benign than, it appears (ibid.:23).

The facts of male control of conversation (through mechanisms that will be detailed in following sections) are best understood within the social context that produces them. But not only are the communicative strategies of men and women created by a system of hierarchy and inequality, the strategies themselves serve to maintain that very system: "One may in fact ask how well male dominance could be maintained if we had open and equally-valued communication between women and men. The construction of miscommunication between the sexes emerges as a powerful tool, maybe even a necessity, to maintain the structure of male supremacy" (ibid.:42).

Power is not abstract, however. It is embodied in people's identities. And those identities are based, in part, on the roles that people expect to have in the society. As Scott Kiesling observed, "When a man constructs a powerful identity, it is usually connected in some way to 'real' power. Thus, the expectation of a 'powerful' identity for men is not symmetrical to the expectation of a 'powerless' identity for women, since a man's powerful identity is *rewarded* (with power), whereas a woman's non-powerless identity may be *punished*" (italics in original; 1997:65–66).

The role women play in this system is, of course, complex. They may at times contribute to maintaining their own subordination by acquiescing to men's control; they may collude with male power by interpreting men's speech as more worthy than their own; and they may counter male prerogatives either through overt objections or covert resistance. Resistance may be demonstrated informally through comment and gossip, or it may be formalized through special speech genres such as women's poetry and songs (see, for example, Lila Abu-Lughod's studies of Beduoin women's genres).

A number of studies have investigated whether cultural stereotypes concerning men's and women's speaking styles have any basis in practice. One such stereotype is that women are more talkative than men. However, an experiment aimed at measuring verbosity (amount of talk) demonstrated the opposite pattern. Male and female college students were presented with three pictures drawn by Albrecht Dürer, a fifteenth-century Flemish artist, and were asked to describe the drawings as thoroughly as possible, taking as much time as they liked (Swacker 1975). Results showed striking gender differences. The mean time for all three pictures was 13.0 minutes for males and only 3.17 for females (ibid.:80). Choosing only the second description, men's speaking length averaged 333.41 seconds, and women's 96.0 seconds. Verbosity differed significantly, but rather than confirming the stereotype of talkative women, the study showed that male speakers talked more. Persistence of the erroneous stereotype has been explained by Cheris Kramer, who suggested that because females are socialized to defer to their co-conversationalists, "perhaps a 'talkative' woman is one who does talk as much as a man" (1975:47). Because men have more rights to talk, they are not considered talkative when they exercise those rights. In contrast, women who speak in moderation are judged to be talkative.

In actual (rather than experimental) settings, men also tend to be more talkative than women. Observation of conversation in university faculty meetings revealed that speaking turns of male teachers were from one and one-quarter to nearly four times longer than those of females (Edelsky 1981:415). When topics and context of meetings were more formal, men's contributions to discussions lengthened and those of women were shortened. In more relaxed, give-and-take exchanges, women's and men's turns were equal.

Extending the meaning of these findings, Jack Sattel (1983) found that although men may be more talkative than women in some settings, they are more silent in regard to discussion of emotions. Sattel contended that men's tendency for emotional inexpressiveness or unwillingness to talk about affect either with women or with other men stems from their desire to maintain and assert power. "What better way is there to exercise power than *to make it appear* that *all* one's behavior seems to be the result of unemotional rationality. . . . Keeping cool, keeping distant as others challenge you or make demands upon you, is a strategy for keeping the upper hand" (italics in original; 1983:120). Silence functions as part of competitive displays of dominance since "to not say anything is to say something very important indeed: that the battle is to be fought by [his] rules and when [he] chooses to fight" (ibid.:122). This tactic is particularly effective when used in interactions with women because of women's tendencies for emotional self-disclosure. Furthermore, Sattel notes that it is women rather than men who have to interpret the other's speech and adjust to it (ibid.:123). Sattel urges that these interactions be understood in the context of male dominance and female subordination:

> Male dominance takes shape in the positions of formal and informal *power* men hold in the social division of labor; greater male prestige includes, and is evidenced by, the greater *reward* which attaches to male than to female activities. What our culture embodies is not simply two stereotypes—one masculine, one feminine—but a set of power and prestige arrangements attached to gender. (ibid.:119–120)

This system, which rests on social power, cannot be changed by "simply changing men's capacity to feel or express themselves" because "men are not oppressed *as men*, and hence are not in a position to be liberated *as men*" (ibid.:123).

In a study of interactions between spouses that substantiated Sattel's insights, Victoria DeFrancisco reported that men's silence had the effect of silencing women. Although men directed topics and their development through interruption and minimal responses, they most often exerted their control by silence, especially in the form of "no response" to their wives' prior statement (1998:179). While women sometimes employed this strategy as well, they did so much less often (68 percent of "no response" were done by men, 32 percent by women). Men's "no response" turns were followed either by their wives' silence (giving up) or attempts to introduce an alternative topic.

Two important studies of gender, by Candace West and Don Zimmerman

(1975, 1983), investigated dyadic (two-person) interactions, focusing on instances of one speaker's turn limited or interrupted by a co-participant. West and Zimmerman recorded casual conversations in public places (coffee shops, stores, university buildings) between people who knew each other and later conducted experiments involving college students who were unacquainted. In both studies, they noted violations of speakers' turns in the form of interruptions, defined technically as an intrusion into current speaker's talk "prior to the last lexical constituent [word] that could define a possible terminal boundary" (Zimmerman and West 1975:114). An "interruption" contrasts significantly with an "overlap," which is "simultaneous speech where a speaker other than the current speaker begins to speak at or very close to a possible transition place in a current speaker's utterance (i.e., within the boundaries of the last word)" (ibid.). Overlaps, therefore, are errors of judgment in transitions and timing to the next turn, whereas interruptions are violations of a current speaker's rights.

Although Zimmerman and West's samples were small, their findings are quite striking and consistent with other research concerning men's and women's status in our society. First, they found a marked difference in patterns of overlap and interruption in same-sex and cross-sex conversations. In the former, overlaps and interruptions were evenly distributed, each speaker contributing approximately the same number. But in cross-sex conversations, almost all errors and intrusions were initiated by men. The following tables present data obtained in the 1975 study (pp. 115, 116).

Interruptions/Overlaps in 20 Same-Sex Conversations

	First Speaker	Second Speaker	Total
Interruptions	43% (3)	57% (4)	100% (7)
Overlaps	55 (12)	45 (10)	100 (22)

Interruptions/Overlaps in 11 Cross-Sex Conversations

	Males	Females	Total
Interruptions	96% (46)	4% (2)	100% (48)
Overlaps	100 (9)	—	100 (9)

In addition to marked gender differences in cross-sex conversations, another significant fact displayed in these tables is that in same-sex interactions, most conversational errors are overlaps (minor mistakes of timing), whereas in interactions between men and women, most intrusions are interruptions (violations of current speaker's turns). Exercise of power by male participants seems to be an operative principle in many cross-sex encounters.

The following table presents findings from West and Zimmerman's 1983 experimental study of unacquainted students (p. 107).

Interruptions in 5 Cross-Sex Conversations

	Amount of Interruption		
Conversation	*Male-initiated*	*Female-initiated*	*Total*
Dyad 1	75%	25%	100% (4)
Dyad 2	100	0	100 (4)
Dyad 3	67	33	100 (6)
Dyad 4	83	17	100 (6)
Dyad 5	63	37	100 (8)

Zimmerman and West's research demonstrates a clear inequality in the rights of women and men engaged in conversation. Men use mechanisms of power and control in interactions with women, whether previously acquainted or not. Interruptions are strategies that disregard the current speaker's talk and attempt to disallow that person an opportunity to express herself fully as she had intended. In so doing, interruptions also function as tactics to exert control over topics of conversation because they frequently lead to changes in topics, establishing the interests of the interrupter. West and Zimmerman concluded:

> When viewed from a perspective encompassing the fate of women in the various institutional domains of society, the many small insults women suffer in face-to-face interaction do perhaps seem trivial. Yet, . . . the gestures of power are an integral part of women's placement in the social scheme of things. These daily gestures are constant "reminders" which help constitute women's subordinate status. (1983:110)

In research designed to test hypotheses concerning relative influences of gender and occupational status on frequency of interruption, Nicola Woods (1988) tape-recorded triadic (three-party) interactions in work settings. Subjects included both male and female supervisors and subordinates. Woods discovered that the two factors of status and gender significantly affected several conversational strategies but that gender was the most important influence on behavior. "Essentially, while the power base of occupational status did influence the way that both men and women organised conversation, nevertheless even when women held high-status occupational positions male subordinates still organised the interaction in a way that allowed them to dominate the floor" (ibid.:149).

Woods found that powerful people (high-status and male) were more likely to interrupt co-participants successfully and were least likely to be interrupted in their turns. And when men intruded on other speakers, they were usually successful in gaining the floor (data indicate 17 out of 20 attempts), whereas women interrupters were not as likely to succeed (only 11 of 21 attempts) (ibid.:151).

The following two tables present Woods's findings on interruptions. The first table displays numbers of interruptions initiated by each speaker; the second presents numbers of times each speaker was interrupted. In both cases, success or lack of success is additionally enumerated. "Occupational status" is rated as 1, 2, or 3, from highest to lowest. In the first set of scores (encounter A), the highest-status

person was a woman, with a second-ranked man and a third-ranked woman; in the second (encounter B), the superior was a man, conversing with female and male subordinates (ibid.:151, 152).

	Encounter A			Encounter B		
Occupational status	1	2	3	1	2	3
Gender	F	M	F	M	F	M
Successful interruption	6	9	4	4	1	4
Unsuccessful interruption	3	1	3	0	4	2

	Encounter A			Encounter B		
Occupational status	1	2	3	1	2	3
Gender	F	M	F	M	F	M
Interrupted successfully	2	6	11	1	7	3
Interrupted unsuccessfully	1	4	1	5	1	0

These data show that men are usually successful in interrupting current speakers. They violate other speakers' turns, even when the men are subordinates and particularly when subordinate to a higher-status woman. And women are the most likely targets of successful interruptions even when they are in higher-status positions. When the double factors of low status and female gender co-occur, women are especially vulnerable, as shown in the second table. The lowest-status woman was interrupted successfully 11 times (encounter A) and the second-ranked woman 7 times (encounter B).

In a study of dyadic conversations between physicians and their patients, West (1998) found that both status and gender were significant factors in the frequency of interruption but, like Woods's findings, gender outweighed status. In interactions between male physicians and their patients, the doctors initiated 67 percent (126) of the interruptions, whereas patients were responsible for only 33 percent (62); but in encounters between female physicians and their patients, the doctors initiated 32 percent (19) of the interruptions, and patients were responsible for 68 percent (40) (1998:399–400). An additional significant finding is that in all dyads involving a male physician, the doctor always interrupted the patient more often than the patient interrupted the doctor, whereas there was variation in dyads involving female physicians. When both doctor and patient were women, both interrupted the other with about equal frequency, whereas male patients interrupted the doctor much more often than the doctor interrupted the patient (ibid.:404–405).

Women and men employ different strategies for conversational interaction in casual and familiar settings as well as in structured contexts. In studies of talk between couples, Pamela Fishman (1983) collected 52 hours of tape recordings made in the homes of three white, middle-class couples (with their approval and ability to censure material if they wished). In her research and analysis, Fishman developed the notion of the "work of conversation" (ibid.:90–91):

Interaction requires at least two people. Conversation is produced not simply by their presence, but also by the display of their continuing agreement to pay attention to one another. That is, all interactions are potentially problematic and occur only through the continual, turn-by-turn, efforts of the participants. . . . In a sense, every remark or turn at speaking should be seen as an attempt to interact. Some attempts succeed; others fail. For an attempt to succeed, the other party must be willing to do further interactional work. That other person has the power to turn an attempt into a conversation or to stop it dead.

Fishman's data revealed a "variety of strategies to insure, encourage and subvert conversation" (ibid.:93). On the whole, women do more of the interactional work, attempting to gain their partner's attention and responding to their partner's talk. The following devices were used to initiate conversation or to introduce topics (ibid.:94–95):

1. *Attention beginnings* (e.g., "this is interesting"). These expressions function to establish the interest or legitimacy of statements or topics to follow. "Attention beginnings" were used twice as often by women as by men.

2. *Asking questions.* Questions help guarantee subsequent talk because they are bound in a paired sequence with answers. Addressees are usually obliged to give at least some response. In Fishman's transcripts, women asked questions two and a half times more often than did men.

3. *Asking "D'ya know what?"* These ritualized questions trigger a three-part exchange of the form: question-question-answer. The initiator asks, "D'ya know what?" addressee asks "What?" and initiator returns with the intended topic. This tactic was used by women twice as much as by men.

A significant ingredient in the work of conversation is the response one gives to co-participants. Responses can encourage speakers to continue or discourage and block interaction. One type of reaction is the "minimal response," often in the form of "umm," "oh," or "yeah," uttered by the listener during or following the current speaker's turn. According to Fishman, men and women used these mechanisms for different purposes. Men's responses tended to occur at the ends of women's turns, taking the place of their own turn. This actually discourages the current speaker because it displays no interest in the speaker's topic, requests no elaboration, and contributes no informational comment that the previous speaker can build on. In contrast, women as listeners tended to place responses within the current speaker's turns, signaling ongoing listener interest and encouraging the speaker to continue (ibid.:95–96).

Finally, Fishman discovered that whereas women suggested nearly twice as many topics as men, they were successful in establishing only about one-third of the accepted topics. Men's topics were almost always accepted, whereas women had a failure rate of nearly 2 to 1. The following table presents relevant data (ibid.:97).

Topic Success and Failure

	Success	Failure	Uncertain	Total
Men	28	0	1	29
Women	17	28	2	47
Total	45	28	3	76

After analyzing the evidence contained in the recordings, Fishman concluded (ibid.:99–100):

> As with work in its usual sense, there appears to be a division of labor in conversation. The people who do the routine maintenance work, the women, are not the same people who either control or benefit from the process. Women are the "shit-workers" of routine interaction, and the "goods" being made are not only interactions, but, through them, realities. . . . But the idea that it is work is obscured. The work is not seen as what women do, but as part of what they are. Because this work is obscured, because it is seen as an aspect of gender identity rather than of gender activity, the maintenance and expression of male-female power relations in our everyday conversations are hidden as well. When we orient instead to the activities involved in maintaining gender, we are able to discern the reality of hierarchy in our daily lives.

GENDER BIAS IN ENGLISH

Language is a vehicle for expressing cultural models, in part through the way people, activities, and ideas are named. In societies with entrenched gender hierarchy, where women and their behavior are disvalued, inequalities in linguistic images are one sign of the denigration of women. By continual usage of words and expressions that demean females, speakers unconsciously (or consciously) reproduce and reinforce negative stereotypes. These stereotypes become internalized symbols for both genders, resulting in male attitudes toward females as deviant and female acceptance of negative self-assessments. In this section we review some of the literature and findings related to gender bias in linguistic form.

Classes of Vocabulary

The English language expresses gender distinctions in many classes of vocabulary, including the labeling of people (nouns), their qualities (adjectives), and actions (verbs). But English does not simply record differences; it covertly (and overtly) demeans or trivializes females, presenting males as normative and females as deviant or secondary.

First of all, English creates a context for the interaction of genders with the term "opposite sex." Certainly the sexes are different, but in what sense are they "opposite"? The word itself connotes a polarity, denying possibilities of overlap or congruence. It also implies conflict and antagonism, as in "they have opposing views" or "the Mayor opposes the new legislation."

Words referring to human beings are often paired for female and male exemplars, but in ordinary usage, males precede and females appear in linguistic "second place." Some instances of this common ordering are male and female, man and woman, he or she, husband and wife. Such pairing denotes primary status of males in two ways. First, order of linguistic components is generally of cognitive importance; that is, more important elements usually occur earlier in sentences. For example, many languages make use of a procedure known as "focus-fronting" through which words and clauses are manipulated to place important or emphasized segments earlier than they would appear in unmarked sentences. English employs passive constructions to accomplish this goal (compare: the child caught the ball/the ball was caught by the child). Therefore, arguing that the first member of a pair carries greater importance is consistent with widespread linguistic processes.

The second kind of evidence supporting the contention of covert inequality in male/female pairs is provided by comparing similar constructions denoting age and status hierarchies. Older or higher-status individuals precede younger or lower-status people: older and younger, parent and child, dominant and subordinate. Other sets of paired words reflect positive connotations given to the first member and negative connotations to the second: good and bad, happy and sad, rich and poor. Gender, then, merges with these constellations of social and semantic categories.

Two counterexamples to the "male + female" ordering are "ladies and gentlemen" and "bride and groom." The first is typically used in public formal situations where polite speech is preferred. Perhaps its use is akin to chivalrous behavior that often masks underlying power. The second, "bride and groom," is also a conventionalized expression relevant in a formal ceremonial context. Note, however, that after the wedding, the couple is transformed from "bride and groom" to "husband and wife." Variation in the usual ordering occurs in kin-term pairs; for example, "mother and father" is as likely as "father and mother." Perhaps this flexibility reflects individual choice based on attitudes toward relatives and may also indicate our society's stereotypes of closer emotional bonds between children and their mothers.

The English language provides evidence of gender hierarchy in marital relationships, first in the traditional, although disappearing, formula "I now pronounce you man and wife" in which the male is labeled by his humanness, but the female is defined in relation to her husband. Second, our culture decrees that women give up their maiden names at marriage and assume their husband's last name. A wife can be referred to by her husband's full name (first + last) with the preposed address term Mrs., as in Mrs. John Smith. The couple can then be called "the Smiths" or even "the John Smiths," depriving the wife of her own identity. Finally, couples are frequently described by the use of the husband's name + "his wife," as in "John Smith and his wife." In such usages, the wife appears almost as a possession or appendage without an autonomous existence. A contrasting construction, "Jane Jones and her husband," has marked meaning and would typically occur only if special attention is given to "Jane Jones" for particular contextual or emotional purposes.

Another symbolic reflection of females' subsidiary status is the possibility of deriving girls' names from male sources. Feminine endings -*a*, -*ette*, -*ine*, -*y* (or -*ie*) are thus added to male names: Roberta, Bernadette, Geraldine, Stephanie. Any male name can idiosyncratically be converted into a girl's name by this procedure. The only boy's name obtained from a female source is Marion, which occurs rarely in contemporary American society but in any case has a special derivation, originating from the religious symbol of Mary.

In a further reflection of the semantics of gender, feminine suffixes -*ette* (or -*et*) and -*y* (or -*ie*) can function as diminutives, that is, as markers of smallness, for example, booklet, itsy-bitsy. Diminutives also carry meanings of endearment, reflected in nicknames and affectionate or youthful versions of personal names: Cathy, Tommy. Although both girls and boys are addressed with these forms as children, males tend to outgrow their diminutive names (except among kin), whereas females often retain them throughout life.

The interaction of age and gender is also differentially marked for males and females in the terms "boy, girl, man, woman." Boys typically become men at roughly the age of adulthood, although exact demarcation of the change is often vague. But girls can remain girls long after they become adults. It is true that this usage is unacceptable today among many people, but it is still frequently employed. Comparable use of the word "boy" to refer to an adult man is restricted to certain regional varieties, as in the American South. These examples demonstrate that although the words "girl" and "boy" have definitions that might appear to be distinguished solely on the basis of gender, they actually have uses and implications that are quite different in recognizing or denying adult status.

Some sets of words for males and females illustrate another process of inequality in images of gender. Consider the following pairs: lord/lady, sir/dame, master/mistress, king/queen, bachelor/spinster, governor/governess. In each of these, there is one level of meaning equating the paired individuals. But a critical process has affected females in a consistent manner. That process is often referred to as semantic derogation, changes in meaning by which negative attributes become attached to senses of words. Semantic derogation of words for women has historically resulted in secondary meanings that demean or trivialize women and their activities or that emphasize their sexuality. The words "mistress" and "dame" are examples of words taking on sexual connotations, whereas "governess" is a trivialization. "Queen" also has a sexual meaning, although it is applied to men, rather than women, in a derogatory fashion. "Spinster" implies negation of sexuality, so that a spinster is not an "unmarried woman" in the same way that a "bachelor" is an "unmarried man." A "bachelor" is a man who is desirable as a potential husband, whereas a "spinster" is an undesirable mate. Because of this negative implication, the expression "bachelor girl" (or even "bachelorette") has evolved.

The word "lady" has special complexities. In one of its uses, it retains polite, respectful implications of its origin. However, it also occurs in casual contexts as a label for a woman whose name is unknown to a speaker: "Hey, lady, move your car!" Perhaps its most interesting function is as a euphemism for "woman." The word "woman" needs a euphemistic replacement because it too has acquired sexual connotations. Compare the following (adapted from Lakoff 1975:26):

She's only twelve, but she already acts like a woman.
She's only twelve, but she already acts like a lady.

These sentences highlight two cultural images of females that our society promulgates. The first suggests her sexuality; the second notes the polite and "proper" behavior expected of her.

The pair woman/man also deserves attention. "Woman" refers specifically and only to females, whereas "man" is used not only for males but for "people" in general, as in "mankind." In addition, "man" appears as a verb meaning "operate" or "control": "We need someone to man the elevator." Finally, the semantics of adjectives and adverbs based on woman and man demonstrate significant contrasts. Compare the following entries from the *Random House Dictionary of the English Language* (1987:1170, 2185) for a succinct rendering of cultural symbols:

MANLY, MANFUL, MANNISH mean having the traits that a culture regards as especially characteristic or ideally appropriate to adult men. Manly is usually a term of approval, suggesting traits admired by society, such as determination, decisiveness, and steadiness. Manful, also a term of approval, stresses courage, strength, and fortitude. Mannish is most often used derogatorily in reference to the traits, manners, or accouterments of a woman that are thought to be more appropriate or typical of a man: a mannish abruptness in her speech.

WOMANLY, WOMANLIKE, WOMANISH mean having traits or qualities that a culture regards as especially characteristic or ideally appropriate to adult women. Womanly is usually a term of approval, suggesting the display of traits admired by society, such as self-possession, modesty, motherliness, and calm competence. Womanlike may be a neutral synonym, or it may suggest mild disapproval. Womanish is usually disparaging; applied to women it suggests traits not generally socially approved. Applied to a man, it suggests traits culturally deemed inappropriate for men and to be found in women: a womanish shrillness in his speech.

In addition, many English words are based on roots or compounds with "man," "master," or other male-oriented sources: bachelor's degree, bedfellow, brotherhood, forefather, fraternize, freshman, manpower, masterful, mastermind, patronize, statesmanship (Nilsen 1977:36).

As Muriel Schulz (1975) pointed out, many words associated with females that began with innocuous or even positive connotations have undergone processes of derogation, most often with sexual implications. For example, "hussy" is derived from Old English "huswife" (housewife), originally meaning "female head of household." It gradually came to mean "a rustic or rude woman" and finally "a lewd, brazen woman or a prostitute." The words "nymph" and "nymphet" were first endearments referring to "beautiful young girls or women" and then became euphemisms for prostitutes, finally meaning "a sexually precocious girl; a loose young woman." Semantic narrowing and derogation also affected the word "whore," which originally was a polite term for "a lover of either sex." It then narrowed its meaning only to women and degenerated as a label for prostitutes (Schulz 1975:66–69).

A more recent expression, "sex object," is a further instance of defining females by their sexuality. The term removes not only females' full personalities and activities but also their very personhood and metaphorically transforms them into inanimates. Similar semantic processes have not affected words for males. In fact, although words referring to male sexuality, such as "stud," are not used in polite speech, they have positive rather than negative connotations.

Terms in African American Vernacular English similarly express derogatory or trivialized meanings for females. In AAVE slang, most words for women emphasize physical characteristics, including variations in skin color—"redbone," "spotlight," "high yaller," "pinky"—or apply animal terms to females—"fox," "filly," "butterfly" (Scott 1974:220).

Female/male differences are also found in adjectives describing people's attributes and in verbs denoting their activities. Most verbs can be used for male or female activities, but others are restricted to refer to actions of females. For example, men/women "yell," but only women "screech" or "shriek"; men/women "talk" and women "chat" or "gossip"; men/women may "laugh," but women "giggle." Notice that all of the specialized "female" verbs have derogatory or trivialized nuances. Adjectives or adverbs derived from these verbs are employed for women with negative meaning: chatty, screechy, talkative, giggly.

Adjectives referring to physical characteristics of females are often used in contexts where comparable modifiers for males would not likely occur. Even public figures and political leaders who are women typically have their appearance or clothing commented upon by the media. This practice reminds women that they are never free from scrutiny and that their physical image is a crucial part of their being.

Analysis of classes of vocabulary, that is, nouns, verbs, and adjectives, uncovers a consistent pattern of segregating males and females and of demeaning or trivializing the latter. Women are restricted, through language, to their roles in relation to men, either as wives or as sexual beings. And their behavior in other spheres of life is disvalued through negative connotations associated with their activities. The English language, then, creates and reinforces cultural models of gender that help maintain social privilege for males and undermine the status and self-worth of females.

Generic "He" and "Man"

One of the most frequently debated examples of linguistic favoritism toward males is the use of the so-called generic "he" and "man" to refer to people without regard to gender. In some contexts, the prescribed pronoun "he" has a singular referent—"A child learns his reading skills in the first grade"—but in others, it has underlying nonsingular semantic referents, as in "Everyone should take his coat." Here, "everyone" may be morphologically singular (lacking the plural suffix -s), but it obviously refers to more than one individual. Insistence by grammarians that "he" is the "proper" pronoun for an indefinite person or people in general dates to the eighteenth century (Bodine 1975). Prior to that time, the pronoun "they" was used for singular or plural indefinites and generics, as shown in writing and presumably in speaking. In a discussion of English pronouns, George McKnight (1928) collected quotations from no less than William Shakespeare's *Much Ado About Nothing:* "God send every one their heart's desire" and "Each leaning on their elbows and their hips." Later authors continued to use "they," as, for example, Jane Austen in *Mansfield Park:* "Nobody put themselves out of the way" and "Each had their favorite." Although people are taught in school to use "he" in formal speech and especially in writing, even casual observation shows that speakers employ "they" in ordinary conversation. Finally, in addition to overlooking semantics and failing to hear actual speech, the grammarian approach ignores the existence of a linguistic context in which only the pronoun "they" can occur. In tag questions, when the subject of a statement is a generic or indefinite person, the underlying pronoun replacement surfacing in the tag is clearly "they":

Everyone left the room, didn't they?

Even when an indefinite noun refers to a single individual, its pronoun is "they":

Somebody left the room, didn't they?

Experimental tests of people's reactions to sentences with "generic he or his" consistently support the contention that "he or his" is never gender-neutral. Rather, it always contains some of its basic masculine sense. This is not surprising; it is even expected in terms of semantic theory in linguistics. That is, every word has a central or focal meaning that is carried with it in all contexts of its extended use. Underlying notions of gender associated with generic pronouns were studied in several experiments conducted by Donald MacKay (1983). One study presented male and female students at UCLA with sentences containing pronouns, such as "When a botanist is in the field, he is usually working." Test sentences were mixed, so that some referred to stereotypically "male-related" antecedents (engineer, doctor), others to "female-related" antecedents (model, secretary), and still others to "neutral" referents (student, musician). Subjects were asked to decide quickly whether or not sentences could refer to females. Results revealed that 95 percent of respondents (ten women and ten men) judged that the sentences could not refer to females. Male and female subjects had similar reactions. And subjects excluded females at constant rates regardless of whether sentences had gender-stereotyped or neutral antecedents (ibid.:41).

In a related experiment, MacKay presented subjects with sentences identical to those in the first test except that pronouns were omitted, for example, "A botanist who is in the field is usually working." Results were strikingly different: 43 percent of the subjects (as compared to 95 percent in the prior study) responded that the sentences could not refer to females. Moreover, identity of antecedents became significant. Subjects thought that 68 percent of sentences with male antecedents could not refer to females, 42 percent with neutral antecedents, and 19 percent with female antecedents. Finally, sex of subject also affected judgments. Men were more likely than women to restrict sentences to male referents. MacKay concluded, "These findings suggest that adding prescriptive he dramatically increases the exclusion of females and washes out effects of subject sex and nature of the antecedent" (ibid.:42).

In another type of experiment, college students (226 male, 264 female) were presented with the task of composing stories based on two themes: "In a large coeducational institution the average student will feel isolated in _____ introductory courses" and "Most people are concerned with appearance. Each person knows when _____ appearance is unattractive" (Moulton et al. 1978). The subject pool was divided into six groups, given alternative versions of the two themes expressed with pronouns "his," "their," or "his or her." Analyses of stories focused on the sex of the main character developed in respondents' compositions. Over all conditions, female characters appeared in 56 percent of stories with "his or her" as the pronoun in the theme statement, 46 percent were female with "their" pronouns, and only 35 percent were female when the pronoun "his" was used (ibid.:1034). Moulton et al. asserted that "our results indicate that using male terms in their 'gender-neutral' sense induces people to think of males even in contexts that are explicitly gender-neutral" (ibid.).

Supposedly neutral interpretations of "man" face similar problems. This word has an interesting history, beginning in Old English to mean "a human being" with no gender association. Separate unambiguous words existed to denote females, *wif,* and males, *wer* or *carl.* "Man" could combine with these to refer specifically to adults of their respective genders: *wifman* and *werman* or *carlman. Wifman* eventually became "woman," and male designators were replaced by semantic narrowing of man to refer to males (Miller and Smith 1977:25). Experimental studies have revealed that even when "man" is used in generic contexts, male images surface.

In one experiment, college students were asked to select and submit illustrations for an introductory sociology textbook (Schneider and Hacker 1973). Each of two groups was presented with alternative titles for chapters, one phrased as "Urban Man," "Political Man," or "Social Man" and the second as "Urban Life," "Political Behavior," or "Society." In the first group, 64 percent of respondents chose photographs of males only, whereas half of those in the second group chose male-only illustrations (ibid.:14). The likelihood of including women in photographs varied for different titles. The only one in which women appeared in a majority of illustrations was "Social Man" in which case a male was typically shown surrounded by females in contexts of social or leisure activities. The title "Urban Man" elicited nearly equal representation, "males only" in 55 percent of illustrations. For the "Political Man," "Industrial Man," and "Economic Man" chapters, women appeared in a small minority of photographs (ibid.:16). On the basis of their study, Schneider and Hacker asserted that uses of "-man" as a label "may serve to 'filter-out' women, largely by suggesting imagery appropriate only or primarily to men" (ibid.:12).

In response to concerns over the symbolic preference for males expressed covertly and overtly by words such as "man," "he," and "his," advocates of gender equality in language have suggested replacing these words with genuinely neutral forms such as "person," "people," and "she or he" and "his or her." However, a curious development has occurred in the case of "-person" when used in compounds such as "spokesperson" or "chairperson." In common usage, there is currently a tendency to restrict "-person" nouns to females, retaining "-man" for males. "Spokesperson," therefore, has replaced "spokeswoman" but not "spokesman."

A similar failure to get the point of an advocated change concerns address designations of Ms./Miss/Mrs. The title "Ms." was introduced in order to eliminate labeling women according to their marital status. Although intended as a replacement for both "Miss" and "Mrs.," it has come to be employed (if at all) to refer solely to unmarried women. The only context in which it is generally used for all women is in business and official letters to address unfamiliar women, thus providing senders with the ability to avoid offending receivers by mistaking their marital status.

All the data uncovered in analyses of English linguistic forms indicate a pervasive, covert ascription of positive and normative qualities to males and negative or secondary ones to females. Continual repetition of English words and expressions, both as speakers and hearers, reinforces cultural evaluations that enhance males' status and disvalue females. These judgments do not originate in the language but arise linguistically to express, supplement, and justify entrenched cultural models.

SUMMARY

In all societies, gender distinctions are expressed through language. They may occur as differences in linguistic form: Women and men use alternatives in pronunciation, word selection, and grammatical construction. Gender-appropriate styles of communicative interaction further mark the separation of women and men. Finally, words and expressions in a language itself may reflect gender differences in how they symbolize males and females.

In the United States and other English-speaking societies, women and men behave differently in several communicative domains. Women tend to use sounds that are marked as standard, correct, and/or prestigeful. Their choice of words and grammatical constructions can be characterized as polite or deferential. And women's interactional moves tend to respect rights of interlocutors. In contrast, men are more likely, given similarities of class, race, and context, to use less formal, less prestigeful, and less polite forms of speech. And through their conversational styles, men more often exert control and dominance.

Explanations for these behaviors should be sought in social systems that not only distinguish between the genders but structure men's and women's relationships in a hierarchical order, endowing men with more valued status and rights and restricting or subordinating women. The English language contributes to gender inequality by the ways that women and men are labeled and their actions are described. Recurrent messages convey derogatory, subsidiary, or disvalued images of women. Through communicative processes, cultural models of gender are both portrayed and reinforced, contributing to the socialization of females and males into their expected roles and also creating their ideas about themselves and each other.

REFERENCES

ABU-LUGHOD, LILA. 1986. *Veiled Sentiments.* Berkeley: University of California Press.

ABU-LUGHOD, LILA. 1990. The romance of resistance: Tracing transformations of power through Beduoin women. *American Ethnologist* 17:41–55.

BAILEY, LEE ANN, AND LENORA TIMM. 1976. More on women's—and men's—expletives. *Anthropological Linguistics* 18:438–439.

BENNET, SUZANNE, AND BERND WEINBERG. 1979. Sexual characteristics of preadolescent children's voices. *Journal of the Acoustical Society of America* 65:179–189.

BODINE, ANN. 1975. Androcentrism in prescriptive grammar. *Language in Society* 4:129–146.

BROWN, PENELOPE, AND STEPHEN LEVINSON. 1987. *Politeness: Some Universals in Language Usage.* New York: Cambridge University Press.

CAMERON, DEBORAH, F. MCALINDEN, AND K. O'LEARY. 1988. Lakoff in context: The social and linguistic functions of tag questions. In *Women in Their Speech Communities,* ed. J. Coates and D. Cameron. London: Longman, pp. 74–93.

CHESHIRE, JENNY. 1982. Linguistic variation and social function. In *Sociolinguistic Variation in Speech Communities,* ed. S. Romaine. London: Edward Arnold, pp. 153–166.

CROSBY, FAYE, AND LINDA NYQUIST. 1977. The female register: An empirical study of Lakoff's hypotheses. *Language in Society* 6:313–322.

DAVIS, HAYLEY. 1996. Theorizing women's and men's language. *Language & Communication* 16:71–80.

DEFRANCISCO, VICTORIA. 1998. The sounds of silence: How men silence women in marital relations. In *Language and Gender,* ed. J. Coates. Malden, MA: Blackwell, pp. 176–184.

DEKLERK, VIVIAN. 1992. How taboo are taboo words for girls? *Language in Society* 21:277–290.

DUBOIS, BETTY LOU, AND ISABEL CROUCH. 1975. The question of tag-questions in women's speech: They don't really use more of them, do they? *Language in Society* 4:289–294.

ECKERT, PENELOPE. 1998. Gender and sociolinguistic variation. In *Language and Gender,* ed. J. Coates. Malden, MA: Blackwell, pp. 64–76.

EDELSKY, CAROL. 1981. Who's got the floor? *Language in Society* 10:383–421.

FISCHER, JOHN. 1958. Social influences on the choice of a linguistic variant. *Word* 14:47–56.

FISHMAN, PAMELA. 1983. Interaction: The work women do. In *Language, Gender and Society,* ed. B. Thorne, N. Henley, and C. Kramarae. Rowley, MA: Newbury, pp. 89–101.

GORDON, ELIZABETH. 1997. Sex, speech, and stereotypes: Why women use prestige speech forms more than men. *Language in Society* 26:47–64.

HENLEY, NANCY, AND CHERIS KRAMARAE. 1991. Gender, power and miscommunication. In *"Miscommunication" and Problematic Talk,* ed. N. Coupland et al. Newbury Park, CA: Sage, pp. 18–43.

HOLMES, JANET. 1984. Hedging your bets and sitting on the fence: Some evidence for hedges as support structures. *Te Reo* 27:47–62.

HUGHES, SUSAN. 1997. Expletives of lower working-class women. *Language in Society* 21:291–304.

JAY, TIMOTHY. 1980. Sex roles and dirty-word usage. *Psychological Bulletin* 88: 614–621.

JESPERSEN, OTTO. 1922. *Language: Its Nature, Development and Origins.* London: Allen and Unwin.

KIESLING, SCOTT. 1997. Power and the language of men. In *Language and Masculinity,* ed. S. Johnson and U. Meinhof. London: Blackwell, pp. 65–85.

KRAMER, CHERIS. 1975. Women's speech: Separate but unequal. In *Language and Sex,* ed. B. Thorne and N. Henley. Rowley, MA: Newbury, 43–56.

LABOV, WILLIAM. 1966. *The Social Stratification of English in New York City.* Washington, DC: Center for Applied Linguistics.

LAKOFF, ROBIN. 1975. *Language and Woman's Place.* New York: Harper & Row.

LEVINE, LEWIS, AND HARRY CROCKETT. 1967. Speech variation in a Piedmont community: Postvocalic r-. In *Explorations in Sociolinguistics,* ed. S. Lieberson. Bloomington: Indiana University Press, pp. 76–98.

MACKAY, DONALD. 1983. Prescriptive grammar and the pronoun problem. In *Language, Gender and Society,* ed. B. Thorne et al. Rowley, MA: Newbury, pp. 38–53.

MALTZ, DANIEL, AND RUTH BORKER. 1982. A cultural approach to male-female miscommunication. In *Language and Social Identity,* ed. J. Gumperz. New York: Cambridge University Press, pp. 195–216.

MCCONNELL-GINET, SALLY. 1983. Intonation in a man's world. In *Language, Gender and Society,* ed. B. Thorne et al. Rowley, MA: Newbury, pp. 69–88.

MCKNIGHT, GEORGE. 1928. *Modern English in the Making.* New York: Appleton.

MILLER, CASEY, AND KATE SMITH. 1977. *Words and Women.* New York: Anchor.

MOULTON, JANICE, G. ROBINSON, AND C. ELIAS. 1978. Sex bias in language use: "Neutral" pronouns that aren't. *American Psychologist* 33:1032–1036.

NICHOLS, PATRICIA. 1983. Linguistic options and choices for black women in the rural South. *Language, Gender, and Society,* ed. B. Thorne et al. Rowley, MA: Newbury, pp. 54–68.

NILSEN, ALLEEN. 1977. Sexism as shown in the English language. In *Sexism and Language,* ed. A. Nilsen et al. Champaign, IL: National Council of Teachers of English, pp. 27–42.

Random House Dictionary of the English Language, 2nd ed. 1987. New York: Random House.

SATTEL, JACK. 1983. Men, inexpressiveness and power. In *Language, Gender and Society,* ed. B. Thorne et al. Rowley, MA: Newbury, pp. 118–124.

SCHNEIDER, JOSEPH, AND SALLY HACKER. 1973. Sex role imagery and use of the generic "Man" in introductory texts: A case in the sociology of sociology. *American Sociologist* 8:12–18.

SCHULZ, MURIEL. 1975. The semantic derogation of women. In *Language and Sex,* ed. B. Thorne and N. Henley. Rowley, MA: Newbury, pp. 64–75.

SCOTT, PATRICIA B. 1974. The English language and black womanhood: A low blow at self-esteem. *Journal of Afro-American Issues* 2:218–224.

SWACKER, MARJORIE. 1975. The sex of the speaker as a sociolinguistic variable. In *Language and Sex,* ed. B. Thorne and N. Henley. Rowley, MA: Newbury, pp. 76–83.

TANNEN, DEBORAH. 1986. *That's Not What I Meant.* New York: Ballantine.

TANNEN, DEBORAH. 1990. *You Just Don't Understand.* New York: Ballantine.

TERANGO, LARRY. 1966. Pitch and duration characteristics of the oral reading of males on a masculinity-femininity dimension. *Journal of Speech and Hearing Research* 9:590–595.

TROEMEL-PLOETZ, SENTA. 1998. Selling the apolitical. In *Language and Gender,* ed. J. Coates. Malden, MA: Blackwell, pp. 446–458.

TRUDGILL, PETER. 1972. Sex, covert prestige and linguistic change in the urban British English of Norwich. *Language in Society* 1:179–195.

UCHIDA, AKI. 1992. When "difference" is "dominance": A critique of the "anti-power-based" cultural approach to sex differences. *Language in Society* 21:547–568.

WEST, CANDACE. 1998. When the doctor is a "lady": Power, status and gender in physician-patient encounters. In *Language and Gender,* ed. J. Coates. Malden, MA: Blackwell, pp. 396–412.

WEST, CANDACE, AND DON ZIMMERMAN. 1983. Small insults: A study of interruptions in cross-sex conversations between unacquainted persons. In *Language, Gender and Society,* ed. B. Thorne et al. Rowley, MA: Newbury, pp. 103–118.

WOLFRAM, WALT. 1969. *A Sociolinguistic Description of Detroit Negro Speech.* Washington, DC: Center for Applied Linguistics.

WOODS, NICOLA. 1988. Talking shop: Sex and status as determinants of floor apportionment in a work setting. In *Women in Their Speech Communities,* ed. J. Coates and D. Cameron. London: Longman, pp. 141–157.

ZIMMERMAN, DON, AND CANDACE WEST. 1975. Sex roles, interruptions and silences in conversation. In *Language and Sex,* ed. B. Thorne and N. Henley. Rowley, MA: Newbury, pp. 105–129.

8

Cross-Cultural Studies of Language and Gender

In the Chukchee language (a native Siberian language), the word for "people" is pronounced /rámkɪčhɪn/ by men and /šámkɪššɪn/ by women. Japanese women use the word /ohiya/ for "water," whereas Japanese men say /mizu/. These are just two examples of a common, but not universal, pattern in which women and men use different pronunciations, words, and/or stylistic devices to distinguish their speech. In some cases, as among the Chukchee, gender marking of pronunciation simply reflects a difference between men and women. In other societies, as among the Japanese, some differences carry a social message of inequality. For example, a Japanese husband can refer to his wife by the term "uti no yatu" or "fellow of my home," whereas a wife can refer to her husband as "uti no hito" or "person of my home." The significant difference here is that the phrase used by husbands is an impolite or informal term used about a person of lower status than the speaker, whereas the phrase used by wives is a polite term used about a person of higher status than the speaker.

Although people in all societies have gender-specific modes of communicating, there are significant cross-cultural differences in both language and style where these distinctions are shown and in prevailing degrees of divergence between the genders. In this chapter we examine data from several cultures in order to understand the range of behavior and to review some hypotheses explaining observed patterns.

Distinctions are sometimes made between languages with "gender-exclusive" patterns, in which women and men always use linguistic alternatives appropriate to their own gender, and languages having patterns of "gender preference," in which men and women exhibit different statistical frequencies in their use of socially marked linguistic forms. We begin by reviewing data of the first type of language and then proceed to the second.

GENDER-EXCLUSIVE PATTERNS

The earliest known documentations of exclusive gender differences in speech are seventeenth-century reports of native Carib people living on the Lesser Antilles. Statements made by Europeans of the period claimed that Carib men and women spoke different languages. This is clearly impossible for, if they did, husbands and wives, parents and children, would not have been able to communicate. It turns out, however, that there were a number of differences in words used by the two genders. The natives evidently explained the linguistic patterns on the basis of their local history. According to their accounts, the Antilles had previously been inhabited by Arawak-speaking peoples who had been defeated by the invading Caribs. The Caribs killed Arawakian men and intermarried with indigenous women. The women taught their own language to their children, but when the boys grew up, they learned words and expressions appropriate to men. Whether this account is historically accurate or a folk explanation, the Carib language did contain a limited number of gender-specific words. Some of these denoted kinship relations; for example, "my father" was *youmáan* in men's speech and *noukóuchili* in women's speech (Jespersen 1922:238). This pattern is not unusual; many languages have distinct kinship terms used by male or female speakers.

Another category of gender-related words referred to some body parts, possibly in recognition of physical differences between women and men. The remaining words denoted the following: friend, enemy, joy, work, war, house, garden, bed, poison, tree, sun, moon, sea, and earth (Jespersen 1922:238, citing Rochefort, *Histoire naturelle et morale des Iles Antilles,* 1665). The linguistic situation that existed among Caribs may have differed in degree from many other languages, but it did not fundamentally differ in kind. However, the origin of Carib gender distinctions, if true according to indigenous sources, does seem to have been unique.

More reliable documentation of gender-exclusive linguistic patterns has been obtained by research beginning in the early twentieth century. Such studies detail pronunciation differences that apply to particular sounds. In Chukchee, consonants č and *r* in male speech are consistently replaced by š in female speech. Similarly, consonant clusters č*h* and *rk* spoken by men are realized as šš by women. Compare the following words (Bogoras 1922:665):

Men	Women	
čūmñáta	šūmñáta	"by a buck"
rámkıčhın	sámkıššın	"people"

From these examples, it appears that male speech is the basic linguistic form and that female speech is derived from it. That is, š in female speech is predictable from either č or *r* in male speech, but the choice of č or *r* by males cannot be predicted from female š. However, another sound pattern in Chukchee indicates the opposite development. Consonants *n* and *t* appearing in basic women's speech are omitted between vowels in derived men's speech, as in the following words (that Bogoras does not translate):

Women	Men
nɪtváqĕnat	nɪtváqaat
tírkɪtir	tírkiir

According to Bogoras, when women and men quote a statement made by a male or female character in storytelling or personal narrative, they use pronunciations appropriate for the character. However, "in ordinary conversation, the pronunciation of men is considered as unbecoming a woman" (ibid.). This comment indicates that Chukchees gave social evaluations to gender-appropriate behavior, although we should be wary of taking the statement at face value inasmuch as Bogoras did not specify his sources or context for the remark. Of perhaps equal interest, Bogoras revealed his own bias regarding gender patterns when he noted in discussing consonant replacements that "the sounds č and r are quite frequent; so that the speech of women, with its ever-recurring š, sounds quite peculiar, and is not easily understood by an inexperienced ear" (ibid.). This kind of statement, taking male behavior as the norm and interpreting female behavior as deviant or "peculiar," is not at all unusual in (male) discussions of gender differences.

Studies of several Native American languages have documented gender distinctions. For example, in Yana, a language spoken in California, complex differences obtain between women's and men's speech (Sapir 1929). Most Yana words have male and female forms, derived through various procedures. If the male form of a word is basic, then females reduce or eliminate the final syllable; if the female form is basic, then males add a final syllable. The system contains different rules for different types of words. A few examples will demonstrate several complexities. In multisyllabic nouns and in verbs ending in short vowels a, i, or u, men's pronunciations are basic and women devoice the final vowel and preceding consonant, unless already voiceless (Sapir 1929:208):

Men	Women	
mô'i	mô'i̥	to eat
imamba	imampḁ	deer liver
mal'gu	mal'ku̥	ear

In monosyllabic nouns, nouns not ending in short a, i, or u, demonstratives, and many verbs, female forms are basic, whereas male forms add a final syllable, the structure of which depends on the type of word involved. The following lists display some alternatives.

Nouns (male adds -na):
Women	Men	
'i	'ina	stick, tree
yā	yāna	person

Demonstratives (male adds -'e):
| aidǰe | aidǰe'e | that one |
| aige | aige'e | to that one yonder |

Verbs (male adds -'a or -'i):

t'ūsi	t'ūsi'i	he will do
nisāk!u	nisāk!u'i	he might go away
mômauk'i	mômauk'i'a	he eats his (another's) food

According to Sapir, male forms of speech are used by men when talking to other men. Female speech is used by women talking to either women or men and by men to women. "Male" speech is, therefore, an exclusive marker of male inter-action, although women use male words when quoting a male speaker. Sapir attempted to explain Yana linguistic differences in sociocultural terms, certainly a laudable goal, but one wonders whether his explanation reveals an American bias rather than a Yana perspective: "Possibly the reduced female forms constitute a conventionalized symbolism of the less considered or ceremonious status of women in the community. Men, in dealing with men, speak fully and deliberately; where women are concerned, one prefers a clipped style of utterance!" (ibid.:212).

Gender differences were documented in Koasati and other languages in the Muskogean family spoken by Native Americans in the southeastern United States (Haas 1944). Male and female pronunciations contrasted in certain classes of words in various ways. Mary Haas established Koasati female forms as basic and derived male forms from them because changes were better described in this direction. Following are lists of rules and examples from Koasati (ibid.:142–144):

1. If the female form ends in a nasal vowel, male forms denasalize the vowel and add -s:

Women	*Men*	
lakawwā·	lakawwa·s	he will lift it
lakawtakkō	lakawtakkos	I am not lifting it

2. If the female form ends with falling pitch on a final short vowel followed by -l, male forms have rising pitch and replace -l with -s:

molhîl	molhís	we are peeling it
lakawhôl	lakawhós	lift it! (you pl.)

3. If the female form ends with falling pitch on a final short vowel followed by -n, male forms retain falling pitch, replace -n with -s, and lengthen the final vowel:

tačilwân	tačilwâ·s	don't sing!
iltočihnôn	iltočihnô·s	don't work!

4. If the female form ends in a vowel followed by one or two consonants, male forms add -s (unless affected by any previously stated rule):

mól	móls	he is peeling it
í:p	í:ps	he is eating it
tačílw	tačílws	you are singing

Koasati men and women used each other's speech when quoting a speaker or formerly when correcting a child's speech in order to reinforce gender-appropriate styles. Women's speech, though, was evidently on the decline by midcentury, because Haas noted that "only middle-aged and elderly women use the women's form, while younger women are now using the form characteristic of men's speech" (ibid.:146). Even so, one of Haas's male informants said that he thought women's speech to be "better" than men's. Because Haas did not pursue this issue in her writing, it is impossible to know precisely what the speaker meant by his remark.

Disappearance of female forms of speech in favor of male forms has been documented in other Native American languages, including Hitchiti (Musko-gean), Biloxi (Siouan), and Gros Ventre (Algonkian) (see Gatschet 1884; Haas 1944; Flannery 1946). This process of replacement, more than the linguistic dif-ferences themselves, indicates gender inequalities. Although gender-specific styles demonstrate social differentiation, they do not necessarily imply a hierarchical rela-tionship between women and men. But when one style is consistently replaced by the other, status and value distinctions between men and women must be assumed. Such distinctions have increased in many native cultures along with other aspects of assimilation to Euro-American society. Gender differentiation certainly existed in earlier aboriginal cultures, but it seems to have stressed complementary roles more often than unequal status relations.

Although differences in sounds have been studied in relatively few languages, it is reasonable to assume that such patterns exist or existed elsewhere. Gender-exclusive usages may have gone unnoticed by linguists, particularly if they dealt only with either male or female speakers. Moreover, processes of change, similar to those documented in Native America, may well have obscured or eliminated gen-der differentiation previously expressed in other languages.

In a few languages, morphological constructions vary, depending on the gen-der of the speaker and/or hearer. For example, in Kūṛux, a Dravidian language spo-ken in North India, verb suffixes are distinguished in a complex pattern in four possible speaker/hearer interactions: man-to-man, man-to-woman, woman-to-woman, and woman-to-man (Ekka 1972). Gender differences occur in a number of ways in Kūṛux verb tenses (past, present, future) and in imperative forms. They also vary for grammatical persons (first, second, third). Some of these contrasts are collapsed in different tenses for some grammatical persons, and others are main-tained. The present-tense paradigm for the verb *bar-* "come" is illustrative (Ekka 1972:26–27):

	Man–Man	*Man–Woman*	*Woman–Woman*	*Woman–Man*
1st sg.	bar-d-an	bar-d-an	bar -e-n	bar-d-an
1st pl.	bar-d-am	bar-d-am	bar -e-m	bar-d-am
2nd sg.	bar-d-ayi	bar-d-i	bar-d-in	bar-d-ay
2nd pl.	bar-d-ar	bar-d-ar	bar-d-ayii	bar-d-ar
3rd sg.	bar-d-as	bar-d-as	bar-d-as	bar-d-as
3rd pl.	bar-n-ar	bar-n-ar	bar-n-ayii	bar-n-ar

Ekka summarized Kū̃rux verb morphology by concluding that stem and suffix forms are basically distinguished according to same-sex man-to-man and woman-to-woman dyads. However, man-to-man forms are used in cross-sex interactions, that is, man-to-woman and woman-to-man. Finally, Ekka stated (ibid.:31)

> The acceptance of [male] grammatical features by women and the rejection of [female] grammatical features by men in Kū̃rux speech system are both linguistically and sociologically interesting phenomena. . . . It may be mentioned that Kū̃rux community is patriarchal where men enjoy higher social status than women. Perhaps it might be that the dominance of [male] grammatical features in three of the four speech contexts reflects men's superiority over women in Kū̃rux speech behavior.

Hints about the possibility of ideological struggle in gender-exclusive styles are provided by Chiquita, spoken by native people in Bolivia. In women's speech, all nouns are treated in identical fashion, but in men's speech, nouns are divided into two classes that are marked morphologically. One class consists of nouns referring to men and supernatural beings; the other consists of all other nouns (reported in Bodine 1975). Men's speech, therefore, links the category of "male" to that of supernatural beings. This style is employed by men only when speaking to other men; women never use it, and the style is never used in speech to them. Ann Bodine speculated that "Chiquita men have tried to use language to symbolically elevate themselves, but . . . Chiquita women have refused to go along with it" (1975:144). Bodine's suggestion is consistent with the fact that social conflicts are often revealed in linguistic forms and styles. Struggle over ideological issues is frequently exhibited in and through language. Use of a particular form can demonstrate a social attitude, just as refusal to use that form can signify a rejection of implied cultural meaning.

All the examples in this section, documenting pronunciation and grammatical and vocabulary differences, are actually rather restricted when viewed in terms of each linguistic system as a whole. They involve either a small number of sounds, a few morphological markers, or a handful of words. They do not alter the fundamental character of a language. No exclusive differences in sentence construction have ever been reported. However, despite the evidence of such patterns, it is well to be cautious about their interpretation. Although discussions of the data label gender usages as "exclusive," the terminology may be misleading. As Bogoras, Sapir, and Haas noted for Chukchee, Yana, and Koasati, respectively, people may use sounds, affixes, or particles regarded as more appropriate for the other gender when quoting another speaker. It may well have also been true that the speech usually associated with the gender other than speaker was used in additional contexts or for additional pragmatic and stylistic functions. Unfortunately, because of the loss of "women's" speech in these communities (or of the extinction of the language altogether), contextual data cannot be retrieved.

Some insights into pragmatic possibilities may be gleaned from a study of Lakhota particles that are inserted after verbs to denote the gender of the speaker (Trechter and James 1994). The particles also carry affective meaning, conveying attitudes of speaker toward self, addressee, and topic. For example, the "opinion/emphasis" particle associated with women (/yele/) connotes nurturance and concern for addressee, whereas the particle associated with men (/yelo/) connotes authority, seniority, and rights to discipline or assert (ibid.:749–750). As in other Native American languages, when quoting other people speakers use the particles of the person who they are quoting. But people may also use particles stereotypically associated with the other gender to convey particular affective and contextual meanings. Sara Trechter and Eli James cite several instances of men's use of "women's" speech: a man talking to his young nephew to indicate affection; an elderly man speaking about a dead relative to indicate his respect for the deceased; and a middle-aged man expressing an opinion that might upset or anger addressee. The researchers also note an example of a woman using a particle associated with men when giving permission to a younger female relative to engage in an activity (singing in public) that contravenes Lakhota mourning observances (ibid.: 752–754). These data uncover a critical distinction between stereotypical ideals and actual usage, a distinction that can presumably be found in most, if not all, societies.

LINGUISTIC AND STYLISTIC PREFERENCES

Because language is situated in culture, and because images of gender are created through culture, it is necessary to analyze the cultural contexts in which speech occurs and is evaluated. And we need to see whether particular gender-linked styles are given different interpretations by members of the society. In this section we review some relevant research concerning language and gender in non-Western societies and attempt to understand both local and common patterns.

Japanese

Japanese society is stratified in terms of class, gender, and age. Class status is marked by deference shown to people of wealth and high position in occupational settings; men receive greater social respect than do women; and seniority within both households and communities bestows prestige to elders. Many aspects of the Japanese language express these status differences between interlocutors. As in other complex societies, factors of region, class, and age, as well as gender, affect speakers' choice of linguistic features. An important distinction in Japanese is that of a speaker's position relative to addressee and his or her attitude toward self and addressee (Clark 1996). As we saw in discussions of Japanese honorifics and polite usages (Chapters 4 and 5), words and grammatical constructions can be altered to reflect the speaker's respect toward the addressee. As noted, women tend to employ these markers with greater frequency than do men. In addition, Japanese men and women tend to employ a number of linguistic features of sound, grammar, and vocabulary at different rates of frequency. Taken together, traits of stereotypical "women's speech" are perceived as more polite and deferential, whereas traits of stereotypical "men's speech" are deemed to be less polite and more assertive.

Gender styles also appear in intonational patterns. As in the speech of American women, Japanese women's intonation is more dynamic than men's, reflected by sharper changes in pitch and stress. Japanese women also tend to use rising intonational contours at the ends of sentences.

In addition to distinctions in pronunciation, Japanese men and women tend to employ separate words for some objects, activities, or ideas. These contrasts are deemed to be more or less polite. Some examples follow (ibid.:28):

	Less Polite Forms	*More Polite Forms*
stomach	hara	onaka
water	mizu	ohiya
delicious	umai	oisii
eat	kuu	taberu

Nouns that contain the prefix {o-} (as in the preceding list) carry connotations of politeness. This prefix is a polite or honorific marker that can be used by either gender but occurs in women's speech with much greater frequency. It can be attached to any noun to render the speaking style more polite or refined. Other politeness prefixes are {go-} and {omi-}, also appearing in women's speech at high rates. However, relative status of speakers in any dyadic interaction is also significant. Both men and women use polite forms to superiors. But because women are socially defined as inferior in status in many intergender interactions, they tend to use polite forms with greater frequency than do men (Clark 1996). For instance (ibid.):

	Less Polite Forms	*More Polite Forms*
box lunch	bentoo	obentoo
chopsticks	hasi	ohasi
book	hon	gohon

In Japan, as in the United States, people stereotypically identify certain syntactic constructions with female speakers and others with male speakers. And in Japan, as in the United States, the validity of some of these stereotypes is questionable. However, it appears that Japanese women tend to use grammatical markers of politeness and deference more frequently than do men.

In order to investigate connections between gender and politeness, the National Language Research Institute of Japan conducted an experimental study of usage of polite speech (reported in Shibamoto 1987:32–33). Subjects were asked how they would make requests, ask questions, and address participants in various situations. Responses were coded as "normally polite" (0), "marked polite" (11), and "rude" (21). Average scores were computed for women and men across situations and showed significant gender differences: 0.27 for men and 2.90 for women.

Additional linguistic evidence of underlying cultural images of gender in Japanese society is the distinctive use of sentence-final particles, that is, morphemes occurring at ends of sentences that mark speakers' attitudes. Common particles in women's speech indicate "femininity" {*wa*}, "childishness" {*no*}, and "uncertainty" {*-te*}. In contrast, particles most often used by men are "emphatics": {*ze*}, {*zo*} (ibid.:33–34). Gender styles in particle usage can thus be compared to patterns of vocabulary or syntactic choices in English. As we have seen, American-Anglo women tend to mark their speech with indicators of mitigation and uncertainty (hedges, tags), whereas men tend to use more direct ("emphatic"?) constructions.

With an understanding of the possibilities of gender distinctions in Japanese, Janet Shibamoto (1987) conducted a study of casual conversations among friends to determine their actual usage. Self-recruited groups of three were observed and recorded. On the basis of these recordings, Shibamoto identified three syntactic features occurring at different frequencies in women's and men's speech (ibid.:36, 38):

1. Women tended to omit subjects, objects, and other noun phrases in sentences.

2. Women tended to transpose subjects from their usual place of preceding verbs (as in English) to positions following verbs, often to the end of sentences.

3. Women tended to omit case markers on subjects and direct objects.

The following tables give percentages of the targeted processes of noun-phrase deletion, subject transposing, and particle deletion occurring in recorded data of women's and men's speech collected by Shibamoto (ibid.:36–38). Women consistently employed the relevant features at much higher rates than did men, providing strong evidence of gender styles.

Noun-Phrase Deletion by Sentence Type and Sex of Speaker

Sentence Type	Males	Females
Nominal	58.6%	69.4%
Adjectival	32.7	51.6
Verbal	65.2	65.0

Sentences with Transposed Elements

Predicate Type	Males	Females
Copular	3.8%	12.6%
Adjectival	9.1	18.7
Verbal	5.0	11.7
Total	5.0	12.7

Deletion of Subject and Object Particles

Case	Males	Females
Subjects	11.0%	24.0%
Direct objects	25.8	40.4
Indirect objects	6.6	6.0

In order to measure the incidence of different kinds of linguistic markers used by women in different contexts, Shibamoto recorded casual conversations among female friends and compared their speech to that of actresses in "home-dramas" on Japanese television. These programs provide players with script outlines but call for improvisation of dialogue. Shibamoto noted occurrences in the data of two types of linguistic indicators that she identified as "stereotyped" (words, sentence particles, honorifics) and "nonstereotyped" (noun deletion, syntactic changes). Shibamoto hypothesized that in the contrived context of "home-dramas," actresses would be able to manipulate stereotypical markers of "womanliness." Because stereotyped features are close to consciousness in speakers, they can be controlled, whereas nonstereotypical features of syntax are not conscious and, therefore, are not consciously controlled (ibid.:39).

All the stereotyped features that Shibamoto examined (polite nominal prefix {o-} and various polite sentence particles) did indeed occur with much higher frequency in the speech of actresses as compared to speech of women in casual conversations. In sharp contrast, no significant differences were found in occurrences of nonstereotypical, nonconscious features (noun-phrase deletion, syntactic changes, and particle deletion). Shibamoto concluded that Japanese speakers are well aware of stereotyped features of female speech and manipulate their use to convey images of femininity (ibid.:48). But, as Shibamoto's study of friends' conversation demonstrated, nonconscious syntactic choices are also made by women and men in their casual communicative behavior to create and transmit messages of gender identity. The messages are linguistic in form but cultural in content.

Evidence indicates changes in usage of gender markers in speech of younger Japanese women. Although the normative reactions of many Japanese people continue to recognize gender-linked styles, actual behavior is not consistent with these images. In order to document young women's speech in informal contexts, Shigeko Okamoto (1995) analyzed tape recordings of dyadic conversations between female college students (ages 18 to 20) residing in Tokyo. The analysis centered on sentence-final particles, auxiliaries, and verb forms that are traditionally classified as "feminine" (used primarily by women), "masculine" (used by men), and "neutral" (used by women and men). The linguistic forms were further identified as "moderately" or "strongly" feminine or masculine. Okamoto found that all ten subjects employed neutral forms most. And eight of the ten used masculine forms more often than feminine forms (ibid.:303). Of the feminine forms used, the majority were "moderately feminine." And, significantly, most of the "strongly feminine" forms used were quotations of the speech of older women. Most of the masculine forms employed were "moderately masculine," although a few speakers used words or expressions perceived as "strongly masculine" or "vulgar" (ibid.:305). In another study, Okamoto and Shie Sato found that middle-aged women tended to use more "feminine" forms than did younger women (1992). Okamoto (1995) cites additional research by Midori Takasaki indicating that women in different occupations employed different levels of "feminine" (or polite) markers: Homemakers used more "feminine" speech than did students, and office workers used more markers of politeness than did professional or self-employed women (1995:307).

The use of "feminine" speech in Japan can be traced historically to the late nineteenth century during the period of state formation and centralization (Inoue 1994). Class and region also played a part in the growth of feminine speech. Its use was encouraged for women of the middle and upper classes in urban areas such as Tokyo. And it co-occurred with the standardization of the Japanese language.

As roles of Japanese women have become more varied and flexible, the emphasis on "feminine" speech has diminished. Young women's use of perceived "masculine" markers may serve to distinguish them from older women and foster solidarity as a group. And the fact that professional women use less "feminine" (polite or deferential) speech may serve both to "express power and to empower themselves" (Okamoto 1995:314). Change may also be taking place in men's use of gender markers. Styles of speaking and use of particles stereotypically identified as "feminine" occur in men's speech with greater frequency than in the past, possibly leading to "neutralization" of these markers. These facts make it clear that gender itself is not the sole contributor to speech styles. Rather, such factors as age, occupation, and class influence linguistic strategies that people employ.

Javanese

The language spoken in Java, an island in the Indonesian chain, contains complex indicators of politeness and deference. These markers occur in both women's and men's speech, but their use by each gender differs significantly. Of equal importance, gender-related usage is evaluated in distinct ways by men and women, raising a critical issue concerning the ability of groups of people to define their own or another's behavior.

Javanese culture contains conflicting notions of gender status. An egalitarian ideology stresses women's and men's autonomy. Women participate in work inside and outside the home with primary responsibilities for managing household income and for hosting social gatherings. An important nationwide reflection of one attitude toward gender is the fact that girls and boys are equally educated. However, other societal norms restrict women's actual participation in public life, as women do not usually become political or religious leaders, although they can occasionally function in place of their husbands (Smith-Hefner 1988:538–539). Javanese culture, then, gives some support for gender equality, but in practice inequality exists in certain areas of life.

The Javanese language has two speech levels, chosen by speakers to reflect their relationship with addressees. One is a familiar style called *ngoko*, used with intimates and people of lower status, and the other is a formal style called *kromo*, for speech to people who are unfamiliar, older, or of higher social status. In addition to this basic distinction, Javanese has some 250 to 300 markers indicating various degrees of honorific attitudes. One class of honorifics (*ki*) is used to "elevate the addressee" in relation to the speaker, and the other class (*ka*) "humbles" the speaker in relation to the addressee (ibid.:540). The two types combine with the familiar and formal speech styles in complex ways in order to express and transmit images of personal status.

In Javanese, gender inequality is reflected in word choices, in differential use of speech levels and honorifics, and in the interactional significance attached to such usage. One manifestation of unequal relationships between women and men is the pattern of address terms used by wives and husbands that indicates the lower status of wives. In Javanese households, a husband generally calls his wife either by her first name, a nickname, or the kinship term *khik* meaning "younger sibling." In contrast, wives address their husbands with the kin term *mas,* "older brother" (ibid.:541). Although Javanese husbands usually are older than their wives, this asymmetric expression of seniority is employed even by couples of similar ages who had addressed each other as equals before marriage, demonstrating that the marital relationship is symbolized as hierarchical. Additionally, wives are expected to speak to their husbands with styles replete with polite and deferential honorifics, whereas husbands use plainer, familiar forms of speech to their wives.

Nancy Smith-Hefner (1988) described a significant contrast in evaluations of women's speech styles given by the two genders. Javanese men interpret women's style as indicating their lower status within the family while women assert that their speech reflects politeness and refinement. As Smith-Hefner remarked, "It is very possible for speakers to interpret their own speech behavior in a given speech interaction as statusful, while the other interlocutor regards it as deferential" (ibid.:540–541). Accepting that women's evaluation of their own behavior is legitimate from their perspective, the question still arises as to why women speak in a polite and refined manner. One possible explanation derives from women's role in socializing children to speak in culturally appropriate styles reflecting a child's junior and subordinate status. Children must learn to use respectful speech to their elders and superiors, including fathers and older siblings. Mothers are the primary teachers of this style. They instruct children by using the desired speech, and the children model their own language after that of their mother (ibid.:542–543). This responsibility compels mothers to employ polite speaking styles. And because women's activities take place predominantly within their households, they are not likely to develop a wide range of speech styles.

Politeness can express several underlying cultural premises and, therefore, can have ambiguous meanings. Both Javanese men and women use polite speech, but they do so in different contexts. Although women employ polite *kromo* styles at home, men use elaborate *kromo* speech in other situations, particularly in public roles as officials or ceremonial leaders. Men, in fact, often develop skilled use of complex honorific markers in order to manipulate and reaffirm their status in personal interactions. Such skill is positively perceived by the community, further enhancing speakers' prestige. According to Smith-Hefner, intricate social messages are transmitted by men's polite speech (ibid.:548):

Humility is given a positive value in Javanese society, but there is a very different feel to an interaction in which the speaker is constrained to speak humbly or politely and one in which the speaker uses artful control of the language to signal linguistic skill and responsiveness to complex linguistic norms. Such speech may sound polite inasmuch as it respects language norms, even while subtly communicating the speaker's skill and status superiority. It is this ambiguity in the social message of the polite forms which renders them powerful. In any single speech interaction they may express deference on the one hand and refinement and power on the other. Deference here can hint—or even openly wink—at social superiority.

Use of polite and respectful language can be coercive in a social system that compels people to act in a deferential manner to their superiors. If a higher-status person speaks politely to someone of lower rank, the latter, in recognition of his actual lowly position, must use language that is even more respectful. "If social inferiors were to respond to a higher status interlocutor in a lower speech level than that with which they were addressed, they would be claiming in effect to be of a higher status than their interlocutor" (ibid.:549). Such behavior would demean one's own position by causing an affront to one's superior.

Javanese language and culture, then, contain complex connections between politeness and gender. In many cultures, where polite speech is most typical of women (e.g., American-Anglo societies, Japan), it is interpreted as a signal of deference and lower status. However, in other societies (e.g., Java), polite speech is manipulated by men to convey messages of power and superiority.

Malagasy

Malagasy is a Malayo-Polynesian language spoken in Madagascar, a large island in the Indian Ocean off the eastern coast of Africa. Studies of Malagasy speech usage reveal similarities to and differences from the Javanese example. Like Javanese, Malagasy has two types of speaking styles. One style is called *resaka*, an everyday or familiar form used in daily interactions, discussions, and informal talk. The other is *kabary*, used in rituals and formal secular situations. In fact, a specific situation becomes ceremonial by the use of *kabary* speech, as, for example, expressing thanks to a host or sympathy to mourners (Keenan 1974:126). Interrelated with the two speech styles are cultural norms that emphasize values of behaving and speaking in nonconfrontational and nonargumentative manners in most social interactions. Social reserve and dignity of speech are positively perceived by both men and women; direct and emotionally expressive language is disvalued.

Indirect speech is favored in everyday behavior, masking potentially unpleasant interactions. For example, commands are rarely issued with imperative constructions because these directly express speakers' authority. Instead, they are mitigated by several linguistic procedures, including use of the passive rather than active voice. Passives focus attention on patients (direct object) of desired actions rather than on agents (subject) and thereby mute the force of an order. Compare the following sentences (ibid.:132):

Active: *Manasa ny lamba amin 'ny savony.*
          Wash the clothes with the soap!

Passive: *Sasao ny lamba amin 'ny savony.*
          Have the clothes washed with the soap! (literally: have washed
          the clothes with the soap)

A directive can also be issued in "circumstantial" form in sentences with nouns denoting the instrument used in an activity. This usage highlights the instrument and further detracts from the action being commanded:

Circumstantial: *Anasao lamba ny savony.*
                  The soap is to be used to wash clothes! (literally: have-
                  washed-with clothes the soap)

Forms of indirection are typical of everyday *resaka* speech, but *kabary* is characterized by even more elaborate use of mitigated means for issuing directives, as well as for performing other speech acts, such as making requests and transmitting unpleasant news.

Gender separation becomes relevant in expectations of and approval/disapproval given to men's and women's behavior. In Malagasy culture, only men are expected to cultivate *kabary* speech. They use indirect styles in daily interactions and learn complex, polite ceremonial speech.

Kabary occasions involve ritualized dialogues between two speakers who competitively use elaborate linguistic and stylistic forms in order to garner audience approval and social prestige. One aspect of this competition is the right for each participant to criticize the other speaker. Because overt criticism is socially disvalued, subtle and indirect speech is used in these confrontations. Mitigated speech, instructive proverbs, and other forms of polite allusion and innuendo are often employed. Following is an example of the use of these strategies in *kabary* speech, quoting a speaker who is developing a criticism of his rival (ibid.:129):

> Thank you very much, sir. The first part of your talk has already been received in peace and happiness. I am in accordance and agreement with you on this, sir. You were given permission to speak and what you said gave me courage and strength. You said things skillfully but not pretentiously. You originate words but also recognize what is traditional. But as for myself I am not an originator of words at all but a borrower. I am more comfortable carrying the spade and basket. You, on the other hand, have smoothed out all faults in the speech; you have woven the holes together. You have shown respect to the elders and respect to the young as well. This is finished. But . . . (criticism begins).

Malagasy women are unable to participate in status-enhancing and socially valued *kabary* displays. Even more telling, they typically employ styles of everyday language that violate cultural norms of nonconfrontation. Women argue in public, criticize the behavior of others, and express anger and disapproval. Although these strategies are socially denigrated, women's freedom to engage in conflict openly is sometimes exploited by men who encourage women to speak for them.

When disputes arise or a man experiences an affront, his wife makes public accusations and criticisms on his behalf. All the while, the husband remains silent and seemingly aloof (ibid.:137–138). Keenan summarized Malagasy gender-related behavior as follows (ibid.:139):

> Women use one kind of power and men another. Women . . . discuss in detail the shameful behavior of others in daily gossip and speak openly of those who *mangala-baraka,* steal honor away from the family. They are associated with direct criticism and haggling in markets. They are able to put others on the spot, to confront others with possibly offensive information where men cannot or prefer not. Women tend to be direct and open in manner. Men tend to conduct themselves with discretion and subtlety. Women dominate situations where directness is called for. Men, on the other hand, dominate situations where indirectness is desirable.

However, if only difference were recognized by Malagasy culture, then a balance or complementarity in roles and powers would be conveyed. But such a potential balance is undermined by asymmetric evaluations given to gender styles. Men receive social rewards in their roles as *kabary* speakers. *Kabary* is associated with learning, skill, and artistry. It is further linked through ceremonial usage to the language and traditions of ancestors. Even in everyday situations, men's style is consistent with norms of indirection and subtlety of expression. In contrast, women's speech does not receive prestige by either gender. Although women's style is used to achieve important interactional goals, and is even exploited by men for these purposes, the speakers, that is, women, are disvalued through criticism of their language. Among the Malagasy, therefore, cultural models of gender are transmitted by evaluations of socially assigned speaking styles in a complex process. First, speech patterns are given differential social rewards, then each pattern is allocated to one or the other gender, and finally the constellation of gender, style, and prestige produces unequal images not only of what women and men do but also of what they are.

Kuna

A complex pattern of gender-differentiated communicative behavior exists among the Kuna, a native people of San Blas, Panama. Kuna society is basically egalitarian both in its social and political structures and in relationships between women and men. In theory, men and women can hold leadership roles in political and ritual activities, although in practice female leaders are rare. Kuna people conceptualize economic and social responsibilities of women and men as distinct yet complementary and harmonious. Men are expected to supply their families with food obtained from farming and hunting; women perform domestic labor, including food preparation, childcare, and other household duties. In addition, women's artistry in making *molas* (appliquéd cloth blouses) for market sale is highly prized and praised. These products are not only important in economic terms but also as valued symbols of Kuna ethnicity (Sherzer 1987:95, 101).

The traditional complementarity of gender roles is expressed in an excerpt from a ritual narrative (ibid.:108):

Rattlesnake says to his wife:
"For you I will go hunting.
For you I will kill an animal."
Rattlesnake's wife responds:
"You are going hunting for me.
You will kill an animal for me.
I will prepare your beverage for you."

Distinctions between women's and men's communicative behavior occur in speech genres associated with each. Some of these genres occur in public or ceremonial contexts, and others take place in private, familial settings. Each is typified by linguistic and topical characteristics that distinguish it from everyday speech. Men's genres include political oratory and ritual incantations. Two types of speaking occur at political gatherings: extemporaneous speeches and debates of community leaders and the formalized chanting of chiefs. These roles are nearly always held by men. Curing chants are performed by (usually) male specialists who gather medicines and administer them in rituals (ibid.:102–103).

There is some overlap between women's and men's speaking roles. Women hold public political gatherings too, mostly concerned with issues related to *mola* cooperatives. At these meetings, women make speeches, engage in debates, and express their opinions. Ritual speech is also performed by some women who recite curing chants taught to them by spirits in their dreams. But women's distinctive genres are lullabies and "tuneful weeping" chanted to dying and deceased relatives. These genres are similar in their focus on individual, family happenings (ibid.:102–105).

According to Joel Sherzer, the egalitarian and complementary division of labor in Kuna society is reflected in the division of speech genres generally performed by women or men. Although the genres are different, no single linguistic style is considered appropriate only to men or women. Each gender has occasion to employ elaborate, rhetorical styles replete with metaphor and symbolic allusions. Each also uses chanting and rhythmic patterns or tunes in certain contexts. Finally, both men and women speak directly and confidently when voicing their opinions (ibid.:110–111).

In Kuna society, women and men are expected to perform different but complementary economic and social duties, and they are versed in different but complementary speech genres. Gifted speakers, whether they be women or men, are equally praised.

Communicative behavior of Kuna people contrasts with that of the Malagasy or Javanese. Whereas the latter sharply differentiate between men's and women's stylistic traits, the former make no absolute separation of linguistic style. In addition, unlike the Malagasy and Javanese, the Kuna do not give more or less favorable evaluations to speech of women or men. Both are highly regarded. It is tempting to conclude that attitudes toward speech and gender are related to the social structure of these societies. Hierarchical organization of status and gender relations among the Malagasy and Javanese is reflected in negative evaluations of women's speech and/or denial of women's access to status-enhancing styles that instead are reserved only for men. In contrast, the egalitarian social system of the Kuna is reflected in positive evaluations and prestige given to skilled verbal performers of both genders.

Samoan

Samoan is a Malayo-Polynesian language spoken by inhabitants of Samoa, a group of islands in the South Pacific. In Samoan society, language and gender are interrelated with the system of social stratification. Differences in social rank are manifested by named titles (*matai*) that can be assumed by either men or women, although in practice most are held by men. Titles are inherited through a system of ambilineal descent, that is, inheritance from either one's father or mother. However, there is a preference for inheritance through fathers. Samoan society recognizes the autonomy of both women and men in theory, but in practice married women are usually subordinate to their husbands. Men's status is dependent on whether they are titled, and if so, on which of the many possible titles they hold. A woman's status is usually measured by the position of her father and, after marriage, her husband. The system of social rank can affect relations between husband and wife if the latter is titled because *matai* women have the same social prerogatives as do men. In addition, married women, whether titled or not, exert some control over their own brothers and participate in making decisions about granting titles within their kinship group.

Age is another important determinant of social status and behavior in Samoan society. Younger people, particularly if untitled, must show deference in speech and demeanor to their elders both within their families and the wider community. The younger person in any interaction is expected to be more attentive to the needs of the older and more accommodating in speech and actions. These norms are learned early in one's family and are demonstrated in hierarchical patterns among siblings.

In order to investigate interconnections among gender, status, and linguistic style, Elinor Ochs (1987) recorded speech of inhabitants of the Samoan village of Falefa, including samples from men and women of various ages and social ranks. She focused on usage of "affect pronouns," pronouns that express affect or attitudes of speakers. The Samoan language contrasts neutral forms for first person as subject, object, and possessor with corresponding affect markers. Affect pronouns for first person are employed by speakers in order to elicit sympathy for oneself from addressees. Neutral forms mean "I, me, my," whereas affect pronouns have meanings such as "poor I, poor me, poor my" (Ochs 1987:53). Affect pronouns replace the final glottal stop + vowel sequence of neutral words with the segment -*ta*, as in *lo²u* → lota "my" (for possession of singular, specific objects) or *ni o²u* →

ni ota "my" (for possession of plural, nonspecific objects). Determiners can also be marked for positive affect, expressing the speaker's sympathy for referents or addressees, for example, *le, se* ("the, a") → *si* ("the dear, a dear"). Additionally, affect can be expressed by various kinds of sentence particles, interjections, and vocabulary choices for verbs and adjectives.

Ochs recorded villagers' conversations containing personal narratives that recount events involving oneself and others. She measured uses of positive, sympathetic affect markers by speakers and also noted listeners' responses, for example, whether they reacted with sympathy toward speaker and referent. Genders, ages, and ranks of narrator-listener pairs in the sample were as follows: untitled young men in their 20s, *matai* men in their 40s and 50s, and untitled women at least 50 years old. These women were all married to titled men (ibid.:60). Ochs found that among narrators, untitled young men used the most affect forms. Age and status, then, surfaced as more important determinants of style than did gender. In contrast, as listeners, both young untitled men and older women employed a high proportion of affect markers, and titled older men expressed least sympathy.

For men, youthful age and lowly rank are consistently reflected in expressions of sympathy toward referents and the elicitation of sympathy for oneself. As listeners, the same social group responds most often with positive affect when sympathy is expressed by other narrators. Older, high-status men demonstrate least affect. Elder women's communicative behavior is more complex, tending to express neutrality as speakers but responding with sympathy to the speech of others.

Explanations for the patterns shown by Samoans may derive from the system of social status. Perhaps elder titled men do not need to employ sympathy markers in their narratives because their high status automatically makes addressees respond favorably to them. In contrast, young men use affect forms as speakers to obtain addressees' empathy. And as listeners, they accommodate to elders by their sympathetic replies. Finally, elder women may show sympathy to others as part of politeness strategies.

The following tables show percentages of narrators' and listeners' use of targeted features. The tables note various classes of affect markers (address terms, sympathy pronouns, interjections, etc.). Groups of narrators are labeled as I

Expression of Sympathy in Narrator's Speech

Affect Form	I	II	III
Address terms	20.8%	2%	0%
Inclusive we	0	2	0
Sympathy lst person	2.6	0	1.4
Symp. determiner	9.1	2	2.7
Symp. referent	10.4	2	1.4
Symp. adj./verb	9.1	2	5.4
Particles	15.6	26	21.2
Interjections	0	0	0.7
Total	67.5%	36%	32.9%

Expression of Sympathy in Listener's Speech

Affect Form	I	II	III
Address terms	6.1%	0%	0%
Symp. determiner	3.0	0	6.8
Symp. referent	6.1	0	1.7
Symp. adj./verb	12.1	2.3	10.2
Particles	33.3	23.3	30.5
Interjections	3.0	4.7	6.8
Agreement (yes/right)	9.1	2.3	5.1
Repetition/paraphrase of narration	18.2	9.3	22.0
Total	90.9%	41.9%	83.1%

(untitled young men), II (titled older men), and III (untitled women married to titled men) (Ochs 1987:61, 63).

Unfortunately Ochs's data do not indicate the composition of each narrator/listener pair, so it is not possible to determine whether the age or gender of the addressee influences the speaker's use of affect markers. Also absent were reports of the speech styles of young women. Had these been included, they might have shown more fully the impact of age and gender on communicative behavior.

IMAGES OF GENDER IN LINGUISTIC FORM

Many languages display images of gender in words and grammar, although the specific linguistic forms that express these images obviously vary. In this section we sample some evidence from a number of languages.

French

French contains a singular pronoun, *on*, that is not marked for gender. It occurs in sentences with indefinite or generic subjects, such as:

Ici *on* parle français.
One, they, people speak French here.

Because French possessive pronouns (comparable to "his" and "her") agree in grammatical gender with possessed nouns rather than sex of possessors, the English problem of using the masculine form "his" or the neutral "his or her" or "their" does not arise. However, even though French expresses neutrality in singular pronouns, bias in favor of males surfaces in plurals. Whereas English has one plural third-person pronoun ("they"), not marked for gender, French has two, distinguishing female and male aggregates, *elles* and *ils,* respectively. Inequality occurs when reference is made to mixed-sex groups. *Elles* is used only if all members are female; *ils* occurs for all-male or male/female groups. Therefore, presence of even one male is enough to tip the semantic balance toward the masculine pronoun.

German

The German language classifies nouns as masculine, feminine, or neuter and marks articles, adjectives, and verbs to agree with the gender of nouns. Whereas grammatically feminine nouns for persons refer only to females, some masculine nouns can be used for either males or females. The following masculine nouns may have male or female referents (Hellinger 1989:275):

der Bürgen	citizen
der Wähler	voter
der Kund	customer

Feminine subjects can co-occur with masculine nouns, but masculine subjects never co-occur with feminine nouns. For example, one can say:

"He/She is a second Einstein."
Er/Sie ist ein zweiter Einstein.

but one cannot say:

*"He is a second Marie Curie."
Er ist eine zweite Marie Curie.

Some masculine nouns can be transformed by feminizing suffixes to refer to females—for example, *der Lehrer* "the teacher" → *die Lehrerin* "the woman teacher" (ibid.:276). The unmarked words symbolize men as neutral or expected exemplars, whereas the marked feminine words symbolize women as derivative or unusual.

Finally, in the few cases where feminine nouns are used for men, they take on derogatory meanings. The words *die Memme, die Tucke,* and *die Tunte,* all meaning "coward," are used as insults in referring to homosexuals (ibid.:275).

Spanish

In some pairs of words having male/female counterparts, the Spanish language expresses sexual meanings for females. Compare the following words and their meanings (Hellinger 1989:277, 284–285):

Masculine	*Feminine*
un reo: "a criminal"	*una rea:* "an impoverished prostitute"
el inocente: "an innocent person"	*la inocente:* "a virgin"
un doncel: "a young nobleman"	*una doncella:* "a virgin"

In addition, when feminine suffixes are added to some masculine occupational terms, the derived word does not refer to a woman of that profession but rather to a wife (ibid.:285):

el médico "doctor"
la médica "doctor's wife"

Both the German and Spanish examples demonstrate a similar theme: Men are neutral, generic, typical persons, whereas women are derived, secondary, or restricted.

Russian

Analysis of the meanings of male/female kinship terms in Russian also shows a restricted representation of females. Roots that occur in kin terms can be extended to name other people or entities, but different patterns obtain for female and male forms. Derivations from female bases generally refer to domesticity and/or sexuality, whereas those derived from male bases have wider "semantic space," referring to activities or qualities of a more social character (Wobst 1981:42–43). And female words tend to acquire negative connotations, most strongly so when applied to men, whereas male terms are positive even when applied to women. For example, roots for "grandmother," *bab-*, and "grandfather," *dyed-*, can both be extended to nonkin. (Note that in reference to one's grandmother, the root word *baba* is never used; rather, it always appears with a diminutive suffix in *babushka*.) Words derived from *bab-* have meanings including "old woman," "wife" (in slang), and scornfully, "stout or loutish woman." Words with *dyed-*, on the other hand, are "ancestors" or "village elders" (ibid.:36–38).

The mother/father pair, *mat-/otyets-* also is extended. Words with *mat-* include "maternity" and "motherhood," in positive tone but others can be applied to males as terms of abuse. Words derived from *otyets* mean "protector, benefactor, leader, founder, and ancestors" (ibid.:38–39).

Finally, the roots for "sister," *syestr-*, and "brother," *brat-*, demonstrate now-familiar patterns. *Syestr-* has limited use, appearing only as a kin term and in restricted contexts as a female friend. In contrast, *brat-* has rich connotations, including "companionship, friendship, someone who loves people as brothers" (comparable forms in English are "brotherhood, brotherly love"). In addition, the root *brat-* can combine with a feminine suffix and be used to refer positively to females, as in expressions for "a sister who is a friend" or a greeting to any woman (ibid.).

Mohawk

In contrast to European languages that restrict feminine meanings, the Mohawk language elaborates feminine semantics. In Mohawk, there are three third-person singular pronoun markers for subjects, occurring as prefixes in verbs. One prefix, {*la-*}, is used exclusively for males (human and animal); another, {*ka-*}, denotes female animals, some female humans, and all inanimate objects; and a third, {*ye-*}, refers to some female humans and all indefinite or generalized persons (Bonvillain 1973:85–87). (Note that the use of {*ye-*} for indefinite or generic persons differs from formal English, where "he" is supposedly the "proper" pronoun for generic persons; see Chapter 7.) The following is a set of Mohawk verbs with human subjects:

layʌ́thos	he's planting it
kayʌ́thos	she's planting it
yeyʌ́thos	she's planting it, someone's planting it

Pronoun prefixes for human females are semantically complex. Speakers can use either {ka-} or {ye-}, the choice depending on context, attitude, and relationship to addressee. Most people employ {ye-} to refer to older women, relatives, and/or any woman toward whom the speaker has a feeling of respect or admiration. {Ka-} is used more often as either a form neutral for attitude or actually negative in affect.

Mohawk speakers use these prefixes somewhat idiosyncratically, as there are no absolute grammatical rules governing their occurrence. Alternatives are selected for personal and contextual reasons. This seems not to have always been the case. Samples of Mohawk spoken in the early twentieth century indicate a different, presumably traditional, pattern in which the semantics of feminine prefixes included a focus on female reproductive capacities. The prefix {ye-} was evidently used to refer to both young girls and older women, whereas {ka-} was selected for women in their childbearing years. The Mohawk language, then, directly symbolized the distinctiveness of women's ability to reproduce.

Remembering that the significance of linguistic form can be understood in specific contexts of culture, Mohawk emphasis on reproduction as expressed by the prefixes was a positive reflection of women's status. The Mohawk kinship system is based on matrilineal clans (i.e., descent traced through women). In addition to their prominence in kinship groups, women had important economic roles in traditional Mohawk culture. They were food producers, providing their families with basic crops of corn, beans, and squash. These crops are symbolized as female, referred to as "The Three Sisters" or "Our Life Supporters." In Mohawk mythology, they are derived from the body of a female mythic personage. Given religious and economic concerns with fertility of the land, kinship groups, and the Mohawk Nation itself, special note of women's childbearing role reflected the acknowledged contributions of women to society.

Meanings of {ye-} and {ka-} have changed, the former now employed to mark respect or positive feeling toward a female, probably as a result of its traditional use for elder women. Although some of the meanings of feminine pronouns have shifted, linguistic attention to females and the use of {ye-} to mark indefinite or generic person can be interpreted as continuing a valued symbolization of women in Mohawk culture.

Japanese

In Japanese, gender inequality within the family is revealed by forms of address employed between spouses and by words used to refer to one's spouse. Husbands typically address their wives by first name or by either of two second-person pronouns: *omae* and *kimi*. *Omae* is the pronoun generally used by status superiors to addressees of lower status; *kimi* is used to subordinates or intimates but not to superiors (Lee 1976:993). In contrast, if a wife addresses her husband by his first name, she adds the honorific suffix *-san*. In addition, she employs the second-person pronoun *anata*, which is used by lower-status people to higher-status addressees (ibid.:996–997).

Differential usage of names and second-person pronouns, therefore, carries symbolic messages of status. A woman addresses her husband with honorifics and with pronouns that indicate her lower status, whereas a man uses a familiar, plain form of address and a pronoun indicating his higher position. Pronouns used by men and women to their spouses are also employed to other interlocutors. Men choose pronoun usage depending on status relationships: *omae* to inferiors, *kimi* to inferiors or equals, and *anata* to superiors. Women generally address all interlocutors with *anata*, thus symbolizing women's social subordination (Shibamoto 1987:29).

In addition to personal names and pronouns, spouses can address each other with parental kin terms, for example, *otoosan* "father" and *okaasan* "mother." Women use *otoosan* to their husbands more often than men use *okaasan* to their wives (ibid.). The use of parent terminology to spouses relates to cultural meanings of seniority and authority, two critical components of inequality in Japanese society. Women are more likely to directly express the elevated position of their husbands than men are to employ symbolically respectful terms for their wives.

In addition to distinctions in spousal address, Japanese patterns for referring to one's spouse indicate gender differentiation as well. For referring to his wife, a man has a number of options (Lee 1976:993–995):

kanai	(derived from *ka* "home, family, house" + *nai* "inside")
tuma	(also meaning "garnishing vegetable served with raw fish; side plank supporting the main part of a roof")
nyoboo	("assistant, secondary person")
gusai	("stupid wife")
uti no yatu	(derived from *uti* "my home" + *no* "of" + *yatu* "fellow")

According to Motoko Lee, these words and expressions connote a secondary person, restricted to the home or participating in a subsidiary capacity. *Gusai*, "stupid wife," is employed to humble a speaker when conversing with someone of higher status. Its use is not meant to insult the speaker's wife but, rather, to honor the addressee by demeaning a person (wife) associated with the speaker (ibid.:995). *Uti no yatu* is an impolite or informal reference to a person of lower status.

Japanese wives can refer to husbands with the expression *uti no hito*, literally "person of my house." This phrase carries polite meaning, used by a lower-status speaker to label a superior. Wives also refer to their husbands as *shujin*, "master." Finally, Lee reported two humorous words used by women: *teishu*, "master of my house," and *yakoroku*, "my lodger." She stated that these words have sarcastic implications but did not specify the contexts of their use (ibid.:998).

Taken as a group, the differentiated pronouns, nouns, and expressions used by Japanese wives and husbands clearly demonstrate gender inequality, directly symbolizing the subordinate status of women.

SUMMARY

Because men and women are socially distinguished in all cultures, contrasts in some of their communicative behavior presumably occur everywhere. But degrees of difference and specific linguistic patterns that display gender distinctions vary cross-culturally. In some languages, rules of gender-exclusive forms prevail, leading to stable divergences between women and men. However, a more widespread pattern is that of preferences for linguistic alternatives, demonstrated through frequencies in use of a range of stylistic variants, including sounds, words, and grammatical constructions.

The existence of differences in men's and women's speech calls for explanations based on the social roles of women and men and the extent of inequality in their relationships. In societies where men have more prestige and rights than women, language and style are used to underscore male privilege. In societies where gender equality exists, communicative behavior and meanings accord value and worth to both genders. Language is thus revealed as a partner in generating cultural models of females and males. It contains images of their "proper" status and behavior by both reflecting in form and reinforcing through use a culture's entrenched symbols of gender.

REFERENCES

BODINE, ANN. 1975. Sex differentiation in language. In *Language and Sex,* ed. B. Thorne and N. Henley. Rowley, MA: Newbury, pp. 130–151.

BOGORAS, WALDEMAR. 1922. Chukchee. In *Handbook of American Indian Languages.* Bulletin No. 40, part 2. Washington, DC: Bureau of American Ethnology, pp. 631–903.

BONVILLAIN, NANCY. 1973. *A Grammar of Akwesasne Mohawk.* Mercury Series No. 8. Ottawa: National Museum of Canada.

BROWN, PENELOPE, AND STEPHEN LEVINSON. 1987. *Politeness: Some Universals in Language Usage.* New York: Cambridge University Press.

CLARK, SCOTT. 1996. Personal communication.

EKKA, FRANCIS. 1972. Men's and women's speech in Kũṛux. *Linguistics* 81:25–31.

FLANNERY, REGINA. 1946. Men's and women's speech in Gros Ventre. *International Journal of American Linguistics* 12:133–135.

GATSCHET, ALBERT. 1884. *A Migration Legend of the Creek Indians.* Philadelphia: Brinton.

HAAS, MARY. 1944. Men's and women's speech in Koasati. *Language* 20:142–149.

HELLINGER, MARLIS. 1989. Revising the patriarchal paradigm: Language change and feminist language policies. In *Language, Power and Ideology,* ed. R. Wodak. Philadelphia: John Benjamins, pp. 273–288.

INOUE, MIYAKO. 1994. Gender and linguistic modernization: A historical account of the birth of Japanese women's language. In *Cultural Performances: Proceedings of the Third Berkeley Women and Language Conference,* ed. M. Bucholtz et al. Berkeley: University of California, Berkeley Women and Language Group, pp. 322–333.

JESPERSEN, OTTO. 1922. *Language: Its Nature, Development and Origins.* London: Allen and Unwin.

KEENAN, ELINOR OCHS. 1974. Normmakers and norm-breakers: Uses of speech by men and women in a Malagasy community. In *Explorations in the Ethnography of Speaking,* ed. R. Bauman and J. Sherzer. New York: Cambridge University Press, pp. 125–143.

LEE, MOTOKO. 1976. The married woman's status and role in Japanese: An exploratory sociolinguistic study. *Signs* 1:991–999.

OCHS, ELINOR. 1987. The impact of stratification and socialization on men's and women's speech in Western Samoa. In *Language, Gender and Sex in Comparative Perspective,* ed. S. Phillips, S. Steele, and C. Tanz. New York: Cambridge University Press, pp. 50–70.

OKAMOTO, SHIGEKO. 1995. "Tasteless" Japanese: Less "feminine" speech among young Japanese women. In *Gender Articulated: Language and the Socially Constructed Self,* ed. K. Hall and M. Bucholtz. New York: Routledge, pp. 297–325.

OKAMOTO, SHIGEKO, AND SHIE SATO. 1992. Less feminine speech among young Japanese females. In *Cultural Performances: Proceedings of the Third Berkeley Women and Language Conference,* ed. M. Bucholtz et al. Berkeley: University of California, Berkeley Women and Language Group, pp. 478–488.

SAPIR, EDWARD. 1929. Male and female forms of speech in Yana. Reprinted in *Selected Writings of Edward Sapir* (1949), ed. D. Mandelbaum. Berkeley: University of California Press, pp. 206–212.

SHERZER, JOEL. 1987. A diversity of voices: Men's and women's speech in ethnographic perspective. In *Language, Gender and Sex in Comparative Perspective,* ed. S. Philips, S. Steele, and C. Tanz. New York: Cambridge University Press, pp. 95–120.

SHIBAMOTO, JANET. 1987. The womanly woman: Manipulation of stereotypical and non-stereotypical features of Japanese women's speech. In *Language, Gender and Sex in Comparative Perspective,* ed. S. Philips, S. Steele, and C. Tanz. New York: Cambridge University Press, pp. 26–49.

SMITH-HEFNER, NANCY. 1988. Women and politeness: The Javanese example. *Language in Society* 17:535–554.

TRECHTER, SARA, AND ELI JAMES. 1994. "Appropriate" gendered speech in Lakhota society. In *Cultural Performances: Proceedings of the Third Berkeley Women and Language Conference,* ed. M. Bucholtz et al. Berkeley: University of California, Berkeley Women and Language Group, pp. 746–756.

WOBST, SUSAN. 1981. Male and female reference in semantic space in Russian. *Russian Language Journal* 35:35–44.

9

Learning Language

ADULT: Adam, say what I say: Where can I put them?

ADAM (3 years old):   Where I can put them?

Adam, a young child learning English, demonstrates a remarkable capacity to acquire language. He accomplishes this, as do all children, not without problems and not in one moment but over a period of years, advancing through stages of linguistic, cognitive, and social development.

Let us first try to understand the complex task facing every human being in the early months and years of their lives. An infant is surrounded by people who make gestures, movements, and noise. The child becomes aware of distinctions between herself and others and develops desires to interact with those others. In some nonconscious manner, she gradually grasps the notion that the behaviors and noises that people make have meaning, that they are purposeful and useful in social interactions. This, in itself, is a profound discovery, made once by each of the billions of people who have ever lived. But this discovery leads to an enormous problem of deciphering the code, of figuring out meanings expressed through sounds and gestures. Young children cannot consult dictionaries or grammar books; they have to construct their own set of rules. In a sense, children are the best linguists, analyzing an unknown language and discovering its grammar based solely on evidence presented by experience.

The process of learning is multifaceted. Children develop knowledge of their language through unfolding and maturing cognitive and linguistic abilities internal to themselves while they are helped by their parents or caregivers, who, in various ways, provide social contexts where these abilities become focused and meaningful. In this chapter we identify linguistic processes of learning in English and then consider comparative data from other types of linguistic systems. Finally, we review some studies of instructional techniques that adults employ to guide children in learning language.

Q1 What are some ideas on how children develop their linguistic ability?

ACQUISITION OF LANGUAGE

A1

Development of linguistic ability is linked to maturation of cognitive processes. It is based on growth of the capacity for symbolic representation, resulting in awareness that sounds that are abstract and arbitrary can be used to stand for both present and absent objects and activities. Increased ability to remember experiences and to associate them with present and future events is also critical to a child's language acquisition. Additionally, language implies an understanding of causality, realizing that people and objects can affect others through their actions or states. Children express relations between objects, people, and/or activities; they do not merely compile a catalog of labels. Finally, interactions with other people lead to a child's understanding that language can be used to express personal attitudes and goals.

Linguistic discovery and creativity are universal processes, inherent in human experience. Children learn language primarily through their own cognitive efforts utilizing the genetic potential that is part of their human endowment. Noam Chomsky has stated that a fundamental question in the study of language is to account for a "speaker's ability to produce and understand instantly new sentences that are not similar to those previously heard. . . . It seems plain that language acquisition is based on the child's discovery of what from a formal point of view is a deep and abstract theory—a generative grammar of his/her language" (1965:57–58). And Chomsky asserted that because all children, regardless of intelligence, motivation, or emotions, learn language, "it seems reasonable to suppose that a child cannot help constructing a particular sort of grammar to account for the data presented. . . . Thus, it may be that the general features of language structure reflect the general character of one's capacity to acquire knowledge—one's innate ideas and innate principles" (ibid.:59).

Speech Sounds

Q2 What must children first realize when acquiring language?

The first step in acquiring language is learning to differentiate and produce sounds occurring in one's language. Children must realize that the stream of noise they *A2* hear is made up of discrete, individual sounds combined in a significant linear order. Then they must learn to control muscular movements in their throat and mouth in order to produce those sounds with consistency so that they are understood by addressees. Before children actually begin to speak, to say words, they go through a period of practicing, or babbling, consonant-like and vowel-like articulations. During the first four months of life, infants demonstrate a rapid increase in the number of sounds that they produce. After the fourth month, there is an abrupt drop in rates of change; relatively few new sounds are introduced into their

Why does a child's expansion of sounds stop by the time he/she turns 1? Q3

A3

repertory. Finally, once a child begins the actual speaking process, normally by the age of 1 year, expansion of sounds stops altogether (McNeill 1987:132). From this point onward, children focus attention on the sounds that are significant in their language. They learn to control their production, make appropriate phonemic contrasts, and follow allophonic patterning.

In addition to forming consonants and vowels, speakers must learn intonational contours specific to their language and follow normative patterns of pitch and rhythm. These are evidently learned quite early. Infants as young as 5 months are sensitive to intonational changes and are able to produce language-appropriate contours in their own babbling (Weir 1966:155–157).

Cross-linguistic studies provide evidence for some universal sequences in acquiring sound systems. Front consonants /p/ and /m/ and the back vowel /a/ are the first to appear in spoken words, although other sounds (back consonants and front vowels) continue to be present in contemporaneous nonspeech babbling. Roman Jakobson (1941) postulated a universal order of differentiation of sounds beginning with a distinction between consonant /p/ and vowel /a/. These two represent extremes of articulation: /p/ is a voiceless stop consonant, formed in the front of the mouth, with complete closure of the vocal channel; /a/ is a voiced vowel, formed in the back of the mouth, characterized by complete opening of the vocal tract. After this fundamental contrast, a child gradually differentiates sounds to fill in articulatory space and/or add complexities in manners of articulation. According to Jakobson and Halle (1956), the first consonantal distinction results from contrast between oral and nasal sounds, that is, oral /p/ and nasal /m/. The next change involves labial/dental differentiation, leading to addition of /t/ to a child's inventory. The first vocalic distinction results from contrasting an open back sound /a/ with a closed, high front vowel /i/. Then distinctions are made in dimensions of frontness/backness (e.g., /i/ and /u/) or in height (e.g., /i/, /e/, and /a/) (ibid.:38–41).

This universal pattern of differentiation explains why children's first words are often made up of sequences like "mama, papa, tata." And it may provide insight into the common, worldwide occurrence of consonants /p, m, t/ in words for "mother" and "father," particularly in address forms. Because parents are the earliest significant people in a baby's universe, it is linguistically and cognitively appropriate to name them with sounds that a baby can most easily produce.

Although children eventually learn all the sounds employed in their language, some sounds present relatively greater difficulty. Consonants requiring more control of muscular movements and timing, such as /θ, ð, s, and r/, are acquired later than simpler sounds such as /p, t, or m/ (Fry 1966:194).

One-Word Utterances

Children are clearly able to understand language before they themselves start to speak. *Passive language* is demonstrated by the fact that children respond appropriately to commands and suggestions made by others. They comply with directives given to them in more complex structures than they themselves are able to produce (Sachs and Truswell 1976). (Although adults do not remember their earliest childhood learning experiences, comprehension of language in advance of performance abilities is familiar to anyone acquiring a second, or "foreign," language. We can all understand native speakers or read textbooks long before we are able to remember words or construct grammatical forms.)

Usually by the end of their first year, children begin to speak single words. These utterances are *holophrastic;* that is, each word expresses broad semantic and contextual meanings. Because earliest utterances are functionally complex, they can only be understood in the context of a child's experience. Goals expressed through children's speech emanate from the interaction of a child with objects and persons in his environment. Children have desires for others to attend to their needs and wants (imperative function), relate emotional states (expressive function), and name objects or people with whom they interact (referential function). Of course, each spoken word may serve several purposes simultaneously.

Studies of holophrastic utterances demonstrate that each word has a complex semantic scope. Many of a child's earliest words are associated with ritualized interactions, as saying "hi" or "bye-bye," or express desires that caregivers can fulfill, as "up," "down," and other demands and refusals (Greenfield and Smith 1976:70). Even young children know that speaking is a human strategy for achieving personal and social goals.

The following table presents data from Patricia Greenfield and J. H. Smith (1976), noting onsets of each semantic function, marking the age at which it first occurred in the speech of one child (age given in months and days), and providing linguistic forms and behavioral contexts.

Onset of Semantic Functions in a Child's One-Word Utterances

Semantic Function	Age	Instance
Performative	7 (22)	*hi*, accompaniment to waving
Performative object	8 (12)	*dada*, looking at father
Volition	11 (24)	*nana*, turning away from stairs in response to mother's "no"
Dative	11 (28)	*dada*, offering bottle to father
Object	13 (0)	*ba(ll)*, having just thrown ball
Agent	13 (3)	*daddy*, hearing father come in door and start up steps
Action or state of agent	13 (16)	*up*, reaching up, in answer to question, Do you want to get up?
Action or state of object	14 (6)	*down*, having just thrown something down
Object associated with another object or location	14 (29)	*caca* (cracker, cookie), pointing to door to next room where cookies are kept
Location	15 (20)	*bo(x)*, putting crayon in box
Animate being associated with object/location	15 (29)	*fishy*, pointing to empty fish tank
Modification of event	ca.18 (1)	*again*, when he wants someone to do something for him again

Two-Word Grammars

[handwritten: Q4 How are utterances one word different than two-word grammars?]

Appearance of two-word combinations marks the beginning of true grammatical constructions. This critical advance is normally made by a child's second year, usually by 18 months. It depends on cognitive growth, learning to differentiate words within classes, and recognizing that sequential ordering of words has meaning. Children realize that grammatical relations must be overtly expressed. This is another remarkable insight made independently by every individual. *[handwritten: A4]*

Emergence of two-word grammars and their continual expansion and refinement indicate a change in the character of a child's thinking. In David McNeill's terms, young children's thought is first *global* and *imagistic* and then becomes *syntactic*. Language acquisition basically involves *unpacking* images through syntactic order. "Unpacking these images into word and morpheme segments and simple linearizations of words are the first steps of language learning at ages one to two years. Children at this age are learning how to think syntactically" (1987:254). The next stage is equally significant: developing abilities to synthesize two kinds of thought, imagistic and syntactic. This kind of thinking "consists of a synthesis in which images are subdivided and linearized without losing sight of the global whole. Thinking in language is not simply subdividing into segments. . . . The synthesis of global and syntactic thinking that we observe in each act of speaking draws on this new form of thinking; and this synthesis appears in the earliest stages of linguistic development" (ibid.:255). *[handwritten: A4]*

McNeill suggested an adaptive advantage in human evolution offered by a synthesis of imagistic and syntactic thinking that may have accounted for the development of human language. "[T]hinking in terms of images that are synthesized with linearly arranged segments of the image—a syntax—could confer adaptive advantages [because] it creates, not a narrow linguistic capacity, but a form of thinking that is necessary for culture and a mechanism for the brain's storage of cultural information" (ibid.:257).

Expressing, or unpacking, experience into linguistic form is a creative process both syntactically and semantically. Children grasp the critical meaning of word order and also understand meanings contained in words themselves. They use this awareness in forming new words and constructions and in comprehending the speech of others.

Research concerned with language in the two-word stage reveals a consistent distinction between two classes of words: a "pivot" class and an "open" class, terms introduced by Martin Braine (1963). The *pivot* category contains a few words used with high frequency in combination with items from the open category. Types of words often occurring as pivots are ritualized greetings or comments (bye-bye, all-gone), demonstratives (this, that), locatives (here, there), possessives (my), and adjectives. The *open* class generally consists of nouns and verbs with which a child communicates his or her referential, imperative, or expressive intentions. Possible two-word constructions consist of combining either two items from the open class or a pivot + an open word. Two pivot words do not co-occur as a complete utterance. This fact gives evidence of a child's developing grammar, involving notions of syntactic restrictions. The following table provides some examples of pivot/open co-occurrences from studies of three different children (McNeill 1966:22).

Pivot and Open Classes from Three Studies of Child Language

Study I		Study II		Study III	
Pivot	Open	Pivot	Open	Pivot	Open
	boy		Adam		arm
	sock		Becky		baby
all-gone	boat	my	boot		dolly's
bye-bye	fan	that	coat		pretty
big	milk	two	coffee	this	yellow
more	plane	a	knee	that	come
pretty	shoe	the	man		doed
my	vitamins	big	Mommy		other
see	hot	green	nut		baby
night-	Mommy	poor	sock	the	dolly's
night	Daddy	wet	stool	a	pretty
hi		dirty	Tinkertoy		yellow
		fresh			arm
		pretty			baby
				here	dolly's
				there	pretty
					yellow

Pivot and open categories are found in many languages with different surface and syntactic characteristics. Thus they appear to reflect a stage in universal cognitive development. Samples are given in Figure 9.1 of two-word sentences from several languages: three Indo-European languages (English, German, and Russian) and three unrelated languages, Finnish, Luo (spoken in Kenya), and Samoan.

Even within restrictions of two-word sequences, children can express varied relations between people, objects, and actions. Although children's speech contains only a limited number of words, young speakers can express complex propositions and intentions. For example, the recorded utterances below are the speech of a young girl (18 months old) in contexts of giving and/or receiving objects (Antinucci and Parisi 1973). The experience of giving/receiving involves several underlying semantic components and their interrelations: an action, an agent performing the act, an object being transferred, and a recipient. The girl's utterances express various combinations of these critical components:

Action: *Give* (giving something to her mother)
Object: *Water* (asking her mother for some water)
Recipient: *To me* (asking for something)
Recipient + object: *To me candies* (asking for candies)
Action + object: *Give ball* (asking for a ball)
Action + actor: *Give mommy* (asking for something from mother)
Recipient + action: *Mommy give* (giving something to mother)

Function of Utterance	English	German	Russian	Finnish	Luo	Samoan
LOCATE, NAME	there book that car see doggie	*buch da* [book there] *gukuk wauwau* [see doggie]	*Tosya tam* [Tosya there]	*tuossa Rina* [there Rina] *vetiä siinä* [water there]	*en saa* [it clock] *ma wendo* [this visitor]	*Keith lea* [Keith there]
DEMAND, DESIRE	more milk give candy want gum	*mehr milch* [more milk] *bitte apfel* [please apple]	*yeshchë moloko* [more milk] *day chasy* [give watch]	*anna Rina* [give Rina]	*miya tamtam* [give-me candy] *adway cham* [I-want food]	*mai pepe* [give doll] *fia moe* [want sleep]
NEGATE[1]	no wet no wash not hungry allgone milk	*nicht blasen* [not blow] *kaffee nein* [coffee no]	*vody net* [water no] *gus' tyu-tyu* [goose gone]	*ei susi* [not wolf] *enää pipi* [anymore sore]	*beda onge* [my-slasher absent]	*le 'ai* [not eat] *uma mea* [allgone thing]
DESCRIBE EVENT OR SITUATION[2]	Bambi go mail come hit ball block fall baby highchair	*puppe kommt* [doll comes] *tiktak hängt* [clock hangs] *sofa sitzen* [sofa sit] *messer schneiden* [cut knife]	*mama prua* [mama walk] *papa bay-bay* [papa sleep] *korka upala* [crust fell] *nashla yaichko* [found egg] *baba kreslo* [grandma armchair]	*Seppo putoo* [Seppo fall] *talli 'bm-bm'* [garage 'car']	*chungu biro* [European comes] *odhi skul* [he-went school] *omoyo oduma* [she-dries maize]	*pa'u pepe* [fall doll] *tapale 'oe* [hit you] *tu'u lalo* [put down]

(continued)

FIGURE 9.1. Functions of Two-word Sentences in Child Speech. (Slobin 1979:8–87)

Function of Utterance	English	German	Russian	Finnish	Luo	Samoan
INDICATE POSSESSION	*my shoe* *mama dress*	*mein ball* [my ball] *mamas hut* [mama's hat]	*mami chashka* [mama's cup] *pup moya* [navel my]	*täti auto* [aunt car]	*kom baba* [chair father]	*lole a'u* [candy my] *polo 'oe* [ball your] *paluni mama* [balloon mama]
MODIFY, QUALIFY	*pretty dress* *big boat*	*milch heiss* [milk hot] *armer wauwau* [poor dog]	*mama khoroshaya* [mama good] *papa bol'shoy* [papa big]	*rikki auto* [broken car] *torni iso* [tower big]	*pypiy kech* [pepper hot] *gwen madichol* [chicken black]	*fiatali'i pepe* [headstrong baby]
QUESTION[3]	*where ball*	*wo ball* [where ball]	*gde papa* [where papa]	*missä pallo* [where ball]		*fea Punafu* [where Punafu]

The examples come from a variety of studies, published and unpublished. Data from the three non-Indo-European languages are drawn from the doctoral dissertations of Melissa Bowerman (Harvard, in progress: Finnish), Ben Blount (Berkeley, 1969: Luo), and Keith Kernan (Berkeley, 1969: Samoan). The examples given here are representative of many more utterances of the same type in each language. The order of the two words in the utterance is generally fixed in all of the languages except Finnish, where both orders can be used freely for some utterance types by some children.

[1] Bloom (1968) has noted three different sorts of negation: (1) nonexistence (e.g., "no wet," meaning "dry"); (2) rejection (e.g., "no wash," meaning "don't wash me"); and (3) denial ("no girl," denying a preceding assertion that a boy was a girl).

[2] Descriptions are of several types: (1) agent + action (e.g., "Bambi go"); (2) action + object (e.g., "hit ball"); (3) agent + object (e.g., "mama bread," meaning "mama is cutting bread"); (4) locative (e.g., "baby highchair," meaning "baby is in the highchair"); (5) instrumental (e.g., "cut knife"); (6) dative (e.g., "throw daddy," meaning "throw it to daddy"). (The use of terminology of grammatical case is suggestive here; cf. Filmore's [1968] discussion of deep cases as underlying linguistic universals.)

[3] In addition to wh-questions, yes-no questions can be made by pronouncing any two-word sentence with rising intonation, with the exception of Finnish. (Melissa Bowerman reports that the emergence of yes-no questions is, accordingly, exceptionally late in Finnish child language.)

FIGURE 9.1. Continued

COMPLEX GRAMMARS

However ingenious and creative a young child can be operating within restrictions of a limited verbal range, two-word utterances soon become too confining. Cognitive development and experiential maturation stimulate children to expand their linguistic abilities. A number of interconnected discoveries and advances are made. A child begins to express additional grammatical relations through expansion in the number of words in a sentence and through employment of morphological processes affecting the structure of individual words. According to McNeill, "Two-word sentences grow to three-word sentences and beyond because a child observes the *relative* position of words. By learning that a word is first in a phrase and that a phrase is first in a sentence, a child learns that the sentence is hierarchically organized. Thus, positional learning, extended through contextual generalization, leads to [complex] sentence structure" (1970:68).

McNeill's statement captures two important themes. First, a child develops awareness that organization within sentences is significant. She recognizes that words are not simply strung along in adjacent slots, but that they combine in functional units (noun phrases, verb phrases) that are affected by rules of placement and movement. Second, a child transfers her learning from one context to others by processes of analogy and rule generalization. These two capacities are demonstrations of human cognitive endowments and are universal in children's learning.

Morphological Development

Morphological processes are employed to express grammatical concepts. Some of the most common concepts are person, number, case, and such verb categories as tense, aspect, and mode. In early stages of speech (one- or two-word constructions), affixes denoting these concepts are generally omitted. With no overt expression of relations, speech is heavily context-bound. As more grammatical information is made explicit in words themselves, speech moves toward freeing itself from immediate contexts. This process is gradual, but its direction is toward increasing the communicative potential available for speakers. Linguistic form that overtly expresses grammatical meanings is informative and can, therefore, be used in interactions with people who do not share all of one's experiences, thus expanding social possibilities for a maturing child. And as a child's cognitive capacities develop, she or he has understandings of the world and of her or his own thoughts that the child wants to express to others. As the child's linguistic abilities progress, she or he is better able to establish satisfying social involvements.

English nouns and verbs contain suffixes to mark certain grammatical categories. Inflections are characteristics of the surface form of words, carrying important information about agents, objects, or recipients associated with activities or states. The following table displays timing and ordering of emergence of nominal and verbal suffixes for two children studied by Ursula Bellugi (1964). Of importance is the fact that both children introduced inflections in the same order, even though ages at their appearance differed considerably.

The Emergence of English Inflections

Inflection	Adam	Eve
Present progressive, -*ing*	28 (months)	19.5 (months)
Plural on nouns, -*s*	33	24
Past on regular verbs, -*ed*	39	24.5
Possessive on nouns, -*s*	39.5	25.5
Third person on verbs, -*s*	41	26

A potentially confusing feature of English inflections is that the same sound, -*s,* appears as a suffix marking number on nouns, possession of nouns, and third-person singular subject of verbs. Ordering of inflections in Adam's and Eve's speech demonstrates that learners differentiate among grammatical functions of -*s,* keeping their applications distinct.

An important process in children's acquisition of morphological features is their extension of rules learned in one context to others through analogy and generalization. They add affixes to newly encountered words by recognizing sounds and applying appropriate morphological rules. In a clever, and now classic, experiment, Jean Berko (1958) developed a test situation to study how children apply plural and possessive suffixes to nouns that they have never heard before and how they apply past-tense and third-person singular suffixes to new verbs. She presented children (ages 4 through 7) with drawings of cartoonlike animals and objects and of men performing various actions. Creatures and activities were named with nonsense words; for example, cartoon characters were labeled "wug" /wʌg/, "kazh" /kæz/, "gutch" /gʌc/; activities were also named with non-English words.

Berko elicited children's selection of affixes to previously unencountered forms through the following kinds of test frames (ibid.:155–157):

Plural: One bird-like animal, then two. "This is a wug (/wʌg/). Now there is another one. There are two of them. There are two____."

Past tense: Man doing calisthenics. "This is a man who knows how to mot (/mat/). He is motting. He did the same thing yesterday. What did he do yesterday? Yesterday he____."

Children were able to apply known affixes to new linguistic material, although a noun's or a verb's sound affected the ease or difficulty of application. Age differences also affected abilities to generalize rules, speakers in the younger group (4–5 years) behaving less consistently than those in the older cohort (5½–7 years). However, relative ease or difficulty of suffix formation was the same at all ages for the different types of inflections. Among nouns, correct plurals were added to words ending in stops, liquids, and vowels. Nouns ending in sibilants (/s, z, š, ž, č, ǰ/) caused more problems. Among verbs, affixation of past-tense markers proved most difficult with verbs ending in -*t* or -*d* (ibid.:159–160). Nouns and verbs that were problematic share the requirement of inserting an "epenthetic" or "filler" vowel between stems and underlying forms of an affix, that is, plural

{-s}→ /-ɨz/ (e.g., /kʌz/ → /kʌzɨz/) and past tense {-d} /-ɨd/ (/mat/ → /mat-ɨd/). On the whole, though, "the picture that emerged was one of consistency, regularity and simplicity. The children did not treat new words according to idiosyncratic patterns. They did not model new words on patterns that appear infrequently. . . . Their best performance was with those forms that are the most regular and have the fewest variants" (ibid.:176–177).

Another significant reflection of children's drive to generalize rules is their tendency to overregularize affixes, very frequently applying allomorphs to nouns and verbs that actually select unusual allomorphs: "mouses" for plural and "comed" or "goed" for past tense. Perhaps the most revealing indicator of children's cognitive process is the fact that they apply analogous rules in a secondary wave after they have already learned irregular forms. This procedure, first described by Susan Ervin (1964), applies to many English verbs common in children's speech environments (as speakers and listeners) and have aberrant past-tense markings, as "came," "went," "did." Children learn these forms first as invariant and unanalyzed wholes. Later they acquire the regular past-tense suffix and extend it to all verbs, resulting in displacement of irregulars: "came" "comed," "did" "doed." Although this process produces forms that are "incorrect" from the viewpoint of adult speech, it demonstrates a child's cognitive and creative capacities. Children generate innovative combinations in order to express newly understood grammatical relations.

Growth in Vocabulary

An obvious aspect of language acquisition is the expansion of vocabulary to include names for people and objects, descriptors of qualities, and indicators of actions and states. Learning new words is based on an interplay of growing cognitive abilities for comprehension, memory, and discrimination and of a widening social environment that presents children with new objects and activities.

Children employ several procedures in developing their vocabularies. From earliest stages of language acquisition, they restructure meanings of words either by broadening or narrowing the senses of individual words. For example, a word can first be used to refer to a large category of similar objects, for example "apple" applied to a pear (Huttenlocher and Smiley 1987:75). Use of object names by young children involves associations between objects and locations or activities, for example, "door" applied to the request to have a door opened (ibid.:78). Later, words are restricted in their usage when children develop awareness of more specific meanings. Changes in semantic ranges of words result when children perceive similarities and contrasts and realize that words are organized into hierarchical categories. This process begins in the one-word stage but continues for many years.

Children also enrich their vocabularies creatively by generating their own words from preexisting words and grammatical material. Anyone who has listened even casually to children speaking can no doubt provide numerous anecdotal examples of such innovations. They arise in order to fill lexical gaps in a child's vocabulary, stimulated by appearance of new objects or involvement in new activities for which the child has no descriptor. In order to study children's spontaneous creation of words, Eve Clark (1982) collected recordings of natural speech and analyzed occurrences of *denominal* verbs, that is, verbs that are derived from nouns. Denominal verbs occur frequently in English to fulfill various grammatical roles. The following list gives examples of legitimate English denominals (ibid.:392):

Placement of object: He *plastered* the ceiling.
Location of object: He *stabled* the horses.
Agent of action: She *authored* the books.
Goals of activity: They *knotted* the rope.
Instrument used: She *wedged* the door open.
Experiencer: They *witnessed* the crime.
Duration of event: He *summered* in Canada.

In Clark's samples of children's speech, young speakers independently created their own denominal verbs based on structural and semantic possibilities provided by words that they heard in adult speech. Some examples follow (ibid.:402–410; ages are given in years;months):

Placement:	(3;11, putting crackers in her soup) *I'm crackering my soup.*
	(5;0, to his mother) *Will you chocolate my milk?*
Location:	(5;0) *I'm going to basket those apples.*
Agent:	(5;1, talking about someone dancing in a ballet) *She's ballerining.*
Goal:	(3;1, watching a cement truck with its back revolving) *That truck is cementing.*
Instrument:	(2;4, wanting to have some cheese weighed) *You have to scale it.*
	(2;11, not wanting his mother to sweep his room) *Don't broom my mess.*
Action:	(2;4, eating soup) *I'm souping.*
	(2;6, seated in a rocker) *Rocker me, Mommy.*
	(3;0, wanting a bell to be rung) *Make it bell.*

These data indicate children's eagerness to express concepts that they newly recognize. If words do not already exist in their limited vocabulary, they spontaneously create their own. In so doing, children utilize their language's operative procedures, learned from other sources. They model innovations on legitimate linguistic forms. Children use their own inherent cognitive processes in a generative sense, demonstrating their creative human intelligence. As the Soviet linguist A. N. Gvozdev aptly remarked:

> The keenness of the child's observations and the artistic clarity of many childish words are common knowledge. They are truly very close to the linguistic creativity of literary artists. We are therefore dealing here with authentic creativity, attesting to the linguistic endowment of children. (cited in Slobin 1966:132)

Syntactic Development

Children's grammars expand by introducing new propositions. Sentence length increases with additional words specifying aspects of an event—for example, adding modifiers or predicates and expressing more complex relations such as negation or dependent clauses. Grammatical development involves ability to understand and express concepts about people/objects and relations to states/activities. Among the best documented areas of propositional growth are the formation of negatives and interrogatives.

When acquiring negation in English, propositions are first negated simply by adding words such as "no" or "not," usually at the beginning of sentences (Klima and Bellugi 1966:192):

No wipe finger.
No sit there.
No the sun shining.
Not a teddy bear.
Wear mitten no.
No fall!

The form of these utterances is syntactically simple. Negative markers are added to otherwise affirmative statements: Neg + S (or less commonly, S + Neg). Children soon progress, usually from two to four months later, to greater complexity by incorporating negation within the internal structure of sentences. For instance (ibid.:194):

He not little, he big.
I no want envelope.
There no squirrels.
That not "O," that blue.

None of these sentences is well formed (from an adult standard), but they show an advance over the earlier stage because negative markers are placed within sentences rather than simply added to them.

The third stage of development, occurring two to six months later, involves more complex incorporation of negation into sentences (ibid.:196):

I not see you anymore.
You didn't caught me.
I didn't did it.
You don't want some supper.
This not ice cream.
I not crying.
Don't touch the fish.
Ask me if I not make mistake.

At this stage, negative marking is productively applied to auxiliaries (can, do). Another feature of this period is that an earlier sentence structure, /Neg + S/, has been omitted from children's grammars. In addition, "no" as an internally positioned marker disappears, replaced either by "not" or by more complex negative forms.

During this stage, several childlike constructions remain, including lack of copulas in some sentences (e.g., "I not crying") and failure to replace affirmative "some" with "any" in negative phrases (e.g., "You don't want some supper"). Also, past-tense forms of main verbs occur in surface structure (e.g., "You didn't *caught* me"), although adult grammar expresses these verbs in present tense ("You didn't *catch* me"). However, children rapidly develop appropriate negative syntax after this phase.

A second area of propositional and linguistic growth is comprehension and expression of *wh-questions*—questions introduced by /what, who, where, why, when/. Children readily make distinctions on both structural and semantic grounds between yes/no and wh-questions. The former are indicated simply by rising intonation. The latter are more complex and involve gradual development of syntactic constructions (Bellugi 1968; Brown et al. 1968; Klima and Bellugi 1966).

In the first stage, a simple wh-word is prefaced to declarative sentences (examples from Klima and Bellugi 1966:200):

Who that?
What that?
What cowboy doing?
Where Mama boot?
Where horse go?

The second stage of development incorporates auxiliaries acquired in declarative contexts and applies them to interrogatives (ibid.:204–205):

Where small trailer he should pull?
What he can ride in?
What did you doed?
Why the kitty can't stand up?
How he can be a doctor?
How they can't talk?
What I did yesterday?

A striking feature of this second stage of wh-formation is that although auxiliaries are properly introduced into sentences, children do not perform subject-auxiliary inversion, that is, in adult English grammar, /NP + aux aux + NP/. If this transformation had affected children's sentences, the question "What he can ride in?" would have been realized as "What can he ride in?" Bellugi suggested that children's difficulties lie in what she termed *performance constraints* on simultaneous operation of multiple transformations. Children obviously comprehend meanings of sentences with inverted subjects and can produce sentences of the same length, composed in fact of identical words. A child begins by adding wh-words to declarative sentences as a first step in transformational cycles and initially can only perform this single operation. Bellugi tested her subjects by asking them to imitate her speech, as in the brief exchange that opened this chapter (ibid.:38):

ADULT: Adam, say what I say: Where can I put them?

ADAM: Where I can put them?

In the next stage, Adam learned to invert subject + auxiliary but was able to do so only with affirmative questions. Negative questions were not inverted. During this period, Adam could perform two operations (wh-word introduction and subject inversion), but when a third proposition was added, his handling of syntax could not incorporate all three simultaneously. Because negation must be included in order to capture the meaning of the sentence, he opted for omitting the subject-inversion transformation. Note the following dialogue from a game in which Adam was directed to ask questions of an "Old Lady" puppet (ibid.:40):

ADULT: Adam, ask the Old Lady where she can find some toys.

ADAM: Old Lady, where can you find some toys?

ADULT: Adam, ask the Old Lady why she can't run.

ADAM: Old Lady, why you can't run?

These exchanges provide further evidence of performance constraints. Significantly, they also support notions in generative grammar of the independent status of transformations. It is obvious that children do not acquire language only from surface phenomena presented in adult speech but also operate on the basis of innate principles that require cognitive maturation. Children develop their capacity to use these principles in distinct stages. Multiple transformations involving multiple propositions present conceptual difficulties resulting in constraints on performance.

Children gradually develop abilities to comprehend and produce complex sentences, including processes of conjoining and embedding. Following are examples of a child's (age 2;4) attempts to imitate some model sentences (Slobin and Welsh 1973):

ADULT: Here is a brown brush and here is a comb.
CHILD: Here's a brown brush an' a comb.
ADULT: The man who I saw yesterday got wet.
CHILD: I saw the man and he got wet.
ADULT: The boy the book hit was crying.
CHILD: Boy the book was crying.

In the first sentence, with a simple conjunction "and," the girl produced an imitation incorporating a regular English transformation (deletion of redundancies) that the model sentence did not apply. She responded in a normal, colloquial style. The second sentence presented difficulties for her in carrying out sentence embedding. She obviously understood the model but could only repeat the semantic content encoded in each underlying sentence separately. Thus, the girl actually disembedded the sentences and produced them in conjoined form, a structure well handled at this stage.

The child's attempt to imitate the third model failed because she did not understand the relations of complex clauses. She merely extracted content words (boy, book, crying) and repeated them without changing their order but did not express underlying semantic roles. One difference between the second and third sentences is that the relative pronoun "who" occurs in the former, providing a clue about underlying structure. It alerts hearers to the existence of an embedded relative clause. In contrast, the third sentence lacks this signal and instead presents a young speaker/hearer with only a string of words.

A significant phenomenon occurring in all imitation-response elicitations is that children do not imitate on demand any linguistic structures that they do not produce spontaneously in their own speech. Thus, there is a lag in expression despite ability to comprehend meaning. Even directed attempts by caregivers in natural settings to "correct" a child's speech fail if they conflict with the child's own grammar. Note the following mother–child exchange as evidence (McNeill 1966:69):

CHILD: Nobody don't like me.

MOTHER: No, say "nobody likes me."

CHILD: Nobody don't like me.
          (eight repetitions of this dialogue)

MOTHER: No, now listen carefully; say "nobody likes me."

CHILD: Oh! Nobody don't like<u>s</u> me.

Examples such as this, as well as those elicited in testing, demonstrate that children do not mimic adults in acquiring language but develop their own grammars. Children refine their grammars by discarding some rules and altering applications of others until they finally arrive at appropriate constructions. But throughout, it is a creative process of observation and production, consistent with maturing cognitive capacities.

COMPARATIVE EVIDENCE

Although researchers concerned with language acquisition accept the notion that children learn through growth of universal cognitive processes, each language presents its own specific structure to be deciphered and reproduced. Studies of many distinct languages confirm hypotheses about universal tendencies but also reveal significant differences in rates of acquisition of various surface phenomena. In this section we review some relevant research in order to understand better both universal and unique processes.

Complex Inflectional Systems

As we have already seen, noun and verb inflections are not included in a child's earliest words. Children first recognize and reproduce the unvarying parts of words (stems or roots), omitting variable segments (affixes). Inflectional affixes are confusing to a child because their occurrence on a word is dependent on semantic roles intended by a speaker; they are not obvious attributes of objects or events. Affixes are omitted because children do not attend to grammatical content and also because a child's simple words are usually understood by her or his caregivers in contexts of ongoing experience. Later, as children become aware of underlying semantic relations, they begin to learn that inflectional affixes express critical concepts.

Many languages have complex inflectional systems that present problems for learners in sorting their forms and meanings. Russian and others within the Slavic family are examples of this type of language. As shown in Chapter 2, Russian nouns are marked for each of six cases: nominative (subject), genitive (possession), dative (indirect object), accusative (direct object), locative, and instrumental. Case suffixes are additionally differentiated for two numbers (singular, plural) and three genders (masculine, feminine, neuter). To complicate matters even further, some suffixes have several allomorphs, conditioned by the shapes of noun stems. Finally, some sounds or combinations of sounds signal multiple case and/or gender and/or number combinations—for example, /-a/ marks feminine singular nominative, masculine singular genitive, neuter singular genitive, neuter plural nominative, and neuter plural accusative.

At first, children omit all case distinctions, using nominative forms in every context (Slobin 1966:136). According to Gvozdev's longitudinal study of his son (cited in Slobin 1966), case suffixes did not appear until age 1 year, 10 months. But then rapid acquisition occurred. In only one month, the boy employed nominative/accusative and gender markers in addition to number and some special diminutive suffixes. Verb inflections for tense also appeared in this same period of morphological blossoming. As Slobin remarked, "Once the principles of inflection and derivation are acquired, the principle is immediately applied over a wide range of types" (ibid.).

Just as an English-speaking child overgeneralizes number and tense inflections, a Russian child similarly applies some case suffixes beyond their appropriate scope. Russian children select the case marker having the most consistent form and the least number of functions. For instance, examine the following suffixes for singular nominative and accusative cases, distinguished for three genders and for animate/inanimate masculines (Slobin 1979:95).

Notice that three of the accusative suffixes have shapes similar to other

	Masculine		Neuter	Feminine
	Animate	Inanimate		
Nominative	Ø	Ø	-o	-a
Accusative	-a	Ø	-o	-u

endings (e.g., {-*a*}: masculine animate accusative/feminine nominative; {-*o*}: neuter nominative or accusative; Ø: masculine nominative/masculine inanimate accusative). Only one suffix, {-*u*}, has a uniquely accusative function. Therefore, it is this suffix that children seize upon and generalize for all nouns in accusative case. It is the one with the clearest stable semantic content.

In a similar process, once instrumental suffixes are learned, children overgeneralize again, this time choosing the masculine/neuter singular suffix {-*om*} to apply to all nouns because this phonological shape has only one other function, whereas the feminine singular instrumental, {-*oy*}, marks five additional semantic roles (Slobin 1966:138).

Russian children first acquire those inflectional suffixes expressing the most concrete semantic content. Number is learned before any of the case markers. Nominative/accusative patterns are acquired next, probably because this distinction reflects a basic dichotomization of action, from agent to acted-upon. Other cases are then added. The last category to be learned is gender, probably because it is the most abstract of the grammatical concepts involved in Russian inflection. It is an arbitrary classification of nouns, having nothing to do with actual perception or experience.

Agglutinating Languages

In agglutinating languages, many morphemes are combined in one word, which can potentially result in long sequences. But rather than presenting unusual difficulties (as an English speaker might assume from the length of words), such languages actually seem to promote easier learning. Turkish is a good example of a highly regular agglutinating language. For instance, note the following list of case inflections applying to nouns in Turkish (Slobin 1982:150):

Nominative	Ø
Genitive	-in / -ın / -ün / -un
Accusative	-i / -ı / -ü / -u
Instrumental/comitative	-le / -la
Dative	-e / -a
Locative	-de / -da
Ablative	-den / -dan

Allomorphic rules selecting variants of suffixes are based on only two principles of vowel conditioning (vowel harmony) and apply consistently. The vowel in stems determines vowels in suffixes. Genitive and accusative suffixes have four allomorphs, varying with four vowels, conditioned by principles of front/back location and of rounding/unrounding. These allomorphs are affected by the following rules:

Vowel in Stem	*Vowel in Suffix*
Front unrounded	i
Front rounded	ü

Back unrounded   ɨ
Back rounded   u

The four remaining cases contain e/a vowels, based solely on a front/back dichotomy: Stems with front vowels select suffixes with /e/; stems with back vowels select suffixes with /a/, as in these examples:

ev-	*ev-im*	*ev-ler-im*	*ev-ler-im-ı*
house	house-my	house-plural-my	house-pl.-my-accusative
house	my house	my houses	my houses (direct object)

According to Slobin, the entire system of noun inflections, including case, number, and possession, as well as much of verb morphology marking subject and tense, is acquired "well before the age of two" (ibid.). Recall that this is the age at which a Russian-learning child is just beginning to use case suffixes. Slobin suggested that several factors contribute to easy acquisition of Turkish: Each suffix has one distinct grammatical role (there are no homonyms); noun and verb paradigms are regular, without exceptions; allomorphs are also conditioned by regular rules; the same set of case suffixes is applied consistently to several word classes; and each suffix has a unique semantic content so that two or more meanings are never collapsed into one form.

Turkish word order is usually SOV (subject + object + verb), but order is not fixed because the inflectional system indicates a noun's grammatical role. Words are shifted within sentences in order to focus on a particular element. Difficulties in acquiring syntax seem to emerge with more complex sentence types, particularly those requiring embedding of relative clauses (ibid.:166).

Research in learning other agglutinating languages indicates similar developmental processes. In a study of children acquiring Tamil, a Dravidian language spoken in southern India, Parimala Raghavendra and Laurence Leonard (1989) focused on the use of verb inflections by young speakers, ages from 2;2 (2 years, 2 months) to 2;7. In Tamil, verbs are inflected for tense (past, present, future), several aspects and moods, and also for person (first, second, third), number (singular, plural), and gender for third person (masculine, feminine). Inflectional suffixes are highly regular; for example, present tense is always {-r}, past {-nd}, future {-v}; person markers are likewise regular. Only neuter singular has some variation.

Raghavendra and Leonard found that children, even the youngest at just over 2 years, applied rules correctly in nearly all instances. The only suffix whose correct appearance did not reach at least 90 percent of possible occurrences was the third-person singular feminine. This suffix has the shape {-a:}, which is identical in sound to two other Tamil suffixes and therefore is the only one not having a unique meaning (ibid.:320). But even the feminine marker was used correctly in 73 to 87 percent of its potential occurrences, indicating that it too was acquired with little difficulty.

Raghavendra and Leonard concluded that, in addition to structural regularity of Tamil's inflectional system, ordering of suffixes attached to stems promotes easy acquisition. That is, they "follow the stem in order of decreasing relevance to the inherent meaning of the stem: verb + tense/aspect + person + number + gender. There is semantic clarity in semantic mapping in Tamil" (ibid.:321). Structural and semantic properties present a conceptually orderly system.

Polysynthetic Languages

Polysynthetic languages differ significantly from other types. They share with agglutinating languages the characteristic of including many kinds of meanings and grammatical forms within a single word, but, in contrast, their affixes are not easily segmented. Several markers collapse into one form that may or may not retain any overt trace of its origin. In addition, each affix can have numerous allomorphs, some of which may be phonologically conditioned, whereas others must be learned separately for specific stems. These languages, then, present problems for children not encountered by learners of morphologically simpler systems.

Mohawk is a polysynthetic, fusional language with complex verb morphology. Verbs contain a large number of prefixes and suffixes having many different kinds of meanings and grammatical functions. The chart in Figure 9.2 indicates structural possibilities. As can be seen, this verbal system creates complexity in terms of both length of words and proliferation of semantic categories.

Data on the acquisition of Mohawk have been obtained by a longitudinal study of one boy, beginning at age 2;10 and ending at 4;1 (Feurer 1980a, 1980b) and by brief observations of five children ranging in age from 1;9 to 4;9 (Mithun 1989). First, because of the length of Mohawk words and children's early inability to produce long sequences, a strategy for word reduction was employed. It was based on reproducing only the stressed syllable of adult words. In Mohawk, most words are stressed on the penultimate (next to last) syllable, and this is the one that appeared in the speech of the youngest child, age 1;9. By age 2;10, two-syllable words occurred, containing the stressed and following syllables (Feurer 1980a:120):

kí:ra	reduced from	*Λkhnekí:ra²*	(I will drink liquid)
sé:ra	reduced from	*Λyethiyatkλ² sé:ra*	(I will see her)

In the first verb, the child by chance reproduced part of the stem, but in the second example, stress falls on a suffix. Children's speech, therefore, is not based on the most informative part of words but, rather, on their acoustic and phonological properties.

After the two-syllable stage, children expand their verbs by moving toward beginnings of words. They first discover the category of pronoun prefixes, the only category that must occur in all verbs. These prefixes often immediately precede verb stems, although other morphemes may intervene. In any case, once children begin to distinguish the pronoun system, they acquire it fairly rapidly. Subject and object pronouns are learned first, followed by transitive markers indicating co-occurences of subject and object, for example, I to him, she to us (ibid.:125).

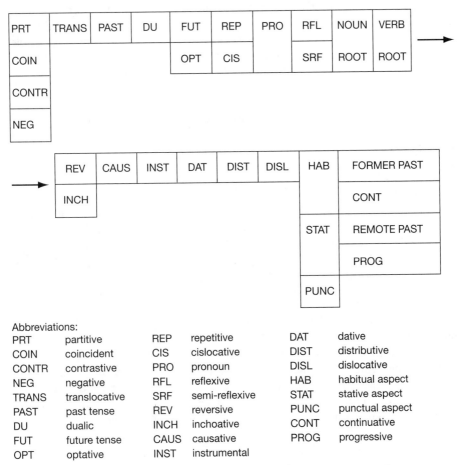

PRT	TRANS	PAST	DU	FUT	REP	PRO	RFL	NOUN	VERB
COIN				OPT	CIS		SRF	ROOT	ROOT
CONTR									
NEG									

REV	CAUS	INST	DAT	DIST	DISL	HAB	FORMER PAST
INCH							CONT
						STAT	REMOTE PAST
							PROG
						PUNC	

Abbreviations:

PRT	partitive	REP	repetitive	DAT	dative
COIN	coincident	CIS	cislocative	DIST	distributive
CONTR	contrastive	PRO	pronoun	DISL	dislocative
NEG	negative	RFL	reflexive	HAB	habitual aspect
TRANS	translocative	SRF	semi-reflexive	STAT	stative aspect
PAST	past tense	REV	reversive	PUNC	punctual aspect
DU	dualic	INCH	inchoative	CONT	continuative
FUT	future tense	CAUS	causative	PROG	progressive
OPT	optative	INST	instrumental		

FIGURE 9.2. Morphological Structure of Mohawk Verbs.   (Mithun 1989:289)

Within the category of grammatical person, first and second are distinguished earliest, followed by third person (Feurer 1980b:35). Mohawk third person is the most complex morphologically and semantically because it also expresses gender (masculine, feminine/indefinite, and feminine/neuter).

Children gradually acquire numerous optional affixes expressing complex grammatical meanings. The boy in Feurer's study did not attempt to combine as many as three prefixes in one verb until age 3;8 (1980a:125). Children observed by Mithun also advanced from ends to beginnings of words and from the most frequent and semantically obvious affixes to those more complex in form and function.

When compared with children learning Turkish or Tamil, these Mohawk speakers seem to take a longer time to acquire fully the verbal affixes of their language. However, once they begin to use the markers, they make very few errors of overgeneralization or confusion of forms (Feurer 1980b:33; Mithun 1989:311). These comments confirm the obvious point that no language can be too complex for its speakers to learn, or, from the other view, every child is innately equipped to decipher whatever complexity a natural language presents.

SOME UNIVERSAL SEQUENCES

Negation

The research by Klima and Bellugi (1966) showed that children's negative constructions begin with Neg + S and end with appropriate application of English transformations. Similar patterns have been documented in other languages. In Russian, adult grammar usually expresses negative propositions with double negation, employing the independent word *nyet* "no" + negative particle *ni* prefaced to a following pronoun or verb, as in *nyet nikavo* "not no-one" (there is no one) or *nyet ni dam* "no, not I-will-give" (I won't give). In the earliest learning phase, children omit the negative particle *ni,* using only the word *nyet* at beginnings of sentences, as in *nyet kavo* and *nyet dam* (Slobin 1966:133).

Children learning Japanese use similar procedures, beginning by using the independent word *nai* as a constant marker of negation. Later, they incorporate negation within sentences themselves, eventually developing the adult system that includes the words *iya* and *iiya* in addition to *nai* (McNeill and McNeill 1968:53–54). Children acquire negative markers in a sequence related to their cognitive function. They learn the proper forms as they are able to understand and express underlying concepts and relations. Examples follow (ibid.:60–61):

1. *nai* (adjective); existence/nonexistence:
   There's not an apple here.
2. *nai* (auxiliary); truth/falsity:
   That's not an apple.
3. *iya;* disapproval or rejection:
   No, I don't want an apple.
4. *iiya;* entailment/nonentailment:
   No, I didn't have an apple, I had a pear.

Children learning the polysynthetic language Mohawk follow processes found in other types of systems. Feurer noted that her subject first employed separate words *yah* "no" (reduced from *iyah*) and *tosa* "don't" (reduced from *tohsa*) prefaced to otherwise affirmative statements. Adult speech marks negation with these words plus a negative prefix attached to verbs. Although Feurer's subject began expressing negation at age 2;10, he did not incorporate negative markers into verbs until age 3;5 (1980a:127). Similarly, among Mithun's subjects, only the oldest child (4;9) used appropriate negation (1989:306).

Wh-Questions

Studies of acquisition of wh-questions in several languages support claims about universal sequences in their development. Children start by employing independent question words at the beginning of declarative sentences (wh + S) and later progress to more complex interrogative structures.

The most striking regularity, though, is the semantic sequencing of wh-propositions. Data from the acquisition of wh-questions in English, German, Serbo-Croatian, Japanese, and Korean show that propositions learned first are "what" and "where," followed closely by "who." The last concepts to emerge are "why" and "when" (Clancy 1989:327, 329).

Age at emergence of various concepts also seems to be roughly comparable for all languages studied. Children learn "what" and "where" questions before the age of 2; "who" questions usually appear by age 2;6, with some variations both earlier and later. Finally, "when" and "why" seem to be most problematic, often not emerging until well beyond the third year (ibid.). Feurer's study of a Mohawk child confirms this pattern. In fact, although the boy expressed "what" and "who" questions by age 2;8, he had not acquired "how" or "why" propositions by the end of the field study, age 4;1 (1980a:128).

Patricia Clancy suggested that cross-linguistic similarities are due to universal cognitive processes in comprehending concepts underlying wh-propositions (1989:337). "What" and "where" questions relate to objects/people in a child's physical sensory experience, referring to his immediate world. They require only that children be able to form and remember mental representations of objects. "What is" simply elicits a label for an object or activity, whereas "where is" depends on an additional ability to understand placement of objects/people in space. Concepts underlying "how," "why," and "when" are more abstract. They involve "notions of means/manner, causality and temporality" (ibid.).

Locative Concepts

Locative expressions refer to placement of objects, persons, and/or events in space or time. According to Dan Slobin, emergence of various locative concepts is based on their cognitive complexity. The concepts are listed below in order of their postulated development (cited in Slobin 1982:160):

IN/ON/UNDER: containment/support/occlusion

BESIDE: spatial proximity

BACK(i)/FRONT(i): proximity to objects with inherent backs and fronts (e.g., cars, houses, people)

BETWEEN: coordinates two proximity relations

BACK/FRONT: proximity to objects without inherent backs and fronts (e.g., trees, blocks, drinking glasses)

Data from acquisition studies of 48 children (aged 2;0 to 4;4) who spoke either English, Italian, Serbo-Croatian, or Turkish supported the developmental sequence outlined above (Slobin 1982:161). Concepts of IN/ON/UNDER were acquired by approximately 80 to 90 percent of the subjects; BESIDE emerged nearly as often (72 to 79 percent). BETWEEN/BACK(i)/FRONT(i) form the next cluster, handled by roughly 20 to 50 percent of the children. The final concepts to be acquired were the more abstract relational notions of BACK/FRONT (for objects lacking inherent backs and fronts). These were found in the speech of relatively few children by age 4.

In sum, the fact that universal processes affect acquisition of negation, wh-questions, and locatives confirms contentions that language learning is interdependent with cognitive maturation. Because growth in ability to comprehend concepts is a natural development of human minds, it is reasonable to expect that expressing these concepts in language will proceed along a common path for all speakers.

INSTRUCTIONAL STRATEGIES

In all societies, caregivers are involved in the linguistic development of their children. Adults often use strategies to help children acquire language. These strategies accomplish several tasks. First, they function as culturally prescribed frames for language-learning situations, directing a child's attention to language as a focus of interaction. Second, they teach children appropriate norms of communicative behavior. Most of this process is covert, but it may be overtly expressed, as in teaching politeness routines such as "Say 'thank you' to the nice lady." Linguistic instruction, then, contributes to overall socialization. Finally, exchanges between adult and child display affect and involve the two in social interaction that can be entertaining and playful as well as instructive.

Strategies in the United States

Caregivers use several techniques in response to children's speech in natural contexts. Adults often repeat children's utterances with an *expansion* of the basic sentence, filling in missing words, as the following examples show (Brown and Bellugi 1968:417):

Child	*Mother*
Baby highchair	Baby is in the highchair.
Eve lunch	Eve is having lunch.
Mommy sandwich	Mommy'll have a sandwich.
Sat wall	He sat on the wall.

Throw Daddy   Throw it to Daddy.

Pick glove   Pick the glove up.

[handwritten margin notes: How do expansions to contribute to linguistic development? Q8 Why is it important for caregivers or parents to use expansions?]

Significantly, when the mother repeats utterances, she maintains the child's word order. The child uses simple nouns and verbs; the mother then provides grammatical elements, including copulas, pronouns, determiners, and locative prepositions. Expansions direct learners to parts of sentences that they have omitted. Although at this stage of development, children are not able to produce extended sequences, these interactions can form a basis for future acquisition. *[handwritten: A8]*

Caregivers also use a technique called *modeling,* commenting on the semantic content of children's words. Here are some examples (Slobin 1968:442):

CHILD: His name Tony.

ADULT: That's right.

CHILD: We got some more.

ADULT: There's a lot in there.

Expansion and modeling contribute to linguistic development in part by supplying additional words and sentences that children can later use as sources of data. Also, instructional techniques ratify a learner's speech. By accepting what a child has said, adults encourage the child to make further contributions to talk.

These styles of adult–child speech have been observed in interactions in middle-class American families. They are based on cultural assumptions that children need to be carefully instructed and socialized and that caregivers have a duty to teach language and conversational skills. These attitudes are not held by all Americans, however. For instance, in a study of adults' interaction with children in a lower-class African-American community in rural Louisiana, Martha Ward (1971) found that adults expect children to naturally learn to speak. In their view, overt adult intervention is not required. Rather than expanding or modeling on children's utterances, adults frequently expanded their own speech, providing both repetitions and alternations in syntax. Repeating and changing syntax indirectly teach children grammatical possibilities. They further demonstrate to a child that dissimilar forms can have similar meanings. Note the following examples of mothers' speech to their children (Ward 1971:48–49):

MOTHER: Tell the lady your name.

                Tell the lady your name.

                What your name?

                Tell Joan what your name.

                Tell her your name.

                Tell Joan your name.

MOTHER: What Scott ate today for dinner?

                What you ate for dinner?

                What did you eat for dinner?

                What you and Warren have for dinner?

Although linguists may debate the relative advantages of each strategy of adult–child verbal interaction, in actual learning processes, none is solely necessary. Children acquire language so long as they are exposed to it in communicative experiences with others.

STRATEGIES IN OTHER CULTURES

In this section we briefly review some studies of instructional interactions in other cultures, demonstrating the effectiveness of many different techniques.

Kaluli

The Kaluli, a small horticultural community of 1,200 people living in New Guinea, believe that it is necessary to begin teaching language to young children as soon as they say their first words. In the Kaluli view, infants are "soft" and need "hardening" or "firming up" of both their physical and mental attributes (Schieffelin 1987:256). Although adults believe that children learn most behavior by observing others, they feel that language must be directly taught or "shown" to a child. Adults teach children with routines that encourage them to repeat adult utterances. An adult makes a statement, followed by the imperative *elema* "say like that." Children are expected to respond with the adult's model sentence. This type of exchange is often used when another person is present. Caregivers tell children what to say to others, thereby teaching norms of communicative interaction.

Elema routines are used by caregivers (usually mothers) with both boys and girls until children are about 3 years old. Differences exist between girls' and boys' participation in *elema* routines. Because girls are socialized very early to take on caregiving responsibilities, they initiate *elema* routines with their mothers. Girls as young as 28 months prompt with *elema* "say like that" and their mothers repeat (ibid.:258). Young girls also use these routines while teaching even younger siblings. Because boys are not expected to be caregivers to children, they do not engage in *elema* routines as initiators but only as recipients.

Kwara'ae

Among the Kwara'ae, people living in the Solomon Islands in Melanesia, a different set of routines is used in intensive teaching of language. Kwara'ae adults begin talking to infants and including them in conversations. Because babies cannot talk, adults speak for them by "translating" their babbling into Kwara'ae words (Watson-Gegeo and Gegeo 1986:18). By the age of 9 or 10 months, various routines are directed to children until they reach their third or fourth year. A common routine involves *calling out* (ibid.:19). This strategy teaches linguistic form and communicative style. Adults instruct children to *ako uana* "call out" to someone, providing the child with sentences to repeat. Children as young as 18 months are able to produce the expected responses.

Adults frequently employ calling-out routines with children to give messages, directives, and instructions to other people. For example, note the following exchange (translated into English) between an adult and a 3-year-old child (ibid.: 21–22):

ADULT: Call out to grandpa.

CHILD: Grandpa!

ADULT: "The rice is done now."

CHILD: The rice is done now.

ADULT: "Come and eat rice."

CHILD: Come and eat rice.

Another instructional technique used by Kwara'ae caregivers is that of *repeating routines,* initiated by the word *uri,* "like this," followed by propositions to be repeated. This routine is first used to teach politeness formulas, such as greetings and farewells (ibid.:25). Adults praise children when they repeat correctly in order to encourage them to learn. Linguistic skills and social etiquette are taught through repeating adult models. In the following routine, an older sister instructs her 27-month-old brother (ibid.:29–30):

SISTER: Then when you're full you just speak like this, "I don't want any more now." "I don't want to eat any more now."

CHILD: I don't want?

SISTER: Then you just speak as I said, like this, "I don't want any more now."

CHILD: I don't want.

SISTER: "I'm full now."

CHILD: Full now.

SISTER: "I'm full, I don't want to eat any more now."

CHILD: Don't want to eat any more now.

SISTER: Then you speak like this, "Put it away now." Then speak like this, "Put the stew away now."

Repeating routines are often used when a third person is present in order to teach children how to make requests, give directives, or convey information. Children are told to repeat a message intended for another person present. As among the Kaluli, Kwara'ae children's compliance with these routines is often used by adults to accomplish their own communicative goals, particularly those of asking favors or expressing opinions because explicit statement of these speech acts by adults is considered inappropriate.

Basotho

The Basotho, the people of Lesotho, an independent country surrounded by South Africa, believe that children must be taught directly so that they will learn to speak properly. Importance of speech is reflected in a Basotho proverb: "A quiet person will perish" (Demuth 1986:54).

Various kinds of *prompting routines* are used in different contexts. Three common prompts are *ere* "say," *echo* "say so," and *juetse* "tell." They can be used separately or together in a single utterance. For instance (ibid.:58):

ere	m-phe	ntho	ena,	*echo,*	mo	*juetse*
say	me-give	thing	this,	say so,	her	tell
Say	"Give me	this thing,"		say so,	tell her.	

In this example, an adult interprets a child's desires, and, through the prompting routine, ratifies the child's rights. Prompts also teach verbal skills for asking questions and making requests. They are especially helpful in instructing children to express polite forms of address and formulas for greetings. And, as elsewhere, Basotho adults use prompting routines with children as intermediaries to transmit messages to other people. In doing so, adults accomplish their own purposes but they also teach children norms of proper communicative behavior. As Katherine Demuth remarked, through prompting "social competence is realized as verbal competence" (ibid.:78).

SUMMARY

Acquisition of language involves a number of complex processes. It is inherently interrelated with cognitive development. As such, language learning proceeds through stages of growth beginning with a child's first awareness that sounds made by others have meaning and that speech can be used to facilitate social interaction. As children develop, they realize that various personal goals are accomplished through language: They can enlist others in satisfying their needs and wants (imperative function), they can convey information (referential function), they can express thoughts and feelings (expressive function), and they can entertain and amuse themselves and others (creative function).

Children begin learning to form sounds and control pitch, rhythm, and volume. They then produce comprehensible words that at first are highly context-bound, referring to multiple aspects of ongoing experience. Later, as children are able to express increasingly complex concepts, their speech becomes free from immediate contexts and can be used for a wider range of functions in varied social situations.

Children in all cultures, learning the language of their society, proceed through similar stages of linguistic and cognitive development. Although languages with different types of morphological and syntactic structures present different kinds of problems for novices, no language presents insurmountable difficulties. All languages are acquired in more or less similar sequences during approximately the same time periods.

Although children acquire language through growth of their own innate cognitive and linguistic skills, adults are involved in the process overtly and covertly as instructors and guides. Caregivers in different cultures employ a variety of strategies to help young learners, often including explicit routines that teach linguistic structures and cultural norms of communicative behavior.

REFERENCES

ANTINUCCI, F., AND D. PARISI. 1973. Early language acquisition: A model and some data. In *Studies in Child Language Development,* ed. C. Ferguson and D. Slobin. New York: Holt, Rinehart & Winston, pp. 607–619.

BELLUGI, URSULA. 1964. The emergence of inflections and negation systems in the speech of two children. Paper presented at New England Psychological Association.

BELLUGI, URSULA. 1968. Linguistic mechanisms underlying child speech. In *Proceedings of the Conference on Language and Language Behavior,* ed. E. M. Zale. New York: Appleton Century Crofts, pp. 36–50.

BERKO, JEAN. 1958. The child's learning of English morphology. *Word* 14:150–177.

BRAINE, MARTIN. 1963. The ontogeny of English phrase structure. *Language* 39:1–13.

BROWN, ROGER, AND U. BELLUGI. 1968. Three processes in the child's acquisition of syntax. In *Contemporary Issues in Developmental Psychology,* ed. N. S. Endler et al. New York: Holt, Rinehart & Winston, pp. 411–424.

BROWN, ROGER, ET AL. 1968. The child's grammar from I to III. In *The 1967 Minnesota Symposium on Child Psychology,* ed. J. P. Hill. Minneapolis: University of Minnesota Press, pp. 28–73.

CHOMSKY, NOAM. 1965. *Aspects of the Theory of Syntax.* Cambridge, MA: MIT Press.

CLANCY, PATRICIA. 1989. Form and function in the acquisition of Korean wh-questions. *Journal of Child Language* 16:323–347.

CLARK, EVE. 1982. The young word maker: A case study of innovation in the child's lexicon. In *Language Acquisition: The State of the Art,* ed. E. Wanner and L. R. Gleitman. New York: Cambridge University Press, pp. 390–425.

DEMUTH, KATHERINE. 1986. Prompting routines in the language socialization of Basotho children. In *Language Socialization Across Cultures,* ed. B. Schieffelin and E. Ochs. New York: Cambridge University Press, pp. 51–79.

ERVIN, SUSAN. 1964. Imitation and structural change in children's language. In *New Directions in the Study of Language,* ed. E. Lenneberg. Cambridge, MA: MIT Press, pp. 163–189.

FEURER, HANNY. 1980a. The acquisition of Mohawk: Preliminary observations of first language development. In *Studies on Iroquoian Culture,* ed. N. Bonvillain. Man in the Northeast, Occasional Publications in Northeast Anthropology No. 6:119–130.

FEURER, HANNY. 1980b. Morphological development in Mohawk. In *Papers and Reports on Child Language Development, No. 18.* Stanford, CA: Stanford University Press, pp. 25–42.

FRY, D. B. 1966. The development of the phonological system in the normal and the deaf child. In *The Genesis of*

Language, ed. F. Smith and G. Miller. Cambridge, MA: MIT Press, pp. 187–206.

GREENFIELD, PATRICIA, AND J. H. SMITH. 1976. *The Structure of Communication in Early Language Development.* New York: Academic Press.

HUTTENLOCHER, JANELLEN, AND P. SMILEY. 1987. Early word meanings: The case of object names. *Cognitive Psychology* 19:63–89.

JAKOBSON, ROMAN. 1941 (1968). *Child Language, Aphasia and General Sound Laws.* The Hague: Mouton.

JAKOBSON, ROMAN, AND M. HALLE. 1956. *Fundamentals of Language.* The Hague: Mouton.

KLIMA, EDWARD, AND U. BELLUGI. 1966. Syntactic regularities in the speech of children. In *Psycholinguistic Papers,* ed. J. Lyons and R. Wales. Edinburgh: Edinburgh University Press, pp. 183–208.

MCNEILL, DAVID. 1966. Developmental Psycholinguistics. In *The Genesis of Language,* ed. F. Smith and G. Miller. Cambridge, MA: MIT Press, pp. 15–84.

MCNEILL, DAVID. 1970. *The Acquisition of Language.* New York: Harper & Row.

MCNEILL, DAVID. 1987. *Psycholinguistics: A New Approach.* New York: Harper & Row.

MCNEILL, DAVID, AND N. MCNEILL. 1968. What does a child mean when he says "no"? In *Language and Language Behavior,* ed. E. M. Zale. New York: Appleton Century Crofts, pp. 51–62.

MITHUN, MARIANNE. 1989. The acquisition of polysynthesis. *Journal of Child Language* 16:285–312.

RAGHAVENDRA, PARIMALA, AND L. LEONARD. 1989. The acquisition of agglutinating languages: Converging evidence from Tamil. *Journal of Child Language* 16:313–322.

SACHS, J. S., AND L. TRUSWELL. 1976. Comprehension of two-word instructions by children in the one-word stage. In *Papers and Reports on Child Language Development, No. 12.* Stanford, CA: Stanford University Press, pp. 212–220.

SCHIEFFELIN, BAMBI. 1987. Do different worlds mean different words? An example from Papua New Guinea. In *Language, Gender and Sex in Comparative Perspective,* ed. S. Philips, S. Steele, and C. Tanz. New York: Cambridge University Press, pp. 249–260.

SLOBIN, DAN. 1966. The acquisition of Russian as a native language. In *The Genesis of Language,* ed. F. Smith and G. Miller. Cambridge, MA: MIT Press, pp. 129–148.

SLOBIN, DAN. 1968. Imitation and grammatical development in children. In *Contemporary Issues in Developmental Psycholinguistics,* ed. N. S. Endler et al. New York: Holt, Rinehart & Winston, pp. 437–443.

SLOBIN, DAN. 1979. *Psycholinguistics,* 2nd ed. Glenview, IL: Scott, Foresman.

SLOBIN, DAN. 1982. Universal and particular in the acquisition of language. In *Language Acquisition: The State of the Art,* ed. E. Wanner and L. R. Gleitman. New York: Cambridge University Press, pp. 128–170.

SLOBIN, DAN, AND C. WELSH. 1973. Elicited imitation as a research tool in developmental psycholinguistics. In *Studies in Child Language Development,* ed. C. Ferguson and D. Slobin. New York: Holt, Rinehart & Winston, pp. 485–497.

WARD, MARTHA. 1971. *Them Children: A Study in Language Learning.* New York: Holt, Rinehart & Winston.

WATSON-GEGEO, KAREN, AND D. GEGEO. 1986. Calling-out and repeating routines in Kwara'ae children's language socialization. In *Language Socialization Across Cultures,* ed. B. Schieffelin and E. Ochs. New York: Cambridge University Press, pp. 17–50.

WEIR, RUTH. 1966. Some questions on the child's learning of phonology. In *The Genesis of Language,* ed. F. Smith and G. Miller. Cambridge, MA: MIT Press, pp. 153–168.

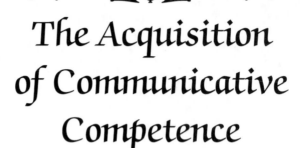

10

The Acquisition
of Communicative
Competence

Compare the following two dialogues. The first is an interaction between a Japanese mother and her child (translated into English):

ADULT: What color is this?

CHILD: No!

MOTHER: What are you saying! You should say, "Green."

CHILD: Green.

MOTHER: There is no one who says things like "No!"

The second dialogue occurred between two 13-year-old boys in Philadelphia, talking about slings they were making for a slingshot fight:

TOKAY: All right we got enough already.

MICHAEL: No—man! *You* must be *crazy. Must* be. Talking about I got *enough.* Boy. You must—I *know* you have never played *now.* Thinkin I got *enough.* Man you need three *thousand* to have *enough.*

Both of these dialogues serve to teach children how to behave with others. In the first, the Japanese mother teaches her child to comply with other people and to avoid direct refusals or rejections. These behaviors are consistent with Japanese norms that stress harmony and agreement in social relations. In the second dialogue, Michael uses insults to emphasize disagreement and to question the competence of his companion.

Through interactions with parents and peers, children acquire *communicative competence,* that is, the ability to function according to cultural models for communicative behavior. In this chapter we focus on children's acquisition of competence as speakers and listeners. We examine research concerned with learning different stylistic strategies. These strategies reflect cultural beliefs about the ways that people achieve communicative goals, for example, issuing directives, reaching agreement, and expressing opinions. Cross-cultural studies enhance our understanding of the diversity of methods employed to obtain desired results.

ACQUIRING COMMUNICATIVE STYLES

Language fulfills diverse functions either separately or simultaneously. M.A.K. Halliday observed that "language is, for the child, a rich and adaptable instrument for the realization of [his or her] intentions" (1973:2). As children mature and have varied social experiences, they develop models of language based on its social functions. In Halliday's terms, these models are the following (ibid.:3–8):

Instrumental: Getting things done, satisfying needs

Regulatory: Controlling others, giving instructions

Interactional: Establishing and maintaining social interactions, defining and consolidating groups

Personal: Expressing one's individuality, emotions, and thoughts

Heuristic: Exploring one's environment, learning about the world, questioning others, and gaining information

Imaginative: Creating and expressing one's fantasies about oneself, others, and the world

Representational: Communicating about ideas, conveying messages

Although these functions of language are universal, methods of achieving them differ in both linguistic form and cultural style. Children acquire communicative behavior through the course of daily experience. Direct instruction or correction is sometimes formalized, as in prompting or repeating routines. Children also extrapolate cultural norms from caregivers' responses to them. And they test their understanding when interacting with others, eventually developing competence in communicative behavior. This competence includes knowledge of how to express intentions in various linguistic forms provided by one's language. For example, one needs to learn appropriate means for issuing commands in different social contexts, whether with bald imperatives, mitigated or embedded directives, or hints. In addition, competence includes knowledge of how to assert one's rights and to respond to the rights of others. Finally, people become sensitive to social distinctions in their community and apply this awareness by choosing among styles of communication.

Learning Politeness

Each culture socializes its members to display behaviors that reflect values that it upholds. Although some basic themes are universal, they receive different emphases among various peoples. For instance, research concerned with ideals of communicative style in Japan reveals the importance of *omoiyari,* or empathy with others (Clancy 1986:214). Speakers and listeners join in negotiating responses to each other's feelings, attitudes, and needs. Indirect expression is favored over explicit statements of opinions and wants. Both speakers and hearers help achieve harmonious relations. Speakers must learn to be sensitive to feelings (or "face") of addressees, to be aware of how their statements might affect others. People learn to express their own attitudes ambiguously so as to avoid potential conflict. Listeners also have a responsibility in negotiating harmony. They must learn to interpret speakers' underlying intentions and opinions from inexplicit surface statements.

Japanese caregivers teach communicative skills to children by example and direct admonition. Children's behavior is commented upon and corrected in order to instill virtues of politeness and attentiveness toward others. Adults often appeal to an explicit value system that classifies certain behaviors as acceptable and just and others as deviant. Corrections are also made by reference to people of higher social status. Caregivers teach children that they must be sensitive to interlocutors' wishes and needs as expressed in questions and directives. Lack of response signals self-absorption that, according to Japanese etiquette, is rude. Note the following exchanges documented in Patricia Clancy's study of Japanese families. In the examples, mothers chastised their children for not responding to an adult's questions (1986:220–221, 235, 233, 237).

1.   (Child, age 2;1, is pretending to eat food from a toy dish)

    ADULT: *Mahochan wa nanika tabeten no? Koko nani ga haitten no?*

                  Are you eating something? What is in there?

    CHILD: [No response]

    MOTHER: *Nani ga haitteru no ka naa. Oneesan nani ga haitten no tte ki-iteru yo.*

                  I wonder what could be in there. Older sister is asking: "What is in there?"

    CHILD: *Purin.*

                  Pudding.

2.   (Child, age 2;3)

    ADULT: *Yotchan no shooboojidoosha misete.*

                  Show me your fire engine.

    CHILD: [No response]

    MOTHER: *Shooboojidoosha da tte.*

                  She said, "Fire engine"

    ADULT: *Shooboojidoosha.*

                  Fire engine.

MOTHER: *Sa, hayaku. Patricia-san misete tte yutteru yo. Isoganakucha. Iso-*
ganaku-cha. A! A!

Well, quickly, Patricia is saying, "Show me it." You must hurry.
You must hurry. Oh! Oh!

Consistent with Japanese emphases on learning to interpret others, mothers
issued directives with rationales based on their own needs and feelings or attributed wishes to others. A total of 45 percent of mothers' stated rationales were of
this type, thus teaching young children to be considerate and responsive.

1. (to child 2;1) *Mama mo nomitai naa.*
Gee, I want to drink too [so give me something to drink].

2. (to child 2;1) *Ano oneechan mo hoshii tte itteru yo.*
That girl is also saying: "I want some."

3. (to child 2;1) *Tottara itaiyo, oneesan itai yo.*
If you pull it [an earring] off, it will hurt, it will hurt her [so don't pull it off].

Because Japanese culture highly values the expression of accommodation and
agreement and the avoidance of overt conflict, children are taught to respond positively regardless of their personal inclinations. One of the mother's directives,
issued to a child (age 2;0) who had refused to lend his toy to a younger child, not
only teaches her child to accede to another's wishes but tells him to make an outright offer of the desired object. And through means of the final tag question, she
asks the boy to join with her in an overt positive assessment of the younger baby
regardless of his inner feelings:

Dame tte yuu no? Hirochan ni mo doozo tte kashite agenakya. Takusan aru kara,
hitotsu doozo tte kashite agenakya. Akachan kawaii deshoo?

Do you say "No!"? You must lend one to Hirochan, saying, "Help yourself."
The baby is cute/lovable, isn't he?

As in all cultures, certain behaviors are considered appropriate, and deviations from them trigger negative reactions. Japanese mothers often evinced somewhat exaggerated responses to a child's nonconformity: (Child, 2;1, was playing
hostess and suddenly began pretending to eat one of the toy dishes)

MOTHER: *Sonna koto shite osara taberu to okashii deshoo? Osara tabeteru hito inai*
deshoo? Ne? Osara dare ga tabeteru no?

Isn't it strange to do that kind of thing, if you eat a plate? No one eats
plates, do they? Who eats plates?

CHILD: *Kore Mahochan.*

Maho [child's name] (eats) this.

MOTHER: *Mahochan ga tabeteru no? Kaijuu mitai. Kowai. Iya. Kowai, obake mitai.*
Mama obake kirai yo.

You're eating it? Like a beast. It's scary. I don't like it. It's scary, like a monster. I hate monsters.

Learning to Express One's Feelings

In contrast to Japanese values, which teach children to guard their feelings and defer to others, Samoan culture encourages discussion and display of emotions, both positive and negative feelings. People openly talk about their own and another's attitudes, reactions, and sentiments. The Samoan language has numerous methods of indicating speakers' emotions and attitudes, including affect particles or interjections signaling anger, *tae* ("shit"), annoyance, *ʔisa,* or disapproval, *aʔa,* or signaling sympathy, *talofae, ota* (Ochs 1986:260). In addition, Samoan has two sets of personal pronouns, one that is semantically neutral for affect and the other that expresses sympathy for the speaker, hearer, or referent, for example, *aʔu* "I," *taʔita* "poor I" (ibid.:268). Neutral and sympathy articles can also be used to express speakers' attitudes toward referents, for example, *le* neutral article, *si* sympathy ("the dear") (ibid.:263).

Children acquire affect markers early in their linguistic development. Significantly, they learn particles and pronouns that express sympathy for oneself before those that indicate empathy for others. Children begin to use affect markers, typically by 20 months of age, prior to their use of neutral pronouns or articles, which often emerges three or four months later (ibid.:266–267).

Affect pronouns are frequently used in formulating directives. By stating sympathy for oneself, a speaker elicits empathy from addressees and obtains compliance with her or his request. The following example is illustrative (ibid.:267):

(child, age 2;5, asking mother for water)

mai	*ua*	*vai*	*deika*
bring	question	water	poor me
"bring	water	for	dear me"

Children acquire most of the positive and negative affect markers before the age of 4 (ibid.). Early learning of this system reflects the emphasis in Samoan culture on expressing and discussing emotions. By encouraging addressees to empathize with speakers, people achieve personal goals, especially in reaching consensus of opinions and obtaining compliance with directives.

Learning to Dispute

In some speech communities, conflict is openly displayed. In a study of preadolescents in a working-class African-American neighborhood of Philadelphia, Marjorie and Charles Goodwin (1987) found that these children did not avoid conflict by deferring to others or mitigating criticisms but instead frequently engaged in open verbal confrontation.

Like all interactions, disagreements are rule-governed events. Children tended to use several stylistic patterns in their disputes. Speakers clearly signaled opposition, often at the beginning of their turn, resulting in explicit, unambiguous rejections or refusals. Note the following examples (ibid.:207, 209–210, 212, 218, 233):

EARL (age 11):   [asking for rubber bands]: Just two.

DARLENE (10):   No! Y'all losin all my rubber bands up.

EDDIE (12):   You didn't have to go to school today, did you.

TERRI (12):   Yes we *did* have to go to school today!

Children repeated part of a previous speaker's talk as a preface to their opposition, highlighting linguistic elements where disagreements are located:

(on reaching a city creek)

PAM (12):   Y'all gonna walk in it?

NETTIE (11):   *Walk* in it, You know where that water come from? The toilet.

Children also focused on disagreement by repeating linguistic sequences and replacing the locus of a verbal challenge with a correction:

DENIECEY (10):   An that happened last year.

TERRI (12):   That happened *this* year.

In these examples, speakers not only do not mitigate their disagreements with the previous speaker's talk, they emphasize opposition both by repeating or substituting for the opposed word and by employing strong stress and changes in pitch. These techniques focus on the source of conflict and additionally "call into question the competence" of the previous speaker. "In essence what is opposed is not simply a position but also an actor responsible for stating such a position" (ibid.:208–209).

Speakers question the interlocutor's competence even more overtly by negative characterizations and insults. For example:

MICHAEL (13):   Me and Huey saw—we saw um: the Witch and the Hangman.

HUEY (14):   The *Hangman* and the *Witch* knucklehead.

Another linguistic technique that maintains and in fact prolongs contradiction is recycling or repeating challenges:

RAYMOND (10):   Boy you broke my skate board.

EARL (11):   No I *didn't*.

RAYMOND: Did *too*.

EARL: Did *not*.

RAYMOND: Did *too*.

All of these strategies were observed in the speech of both girls and boys. However, some gender differences occurred in topics for dispute and by some styles of confrontation. Boys' arguments typically involved assertions of power and challenges to others:

(initial talk refers to an incident in which Cameron was reported to have cried because he lost a key)

JOEY (7):	He—he was gettin ready to cry.
CAMERON (6):	But that wasn't mine.
CAMERON:	Mole!
JOEY:	Mole.
CAMERON:	Ah shud up.
JOEY:	Ah shud up.
CAMERON:	*Make* me.
JOEY:	*Make* me!
CAMERON:	Why donchu make *me*.

In contrast, girls tended not to confront each other directly but to make negative assertions about someone's behavior to a third party. Disputes often took the form of reporting other people's statements, engaging in "he-said-she-said" arguments (ibid.:230). In the process of reporting previous episodes, speakers attempted to justify their actions or statements and to seek support from co-participants in their dispute with others. The following is an illustrative interaction:

PAM (12):	Terri said you said that I wasn't gonna go around *Poplar* no more.
DARLENE (10):	You *said* you weren't.
NETTIE (11):	She—Terri say—
PAM:	And Terri said that um that you said that *Pam* wasn't gonna go around *Poplar* no more.
DARLENE:	That's what Terri said.
PAM:	Well, I *know* what Terri said that you said. She said—She sat there and looked at you. And Terri—And *she* said—And if you have anything to *say* about *me* you come and say it in front of my *face*. And *here* and *right here* you say whatever you got to say cuz *everytime* you go around Poplar you always got something to say.
NETTIE:	Terri *said* it *too*.
PAM:	And I'm telling Terri *too* that she said it.
DARLENE:	I gotta go somewhere.

LEARNING STATUS AND ROLE

Children learn through socialization that people's rights and obligations differ, depending on their status and the kinds of roles they perform. Status is a concept applying to relations in society, but it is manifested within families as well. It is in familial interactions that children first become aware of different categories of people based on characteristics such as age and gender. In a society stratified by age, gender, and status, a child eventually learns that social rights are unequally distributed, that certain types of people have more rights or powers than others. Unequal status within families, then, is a reflection of inequality in the larger society. And it is a necessary component in the continual reproduction of social segmentation. People must learn as children how to order themselves hierarchically as adults. Language usage is one means of transmitting this knowledge. Children observe, as onlookers and participants, the varied interactions among family members. They formulate conceptions of themselves and of their place in the world in accordance with cultural models that are enacted on a daily basis in their households.

Status and Role in American English

Communicative competence related to social stratification is acutely displayed in people's rights to speak and obligations to defer to or comply with others. On the basis of age, children have restricted rights and limited ability to control others. Children's lack of power is shown in several ways. First, they are often unsuccessful in getting the attention of adult addressees. This is obviously a critical problem because desired social interaction is blocked without some attentive response by potential co-participants. In a study of language use in family settings, Susan Ervin-Tripp et al. found that when children of ages 2 to 4 tried to get the attention of someone already engaged in conversation, they were unsuccessful 94 percent of the time. Older children, ages 4 to 7 years, fared somewhat better but still met with overwhelming failure at a rate of 79 percent (1984:124).

Second, children's lack of power is shown by the fact that adults often interrupt their speaking turns. Although our cultural stereotypes portray children as talkative and likely to interrupt others, laboratory and natural observations of familial interactions demonstrate just the opposite. Children are more often interrupted by their parents (Gleason 1987:197). Age, then, confers abilities to demand and maintain the floor. Gender of adult and child also emerges as significant. A number of experimental and home studies indicated that fathers interrupted children more than did mothers and both parents interrupted daughters more often than sons (ibid.). Children themselves replicate this gender-differentiated pattern quite early. In a study by Anita Esposito of children ages from 3;6 to 4;8 who were observed in male/ female encounters, boys interrupted girls twice as frequently as the reverse. In fact, in each of the 10 pairs in Esposito's study, boys were the most frequent interrupters (1979:218).

Esposito's findings on interruption among children differ in an important respect from studies of adults (Zimmerman and West 1975; West and Zimmerman 1983; see Chapter 7). Among adults, women tend to become silent when interrupted by men (Zimmerman and West 1975:123), but in Esposito's observations of children, girls did not react to interruptions in this way (1979:219). Young girls appear not to defer to boys to the same extent that women do to men. However, studies of children indicate that even at very early ages they are already socialized to produce and/or experience unequal encounters.

Power is also displayed in the context of giving and receiving directives. Frequency of issuing directives is correlated with social rights to control others. Linguistic styles chosen to issue commands are sensitive indications of the speaker's rights. Bald imperatives assert power overtly, whereas mitigated expressions, questions, and statements of rationales soften the speaker's control and acknowledge the addressee's feelings or "face." Studies of parent–child interactions indicate that adults consistently issue more directives to children than they receive. Gender differences are relevant too, especially in the type of directive issued. In studies of behavior in natural home settings, Gleason (1987) found that fathers produced bald imperatives twice as often as did mothers. A total of 38 percent of all fathers' utterances were overt commands. Mothers, in contrast, tended to issue requests with mitigating polite constructions and questions. In laboratory observations, parental gender differences were minimal; fathers evidently were sensitive to the public nature of the context and, therefore, demonstrated less explicit power (1987:195). But in daily encounters, children experienced adults' lack of concern for their autonomy.

Fathers socialize sons into competitive behavior not only by issuing direct imperatives but also by adding threats or insults. Commands such as "Don't go in there again or I'll break your head" and references such as "wise guy" and "nutcake" were addressed to sons (ibid.). These encounters no doubt serve as "training grounds" for boys when they interact with other boys in competitive displays and challenges. Later, when they become parents, they reproduce the same hierarchical system with their children.

Children themselves acquire gender-sensitive patterns for expressing directives. Gleason found that by the age of 4, girls and boys issued directives in a similar style to those given by same-sexed parent (ibid.:198). Ervin-Tripp et al. reported that children recognize addressee's gender because they issued less polite directives to their mothers but made mitigating rationales when making requests of fathers (1984:131).

Results of laboratory studies conducted by Elaine Andersen (1986) revealed children's keen awareness of prerogatives of age and gender. Andersen observed 24 children in play sessions in which 5-year-old subjects were given family-role puppets, Mother, Father, and Baby, and were asked to make up stories, speaking the roles of the characters. In the dialogues, Father-puppets issued direct commands, rarely providing rationales or explanations, whereas Mother-puppets mitigated or explained most of their requests. For example (ibid.:155):

MOTHER-PUPPET: Gotta get the baby tucked into beddy bye. She's not a sleepy. [To baby] Go to sleep, sleep, sleep, darling. Go to sleep. [Turns to father] Don't you think it's time to go to bed? It's midnight—we should go to bed.

Mothers' and Babies' style of commanding differed from that of Fathers, par-alleling Gleason's findings of actual speech behavior. But Mothers and Babies also exhibited contrasts. Mothers commonly phrased indirect commands as hints such as "Dinner's ready" (come and eat) or "Now it's time for your naptime" (go to sleep). Babies employed statements of need to soften their commands: "I need breakfast" or "I want to go to the park and play" (ibid.:159, 156).

Various styles of issuing directives imply differences in the rights of the speaker and the addressee. Bald imperatives assert the speaker's power to control actions of others. Hints are expressed as declarative propositions that leave open possibilities of compliance or noncompliance with underlying requests. They are, therefore, sensitive to the addressee's autonomy. Finally, rationales of needs and wants imply that addressees have some obligations to satisfy speakers, as parents have to care for children.

In another study of experimental play, 5-year-olds were asked to enact roles of doctor and patient (Sachs 1987). Observations of pairs of same-sexed children focused on the incidence of "obliges" in children's speech. An *oblige* is a linguistic construction that obligates the addressee to respond. It includes imperatives, pro-hibitions, directives, and questions. The following are some examples from Sachs (ibid.:182):

Oblige	Example
Imperative	Bring her to the hospital.
Prohibitive	Don't touch it.
Declarative directive	You have to push it.
Pretend directive	Pretend you had a bad cut.
Question directive	Will you be the patient?
Tag question	That's your bed, right?
Joint directive	Now we'll cover him up.
State question	Are you sick?
Information question	What does she need now?
Attentional device	Lookit.

Girls and boys expressed obliges with different linguistic structures. The fol-lowing table presents percentages of each type in children's speech (ibid.).

Percentage of Obliges for Boys and Girls

Category	Boys	Girls
Imperative	25%	10%
Prohibition	11	2
Declarative directive	6	5
Pretend directive	4	11
Question directive	0	2
Tag question	16	35
Joint directive	3	15
State question	11	2
Information question	22	16
Attentional device	2	2

Girls and boys used approximately the same absolute numbers of obliges (174 and 186, respectively), but differences in stylistic choice are clear. Boys produced more than twice the percentage of unmitigated (direct and overt) obliges that girls did (42 versus 17 percent), whereas girls used mitigated forms (polite, indirect, implied, explained) nearly twice as often as did boys (65 versus 34 percent) (ibid.:183).

Responses made by recipients of directives have also been studied. Research with four middle-class white families revealed that girls and boys exhibited different kinds of reactions to directives (Ervin-Tripp et al. 1984). Although boys and girls (ages 3 and 4 years) complied with directives at approximately the same rate, they used contrasting modes of noncompliance. Boys were more likely than girls to refuse directives overtly (54 percent versus girls' rate of 35 percent). Girls, however, more often than boys used the strategy of ignoring directives (33 percent for girls and 16 percent for boys) (ibid.:126). This gender difference indicates boys' greater power because an outright refusal is an assertion of autonomy, implying rights to control oneself and challenging the authority of an issuer of commands. Ignoring directives is also an act of self-assertion but in a covert manner. It may not be any more compliant than a refusal, but it is deferential to the issuer's authority.

Communicative competence includes knowledge of interpretive norms that listeners can use to evaluate speech. Speech informs listeners in two respects. First, it transmits speakers' knowledge, intentions, and attitudes. Second, it provides listeners with data from which to make judgments about speakers. When people listen, they learn more than simply the content of messages addressed to them; they also learn something about a speaker's social identity. Cultural stereotypes abound concerning the way different categories of people are thought to communicate. Children acquire these stereotypes as part of their cultural knowledge. And, like any other learning process, children's interpretive rules develop gradually over time with increased experience and exposure to community norms.

One basic feature of a person's social identity is gender. As we have seen, gender is amply reflected in communicative style. It is also subject to beliefs about people's behavior. In order to study degrees of gender stereotyping among different age groups, Carole Edelsky (1977) conducted experiments with four cohorts: first-grade children, third-graders, sixth-graders, and adults. Subjects were presented with 24 sentences containing variants of modifiers, intensifiers, and directives and were asked to decide whether each sentence would likely be spoken by men only, women only, or by men and women with equal likelihood. The following sentences were used, although their order was mixed in presentation so that similar sentences were not sequential (ibid.:228):

1. That's an *adorable* story.
2. That's an *adorable* movie.
3. *Oh dear,* the TV set broke!
4. *Oh dear,* I lost my keys!
5. *My goodness,* there's a friend of mine!
6. *My goodness,* there's the president!

7. *Won't you please* get me that pencil?
8. *Won't you please* close the door?
9. I was *just* exhausted.
10. I was *just* furious.
11. I was *so* mad.
12. I was *so* tired.
13. I was *very* mad.
14. I was *very* tired.
15. That was a great show, *wasn't it?*
16. They did the right thing, *didn't they?*
17. *Close* the door.
18. *Get* me that pencil.
19. *Damn it,* the TV set broke!
20. *Damn it,* I lost my keys!
21. *I'll be damned,* there's a friend of mine!
22. *I'll be damned,* there's the president!
23. I was *damn* mad.
24. You're *damn* right.

The youngest children (first-graders) were not sensitive to vocabulary markers of gender, showing only a low consensus to associating "adorable" with women and "damn it" with men. By third grade, children agreed on assignment of gender for two-thirds of the variables. Responses of sixth-graders were the most interesting when compared to adult interpretations. Sixth-graders assigned gender consistent with adult judgments but actually reflected even stronger consensus about some of the variables than did adults. The table below presents relevant data (ibid.:233).

The three items for which sixth-graders' judgments differed from adults were

| | Age Groups | | | |
Variable	First Grade	Third Grade	Sixth Grade	Adults
Adorable	W	W*	W*	W*
Damn it	M*	M*	M*	M
Damn + adjective	—	M*	M*	M
I'll be damned	—	M*	M*	M*
Oh dear	—	W*	W*	W*
My goodness	—	W	W*	W*
Won't you please	—	W	W*	W
Tag question	—	M/W	W	W
So	—	—	W	W
Very	—	—	W	W
Just	—	—	W	W
Command	—	—	M	M/W

W* = female, high consensus; W = female, low consensus;
M* = male, high consensus; M = male, low consensus; M/W = neutral;
— = not meeting criteria.

higher consensus on "damn" and "damn it" associated with men, higher consensus on "won't you please" attributed to women, and exclusive assignment of commands to men. When Edelsky asked children to explain their judgments, a frequent comment was "Men swear but ladies don't" (ibid.:235). Although this cultural stereotype is prevalent in our society, adults certainly know that women do swear, and therefore they are less likely to assign profanity exclusively to men. Two children's remarks about directives and politeness are relevant to the other variables for which children had stronger reactions than adults did. In discussing home situations, they observed that "She *has* to be polite because we won't do it if she doesn't say 'please,' but if a man doesn't say it, we sure will anyway" and "The man is thought of as the king of his house or something and he can tell you what to do, and the lady just *wants* you to close the door while the man tells you to and expects you to do it" (ibid.:238; emphasis in original).

The results of Edelsky's study and the comments of the children themselves provide rich evidence of the strength of gender categorization and of the acquisition of knowledge about social meanings of language. Children learn these meanings as part of their enculturation. Once learned, their judgments appear to be more constrained by stereotypes than are adults'. Perhaps because children have less real-life experience with actual variation among speakers, they are more influenced by idealized models.

One of the ways that children acquire models of gender and social relations is through their exposure to and incorporation into family interactions. In their study of dinnertime narratives, Elinor Ochs and Carolyn Taylor observe that "certainly from the point of view of a child, routine moments of family communication are the earliest and perhaps the most profound medium for constructing gender understandings" (1995:98). Rights of family members were constructed and enacted through their participation in various roles in accounts of past and present activities. Based on recordings of 100 spontaneous narratives, Ochs and Taylor describe a "Father knows best" family dynamic in which "father is set up to be primary audience, judge and critic of family members' actions, thoughts and feelings" (ibid.:99). Children figured as "protagonists" (person who the story was about) in 60 percent of narratives, mothers were protagonists in 23 percent and fathers in 19 percent. Therefore, children's actions and thoughts were most open to the scrutiny of others, whereas fathers were the "least vulnerable family members" (ibid.:102). The preponderance of children as protagonists was reversed by their rarity as narrative "introducers" (the person selecting the topic). Only about one-third of the stories about the children were introduced by the child him- or herself. Instead, parents (especially mothers) focused the narrative on the child's actions, thus reflecting and reinforcing the child's lack of privacy and powerlessness by exposing the child to the scrutiny of others. Finally, stories were most often oriented to fathers as "primary recipients," thus setting up father as the "family judge" with rights to evaluate others. Although fathers sometimes held this role by virtue of self-selection, most often mothers introduced narratives with fathers as recipients. And while protagonists were most often children, mothers were more likely to orient stories about themselves to fathers than fathers were to orient stories about themselves to mothers. By doing so, women not only set up fathers as judges but also set themselves up as targets of fathers' evaluation and criticism.

A complex play of family and interactional power is enacted through the narrative dynamics. In the most frequent pattern, women hold the powerful role of selecting narrative topics and protagonists, but they then transfer family power to fathers, who act as judges of members' actions and thoughts. Ochs and Taylor, therefore, conclude that mothers' "exercise of power is ephemeral and may even be self-destructive by giving fathers a platform for monitoring and judging wives and children. . . . Women may wittingly or unwittingly contribute to—and even set up—the daily reconstruction of a "Father knows best" ideological dynamic" (ibid.:116–117). Children are socialized into the ideology of asymmetric gender relations both because they are witnesses to it as audience and because they are engulfed in it when they are chosen (usually by others) as protagonists in the drama.

Status in Samoan

Children in all cultures are sensitive to status of individuals in their households and their society and need to learn to recognize people's rights. Every society expresses meanings related to social status in specific linguistic form. In the speech of Samoan children, use of two imperatives, *aumai* "bring/give" and *sau* "come," is correlated with status and expresses a child's understanding of the status differences between speaker and addressee (Platt 1986). These verbs are significantly distinguished in Samoan speech in terms of hierarchical orderings between speaker and addressee. The verb *aumai* "bring/give" implies the speaker's right to expect and demand a portion of available objects, goods, and resources. All members of a household, including children, reciprocally share these rights. In contrast, *sau* "come" expresses social power to direct and control another's actions. This power is not evenly distributed among people but is given to those of high status. Within households, people's status is based on age; children, therefore, are of lower rank than adults; older children have higher status than younger ones. *Sau* "come" is appropriately used by higher-ranked people to those of lower status because the former have authority to control the latter. It is, therefore, seldom used by children. The verb *aumai* "bring/give" is not restricted in this way and is commonly employed by lower- to higher-status people (Platt 1986:141–142).

Samoan children learn the culturally prescribed social meanings of *sau* and *aumai* at a very early age. As might be expected, they acquire *aumai* much earlier than *sau* because they most often interact with older, that is, higher-status, people. The authority expressed in *sau* is not available to children in most daily encounters. Children use *sau* mainly to infants or to domesticated animals (ibid.:142).

Relationships in Hungarian

Terms of address are sensitive indicators of social status and interpersonal relationships. In languages with complex pronoun systems based on participants' identity, children need to learn social meanings expressed by these linguistic forms. In Hungarian, adult speakers select among four possibilities: familiar (T), formal (V), polite (P), and formal-polite (VP). Children typically use either familiar T or polite P (Hollos 1977:213). Hungarian address is marked in pronouns and verbs according to the following conventions (ibid.:222):

> Familiar T: *te* + second-person singular verb
>
> Formal V: *maga* + third-person singular verb
>
> Polite P: title/honorific + last name or title/honorific + first name + third-person singular of verb "to wish, like, please" + infinitive of main verb
>
> Formal-Polite V/P: *on* + third-person singular verb

Adults use these forms depending on similarities or differences in age, gender, status, and familiarity in relation to addressees. Pronoun use is an elaborate system, requiring awareness of both social relations and complex linguistic rules. Familiar T is exchanged between kin of similar ages and between same-sexed nonkin with whom one has a close friendship. Formal V is exchanged between status equals who are socially distant. Nonreciprocal P/T is used by participants who are of markedly different ages or statuses; the younger/lower-status individual employs Polite P and receives Familiar T. Children use reciprocal T with other children or young people and nonreciprocal P/T with their elders (ibid.:223).

In a study of children's knowledge of social meanings in address forms, Marida Hollos (1977) presented subjects (ages 7 through 9) with two sets of tasks. In one task, Hollos showed children pictures of scenes with figures engaged in daily activities, such as shopping and visiting. Subjects were asked to play the roles of various figures. They were directed with such questions as: "How does your mother greet the shopkeeper when she goes shopping? Ask for some eggs, as your mother would." In a second task, Hollos again presented children with pictures of scenes, but dialogue was supplied; the children were asked to decide which of three addressees would be the appropriate recipient of each question or command. The utterances contained three kinds of pronominal usage: familiar T, formal V, and polite P; for instance, Mother, using P, asks: "Did you leave the door open?" The choices were [a] grandfather (appropriate form P); [b] child (T); and [c] veterinarian (V). In another example, Doctor, using V, states: "You have to take this medicine three times a day." The choices were: [a] a stranger from the city (appropriate form V); [b] grandmother (P); and [c] teacher (V) (ibid.:217).

Children at all ages in Hollos's study recognized and used appropriate pronouns in depicted interactions between children (mutual T) and between children and adults (nonreciprocal P/T). They also correctly employed mutual T between familiar adults (ibid.:218). Children's ability in these tasks is based on the scenes' compatibility with daily life. Because they interact with other children and with adults and because they observe conversations between familiar adults in their households, they easily comprehend and apply the underlying social meanings of T and P pronouns.

Children had the most difficulty in assigning or producing appropriate forms of address for encounters between unfamiliar adults. They erroneously assumed that unfamiliar adults consistently exchange P because this is the address form that a child would use to an adult. In other words, children's judgments are influenced by their own experience. Nine-year-olds made fewer errors than younger subjects, demonstrating that they were acquiring keener sensitivity to the social semantics involved. As Hollos observed, they were also developing the cognitive ability to "switch perspectives with others" (ibid.:222).

LEARNING TO CONVERSE

Speaking is a social activity, involving intentions related to co-participants. The speaker's competence includes knowledge of rules for beginning, maintaining, and ending conversations. Because talk occurs in specific speech events, it must, therefore, be relevant to the context that includes topics, participants' interests, and ongoing activities. Children need to learn how to converse in a relevant, coherent manner. They need to learn the complex rules that organize talk. A child's ability to perform successfully depends on cognitive, linguistic, and social maturation. These three aspects of development are interrelated, each one aiding the others in progressing toward full social engagement.

Knowledge of Structure

As we saw in Chapter 5, conversation is based on alternation of turns. In two-party encounters, roles of speaker and listener are continually exchanged. Turns to speak are automatically assigned, so that when one speaker ends, the next turn belongs to the listener. Even infants are exposed to this rule when adults carry on "dialogues" with them. Adults talking to babies typically pause at the end of each discourse unit, leaving an empty turn for the infant. An adult may continue with another statement or may fill in a baby's turn by "translating" the latter's intentional or unintentional vocalizations.

It is not until children are nearly 3 years old that they learn to take speaker turns. By then they know that they need to make some response, even if just with audible sound fillers such as "mm," when the previous speaker has ended. They also know to wait to speak until the interlocutor has completed her or his turn. In studies of young children's conversations, Catherine Garvey (1984) observed very few overlaps in children's conversation (only about 4 to 5 percent of utterances), indicating that these young speakers had acquired the "one-turn-at-a-time" rule (ibid.:55).

Children also learn quite early that when questions are asked, addressees are obliged to respond. Through prompting and other routines, they realize that when questioned, they must answer or at least make a minimal response. As speakers, children strategically employ questions to engage others in talk. Children often issue a rapid sequence of questions in order to secure responses from otherwise uncooperative addressees. Another ploy children use to gain the floor is the "Y'know what?" or "Guess what?" gambit. The addressee's automatic response ("What?") gives the turn back to the child. The fact that children resort to these tactics indicates their relative difficulties in social encounters and their creativity in persevering to establish their right to talk.

Young speakers do encounter obstacles, however. First, as already discussed, their turns are often interrupted by adults (Gleason 1987:197). Second, although they manage well in two-party encounters, they have problems with multiparty interactions, particularly those involving older children or adults. Their problems are both linguistic and social. Because of the fast pace of conversation, young children are not always able to ask for explanations or clarifications of words that they do not understand. Even when a child is given an opportunity to ask for clarification, she needs to learn how to focus on the troublesome element. This is not as simple as it might appear. We can recall David McNeill's characterization of children's early thinking as "imagistic" (1987:254). But language is linear and requires segmenting (or "unpacking") thought into units that are arranged syntagmatically. Just as a young child's thought is holistic, so is his comprehension. Therefore, when children do not understand an utterance, it is difficult for them to locate the specific segment causing problems.

Children encounter additional difficulties in conversing. Because young children have not developed the skill needed to time their turn to the end of the previous speaker's, their intention to speak next may not be recognized by co-participants. Additionally, children have trouble retaining the floor even after it has been allocated to them. A helpful strategy is usage of fillers such as "y'know" or "um," "uh," and the like. These allow the current speaker to maintain his or her turn while pausing to check thoughts or wordings. Children need to acquire this tactic because "empty" pauses are quickly colonized by interlocutors. Very young children do not employ sophisticated means but resort to simple repetition of sounds or words while trying to organize their speech. Note the following utterance of a boy (age 2;8) trying to explain why his stomach hurt: "Cause i-/i-/i-/i-/i-/ it was hurting cause i-/ it was hurting because it was hurting/ . . . and/ . . . and it feels all better now" (Garvey 1984:38). By the age of 4 or 5, however, children begin to use more conventional fillers.

A child also learns to give appropriate signals to speakers indicating active listenership. These signs, or backchannel cues, include such behaviors as nods and smiles and vocalizations like "um," "yeah," or "uh huh." In adult interactions, backchannel cues need to be well timed to the speaker's utterances. Because they involve attention to linguistic units as well as to content, their appropriate use depends on more complex processing than young children can manage. Not surprisingly, they do not appear until late in childhood and are not well utilized until adolescence (ibid.:37).

Cohesion in Conversation

Another important feature of conversation is its cohesion across speaker turns. Talk is linked to prior talk not only within turns but also to one's previous statements and to those of other speakers. Directive-response pairs (e.g., question-answer, command-action) obviously depend on this association. A response must be related to the directive, either by supplying/performing appropriate information/actions or by explaining one's noncompliance. Children recognize this cohesive bond in their use of serial questioning as a conversational strategy.

Declarative propositions exhibit cohesion within and across turns as well. Cohesion is achieved through content and linguistic form. First, conversations are about something, about topics. Topics normally shift during encounters, but the content of talk should be focused or relevant to current issues. More complex, however, are the linguistic devices used to organize discourse. Lack of skill in employing such markers is, in fact, a distinctive trait of young children's speech.

In English, cohesion is achieved through various means, including use of pronouns and demonstratives (this, that) and processes of substitution, comparison, conjunction, and clausal dependency. Pronouns and demonstratives relate or refer to previously mentioned entities. Comparatives (same, other, more) have similar functions. These devices also serve to eliminate redundancies that could potentially overwhelm verbal output. They are an aspect of language's economy, allowing speakers to delete long sequences and replace them with single words. Conjunctions serve a similar function, permitting omission of portions of underlying sentences. Children acquire these basic cohesive devices quite early. In fact, experiments asking for imitation reveal children's drive to produce naturally efficient speech in their occasional nonimitation of models. Recall Dan Slobin's dialogue (see Chapter 9) in which an adult prompted with "Here is a brown brush and here is a comb" and the child (age 2;4) responded, "Here's a brown brush an' a comb."

Garvey's research indicated that children acquire some cohesive devices by the age of 2;6 to 3 years. The most commonly used forms were pronouns (56 percent), followed in frequency by demonstratives (21 percent); comparatives were rare (1984:86). The conjunction "and" is learned even earlier, usually by age 2, although its first uses are somewhat indiscriminate. For example, a child (age 2;3), wanting her mother to read a book, said, "Would you read it to me? And I'll listen." Another use occurred in "Hold the ladder and it won't fall down."

Cohesion is also achieved through substitutions of words. One type is use of synonyms or paraphrases that minimize the appearance of repetitiveness but link current to prior talk. Young children's substitutions are at first global—"thing," "stuff," "do"—but gradually they become more selective and informative.

Another cohesive process that reduces output is ellipsis. Ellipsis involves omission of textual material that is assumed to be shared by co-participants (e.g., "What's in there?"/"Cookies" (are in there). Sharing of knowledge, or presupposition, is based on expectations that participants recall and can refer to prior talk. Young children begin to use ellipsis systematically by the age of 3. The following table presents Garvey's data for incidence of elided segments in speech of 3- to 5-year-olds (ibid.:83–84). Note that percentages indicate proportion of all elided utterances in the corpus (accounting for 22 percent of all of the children's speech).

Type of Signal Retained	Example	Percentage
1. Polarity marker	Are you ready? Yes (I am ready).	40
2. Modal element	Can you see it? I can (see it).	13
3. Wh- component	There's only one thing to do. What? (is the one thing to do).	11
4. Logical connective	Why don't you want to do anything? (I don't want to do anything) 'Cause I'd rather be back in school.	9
5. Complement	What do we have to use? (We have to use) A raincoat.	7
6. Subject	What's in there? Cookies (are in there).	6
7. Matrix clause	Where did the table go? I'll show you (where the table went).	6
8. Adjunct of clause	Where's the man? (Is the man) At the factory?	2
9. Lexical verb	I go get some ice cream after my mommy comes. You won't go (get some ice cream after your mommy comes).	2
10. Simple verb	There's no play houses. Yes, there is (play houses).	2

Interactional Cooperation

In order to converse appropriately, children need to learn that communicative interaction is cooperative. Participants normally signal their attentiveness not only to each other's talk but also to each other as people through markers of politeness, including such phrases as "please" and "thank you," forms of address, ritualized greetings and partings, and apologies. Many of these are overtly taught to children as part of their socialization. Polite signals indicate one's concern for participants and help minimize potential conflict because they recognize addressees' rights to fair treatment.

Interactions often involve requests between co-participants. In children's encounters, a frequent type of request is a request-for-permission, including entreaties for use of toys and play areas or admission to play groups. To obtain one's goals, speakers need to phrase their desire in an appropriate form. A request that is too abrupt and demanding may be rejected, although one that is too unobtrusive risks being ignored. Children learn a multitude of strategies, adjusting their choice to perceived situations and interlocutors. In the following dialogue, two children, Judy (age 2;8) and Tom (2;9) mutually construct their play (Garvey 1984:112).

Tom	*Judy*
Can I play here?	
	Yeah, you can.

(Sits down by Judy and
points to a plate.) Can I
have some muffins?

> Don't touch them, 'cause
> they're very hot.

I'm gonna put a little sugar
in your muffins, all right?

> (Judy watches as Tom pretends
> to sprinkle sugar on the
> imaginary muffins.)

In this delicate situation, Tom requests permission while recognizing Judy's prior claim to space and objects. Although Judy denies Tom access to the muffins, she acknowledges the legitimacy of his wishes by justifying the denial. Tom obeys Judy's prohibition against touch but interacts with the imaginary muffins nonetheless, after again asking permission, that is, "all right?"

When their desires are blocked by others, children try to achieve their goals by resorting to repetitions, rephrasings, explanations, and additional claims. The following encounter between Judy and Tom is an example of request and response moves (ibid.:124).

Judy	Tom
(Stands beside wooden car) Can I have a turn now?	(Driving wooden car)
	(No response.)
I have a turn now?	I'm doing it right now.
When you finished?	I'm not finished yet.
Awright. (Continues to stand by car and look at Tom)	(Drives for seconds) Now I'm finished. (Climbs off car)
(Gets on car)	

Children frequently seek permission to join play groups. When groups are already established, children need to use various strategies in order to gain admittance. For example, examine the following scene of nursery-school children (Corsaro 1979:320–321):

Two girls, Jenny (4;0) and Betty (3;9) are playing around a sandbox, putting sand in pots, pans, and bottles. Another girl, Debbie (4;1), approaches. Neither J nor B acknowledges her presence. D doesn't speak to them and no one speaks to her. After watching for five minutes, she circles the sandbox three times and stops. After a few more minutes of watching, D moves to the sandbox and reaches for a teapot in the sand. J takes the pot away from D and mumbles "No." D backs away and again observes J and B. She then walks over next to B, who is filling the cupcake pan with sand. D watches B for just a few seconds, then says:

D–B: We're friends, right? We're friends, right, B?

        (B, not looking up at D, continues to place sand in pan and says:)

B–D: Right.

        (D now moves alongside B, takes a pot and begins putting sand in it.)

D–B: I'm making coffee.

B–D: I'm making cupcakes.

B–J: We're mothers, right, J?

J–B: Right.

D employs several strategies in this encounter. Although her first overt attempt at admission is rebuffed, she had carefully prepared the way through nonverbal cues. After an interval of time, she changes moves and begins with a personal appeal to prior status as a friend of B. When this is acknowledged, she engages in independent but parallel activity (making coffee). B responds with a correlated action and explanation (making cupcakes). Finally, the triad is completed by placating and reaffirming bonds with J.

In his study of nursery-school encounters, William Corsaro isolated a large number of "access strategies," some of which proved more successful than others (ibid.:324). Among the more helpful were these:

1. Producing a variant of ongoing behavior
2. Questioning participants
3. Offering of object
4. Greeting
5. Reference to affiliation

In contrast, the least likely to achieve positive results were

1. Disruptive entry
2. Reference to adult authority
3. Claim on area or object

Children typically do not abandon their attempts to gain entry when they receive a negative response. Instead, they often try again (as in the scene above), selecting an alternative tactic. On the whole, indirect strategies tend to be more successful than direct or intrusive moves. Indirection in verbal and nonverbal behavior is considered a feature of politeness and thereby acknowledges people's rights and claims. Politeness on the part of one actor tends to be answered by polite responses by others.

Narratives

Conversations frequently include reportings of previous experiences. These personal narratives recount events having immediate relevance to the speaker as part of her life. Narrators are obligated to make their stories relevant to addressees as well. Events reported should be shown to exemplify a more general point or to have some extra-situational value, to be entertaining or enlightening. In other words, they should be "newsworthy."

Reporting one's experiences is a skill that develops gradually in children. Young children encounter a range of difficulties. First, they often choose to relate events that are not particularly interesting to listeners, especially to adult listeners. And children have trouble making their stories engaging on the basis of other criteria, for example, by being dramatic or enlightening. A child's limited experiences naturally restrict the kinds of events he or she can report. But more important is his or her inability to employ narrative devices that contribute linguistically to a story's appeal.

Personal narratives are constructed with six different components (Labov and Waletzky 1967):

1. *Abstract:* Summarizes the main point or result of the story
2. *Orientation:* Identifies time, place, characters
3. *Complicating action:* Recounts events, in chronological sequence
4. *Evaluation:* Transmits attitudes or emotions of speaker and/or other characters
5. *Result or resolution:* Provides point of story
6. *Coda:* Terminates story, so that listeners do not ask: "And then what happened?"

Narratives must contain complicating action and resolution, but the other components are optional. Even if all segments are included, speakers may elaborate certain sections while providing scant treatment of others. Very young children tend to relate actions but omit orientations and codas. A serious flaw in their narratives is the lack of evaluative material. Young children evidently assume that actions are important or newsworthy enough to maintain audience interest.

Research by Keith Kernan (1977) on narratives produced by African-American girls in an urban California community revealed differences in structural and linguistic devices used by younger and older speakers. Stories told by young girls (ages 7–8) were predominantly composed of complicating action. Only one story in this group contained an abstract. Orientations did introduce the texts but were quite short and typically were confined to brief note of characters or places. Young children often mentioned the names of characters, giving no other identifying features, even though their audience was unfamiliar with the people named (ibid.:94–95).

Older girls (ages 10–14) usually began their stories with abstracts or introductions, such as:

1. We almost drowned in L.A.
2. First time I ever got scared is when, when you know, that them two mens got killed down there.

Orientation sections by older children were elaborate, making up roughly 20 percent of an entire story. Girls included statements of mood and motivation as well as characters and places in making their narratives relevant and appealing to audiences. Within stories, older speakers effectively evaluated or attributed evaluations of ongoing events to others. They also used stylistic devices such as repetition, paraphrasing, or exaggeration in order to capture and maintain audience interest. For instance (ibid.:98):

> An girl, you know, half of the cake was gone. I was so mad I almost cried, girl. I say "Mama, I told you Tommy was gonna eat all that cake," I mean, Tommy had him a big, giant piece, girl. That cake was gone.

Finally, older girls were more skilled at terminating their stories. Some simply brought the narrative to a concise close, and others ended with condensed statements of the moral point of the text (ibid.:96):

1. And they still letting her play no matter what they say.
2. I felt sorry. I shouldn't did that in the first place.
3. That's how they get killed. By going in other people's business.

Linguistic framing is an important element in any kind of communicative activity. Co-participants have to signal their awareness of an event's beginning and ending. Young narrators are not aware of this necessity. Their interactional strategies tend to be oriented toward their own interests and needs, whereas older speakers understand that they have to make personal experiences relevant to listeners.

In a collection of narratives produced by boys and young men living in Harlem, younger speakers described events in simple chronological order with little or no introduction, identification of characters, or evaluation. For example, the following story was told by a young child about an episode in a television program (Labov 1972:367):

> This kid got shot and he had to go on a mission. And so this kid, he went with Solo. So they went and this guy—they went through this window, and they caught him. And then he beat up them other people. And they went and then he said that this old lady was his mother and then he—and at the end he say that he was the guy's friend.

Older children were able to dramatize and evaluate events, as in the next story, told by a boy of 11 (ibid.:368):

> When I was in fourth grade—no, it was in third grade—This boy he stole my glove. He took my glove and said that his father found it downtown on the ground. I told him that it was impossible for him to find downtown 'cause all those other people were walking by and just his father was the only one that found it? So he got all mad. Then I fought him. I knocked him all out in the street. So he say he give. And I kept on hitting him. Then he started crying and ran home to his father. And the father told him that he ain't find no glove.

The first story is hard, if not impossible, for a listener to follow. Pronouns are used without previous mention of referents. It is a skeletal recounting of facts. In striking contrast, the second narrator provides enough contextual information so that listeners can easily understand events. In addition, the speaker uses stylistic devices to continually highlight the story's major point. Each statement develops the theme by adding new and pertinent information. Finally, the story ends with reference to the antagonist's father, succinctly justifying the narrator's actions.

Use of evaluative comments increased with the age of storytellers, and older speakers employed more elaborate embedding of evaluation into their stories. They effectively used quantifiers ("he had cuts all over") and repetition ("You bleedin', you bleedin', Speedy you bleedin'!") to intensify the impact of actions (ibid.:379).

Both Kernan's and Labov's research demonstrate that older children acquire sophisticated linguistic techniques in narration. But employment of these skills rests on social maturity. Older speakers realize that they must attract and maintain listener interest on the basis of shared assumptions about relevance existing outside the narrative itself.

SUMMARY

Communicative competence is the knowledge of cultural rules for appropriate use of language in social interaction. It includes ability to utilize these rules in situated speech events, recognizing the intentions of speakers and the needs and rights of listeners. As part of socialization processes, children learn that language can fulfill a variety of functions. Through example, prompting, and correction, they are encouraged to adopt communicative behaviors consistent with prevailing values about the propriety of expressing one's opinions, directing another's actions, or deferring to co-participants.

Children become aware of the social order of their community through daily interactions within their households. They learn that classifications of people based on factors such as age, gender, and status are reflected in styles of conversational interaction. These styles manifest and maintain cultural models of people's differentiated claims to rights and authority in relation to others. Children acquire communicative competence through development of linguistic and sociolinguistic skills. They improve their ability to employ formal rules of their language, and they learn that stylistic variants have social and situational meaning. This learning takes place in the context of increasing interpersonal maturity, recognizing that speaking is a social activity and must be attuned to the expectations, assumptions, and needs of others as well as of oneself.

REFERENCES

ANDERSEN, ELAINE. 1986. The acquisition of register variation by Anglo-American children. In *Language Socialization Across Cultures*, ed. B. Schieffelin and E. Ochs. New York: Cambridge University Press, pp. 153–161.

CLANCY, PATRICIA. 1986. The acquisition

of communicative style in Japanese. In *Language Socialization Across Cultures,* ed. B. Schieffelin and E. Ochs. New York: Cambridge University Press, pp. 213–250.

CORSARO, WILLIAM. 1979. "We're friends, right?" Children's use of access rituals in a nursery school. *Language in Society* 8:315–336.

EDELSKY, CAROLE. 1977. Acquisition of an aspect of communicative competence: Learning what it means to talk like a lady. In *Child Discourse,* ed. S. Ervin-Tripp and C. Mitchell-Kernan. New York: Academic Press, pp. 225–243.

ERVIN-TRIPP, SUSAN, M. O'CONNOR, AND J. ROSENBERG. 1984. Language and power in the family. In *Language and Power,* ed. C. Kramarae, M. Schulz, and W. O'Barr. Newbury Park, CA: Sage, pp. 116–135.

ESPOSITO, ANITA. 1979. Sex differences in children's conversation. *Language and Speech* 22:213–220.

GARVEY, CATHERINE. 1984. *Children's Talk.* Cambridge, MA: Harvard University Press.

GLEASON, JEAN B. 1987. Sex differences in parent-child interaction. In *Language, Gender and Sex in Comparative Perspective,* ed. S. Philips, S. Steele, and C. Tanz. New York: Cambridge University Press, pp. 189–199.

GOODWIN, MARJORIE, AND CHARLES GOODWIN. 1987. Children's arguing. In *Language, Gender and Sex in Comparative Perspective,* ed. S. Philips, S. Steele, and C. Tanz. New York: Cambridge University Press, pp. 200–248.

HALLIDAY, M.A.K. 1973. *Explorations in the Functions of Language.* Hawthorne, NY: Elsevier North-Holland.

HOLLOS, MARIDA. 1977. Comprehension and use of social rules in pronoun selection by Hungarian children. In *Child Discourse,* ed. S. Ervin-Tripp and C. Mitchell-Kernan. New York: Academic Press, pp. 211–223.

KERNAN, KEITH. 1977. Semantic and expressive elaboration in children's narratives. In *Child Discourse,* ed. S. Ervin-Tripp and C. Mitchell-Kernan. New York: Academic Press, pp. 91–102.

LABOV, WILLIAM. 1972. The transformation of experience in narrative syntax. In *Language in the Inner City,* ed. William Labov. Philadelphia: University of Pennsylvania Press, pp. 354–396.

LABOV, WILLIAM, AND J. WALETZKY. 1967. Narrative analysis. In *Essays on the Verbal and Visual Arts,* ed. J. Helm. Seattle: University of Washington Press, pp. 12–44.

MCNEILL, DAVID. 1987. *Psycholinguistics: A New Approach.* New York: Harper & Row.

OCHS, ELINOR. 1986. From feelings to grammar: A Samoan case study. In *Language Socialization Across Cultures,* ed. B. Schieffelin and E. Ochs. New York: Cambridge University Press, pp. 251–272.

OCHS, ELINOR, AND CAROLYN TAYLOR. 1995. The "Father knows best" dynamic in dinnertime narratives. In *Gender Articulated: Language and the Socially Constructed Self,* ed. K. Hall and M. Bucholtz. New York: Routledge, pp. 97–120.

PLATT, MARTHA. 1986. Social norms and lexical acquisition: A study of deictic verbs in Samoan child language. In *Language Socialization Across Cultures,* ed. B. Schieffelin and E. Ochs. New York: Cambridge University Press, pp. 127–152.

SACHS, JACQUELINE. 1987. Preschool boys' and girls' language use in pretend play. In *Language, Gender and Sex in*

Comparative Perspective, ed. S. Philips, S. Steele, and C. Tanz. New York: Cambridge University Press, pp. 178–188.

WEST, CANDACE, AND DON ZIMMERMAN. 1983. Small insults: A study of interruptions in cross-sex conversations between unacquainted persons. In *Lan-* *guage, Gender and Society,* ed. B. Thorne, C. Kramarae, and N. Henley. Rowley, MA: Newbury, pp. 103–118.

ZIMMERMAN, DON, AND C. WEST. 1975. Sex roles, interruptions and silences in conversation. In *Language and Sex,* ed. B. Thorne and N. Henley. Rowley, MA: Newbury, pp. 105–129.

11

Multilingual Nations

Note the contentious language in the following dialogue between two bilingual Canadians, one (the man) a native speaker of English and the other (the receptionist) a native French speaker:

MAN:	Could you tell me where the French test is?
RECEPTIONIST (IN FRENCH):	Pardon? ("Pardon?")
MAN:	Could you tell me where the French test is?
RECEPTIONIST:	En français? ("In French?")
MAN:	I have the right to be addressed in English by the government of Quebec according to Bill 101.
RECEPTIONIST (TO A THIRD PERSON):	Qu'est-ce qu'il dit? ("What's he saying?")

Both speakers are bilingual in English and French, so they can well understand each other. Either speaker could have chosen to use the language preferred by the interlocutor. Because the man spoke first, in English, the receptionist could have responded in English. Failing that, the man could have next repeated his question in French after the receptionist's French response. But neither speaker was willing to accommodate the other. Instead, they both insisted on continuing to use their own native language. Such an interaction is symbolic of linguistic and, as we shall see later in the chapter, social, economic, and political conflicts in Canada. It is commonly played out elsewhere in the world as well where different ethnic groups compete for economic and political control in their communities and nations.

All modern nations are multilingual in the sense that some sectors of their population speak more than one language. Presumably even in earlier, small-scale societies, at least some members were bilingual or multilingual. Because trade, travel, and intermarriage between neighboring or distant peoples have always occurred, the convenience and/or need to speak the language of another group has been an obvious social fact.

In this chapter we begin by examining relations of languages in two multilingual countries, India and Canada. We then describe and analyze linguistic diversity, public policies, and attitudes concerning languages in the United States.

In multilingual communities, each language has a particular status, one (or some) having greater prestige than others. Many factors contribute to linguistic ranking, including the social status of native speakers and economic, political, and social contexts of contact. In some cases relatively benign attitudes are maintained, but elsewhere, conflict among members of different linguistic groups disrupts societal cohesion. We now turn to a discussion of these issues in the context of India and Canada.

INDIA

Linguistic Diversity

Linguistic diversity in India is enormous. Hundreds of different languages are spoken, distributed among four distinct language families: Indo-Aryan, Dravidian, Austro-Asiatic, and Tibeto-Burman. These families are represented among Indian speakers as follows: Indo-Aryan, 74 percent; Dravidian, 24 percent; Austro-Asiatic, 1.5 percent; and Tibeto-Burman, 0.70 percent (Census of India 1981). The map in Figure 11.1 on page 301 illustrates areas of concentration of the language families.

Prior to India's independence in 1947, English was the country's governmental language. Its prominence originated from Great Britain's economic and political control from the eighteenth century until independence. English was the language of the colonizers and became a second language of indigenous elite classes. After independence, as part of a rejection of India's colonial era, the governing Congress Party gave "official" status to Hindi, an Indo-Aryan language presently spoken by more than 260 million people. The government also hoped that establishing one official language would help to integrate the hundreds of ethnic groups living in India.

India's constitution of 1948 recognized linguistic diversity by granting "national" status to the following 15 languages (Census of India 1980; note that a census was not taken in the state of Assam; therefore, the figure for speakers of Assamese is far from complete; Census of India 1981).

In the early 1950s, the Indian government began to reorganize its internal polities and confronted the serious problem of linguistic and ethnic diversity within its borders. A principle of linguistic homogeneity was used to establish states. In all but 2 of India's 18 states, a majority of residents speak a common language. However, "homogeneity" is a misleading term, implying complete or near complete similarity. Such a situation does not exist in any Indian state. Rather,

Language	Number of Speakers (in millions)	Percentage
1. Assamese	0.07	0.01
	(8.95, Census of 1971)	
2. Bengali	51.50	7.79
3. Gujarati	33.19	5.02
4. Hindi	264.18	39.94
5. Kannada	26.89	4.06
6. Kashmiri	3.17	0.48
7. Malayalam	25.95	3.92
8. Marathi	49.62	7.50
9. Oriya	22.88	3.46
10. Punjabi	18.59	2.81
11. Sanskrit	0.003	
12. Sindhi	1.95	0.29
13. Tamil	44.73	6.76
14. Telugu	54.23	8.20
15. Urdu	35.32	5.34

although states may have a majority of speakers of a single language, percentages vary from just over 50 percent (Assamese in Assam) upwards to 95 percent (Malayalam in Kerala). And despite goals of linguistic uniformity, some states have no numerically dominant language (e.g., Himachal Pradesh) (Apte 1976:155).

Conflicts over boundaries between states have continued. As late as 1966, the former state of Punjab was subdivided into Hindi-speaking Harayana and Punjab-speaking Punjab. Some regional border disputes are still ongoing, for example, between Kannada-speaking Mysore and Marathi-speaking Maharashtra. A number of areas in dispute between two states have become "union territories" and are administered by the central government. For example, Goa declined to become merged with the neighboring state of Maharashtra. Both the states of Punjab and Harayana have claimed the city of Chandigarh, but the city has so far remained independent (ibid.:147). These conflicts indicate the complexity of ethnic and linguistic divisions in India and the difficulties in reaching compromise.

In addition to Hindi (the country's "official" language) and 14 other "national" languages, each state can choose its own "regional" language. A state can adopt Hindi as its regional language, or it may select another code from among those spoken in its territory for use in local government affairs and in education. India's constitution further guarantees rights of all citizens to communicate in their own language and allows them to interact with any government agency in a code of their choice (ibid.:144).

Of the 18 states, 6 have selected Hindi as their sole regional language (Bihar, Haryana, Himachal Pradesh, Madhya Pradesh, Rajastan, Uttar Pradesh); 1 state (Gujarat) has chosen Hindi and an indigenous code (Gujarati); English is the regional language of 3 states (Kerala, Mysore, Nagaland); English and Oriya are the languages of the state of Orissa; in the remaining 7 states, indigenous regional languages have been designated (Andra Pradesh: Telugu; Assam: Assamese;

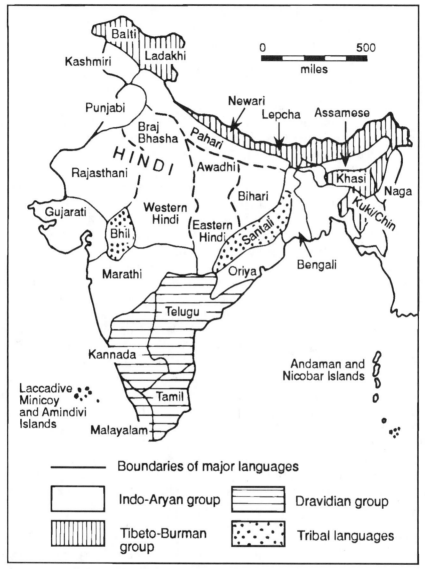

FIGURE 11.1. Linguistic Divisions in India. (Apte 1976:143, from Baldev Raj Nayar, *National Communication and Language Policy in India*, New York: Praeger Publishers)

Jammu/Kashmir: Urdu; Maharashtra: Marathi; Punjab: Punjabi; West Bengal: Bengali). Of 10 union territories, 5 have English as their regional language; 2 have English and Hindi; 1 has English and French; and only 1 has a local language (Bengali) as its regional code (ibid.:161–163).

Not only are there problems in state boundaries and selection of regional languages, but there are also controversies in choosing writing systems for local and national languages. Eleven different scripts are in use in India. Minority languages that historically have not been associated with a written form have particular problems adopting scripts. To illustrate possible complexities, consider the situation of Santhali, a language spoken in four states (Assam, Bihar, Orissa, West Bengal). Each of the four states uses a different script for its own regional code. Therefore, if Santhali is written in the script of its state, four versions would coexist. The central Commission of Linguistic Minorities has tried to solve the problem by suggesting adoption of either Devangari, the script in which Hindi is written, or the Roman alphabet, but the states involved have been unable to reach agreement (Dua 1985:362).

English remains an optional language in several societal domains throughout most of India. It is the mother tongue of only 200,000 people in India but is known to some degree by approximately 25 million. Despite the Congress Party's desire to establish Hindi as the sole official language, either Hindi or English is used in the Indian Parliament and in communication between states and with the central government. In addition, English is sometimes used as a medium of instruction in schools, particularly in universities. In fact, knowledge of English has become a marker of advanced education and elite social status. Finally, courts function primarily in English, especially at higher levels of adjudication. In town courts, proceedings are often conducted in local languages, although official records are maintained in English. In High Courts and the Supreme Court, lawyers and judges employ English even though it may not be understood by other participants (Kidder 1976:238–239). Use of English creates a language barrier or "blackout" (ibid.:247) that helps maintain the privileged position of lawyers and other professionals. By translating proceedings for their poorly educated clients, lawyers may filter information in a way that secures their advantages and the disadvantages of their clients.

Although speakers of Hindi constitute the largest single linguistic group (approximately 40 percent of the population), and Hindi is strongly endorsed by the central government, several sectors of the Indian populace oppose its use as the official language and instead advocate English. Members of elite classes, most of whom are proficient in English, prefer English because its use enhances their prestige and control over governmental, technological, and educational institutions. Opposition to Hindi is also voiced by people in South India where Hindi is sparsely represented or absent altogether. These people resent economic and political control by Hindi-speaking regions and, therefore, resist Hindi linguistic dominance (Apte 1976:148).

Rivalry among the numerous and diverse ethnic and linguistic groups in India has blocked the smooth adoption of Hindi. Governmental and educational institutions have had little effect on encouraging employment of Hindi. In fact, according to S. N. Sridhar (1988b:312–313), the spread of Hindi throughout India is attributable more to its use in the popular cinema and television than to official policies.

Standardization

The ascendancy of Hindi is complicated by the factor of linguistic standardization. Standard Hindi differs from colloquial speech in pronunciation and vocabulary, borrowing many words from Sanskrit, India's ancient literary and ceremonial language. Hindi's social prestige is strengthened by its incorporation of Sanskrit vocabulary, "showing that an Indian language can be independent of English and other international languages" (Southworth 1985:232). But this process of Sanskritization also separates standard Hindi from the speech of ordinary people. Most Indians in all regions speak colloquial or vernacular styles of their languages, so even native speakers of Hindi have problems understanding standardized, literary Hindi.

Similar processes of standardization have affected regional languages in each state, resulting in problems for native speakers and other state residents. For instance, a survey of speakers of Malayalam, the majority language of Kerala, a state having the highest literacy rate in India, revealed only slight ability of respondents to understand standardized Malayalam (Southworth 1985). Franklin Southworth prepared two levels of written text, administering one to adults with an average of eight years' education and a simpler version to adults with 4.4 years of schooling. On a comprehensibility scale from 0.0 to 5.0, the first group averaged 1.5 and the second, 2.0. Although the sample was small, results clearly showed that speakers had difficulty understanding standardized forms of their native tongue (ibid.:234). Only well-educated elites are functionally fluent in standardized literary forms of language and, therefore, are able to maintain their status over an uneducated or poorly educated populace through the medium of linguistic code.

Many Indian languages are in the process of "modernization," that is, adapting or expanding their vocabularies to include new items or activities. This linguistic process is accelerated by socioeconomic trends toward increased urbanization, industrialization, and access to education. It is furthered as well by the use of borrowed and coined words in mass media (Daswani 1989:85). Modernization includes borrowing words from other languages, especially from Hindi, Sanskrit, English, or another of the major Indian languages (Sridhar 1988a:356). Borrowed words are often integrated into compounds with native words to label modern entities. For example, the following expressions are used in Kannada, a Dravidian language of South India (ibid.:357):

aspirin matre: "aspirin tablet"
cancer roga: "cancer" (literally: cancer disease)

Another common process involves compounding two (or more) native words to form a new construction:

vicara sankirana: "symposium" (literally: thought confrontation)

Finally, meanings of existing words are sometimes reinterpreted to apply to innovations:

akasavana: "radio" (literally: voice from the sky)

Linguistic procedures such as these expand a language's contextual usefulness. However, they can also result in development of "style strata" (ibid.:359), which segments a linguistic community into unequal groups based on degrees of familiarity with a more technical or educated variety.

In some cases, modernization of local languages has led to rapid linguistic changes affecting not only incorporation or creation of new words for technological innovations but also replacement of indigenous words by others derived from a language with higher societal status. For instance, Tripuri, a local language spoken in West Bengal, has adopted many Bengali words, including labels for colors and numbers as well as grammatical indicators such as "who, which, until" (Dua 1985:363). If this process gains momentum, it could potentially erode the distinctiveness of some local languages under pressure from competing regional or national codes.

Linguistic Minorities

All Indian states contain linguistic minorities, people who speak neither Hindi nor the official state language. Some of these minorities constitute large sectors, numbering in the millions, whereas others are members of small, isolated, mostly rural tribal enclaves. Languages having large numbers of speakers are more likely to receive public recognition and be used as mediums of instruction and mass communication than are those spoken by only a few.

Each state government determines which of its languages can be used in education. A state's regional language and/or Hindi are always options. Many people throughout India oppose instruction in Hindi because native speakers of Hindi have an advantage in schooling because they already command the official code, whereas speakers of other languages (who constitute the majority of Indians) must learn a second language. In response, the national government proposed a "three-language formula" in 1961 requiring students to develop literacy and fluency in three languages: their regional language, Hindi (or, in Hindi-speaking regions, another Indian language), and English (or another modern European language) (Sridhar 1988b:311). This solution still burdens speakers of minority tribal languages whose native code is rarely recognized for use as a regional or instructional language. The government's proposal was rejected by many states. Because the Indian constitution assigns control over education to states rather than to the central government, most states have developed their own instructional policies.

Minority languages receive support for schooling in some states, but in others they do not. In states where minority languages are used in school, they typically are employed only in early grades. Students are later required to learn the regional language or Hindi (Dua 1985:364). Lack of national guidelines results in seemingly inconsistent decisions. For example, Garo is used in education in the state of Assam, although its speakers (approximately 10,000) constitute less than 1 percent of the population; but it is not a medium of instruction in Meghalaya, where it is spoken by 32.48 percent of residents (ibid.:361).

Practical problems undoubtedly exist in supporting minority languages because educational uses necessitate economic investments in teacher training and preparation of texts and other instructional materials. However, pedagogical decisions are often based on societal attitudes toward speakers of each language. Refusal to acknowledge minority or tribal languages is tantamount to asserting economic and/or political control over their speakers. But minority linguistic communities are not united on issues of language choice because class or caste differences affect people's goals. Elites may choose not to advocate their own native language for state recognition and instead favor Hindi or English because these have national and international stature. Inasmuch as elites are likely to be well educated, their fluency in Hindi and/or English enables them to participate in national culture while at the same time separates them from others in their linguistic community who are subordinate.

Mass communication also promotes marginalization of minority linguistic communities. Print and broadcast media are rarely available in local languages. Even when available, most sectors of minority groups do not support these media because topical coverage is generally limited to local events. In most cases, newspapers printed in minority languages have circulations of under 3,000 (Dua 1985:368). Thus, because minority media have only narrow appeal, they cannot adequately legitimate or strengthen local identities.

However, despite obstacles, hundreds of minority languages continue to be spoken in India. Even languages spoken by very few people can maintain their vigor. In a review of minority languages in the state of Kerala, V. I. Subramoniam identified the following circumstances favoring continued use of local codes in a small community: (1) little or no job contacts with speakers of dominant languages; (2) low levels of formal education; (3) tendency for marriages to take place between people of the same community; and (4) lack of migration to other areas either for work or schooling (1977:23–26). For example, a group known as Kudumbis, numbering only 800, speak Konkani in an overwhelmingly Malayalam-speaking area. Kudumbis live in a small suburb of a major city. Economic pursuits are limited: Women are engaged in selling rice; men work as day laborers. The community is isolated from prolonged contacts with other groups and, thus, is able to maintain its distinctive ethnic and linguistic identity. Most adults speak only Konkani, although some younger people have been educated in Malayalam and are able to use it with varying proficiency. Konkani remains the language of Kudumbis' homes. Older people of both genders, most women, and all preschool children are monolingual Konkani speakers (ibid.:21–22).

Although such communities exist by the thousands throughout India, the people pay a price for their isolation because they have few educational and economic opportunities that could potentially lead to improved standards of living.

Finally, nationalist philosophies often relegate minority languages and their speakers to peripheral status. Expansion of standardized codes through mass communication, education, and government encourages uniformity not only of language but also of "ideology and culture" (Dua 1985:370). The government advocates linguistic uniformity as a necessary adjunct to centralization and coordination of economic development and modernization. Minority languages and their speakers, thus, become stigmatized as obstacles to societal integration and advance.

CANADA

Language in Canada

The linguistic situation in Canada, although apparently simpler than in India, is replete with long-standing ethnic tensions that finally erupted into political conflicts. Canada was colonized by French and British traders and settlers beginning in the sixteenth and seventeenth centuries. French settlement was concentrated around ports along the St. Lawrence River from Montreal eastward to the Atlantic Ocean. British control expanded westward, eventually reaching the Pacific coast. In 1762, France's colony of Quebec was ceded to the British after France's defeat in the Seven Years' War. Rural French farmers were geographically, economically, and linguistically separated from urban English workers, business owners, and politicians in Quebec. Members of French upper classes, though, entered professions such as medicine, law, and the clergy. After Canadian independence from Great Britain in 1867, these francophone elites controlled provincial government as anglophone Quebecers turned their interests to federal politics (Heller 1985:76). (Note that anglophone refers to a monolingual English speaker or a bilingual with English dominance; francophone refers to a speaker who is monolingual in French or a French-dominant bilingual.)

The fairly stable separation of French and English speakers in Quebec began to change after World War II. A growing French middle class was absorbed first by the expanding provincial bureaucracy. In the 1960s, this group entered private business sectors previously monopolized by anglophones. According to Monica Heller, as French prominence increased, francophone politicians championed the cause of Quebec nationalism in part to strengthen their control over the political apparatus. They wanted to keep Quebec's anglophones out of provincial politics and to block inroads by the immigrant populace, most of whom ally themselves with anglophones and adopt English rather than French as their second language (ibid.:77).

Many of Quebec's francophone residents continued to resent the fact that the province's economy was controlled by anglophones, often by corporations located in English-speaking provinces. As a result, calls for Quebec's independence from Canada increased throughout the 1960s and led to urgent responses by federal authorities, including passage of the Official Languages Act in 1969. As stated in the act's Declaration of Status of Languages, "the English and French languages are the official languages of Canada for all purposes of the Parliament and Government of Canada, and possess and enjoy equality of status and equal rights and privileges as to their use in all the institutions of the Parliament and Government of Canada" (quoted in Grosjean 1982:16–17).

This policy means that Canada is a bilingual country in the sense that services must be provided in two languages so that any (monolingual) resident can benefit. It does not specifically advocate individual bilingualism, that is, that people should speak two languages. In accordance with the law, all government documents are published in both languages and speakers of either have rights to interact with agencies in a language of their choice. In the opinion of Frank Vallee and John de Vries (1978), this approach accomplishes two goals. First, by granting symbolic recognition to French and its speakers, it blunts the appeal of francophone nationalism. Second, by attracting francophones into federal employment, it offers an economic lure to weaken Quebec separatism (ibid.:765).

In the domain of education, the federal government provides funds to help provinces set up bilingual education programs in districts where at least 10 percent of the population speaks the minority language (English in Quebec; French elsewhere). This goal has not been uniformly or adequately met, however (Grosjean 1982:17).

Federal attempts at reconciliation did not succeed. Most of Canada remained indifferent or hostile to Quebec's grievances. In Quebec, francophones rejected official bilingualism and instead established French monolingualism in the province. In 1977, Quebec's government enacted the Chartre de la Langue Francaise (Charter of the French Language), known as Bill 101, which recognizes French as the only official language of Quebec. Official documents are published in French only. French is the language of education for the francophone majority and for immigrants speaking other languages. Anglophones may send their children to English-speaking schools if the parents had been educated in English in Quebec (ibid.:18). In addition, French has become the routine language of public and private employment. All job seekers must speak French, as must current employees who apply for promotions (Heller 1985:77). These provisions for language use in education and at workplaces at first applied to Native Canadian communities as well, but Native Canadians succeeded in establishing their rights to use either their native language or English or French as they see fit.

This historical review provides a background for examining language abilities, situational usage, and attitudes toward speakers of French and English. Canadians' linguistic proficiencies remained stable throughout most of this century. Since the 1970s, some significant changes have occurred in proportions of those speaking only French and in rates of bilingualism. The following table compares figures from the 1971 census as reported by Vallee and de Vries (1978:776) and the census of 1991 (*Statistics Canada* 1995, Cat. No. 93–318:8):

Proportions of Speakers of Official Languages

	1971	*1991*
English only	67.1%	66.6%
French only	18.0	15.4
Both English and French	13.4	16.3
Neither	1.5	1.6

Although the proportion of Canadians who speak only English has remained relatively constant, fewer Canadians speak only French. It is, therefore, French speakers who have primarily contributed to the increase in bilingualism. Another reflection of English prominence in Canada is the fact that most people who speak a nonofficial language and only one of the official languages choose English rather than French. Figures from the 1986 census indicate that 2.1 percent of Canadians speak English and a language other than French, whereas only 0.1 percent speak French and a language other than English (*Canada Year Book* 1990:2.25).

Rates of French/English bilingualism are highest in Quebec and neighboring New Brunswick (34.3 and 28.6 percent, respectively). In other provinces, bilinguals account for much smaller proportions of the population: Ontario is highest with 11.1 percent, the Prairie provinces average 6.0 percent, and Newfoundland is lowest with 2.9 percent (*Statistics Canada* 1995, Cat. No. 93–318:8). These figures indicate some slight increases in bilingualism throughout Canada since 1971.

Across Canada, percentages of francophone bilinguals significantly outnumber anglophone bilinguals. Based on 1971 figures, approximately one-third of native speakers of French also speak English, whereas only 7.6 percent of anglophones speak French. In Quebec's neighboring provinces, rates of francophone bilingualism are highest: 53.2 percent of francophones in New Brunswick and 80.7 percent in Ontario speak English. These figures contrast dramatically with the incidence of anglophone bilingualism, merely 5.1 percent and 5.5 percent in New Brunswick and Ontario, respectively. The only province where anglophone bilinguals outnumber francophone bilinguals is in Quebec (59.1 to 24.6 percent) (Vallee and de Vries 1978:781–782). In sum, then, it is the high incidence of anglophone bilingualism in Quebec (59.1 percent) that pulls up the national average to as small a figure as 7.6 percent.

In Canada there is concern over the strong separation of French and English communities. Surveys of personal values, political opinions, and voting patterns indicate a consistent difference between these populations (Meisel 1978). And when respondents were asked to assess diverse ethnic groups, English Canadians gave lowest ratings to French Canadians, preferring members of other non-English ethni-cities. French Canadians, though, rated English Canadians higher than other non-French groups (ibid.:687). Although language is not the only cause of these attitudes, it can be used as a signal of and catalyst for arousing prejudicial stereotypes.

The attitudes of the Quebecois about language and linguistic groups were heightened following passage of Bill 101 (Charter of the French Language) in 1977. Surveys conducted in Quebec revealed that both anglophones and francophones recognized the existence of two ethnic/linguistic blocks whose opinions and interests diverged sharply. Members of both groups thought that francophones favored Bill 101 and that anglophones opposed it, and both thought that anglophones felt threatened by the legislation (Taylor and Dube-Simard 1985). In addition, although Quebec's anglophones claimed that the bill's provisions were unjust, they reported that they had not received unfair treatment. Donald Taylor and Lise Dube-Simard suggested that media accounts of fears and problems of a few individuals may have contributed to the widely held perception of injustice even though that perception is not validated by personal experience (ibid.:165).

The media in Canada (as elsewhere) play a key role in either strengthening national consensus or in expressing divergent perspectives. Analyses of the French and English press uncovered significant differences in their orientations. For example, an examination of press coverage of a critical incident in 1970 revealed that French and English newspapers focused on markedly different aspects of the episode (Siegel 1983). The crisis began when a Quebec separatist group in Montreal kidnapped the British trade commissioner and the Quebec minister of labour, the latter of whom was subsequently killed. French media stressed themes of negotiation and compromise while discussing the complexities of Canadian federalism and grievances of the French community. English media, in contrast, stressed efforts to apprehend the kidnappers and free their hostages. Whereas the French press gave prominence to government officials attempting to resolve the crisis, the English press highlighted police activities (ibid.:212–213). In sum, the media transmitted divergent views of events, helping to construct socially derived and socially maintained portrayals of reality. As these different constructions become widely disseminated and accepted, they contribute to societal divisions and hostilities.

Situational Use

In the current context of political strife concerning rights of linguistic minorities in Canada and rights of the linguistic majority in Quebec, situational language choice assumes symbolic and personal meanings. In Montreal, a predominantly French-speaking city but with the largest percentage of anglophones in Quebec, selection of code between bilingual speakers may reflect underlying attitudes about each language. By choosing one language over another, speakers assert their identity and show their sensitivity to the linguistic rights of others. For instance, in the dialogue quoted at the beginning of this chapter, a receptionist in a government agency and an anglophone who wanted to take an official French test made symbolic statements with their choice of code in a clearly confrontational encounter. Recalling the interaction, one can assume that the anglophone applicant had some ability to speak French because he planned to take (presumably with hopes to pass) a test in French, yet he demanded his right to use his native language. The francophone bilingual receptionist countered his challenge by pretending not to understand English.

A decidedly nonconfrontational interaction is illustrated in the following telephone conversation between a hospital clerk and patient. Both speakers attempted to accommodate to each other. The clerk answered the telephone in English, noticed the patient's French response, and proceeded to match her language to the code of the patient's prior turn. However, this strategy did not lead to an entirely trouble-free interaction because the patient was uncomfortable not knowing the clerk's ethnic identity (Heller 1985:80–81):

CLERK: Central Booking, may I help you?

PATIENT: Oui, allô?   ("Yes, hello?")

CLERK:	Bureau de rendez-vous, est-ce que je peux vous aider?	("Appointments Desk, may I help you?")
PATIENT:	(French)	(The patient begins to try to make an appointment)
CLERK:	(French)	
PATIENT:	(English)	
CLERK:	(English)	
PATIENT:	(French)	
CLERK:	(French)	
PATIENT:	Êtes-vous française ou anglaise?	("Are you French or English?")
CLERK:	N'importe j'suis ni l'une ni l'autre.	("It doesn't matter, I'm neither one nor the other.")
PATIENT:	Mais . . .	("But . . .")
CLERK:	Ça ne fait rien.	("It doesn't matter.")
PATIENT:	(French)	

(The conversation continues in French.)

In conversations between friends and colleagues who are aware of each other's linguistic abilities, various adjustments can be made. Some speakers repetitively translate previous statements in order to include all interlocutors in multiparty discussions. In the following excerpt, three coworkers are conversing, two francophone bilinguals (Albert and Claude) and an anglophone (Bob) with slight French proficiency (ibid.:85):

ALBERT:	. . . il nous reste plus de temps après ça pour discuter les problèmes majeurs t'sais les choses qui vraiment you understand that Bob? I say if we lose less time in going over the routine we have more time to discuss the important uh . . .	("We'll have more time after that for discussing major problems you know the things that really . . .")

A final example illustrates another option, that each speaker uses the native language of her or his preference in an exchange of autonomous turns (ibid.:88):

HÉLÈNE:	Va-t-on manger de la soupe aujourd'hui?	("Are we going to have soup today?")
IAN:	I'm going to, I don't know if anyone wants to join me.	

HÉLÈNE: Je veux bien, qu'est-ce   ("Sure, I do, what will
          qu'on mange?   we have?")

IAN: Oh, I'll take care of it.

Attitudes Toward Languages and Speakers

Although overt behavior reflects speakers' adjustments to interlocutors, covert attitudes also significantly affect both personal interactions and community-wide relations. Canadians' reaction to French and English speakers and their behavior in interlinguistic encounters have been studied using several techniques. Results of research in the 1950s and 1960s will be discussed first, followed by comparison with later studies. The first experiments employed the *matched-guise technique* (Lambert et al. 1960) in which subjects listen to tape-recorded speech in two versions of the same content, both spoken by the same fluent bilingual person. In one version, the bilingual speaks French and in the other, English. Subjects are asked to rate speakers (thinking they are different people) according to various dimensions of personality, intelligence, competence, and sociability.

Studies by Wallace Lambert et al. in the 1950s and 1960s revealed consistent patterns. In their experiments, using male guises and male and female judges, anglophone subjects, as expected, rated guises more favorably when they spoke English rather than French. But, surprisingly, francophone subjects expressed similar preferences for English speakers except on ratings for kindness and religiousness. On other measures (intelligence, leadership, self-confidence, dependability, attractiveness, ambition, sense of humor), francophone subjects preferred English speakers. Moreover, francophones gave significantly higher ratings to English speakers than did anglophones for qualities of leadership, intelligence, and self-confidence (ibid.:47).

The various dialects of French spoken by the four bilingual guises in Lambert et al.'s experiments had an effect on subjects' assessment. Two spoke standard Canadian French, one a rural, heavily accented Canadian French, and the fourth Parisian French. All subjects rated the Parisian French guise most favorably and the rural Canadian guise most negatively (ibid.:50). These results indicated that both anglophones and francophones hold strong negative stereotypes of French Canadians.

A subsequent study used male and female guises in order to assess the variable of speaker's gender on hearer's attitudes. Among anglophone subjects, both men and women attributed more negative characteristics to French-speaking male guises but more positive traits to French-speaking females. Among francophone judges, men consistently rated English speakers (male and female) more positively than French speakers. Francophone women, though, preferred French-speaking men on certain measures, rating them as more competent and sociable (Lambert 1967:95–97).

Matched-guise experiments with children as speakers and judges revealed the age at which socially derived stereotyping begins. One study involved 10-year-old subjects, half of whom were monolingual French speakers and half were bilingual francophones. They were told that the purpose of the experiment was to see how well people can evaluate personalities of speakers solely on the basis of their voice. Speaker guises were all 10-year-old bilingual girls. The results of this study indicated a split between reactions of monolingual and bilingual subjects. Monolinguals rated French-speaking guises much more favorably on all personality traits, demonstrating strongly negative attitudes toward English speakers. In contrast, bilinguals did not show any significant preference for either speaker (Anisfeld and Lambert 1964:91–92). They exhibited no prejudice toward other groups and no strong preference for their own group. By around age 12, however, negative attitudes on the part of francophone bilinguals toward French speakers were found in further research. Social class of respondents influenced these ratings: Middle- and upper-class children had stronger biased reactions than did children from working-class families (Lambert 1967:98–99).

Employing a different research strategy, a series of experiments applied speech accommodation theory to Canadian linguistic performance and its evaluation. *Speech accommodation theory* basically suggests that when speakers have positive attitudes toward interlocutors, they accommodate or converge to the latter's speech styles. In contrast, they maintain their own style, and possibly even exaggerate it, if they have negative opinions about co-participants (Giles, Taylor, and Bourhis 1973:179).

In tests of speech accommodation theory with Canadian bilingual subjects, anglophone bilinguals listened to the recorded speech of a francophone bilingual man giving directions from a map of Montreal. Subjects were informed that the speaker knew his hearers would be English-dominant and that he was free to speak whatever language he wished. Each subject heard one recording, although four different versions were distributed among them. The versions were spoken in French, mixed French and English, fluent English, and nonfluent, hesitant, heavily accented English. After listening to a tape, anglophone subjects were asked to make recordings of their own descriptions of a city route, intended to be played later to the francophone speaker they had heard.

The study revealed that subjects who had heard the French version responded in English, whereas those hearing nonfluent English replied in French or apologized for their lack of French proficiency (ibid.:187). According to Giles et al., when the speaker on tape used French he was seen as nonaccommodating to his anglophone hearers; subjects responded by refusing to accommodate to him. When he spoke English with difficulty, subjects thought he was making a great effort to accommodate to them and they reciprocated his effort by trying to reply in French (ibid.). Another possible factor explaining this behavior, though, is that subjects hearing nonfluent English might have assumed the speaker had difficulty comprehending English and so they tried to reply in French simply to be understood.

A subsequent study of francophone bilingual subjects hearing a taped message from an anglophone speaking in French added a further manipulation to the same basic procedure. This time, one group of subjects was informed that the anglophone bilingual speaking French had been permitted to speak whatever language he wished, whereas another group knew that he had been told to speak in

French. Subjects evaluated speakers more positively when they assumed they were hearing a voluntary French taping (voluntarily accommodating to them) than when they heard a speaker who had been instructed to speak French (Simard, Taylor, and Giles 1976:382–383).

All the various reactions to speech exhibited in these experiments can be understood in the sociopolitical context of language in Canada in the 1960s and early 1970s. Attitudes toward language are not in their origin linguistic but, rather, social. People attribute qualities to speakers of particular languages as a reflex of their opinions about members of given linguistic or ethnic communities. In some cases, prejudice against outgroups is uniform, for example, anglophone negative stereotyping of francophones. But members of stigmatized groups may themselves adopt self-denigrating bias, although in these cases, attitudes frequently are mixed, approving of ingroup people on certain measures.

Studies by Lambert et al. and Giles et al. were conducted prior to the 1977 passage of Bill 101 that established French as the only official language of Quebec and that promotes French usage in education and business as well as in government. Surveys and experiments conducted since 1977 are important indicators of both change and stability in Canadian attitudes toward language and language users. Richard Bourhis (1985) reported three types of studies designed to investigate different aspects of linguistic and social interconnections. First, Bourhis administered a questionnaire to francophone undergraduates at the University of Montreal and to anglophones at McGill University (also in Montreal). Respondents were asked a number of questions concerning their linguistic behavior in situations of interlinguistic contact. They were specifically queried about which language they used in conversing as customers to "outgroup" clerks in stores and restaurants (an outgroup clerk is an English speaker to a francophone, a French speaker to an anglophone).

Although both groups reported initiating conversations in their native language in such settings, adhering to the traditional norm that "the client is always right," anglophones claimed that they were more likely to change to French with francophone clerks "today" than they had been "in the past" (i.e., prior to Bill 101). These respondents also noted that francophone clerks were less likely to switch to English than had been characteristic of past encounters. In contrast to anglophone respondents, francophones did not report a changed pattern in their choice of language in these interlinguistic contacts; they still maintained French or changed to English at the same rates as in the past.

In a finding with similar implications, anglophone respondents said that francophone clerks were less likely today to accommodate to an English-speaking client than in the past, whereas francophones reported that anglophone clerks were currently more likely to converge to French-speakers than in previous years (ibid.:182).

This survey documents a change in expectations, attitudes, and experiences of young people in Montreal since discussion of language issues has become public and governmental intervention has created a legal and social climate encouraging the use of French.

However, overtly expressed sentiments are not always consistently reflected in actual behavior. Bourhis reported two related experiments asking subjects (ages 16 and 17 years) to evaluate speakers on tape recordings of three-part dialogues in which two male actors portrayed clerks and customers. In both tests, dialogues had the same format of turns: salesperson/customer/salesperson. In the first study, the following language choices were employed: (1) F-E-F, (2) F-E-E, (3) F-F-F, and (4) F-F-E. Both anglophone and francophone respondents rated ingroup speakers more positively than outgroup speakers (ibid.:186). This is an important finding because it demonstrates a significant change from earlier studies (e.g., Lambert 1967) in which francophones had negative biases against speakers of French. In addition, francophone subjects were positively impressed by anglophone customers who converged to the French-speaking clerk. Finally, all subjects reacted negatively to the francophone clerk when he failed to switch to English in response to an anglophone customer and thus violated norms of politeness to customers.

In the second study, the same procedure was followed in dialogues beginning with an English-speaking clerk: (1) E-F-E, (2) E-F-F, (3) E-E-E, and (4) E-E-F. Here, all subjects reacted favorably to the anglophone clerk when he switched to French in his response (ibid.:188–189). Positive responses were greater toward the anglophone clerk converging to French (study 2) than for a francophone converging to English (study 1). Perhaps such reactions imply that some degree of hierarchical relations continues between English and French. That is, a speaker of a higher-status language (English) is especially rewarded for switching to a lower-status language (French).

A further series of studies by Bourhis was aimed at eliciting actual language use by interlocutors in natural settings. In this research, a perfect bilingual asked directions of pedestrians in Montreal. In encounters conducted in 1977 (shortly after passage of Bill 101), 95 percent of francophone pedestrians converged to English when the experimenter spoke English, whereas only 60 percent of anglophones converged to French when the experimenter spoke French (note that a response was counted as convergence if it contained even as little as one word of the "foreign" language) (ibid.:193).

This study was followed in 1979 by an identical procedure to test whether changes in behavior had occurred. Experiments were conducted with middle-aged subjects chosen at random in downtown Montreal and with young university students at McGill and the University of Montreal. Among older subjects, 100 percent of francophones switched to English when queried in English, and 70 percent of anglophones switched to French in response to a question in French. In contrast, young francophone university students converged to English at a rate of 83 percent, matched by 84 percent of anglophone students who converged to French (ibid.:196–197).

A number of important conclusions can be drawn from studies by Bourhis and his colleagues. Overt attitudinal responses by francophones have changed markedly from earlier studies by Lambert and others. By the late 1970s, francophones were at least consciously demonstrating positive reactions to their own group as shown by students' claims to maintain their own language in interlinguistic contacts. In addition, anglophone students claimed a current greater tendency than in the past to converge to French.

Covert attitudes, as revealed by the "dialogue" experiments, show some shift from earlier reactions but also demonstrate that English continues to have some prestige. In addition, the fact that older anglophones resist converging to French and that older francophones are willing to converge to English, as elicited in the "asking directions" studies, similarly indicates inequalities between the two linguistic communities. However, future trends may be indicated by the fact that younger respondents, both francophone and anglophone, were equally willing to converge to the outgroup language (at rates of 83 and 84 percent). Although this last point may auger well for possibilities of linguistic tolerance on a nonconscious level, recent political developments in Quebec indicate sharpening differentiation among various linguistic/ethnic groups.

A historic referendum on the question of sovereignty for the province of Quebec was held on October 30, 1995. Since the 1960s, a separatist movement had grown in Quebec, organized since the 1970s as a political party (Parti Quebecois) whose goal was independence for Quebec. Along with demands for political and economic ascendency of francophones in Quebec, the Parti Quebecois spearheaded the campaign for passage of Bill 101, making French the only official language of the province. In recent years, as francophone political and economic control was consolidated, cultural and linguistic issues that were always present took center stage, at least in rhetorical efforts to gain public favor for independence. Several referenda on the question were easily defeated in earlier years, but in 1995 proponents of sovereignty came within one percentage point of achieving their goal, in part by rallying people around the issue of their cultural and linguistic distinctiveness—a distinctiveness that is readily apparent and elicits emotional as well as intellectual reactions.

The final vote (50.5 percent against separation, 49.5 percent in favor) indicates a divided province, but the specific figures for diverse linguistic groups are even more revealing; 60 percent of francophones voted for independence, while only 10 percent of anglophones and a mere 5 percent of "allophones" (native speakers of neither French nor English) did so. Indigenous peoples, called the First Nations in Canada, were especially opposed to Quebec independence. In fact, a week before the provincial vote, the Crees and Inuits held a referendum in their communities in which the Native groups voted nearly unanimously that if Quebec has the right to separate from Canada, they have the right to remain. Regional diversity among francophones also surfaced. Pro-sovereignty voting was lower in the city of Montreal and in areas of Quebec that border other provinces (Ontario to the west, New Brunswick to the east) or the United States than elsewhere.

Leaders of the separatist movement vowed to renew their efforts and seek another referendum in a few years. The issue of linguistic and political distinctions in Canada, begun more than 400 years ago, will obviously not be resolved immediately.

THE UNITED STATES

Language in the United States

The United States is a multilingual nation inhabited by millions of people who speak more than one language. Although English is the country's dominant language, it is not the first language of many native-born citizens. And, of course, numerous immigrants continue to use their original language in most social interactions. No federal legislation specifically grants official status to English, but a "complex web of customs, institutions and programs has long fostered well-nigh exclusive reliance upon English in public life" (Fishman 1981:517). This was not always the case. From the late eighteenth through the mid-nineteenth centuries, political leaders and prominent citizens contended that all Americans should be encouraged to learn English but not be hindered from maintaining whatever other languages they spoke. These leaders understood that different languages express different thoughts and cultural orientations, and thus they believed that linguistic diversity strengthened the development and exchange of ideas (Heath 1977:272). In this period, some states promoted languages other than English by publishing laws in additional codes, for example, German in Pennsylvania and French in Louisiana. Furthermore, some laws affecting Native Americans were printed in indigenous languages in the nineteenth century (ibid.:273).

Change in attitudes toward multilingualism came in the latter half of the nineteenth century. Policies promoting or protecting other languages were repealed. Educators and public figures stressed the necessity for all to learn "correct," standard English. Many states enacted laws requiring sole use of English in schools and mandated fines for teachers who spoke other languages in the classroom. Children were often punished for speaking non-English mother tongues. The U.S. Supreme Court, however, ruled in 1923 that minority communities have a constitutional right to speak their own languages in private, but not public, schools if they so wish (Grosjean 1982:69–70). Because most people attend public schools, they are subject to public restrictions on the use of their native language. Standardization of code was increasingly stressed. "Textbooks emphasized the co-occurrence of 'good talk' with good behavior, a moral character, and an industrious nature. . . . The way of dealing with 'strangers' and their differences was to educate them to use 'good American speech' and motivate them to conform in the Americanizing process" (Heath 1977:274). This trend was strengthened in the twentieth century, especially during World War I and World War II when speakers of some foreign languages were suspected as traitors.

Despite social pressures and the prominent image of English as the code of U.S. residents, the reality of linguistic diversity continues. According to statistics collected by the U.S. Bureau of the Census in the census of 1990 (CPH-L-133), 31.8 million people (14 percent of the total population age 5 and over) reported non-English mother tongues. This figure represents an increase since 1980, when 23.1 million residents (11 percent of the population) were native speakers of a language other than English. The census reported that 380 languages were spoken in homes in the United States, including 120 Native American languages.

Of all non-English languages, Spanish was spoken at home by the largest number of people, having 17.3 million speakers, or somewhat more than half of all people claiming a non-English mother tongue. This figure, too, represents an increase from 1980 when there were 11.1 million Spanish-speaking residents. In addition to Spanish, the most frequently spoken non-English languages were French (1.7 million speakers), German (1.5 million), Italian (1.3 million), and Chinese (1.2 million). Taken as a group, Asian and Pacific Island languages had 4.5 million speakers; and Native American languages were spoken by some 332,000 people.

The ability of speakers of non-English mother tongues to speak English varied considerably. Approximately 56.1 percent reported that they spoke English very well, 23 percent answered that they spoke English well, 15.2 percent said they did not speak English well, and 5.8 percent did not speak English at all.

Although Spanish dominates as a non-English home language in the nation, some regional variation exists. Among speakers of non-English languages, French is the most frequently spoken language in Louisiana, Maine, New Hampshire, and Vermont. German is most used in Montana, Minnesota, and North and South Dakota. Portuguese is first in Rhode Island. The Native American language called Yupik dominates in Alaska, and Japanese is most commonly spoken in Hawaii.

States varied in their numbers and proportions of speakers of non-English languages. The four states having at least 2 million such residents were California (8.6 million), New York (3.9 million), Texas (3.9 million), and Florida (2 million). However, New Mexico had the highest proportion of speakers of non-English languages (36 percent), followed by California (32 percent). Areas with the smallest ratios of people with non-English mother tongues are in the South (except Louisiana and Florida), the Central and Mountain states, and the Northwest. The map in Figure 11.2 presents percentages of speakers of minority languages based on 1976 figures. It also highlights prominent languages in each state.

Bilingual Education

Recognizing the reality of multilingualism in the United States, public policies shifted in the direction of protecting the rights of linguistic minorities. First steps were taken in the domain of education. In 1963, the Coral Way School in Dade County, Florida, established a federally funded bilingual education program for Spanish-speaking immigrants from Cuba. The next year, Texas's Webb County schools began operating bilingual classes for Spanish speakers. Congress encouraged such programs by passing the Bilingual Education Act of 1968, or Title VII of the 1965 Elementary and Secondary Education Act. This act provides federal funding for bilingual education in public schools. Congress periodically updates the act, most recently in 1979–1980, to give additional funding for increased services. Under the law, federal monies are given to state education departments and

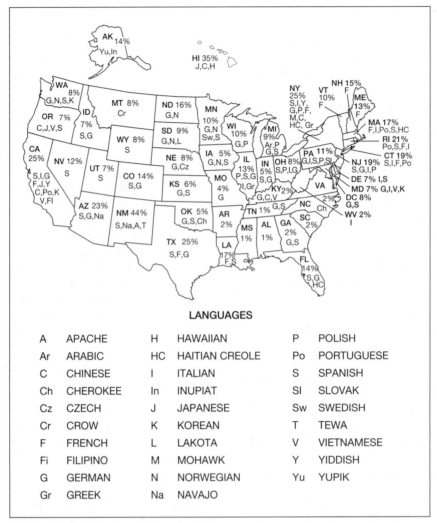

FIGURE 11.2. Distribution of Minority Languages. (Grosjean 1982:47, based on 1976 Survey of Income and Education, *National Center for Education Statistics Bulletin* 78, B-5)

local school districts to provide bilingual education programs for students of limited English-speaking ability. The current statement of eligibility specifically includes Native Americans and others who may be native speakers of English but "who come from environments where a language other than English has had a significant impact on their level of English language proficiency" (quoted in Leap 1986:601).

Federal legislation did not spell out characteristics of programs or length of time students should remain in bilingual classes. It encouraged states and local districts to develop curricula and train teachers. Seventy-six programs were funded during the first year of applicability, nearly all for Spanish-speaking students. Massachusetts was the first state to implement mandatory bilingual education with passage of its Transitional Bilingual Education Act in 1971, providing that school districts with at least 20 children of one language group who have limited English proficiency must institute bilingual programs (Grosjean 1982:72).

Bilingual education in the United States is usually based on a "transitional" model, oriented toward assimilation of foreign-speaking communities. Its goal is to encourage speakers' shift to English, eliminating reliance on their native languages. For example, the Massachusetts law specifies that a child remain in a bilingual program for a maximum of three years. During the first year, the native language is used in 95 percent of class time, reduced to 50 percent in the second year and 5 to 10 percent in the third (ibid.:73). In contrast to transitional programs, some countries such as India adopt "maintenance" models that encourage acquisition of fluency and literacy skills in both native and second languages. Therefore, although the Bilingual Education Act is a progressive step in recognizing difficulties for children in classrooms dominated by what for them is a foreign language, it does not actually promote multilingualism. According to Joshua Fishman, "the Act was primarily an act for the Anglification of non-English speakers and not an act for bilingualism. . . . Thus, it is basically an act against bilingualism" (1981:517–518).

In 1974, the U.S. Supreme Court handed down a landmark decision in the *Lau* vs. *Nichols* case that resulted from an action brought by members of the Chinese community in San Francisco who alleged that school systems without bilingual programs effectively deny non-English-speaking students an equal education. The Court agreed that such systems violate the 1964 Civil Rights Act. Although remedies were not specified by the Court, the Department of Health, Education, and Welfare subsequently issued guidelines for corrective actions, including bilingual instruction and teaching English as a second language. Generally, school districts with at least 20 children of the same language group must institute bilingual programs (Grosjean 1982:73–74).

Through federal funding, more than 1,000 bilingual projects are in operation. They are concentrated in California (287), New York (115), and Texas (96), but nearly all states and U.S. trust territories participate. Although most bilingual programs are geared for speakers of Spanish (80 percent), other languages include French, Greek, Yiddish, Haitian Creole, Armenian, Japanese, Vietnamese, Chinese, Ilocano (of the Philippines), and several Native American languages such as Navajo, Apache, Algonquin, Ojibwa, and Oneida (U.S. Department of Education 1990).

These programs enable many children with limited English proficiency to benefit from schooling. However, they do not reach the majority of children who need them. Grosjean reports that 3.6 million children are eligible but that less than 40 percent receive bilingual education (ibid.:78). Reasons for the discrepancy between needs and services include lack of adequate funding, low priority given to these programs by some states and local districts, and the possibility that numbers of eligible children in any one school do not reach the required threshold of 20.

Debates continue among professionals and the public about the effectiveness of bilingual education. Detractors claim that it is unnecessary, that children will learn by being "immersed" in a second language (English), and/or that it is harmful to their educational advancement. In contrast, supporters cite advantages to a minority child's self-esteem by recognizing the worthiness of her or his language and culture. They also point to numerous studies that demonstrate enhanced learning not only of English but also of other academic subjects by students in bilingual programs.

Research by Beverly McConnell (1985) among children of migrant Mexican workers in two parallel bilingual programs showed that bilingual schooling aids learning abilities. One school was located in southern Texas and the other in Washington State. Both programs, beginning in preschool and extending through third grade, include teaching math and oral and written Spanish and English. Although these programs are identical, the communities served are vastly different. In Texas, most extrafamilial contacts (e.g., in stores, churches, and through the media) are conducted in Spanish, whereas in Washington, English dominates. McConnell compared achievement scores over a seven-year period of some 700 children in the two bilingual programs with similar groups of Spanish-speaking children in Washington who were in monolingual English classes and found significant differences in performance in all subjects. At earliest ages, the Washington bilingual group acquired English vocabulary more rapidly than did the Texas group, but this distinction disappeared by age 7. A major finding was that children in either of the bilingual programs learned English vocabulary at a much faster rate than did the children educated monolingually in English. McConnell explained:

> When Spanish-speaking children enter a traditional classroom where the teacher does not understand Spanish, the children often become silent, and are not expected to respond by a teacher unable to communicate with them. Without practice they do not learn either Spanish or English very fast. With a bilingual teacher, communication is never lost—what is said in Spanish is understood and responded to, and the teacher is able to help the child rephrase the question or comment into English so that there is more language practice in both languages and more active learning. The result is significantly greater learning of English by children in the bilingual program than for children from traditional, English immersion classrooms. (1985:205)

Children in Texas made greater improvements in their Spanish linguistic skills than did those in Washington, undoubtedly because their use of Spanish was reinforced in their homes and communities. These children demonstrated greater competence in math as well. McConnell suggested that for the Washington children, "the process of language shift [away from their Spanish mother tongue to English] is somewhat detrimental to the learning of math" (ibid.:210).

Another study compared cognitive functioning of sixth-grade monolingual children in Pennsylvania with Spanish/English bilingual students in Texas (Kessler and Quinn 1985). The latter had been in bilingual programs through third grade and were fluent and literate in both Spanish and English. Carolyn Kessler and Mary Quinn devised an experiment to test children's ability to formulate their own scientific hypotheses after viewing films dealing with science problems. Both the monolingual and bilingual children were divided into two groups, an experimental and a control. Those in experimental groups were taught to distinguish between types of scientific hypotheses, for example, differences between explanations such as "Magic did it" and "I could test my idea by putting several little bottles with different amounts of water in them in a tub and then see which ones would sink." Children in control groups were not given overt instruction of this sort. All students were told to devise hypotheses to explain the science problems they had seen on film. Although both experimental groups formed much more complex hypotheses than did the controls, bilingual children far surpassed monolinguals. Based on a standardized rating system, the mean for the monolingual experimental group was 53.3, but for bilinguals it was 176.0 (ibid.:289–290).

Kessler and Quinn relate bilingual children's achievement to superior cognitive functioning. They contend, along with other researchers, that "bilingual children have a cognitive flexibility and a more diversified set of mental abilities than monolinguals" (ibid.:283). Consistent with the notion that intellectual development is triggered by exposure to "discrepant events," "bilingualism presents an additional element of conflict within the linguistic environment since the child must adapt to two languages. In learning to manipulate language structures, the child may develop a general cognitive skill useful in other domains." Finally, "it may be that certain relevant aspects of the problem situations may be brought to the bilingual child's attention by the availability of two different linguistic perspectives" (ibid.:285–286). This conclusion is compatible with Sapirian-Whorfian insights about relationships between language systems and thought processes. Monolinguals speak and, therefore, think primarily within frameworks provided by a single language, whereas bilinguals inherently have at their ready disposal a wider range of alternative linguistic and cognitive options.

A small number of schools in the United States are dedicated to achieving "two-way" bilingualism, teaching English to children from non-English-dominant homes and teaching Spanish to English-speaking children. The Oyster Bilingual School in Washington, D.C., has the oldest such program. The school's population represents more than 25 countries and is racially and ethnically diverse: 58 percent Hispanic, 26 percent white, 12 percent African American, and 4 percent Asian (Freeman 1996:558). Although the two-way language program is successful in teaching children both English and Spanish, the ways in which children employ the languages differ. They are more likely to switch from Spanish to English than from English to Spanish. Furthermore, the fluency of Spanish-dominant students in English is better than that of English-dominant students in Spanish. These facts indicate an English orientation that underlies the school culture, obviously reflecting societal values and norms.

Recent Trends in Law

Laws protecting the rights of linguistic minorities affect several societal areas in addition to education. In 1975, Congress passed voting rights amendments containing provisions that mandate distribution of information for registering and voting in languages of minority ethnicities if these people make up at least 5 percent of the voting age population in a district (Rubin 1985:144). In 1978, Congress passed the Court Interpreter's Act to provide court interpreters in cases where defendants, plaintiffs, and/or witnesses "speak only or primarily a language other than English" (quoted in Rubin 1985:136). Deaf people who use American Sign Language are also protected by this act, guaranteeing them the services of an interpreter in court proceedings in which they are a witness, defendant, or party to a dispute (*Gallaudet Encyclopedia* 1987:212). The act sets guidelines for determining and certifying the qualifications of bilingual interpreters.

Numerous federal and state agencies have also instituted policies to help non-English speakers and people with limited English proficiency avail themselves of public services. For example, the New York City Department of Social Services hires bilingual workers to aid clients who apply for welfare benefits. In the health field, the California Department of Health Services recommends dissemination of bilingual material concerning hospital procedures. And the U.S. Department of Labor regulates provision of bilingual services to people seeking unemployment compensation (ibid.:146, 138).

Although these laws and administrative regulations safeguard rights of citizens and residents who lack full English proficiency, efforts began in the 1980s to reverse these protections. In 1981, a constitutional amendment was introduced to make English the nation's official language, but it has not been enacted despite repeated reintroductions in both the House and Senate (Baron 1990). Working in the legislative forum, in 1996 the House of Representatives passed the Language in Government Act (HR-123) that would mandate the use of English by "all employees and officials of the Government of the United States while performing official business" (quoted in Hornberger 1998:446–447). The legislation has not become law, however, because of its repeated failure to be enacted by the Senate. In the words of one senator, Paul Simon of Illinois, it is a "not very subtle symbolic attack" on Hispanic and Asian Americans (ibid.:447). Using local strategies, numerous states, either through legislatures or voter referenda, have passed laws that establish English as the official language of the state and do not allow use of public monies to prepare, print, or distribute information, forms, or brochures in languages other than English. Such regulations are in force in 17 states, mostly in the South and West. Many of these are states with relatively small immigrant populations (Kentucky, Mississippi, Nebraska), but others have high proportions of foreign-born residents (California, Hawaii, Illinois, Florida) (US English 1990). Laws supporting English as an official language are pending in another nine states, most in the Northeast; and they have been proposed and rejected in eight states (Baron 1990:201).

In California, voters approved a ballot initiative in 1998, called Proposition 227, that aims to reverse bilingual education policies. Under the plan, "nearly all" bilingual classes must be conducted in English rather than in the children's native language, usually Spanish. However, since the law does not define what "nearly all" means, school districts have interpreted the plan in diverse ways. Some districts use a formula of 20 percent Spanish/80 percent English, others use a 30–70 percent formula, and some have classes taught 40 percent in Spanish and 60 percent in English (*New York Times* 1998). In any case, only about 30 percent of foreign-language-speaking children are actually enrolled in bilingual programs because of the scarcity of qualified teachers.

The diversity of policies and attitudes concerning language and multilingualism indicates the complexity of these issues. Unfortunately, the facts of language use in the United States are often obscured or even ignored in the debate. While 15 percent of Americans either speak a language other than English or live in a household where one is spoken, more than 97 percent of all U.S. residents speak English. And about 90 percent of Americans are monolingual speakers of English (Baron 1990:177). Despite the rhetoric that arouses totally unfounded fears of the future shrinkage of English use, in fact fewer U.S. residents do not speak English today than at the beginning of the nineteenth century. The shift to greater English dominance currently than in the past can be accounted for by gains in educational achievement and by the decline in the proportion of immigrants to the total population. That is, while the proportion of foreign-born residents was 14 percent in 1920, it was only 7 percent in 1990 (ibid.:189).

Native American Languages

Many speakers of non-English languages come from communities that have resided in this nation for decades or centuries. In the case of Native Americans, their ancestors have lived here for millennia. Analysis of 1971 census data indicates that 250,000 American Natives speak an indigenous language as their mother tongue. Approximately half of these people live on reservations and the others live in off-reservation towns and cities (Leap 1981:126–127). Native American speakers of indigenous languages represent numerous linguistic families. Some languages are currently spoken by only a small number of people, whereas others are well represented. Navajo has more than 100,000 speakers. According to federal statistics, the following linguistic families have at least 10,000 speakers: Algonkian, 48,000; Athabaskan (non-Navajo), 17,000; Iroquoian, 17,500; Muskogean, 16,500; Uto-Aztecan, 30,000; and Siouan, 28,000 (Leap 1981:126; Young 1978:162).

Figures available from the 1990 U.S. Census are not exactly comparable because of differences in the questions asked. However, some 332,000 people reported that they speak a Native language at home (note that others may be speakers of indigenous languages but do not use the language "at home"). By far the most frequently spoken language is Navajo (148,530 people reporting it as their home language). Other languages with more than 10,000 speakers include Dakota/Lakhota, Yupik, Apache, Cherokee, and Pima and Papago. Those with between 5,000 and 10,000 speakers are Choctaw and Chickasaw, Keres, Zuni, Muskogee/Creek, Hopi and Ojibwa (Broadwell 1995:146–147). In addition, some 17,000 respondents reported their home language as "Indian" or "American Indian." And approximately 10,000 people stated that they were monolingual speakers of an indigenous language.

The linguistic needs of Native American children are addressed by several federal laws, including the Bilingual Education Act of 1968, amended specifically for Native Americans in 1972 as the Indian Education Act. This law provides funds for programs serving Native American communities (Spolsky 1977:59). Extension of the Bilingual Education Act in 1979–1980 also benefits Native Americans even if they do not speak their tribal language.

Various reservations have developed educational programs designed to meet their specific needs. Some groups accept a transitional model advocated by the federal government. Among the Northern Cheyenne, Choctaw, Ute, and Zuni, bilingual programs seek to teach students English in early grades and switch exclusively to English in third grade. Other Native American peoples employ a maintenance model of bilingual education, stressing acquisition of skills in English while simultaneously developing literacy and fluency in their indigenous language. For example, the Navajo, Yupik, and Cree continue instruction in their native language in elementary school (ibid.:65). In addition, Navajo is spoken in community colleges on the reservation. For groups whose native language is no longer spoken as a first language, linguistic programs aim at revival, usually in conjunction with instruction in other aspects of traditional culture.

In an important statement of policy, in 1990, the U.S. Congress recognized the importance of languages to the continuation of distinctive Native American cultural identity. The Native American Languages Act (PL 101–477) states:

> The status of the cultures and languages of Native Americans is unique and the United States has the responsibility to act together with Native Americans to ensure the survival of these unique cultures and languages. The traditional languages of Native Americans are an integral part of their cultures and identities and form the basic medium for the transmission, and thus survival, of Native American cultures, literatures, histories, religions, political institutions, and values.

In addition to generally encouraging use of Native American languages, the act specifically endorses use of these codes as "mediums of instruction in order to encourage and support Native American language survival, educational opportunities, increase student successs and performance, increase student awareness and knowledge of their culture and history and increase student and community pride."

Efforts to protect and promote the use of Native American languages are especially critical, given the fact that many of these languages have few speakers at this time. The paucity of speakers has resulted from many factors, not the least of which was the federal government's policies, lasting from the nineteenth until the middle of the twentieth century, that banned the use of Native American languages in schools and dormitories for Native American children. Officials targeted the maintenance of indigenous languages as impediments to the "assimilation" of Indians into American society. The government, in collusion with missionaries and secular teachers, established boarding schools for Native American children in order to separate children from their families and break their emotional and cultural ties with their communities. In the words of John Atkins, Indian commissioner in 1887, "The instruction of Indians in the vernacular is not only of no use to them, but is detrimental to the cause of their education and civilization, and no school will be permitted on the reservations in which the English language is not exclusively taught" (Commissioner of Indian Affairs 1887:xxii).

Strong social and political pressures have been exerted for centuries to compel Native Americans to abandon their traditional cultures. In addition to forcing children to speak English, American authorities had two important goals. They wanted Indians to abandon traditional religious beliefs and practices and convert to Christianity. And governments wanted to indoctrinate Native American children into sharing American values and finally acquiesce to American authority and control. As a result of decades of such pressures, many Native American languages were forgotten. And many of those still spoken today have uncertain futures even though the direct assault on them has ended. Of course, some remain strong, especially Navajo (in the Southwest), Inuit-Inupiat (in Arctic Canada and Alaska), Cree (in subarctic Canada), and Lakhota (in the Great Plains), among others. In the context of the history of U.S. (and Canadian) policy toward Native American languages, the recent statement by Congress is most welcome, although its practical effect is yet to be seen.

Creole Languages in the United States

Three unique languages developed in the United States in the past several hundred years. These are Gullah (spoken mostly on the Sea Islands off the coast of South Carolina), Louisiana Creole, and Hawaiian Creole. As are all creoles, these languages are amalgams of sounds, grammatical forms, and vocabularies from several linguistic sources. Creoles arise in contact situations where speakers of different languages interact and need to develop a mutually intelligible code. Gullah and Louisiana Creole are derived from various African languages and English or French, respectively. Hawaiian Creole is a complex mixture of English, Native Hawaiian, and several Asian and Pacific languages.

Gullah. Gullah is spoken by possibly as many as 300,000 people on the Sea Islands and along the mainland Atlantic coast from southern North Carolina to northern Florida. Most speakers of Gullah are descendants of Africans whose languages contributed to this creole. Figure 11.3 depicts the relevant area.

Gullah changed significantly in the twentieth century because of increasing contact with speakers of standard English and southern regional dialects. As English elements have been incorporated into Gullah, many creole features have become attenuated. Although no "pure" Gullah speakers remain, the language retains many distinct forms and rules, differing considerably from standard English. The following sample of Gullah is taken from the speech of a 9-year-old girl (Nichols 1981:74; text is written in standard English orthography, with added underlining of distinctive Gullah traits):

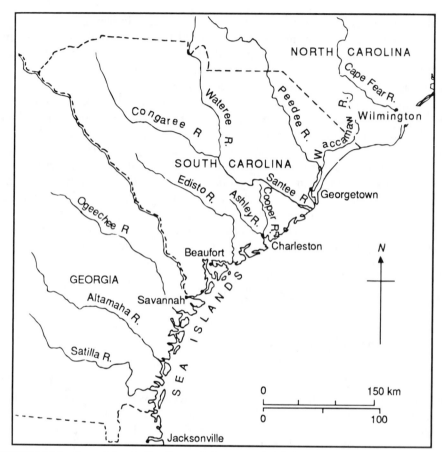

FIGURE 11.3. Coastal South Carolina and Georgia.   (Nichols 1981:72)

When Christmas <u>come</u> I had gone to my <u>Aunt</u> house. Then my aunt
<u>say</u> have to beat my little sister 'cause she had, she had broke a glass,
with the cocoa in <u>um</u>. And then we had gone up to <u>we</u> other <u>cousin</u>
house name ____. And then we had see-then we-then that night we
had gone up to Jerome. Then when we <u>come</u> from there, the dog had
come and <u>bite</u> my little sister and my little sister <u>say,</u> "Owww, Ooooo."
And then <u>ee</u> say, "Unnn." And then she-and then after that-Monday,
we-I had gone to my <u>aunt</u> house <u>fuh</u> see my baby sister. And then we
had gone and <u>play.</u> And then I <u>had ride</u> her bicycle. And <u>she</u> bicycle had
broke. And ____ say, "Oh, ____, see what you <u>done do</u>; broke that <u>girl</u>
bicycle."

I <u>say,</u> "I ain't do <u>um;</u> you do <u>um</u> 'cause you want me <u>fuh tote</u> you."

Characteristic grammatical features of Gullah include the following (unless otherwise specified, examples are from ibid.:74–75):

1. Third-person subject pronouns are not distinguished for gender. The original Gullah form for all third-person singular subjects was *ee*, /i/. Among some speakers there is a tendency now to include aspiration, /hi/, but its occurrence is unstable. Some speakers employ the standard feminine pronoun /ši/ ("she"), using it contrastively with /i/ or /hi/ for masculine and neuter subjects. This pattern, too, is currently unstable (Jones-Jackson 1984:355). In the sample above, for example, the girl uses both *she* and *ee* as pronouns for female subjects.

2. The third-person possessive pronoun *ee* /i/ is used for all three genders (masculine, feminine, neuter). Again, variation is found, with use of /i/ or /ši/ for feminine possessors, and occasional adoption of standard "her." Examples are "he took *ee* mother long with um" (his); "but I ain't see *she*" (her). Also note in the quoted story: "And then I had ride *her* bicycle. And *she* bicycle had broke."

3. The third-person objective case pronoun is *um* /ʌm/ for all three genders: "but I ain't see she fuh tell *um* nothing" (her); "I ain't know fuh get *um* off" (it). Current variation includes /ši/ for feminines: "but I ain't see *she*" (her); "she took *she* time for get here" (Jones-Jackson 1984:358).

4. Nouns are not inflected for possession; e.g., in the girl's story: "I had gone to my *aunt* house." Similarly, plural objects are not marked for number: "there was this big snake with two horn."

5. Simple past tense is usually not marked: "Then my aunt *say* have to beat my little sister."

6. Several verbal aspects are overtly marked:
    a. Habitual: "This summer, when my daddy *be working*, they always have lot of peaches."
    b. Progressive, marked by *duh:* "Gregg *duh* hide."
    c. Perfective, marked by *done:* "I *done* know."

7. Clauses with infinitive verbs are introduced by *fuh*, as in: "I come *fuh* get my coat" or in the narrator's "you do um 'cause you want me *fuh* tote you."

8. Embedded sentences are introduced by sɛ, as in the following excerpt quoted by Dreyfuss (1978:66) from Lorenzo Turner's transcription of Gullah (1949:211): /dɛn di čɪ/ɛn dɛ ɪn nyu yak s ɛ n wʌd sɛ de ē gain gɪt nʌtn/ "Then the children in New York sent word <u>that</u> they weren't going to get anything."

Gullah's distinctive grammatical features are similar to those of several West African languages. For instance, just as Gullah does not mark gender differences, neither do Yoruba, Igbo, and Efik (Jones-Jackson 1978:426). Unlike English, West African languages contain highly developed aspectual systems, a characteristic also found in Gullah. Finally, the particle <u>sɛ</u> occurs with identical functions in Gullah and some West African languages such as Twi (Dreyfuss 1978:66). (On a comparative note, recall that s̲e̲ appears in Jamaican English or patois spoken by people of Jamaican descent in Great Britain; see Chapter 6.)

Gullah's inventory of sounds is similar to that of English, but it contains some distinctive elements:

1. Gullah replaces English interdental fricatives /θ/ and /ð/ with corresponding alveolar stops /t/ and /d/, respectively (Jones-Jackson 1978:427–428).

2. Gullah contains bilabial fricatives /ɸ/ and /ʙ/. Voiceless /ɸ/ appears in place of English labiodental /f/, whereas voiced /ʙ/ replaces English labiodental /v/ and bilabials /b/ and /w/. Bilabial fricatives do not occur in standard English, although they are common sounds in West African languages (ibid.:427).

3. Vowels /i/, /e/, /o/, and /u/ are monothongs in Gullah, whereas they are dipthongs in English, that is, /iy/, /ey/, /ow/, and /uw/ (Dreyfuss 1978:66).

Finally, although Gullah vocabulary is primarily derived from English, Turner reported some 250 words in Gullah that originated from 20 West African languages (Turner 1949; Dreyfuss 1978:65). The following examples were recorded in Jones-Jackson's study of Gullah in the 1970s (1978:425–426).

Gullah	*English*	*Source Language*
gulu	pig	gula "pig, hog" (Kongo)
guba	peanut	ŋguba "peanut" (Kimbunda)
gɔmbo	okra	tšιŋgɔmbɔ "okra" (Tshiluba)
jiga	small flea	ɟiga "insect" (Wolof)
nansi	spider	anansi "spider" (Twi)
tot	to carry	tota "to pick up" (Kikongo)
cikabod	a see-saw	cika "to lift" (Mandingo)
hudu	bad luck	húždužba "to arouse resentment" (Hausa)

Louisiana Creole. Louisiana Creole is derived from French and from African languages spoken by slaves brought to the area principally from West Africa. Creole coexists today with two varieties of French, a rarely spoken dialect descended from the speech of colonial settlers and a widely used Acadian, or "Cajun," dialect originating with eighteenth-century émigrés from Nova Scotia. Regional and standard English are now spoken in Louisiana as well. The number of creole speakers is unknown, but estimates of 80,000 have been suggested (Dreyfuss 1978:67). Most speakers of creole are African American, although many whites also speak the language. Speakers of creole are often bilingual in Cajun French or multilingual speakers of Cajun, standard French, and/or English. As expected in a situation of such constant contact, changes in all these varieties have taken place.

Distinctive traits of Louisiana Creole include the following (examples compiled from Dreyfuss 1978:68–70 and Nichols 1981:79–80):

1. Replacement of standard French rounded front vowels by unrounded vowels:

French				Creole	
ü	fumer	/fümé/	→	i /fimé/	"to smoke"
ɔ̈	seul	/sɔ̈l/	→	ɛ /sɛl/	"alone; only"
ö	peu	/pö/	→	e/pe/	"a little"

2. Use of feminine definite article *la* for all nouns, including nouns that are masculine in standard French. Definite articles either follow or precede their nouns in creole, whereas they always precede in standard French:

Creole	French	
Fɔm-la	la femme	"the woman"
la-kɔrd	la corde	"the string"
ti-košõ-la	le petit cochon	"the little pig"

3. Gender is not distinguished for third-person subjects, both marked by the pronoun *li:*

li vini pu-mõte āho-là
she/he managed to climb up there

4. Standard third-person plural pronouns *ils/elles* ("they" masculine/feminine) are replaced by *ye. Ye* also occurs following nouns to mark plurality:

Creole: /sa fɛ trwa lapɛ̃-*ye* ki muri. m-alɛ šarše *ye*/
French orthography: ça fait troit lapin-*ye* qui mouri. Moi aller chercher *ye*
"That makes three rabbits who are dead. I'll go look for *them*."

5. Tense is not marked on verbs. Particles indicating aspects precede verbs:

mo fini	I finish, I finished, I will finish
mo te-fini	I have finished (completive)
m-ape-fini	I am finishing (progressive)
m-ape-kupe	I am running (progressive)
mo te-pe kupe	I was running (progressive)
m-ale-kupe	I will run

6. Embedded sentences are introduced by sɛ (note the similarity to Gullah):

Creole: /buki tɛ krwa sɛ ɛ̃ nɔt lapɛ̃/
French orthography: Bouki te croire <u>se</u> un autre lapin.
"Bouki believed that it was another rabbit."

Due to multilingualism and dialect mixing in Louisiana, creole has had an impact on local varieties of English. The following constructions in English are derived from Louisiana Creole (Marshall 1982:314–315):

1. Omission of tense markers:
He come and see you. (past)
She expect in September. (present)

2.   Omission of noun plurals:
     sixty-two stitch
     in other word

3.   In interrogative sentences, the auxiliary "do" (or "did") is not included:
     How she write dat?
     What he used to do?

4.   Shifts in meaning (translations of creole constructions):
     I made $200 worth of damage. (from creole/French *faire* "to make, do")
     What he used to do for a life?
     She remarried back.

Hawaiian Creole. Hawaiian Creole is one of many languages spoken in
Hawaii. The complex linguistic situation in that state is a result of contact among
indigenous Hawaiians, American colonizers, and Asian, Pacific, and European
immigrant workers. American colonization of the Hawaiian islands began in the
late eighteenth century and intensified in the nineteenth. The Hawaiian monarchy
was overthrown in 1893 and the territory was annexed by the United States in
1898. During this era, American plantation owners and traders brought in workers from many countries, principally China, Japan, the Philippines, and Portugal.
In this multilingual context, a Hawaiian pidgin language developed for use among
workers, merchants, and residents of diverse linguistic backgrounds (Sato
1985:255–258).

Pidgins are similar to creoles in their origin, arising in contact situations
among speakers of varied languages. They differ in that pidgins have simplified
grammatical structures and a limited vocabulary, containing primarily those words
necessary to carry on restricted conversations between people who interact in specific contexts, as in work or trade. Pidgins are not first languages of any speaker
but are acquired for use with limited functions. Pidgins sometimes eventually
develop into creoles, that is, full languages, through expansion of grammatical elements and vocabulary. They then can be learned as first languages by children, possibly beginning with offspring of interethnic marriages. Such a potential situation
arose in Hawaii and probably accounts for the origin of Hawaiian Creole
(ibid.:261).

Creole is currently spoken by nearly half of the 800,000 residents of the state.
Most speakers are bi- or multilingual, speaking variants along a creole-standard
continuum (Nichols 1981:82).

Distinctive traits of Hawaiian Creole include the following (examples compiled from Nichols 1981:85–86; Dreyfuss 1978:72):

1.   Absence of definite articles. Indefinite article is expressed as *wan:*
     I go see *wan* movies. (I went to see a movie.)

2.   Past tense is either not marked or signaled by *wɛn* preceding a verb:
     My cousin go. (past)
     I *wɛn* go climb up when I was *wan* baby. (I climbed up when I was a baby.)

3. "Neutralization" or elimination of past-tense markers occurs in two syntactic contexts (Day 1973:307–308):
   a. In sentences containing multiple past-tense verbs, only the first verb is marked; subsequent verbs are not marked:
   So he went down there and open the door and trying to drag the guy out.
   b. In sentences containing adverbs referring to past times, verbs are not marked for tense:
   In those days, when I get only one two baby I go with Papa all over. (In those days, when I had only one or two babies, I went with Papa all over.)

4. Future tense is signaled by *gon* preceding a verb:
   I *gon* see wan movie.

5. Progressive or habitual aspect is marked by *stay* preceding a verb:
   Us *stay* playing basketball over there.

6. Negation is marked by:
   a. *no* or *not* in nonpast tenses:
   I *not* joking.
   b. *never* in past tense:
   He *never* go. (He didn't go.)

7. Clauses with infinitive verbs are introduced by *for:*
   Ask him *for* iron my shirt.

The following passage illustrates many features of Hawaiian Creole. It was spoken by a 45-year-old man who resided on one of the most remote islands in the chain (Sato 1985:262):

/luk nau, a bin go si Toni abaut go spansa da kidz, ae, da b skitbawl tim, da wan ai ste koch fo—ai tel, e. Toni, hauz abaut, a, spansa da kidz, boi, yu no æfta awl iz awl Puhi kidz, yu no—æn awl as gaiz awl y unyen membaz, ae? a tel am yu—yu gaiz kæn spansa ada gaiz—ai no si wai yu gaiz no kæn spansa da kidz/

look-now, I-been-go-see-Tony-about-go-sponsor-the-kids, eh, the—basketball-team, the-one-I-stay-coach-for—I-tell, hey, Tony, how's-about, uh, sponsor-the-kids, boi. you-know-after-all-it's-all-Puhi-kids-you-know—and-all-us-guys-all-union-members, eh? I-tell-him-you—you-guys-can-sponsor-other-guys—I-no-see-why-you-guys-no-can-sponsor-the-kids

"Look now, I went to see Tony about [their] sponsoring the kids, eh, the basketball team that I'm coaching. I said, 'Hey, Tony, how about sponsoring the kids, boy? You know after all they're all Puhi [name of a town] kids, you know—and all of us [parents] are union members, eh?' I told him, 'You—you guys can sponsor other guys—I don't see why you can't sponsor the kids.'"

All three American creoles share certain structural similarities. Morphological complexities are minimal because of an absence of markers for plurality on nouns, gender on pronouns, and tense on verbs. Aspectual distinctions, however, are well developed.

In all three speech communities, speakers of creoles are rarely, if ever, monolingual. They employ various dialects and/or languages on a continuum from heavily creolized to regional standards. Speakers of creoles tend to be among the poorest, least educated sectors of their communities, usually living in rural or isolated regions. Because of a combination of their class, limited education, and, often, race, and influenced by dominant societal attitudes favoring standard English, these speakers are generally stigmatized. Their language is denigrated as ungrammatical or incorrect. Needs of creole-speaking children in schools are ignored; they are expected to learn standard English with no special instruction in bilingual programs. Negative stereotypes no doubt contribute to the erosion of some distinctive characteristics of the creoles, yet they remain fully functional languages spoken by substantial numbers of people.

SUMMARY

In all societies, some people speak more than one language. Multilingualism results from universal experiences of meeting and living with people of diverse linguistic and ethnic backgrounds. In modern nations, conflicts based on economic and/or political conditions often surface as conflicts over languages spoken by different groups. The language one speaks is an important aspect of individual identity and can be used to galvanize and focus group consciousness. We have examined aspects of these issues in India, Canada, and the United States, each having its own specific problems and outcomes.

In India, linguistic diversity reflects a complex history of uniting many distinct cultural groups into a modern political entity. In Canada, two large ethnic divisions compete for economic and political status. Finally, multilingualism in the United States stems from past and present immigration. Immigrants have continually interacted with previously established communities, whether native or themselves descendants of prior immigrants.

Government policies in the United States have undergone historical changes regarding support or nonsupport of minority language rights. These policies, and public opinion, are still in flux and will undoubtedly continue to arouse controversy. But the fact remains that millions of people in the United States are speakers of languages other than English. Native-born and immigrant, monolingual and multilingual, all add to society's complexity and diversity.

REFERENCES

ANISFELD, ELIZABETH, AND WALLACE LAMBERT. 1964. Evaluational reactions of bilingual and monolingual children to spoken languages. *Journal of Abnormal and Social Psychology* 69:89–97.

APTE, MAHADEV. 1976. Multilingualism in India and its socio-political implications: An overview. In *Language and Politics,* ed. W. O'Barr and J. O'Barr. The Hague: Mouton, pp. 141–164.

BARON, DENNIS. 1990. *The English-Only Question: An Official Language for Americans?* New Haven, CT: Yale University Press.

BOURHIS, RICHARD. 1985. The Charter of the French Language and cross-cultural communication in Montreal. In *Conflict and Language Planning in Quebec,* ed. R. Bourhis. Avon, England: Clevedon, pp. 174–204.

BROADWELL, GEORGE. 1995. 1990 census figures for speakers of American Indian language. *Language in Society* 61:145–149.

Canada Year Book. 1990. Ottawa: Statistics Canada.

CENSUS OF INDIA. 1980, 1981.

COMMISSIONER OF INDIAN AFFAIRS. 1887. *Annual Report.* Washington, DC.

DASWANI, C. J. 1989. Aspects of modernization in Indian languages. In *Language Adaptation,* ed. F. Coulmas. New York: Cambridge University Press, pp. 79–89.

DAY, RICHARD. 1973. Tense neutralization in the Hawaiian post-creole gradatum. In *New Ways of Analyzing Variation in English,* ed. C. Bailey and R. Shuy. Washington, DC: Georgetown University Press, pp. 306–312.

DREYFUSS, GAIL. 1978. Pidgin and creole languages in the United States. In *A Pluralistic Nation,* ed. M. Lourie and N. Conklin. Rowley, MA: Newbury, pp. 61–77.

DUA, HANS. 1985. Sociolinguistic inequality and language problems of linguistic minorities in India. In *Language of Inequality,* ed. N. Wolfson and J. Manes. The Hague: Mouton, pp. 355–372.

FISHMAN, JOSHUA. 1981. Language policy: Past, present and future. In *Language in the USA,* ed. C. Ferguson and S. Heath. New York: Cambridge University Press, pp. 516–526.

FREEMAN, REBECCA. 1996. Dual-language planning at Oyster Bilingual School: "It's much more than language." *TESOL Quarterly* 30:557–582.

Gallaudet University Encyclopedia of Deaf People and Deafness. 1987. New York: McGraw-Hill, vol. I.

GILES, HOWARD, DONALD TAYLOR, AND RICHARD BOURHIS. 1973. Towards a theory of interpersonal accommodation through language: Some Canadian data. *Language in Society* 2: 177–192.

GROSJEAN, FRANCOIS. 1982. *Life with Two Languages.* Cambridge, MA: Harvard University Press.

HEATH, SHIRLEY. 1977. Language and politics in the United States. In *Linguistics and Anthropology,* ed. M. Saville-Troike. Georgetown University Round Table on Languages and Linguistics. Washington, DC: Georgetown University Press, pp. 267–296.

HELLER, MONICA. 1985. Ethnic relations and language use in Montreal. In *Language of Inequality,* ed. N. Wolfson and J. Manes. The Hague: Mouton, pp. 75–90.

HORNBERGER, NANCY. 1998. Language policy, language education, language rights: Indigenous, immigrant, and international perspectives. *Language in Society* 27:439–458.

JONES-JACKSON, PATRICIA. 1978. Gullah: On the question of Afro-American language. *Anthropological Linguistics* 20:422–429.

JONES-JACKSON, PATRICIA. 1984. On decreolization and language death in Gullah. *Language in Society* 13:351–362.

KESSLER, CAROLYN, AND MARY QUINN. 1985. Positive effects of bilingualism on science problem-solving activities. In *Perspectives on Bilingualism and Bilingual Education,* ed. J. Alatis and

J. Staczek. Washington, DC: Georgetown University Press, pp. 283–296.

KIDDER, ROBERT. 1976. Language and litigation in South India. In *Language and Politics,* ed. W. O'Barr and J. O'Barr. The Hague: Mouton, pp. 235–251.

LAMBERT, WALLACE. 1967. A social psychology of bilingualism. *Journal of Social Issues* 23:91–109.

LAMBERT, WALLACE, R. C. HODGSON, R. C. GARDNER, AND S. FILLENBAUM. 1960. Evaluational reactions to spoken languages. *Journal of Abnormal and Social Psychology* 60:44–51.

LEAP, WILLIAM. 1981. American Indian languages. In *Language in the USA,* ed. C. Ferguson and S. Heath. New York: Cambridge University Press, pp. 116–144.

LEAP, WILLIAM. 1986. American Indian English and its implications for bilingual education. In *Dialect and Language Variation,* ed. H. Allen and M. Linn. New York: Academic Press, pp. 591–603.

MARSHALL, MARGARET. 1982. Bilingualism in southern Louisiana: A sociolinguistic analysis. *Anthropological Linguistics* 24:308–324.

MCCONNELL, BEVERLY. 1985. Bilingual education and language shift. In *Spanish Language Use and Public Life in the US,* ed. L. Elias-Olivares et al. The Hague: Mouton, pp. 201–215.

MEISEL, JOHN. 1978. Values, language and politics in Canada. In *Advances in the Study of Societal Multilingualism,* ed. J. Fishman. The Hague: Mouton, pp. 665–717.

New York Times, 1998. California bilingual teaching lives on after vote to kill it (Don Terry). October 3:A1,7.

NICHOLS, PATRICIA. 1981. Creoles of the USA. In *Language in the USA,* ed. C. Ferguson and S. Heath. New York: Cambridge University Press, pp. 71–91.

RUBIN, JOAN. 1985. Spanish language planning in the US. In *Spanish Language Use and Public Life in the US,* ed. L. Elias-Olivares et al. The Hague: Mouton, pp. 133–152.

SATO, CHARLENE. 1985. Linguistic inequality in Hawaii: The post-creole dilemma. In *Language of Inequality,* ed. N. Wolfson and J. Manes. The Hague: Mouton, pp. 255–272.

SIEGEL, ARTHUR. 1983. *Politics and the Media in Canada.* Toronto: McGraw-Hill Ryerson.

SIMARD, LISE, DONALD TAYLOR, AND HOWARD GILES. 1976. Attribution processes and interpersonal accommodation in a bilingual setting. *Language and Speech* 19:374–387.

SOUTHWORTH, FRANKLIN. 1985. The social context of language standardization in India. In *Language of Inequality,* ed. N. Wolfson and J. Manes. The Hague: Mouton, pp. 225–239.

SPOLSKY, BERNARD. 1977. American Indian bilingual education. *International Journal of the Sociology of Language* 16:57–72.

SRIDHAR, S. N. 1988a. Language modernization: Structural and sociolinguistic aspects. In *Conference on the Basque Language.* Lisbon, Portugal, pp. 351–368.

SRIDHAR, S. N. 1988b. Language variation, attitudes and rivalry: Spread of Hindi in India. In *Language Spread,* ed. P. Lowenberg. Georgetown University Round Table in Languages and Linguistics 1987. Washington, DC: Georgetown University Press, pp. 300–319.

Statistics Canada. 1995. Cat. No. 93–318. Ottawa.

SUBRAMONIAM, V. I. 1977. A note on the preservation of the mother tongue in Kerala. In *Indian Bilingualism,* ed.

P. G. Sharma and S. Kumar. Agra, India: Kendriya Hindi Sansthan, pp. 21–33.

TAYLOR, DONALD, AND LISE DUBE-SIMARD. 1985. Language planning and intergroup relations: Anglophone and francophone attitudes toward the Charter of the French Language. In *Conflict and Language Planning in Quebec,* ed. R. Bourhis. Avon, England: Clevedon, pp. 148–173.

TURNER, LORENZO. 1949. *Africanisms in the Gullah Dialect.* Chicago: University of Chicago Press.

U.S. BUREAU OF THE CENSUS. 1993. *Language Spoken at Home and Ability to Speak English for United States Regions and States: 1990* (CPH-L-133). Washington, DC.

U.S. CONGRESS. 1990. Native American Languages Act. PL 101-477.

U.S. DEPARTMENT OF EDUCATION. 1990. Office of Bilingual Education. Printout. Washington, DC.

US ENGLISH. 1990. Filefacts. Washington, DC.

VALLEE, FRANK, AND JOHN DE VRIES. 1978. Trends in bilingualism in Canada. In *Advances in the Study of Societal Multilingualism,* ed. J. Fishman. The Hague: Mouton, pp. 761–792.

YOUNG, ROBERT. 1978. English as a second language for Navajos. In *A Pluralistic Nation,* ed. M. Lourie and N. Conklin. Rowley, MA: Newbury, pp. 162–172.

12

Bilingual Communities

In the following two examples from the speech of bilinguals, the speakers combine elements from each of their two languages for stylistic and emphatic effect:

(Mother to child, using English and Spanish):
"Go sit down, go. SIEN-TA-TE (SIT DOWN)!"

(Father to child, using English and French):
"Now it's really time to get up. Lève-toi! (Get up.)"

These are two simple examples of the ways that bilinguals exploit the resources of their languages to convey thoughts and emotions. The speakers here are members of bilingual communities, one in the United States and the other in Canada. Bilingual communities exist throughout the world, wherever members of different ethnic groups meet, interact, and exchange ideas.

Contact between speakers of different languages has diverse linguistic and societal consequences. In order for people in contact situations to communicate, at least some of them must be bilingual. These bilinguals are often catalysts for language change. Exposure to different languages may lead bilingual speakers gradually to incorporate new linguistic material into their primary languages. Innovations eventually spread beyond bilingual communities so that new sounds, morphemes, and/or syntactic constructions can be incorporated into an indigenous system. In addition, words are often borrowed or old meanings adjusted because of influences from foreign sources. Over a period of time, languages can thus be altered as a result of linguistic and social contact.

In bilingual (or multilingual) communities, speakers develop strategies for use of their languages. They may restrict each language to particular contexts, participants, or topics. Each language then performs distinct situational or social functions. This division of roles can remain stable for centuries, or it can lead to shifts in statuses of languages spoken.

In this chapter we begin by discussing a number of changes in languages derived from foreign cultural and linguistic influences. We then turn our attention to examining functional uses of and attitudes toward languages in bilingual communities. Finally, we discuss several conversational strategies used by bilinguals and some consequences of interlinguistic or interethnic communication.

LINGUISTIC CHANGE

Languages change over time. Change sometimes results from processes internal to a language itself. For instance, a language may gradually eliminate case markers on nouns or reorder words within phrases. Evidence of such patterns can be found in the history of English. Old English had noun suffixes that indicated three genders (masculine, feminine, neuter) and four cases (nominative, genitive, dative, accusative), but Modern English nouns lack these markers.

Languages also change as a result of influences from other linguistic systems. All languages contain elements derived from other codes—a normal universal process because no language is a completely closed system. A few examples from English sounds, grammar, and vocabulary will suffice to illustrate this process.

The Modern English consonant /ž/ was not present in the sound system of Old English (or Anglo-Saxon). It is a sound derived from French, heard by eleventh-century inhabitants of the British Isles in speech of Norman invaders after A.D. 1066. At first, when Anglo-Saxons borrowed French words, they replaced the foreign, and to them unpronounceable, /ž/ with their native sound /ǰ/. Compare the following French and English words written phonemically:

	English	French
just	ǰʌst	žüst
judge	ǰʌǰ	žüz
Jack	ǰæk	žak

The English consonant /ǰ/ replaced French /ž/ because it is the native sound closest to the French one. Both /ǰ/ and /ž/ are voiced, palatal consonants, although they differ in their manner of articulation: /ǰ/ is an affricate, whereas /ž/ is a fricative. As a result of centuries of contact between English and French speakers, the French /ž/ was eventually incorporated into the sound system of Modern English. It currently occurs in some words of recent French origin—for example, "lingerie" (/lʌžeri/), "rouge" (/ruž/)—as well as in a few other words such as "pleasure" (/pležɤ/) and "casual" (/kæžual/).

French influence on English grammar occurs in some comparative and superlative adjectival constructions. Old English employed the suffixes *-er* and *-est* as in fair/fairer/fairest. Modeling on French *plus* ("more") and *le plus* ("most") is reflected in sets like beautiful/more beautiful/most beautiful.

Syntactic change is another possible result of linguistic contact. English syntax has been modified by Latin and French sources. G. L. Brook suggested that influence from Latin, and to a lesser extent from French, became particularly strong because these languages were important in British schooling. Because educators believed that Latin was a superior language, they used it as a model (1958:147–148). Examples of Latinate origin include use of infinitve verbs following accusative constructions, as, for example, "I know him to be a good person" or "I told her to arrive by noon." Additionally, grammarians copied Latin structure in their opposition to ending sentences with prepositions. Brook noted the fact that John Dryden, a seventeenth-century writer, revised some of his own works to fit the preferred style, altering his original "the age I live in" to "the age in which I live" (ibid.:148).

Borrowing foreign words is the most widespread result of linguistic and cultural contact. Although rates of borrowing vary, all languages incorporate words of foreign origin. When new items or activities are introduced from other cultures, donors' labels for these entities or events are often added to native lexicons. Hundreds of words in Modern English are derived from Latin and French, the two most frequent sources. English has also borrowed words from dozens of other languages. The following list contains only a handful of *loanwords,* representing a variety of origins (collected from Pyles and Algeo 1982:297–316):

Source	*Loanwords*
Greek	agnostic, chlorine, idiosyncrasy, telephone
Irish Gaelic	brogue, leprechaun, shamrock
Scots Gaelic	clan, plaid, slogan, whiskey
Scandanavian	muggy, rug, ski
Spanish	bonanza, canyon, patio, ranch
Portuguese	albino, flamingo, molasses
Italian	balcony, bandit, studio, umbrella
Dutch	boss, cookie, pit (of fruit), sleigh
German	hamster, pretzel, semester
Yiddish	kibitzer, nebbish, phooey, schlep
Russian	czar, mammoth, tundra, vodka
Turkish	fez, tulip, turban
Arabic	candy, mattress, orange, sugar
Hebrew	cherub, hallelujah, jubilee, kosher
Persian	caravan, bazaar, shawl
Sanskrit	karma, yoga
Hindi	bungalow, dungaree, jungle, pajamas
Chinese	tea, kowtow, tycoon
Japanese	hara-kiri, samurai, soya
Pacific languages	bamboo, kangaroo, launch, tattoo
African languages	gorilla, jazz, tote, yam

| Native North American languages | bayou, mocassin, moose, pecan |
| Native Central American languages | chocolate, maize, tomato, potato |

In some cases, foreign words whose meanings are similar to native words are borrowed, but each takes on specialized usage. For example, indigenous Anglo-Saxon animal terms are now complemented by French words to refer to foods:

Animal	*Food*	*French Source*
steer	beef	boeuf
pig	pork	porc
calf	veal	veau
sheep	mutton	mouton
chicken	poultry	poulet

Finally, foreign influences sometimes result in contrasting stylistic uses for native or borrowed words. In English, some words of French origin are considered more formal or polite than their Anglo-Saxon equivalents:

Anglo-Saxon Source	*French Source*
smell	odor
sweat	perspiration
eat ·	dine
dead	deceased
want	desire
look at	regard
go away	depart
come back	return

Processes of linguistic change can be easily and abundantly demonstrated in all languages of the world, although the locus and extent of modification vary depending on duration, context, and intensity of contact between speakers of different languages. Just as hundreds of English words are borrowed from foreign sources, other languages have loans from English. And just as English has modified foreign words to fit native phonological patterns, so other host languages have altered sounds of English words to fit their systems. A few examples are offered on page 340 to illustrate this process, with explanations of changes.

LANGUAGE USE IN BILINGUAL COMMUNITIES

In bilingual or multilingual communities, particular languages can become associated with particular contexts and invoke distinct social and personal meanings. Such functional specialization and related social attitudes may remain stable or they may result in shifts in linguistic preference, possibly even in the loss of one language entirely. In this section we describe several examples of language use in bilingual communities. The cases discussed illustrate different sets of features and patterns of linguistic choice.

English Donor		Host Language		
Spelling	Pronunciation	Language	Loanword	Change
roof	ruf	Spanish (Puerto Rico)	rufo	add final vowel
ginger beer	jɪnjɚ bir	Spanish (Costa Rica)	čɪnčɪbi	replace voiced /ǰ/ with voiceless /č/; delete syllable-final /r/
police	pʌlíys	Swahili	polisi	add final vowel
car	kar	Swahili	kaa	delete final /r/
ruler	rulɚ	Ganda	luula	replace initial /r/ with /l/
railway	reylwey	Ganda	leerwe	replace initial /r/ with /l/; replace medial /l/ following a front vowel with /r/
thumbtacks	θʌmtæks	Mohawk	tamtaks	replace fricative /θ/ with stop /t/
matches	mæčɪz	Mohawk	maǰis	replace voiceless /č/ with voiced /ǰ/; replace voiced /z/ with voiceless /s/
number	nʌmbɚ	Navajo	nóomba	delete final /r/
Christmas	krɪsmɪs	Navajo	késmiš	simplify initial consonant cluster; replace alveolar /s/ with palatal /š/
elevator	ɛlɪveytor	Japanese	erebeta	replace /l/ with /r/; replace /v/ with /b/; delete final /r/
baseball	beysbɔl	Japanese	beisuboru	add epenthetic vowel; replace /l/ with /r/; add final vowel
casual	kæžual	Tagalog	kazwal	replace /ž/ with /z/; simplify vowel cluster
budget	bʌǰɛt	Tagalog	badyɛt	replace affricate /ǰ/ with stop /d/ + glide /y/

SOURCES: Puerto Rican Spanish: Zentella 1985:45; Costa Rican Spanish: Appel and Muysken 1987:169; Ganda: Halle and Clements 1983:51; Mohawk: Bonvillain 1978:37; Navajo: Young and Morgan 1987:7; Swahili, Japanese: Berlitz 1982:299–300; Tagalog: Molony 1977:141–142.

An *ethnography of communication* among bilinguals includes analysis of their choice of language in various speech events. Factors such as context, participant, topic, and goal influence bilinguals' decisions. For instance, two speakers of Spanish and English in the United States may converse at work in English but speak Spanish to each other on their way home. They may talk about a current international crisis in English but gossip about their neighbors in Spanish. And they may use Spanish to signal their mutual solidarity as members of a Hispanic ethnic group.

The term *diglossia* refers to situations where each language is systematically employed in certain domains or events. The term was introduced by Charles Ferguson (1959) to apply to circumstances where two varieties of the same language coexist in a community, for example, a national standard and a regional form; however, diglossia currently includes both bilingual and bidialectal conditions. Ferguson referred to the sets of contexts and values assigned to each language as high or low (1959:327). A *high language* is used in public arenas, such as school, church, and government. It has a long literary tradition and may be linked to prestigeful social groups. In contrast, a *low language* is used in private or informal domains with family and friends. It may have less social prestige than the high variety, but it often is associated with strong emotional loyalty and can be used to signal in-group membership.

Bilingualism in Paraguay illustrates such divergent associations demarcating Spanish and Guarani, an indigenous language spoken by more than 90 percent of the population. Paraguay's 1967 constitution recognized Guarani and Spanish as "national" languages, although Spanish is given status as the "official" language. Nearly everyone living in rural areas speaks Guarani, but even in Paraguay's capital, Asuncion, 76 percent of the populace are bilingual. Monolingual Guarani speakers usually reside in rural villages, whereas monolingual Spanish speakers typically live in large cities (Rubin 1985:112).

Among bilinguals, who constitute the overwhelming majority of Paraguayans, a diglossic pattern obtains. According to Joan Rubin, four contextual factors influence a bilingual's choice of code: location of interaction, degree of formality, degree of intimacy, and seriousness of discourse (ibid.:116). In general, Spanish is the language of urban life and is used in formal situations such as speaking to officials, doctors, teachers, and others with whom a speaker is socially distant. Guarani predominates in rural areas but is spoken throughout Paraguay in interactions with family and friends, especially when conversing about informal or personal topics (ibid.:116–117).

Attitudes toward the two languages are somewhat contradictory, particularly regarding Guarani. Spanish has prestige because of its association with an international culture and an important literary tradition. Guarani is favorably perceived as a symbol of Paraguayan nationalism. But it is also sometimes disparaged as unsophisticated. For this reason, young men in the countryside reported that they try to use Spanish when initiating courtship, although couples tend to switch to Guarani when they become better acquainted (ibid.:117). Despite some negative attitudes toward Guarani, it is thought to be emotionally expressive. Finally, Rubin noted that Paraguayans traveling abroad typically speak Guarani to each other "in order to establish their solidarity by the use of the more unusual and intimate language" (ibid.).

Patterns of language use in many African countries illustrate the coexistence of local tribal codes and international lingua francas, each assigned various communicative functions. A *lingua franca* is a language that is used by nonnative speakers when interacting with speakers of different codes. It thus enables members of diverse ethnic and linguistic groups to communicate with one another. In many parts of Africa, an indigenous language, Swahili, has functioned for centuries as a lingua franca. During the era of European colonization in Africa, European languages, principally English and French, assumed roles as international and interethnic languages. Even though African nations are now independent, English and French often continue to function as codes for administration, business, advanced education, and elite discourse. Therefore, despite the small ethnic base of European languages in Africa, they are frequently employed in public domains.

In addition to the lingua francas, linguistic usage in Africa is complicated by the multitude of codes spoken within each nation. These languages are native to different indigenous ethnic or tribal groups, each of which uses its own code among co-members. The languages all maintain their vitality in a social context of ethnic diversity.

Linguistic choices are made on both the societal and interpersonal levels. Since independence from colonial rule, African governments have developed their own policies regarding language use in educational and administrative contexts. Kenya and Tanzania provide instructive contrasts in linguistic policies. The Tanzanian government recognizes Swahili as its official code, and it is used in all public domains, including schools and government institutions. Although it is not the first language of most Tanzanians, Swahili is a member of the Bantu linguistic family, as are the native codes of 90 percent of the population (Appel and Muysken 1987:56). Therefore, because of the linguistic similarities between Swahili and the vast majority of languages spoken in Tanzania, Swahili is acceptable as a lingua franca for use in public encounters and in interactions between people from different ethnic groups.

The government in Kenya also acknowledges Swahili as an official language, but in practice English is employed in many societal domains. English is the language of business, legal proceedings, and most government administration. The first three years of schooling are conducted in local native languages, but beginning in the fourth year, instruction is given in English (Zuengler 1985:244).

A critical difference between language policies in Tanzania and Kenya is the use of Swahili in Tanzanian schools and of English in Kenyan education. According to Jane Zuengler (1985), the Kenyan government chooses English because it wants to encourage a select minority to pursue advanced education and participate in economic development projects in conjunction with international business groups. In contrast, Tanzania selects Swahili because it wants the entire population to achieve an adequate level of literacy and education as preparation for either rural or urban employment (ibid.:246–248).

When members of different ethnic groups interact, they must select an appropriate code. Choice of the tribal language of one participant obviously carries social messages concerning relative status, prestige, or authority. Because such messages can potentially lead to antagonism, interethnic interactions often take place through the medium of a neutral language. Carol Scotton's study of language usage in workplaces in the capitals of Kenya, Uganda, and Nigeria showed that although coworkers may be multilingual and share one or more tribal languages, they often choose to speak a nontribal lingua franca as a "strategy of neutrality" (1976:919). In West Africa, English and/or pidgin English predominate as such languages, whereas in East Africa, Swahili is often selected. A neutral code is "nobody's language," so its use does not transmit messages of inequality between interlocutors. Speakers thus engage in "reciprocal accommodation" (ibid.:920) by implicitly recognizing the affront people may feel when their own code is disparaged.

Despite the use of English as a neutral language in public domains, attitudes toward it may be mixed. For instance, people who speak English with a British or American accent rather than with the local African accent may be resented because they are negatively viewed as "putting on airs" and flaunting their wealth and access to education abroad (Saah 1986:372).

In some countries, linguistic choices in bilingual communities indicate a clear, permanent shift away from a local language. For example, Susan Gal's (1978) research in an eastern Austrian province near Hungary uncovered a changing preference away from Hungarian, favoring German. Gal's study concentrated on the town of Oberwart (Felsoor in Hungarian), located in an area that was originally part of Hungary but has been in Austria since 1921 when boundaries were realigned after World War I. Following World War II, Oberwart became a county administrative and commercial center, populated by immigrant monolingual German speakers from Austria and an indigenous community of Hungarian/German bilinguals and Hungarian monolinguals. The latter two groups constitute approximately one-quarter of the town's more than 5,000 residents.

Austrians and Hungarians are differentiated economically and socially. Austrians tend to hold professional, administrative, and commercial positions. Hungarians were previously peasant farmers but currently most are industrial workers (ibid.:3). Because of economic changes, Hungarian has become disparaged as the language of peasants, associated with a way of life that is now negatively perceived.

Gal found that several factors were reliable predictors of language choice among bilinguals in Oberwart, including speech situation, age and gender of the speaker, and the speaker's usual social networks. When conversing with doctors, government officials, and young people, most bilinguals chose German. When talking to parents and elders, most spoke Hungarian. Interactions with siblings and age-mates varied, depending on age of speaker. Older people tended to speak Hungarian with familiars, whereas younger residents spoke German. Bilinguals who regularly associated with monolingual German speakers were more likely to use German in their encounters with other bilinguals than were those whose social networks consisted mainly of monolingual Hungarian peasants and farm workers (ibid.:6–7).

Gender was an important factor in shifts of language preference in Oberwart. Women and men made different linguistic choices based on differing economic alternatives. Although some young men continue to value peasant life, most young women reject it entirely. Farming retains some traditional prestige for a man and gives him economic independence, but for a woman it is burdensome and allows her little autonomy, given male-dominated gender relations in traditional farm households (ibid.:10). Young women, therefore, opt for industrial employment and/or marriage to industrial workers. Whereas farming families tend to be Hungarian monolinguals or Hungarian-dominant bilinguals, industrial workers and their families tend to be German speakers. Women, therefore, use the German language as a symbol of their social values. Shifts to German will no doubt become even stronger in the future because children in households with at least one German-speaking parent are always monolingual German speakers.

A fourth possible social and linguistic configuration is exemplified by many Hispanic communities in the United States. Research among Puerto Ricans, for example, reveals several trends regarding use of and attitude toward Spanish and English. Studies in New York City indicate shifts toward English usage and simultaneous approval of Spanish maintenance (Pedraza 1985). In the community known as El Barrio, an area of 125 square blocks with a population of 175,000 approximately 60 percent of whom are Hispanic, age and length of residence are factors in language choice. Older people and recent immigrants continue to use Spanish in all or nearly all contexts. In contrast, second- and third-generation Puerto Ricans lose their ability to speak Spanish, although they may retain passive comprehension. But the community is united in strongly favoring acquisition of skills in both Spanish and English (ibid.:61, 63).

Although a shift toward English is discernible, the community as a whole remains solidly bilingual. This pattern results from a high level of individual bilingualism and from a continual influx of Hispanic immigrants. In communities in other parts of the United States where Hispanic people are not as heavily concentrated as in large urban centers, shifts toward English are more pronounced. For instance, among members of Hispanic groups living in Indiana, 46.2 percent report English as their best language, 35.4 percent claim to be equally fluent in both languages, and only 18.4 percent report Spanish as their best language. These figures contrast with statistics from New York City Hispanics, where 29.7 percent of a sample reported English as their best language, 39.6 percent were fluently bilingual, and 29.7 percent considered Spanish their dominant code (Attinasi 1985:45).

Even though the two communities differed in language usage, positive attitudes toward Spanish maintenance were just as strong in Indiana as in New York. In both areas, people recognize the value of Spanish as an indicator and symbol of ethnicity. Among Hispanics in Indiana, 98.5 percent believed that being bilingual is advantageous, 92.3 percent wanted Spanish to be maintained in their community, and 89.2 percent advocated bilingual education for their children (ibid.:49). These attitudes indicate robust continuation of Spanish in Hispanic communities even in the context of individual shifts to English dominance.

The situation of native peoples in Guatemala and Mexico illustrates tendencies to limit use of indigenous languages in favor of the language of a dominant national culture. In both Mexico and Guatemala, speakers of Mayan languages whose ancestors developed the powerful Mayan states of pre-Columbian times have come under increasing social and economic pressure to shift to usage of Spanish. However, degrees of shift vary, depending upon a community's isolation from or integration into the nation in which they reside. Several Mayan communities exemplify distinctive choices of language use.

The Chol Maya, who live in the southern Mexican state of Chiapas, are one of the most traditional groups in the region. They have been able to maintain their indigenous culture and language because of their location in rural towns isolated from main transportation routes. In addition, their participation in Mexico's economy is marginal, limited to growing a small amount of coffee as a cash crop. The Native language, Chol, is employed by nearly all community members, two-thirds of whom are monolingual speakers. Use of Spanish is common only among some young men who have desires to leave their towns and migrate to Mexico City or other cities in the country (Fought 1985:28–29).

More heavily influenced by Spanish language and culture are the Chorti Maya, who live nearby in eastern Guatemala. They reside in small, dispersed hamlets outside of towns inhabited by Guatemalan Ladinos, who are Spanish speakers. Most Chorti are bilingual; monolingual Chorti speakers are found only among very young children. Whereas Chorti is the primary language used in native homes, Spanish is necessary for public interactions in towns. Interethnic contacts are generally conducted in Spanish despite the fact that the Chorti outnumber Ladinos by nearly 10 to 1 (ibid.:24). Therefore, the relative social and economic power of participants determines choice of language. It is the Chorti rather than the Ladinos who become bilingual. Knowledge of Spanish is essential for upward social mobility, as well as for daily contacts with Ladino storekeepers and with authorities in government agencies and schools.

Although the Chorti language has little social prestige, it is used in the domain of religion. Resident missionaries of both the Roman Catholic and Quaker faiths have learned Chorti and employ it in religious services and instruction. They recognize that people have strong emotional ties to their native language (ibid.:27).

Among a third Mayan group, the Chontal of Chiapas, linguistic shift is most marked. The Chontal live in an area of recent industrial development. Oil refineries employ some Chontal as well as Spanish-speaking Mexicans. Networks of highways have been built to link the area to other centers. Although most Chontal speak their native language, nearly all are bilingual in Spanish as well. The only societal domain in which Chontal predominates is in the home, but even there many bilingual speakers employ Spanish rather than their native code (ibid.:23).

In addition to different patterns of linguistic use in these three Mayan communities, the languages themselves reflect varying degrees of influence from Spanish. All three languages contain many loanwords from Spanish, a result of incorporating numerous features of Mexican and Guatemalan culture. In Chol Mayan, spoken by the least assimilated group, loanwords are limited to these cultural borrowings. In contrast, Chontal Mayan, spoken by the most assimilated group, contains Spanish words that have replaced native labels for many indigenous objects as well as for borrowed items. Spanish grammar has also influenced Chontal Mayan, resulting in displacement of conjunctions and prepositions and in reformulation of sentence structure (ibid.:23, 28). The extent of linguistic change in Chontal Mayan is a clear and direct effect of extensive contact between natives and speakers of Spanish. It is also a clear and direct reflection of social and economic pressure experienced by the Chontal in their subordinate position relative to the dominant culture.

Patterns of language use and shift exemplified by Mayan peoples are by no means unique. Similar restrictions on functions of indigenous languages in situations of expanding national cultures and their codes occur throughout Latin America and, indeed, throughout the world. However, in some countries where large populations of indigenous peoples are concentrated, governments have occasionally attempted to address problems of speakers of native languages. For example, such attempts have been made in Peru. Although Peru is officially a Spanish-speaking country, it has an estimated 3.5 million speakers of indigenous languages, accounting for one-third of the country's total population (Briggs 1985:297). In the 1960s and 1970s, the Peruvian government established bilingual education programs for speakers of Quechua, who constitute the largest native group, numbering more than 3 million. Although these programs have not received consistent governmental support (ibid.:302), they do acknowledge the strength of native languages. The large numbers of speakers of Quechua in Peru and of other indigenous languages elsewhere help ensure their survival despite overall trends toward assimilation of native peoples and the spread of national languages.

Finally, languages that have experienced constriction in usage and loss of speakers can be revitalized when particular attention is focused on the association between linguistic and ethnic identity. The resurgence of Basque in Spain since the 1960s is a telling example of the strength of a once-forbidden language when its speakers reassert their rights to cultural autonomy. Basque (or Euskera, also spelled Euskara) is spoken in seven provinces of northern Spain (and one in southern France) that are referred to as "Euskal Herria" ("Basque Country"). The link between land and language is explicit in the designation of the region since Euskal Herria literally means "land of the Basque language." Ethnicity and language are also made explicit by the term for a Basque person, *euskaldun,* meaning "someone who possesses the Basque language ("euskera") (Hoffmann 1996:78). Basque was the majority language of the region until the eighteenth century but has since been marginalized by the spread of Castilian (and French in France). According to Spanish government estimates for 1991, of some 2,900,000 residents of Euskal Herria, there were approximately 660,000 fluent speakers of Basque and an additional 455,000 people with some knowledge of the language (Zuazo 1995:5).

The shift away from Basque was intensified during the rule of General Francisco Franco, beginning at the end of the Spanish Civil War in 1939 and ending with his death in 1975. The use of Basque was forbidden because of its association with political radicalism and agitation against the central government. A gradual lessening of official restrictions began in the 1960s, leading to the development of Basque-language schools for children as well as programs aimed at teaching Basque to adults (ibid.:21).

Promoters of Euskera had to grapple with the complexity of dialectal differences, as the language had evolved in different communities. Some dialects are mutually intelligible but others are not. Therefore, efforts were undertaken to develop a standardized form that could be used throughout the region. In 1968, a basic text of *euskera batua* ("unified Basque") was published by the Academy of the Basque Language. Euskera batua is based primarily on an educated variety of one of the regional dialects but it is not understood by all speakers of other regional forms. For some speakers, "it is almost a new language" (Hoffmann 1996:77). Still, it is the variety now taught in schools and used in public domains while regional dialects continue to be spoken in home and community settings.

Use of Basque has grown considerably, especially since the establishment of Basque autonomy in 1979. Euskera is taught at all levels of education beginning in the primary grades and continuing through the universities. The numbers of speakers have risen steadily. According to surveys conducted in 1986, 26.7 percent of Basques understood Euskera while 24.6 percent were able to speak it. Smaller percentages of people were able to read it (18.7 percent) or write (16.2 percent) the language (Artigal 1993:32). The Autonomous Community of the Basque Country, or Euskadi (established in 1979), is officially bilingual. Newspapers, other public media, government documents, and street and business signs are bilingual. Public sector employees must be bilingual. Religious services are held in Spanish and Euskera. And a growing literature of prose and poetry is published in Basque. Throughout the region, governmental, educational, and cultural agencies actively promote the use of Basque in ever-widening social contexts. Members of the Basque community recognize the direct link between the political autonomy of Euskadi and the maintenance of their linguistic and cultural heritage.

Endangered Languages

In many parts of the world, speakers in bilingual communities have abandoned their native language in favor of their second language. When an entire community does so, the native language dies as an effective means of communication. This process of *language obsolescence* or *language death* is a worldwide phenomenon affecting different types of communities. In some cases, indigenous peoples abandon their native language after being subjected to invasion, conquest, and subsequent control by an overwhelming power. For example, many Native American societies throughout North and South America have stopped speaking their own languages and have replaced them with the dominant national code in their countries. Many indigenous peoples of Australia and of small islands in the Pacific have also ceased using their native languages. Similar processes have taken place in Africa, Asia, and Europe. Replacement of native codes by dominant languages is usually a gradual process, first restricting native languages to limited interactional spheres and eventually leading to their complete abandonment. Once replacement is complete, the indigenous language disappears from the human scene, the classic case of language death.

The future of the majority of the world's languages is very much in doubt. According to Michael Krauss's estimates, about half of the world's current 6,000 languages will no longer be spoken by the end of the twenty-first century (1992:6). In an even more dire prediction, Krauss suggests that as many as 90 percent of the world's languages will be either extinct or on their way to extinction by that time (ibid.:7). Many languages spoken today are what Krauss calls "moribund" (ibid.:4). These are languages that are spoken by adults but are no longer being learned as the mother tongue by children and are, therefore, "no longer viable." It is their lack of generational continuity that dooms these languages unless steps are taken to promote their use through education and encouragement in familial and informal settings. In the United States and Canada, of some 187 languages still spoken by Native Americans, 149 are no longer being learned by children. Conditions are somewhat better in Central America, where 50 of 300 (17 percent) indigenous languages are likely to die out and in South America where 110 of 400 (27 percent) Native languages probably face extinction. According to Krauss, the worst conditions are found in Australia, where 90 percent of the 250 aboriginal languages are moribund (ibid.:5).

In an attempt to focus on issues of language in the international arena, the Working Group on Indigenous Populations of the United Nations Commission on Human Rights is drafting a Universal Declaration on Indigenous Rights for Native peoples that includes "the right to maintain and use their own languages, including for administrative, judicial, and other relevant purposes; the right of children to have access to education in their own languages, and to establish, structure, conduct, and control their own educational systems and institutions" (Alfredsson 1989:258). Education in one's native language and the promotion of its use in society are clearly key to maintaining a language's vitality and averting the worldwide trend that Krauss warns against. As Nancy Hornberger notes, where languages are in danger, bilingual communities should undertake "bottom-up revitalization efforts" that encourage the transmission of a language from one generation to the next because of its usefulness in the widest possible range of communicative contexts. "Such revitalization efforts are not about bringing the language back, but rather about bringing it forward" (1998:453).

Processes of language shift and loss are exemplified in many Native American communities in the United States. Jeffrey Anderson's (1998) study of the Northern Arapaho at the Wind River Reservation in Wyoming demonstrates complexities in attitudes and behaviors associated with the indigenous code and with English. In the middle of the nineteenth century, knowledge of English began to be valued as a means of communicating with federal officials who came to have increasing influence and control over reservation communities. Those few Arapahos who spoke English became interpreters and brokers in relations between the Native people and outsiders. By late in the century, federal education policies restricted or even eliminated the use of Native languages in schools, thus limiting young people's fluency in their own code. People who were most proficient English speakers eventually rose to positions of tribal leadership in part because of their linguistic skills. Bilingualism was considered an asset. For much of the twentieth century, both Arapaho and English were valued for their usefulness in different contexts. Arapaho was spoken in homes, at community meetings and celebrations, and in religious contexts, whereas English was used in school, business, and government domains. Gradually, however, the pattern of stable bilingualism "gave way to language loss when the speech community could no longer maintain the boundaries between the two languages" (1998:57).

Beginning in the 1950s, most children learned English as their first language. The change was so abrupt that many families were divided between older siblings who were fluent speakers of Arapaho and younger siblings who spoke only English (ibid.:55). As a result of these processes, by the 1990s, only about 500 or 600 people out of a reservation population of approximately 5,000 are fluent speakers of Arapaho. Most are more than 60 years of age. As a further indication of the future, few parents speak Arapaho to their children (ibid.:54). Arapaho is typically employed only in "speech situations involving elders (e.g. meetings of elders as consultants, ceremonial speech acts, and informal gatherings)" or in educational settings specifically aimed at teaching the language (ibid.).

Members of the Arapaho community have diverse attitudes toward the changes that have taken place. Elders view the loss of Arapaho as "one stream in a larger shift in everyday social relations—that is, in ways people talk to each other, . . . in the loss of respect, hospitality, and modes of visiting" (ibid.:101). Perhaps in an attempt to regain a traditional sense of community, many young people are trying to learn the indigenous language in concert with renewed interest in Arapaho ceremonial and social practices.

The role of parental (or other caregivers') use of indigenous languages in the maintenance of the native code is demonstrated in a study conducted at the Alabama-Coushatta Reservation in eastern Texas (Halmari 1998). While people age 45 years or older were likely to be fluent in Alabama or Coushatta (or both) and to consider one of the native languages to be their "dominant" language, people younger than 45 varied in their fluency. Among the younger tribal members, 55 percent stated that English was their dominant language, 21 percent noted equal dominance of English and one of the indigenous languages, and the remaining 24 percent reported that they were dominant in either Alabama or Coushatta (ibid:415). Age differences were also significant in language usage patterns. Older speakers typically employed an indigenous language when conversing with peers, whereas younger speakers were more likely to speak English to siblings and age-mates (ibid.:419). Furthermore, parental language use was the prime predictor of linguistic abilities of younger speakers. Young tribal members who were bilingual (or trilingual) typically grew up in households where one or both parents regularly spoke a Native language to their children (ibid.:423). On the basis of findings such as these, Halmari notes the importance of "community language planning" that encourages parents to speak indigenous languages to their children and that creates other "opportunities for younger and older members of the community to interact with each other in native languages in natural and mutually rewarding speech situations" (ibid.:423–424).

Immigrant populations often give up their native language in favor of the language of the society into which they have moved. Immigrant groups in the United States are good examples of this process. In general, many immigrant families in the United States retain some knowledge of the parental language in the second generation, but by the third generation, much, if not all, of that knowledge is lost. Social pressure toward English monolingualism is an important factor in this trend, supported and encouraged by an educational philosophy that often disparages bilingualism and claims, contrary to the findings of most academic research, that children who speak two languages have difficulty learning either one well (see the discussion in Chapter 11). The loss of native languages in immigrant communities, however, does not mean that the language itself is undergoing language death, because it continues to be spoken by people remaining in the country of origin.

Gaelic, the indigenous Celtic code of Scotland and Ireland, exemplifies the process of loss and restriction. Gaelic is an endangered language whose eventual fate is uncertain. Once spoken by the entire population of these countries, Gaelic is now in active use only in isolated areas in the northern and western edges of the territories. This restriction has been a long-term process, beginning centuries ago when the English invaded and conquered the native Celts. The English language then gradually replaced the local code. Although Gaelic is still spoken in some rural areas, even there its use is limited, becoming more so with each generation. In fact, since the 1970s, few parents speak Gaelic to their children (Watson 1989:42).

Attitudes toward Gaelic are somewhat mixed. In Ireland, Gaelic is officially recognized by the constitution as the "national language" and the "first official language" (Constitution of Ireland, Article 8). The Irish government promotes a standardized form of Gaelic that is taught in schools and used in published official documents. Gaelic is also promoted through radio programs and other cultural outlets (ibid.:47). Still, its actual use is decreasing despite government support for its revival (ibid.:44). Many factors contribute to its decline, notably the influx of English-speaking people, incorporation of isolated areas into regional and national economies, and desires of young rural residents to leave the area for economic opportunities elsewhere. These trends result in the association of Gaelic with an uneducated, poor, rural population that translates into a negative attitude toward maintaining the language.

In Scotland, Gaelic is not given official recognition and support as it is in Ireland. And it is generally disparaged by nonspeakers as representing a backward, traditional past. However, those few people who still speak the language are strongly loyal to it and have high regard for other speakers. As one elderly Gaelic speaker commented to Seosamh Watson, "Because we have a side [a liking] to anyone that'll speak the Gaelic. It draws us like a magnet. Anybody that'll speak the Gaelic I've a side to them and I'll trust my life to them" (ibid.:45). But despite such positive associations, older speakers rarely employ Gaelic with their children, and its use is declining rapidly in Scotland.

English is replacing Gaelic in Scotland and Ireland because of social and economic pressures that have accelerated during the twentieth century. As traditional economic pursuits such as fishing and sheepherding have declined, many rural people have had to seek employment away from their isolated communities. Knowledge of English has become a requirement for successful out-migration and integration into national labor markets. In addition, the prestige of English filters throughout the educational establishment in Ireland and Scotland regardless of official policies that promote Gaelic in Ireland. Speaking English carries social prestige, especially for the young who associate it with pop music, sophisticated fashions, and sports. The spread of English is also enhanced by its exclusive use in the mass media (ibid.:49).

In contrast to English, Gaelic has no prestigious written tradition but is associated with folk culture, which is often disparaged in modern society, especially by the young. A further sign of Gaelic's vulnerability is the fact that it has borrowed many English words not only for innovations in technology and science but also as replacements for indigenous Gaelic nouns, adjectives, and verbs (ibid.:50). As a result of a lack of native words for modern objects and activities, speakers of Gaelic often switch to English in order to talk about "subjects more complicated than the weather, community news, or basic farming or fishing" (ibid.:55).

Given Gaelic's limited usefulness and the high rates of English monolingualism among the young, it is unlikely that Gaelic will survive as a vibrant, living language for much longer unless official policies have more than a superficial effect. It may well suffer the language death all too typical of codes of indigenous peoples throughout the world whose lands and cultures have been overwhelmed by conquering nations.

The fate of Gaelic as an indigenous language in Ireland and Scotland is matched by its fate as the language of Celtic immigrants to other countries. Gaelic is still spoken by small groups of people whose ancestors migrated from Scotland to Nova Scotia, Canada, in the eighteenth and nineteenth centuries, but its use is highly restricted and the number of Gaelic speakers has fallen sharply since the 1930s and 1940s. According to researcher Elizabeth Mertz, the case of Gaelic in Cape Breton is an example of what Nancy Dorian has termed a linguistic tip, a situation in which "a language which has been demographically highly stable for several centuries may experience a sudden 'tip,' after which the demographic tide flows strongly in favor of some other language" (Dorian 1981:51). In two communities studied by Mertz, residents were bilingual in English and Gaelic until the 1930s and 1940s, but thereafter Gaelic was no longer transmitted to the younger generations. Currently there are no fluent Gaelic speakers under 40 years old. And many people in their 40s who speak Gaelic are not fluent facile speakers but, rather, use the language rarely and with difficulty (Mertz 1989:105–106).

Although Gaelic was spoken by most residents in the 1930s, it had already become a language of private, familial contexts and was rarely used in public. But at that time a dramatic change occurred when parents no longer spoke Gaelic to their children. Mertz explains this sudden shift, or "tip," in economic, social, and ideological terms. The economy of Cape Breton had been marginal for centuries, dependent on small-scale fishing and farming. During the economic depression of the 1930s, residents' livelihood deteriorated even further. People realized that the economic potential of isolated areas was severely limited and responded by trying to seek occupations elsewhere in Nova Scotia and Canada. Their desire to disassociate themselves from their isolated background was reflected in their pejorative attitudes toward speaking Gaelic, a language that had long suffered from a lack of prestige as compared to the high status of English.

The educational system contributed to the decline of Gaelic by promoting the notion that bilingual speakers are at a disadvantage because each of their languages interferes with their ability to learn either one well. One of Mertz's consultants recalled: "Parents thought teaching Gaelic would sort of confuse the two languages in their minds" (ibid.:111). This ideology, erroneous though it was, convinced parents to stop speaking Gaelic to their children in order to better the youngsters' chances of speaking "good" English, assimilating into mainstream Canadian society, and advancing socially and economically.

Older Cape Breton speakers continue to employ Gaelic with friends and families in informal settings. Greetings, affectionate names, and exclamations are often expressed in Gaelic. And its use can succinctly mark the distinction between insiders and outsiders. But with the passing of older generations, Gaelic will soon die out as an immigrant language of Nova Scotia.

The International Dominance of English

One consequence of the historic colonial experience has been the spread of the languages of colonizers far beyond their own national boundaries. The expansion of European languages to other parts of the globe is but the latest example of this process. The worldwide prominence of specific European languages has risen and fallen with their colonial fortunes. Presently, although direct imperial control has disappeared or at least weakened, linguistic dominance of former colonial languages has survived. French is still spoken in many countries of Africa, the Caribbean, and the Pacific. Spanish is the major language of most of South and Central America. And English is spoken by residents of former British and American colonies or possessions in the Americas, the Pacific, and Africa. Use of English has spread to many additional countries because of the economic, political, and cultural influence of the United States. In fact, as such influence has accelerated since World War II, the English language too has gained increasing worldwide dominance. Some 350 million people are native speakers of English and an estimated additional 300 million use English as their second language (Finegan 1989:298; Baron 1990:178). English is the most frequently taught foreign language in the world's schools. It is the sole official language of more than 25 countries and functions along with others as official languages in some 35 more. Finally, English dominates as the primary language of international business. An estimated 75 percent of all mail and 80 percent of computer data are written in English (Baron 1990).

Reflecting the deepening influence of the language, varieties sometimes called "New Englishes" have developed. According to John Platt et al. (1984), New Englishes are "localized" or "nativized" dialects that have adopted "language features of [their] own, such as sounds, intonation patterns, sentence structures, words, expressions, . . . [and] different rules for using language in communication" (1984:3). These are not creoles because they have not developed from pidgins but, rather, from a form of English disseminated through formal education. New Englishes are in use in numerous countries throughout the world. They have developed in Africa (Ghana, Liberia, Nigeria, Sierra Leone, Cameroon, Kenya, Tanzania, Uganda, Zimbabwe), the Caribbean (Barbados, Guyana, Jamaica, Puerto Rico, Trinidad and Tobago), Asia (Bangladesh, Hong Kong, India, Malaysia, Philippines, Singapore, Sri Lanka), and the Pacific (Fiji, Guam, Hawaii, Samoa, Papua New Guinea) (ibid.:15). Platt et al. apply the term to varieties of English that are spoken in areas where English is typically used as a medium of instruction, especially in higher education, and has important societal functions in government, business, high-status professions such as law and medicine, and mass communication. Some speakers of New English also employ it in familial and casual settings. The language typically is perceived by the speech community as a neutral language and/or a language of high status. Its neutrality derives from the fact that it is not associated with any particular native ethnic or regional group, and its high status comes from its association with advanced education and public uses. These latter features obviously imply privileges of class and social power as well. Remarking on the social clout of English, a Zambian reported that "in Tanzania and Zambia people carry English newspapers just to be seen . . . even if they cannot read it and hold it upside down" (ibid.:29).

New Englishes are characterized by unique local features of sound, syntax, lexicon, and style. There are, however, a number of general patterns that distinguish these varieties. Among the distinctive phonological traits, the most common is the replacement of the interdental fricatives /θ/ and /ð/ with the corresponding stops /t/ and /d/ because of the lack of the fricatives in most languages. Consonant clusters are often simplified, again in accordance with phonotactic rules of the dominant language spoken in the area. Nouns in many New Englishes are typically not marked for number. In addition, markers or separate words denoting definite or indefinite are also generally omitted. And third-person subjects or objects are often not distinguished for gender. New Englishes often rework or omit markings on verbs, particularly for events in the past. For example (all examples are from Platt et al. 1984):

> I *graduate* there in 1975 (Papua New Guinea)
> I was new here and I *don't know* where to go (Philippines)
> My wife, she *pass* her Cambridge (Singapore)

Instead, some New Englishes indicate tense with adverbs or special words:

> *Before* I always go to that market (Malaysia)
> My father *already* pass away (Singapore)
> You *eat finish,* go out and play (Singapore)
> (When you've finished eating, go and play)

In addition, New Englishes may use the "be + verb + ing" construction for stative verbs, as well as for action or process verbs:

> Mohan *is having* two houses (India)
> I *was doubting* it (India)
> She *is knowing* her science very well (East Africa)

The lexicons of New Englishes often borrow from the "background" languages of the area:

> When we get home, we ask daddy to *changkol* the garden
> (Singapore: *changkol* "hoe")
> If you don't like, *yaya* will give you water (Philippines:
> *yaya* "nursemaid")
> Don't *kacho* (or *kacau*) me when I want to work! (Malaysia:
> *kacau* "disturb")

New Englishes also contain locally coined words:

> dry coffee (coffee without milk and sugar: East Africa)
> change-room (dressing room: India)
> bed-spacer (someone who rents a bed in a room or dormitory: Philippines)

Some words exemplify processes of shifts in word classes:

> to friend (to be friends with: Malaysia, Jamaica)
> to be aftering something (to look for something: Papua New Guinea)
> My gentleman naked himself (Singapore)
> (got undressed, undressed himself)

And words may change their meanings:

> You did not give me any *balance* (change: West Africa)
> Take some water to the *stranger* (guest: Nigeria)
> You can *drop* here (get out: Singapore)

BILINGUAL CONVERSATIONAL STRATEGIES

Bilingual speakers have more linguistic resources at their disposal than do mono-lingual speakers. Words in each language express somewhat different meanings, either because they refer to different entities or activities or because they express divergent perspectives. Bilinguals, therefore, often employ strategies for maximizing the potential expressiveness of their linguistic repertory.

Code Switching

When bilingual speakers converse, they frequently integrate linguistic material from both of their languages within the same discourse segment. This process, called *code switching*, differs significantly from borrowing. When words are borrowed, host languages adapt sounds and intonation patterns to suit their native rules. In code switching, alterations do not occur. Instead, switched elements retain the sound patterns of their origin.

Code switching has a variety of linguistic and interactional functions. It can have simple uses in expanding vocabulary. Bilingual speakers may employ a word from one language in sequences spoken in another because the latter lacks a comparable word expressing the desired meaning. In some cases, both languages may actually have words with similar meanings, but the structure of one may be more cumbersome than the other. Speakers often opt for the simpler expression.

Some examples from Mohawk can illustrate switching for ease of vocabulary. The indigenous Mohawk language did not contain specific words for each day of the week and month of the year. After contact with Europeans, Mohawks constructed their own native labels for 7 days and 12 months, but in current usage, most speakers switch to English even though a word exists in their vocabulary. In the following sentences, the speaker incorporated English "Sunday morning" in place of Mohawk *awʌtatokʌ htí:keʔ* "holy day" and "July" in place of *ohyaliʔ kó:wa* "the fruit ripens a lot" (Bonvillain 1988:15, 13):

1. *ó:nʌ*   *kiʔ*   *kiʔ*   Sunday morning   *wà:kye*
   (then   this   this)   (I woke up)
   "Then I woke up Sunday morning."

2. *yà:yak niwáhsa*   *wisk yakoyelí:tu*   July
   (sixty-   five she turned)
   "She turned sixty-five in July."

In subsequent examples throughout this section, abbreviations are used to indicate languages: E = 5 English, F = 5 French, H = 5 Hindi, M = 5 Mohawk, S = 5 Spanish. English translations are given in parentheses of segments spoken in other languages. Sources of examples are not indicated in the text but have been obtained from Bonvillain 1988 (Mohawk); Grosjean 1982 (French); Gumperz 1982 (Hindi, Spanish); Kachru 1978 (Hindi); McClure 1977 (Spanish); Pandit 1986 (Hindi); Pfaff 1979 (Spanish); Sridhar 1978 (Kannada); and Zentella 1985 (Spanish).

Instances of using the more accessible word may depend on speakers' linguistic abilities in their two languages or momentary lapses of memory:

3. [S/E]:   *Necesito un* string   *para la* kite
             (need a)   (for the)
             "I need a string for the kite."

Words may be transferred from one language to another because of social values associated with knowledge of a prestige code. Switches from Hindi to English exemplify this tendency:

4. society *hii aisii hai*
   "The society is like that."

5. *itanaa* money *aayaa kahaan se?*
   "Where did so much money come from?"

Code switching has numerous discourse and interactional functions, such as emphasizing, marking discourse boundaries, expressing emotions or opinions, and signaling in-group/out-group membership. Some of these functions are exemplified in the remainder of this section.

Code switches sometimes involve use of routine phrases or markers of politeness and solidarity:

6. [S/E]: *Dale un beso a Pucho* (Give Pucho a kiss). Julie, please.

7. [E/S/E]:   A. Well, I'm glad I met you.
               B. *Andale pues* (O.K. Swell) And do come again. Mm?

Tag questions also make use of switched elements:

8. [E/S]: She is, *verdad?* (right?)

Because code switching involves two languages, it inherently results in contrast and, therefore, can be used as an attention-getting device. In the following two examples, from the speech of a 9-year-old Mexican-American girl, equivalent words, "look/*mira*" are switched, depending on the base language; that is, "look" is switched into Spanish, whereas "*mira*" is transferred into English. Thus, it is the fact of switching itself that carries contrastive meaning:

9. Now let me do it. Put your feets down. *Mira!* (Look!) It's Leti's turn again. Hi Leti.

10. *Yo me voy a bajar, Teresa* (I'm getting down, Teresa.) Look!

Code switching within sentences or discourse highlights transferred elements and can be used as a dramatic device in narrative. In the next extract from a personal story, the narrator switches from Mohawk to English to focus on her father's formal attire and demeanor:

11. *tehoji?jahlʌ́hhoh*   *ki? ná:?* a blue suit   *lótstũ*   *tanú?* white shirt
    (he was all dressed up   this)   (he wore   and)

kwah ki? na? it was starched, the collar was starched, necktie *lótstū*
(very   this)   (he wore)

"He was all dressed up, he wore a blue suit and a white shirt, it was very
starched, the collar was starched, he wore a necktie."

Speakers may express the same meaning in both languages sequentially, using
repetition as an emphatic device. Such switches are particularly effective in issuing
directives:

12. (Mother to child; S/E): *Callate* (shut up). Shut up!

13. (Mother to child; E/S): Go sit down, go. *SIEN-TA-TE* (SIT DOWN!)

Repetitions sometimes include expansions or clarifications:

14. (Child to younger child; E/S): Roli, you stay here. *Tu quedate 'jito con Suzy.*
(Stay with Suzy, Honey!)

15. (Father to son learning to swim in a pool; H/E): *Baju-me jao beta, andar mat*
(Go to the side son, not inside.) Keep to the side.

Switches are sometimes used to signal changes in types of syntactic constructions occurring within a speaker's turn:
From statement to command: [E/F]:

16. Now it's really time to get up. *Lève-toi!* (get up!)

From statement to question: [E/S]:

17. I wiggle my fingers. *Qué más?* (what else?)

Speakers frequently switch at boundaries of internal quotes within narratives:

18. [S/E]: *El me dijo,* (he told me) "Call the police."

19. [E/H/E]: I went to Agra, *to maine ʌpne bhaiko bola ki* (then I said to my
brother that), if you come to Delhi you must buy some lunch.

20. [H/E]: *parhne mee siimaa kii bahut rucii hai, vah kahtii hai* (Sima is very
much interested in studies, she says) education is necessary for life.

Switching can occur within a sentence to segment phrases or clauses that
mark qualification, explanation, or elaboration:

21. [E/H]: The public is mad because *saalon se* repression *cal rahaa hai* (the
repression has been going on for years).

22. [H/E]: *mujhe duusaron se acchii hindii bhii aatii hai lekin phir bhii main
samajhatii huun* (I know Hindi better than others, even then I feel) that it is
not up to the mark.

23. [E/S]: That has nothing to do *con que hagan ese* (with the fact that they're
doing this).

24. [E/S]: Those are friends from Mexico *que tienen chamaquitos* (who have little children).

25. [F/E/F/E]: *Va chercher Marc* (go fetch Marc) and bribe him *avec un chocolat chaud* (with a hot chocolate) with cream on the top.

Code switching may perform several kinds of shifts within discourse. Shift of focus: from action to a comment or evaluation:

26. [S/E]: *Lo pegó aqui* (he hit him here). I saw it.

27. [S/E]:   A: *Donde vive María?* (Where does Maria live?)
         B: *María vive en mi casa* (Maria lives in my house).
            Really she is.

28. [H/E/H] [Narrator telling a traditional story]: *sharmishthaa ye sun letii hai to sharmishthaa kahatii hai* (Sharmishtha overhears this and says) I like this sentence very much, *pitaajii jab raajpuut laraaii men jaate hain to pitaa aashiir-vaad dete hain kii tum laraaii men* successful *ho.* (When the Rajputs go to the battlefront their fathers bless them by wishing them success in the battle.)

Shift of addressees:

29. [E/S]:   A (speaking to B): Why you cry baby?
         A (speaking to C): *Esta llorando* (he is crying).

Shift of topic within conversations: Next speaker switches code to mark discontinuity with previous speaker's topic:

30. [S/E]:   A: *Dile que es una casa sin techo* (tell her that it's a house without a roof).
         B. We have a pretty, uh, Christmas tree.

The following example, from Hindi to English, demonstrates the speaker's internal comment and topical shift:

31. *yah ek nazuk mamla hai* (it is a delicate matter); let's not talk about it.

Code switching may separate a speaker's turn into segments that fulfill contrasting functions. In the following telephone conversation, both speakers switch for a variety of interactional and emotional purposes [S/E]:

32. A: *Qué pasa?* (what's happening?) Can't you come over today?
   B: I would love to, but I don't know if we can for sure. *Dejame hablarte despues que llegue Joe* (let me talk to you later after Joe arrives). I don't know what to tell you right now.
   A: Okay *y* don't forget, *llamame despues* (call me later).

In A's first turn, she switched to English after the routine opening *Qué pasa?* Her friend responded in English, switching internally to Spanish to set apart her explanation for not making definite plans.

    Another contrastive use of switching within an exchange between a 9-year-old girl and her 3-year-old brother illustrates an emotional function [E/S]:

33. P: Stop it Roli. You're stupid.
    R: You stupid Pat.
    P: Don't hit me! (laughing and holding R off)
    R: (trips and begins to cry)
    P: *Ay Roli! Mi hijito qué paso?* (Oh Roli! Honey, what happened?)

The following example reflects emotional attitudes expressed in a bilingual's two languages. The speaker, whose native language is Spanish, is discussing her attempts to stop smoking:

34. . . . they tell me "How did you quit Mary?" I don't quit . . . I just stopped. I mean it wasn't an effort that I made *que voy a dejar de fumar por que me hace dano o* (that I'm going to stop smoking because it's harmful to me or) this or that uh-uh. It's just that I used to pull butts out of the waste paper basket, yeah. I used to go look in the . . . *se me acababan los cigarros en la noche* (my cigarettes would run out on me at night). I'd get *desperate y ahi voy al basarero a buscar, a sacar* (and there I go to the wastebasket to look for some, to get some), you know.

According to John Gumperz's analysis of this text, code switches symbolize the speaker's "involvement in the message. Spanish statements are personalized while English reflects more distance. The speaker seems to be talking about her problem in English and acting out her problem through words in Spanish" (1982:81).

Such emotional associations with one's native language are common. Bilingual speakers often feel more emotionally attuned to their first language and more apt to express feelings through it. In some cases, however, speakers may switch from their native language in order to avoid sensitive issues and to adopt emotional distance or neutrality. In the next extract, from an Indian woman's discussion of her opposition to traditional arranged marriages, the speaker switches from Hindi to English:

35. *mere saath to kabhii aisaa nahiin ho sakataa* (it can never happen to me). I feel very odd *kii* how can you share the bed, share the feelings with the boy whom you don't know.

Because words and expressions often presuppose underlying cultural values, speakers sometimes switch from their primary language in order to avoid expectations associated with native norms. In an example from another Indian language, Kannada, the request "*nanagondu* favor *ma:dti:ra?*" (will you do me a favor?) involves a switch to English "favor" from Kannada *upaka:ra*. Use of English here distances speakers from the strength of obligations to return favors that are basic to Kannada customs (Sridhar 1978:116).

Code switching sometimes appears to be motivated or triggered by words within sentences. If a foreign word is transferred into the base language, it often triggers subsequent switches of words or clauses. In the next examples, words, titles, or names spoken in English lead to a complete change to English:

36. [S/E]: *Porque allí hay* (because here are some) cashews. You don't like them?
37. [S/E]: *la historia que el* (the story that) "Exorcist" is based on . . .
38. [M/E]: *tkathé:thahkwe?* (there used to be a gristmill at) Millrush; he was talking way back fifty years ago.

In some cases, use of a particular language by one bilingual speaker can trigger another bilingual speaker to match the language choice of the first. Research by Guadalupe Valdes-Fallis (1978) indicated that this kind of switching may be influenced by the interlocutors' gender. In a sample of Mexican-American women recorded in same-sex and cross-sex conversations, the women matched the language of their male interlocutors more frequently than of female co-participants. Valdes-Fallis concluded that these women switched to the language of males as a sign of their deference or accommodation to addressees. The fact that women accommodated more to men than to other women can be interpreted as their recognition of gender inequality.

In sum, code switching is a complex process having many grammatical and interactional functions. It requires a firm knowledge of the formal grammars of both languages because of the structural constraints in each language that determine what kind of elements can and cannot be switched and where (and where not) they can be placed. Additionally, switching requires communicative competence, learning how to use linguistic devices as emphatic, contrastive, and/or emotional signals. Studies of Mexican-American children (ages 3 to 13) found that linguistic proficiency must be fairly advanced before code switching can occur (McClure 1977). Fluent bilinguals (usually older) switched more often, in more complicated structural environments, and with greater interactional sophistication than did less linguistically competent (usually younger) children (ibid.:99, 111). Erica McClure concluded by commenting that "the adept use of code-switching by the bilingual can be viewed as analogous to the creative use of language by a skilled monolingual author or orator" (ibid.:112).

Code Mixing

Code mixing is a linguistic process that incorporates material from a second language into a base language, adding morphological markers of the base to introduced elements. It differs from code switching by more deeply integrating mixed material into the host's linguistic system. For instance, consider the following extract from Kannada, a Dravidian language of South India. In the text, the speaker employs many English words despite the fact that Kannada contains equivalents. English elements obey English grammatical rules within mixed units (e.g., commercial-minded, holy alliance of marriage), but English units obey Kannada rules in their placement within larger clauses. For example, the construction translated as "the sacred occasion of arranging the holy alliance of marriage" is governed by Kannada order placing relative clauses before head nouns (i.e., holy alliance of marriage + sacred occasion (Sridhar 1978:111). The sample is from a contemporary play, spoken by a father angered by his prospective son-in-law's demand for dowry (ibid.:110):

> . . . kshamisu, *dear boy,* na:nu use ma:dida *strong language*-u eshto: *control*-ma:do:k no:dde. a:dre na:nu *educated*-u, man of *culture*-u, *broad-minded*-u, ambo:dnella mar-tubittu nannello: halli:kade:l huttid *commercial-minded* gama:ra anta tilkondu *holy alliance of marriage arrange*-ma:do: *sacred occasion*-nalli *dowry* eshtu anta ke:lti:yalla, nan *blood*-u *boiling point*-ge barde iddi:te?

> (. . . Forgive me, dear boy, I tried so much to control the strong language that I used. But, on this sacred occasion of arranging the holy alliance of marriage, forgetting that I am educated, a man of culture, broad-minded, and taking me for a village-born, commercial-minded rustic, you ask me how much "dowry" I would give! Wouldn't my blood come to a boiling point?)

Another instance of code mixing in the text is the application of Kannada morphological markers on transferred material. Suffixes *-u, -ma, -ge,* and *-nalli* are added to appropriate English words: educated-*u*, control-*ma*, boiling point-*ge*, sacred occasion-*nalli.*

Like code switching, code mixing has social functions. In India, speakers who use English are perceived as well educated, sophisticated, and refined. In the quoted text, the speaker employs English to contrast his own enlightened opinions with those of traditional, backward people (ibid.:114).

The Navajo language provides some further examples of code mixing. Two processes operate to integrate English material into Navajo structure. First, English verbs occur in conjunction with Navajo helping verbs: "make" with transitives and "do/be" with intransitives. Navajo verbs then carry obligatory markers for person, number, mode, and aspect (Canfield 1980:219). For instance:

1. Nancy *bich'í?*   show *ánílééh*
    3rd p.:to   2nd p.:make
    "Show it to Nancy."

2. Swimming *asht'í*
    1st p.:do/be
    "I'm swimming."

A second type of mixing is characterized by substituting an English word in place of a Navajo verb stem. In this case, Navajo affixes are added to transferred forms:

3. *shil*   *naweasy* (from "queasy")
    1st p.:with   3rd p.:sick
    "I feel sick."

4. *shiléechãã?i*   *anáyíílturn* (from "turn")
    my dog   3rd p.:died
    "My dog died."

Navajo/English code mixing occurs in the speech of bilinguals, often young speakers, reflecting their exposure to the English language and to Anglo culture.

Finally, in the following examples from Canadian francophone speech, speakers embed English words into French morphological and syntactic structure. In the first utterance, French suffixes are added to an English adjective; in the second, an English unit, "high-rise building," is adjusted to French word order that places a modifier after, rather than before, its head noun (Poplack 1988:97):

1. Sont *spoilés* rotten.
   "They're spoiled rotten."
2. A côté il y en a un autre gros *building high rise.*
   "Next door there's another big high-rise building."

INTERETHNIC MISCOMMUNICATION

Because cultural expectations are part of communicative competence, interlocutors who come from the same culture are likely to operate with the same rules for speaking and interpreting speech. In contrast, interlocutors of different cultural backgrounds may misinterpret each other's messages despite the fact that they comprehend the language spoken. Quoting Susan Gass and Evangeline Varonis, "No natural speech utterance is ever made in a linguistic vacuum. Each is enriched and empowered by a social history that considers the relationships of class, status, power, and solidarity, and a linguistic history that includes culturally specific rules of discourse, politeness, conversational maxims, conversational inference, and patterns of interpretation" (1991:121). When people converse, they use their own culture's norms to interpret messages and to evaluate interlocutors. Positive or negative judgments are often made, based not necessarily on speakers' actual intentions but on hearers' own culturally derived norms about how social and personal meanings are expressed in language. Listeners attribute to speakers the kinds of motives they would have if they had expressed themselves with the linguistic forms they are hearing. Because most cultural and linguistic presuppositions are nonconscious, interlocutors most often interpret each other's speech subjectively. Exposure to another culture or frequent interethnic contacts may modify subjective reactions. However, misinterpretations may become entrenched and contribute to creating and maintaining stereotypes about other people.

Miscommunication can occur in any encounter, even between people of the same culture, or, for that matter, the same family. But cultural differences increase the chances of divergent understandings. Problems can arise when participants attribute direct or indirect meanings to each other's speech. Consider the following exchanges between wives and husbands. In both cases, the wives are American and the husbands are Greek (Tannen 1982:220, 222):

1. WIFE: John's having a party. Wanna go?
   HUSBAND: OK.
   (Later)
   WIFE: Are you sure you want to go to the party?

	HUSBAND:	OK, let's not go. I'm tired anyway.
2.	HUSBAND:	Let's go visit my boss tonight.
	WIFE:	Why?
	HUSBAND:	All right, we don't have to go.

In both episodes, spouses misinterpreted questions and statements. American wives intended their questions as straightforward requests for confirmation or clarification. But Greek husbands interpreted them as indirect expressions of hesitation or disinterest. Even though participants obviously knew each other well, they were incorrect about interactional meanings implied by assertions and questions. Such lack of synchrony can become a way of life and lead to deeper conflicts. Quoting Deborah Tannen on this issue, "Misjudgment is calcified by the conviction of repeated experience" (ibid.:220).

When people of different ethnic backgrounds interact frequently, they can become aware of their divergent interpretations, possibly as a result of arguing about each other's meanings. But when interethnic encounters are brief, routinized, or limited to specific contexts, miscommunication can easily lead to negative stereotypes. For example, in a study of speech of Chinese businesspeople, Linda Young (1982) identified linguistic features that render their style problematic for American interlocutors. The structure of Chinese sentences and discourse differs fundamentally from that of English. English sentences are based on a subject-predicate order, whereas Chinese follows a topic-comment format. Compare the sentences below (Young 1982:74):

English:	A giant squid	ate the blue surfboard.
	Subject	Predicate
Chinese:	Blue surfboard	giant squid ate.
	Topic	Comment

Chinese structure also contains subordinate clauses that evaluate assertions made in main clauses. Subordinate clauses precede main clauses, each introduced by specific markers, described by Young as causal (because . . . , therefore; since . . . so); conditional (if . . . , then); and concessive (although . . . , yet or but) (ibid.:75).

These linguistic patterns apply not only to sentences but to the organization of discourse as well. Chinese speakers use a topic-comment format in ordering the presentation of their opinions, judgments, and requests. Chinese speakers respond to questions by first stating their reasons or explanations and ending with their judgments. Consider the following two exchanges (ibid.:76):

AMERICAN: How does the Nutritional Institute decide what topics to study? How do you decide what topic to do research on?

CHINESE: *BECAUSE*, now, period get change. It's different from past time. In past time, we emphasize how to solve practical problems. Nutrition must know how to solve some deficiency diseases. In our country, we have some nutritional diseases. But now it is important that we must do some basic research. *SO,* we must take into account fundamental problems. We must concentrate our research to study some fundamental research.

(In response to question about qualifications for salespeople):

My business is textile. The salesman is. . . . The quality of the salesman, need something different. *BECAUSE* the volume of making a sales in textiles is at least over ten thousand US dollars, sometimes. Whenever anybody who makes a decision to buy such . . . willing to pay such amount, we'll make sure their financial aid is strong. And, then, . . . sometimes the market may suddenly drop in textile. Maybe we're willing to buy one month ago, but may not be buying . . . want to buy now. Things like that. *SO,* for a salesman, also have to understand about the financial situation and things like that.

When Americans listened to tapes of these conversations, they had difficulty following the arguments or understanding the points being made. They described the Chinese speakers as hesitant, unclear, and evasive. Americans prefer a concise presentation of views, stating conclusions first and then, if necessary, proceeding to explanations. In contrast, Chinese people prefer to provide their reasoning initially, gradually developing shared knowledge so that when a conclusion is finally stated, its legitimacy will be mutually recognized. Chinese speakers intend this style as a display of cooperation and a desire to avoid confrontation (ibid.:80). Americans typically failed to appreciate underlying Chinese social values and instead became impatient with surface forms. In comparing these ethnic differences, a bilingual Chinese student living in the United States commented that Chinese speakers

at the same time as [they] are speaking, are reasoning with the listener to allow the listener to see whether what they say makes sense or not. This Chinese speech style is more open-minded, less biased, not constrictive as the American style, where it immediately sets you up to a particular frame of mind. You see, with the American style, you can react immediately to what the speaker says without listening to the rest of their explanation. (ibid.:82–83)

When participants have divergent interpretations of underlying intentions, serious consequences can ensue, especially in situations where one participant has authority over another. In these cases, dominant people can discriminate against subordinates with justifications based, in part, on stereotypes triggered by communicative styles.

In complex, multiethnic societies, ethnic stratification is interwoven with other kinds of unequal relationships. Although ideally all participants help construct social meanings of encounters, in situations of inequality, meanings and interpretations given by high-status people override those of low-status participants. For instance, analyses of interactions and outcomes in job interviews reveal that divergent assumptions about meanings of questions and answers can work against the ability of minority people to be understood and taken seriously. Consider the following extract from an interview for a job as a librarian in a college in Great Britain. The interviewers are British and the applicant is a South Asian man with a British professional degree (Jupp et al. 1982:252–253):

INTERVIEWER: One last question, Mr. Sandhu, why are you applying for this particular type of job in a college—a librarian's job in a college?

APPLICANT: Well, in fact, I have, up till now—um—previous to my—this job which I'm at present doing, I did send about 150 applications and my present job that was the only interview I got and I was accepted there and I was given that job doing and that is a temporary job as you know. Job is going to finish next December—so I desperately need another job—I've already sent about 50 applications but this is my second interview.

INTERVIEWER: I see, thanks very much.

SECOND INTERVIEWER: What attracts you to this particular librarian job and, in particular, why do you want to come to Middleton College?

APPLICANT: Well, as I have said, I have already applied for 50 other jobs, you know, sent 50 applications and—er—this is my second interview. I'm not particularly interested in this particular job. I'm interested in a job maybe in an academic library maybe in a public library—any job in this field, you know—I'm qualified for this and I desperately need one.

SECOND INTERVIEWER: Um—well, we, I think, perhaps might be looking for someone who's really committed to working for the college for the next at least three or four years.

The critical problem faced by the applicant has nothing to do with his linguistic skills; he is a fluent speaker of English. His handicap is his lack of knowledge about underlying sociolinguistic rules for conducting interviews. According to British (and American) norms, interviewers often ask indirect questions and expect applicants to respond by focusing on their special qualifications and interests. The candidate here did not recognize implied meanings of interviewers' questions. In discussing the episode afterward with researchers, Mr. Sandhu "confirmed that he was puzzled and somewhat insulted by being asked a question that he interpreted as meaning, 'Why do you want a job?'" (ibid.:252).

This exchange was obviously problematic for all parties. Interviewers were confused by Mr. Sandhu's response, as shown by the fact that the second interviewer pursued the question of the candidate's specific qualifications and interests. Because this inquiry was also stated indirectly, Mr. Sandhu again failed to respond according to British norms. The applicant made two errors of interpretation and reply. First, he responded to surface forms of questions rather than to their indirect, implied meanings, and second, he answered directly and perhaps too honestly. His basic message was that he is qualified for this (and any comparable) job and therefore ought to be hired. Because the interviewers did not directly state their confusion or dissatisfaction with Mr. Sandhu's replies, they did not give him any clues that he could use to satisfy their concerns. Each subsequent turn only served to deepen and solidify or (to use Tannen's term) "calcify" misinterpretations by all participants. These are serious problems because interviewers are in a position to make decisions that critically affect applicants' lives. Thus, members of ethnic minorities may be discriminated against, albeit unconsciously, because they and dominant decision makers, or gatekeepers, rely on divergent behavioral and interpretive frameworks.

The likelihood of cultural misinterpretation actually increases with the greater linguistic fluency of nonnative speakers. When conversing with someone whose knowledge of the language of discourse is clearly limited, people are more likely to make allowances for their performance, but when the interlocutor demonstrates linguistic competence, people tend to ignore possible cultural causes of divergent meanings.

SUMMARY

Language contact frequently results in changes in linguistic systems. New sounds may be introduced and/or grammatical constructions may be altered. In addition, all languages borrow words from foreign sources to name introduced items, activities, or ideas.

Within multilingual communities, speakers adjust to their languages and to each other in several ways. They often employ each language in certain situations, sensitive also to topics or participants. Stable patterns of language use can become established, but shifts in values and preferences may occur as a result of changing economic, social, and/or political conditions. In such situations, some languages may gain ascendancy because members of the community employ them in more contexts while others may become limited in their communicative functions. In the most extreme cases, some languages may die out.

Common strategies of bilingual interlocutors include code switching and code mixing, techniques of blending material from each language. Use of these devices enables bilingual speakers to maximize both their available linguistic inventories and their methods of signaling personal, interactional, and social meanings.

Although contact with members of diverse ethnic and linguistic groups is a culturally and individually enriching experience, it can result in miscommunication. Interlocutors interpret messages on the basis of their own socialization about linguistic and sociolinguistic cues. People enculturated into different systems have learned divergent normative cultural models and, therefore, may misinterpret the behavior and speech of others.

REFERENCES

ALFREDSSON, GUDMUNDUR. 1989. International discussion of the concerns of indigenous peoples. *Current Anthropology* 30:255–259.

ANDERSON, JEFFREY. 1998. Ethnolinguistic dimensions of Northern Arapaho language shift. *Anthropological Linguistics* 40:43–108.

APPEL, RENE, AND PIETER MUYSKEN. 1987. *Language Contact and Bilingualism.* London: Edward Arnold.

ARTIGAL, JOSEP MARIA. 1993. Catalan and Basque immersion programmes. In *European Models of Bilingual Education,* ed. H. Beardsmore. Philadelphia: Multilingual Matters, pp. 30–53.

ATTINASI, JOHN. 1985. Hispanic attitudes in northwest Indiana and New York. In *Spanish Language Use and Public Life in the US,* ed. L. Elias-Olivares et al. The Hague: Mouton, pp. 27–58.

BARON, DENNIS. 1990. *The English-Only Question.* New Haven: Yale University Press.

BERLITZ, CHARLES. 1982. *Native Tongues.* New York: Grosset and Dunlap.

BONVILLAIN, NANCY. 1978. Linguistic change in Akwesasne Mohawk: French and English influences. *International Journal of American Linguistics* 44:31–39.

BONVILLAIN, NANCY. 1988. Dynamics of personal narrative: A Mohawk example. *Anthropological Linguistics* 30:1–19.

BRIGGS, LUCY. 1985. Bilingual education in Peru and Bolivia. In *Language of Inequality,* ed. N. Wolfson and J. Manes. The Hague: Mouton, pp. 297–310.

BROOK, G. L. 1958. *A History of the English Language.* New York: W. W. Norton.

CANFIELD, KIP. 1980. A note on Navajo-English code-mixing. *Anthropological Linguistics* 22:218–220.

DORIAN, NANCY. 1981. *Language Death: The Life Cycle of a Scottish Gaelic Dialect.* Philadelphia: University of Pennsylvania Press.

FERGUSON, CHARLES. 1959. Diglossia. *Word* 15:325–340.

FINEGAN, EDWARD, AND NIKO BESNIER. 1989. *Language: Its Structure and Use.* New York: Harcourt, Brace.

FOUGHT, JOHN. 1985. Patterns of sociolinguistic inequality in Mesoamerica. In *Language of Inequality,* ed. N. Wolfson and J. Manes. The Hague: Mouton, pp. 21–39.

GAL, SUSAN. 1978. Peasant men can't get wives: Language change and sex roles in a bilingual community. *Language in Society* 7:1–16.

GASS, SUSAN, AND EVANGELINE VARONIS. 1991. Miscommunication in nonnative speaker discourse. *"Miscommunication" and Problematic Talk,* ed. N. Coupland et al. Newbury Park, CA: Sage, pp. 121–145.

GROSJEAN, FRANÇOIS. 1982. *Life with Two Languages.* Cambridge, MA: Harvard University Press.

GUMPERZ, JOHN. 1982. *Discourse Strategies.* New York: Cambridge University Press.

HALLE, MORRIS, AND G. N. CLEMENTS. 1983. *Problem Book in Phonology.* Cambridge, MA: MIT Press.

HALMARI, HELENA. 1998. Language maintenance on the Alabama-Coushatta Reservation. *Anthropological Linguistics* 40:409–428.

HOFFMANN, CHARLOTTE. 1996. Monolingualism, bilingualism, cultural pluralism and national identity: Twenty years of language planning in contemporary Spain. In *Monolingualism* and Bilingualism: Lessons from Canada and Spain, ed. S. Wright. Philadelphia: Multilingual Matters, pp. 59–90.

HORNBERGER, NANCY. 1998. Language policy, language education, language rights: Indigenous, immigrant, and international perspectives. Language in Society 27:439–458.

JUPP, T. C., CELIA ROBERTS, AND JENNY COOK-GUMPERZ. 1982. Language and disadvantage: The hidden process. In Language and Social Identity, ed. J. Gumperz. New York: Cambridge University Press, pp. 232–256.

KACHRU, BRAJ. 1978. Toward structuring code-mixing: An Indian perspective. International Journal of the Sociology of Language 16:27–46.

KRAUSS, MICHAEL. 1992. The world's languages in crisis. Language 68:4–10.

MCCLURE, ERICA. 1977. Aspects of code-switching in the discourse of Mexican-American children. In Linguistics and Anthropology, ed. M. Saville-Troike. Georgetown University Round Table on Languages and Linguistics. Washington, DC: Georgetown University Press, pp. 93–116.

MERTZ, ELIZABETH. 1989. Sociolinguistic creativity: Cape Breton Gaelic's linguistic "tip." In Investigating Obsolescence: Studies in Language Contraction and Death, ed. N. Dorian. New York: Cambridge University Press, pp. 103–116.

MOLONY, CAROL. 1977. Recent relexification processes in Philippine Creole Spanish. In Sociocultural Dimensions of Language Change, ed. B. Blount and M. Sanches. New York: Academic Press, pp. 131–159.

PANDIT, IRA. 1986. Hindi English Code-Switching: Mixed Hindi English. Delhi: Datta Book Centre.

PEDRAZA, PEDRO. 1985. Language mainte-

nance among New York Puerto Ricans. In Spanish Language Use and Public Life in the US, ed. L. Elias-Olivares et al. The Hague: Mouton, pp. 59–71.

PFAFF, CAROL. 1979. Constraints on language mixing: Intrasentential code-switching and borrowing in Spanish/English. Language 55:291–318.

PLATT, JOHN, HEIDI WEBER, AND HO MIAN LIAN. 1984. The New Englishes. London: Routledge and Kegan Paul.

POPLACK, SHANA. 1988. Language status and language accommodation along a linguistic border. In Language Spread, ed. P. Lowenberg. Georgetown University Round Table in Languages and Linguistics, 1987. Washington, DC: Georgetown University Press, pp. 90–118.

PYLES, THOMAS, AND JOHN ALGEO. 1982. The Origins and Development of the English Language, 3rd ed. New York: Harcourt Brace Jovanovich.

RUBIN, JOAN. 1985. The special relation of Guarani and Spanish in Paraguay. In Language of Inequality, ed. N. Wolfson and J. Manes. The Hague: Mouton, pp. 111–120.

SAAH, KOFI. 1986. Language use and attitudes in Ghana. Anthropological Linguistics 28:367–377.

SCOTTON, CAROL. 1976. Strategies of neutrality: Language choice in uncertain situations. Language 52:919–941.

SRIDHAR, S. N. 1978. On the functions of code-mixing in Kannada. International Journal of the Sociology of Language 17:109–117.

TANNEN, DEBORAH. 1982. Ethnic style in male-female conversation. In Language and Social Identity, ed. J. Gumperz. New York: Cambridge University Press, pp. 217–231.

VALDES-FALLIS, GUADALUPE. 1978. Code-switching among bilingual Mexican-American women: Towards an understanding of sex-related language alternation. *International Journal of the Sociology of Language* 17:65–72.

WATSON, SEOSAMH. 1989. Scottish and Irish Gaelic: The giant's bed-fellows. In *Investigating Obsolescence: Studies in Language Contraction and Death,* ed. N. Dorian. New York: Cambridge University Press, pp. 41–60.

YOUNG, LINDA. 1982. Inscrutability revisited. In *Language and Social Identity,* ed. J. Gumperz. New York: Cambridge University Press, pp. 72–84.

YOUNG, ROBERT, AND WILLIAM MORGAN. 1987. *The Navajo Language,* rev. ed. Albuquerque: University of New Mexico Press.

ZENTELLA, ANA. 1985. The fate of Spanish in the US: The Puerto Rican experience. In *Language of Inequality,* ed. N. Wolfson and J. Manes. The Hague: Mouton, pp. 41–59.

ZUAZO, KOLDO. 1995. The Basque country and the Basque language: An overview of the external history of the Basque language. In *Towards a History of the Basque Language,* ed. J. Hualde et al. Philadelphia: John Benjamins, pp. 5–30.

ZUENGLER, JANE. 1985. English, Swahili, or other languages? The relationship of educational development goals to language of instruction in Kenya and Tanzania. In *Language of Inequality,* ed. N. Wolfson and J. Manes. The Hague: Mouton, pp. 241–254.

13

Language
and Institutional
Encounters

Note the italicized words in the following excerpt from a doctor's advice to a patient seeking to choose a method of birth control:

> "If you take them *right*, you are going to be in *pretty good shape* . . . and of course, *everybody uses birth control pills.*"

Were the doctor's words neutral? Or did they reveal the doctor's attitudes? When patients seek advice from doctors, they usually assume that the doctor has impartial information and expertise that they themselves lack. But a patient's ability to make an informed, independent decision is often undermined by the words doctors use to convey covert messages and assert their authority.

Talk is situated in interactions that are themselves situated in social contexts within an overall framework of cultural meanings. In addition to the words spoken in encounters, messages about people's worthiness and rights are communicated. These messages are the subtexts of human interaction. We have already seen that societal divisions into categories of gender, class, race, age, and ethnicity affect speaking styles and conversational strategies. In this chapter we focus on interconnections between language and hierarchical roles. We begin with a general discussion of this issue and then proceed to analyses of institutional settings where power and control versus powerlessness and constraint are systematically actualized. We will discuss institutional interactions in the United States and Great Britain. Examination of behavior in other societies might demonstrate the extent to which comparable institutional controls are exerted.

LANGUAGE IDEOLOGIES

Every culture has systems of beliefs about the world, including ideas about human beings, their abilities and rights, and the ways they interact with each other. These are not abstract or immutable systems arising purely from human minds. Rather, they are contextually created and serve specific social functions. As conditions change through historical processes, cultural beliefs change too and so do the linguistic behaviors that reflect them.

Belief systems not only explain but also legitimate social orders and constructions of reality. In stratified societies, for example, beliefs about the inherent superiority of some groups and inherent inferiority of others (potentially classified according to gender, class, race, age) are maintained and reproduced through linguistic messages. Meaning is never divorced from the society that creates it. And once created, it becomes part of the consciousness of individuals. This consciousness is formed in a reflexive process, interacting with the view of reality that society constructs, according to V. N. Volosinov (1973:12–13):

> The individual consciousness is a social-ideological fact. . . . The only possible objective definition of consciousness is a sociological one. Consciousness takes shape and being in the material of signs created by an organized group in the process of its social intercourse. The individual consciousness is nurtured on signs; it derives its growth from them; it reflects their logic and laws.

Belief systems, or ideologies, are transmitted through many social modes, such as religious rituals, moral and aesthetic values, political displays, and the like. And they are expressed in and through language. Words in themselves are neutral, but their use gives them social and symbolic content. Words and the beliefs they express form a coherent cultural system, or, as Volosinov stated, "a unity of the verbally constituted consciousness" (ibid.:15).

Linguists and anthropologists have increasingly focused on the ways that social power and control are reflected in language, language use, and language ideologies. Speech communities, whether small homogeneous villages or large heterogeneous state societies, develop ideologies about language, about what constitutes a language, about what is acceptable or appropriate language use. These ideologies are transmitted through communicative behavior and through how people talk about language and linguistic activities. In most modern nations, language ideologies entail practices that select and promulgate a standard or "legitimate" language for use in public contexts, for example, in schools, the media, and political, economic, and religious life. Other varieties or dialects are then evaluated negatively in relation to the standard and their speakers are stigmatized. The selection of a particular dialect as a standard is the result of complex linguistic, social, economic, and political processes. The variety chosen as standard is usually one associated with an elite segment of society. In Great Britain, the standard (now usually referred to as Received Pronunciation or RP) was a dialect originally associated with upper-class speakers regionally centered around London. By the late nineteenth century, that regional elite dialect spread through the English public school system (in U.S. terms, private schools). Any young man desiring to advance his education at a prestigious university was well advised to adopt the accent as well (Milroy 2000:72). Although RP was at first a regional dialect, once it became the standard it was redefined on the basis of class. RP speakers were perceived as upper class, whereas speakers of other dialects were stigmatized because of their language and its class associations. In the United States, in contrast, issues of class were publicly less salient than in Great Britain, and instead, racial and ethnic distinctions were more prominent. Until the late nineteenth century, bilingualism and multilingualism were accepted as normal features of language life, and, indeed, several states officially recognized bilingualism by publishing statutes in languages other than English (French in Louisiana; German in Pennsylvania). By the early twentieth century, however, the tide had turned against an official view of the United States as a multilingual nation. Increasing immigration from Europe and elsewhere aroused antagonism on the part of the American citizenry, resulting in a general pattern of loss of foreign mother tongues by the second or third generation. Influences from other languages into American English pronunciation were disparaged. Racial distinctions became especially marked, leading to the strong stigmatization of African-American English that continues into the present times. The dialect recognized as standard in the United States is perceived to have the least distinguishing features and, therefore, thought to be the most easily understood no matter what the regional background of the hearer. In contrast to the situation in Great Britain where most people are able to identify the standard Received Pronunciation whether they speak it or not, in the United States there is a much lower degree of consensus about exactly what standard pronunciation is. In fact, it is more readily identified by what it is not—that is, it is not the speech of regional stigmatized groups, especially Southerners, New Yorkers, and Appalachian dwellers, and not the language of racially or ethnically marginalized groups, especially African Americans and Hispanics. There is no general agreement, even among professional linguists, about the regional origin of the U.S. standard (ibid.:59). But in both the United States and Great Britain, there is strong adherence to standard language ideology, a belief that there is only one correct form of spoken and written language. Deviations from the given standard are wrong and in need of correction. Positive and negative attitudes toward standard or nonstandard speech are extended to the speakers themselves. Speakers of nonstandard forms are thought to be stupid, lazy, or even morally deficient.

The emergence of a dominant and dominating standard language in the United States and Great Britain is indicative of a widespread process. Bourdieu has written extensively about a similar generation of standard or "legitimate" language in France (1991:46–48). There the dialect of French spoken by the social and political elite was elevated to official status beginning in the sixteenth century, relegating other regional varieties to the status of "patois." Before their subordination to the standard, regional dialects had both oral and written uses. Local ordinances, contracts, and literary forms, especially poetry, were written in the regional dialects, but these gradually gave way to the dominance of the standard and lost their deep traditions, becoming marginalized forms of speech.

Struggles over standard language choice are attested in many former colonial nations of Africa where the focus is not so much on dialects within a language but on choices among separate languages. Decisions about which language to use as the official or national language, whether to choose a colonial language (English or French) or whether to select an indigenous language, are often fraught with conflict based on class and ethnicity as well as prevailing social, economic, and political goals of the central government.

The development of a standard language often coincides with processes of state formation and centralization through which the state exerts both linguistic and cultural control. Such is the case of the development and spread of the language known as Indonesian in the modern state of Indonesia. Indonesian has roots in several Malay dialects indigenous to some areas of the collection of islands known as Indonesia as well as several varieties of lingua francas that were spoken throughout the islands before European colonial encounters in the sixteenth century (Errington 2000:207). The origin of Indonesian dates to the period of Dutch colonial occupation. Because the Dutch avoided using their own language with their native clients, they sought to select an indigenous dialect for use in trade, missionary, and other colonial enterprises. Dutch efforts to deepen their control in the islands led to further attempts to standardize a native language. By the beginning of the twentieth century, a standard Malay orthography was introduced, leading to codification of a "general, cultured Malay" (ibid.:207). The language was formally given the name of "Indonesian" in 1928 at a meeting of Dutch-educated native intellectual and political elites in a declaration of purpose, stating the goal of creating a "unified people" speaking "one language" in a "single homeland" (ibid.:208).

Through its promulgation in schools and its use in public governmental and economic contexts, Indonesian has become the dominant language of Indonesia. As is common in many colonial and postcolonial nation-states, the national language is the mother tongue of relatively few people but its dominance and authority are acknowledged by all. Indeed, the state can hardly conceive of itself without a dominant language ideology. In the words of a government publication, "the concept of national society cannot be fully understood if one national language does not exist. A country that has one general/common language known throughout society will be more advanced in development and its political ideology will be safer and stable" (Burhan 1989; quoted in Errington 2000:211). Indonesian has, thus, become associated inextricably with the identity of Indonesia as a nation and, therefore, the language has become part of the identity of the nation's citizens.

As currently spoken, Indonesian has incorporated numerous borrowings from English. This tendency is applauded by some of the country's language commentators and authorities who, at the same time, are critical of the use of words derived from archaic Old Javanese and Sanskrit. Attitudes favoring English words reflect the desire to appear "modern" while the use of Old Javanese and Sanskrit words is criticized as "nativistic" and "traditional" (ibid.:216). The extent of English influence on Indonesian is evident not merely in the number of borrowed words but also in their meanings. English borrowings have been adopted into Indonesian for new items of modern technology, a process that is nearly worldwide in its scope. But, in addition, English borrowings have replaced some perfectly adequate Indonesian words. English has, therefore, exerted its dominance as the major international language, infiltrating the local dominant language of Indonesia.

In all modern countries, the educational system is one of the prime arenas for the promulgation of standard languages and standard language ideologies. Dell Hymes's observations about language dynamics in the United States applies equally well elsewhere:

> Language has been a central medium of cultural hegemony in the United States. Class stratification and cultural assumptions about language converge in schooling to reproduce the social order. A latent function of the educational system is to instill linguistic insecurity, to discriminate linguistically, to channel children in ways that have an integral linguistic component, while appearing open and fair to all. All have equal opportunity to acquire membership in the privileged linguistic network. If they fail, it is their fault, not that of the society or school. (1996:84)

The insistence on linguistic uniformity, coupled with criticisms of any deviation, is among the building blocks of educational systems in most modern state societies. Linguistic hegemony is manifested both in the use of the standard and the recognition of its prestige and authority even by people who do not themselves employ it. And failure to conform, whether due to choice or to lack of access, justifies the exclusion of marginalized groups. As Bourdieu observed:

> Produced by authors who have the authority to write, fixed and codified by grammarians and teachers who are also charged with the task of inculcating its mastery, the language is a *code,* in the sense of a cipher enabling equivalences to be established between sounds and meanings, but also in the sense of a system of norms regulating linguistic practices. (1991:45)

However, the fact that nonstandard, nonprestige varieties continue with great vigor should be understood, not in negative terms but as a positive reflection of individual and group values. Nonstandard varieties must have "covert prestige" (Trudgill 1972) or they would eventually disappear. Discovering what these competing values are is a complex matter. As Kathryn Woolard observes, "Competing sets of values exist, creating strong pressures in favor of the 'illegitimate' languages in the vernacular markets, and not just an absence of pressure against them" (1985:744). Nonstandard varieties may be supported by in-group membership identification, especially in close and dense networks in which members exert strong pressures toward conformity as an emblem of their group. Group solidarity may have meanings of opposition to domination by elite segments of society. Quoting Woolard again, "It is critical to understand that vernacular practices are productive, not merely reproductive, that they arise not from a mere bending to the weight of authority, but are paradoxically a creative response to that authority, mediated by the opposition value of solidarity" (ibid.:745). The continuation of "devalued linguistic strategies and genres" (Gal 1989:349) can be seen as forms of resistance by their very survival and also by their transmitting "alternate models of the social world" (ibid.).

Studies of language ideologies and resistance to dominant varieties can attempt to connect the processes of face-to-face interaction with social, economic, and political orders. Members of some stigmatized communities may sharpen or exaggerate their differences from the dominant forms. For example, a dialect of Caribbean immigrants and their descendents in Great Britain, called Afro-Lingua, turns the tables on standard English, opposing some widespread metaphoric constructions that transmit negative images of "black" and positive images of "white" (see Chapter 6 for a discussion of Afro-Lingua and other Black dialects in Great Britain and the United States). Afro-Lingua originated and spread with the popularity of the Rastafarian movement and especially with the reggae music closely identified with it. Rastas, as they are often known, challenge some basic cultural models transmitted through standard English metaphors:

> For example, black is depicted as bad or dangerous. "A black day" means that on a particular day things have gone badly for the whites. "A black sheep" in the family means the worst or most detested member of the family. One sees, quite clearly, that black is associated with the devil and hell and with death. At the same time the assumption is that white is good, right, pure. There is no doubt that the black/white opposition is racial and racist. (Bones 1986:46)

Some English words are altered in Afro-Lingua by changing syllables to highlight cultural and political meanings. For example, the word "politics" is transformed into "politricks," the word "system" becomes "shitstem," and "oppression" becomes "downpression" (Wong 1986:119). By transforming these words, speakers of Afro-Lingua deliberately attack underlying meanings that exemplify the control of dominant language ideology on subordinate and stigmatized peoples.

In societies with standard language ideologies, the standard becomes naturalized; that is, community members regard the standard as natural, commonsense, and unquestioned. They accept the fact that any variation from the standard is either ignored or discredited. Language ideologies develop and are maintained in specific cultural contexts. It is appropriate to ask whose interests are served by the dominant ideologies, who benefits from the beliefs that are promulgated, and who is disadvantaged. Languages and beliefs about language have social and political implications. Beliefs about the correctness of the dominant language become so much a part of people's everyday thinking that they fail to see that these beliefs are socially constructed. Rather, the dominance of the standard becomes part of their everyday consciousness, unexamined and naturalized. As Michael Silverstein remarked,

> Many speakers of languages in such cultural orders [where dominant languages are standardized] cannot even conceive of any other kind of linguistic phenomena, for instance, unwritten languages, languages without standards, and so on . . . The very

concept of language rests upon finding the various institutional paraphernalia of standardization, for example, literacy in relation to standard register, grammars and dictionaries, authoritative judgment of correctness enforceable in certain institutional rights of power over discourse, and so forth. Within cultures of standard, forms of language that lack these to some significant degree are relegated to some classificatory category other than language. (2000:122–123)

In addition to its role in the development of a standard language, state control exerts its influence in language practices that impose social and cultural values and promulgate particular dominant language ideologies. For example, although literacy is usually seen as a positive process, or at worst a benign one, in fact literacy may be embedded in social and political processes that are detrimental to the survival of an indigenous culture.

Bambi Schieffelin's study of the introduction of literacy among the Kaluli of Papua New Guinea demonstrates the ways that literacy practices contributed to transforming Kaluli identity. Although Kalulis first met white people in 1935, it was not until the early 1970s that Australian missionaries entered their territory, bringing Christianity, education, and literacy in an attempt to alter Kaluli society. The missionaries, soon joined by others, produced grammatical sketches and readers that introduced Christian and European concepts and values. New ideas were transmitted with sample verbs and nouns such as "write," "book," "wireless radio," "letter," and "do school." In some cases, Kaluli words were expanded in their meanings to fit borrowed concepts, whereas in others the missionary linguists created new words out of native morphemes (2000:302–303). Christian concepts and characters were introduced in sentences given to illustrate Kaluli vocabulary: "Do you pray to God every day?" and its accompanying response "Yes, I pray every day" (ibid.:304). Other sentences included vocabulary and concepts depicting European activities that were presented to Kalulis in a positive light. Especially common were sentences about buying goods such as cloth, beads, and tinned fish that could be purchased at mission stores. Stories in primers and readers depicted Kaluli families in traditional subsistence activities but also included foreign activities such as going to the mission store, church, or school. One of the most startling introductions is the word employed for the Kaluli themselves. Instead of using an indigenous name for the people, the readers employ the term *ka:na:ka,* derived from the New Guinean trade pidgin Tok Pisin. Although the formal definition of *ka:na:ka* is "native, nonindentured person," it has long been used with derogatory connotations to mean "uncivilized, backward" (ibid.:308). Through the introduction of this word for the Kaluli, the books "(re)formulate, (re)present, (re)construct" Kaluli social identity and present the Kaluli themselves in negative terms (ibid.:309).

Literacy practices have also transformed Kaluli modes of acquiring knowledge and forming opinions. Traditionally, knowledge was imparted through oral learning, dialogue, and conversational feedback, whereas consensus was built through open discussion with the participation of all interested parties. In contrast, the literacy practices imparted to the Kaluli are authoritative, regimented, and controlled through the printed text and through a new group of local experts such as teachers and missionaries. Replacing patterns of egalitarian discussion and community involvement, a hierarchical system wielded by foreign experts and their students has taken shape in indigenous communities.

Language ideologies entail beliefs and practices about the use of authoritative speech, that is, the speech of culturally validated voices of authority. Quoting an authority (or what M. M. Bakhtin [1981:342] referred to as "authoritative discourse") creates distance between the narrator, the text quoted, and the listener. According to Bakhtin,

> . . . the authoritative word demands that we acknowledge it, that we make it our own; finds us, quite independent power it might have to persuade us internally; we encounter it with its authority already infused to it. The authoritative word is located in a distant zone, organically connected with a past, that is felt to be hierarchically higher. Its authority was already acknowledged in the past. It is a prior discourse. It is therefore not a question of choosing it from among other possible discourses that are its equal. (ibid.)

Reported speech, especially that of authority, can be used to manipulate an audience for a desired end. Quoting authoritative sources can be a move to legitimate one's own position and persuade an audience to accept one's word without question. However, depending on the cultural and situational context, use of authoritative speech can be controversial and may not necessarily achieve the desired ends. In societies like our own, authorities quoted may be from a variety of sources: so-called experts (scientists, doctors); public, political, or media figures; historical personages who have come to be considered near-legendary (for example, most prominently, our founding fathers).

In many other societies, traditional lore, proverbs, and mythological characters may be cited as authorities for everyday experience. In a study of the use of authoritative speech in a political controversy on the Micronesian island of Belau, Richard Parmentier (1993) demonstrated the ways in which language use signaled changing norms associated chiefly with language. During a village meeting prompted by political disputes over a new constitution, a middle-aged woman suddenly began to scream, stomp her feet, repeat the names of the two chiefs present, adding, "I hate it, I hate it, I hate it!" (1993:266). The woman later claimed to have been speaking the words of one of the community's traditional gods. This claim proved to be controversial; some villagers accepted it as valid, while others (including the chiefs) questioned the woman's right to speak for the gods, noting that she did not have the proper cultural credentials to use the divine authoritative voice. During the uproar that followed this outburst, a villager asked one of the chiefs whether he would in fact support the new constitution. The question itself violated traditional norms because high-ranking chiefs are never asked to publicly state their opinions. Overhearing the question, another chief interjected, "Who was it that asked this? I cannot approve of this *boy* asking Ngirtur for his thoughts" (ibid.:267). Another meeting was soon held to discuss the political turmoil and events of the previous meeting. After several attempts to be recognized as a speaker, the high-ranking chief referred to the past incidents and spoke at length about his reactions to the political controversy, quoting traditional proverbs to substantiate his interpretation of events and the need for traditional norms of interaction and procedure. As Parmentier observed,

> [the chief] is using his authority as a high-ranking title holder and as an accepted expert on Belauan tradition and village history to typify rather than to merely report discourse. The function of citing traditional proverbs can be understood in terms of the speaker's need to legitimize his own position as an authoritative voice. In attempting to remind the village of certain traditional norms of language use and to perform a resolution of political tension exacerbated by recent violation of these rules, the chief obviously places great store not only in his own political weight but also in the power of speech to affect the goals sought. For some people in the village, however, the speech accomplished an unintended purpose—that of standing as a historical marker of the demise of chiefly authority and respect. (ibid.:284)

In the traditional view, "high-ranking chiefs have little need to persuade others of their views through public oratory, since their final decisions were not subject to questioning or even debate. In fact, passive silence was one of the hallmarks of presupposed chiefly authority. So the chief's highly persuasive speech about the relevance of traditional rules of speaking belies its own message" (ibid.:284).

LANGUAGE AND STATUS

Differences in rights and values given to various categories of people are manifested in several features of language. First is the ability to name and classify:

> The ability to bestow meanings—to "name" things, acts and ideas—is a source of power. Control of communication allows the managers of ideology to lay down the categories through which reality is to be perceived. Conversely, this entails the ability to deny the existence of alternative categories, to assign them to the realm of disorder and chaos, to render them socially and symbolically invisible. (Wolf 1982:388)

Examples of how society labels people demonstrate this process. For instance, many English words for females tend to take on derogatory, limiting, and often sexual meanings. Similarly, members of nonwhite racial groups are negatively labeled. The right to name and thereby either legitimate or trivialize others is not only expressed in vocabulary, it is enacted in daily encounters whereby it reflects and reproduces the prevailing social order. The following episode is recalled by Alvin Poussaint, an African-American doctor (1967:53):

> "What's your name, boy?" the policeman asked.
> "Dr. Poussaint, I'm a physician."
> "What's your first name, boy?"
> "Alvin."

These four utterances poignantly give witness to conflicts inherent in many unequal social interactions, made overt here although generally enacted covertly. In struggles for the right to name, powerless individuals lose the ability even to name themselves.

In stratified societies, elites or majorities often employ derogatory words for subordinate groups. Use of these words "may promote prejudice by enhancing the perception of out-group members as like each other and unlike in-group members" (Greenberg et al. 1988:76). Derogatory labels express negative attitudes by speakers toward members of targeted groups and produce negative stereotypes about people defined as "other." In statements reminiscent of ethnolinguistic discussions of relationships between language and thought, Jeff Greenberg et al. contend:

> Because DELs [derogatory ethnic labels] have the power to communicate all the negative beliefs about a given group in a single word, they are likely to be especially potent communicative devices. Words have the power to make a concept seem like something that actually exists in the world. [They] crystallize [negative] beliefs into concept or prototype that has a sense of concrete reality to those who use the term. Essentially, the DEL is a cultural legitimization of a negative conception of members of a particular out-group; the mere existence of the term implies at least some cultural sanctioning of the concept it represents. (ibid.:77)

Use of derogatory labels for people based on their gender, ethnicity, or race is an example of expressing and imposing social beliefs through rights to name and refer. Subordinate groups are thus demeaned and depersonalized.

Interrelationships between language and hierarchical social models can also be demonstrated by contrasts in evaluations of speaking styles associated with different groups. For example, women's speech is negatively judged because of its reputed use of numerous devices to hedge or disclaim speakers' opinions and generally to show deference to interlocutors. Although it is positively perceived as "polite," women who employ this style are dismissed as inconsequential. But women who use direct ("masculine") speech are criticized for being abrasive and aggressive. A cross-cultural view, though, quickly demonstrates that it is the speakers, female or male, who are socially evaluated and not their linguistic output in the abstract. For instance, recall that among the Malagasy (Keenan 1974; see Chapter 8), women's direct and sometimes confrontational style is denigrated, whereas men's inexplicit, vague, and deferential speech is praised, in fact, likened to that of the ancestors.

Differences in status are not only expressed in words and speech patterns but are also demonstrated in assignment of rights to speak and determine topics of talk. Rights or constraints are displayed in interpersonal encounters on a daily basis where high-status people can exert their influence. We have seen examples of this process in relation to male/female and adult/child interactions where higher-status individuals often interrupt or disregard contributions of lower-status interlocutors. The latter learn strategies of indirection, mitigation, or manipulation in order to eke out some communicative space. According to Bonnie Erickson et al., low-status speakers react to their situation by developing a style that the researchers identify as "powerless." It is characterized by use of intensifiers, hedges, hesitations, rising intonations, and polite forms (1978:267–268). These examples are appropriate illustrations of Bourdieu's observation that ". . . the competence adequate to produce sentences that are likely to be understood may be quite inadequate to produce sentences that are likely to be *listened to,* likely to be recognized as *acceptable* in all the situations in which there is occasion to speak" (1991:55).

Immediate contexts of encounters shape the behavior taking place within. As Volosinov stated, "We [can] see what enormous significance belongs to the *hierarchical factor* in the processes of verbal interchange and what a powerful influence is exerted on forms of utterance by the hierarchical organization of communication" (1973:21). Volosinov applied this insight to understanding the forms and functions of all utterances. "Indeed, [they are] socially oriented in [their] entirety. [They] are determined immediately and directly by the participants of the speech event in connection with a specific situation. That situation shapes the utterance, dictating that it sound one way and not another—like a demand or request, insistence on one's rights or a plea for mercy, in a style flowery or plain, in a confident or hesitant manner, and so on" (ibid.:86–87).

A Non-Western Comment

As with all aspects of language use, cultural models of behavior may give alternative interpretations of similar stylistic variants. Although differentiation of status exists to some extent in most, if not all, societies, whether within households, communities, or wider social systems, linguistic and sociolinguistic forms that reflect inequality may vary. Behavior exemplifying high or low status in one culture may have quite different social meanings in another. For instance, in Japan, the so-called "powerless" style, identified by Erickson et al. (1978), is valued for all Japanese speakers (Wetzel 1988). Within Japanese culture these behaviors are not markers of powerlessness but, rather, are indicators of the speaker's basic humanness, expressed by *ningen-rashii* and *yutaka,* concepts stressing interpersonal harmony and empathy (ibid.:560). Favored models of interaction and communication emphasize "sensitivity to the other, demonstrations or signals of empathy, solicitation of agreement, concern about what others are thinking, silent protest as a strategy for signalling disagreement or displeasure" (ibid.:561). In contrast, Japanese speakers view communicative behaviors that are considered signals of power in our society (control through interrupting, challenging, or ignoring another's comments; direct assertions of opinions) as "immature or childish" (ibid.).

This comment does not negate the relevance of analyzing interactions between social structures and language. Indeed, it cautions us to attend to the continually interconnected nature of linguistic form and cultural context that gives talk its meaning and potency.

INSTITUTIONAL CONTEXTS

In our society, institutional settings, wherein roles are distributed and interactions are managed in terms of preassigned rights and constraints, are important in orienting, explaining, and influencing our lives. Jurgen Habermas (1970) referred to development of a "technocratic consciousness" that affects our ways of thinking (our worldview) in institutional spheres and is extended to other interactional contexts. It has become a "background ideology," replacing interpersonal and symbolic understandings of experience with its own emphasis on "purposive-rational action." We accept this mode of thought and behavior as normal, natural, and legitimate. In fact, "the concealment of the difference [between alternate modes of thinking] proves the ideological power of the technocratic consciousness" (ibid.: 105–107).

Numerous institutions affect our lives and through their hierarchical structure elicit characteristic kinds of behaviors within them. Two prominent examples are institutions that provide education and health care. Everyone has direct experience with schools and medical providers, coming under their authority for extended periods of time and/or in critical periods of life. A third major institution in American society is that of the legal establishment. Although many people do not have direct contact with courts, courtroom behavior is so explicitly linguistic and controlling that it deserves attention as an exemplar of the ways that communicative contexts affect behavior.

We will presently turn to analyses of communicative norms prevailing within these institutions, attempting to uncover their impact on individuals and their role in maintaining hierarchical organizations of society. Social relations are enacted on both the societal ("macro") level and the interpersonal ("micro") level. Human behavior in even the most personalized encounters is affected by wider social meanings. Although people may not be consciously aware of hidden constraints, they nonetheless act in accordance with unstated rules of behavior and communication. Encounters within institutional frameworks are influenced by the overall authority of institutions themselves, expressed interpersonally by specific participants through specific ways of speaking.

Following discussion of these structured settings, we end the chapter by considering the role of mass media in constructing, reflecting, and reinforcing social beliefs.

EDUCATION

Educational settings provide excellent demonstration of the role of hierarchy in allocating rights to direct encounters. Authority of teachers in the classroom is not only based on their institutional position but is further compounded by the status of age (adult/child) and often as well by that of class (middle/working class). Parents, too, are constrained in their interactions with school professionals because of institutionally derived rights of the latter to make decisions and dispense or with-hold rewards.

Communicative behavior in classrooms in the United States is typified by question-answer sequences. Individual children are either chosen to respond or compete with each other through calling out or raising their hands for the right to respond. Such insistence on individualized answers, which seems so "natural" to those of us socialized in this system, creates difficulties for some groups of children. For instance, many Native American children are socialized to refrain from behavior that isolates their performance in a competitive manner in front of peers. In a comparison of classroom behavior of Native American children from the Warm Springs Reservation in Oregon with that of nearby non–Native American students, Susan Philips found that Native Americans were extremely reluctant to answer teachers' questions or to speak out in class. In contrast, in situations where they could have individual access to teachers, they were more likely than non–Native Americans to seek help, initiate questions, and engage in dialogue (1978:397). Thus it was the structure of settings, not inherent interest, that affected their responses.

People in other Native American cultures think of instruction as a process of discovery through observation by learners who arrive at conclusions based on information given to them from which they deduce generalizations or applications. For instance, consider the following episode of a Cree elder speaking with a class of elementary school children in Alberta, Canada (Darnell 1985:69):

> An old man discussing number words in Cree and English first established with the children that one cannot say "one *moswa*" or "*peyak* moose." The students were left to make the general observation that both words have to be in the same language. The old man then showed them the symbol 1 and asked them which language that was in. The unanimous response was "English." The old man appeared startled but recovered quickly and began to make his point in a different way. He asked the children if the Ukrainians had a word for one and, after a moment of silence, was told that they did. He then asked about the Chinese and the children agreed that they too had a word for one. One boy then said, "I guess everybody has a word for one." The old man acknowledged that statement by saying, "Oh, I see."

In contrast to this kind of interaction, in most American classrooms, questions are used explicitly to measure pupils' attentiveness and absorption of knowledge. Contextual examination of these speech events reveals that questions function as control mechanisms as well. According to Elliot Mishler, "Through the act of questioning, one speaker defines the way in which the other is to continue with the conversation and thus defines their relationship to each other along a dimension of power and authority" (1975:105).

In his study of adult/child interactions in first-grade classrooms, Mishler identified two types of "interrogative units" each composed of a sequence of three utterances including a question, a response from addressee, and a confirmation from initiator (ibid.:100–101):

I. Chaining:
    1. Initial question
    2. Response/answer
    3. Confirmation/question (i.e., confirmation contains a further question)
        Q: s1:   Did you really finish all your work before everybody else?
        R/A: s2:   Yeah.
        C/Q: s1:   What kind of work was it?
        R/A: s2:   Well. We just had a piece of paper and it had all the
                   names on it. And we had to see if it was odd or even.
        C/Q: s1:   Do you know all the odd numbers and all the even
                   numbers?
        R/A: s2:   Uh huh.
        C/Q: s1:   How far up can you count?

II. Arching:
    1. Initial question
    2. Response/question
    3. Confirmation/response (i.e., response contains a question and
        confirmation is a response)
        Q: s1:   Whaddya mean? He is (S) He's
        R/Q: s2:   (S) Is he under water?
        C/R: s1:   He is. See now here's a scuba suit on him.
        C: s2:   I think he's dead.

Chaining was the predominant mechanism in all interrogative units in class-rooms, but rates of chaining and arching differed, depending on the status of initiators. Adults employed *chaining,* asking another question after the child's response, in 84 percent of discourse series that they initiated, whereas *arching,* child responding to the adult's question with a question, occurred in only 30 percent of these interactions. In contrast, although chaining occurred in 69 percent of child-initiated sequences, arching had a higher frequency rate, at 78 percent (ibid.:107).

In sum, adults employ two methods of control: When initiating a discourse series, they use chaining (asking further questions) to regain control after a child's response; when children initiate a series, adults use arching (responding to questions with own questions) to make a countermove, taking control from the child. Children do employ chaining at a substantial rate (69 percent) when initiating sequences with adults, but they seldom use arching (30 percent) to counter an adult's claim of control. Status, then, gives rights to determine the content and direction of talk, as well as rights to assert control over or take control away from interlocutors. Children learn these covert social lessons through the structure of their formal schooling.

Children also learn lessons about gender through classroom interactions. Although they are exposed to gender roles and associated conversational strategies in their homes (see Chapters 7 and 10), they become direct participants in the classroom when they engage in discussions and question-answer sequences. Boys tend to dominate classtime by more frequent responses and lengthier turns. But since teachers are the primary controllers and facilitators of talk in class, they are responsible for constructing and reinforcing gender roles. In a study of classroom sequences, teachers (in this case, female teachers) helped boys dominate talk by more often turning toward them, gazing at them, and selecting boys to answer questions (Swann 1998).

Language plays a critical role in the micropolitics of interactions within educational institutions. Context, as always, provides the key to understanding the meaning of any utterance or series of utterances. Analyses of transcripts of school meetings having the purported goal of making decisions about placing a child in special education programs reveal some ways that authority and order are managed (Mehan 1986). Participants included a school psychologist, principal, special education teacher, classroom teacher, and parent (usually the mother). Despite the overt goal of group involvement, decisions had actually been made by authorities (psychologist, principal, special-ed. teacher) prior to meetings. The meetings' real purpose, then, was to publicly ratify those decisions.

Numerous linguistic mechanisms were used by authorities in the process of "routinely inducing" others (teacher, parent) to agree (Mehan 1986:141). Committee meetings began with lengthy presentations of information about the child, followed by brief segments of decision making (or decision affirming). In the first phase, high-status professionals spoke first. They presented data in "objective" terms, giving results of batteries of tests, filled with statistical percentages and technical terminology. The words chosen were dispassionate, global, and categorical. Authorities used professional terms and jargon without clarification. The effect is one of mystification, surrounding presentations in a linguistic mode of science, or, repeating Habermas's phrase, a "technocratic consciousness." And, as Habermas predicts, this mode is not questioned or challenged by others, particularly not by lower-status participants.

In addition, psychologists often spoke in platitudes, for example, "He has difficulty applying himself" or "She does possibly have some fears and anxieties" (ibid.:149). Again, no one questioned the standards by which a child's "applying" himself was measured, nor the relevance of "fears and anxieties" to the issue at hand.

The tapes further demonstrate that high-status participants often interrupted teachers' and parents' speaking turns by asking questions or commenting upon prior statements. According to Mehan, the contributions of parents and teachers focused on "contingent" explanations of children's performance, providing background and contextual information (ibid.:155–156). These were dismissed by professionals as irrelevant because they are not measurable and comparable.

Authorities used specific linguistic devices to create a (false) impression of solidarity and reciprocity. Consider the following excerpt from the opening of a session (analysis based on data from Mehan 1986:147–149):

PSYCHOLOGIST: Um. What we're going to do is, I'm going to have a brief, an overview of the testing because the rest of, of the, the committee has not, uh, has not an, uh, been aware of that yet. And uh, then each of us will share whatever, whatever we feel we need to share.

PRINCIPAL: Right.

PSYCHOLOGIST: And then we will make a decision on what we feel is a good, oh placement for an, Shane.

Note especially the use of "we" in the very first sentence, setting the scene of a communal effort. "We" and "us" occur in nearly all of her utterances. A similar effect is achieved with repetitive uses of "share." Finally, the principal's contribution, "right," serves to ratify the proceedings, affirming their legitimacy and expressing consensus.

The decision-making phase of meetings tended to be short and succinct. Two examples follow:

PSYCHOLOGIST: Does the uh, committee agree that the, uh learning disability placement is one that might benefit him?

PRINCIPAL: I think we agree.

PSYCHOLOGIST: We're not considering then a special day class at all for him?

SPECIAL-ED. TEACHER: I wouldn't at this point.

MANY: No.

PSYCHOLOGIST: Okay. Now, okay, now then, let's, why don't we take a vote. Um, for the Learning Disabilities Group pullout program. Um, is there anyone, anyone who does not agree? Okay. I think that was unanimous. (soft laughter) All right.

Decisions clearly are not being negotiated; rather, they are presented. There is little room for disagreement, particularly given overall institutional contexts and status imbalances among participants. Those with authority present conclusions and request (in fact, assume) compliance of subordinates. The latter, recognizing institutional rules, accept and thereby maintain their subordination. Their collusion may appear to be voluntary, but they are actually constrained by the hierarchical order of context.

The decision-making process in the school is not inconsequential but in fact may have lifelong implications for a student. In a later work, Mehan (1996) shows in detail the discourse processes that result in a child, a complex human being, receiving a label of learning disabled. At the end of a lengthy process of abstracting particulars from the density and ambiguity of experience, the child becomes an object in an official version of his or her life experiences and coping strategies. The institutional processes of "referral," "educational testing," and "placement" each generate a different sequence of discourse that is decontextualized and subsequently recontextualized in another setting. The complexity of experience is distilled into technical jargon that is then used to justify submitting the child to the next step in the procedure, eventually leading to a label and a consequent placement. A teacher makes a decision based on interactional and pedagogical facts that a particular student may need assistance of some kind, the teacher's report is discussed at a meeting of a "school appraisal team," the meeting generates a summary recommendation, the school psychologist conducts educational testing and writes a report that is part of the discussion at a placement committee meeting that makes the final placement decision. The forms and reports generated at each stage "are decentered and indeed de-voiced" in that as they move through the system, they become "institutionally isolated from the interactional practices that generated them in the preceding events" (ibid.:259). In a final placement meeting analyzed by Mehan, the "expert" (i.e., school psychologist) presented supposedly objective data using professional, technical jargon, while the child's teacher and mother spoke an ordinary, plain language. Despite, or rather because of, the fact that the psychologist's report was difficult to understand, she was never questioned for clarification, whereas the mother and teacher were frequently interrupted and asked to clarify their statements. As Mehan notes,

> The psychologist's report gains its authority by the very nature of its construction. The psychologist's discourse obtains its privileged status *because* it is ambiguous, *because* it is shot full of technical terms, *because* it is difficult to understand. When technical register is used and embedded in the institutional trappings of the formal proceeding of a meeting, the grounds for negotiating meaning are removed from under the conversation. To request a clarification from the psychologist, then, is to challenge the authority of a clinically certified expert. (ibid.:269–270; emphasis in original)

At the end of this process, the ambiguities and inconsistencies in a child's behavior, some indicating problems and others indicating great strengths, are all equally submerged under a label that contributes to constituting the child's educational and social identity. Labeling has far-reaching consequences for children's future educational experiences and for their life choices.

MEDICAL ENCOUNTERS

In medical encounters, doctors routinely exert authority and control and patients acquiesce to their authority. Medical encounters are speech events in which the legitimacy of technocratic consciousness is taken for granted. In this context especially, Habermas's assertion is pertinent that the "dominant, rather glassy background ideology, which makes a fetish of science, is . . . irresistible and far-reaching" (1970:111).

Analyses of transcripts of medical interviews reveal several important recurrent themes. First, doctors direct encounters through use of questioning, establishing relevant topics and their development. Second, their reactions to patient contributions validate or invalidate responses and thereby reassert control. Third, they dismiss, by ignoring or redirecting, patients' talk if it is not consistent with the scientific medical model upheld by the doctor. Finally, by controlling and interpreting information dispensed to patients, doctors influence decisions that patients ostensibly have a right to make for themselves.

Medical interviews typically begin with open-ended questions, such as "What's the problem?" "What's bothering you?" "What brings you here today?" Initial inquiries do the work of setting boundaries to encounters, providing frames of relevance. Afterward, doctors typically refine their focus by asking sequences of questions related to patients' knowledge and experience. In the following excerpt from the beginning of an interview, the doctor directs and limits patient responses. He uses chaining to maintain control and interrupts the patient's responses (e.g., when the patient discusses fever, the doctor interrupts to ask about other symptoms). The doctor also issues perfunctory ratifications ("Okay") or vocalizations ("uhm"). These do not function as supportive backchannel cues to indicate active listenership but are used instead to limit the patient's contributions (Mishler 1984:65–66):

D: What's the problem?

P: (. . .) had since last Monday evening so it's a week of sore throat

D: hm hm

P: which turned into a cold . . . uhm . . . and then a cough.

D: A cold you mean what? Stuffy nose?

P: uh Stuffy nose yeah not a chest cold.

D: hm hm

P: uhm

D: And a cough.

P: And a cough . . . which is the most irritating aspect.

D: Okay. (hh) uh Any fever?

P: Not that I know of. I took it a couple of times in the beginning but haven't felt like—

D: hm. How bout your ears?

P: uhm . . . Before anything happened . . . I thought that my ears . . . might have felt a little bit funny but . . . I haven't got any problems.

D: Okay. Do you have any pressure around your eyes?

P: No.

D: Okay. How do you feel?

P: uhm . . . Tired. I couldn't sleep last night uhm

D: Because of the cough.

The following, extended excerpt from another episode reveals strategies used by a doctor to direct the patient's talk into the "scientific" mode (Mishler 1984: 84–85):

D: Hm hm. Now what do you mean by a sour stomach?

P: What's a sour stomach? A heartburn like a heartburn or something.

D: Does it burn over here?

P: Yeah. I think it like—if you take a needle and stick ya right . . . there's a pain right here.

D: Hm hm hm hm

P: and and then it goes from here on this side to this side.

D: Hm hm Does it go into the back?

P: It's all up here. No. It's all right up here in the front.

D: Yeah. And when do you get that?

P: Well when I eat something wrong.

D: How soon after you eat it?

P: Well probably an hour . . . maybe less.

D: About an hour?

P: Maybe less . . . I've cheated and I've been drinking which I shouldn't have done.

D: Does drinking make it worse?

P: Ho ho uh ooh Yes . . . Especially the carbonation and the alcohol.

D: Hm hm How much do you drink?

P: I don't know. Enough to make me go to sleep at night . . . and that's quite a bit.

D: One or two drinks a day?

P: Oh no no no humph it's more like ten . . . at night.

D: How many drinks—a night.

P: At night.

D: Whaddya ta—What type of drinks?

P: Oh vodka . . . yeah vodka and ginger ale.

D: How long have you been drinking that heavily?

P: Since I've been married.

D: How long is that?

P: (giggle) Four years. (giggle) Huh. Well I started out with before then I was drinkin beer but um I had a job and I was . . . ya know . . . had more things on my mind and ya know I like—but since I got married I been in and out of jobs and everything so . . . I—I have ta have something to go to sleep.

D: Hmm.

P: I mean I'm not gonna— . . . It's either gonna be pills or it's gonna be . . . alcohol . . . and uh alcohol seems to satisfy me moren pills do . . . They don't seem to get strong enough . . . pills that I have got I had—I do have Valium . . . but they're two milligrams . . . and that's supposed to quiet me down during the day but it doesn't.

D: How often do you take them?

Of particular significance in this encounter is the doctor's reaction to the patient's insertion of personal content in her responses about her drinking. The doctor does not ask for clarification of implied connections between the patient's marriage and her drinking problem. Rather, he refers to the objectivity of numbers: "How long is that?" The doctor does allow the patient to elaborate on her personal message, but he does not comment on it. Instead, at the end, he returns again to scientific inquiry: "How often do you take them?" All of the patient's attempts to individualize her problem are diverted into and subsumed by a medical perspective. We do not know her motives, but if she were seeking support or help with her life situation, this goal was unfulfilled.

Moral messages are frequently uttered by doctors in the guise of scientific objectivity. For instance, in an interview recorded by Howard Waitzkin (1983), a doctor responded to a patient's anxiety about returning to work after a heart attack by moralizing about the benefits of working. Even assuming that the patient was well enough to return to work, the point is that doctors can influence patients' behavior through implied communicative messages as well as through overt medical explanations (ibid.:152):

> I would think that maybe we would plan on getting you back, say mid-June, to work, which I think is the best thing in the world for you, to get back to work . . . there's no reason why we can't get you back in the middle of things.

Doctors also exert their influence by providing or withholding information requested by patients who are in the process of making medical decisions. For example, a study of doctors' advice about contraceptive methods shows that medical professionals use their expert authority to steer patients toward decisions that they themselves endorse (Fisher and Todd 1986). In transcripts of medical interviews, the doctors, who all advocated use of birth-control pills, stressed the efficiency and reliability of pills and the inconvenience and uncertainty of other methods. Conversely, negative consequences of the pills and the advantages of barrier devices were downplayed.

Many linguistic techniques employed by doctors had subtle rather than obvious effects and contributed to supporting their preferences. The following analysis is based on an interview (Fisher and Todd 1986) between a doctor and a patient who requested advice about all contraceptive methods in order to choose the one best for her. The doctor began with a long discourse on options, starting with the pill (his favorite), then proceeding to IUDs, diaphragms, and over-the-counter aids. The order of listing itself is significant, beginning with his preference and continuing through less and less desired choices. Not only did he selectively present scientific information about each option, he also used specific wordings to convey his message subtly. He made the following comments about pills (emphasis added):

> "If you take them *right,* you are going to be in *pretty good shape . . .* and of course, *everybody uses birth control pills."*

He described some "short-term side effects," including the occurrence of blood clots, and further claimed:

> "All side effects [are] *short term . . .* but there are a lot of *little nuisance* problems" (e.g., headaches, skin rashes, and bad moods).

Throughout his discourse, the doctor made several switches of personal pronoun reference that had the effect of confounding the distinction between himself and the patient. While talking about birth-control pills and risks of cancer, he said:

> "Now if *you* told me *your* mama had cancer of the womb and *my* aunt had breast cancer and *my* grandmother died of female cancer, then maybe *we* should talk a little bit more."

Because the patient had no such medical history, he continued,

> "I think *we* can feel safe on birth control pills."

And, finally,

> "When *you* decide, *I* want a child, *I* think it's good to get off them six months before *you* wanna start trying because there's such a thing called post-pill amenorrhea."

This use of language is undoubtedly not conscious, but it nonetheless contributes to the appearance of a jointly negotiated decision. By switching reference, the doctor adopts the patient's perspective, making her feel that their interests are identical.

In another interview, when a patient taking birth-control pills wanted to change methods and asked about alternatives, the doctor responded in an extended monologue about the dangers of IUDs and ended by asserting, "So it sounds like maybe the pill really is the right thing" (ibid.:14). The surface form of this sentence implies input from both interlocutors, but in fact only the doctor has contributed and, therefore, actually directs the decision-making process.

In all of these medical encounters, it is true that patients have a role to play, contributing to and colluding with doctors' authority. Neither patient nor doctor acts independently of one another. However, a critical difference between the two is that the behavior of the former is primarily reactive, whereas that of the latter is largely determining. Professionals and clients in this institutional setting accept and adopt cultural models of rights that individuals have in their diverse roles. People with structural authority exert their influence through communicative strategies, whereas subordinates accede to institutional constraints.

Despite the constraints on patients to accede to doctors' agendas, patients are not totally powerless. Nancy Ainsworth-Vaughn's (1998) examination of interactions between 30 patients and 6 physicians in hematology-oncology practices in two midwestern communities revealed several strategies patients used to claim power. Patients introduced or shifted to topics of concern to themselves through statements and questions posed to doctors. They also suggested diagnoses for their own conditions or challenged diagnoses offered by physicians, citing evidence from their own experiences. In addition, patients sometimes proposed treatments through declarative statements or questions. Through these and other mechanisms, patients were able to use narratives, personal interpretations, and suggestions to work with their physicians in co-constructing diagnoses and treatments (1998:180–182). In general, patients attempted to make sense of their illnesses and cope with their changed way of life by grounding their experience in narratives of their world. Physicians sometimes attempted to avoid engaging in too much conversational talk with patients, possibly to save time, to avoid questions of their competence, or to avoid emotional involvement and identification with patients. But patients were often successful in adopting strategies that claimed power for themselves.

LEGAL SETTINGS

Legal proceedings are among the most highly structured interactional events in our culture. As outlined in Chapter 4, many aspects of behavior in legal settings, especially in courtrooms, are formalized: The physical environment and spatial positioning of participants are predetermined, rights and obligations to speak are given according to role, and relevance of topics is narrowly defined. Each type of participant—judges, lawyers, and witnesses—has different speaking styles.

Language used in legal proceedings, in both written and oral form, maintains its prestige because of its dissimilarities with colloquial English. The fact that legal language (or "legalese") is not well understood by laypeople enhances the authority of attorneys and judges because they are familiar with the code of encounters. Lawyers frequently become interpreters or translators of legal proceedings for their clients, a role that both adds to their status and renders clients dependent.

Some characteristics of legal language include the following (Mellinkoff 1963:11–29):

1. Common words used with specialized meanings:
   instrument "legal document"; *serve* "deliver legal papers"

2. Rare words from Old and Middle English:
   aforesaid, forthwith, hereafter

3. Latin words and phrases:
   corpus delicti, nolo contendere, res judicata

4. French words not in the general lexicon:
    fee simple, voir dire, tort

5. Legalistic jargon:
    order to show cause, pursuant to stipulation

As an example of the mystifying effect of special terminology and complex syntactic constructions, consider the following formulation of instructions to a jury in a personal injury case. Most Americans, including well-educated speakers of English, would have difficulty understanding that the judge is telling the jury that if the plaintiff's injury was partly caused by his own negligence, he cannot recover damages. The wordiness and complexity of legal phrasings create a density that is hard to decipher. This density produces an aura of distance and secrecy, further contributing to the prestige of its speakers (ibid.:26):

> You are instructed that contributory negligence in its legal significance is such an act or omission on the part of the plaintiff amounting to a want of ordinary care and prudence as occurring or co-operating with some negligent act of the defendant, was the proximate cause of the collision which resulted in the injuries of damages complained of. It may be described as negligence on the part of the plaintiff, if found to exist, as helped to produce the injury or the damages complained of, and if you find from a preponderance of all the evidence in either of these cases that plaintiff in such case was guilty of any negligence that helped proximately to bring about or produce the injuries of which plaintiff complains, then and in such place the plaintiff cannot recover.

The construction of lawyers and of the speech of law as privileged begins in law schools where the education of future lawyers is highly regimented. Law school classrooms are characterized by the professor's rigid control over the students. Law professors typically call on students without their volunteering. The students must be ready to perform to the specifications of a formalized mode of interaction. They are trained in the strategic use of technical jargon and the citation of case law and legal precedents that function as authoritative sources. Through tight control of turn-taking, encouragement of the use of technical legal terms, and the insistence that students perform when called upon, "a highly regimented discourse style contributes to an authoritative approach to language, as law students are trained to read and speak about the texts that they will call upon for authority in the practice of their profession" (Mertz 1996:245).

Authority and control are paramount recurring themes in legal settings. These social principles are not enacted covertly, as is often the case in educational and medical contexts. Rather, they are made explicit in the functioning of courts. The overt purpose of court proceedings is establishment of innocence or guilt and determination of fines or punishments. Interactions are typically based on adversarial principles: attorneys representing inherently conflictual positions (for the "defense" or the "prosecution") "argue their cases" before a neutral "judge" in order to persuade members of a jury to render a "verdict" favoring their side. Attorneys' styles of speaking are critical influences on a jury's decisions. Witnesses, too, are assessed by both what they say and how they say it.

Researchers in the study of courtroom behavior have discovered stylistic attributes of witnesses and lawyers that influence the ways that their statements are assessed. Bonnie Erickson et al. (1978) identified two styles of speaking, referred to as powerless and powerful. *Powerless* speech, used by low-status witnesses, is characterized by frequent use of intensifiers (so, very), hedges (kinda, I think, I guess), hesitation forms (uh, well, you know), questioning forms (rising intonation in declarative contexts), and polite forms (please, thank you). *Powerful* speech, used by high-status witnesses (e.g., parole officers, doctors, and other expert professionals), tends to be free of these markers and to result in a "more straightforward manner" (ibid.:267–268).

The following dialogue exemplifies the relevant linguistic contrasts (ibid.: 270):

Q: Then you went next door?

A: (POWERLESS): And then I went immediately next door, yes.

   (POWERFUL): Yes.

Q: Approximately how long did you stay there before the ambulance arrived?

A: (POWERLESS): Oh, it seems like it was about uh, twenty minutes. Just long enough to help my friend Mrs. Davis, you know, get straightened out.

   (POWERFUL): Twenty minutes. Long enough to help get Mrs. Davis straightened out.

Q: Now how long have you lived in Durham?

A: (POWERLESS): All my life, really.

   (POWERFUL): All my life.

Q: You're familiar with the streets?

A: (POWERLESS): Oh yes.

   (POWERFUL): Yes.

Q: You know your way around?

A: (POWERLESS): Yes, I guess I do.

   (POWERFUL): Yes.

Erickson et al. presented testimony in the two styles to evaluators who rated witnesses on various scales. Witnesses who used powerful speech were perceived to be more credible (believable, convincing, trustworthy, competent) and attractive (strong, active, likable, intelligent, and powerful) than those speaking in a powerless style (ibid.:274–275). Credibility of witnesses is obviously crucial when juries deliberate and arrive at verdicts. Hearers attribute positive characteristics to speakers of powerful speech for several interrelated reasons. First, such speech is generally associated with high-status people, who, by social position, receive deference and respect. The fact that powerful witnesses are often professionals with scientific or other technocratic expertise adds to their credibility. Second, the comparative lower social status of most members of juries makes them vulnerable to the influence of authorities. Third, powerful speech, with its use of technical terminology and direct formulations, implies the speaker's certainty and self-assurance. In contrast, powerless speakers, who use qualifiers, hesitations, and hedges, unconsciously transmit messages of uncertainty about their own assertions. They are less likely to be believed, partly because they themselves seem unsure of their beliefs.

The overall structure of witnesses' discourse also has an impact on how they are perceived (Lind and O'Barr 1979). When witnesses give "fragmented" testimony, that is, are asked frequent, direct, and limiting questions, they are evaluated as less competent than when giving "narrative" testimony, that is, allowed to give longer responses (ibid.:76–77). When witnesses are permitted long, self-directed turns, listeners (juries) understand that the lawyer respects them. In contrast, when lawyers interrupt and repeatedly question a witness, the witness is seen to be held in low esteem.

The primary mode of linguistic interaction in courts is the question-answer sequence. In a study of British courts, Sandra Harris (1984) found that magistrates and clerks used various types of questions to control the contributions of defendants and make subtle accusations against defendants. Magistrates' proceedings involve defendants, usually of low socioeconomic status, who are in court because they failed to pay previously imposed fines. The goal of magistrates is to question defendants, ascertain reasons for noncompliance, and impose a court-ordered schedule of payments. Questions are not isolated linguistic utterances but, rather, function within specific contexts of the court and its purposes. Therefore,

> it is difficult for the person with higher status in a clearly defined authority role (magistrate, clerk, lawyer) to ask a question which is perceived by the defendant or witness as simply an information question and not about fixing responsibility or ascribing blame. The securing of information often becomes secondary in this context to the maintenance of status relationships, where the questioner has the power to reject both topics and answers as inappropriate and to structure the course the discourse will take. (ibid.:7)

Magistrates' and clerks' questions fall into several categories based on syntactic form (ibid.:10–11):

1. Interrogatives:
   a. Polar interrogatives:
      Do you work?
      Are you fit again now?
   b. Disjunctive interrogatives:
      Are you married or single?
      Did you say five pounds or nine pounds?
   c. Declaratives + interrogative frame:

Is it true that . . .
Are you asking the Court to . . .
d.   Declaratives + interrogative tag:
That means you've to pay thirteen pounds, doesn't it?
You'd better not argue with any foreman in the future, had you?
e.   Interrogative request:
Will you stand up, Mr. B., please?
2.   wh-interrogatives:
How much do they earn per week?
Where are your children now?
When were you taken sick?
Which solicitor have you been to?
Who wrote this letter for you?
What are you going to do about it?
How are you going to pay it then?
Why is it you're suddenly flush with money?
3.   Declaratives calling for confirmation:
You're unemployed. (Yeah.)
And then you did two weeks' work. (During May sir—yes.)
You mean a total of five pounds. (A total of five—that's two pounds off my arrears.)

Types of questions were not randomly distributed but occurred with different frequencies, as displayed in the following table (ibid.:13).

Classification of Questions by Type

Type	Number	Percentage
Interrogatives	130	69.1%
a. Polar, tag, disjunctive	59 (45.4% of interrogatives; 31.4% of all questions)	
b. wh-interrogatives	71 (54.6% of interrogatives; 37.8% of all questions)	
Declaratives for confirmation	58	30.9
Total	188	100.0

The syntactic form of questions triggers particular kinds of responses. Polar interrogatives require a yes/no answer, tag questions ask for yes/no confirmations, and disjunctives provide two alternatives, constraining the addressee to choose one. Many wh-questions also are highly conducive and lead to narrow response alternatives. For instance, questions of "how much" or "what" require minimal responses, as do those of "where," "when," and "who." Only "why" and "how" questions allow some latitude and elaboration of replies. In Harris's transcripts, of all questions asked, 62.2 percent were either yes/no or disjunctive interrogatives. The following table presents a classification by response (ibid.:14).

Classification of Questions by Response Required

Response	Number	Percentage
Answered by yes/no or disjunctive	117	62.2%
Answered by naming set amounts	39	20.7
Answered by restrictive responses	21	11.2
"Why" and "how" questions	11	5.9
Total	188	100.0

The data reveal that, taken together, 94 percent of the questions call for limited or restricted replies. When defendants attempted to give more than minimal responses to questions, they were interrupted with subsequent questions (i.e., chaining), having their explanations ignored and dismissed, as demonstrated in the following example. Whenever the defendant tried to explain his circumstances, the magistrate routinely interrupted, cutting off his attempts. By this technique, the magistrate exerted his authority to validate or invalidate the scope of responses (ibid.:15–16):

M: Um—and what is you—what are your three—your children living on—and your wife?

D: Well I do know they uh receive supplementary benefits sir—I realize entirely that it's up to me to counterbalance that by paying you know I know ( ).

M: Are you paying anything at all?

D: No. I haven't been able to—at all sir—no I get ( ).

M: Are you supporting anyone else?

D: Not at all—no—I live on my own sir.

M: And how much do you receive then?

D: Fourteen pounds thirty-five.

M: Well, can't you spare something of that—for your children?

D: Yes—I would do ( ).

M: When did you last pay—anything?

Questions in courts are understood within their institutional context, one that assigns rights of control to certain participants and denies those rights to others. Harris noted that magistrates and defendants come to these interactions with different views of reality. Magistrates assume defendants to be unwilling to pay, whereas defendants must try to convince the court that they are unable to pay. Due to the institutional framework, it is the magistrates' perspective that dominates and thereby leads to the underlying accusatory semantics of many questions. For example (ibid.:20):

M: Are you supporting anyone else? (= You don't support your ex-wife but you choose to support someone else when your wife should have priority.)

M: How many jobs have you applied for in the last two weeks, Mr. B.? (=You've not been trying to get a job because you don't want to work.)

M: How much did the carpet cost? (= You spend money on carpets which should be used to pay your fine.)

Form, content, and context are clearly relevant to the ways that addressees respond. The institutional context has a determining effect on interpretations of linguistic structure. Defendants comply with the directive nature of questions not only because of their conducive form but also because of power relationships emanating from the structural authority of court officials.

Despite the strong pressures exerted by officials and lawyers in courts, ordinary people can assert their rights to be heard if they feel that they have legitimate knowledge and expertise. Data from a study of interactions between lawyers and "expert witnesses" in a land claims case involving Native Americans in the Southwest showed that some Native American witnesses did not accommodate to the demands of lawyers but responded in ways consistent with their own cultural norms (Bunte and Franklin 1992). For example, in the encounters transcribed below, between a Paiute elder and an Anglo lawyer, the Paiute (speaking through a translator) gave testimony appropriate to his knowledge and position in the Paiute community. That is, among the Paiute, elders are respected for their experience and wisdom. According to Bunte and Franklin, "the elders have the dominant role. They decide the topic, as well as when and how long they will talk. The listeners/learners listen" (ibid.:21). Such a style of imparting knowledge differs considerably from courtroom encounters where the witness "is treated as a passive source of knowledge, rather than as a partner in the local management of talk. The goal is to get at the 'facts'—objectified, decontextualized knowledge" (ibid.:20). In the question/answer sequences, the Paiute elder, Joe Norman, voiced his annoyance at the attorney, whose demeanor contradicted Paiute norms of respectful listenership by directing, interrupting, and repeating questions (ibid.:22):

ATTORNEY: In the year that Na'aintsitsi was born, did you see him [a Navajo] grazing his sheep?

NORMAN: I just see him.

ATTORNEY: Did you see him grazing his sheep?

NORMAN: Yes, I used to see him. What's wrong with that [answer]?

ATTORNEY: Do you know the year you were born?

NORMAN: What's he going to do with that? (said to interpreter)

ATTORNEY: I just want to know what year you were born.

NORMAN: I'm 72 years old.

In these interactions, the witness refuses to totally acquiesce to the demands of the attorney. He adheres to Paiute, rather than Anglo, norms of behavior.

Although the attorney is no doubt annoyed with Norman's responses, he must try to modify his own questioning because Norman is an "expert witness" whose knowledge is relevant and necessary to the case being heard. Had Norman's expertise not been so highly valued, or had he been a defendant rather than a witness, the attorney's style would probably not have been at all accommodating.

THE MEDIA

The importance of the media in contemporary society is undeniable. Print and electronic sources provide us with nearly continual news, information, and entertainment. Their ubiquity and our reliance on them help produce and disseminate particular constructions of reality. Because the mass media often promulgate views consistent with prevailing beliefs, they participate in the maintenance of the social system.

All media have the potential for expanding people's awareness of how local, national, and international events affect individual lives, but in actual practice they usually fall short of fulfilling this function. News articles and programs are selective in scope and perspective. They choose some topics as "newsworthy" and highlight certain aspects of events; other topics and viewpoints are ignored. This process derives from and expresses bias, providing receivers with only partial understandings. Without our conscious awareness, the media influence our opinions and our social knowledge. Of course, no account, whether on a mass scale or in personal narrative, is all-inclusive, but, unlike face-to-face conversations, the media's portrayal of events cannot be immediately questioned, challenged, or countered by recipients. Moreover, people in our society tend to accept what they read, see, or hear through the media. The formats themselves contribute to this tendency, as reports come to us in a highly technologic fashion from supposedly dispassionate and objective sources.

The media (and other instruments of public knowledge) operate on the basis of shared cultural myths, central among them the myth of neutrality (Schiller 1973:11). (Mis-)perceptions of the neutrality of news reports are furthered by the manner in which they are offered. Two seemingly contradictory but in fact complementary approaches predominate. Television newscasts are often given by people who are familiar to and, therefore, trusted by their audiences. This familiarity is obviously false, but it nonetheless leads audiences to accept speakers' accounts. In contrast, print media create an aura of impartiality by the anonymity of most sources and writers.

In all media, specific linguistic devices are used to create and sustain points of view. The fact that certain forms of language are repeatedly employed indicates that the process is systematic, although not necessarily consciously manipulated. Linguistic analyses uncover recurring features of vocabulary and grammar. Of obvious importance are the words chosen to name (nouns) and describe (adjectives) participants and to depict actions (verbs and adverbs). Equally critical, but much less obvious, are syntactic constructions that relate participants to events. For example, sentence constructions can be changed to focus on different words. English sentences typically express agents of actions as grammatical subjects, but they can be made passive by transposing words and placing recipients of actions in subject positions. Agents then are expressed instrumentally:

The child broke the toy.
The toy was broken by the child.

This technique places focus on recipients rather than agents. A further grammatical step optionally omits agents entirely, resulting in even stronger emphasis on recipients:

The toy was broken.
The toy was broken when the child stepped on it.

With this linguistic background, we can analyze British press reports of a 1975 incident in (then) Rhodesia, now Zimbabwe, in which Rhodesian police killed 11 unarmed African demonstrators (Trew 1979:94–95). Compare the following two headlines and lead sentences of accounts, the first from *The Times* and the second from *The Guardian:*

RIOTING BLACKS SHOT DEAD BY POLICE AS ANC LEADERS MEET

Eleven Africans were shot dead and 15 wounded when Rhodesian police opened fire on a rioting crowd of about 2,000 in the African Highfield township of Salisbury this afternoon.

POLICE SHOOT 11 DEAD IN SALISBURY RIOT

Riot police shot and killed 11 African demonstrators and wounded 15 others here today in the Highfield African township on the outskirts of Salisbury.

The contrasting headlines illustrate the processes of passivization. Newspaper headlines are pivotal features of print media, playing a key role in influencing readers' opinions. As titles, headlines are "conventionalized expressions of the highest proposition in the macrostructure" of the text (van Dijk 1988:226). They summarize topical focus and condense comments. In practice, readers often do not continue beyond headlines and lead sentences, so their style and content are especially critical.

The lead sentences in the two British reports also contain significant contrasts. In *The Times*'s account, the lead sentence not only focuses on recipients by use of a passive construction, it entirely deletes agents as instruments and only implies their role through a temporal, circumstantial clause, "when Rhodesian police opened fire."

Subsequent sentences in opening paragraphs from each newspaper further indicate manipulative uses of linguistic content and form:

Times: The shooting was the climax of a day of some violence and tension during which rival black political factions taunted one another while the African National Council executive committee met in the township to plan its next move in the settlement issue with the government.

Guardian: Disturbances had broken out soon after the executive committee of the African National Council met in the township to discuss the ultimatum by the Prime Minister, Mr. Ian Smith, to the ANC to attend a constitutional conference with the government in the near future.

Several key contrasts of vocabulary emerge, illustrated in the following lists:

	The Times	The Guardian
Agents:	Rhodesian police	Riot police
Recipients:	Rioting blacks	African demonstrators
Events:	(Africans) were shot dead	(Police) shot and killed
Location:	African Highfield township of Salisbury	Highfield African township on the outskirts of Salisbury
Circumstances:	Rioting crowd, day of violence, rival black factions, taunted one another, settlement issue	Disturbances, constitutional conference

The focus of *The Times* is clearly on recipients rather than agents and casts them in unsympathetic terms. This is accomplished by use of passive syntax and by proliferation of descriptors with negative connotations: rioting crowds, violence, rival factions, taunted one another. *The Guardian,* in contrast, employs active constructions that include the police as agents and uses less sensational words: demonstrators, disturbances. The incident is located differently also. *The Times* describes the site as "African Highfield township of Salisbury," which seems innocuous enough until compared to *The Guardian's* wording, "Highfield African township on the outskirts of Salisbury." The latter presupposes readers' knowledge of Rhodesia's segregationist policies that barred black settlements from white cities. This fact of life is completely ignored by *The Times*. Finally, whereas *The Times* gives vague mention of background political contexts (e.g., "settlement issue"), *The Guardian* grants more legitimacy to the ANC in its participation in a "constitutional conference."

This contrast of precise words and phrasings reveals the specific options that newswriters can select and demonstrates that actual choices are not trivial but, rather, convey different impressions and opinions.

News reports also influence consumers by appealing to emotions and relying on presupposed cultural symbols. Florian Menz (1989) analyzed accounts concerning conflict over the construction of a hydroelectric plant in an Austrian forest in 1984, resulting in occupation of the site by conservationists and subsequent police intervention. Reports in the largest Austrian tabloid, *Neue Kronenzeitung*, made use of symbolic meanings to support its stance favoring the environmentalists and opposing government actions. For instance, the paper exploited the fact that the incidents occurred at Christmastime by evoking religious images and pervasive cultural symbols. Note the following excerpts from *Neue Kronenzeitung*'s coverage (ibid.:238–240):

1. Christmas in Au Forest. Campfires crackle with devout conviction.
2. They made a pilgrimage into Au Forest with torches and candles in their hands.
3. Fog came down and covered the crowd like the dome of a cathedral.
4. To talk together, to eat together, to believe together.

Such wordings transmit cultural meanings that are shared but unstated. They are what Peter Moss has described as "culture triggers" that "facilitate the drawing of conclusions in a more familiar frame of reference" (1985:49).

Television news employs linguistic devices similar to those in print media. Visual images, though, supplement and reinforce messages. Citing an example from Peter Dahlgren (1987:38), "If birds-eye shots of 'demonstrators' in the street are followed by medium close-ups of 'officials' in their offices, presented with names and titles, the relative legitimacy of the two groups has been signified by the codes at work in the television news discourse." Furthermore, "We know the codes so well—they are so familiar—that we rarely notice them. Yet they prestructure our signification process as viewers." These communicative codes rely on and transmit cultural meanings that are taken for granted, but are all the more influential in both their systematic and localized effects.

SUMMARY

Status and authority are not impersonal forces of nature. They are created and valued by people. In order to be valuable they must be exercised, and to be exercised they must be expressed. Talk and writing are major means of communicating status and influencing ideas and systems of belief.

Institutional settings provide contexts for repeated exposure to and maintenance of societal inequalities. Authority is manifested not in obvious displays of force, which themselves would be disruptive, but in the much more efficient means of seemingly benign interactions. Through influence over what is said, what is not said, and by whom and to whom, privileged people are able to perpetuate their status. It is certainly true that ordinary people can challenge the talk of authorities, but they are usually so thoroughly socialized about the legitimacy of the social system that they collude with it in maintaining their own subordinate position.

Authorities within institutions of education, medicine, and law foster compliance through various strategies, such as making supposedly dispassionate assertions, directing topics by interrupting or ignoring unwanted contributions, and generally usurping the rights of others to interact equally. The media, too, contribute to social meanings by the way they select "newsworthy" events and describe participants. These processes are not tangential to society but form its very essence. And, throughout, language is used to construct and reconstruct the system.

REFERENCES

AINSWORTH-VAUGHN, NANCY. 1998. *Claiming Power in Doctor-Patient Talk.* New York: Oxford University Press.

BAKHTIN, M. M. 1981. *The Dialogic Imagination, Four Essays.* Austin: University of Texas Press.

BONES, JAH. 1986. Language of the Rastafaris. In *Language & the Black Experience,* ed. D. Sutcliffe and A. Wong. London: Blackwell.

BOURDIEU, PIERRE. 1991. *Language and Symbolic Power.* Cambridge: Harvard University Press.

BUNTE, PAMELA, AND ROBERT FRANKLIN. 1992. You can't get there from here: Southern Paiute testimony as intercultural communication. *Anthropological Linguistics* 34:19–44.

DAHLGREN, PETER. 1987. Ideology and information in the public sphere. In *The Ideology of the Information Age,* ed. J. Slack and F. Fejes. Norwood, NJ: Ablex, pp. 24–45.

DARNELL, REGNA. 1985. The language of power in Cree interethnic communication. In *Language of Inequality,* ed. N. Wolfson and J. Manes. The Hague: Mouton, pp. 61–72.

ERICKSON, BONNIE, E. A. LIND, B. JOHNSON, AND W. O'BARR. 1978. Speech style and impression formation in a court setting: The effects of "power-ful" and "powerless" speech. *Journal of Experimental Social Psychology* 14:266–279.

ERRINGTON, JOSEPH. 2000. Indonesian(s') authority. In *Regimes of Language: Ideologies, Polities, and Identities,* ed. P. Kroskrity. Santa Fe, NM: School of American Research Press, pp. 205–228.

FISHER, SUE, AND ALEXANDRA TODD. 1986. Friendly persuasion: Negotiating decisions to use oral contraceptives. In *Discourse and Institutional Authority: Medicine, Education and Law,* ed. S. Fisher and A. Todd. Norwood, NJ: Ablex, pp. 3–25.

GAL, SUSAN. 1989. Language and political economy. *Annual Review of Anthropology* 18:345–367.

GREENBERG, JEFF, S. L. KIRKLAND, AND TOM PYSZCZYNSKI. 1988. Some theoretical notions and preliminary research concerning derogatory ethnic labels. In *Discourse and Discrimination,* ed. G. Smitherman-Donaldson and T. van Dijk. Detroit: Wayne State University Press, pp. 74–92.

HABERMAS, JURGEN. 1970. *Toward a Rational Society.* Boston: Beacon Press.

HARRIS, SANDRA. 1984. Questions as a mode of control in magistrates' courts. *International Journal of the Sociology of Language* 49:5–27.

HYMES, DELL. 1996. *Ethnography, Linguistics, Narrative Inequality: Toward an Understanding of Voice.* London: Taylor & Francis.

KEENAN, ELINOR OCHS. 1974. Normmakers and norm-breakers: Uses of speech by men and women in a Malagasy community. In *Explorations in the Ethnography of Speaking,* ed. R. Bauman and J. Sherzer. New York: Cambridge University Press, pp. 125–143.

LIND, E. ALLAN, AND WILLIAM O'BARR. 1979. The social significance of speech in the courtroom. In *Language and Social Psychology,* ed. H. Giles and R. St. Clair. London: Blackwell, pp. 66–87.

MEHAN, HUGH. 1986. The role of language and the language of role in institutional decision making. In *Discourse and Institutional Authority: Medicine, Education and Law,* ed. S. Fisher and A. Todd. Norwood, NJ: Ablex, pp. 140–163.

MEHAN, HUGH. 1996. The construction of an LD student: A case study in the politics of representation. In *Natural Histories of Discourse,* ed. M. Silverstein and G. Urban. Chicago: University of Chicago Press, pp. 253–276.

MELLINKOFF, DAVID. 1963. *The Language of the Law.* Boston: Little, Brown.

MENZ, FLORIAN. 1989. Manipulation strategies in newspapers: A program for critical linguistics. In *Language, Power and Ideology: Studies in Political Discourse,* ed. R. Wodak. Amsterdam/Philadelphia: John Benjamins, pp. 226–249.

MERTZ, ELIZABETH. 1996. Recontextualization as socialization: Text and pragmatics in the law school classroom. In *Natural Histories of Discourse,* ed. M. Silverstein and G. Urban.

Chicago: University of Chicago Press, pp. 229–249.

MILROY, LESLEY. 2000. Britain and the United States: Two nations divided by the same language (and different language ideologies). *Journal of Linguistic Anthropology* 10, no. 1:56–89.

MISHLER, ELLIOT. 1975. Studies in dialogue and discourse. II. Types of discourse initiated and sustained through questioning. *Journal of Psycholinguistic Research* 4:99–121.

MISHLER, ELLIOT. 1984. *The Discourse of Medicine: Dialectics of Medical Interviews.* Norwood, NJ: Ablex.

MOSS, PETER. 1985. Rhetoric of defense in the United States: Language, myth and ideology. In *Language and the Nuclear Arms Debate: Nukespeak Today,* ed. P. Chilton. London/Dover, NH: Frances Pinter, pp. 45–63.

PARMENTIER, RICHARD. 1993. The political function of reported speech: Of Belauan example. In *Reflexive Language: Reported Speech and Metapragmatics,* ed. J. A. Lucy. New York: Cambridge University Press, pp. 261–286.

PHILIPS, SUSAN. 1978. Participant structures and communicative competence: Warm Springs children in community and classroom. In *A Pluralistic Nation,* ed. M. Lourie and N. Conklin. Rowley, MA: Newbury, pp. 390–407.

POUSSAINT, ALVIN. 1967. A Negro psychiatrist explains the Negro psyche. *New York Times Magazine,* August 20, 1967.

SCHIEFFELIN, BAMBI. 2000. Introducing Kaulali literacy: Of chronology of influences. In *Regimes of Language: Ideologies, Polities, and Identities.* Santa Fe, NM: School of American Research Press, pp. 293–328.

SCHILLER, HERBERT. 1973. *The Mind Managers.* Boston: Beacon Press.

SILVERSTEIN, MICHAEL. 2000. Whorfianism and the linguistic imagination of nationality. In *Regimes of Language: Ideologies, Polities, and Identities,* ed. P. Kroskrity. Santa Fe, NM: School of American Research Press, pp. 85–138.

SWANN, JOAN. 1998. Talk control: An illustration from the classroom of problems in analyzing male dominance of conversation. In *Language and Gender,* ed. J. Coates. Malden, MA: Blackwell, pp. 185–196.

TREW, TONY. 1979. Theory and ideology at work. In *Language and Control,* ed. R. Fowler et al. London: Routledge and Kegan Paul, pp. 94–116.

TRUDGILL, PETER. 1972. Sex, covert prestige and linguistic change in the urban British English of Norwich. *Language in Society* 1:179–195.

VAN DIJK, TEUN. 1988. How "they" hit the headlines. In *Discourse and Discrimination,* ed. G. Smitherman-Donaldson and T. van Dijk. Detroit: Wayne State University Press, pp. 221–262.

VOLOSINOV, V. N. 1973 (1929). *Marxism and the Philosophy of Language.* Cambridge, MA: Harvard University Press.

WAITZKIN, HOWARD. 1983. *The Second Sickness: Contradictions of Capitalist Health Care.* New York: Free Press.

WETZEL, PATRICIA. 1988. Are "powerless" communication strategies the Japanese norm? *Language in Society* 17: 555–564.

WOLF, ERIC. 1982. *Europe and the People Without History.* Berkeley: University of California Press.

WONG, ANSEL. 1986. Creole as a language of power and solidarity. In *Language & the Black Experience,* ed. D. Sutcliffe and A. Wong. London: Blackwell, pp. 109–122.

WOOLARD, KATHRYN. 1985. Language variation and cultural hegemony: Toward an integration of social linguistic and social theory. *American Ethnologist:* 738–748.

Glossary

Accusative case: Grammatical case indicating the direct object of a transitive verb; e.g., Amy wrote *a letter.*

Action/process verb: A verb denoting an action performed by an agent that also entails a process affecting a patient; e.g., Amy *wrote* a letter.

Action verb: A verb denoting an action performed by an agent; e.g., The dog *ran.*

Adjacency pair: A set of two linked turns in conversation. The first, said by one interlocutor, automatically triggers the second, said by another interlocutor; e.g., greeting/greeting; offer/acceptance or refusal.

Affix: A bound morpheme that attaches to a root, stem, or free morpheme; e.g., English plural noun markers: roots; negative markers on adjectives: *im*possible.

Affricate: A consonant beginning with complete blockage of air, followed by release of air as the sound continues; e.g., in English, /c, j, s, z/.

Agency: Ability of referent to initiate, control, direct, or affect actions or events.

Agglutinating language: A language characterized by complex word formation in which many morphemes can combine within a word; e.g., Turkish, Tamil.

Allomorph: A variant of a morpheme. Allomorphs of the same morpheme have identical meanings but differ in phonological form. Allomorphs occur in predictable environments, selected by allomorphic rules; e.g., plural noun markers in English: -z follows sibilants (/kl sz/ classes); -s follows voiceless consonants (/ruwts/ roots); -z follows voiced consonants (/dɔgz/ dogs) and vowels (/biyz/ bees).

Allophone: A variant of a phoneme. Allophones of the same phoneme have different sounds. They occur in predictable environments, selected by allophonic rules. In English, voiceless liquids follow voiceless stops, voiced liquids follow voiced stops, e.g., truy/druy (true/drew); plat/blat (plot/blot).

Anglophone: A monolingual speaker of English or a bilingual with English dominance.

Arching: Conversational strategy in which a person who is questioned responds by asking the first speaker another question rather than answering the initial question.

Articulatory phonetics: The formation, or articulation, of sounds by speakers, including places of articulation of sounds in the vocal apparatus and manners of modifying or affecting the airstream as it passes through the vocal system.

ASL: American Sign Language, a system of communication using hand configurations and their placement and movement in order to convey meaning. ASL is employed primarily by deaf people in the United States.

Aspect: A grammatical category of verbs that distinguishes the ways that an action or event occurs in time; e.g., punctual, repetitive, continuous.

Aspirated sound: A sound produced with a strong release or puff of air.

Backchannel cue: A verbal or nonverbal signal given by interlocutors to register their continued attention to each other's talk. Verbalized signals include such utterances as "yeah," "right," and "hmmm"; nonverbal signals include head-nods, smiles, and eye contact.

Bilingualism: Knowledge and use of two languages. The term applies both to individual speakers who know two languages and to communities in which two languages are employed by many, most, or all members.

Case: A grammatical category of nouns and pronouns indicating their grammatical relations with other nouns or verbs within a clause. Cases may express such relations as subject (nominative), direct object (accusative), indirect object (dative), possessor (genitive), and instrument (instrumental).

Caste: A system of social stratification that assigns people to a grouping (caste) by birth. Castes are hierarchically ordered. Members of a given caste usually are not able to alter their status and generally marry within their group.

Chaining: A conversational strategy in which a speaker first asks the interlocutor a question, is given an answer, and then proceeds to ask another question.

Code mixing: Incorporation of linguistic material from a second language into a base or matrix language. Morphological markers and/or grammatical rules of the matrix language are applied to the incorporated material.

Code switching: A process employing linguistic material from two (or more) languages within a conversational segment. Switched material retains its own phonological and grammatical patterns and constraints.

Communicative competence: Knowledge of rules of language and language use. Communicative competence entails ability to speak a particular language and knowledge of cultural and social norms of appropriate language use in given interactional contexts.

Componential analysis: A method of analyzing words within a semantic domain in order to isolate underlying semantic features or components. This method has been applied to such domains as kinship—for example, analyzing words for relatives in terms of such components as sex of relative, generation, and lineal or collateral descent.

Covert prestige: Implicit, but not overtly stated, prestige accruing to a particular speech style. Covert prestige may be demonstrated, for example, by some men's claims to employ more nonstandard speech than they actually do. Thus, standard speech has overtly recognized prestige, but for these speakers, nonstandard speech has covert prestige.

Creole: A language historically derived from two or more languages in a context of cultural and linguistic contact. Creoles develop when speakers need a code to enable them to communicate with each other.

Crossover pattern: A statistical pattern in which lower-middle-class speakers employ standard or prestige forms at higher rates than do upper-middle-class speakers.

Cultural model: An implicit, often non-conscious, construction of reality that is created, shared, and transmitted by members of a group.

Dative case: A grammatical case expressing the indirect object of a verb; e.g., They gave the book to *the student.*

Deep structure: The underlying order of words as they are generated by basic phrase structure rules.

Denominal verb: A verb that is derived from a noun; e.g., They *summered* in Canada.

Diglossia: A pattern of language use in a bilingual community in which two languages (or two dialects of the same language) are systematically employed in different social contexts.

Dipthong: A vowel whose articulation begins with the tongue in one place in the mouth and then shifts or glides during its production; e.g., b*iy*t ("beet"), b*ow*t ("boat").

Directive: An utterance used to direct an addressee to perform some action; e.g., commands.

Elaborated code: A style of speaking that expresses "universalistic" meanings by use of nouns, adjectives, and verbs with explicit meanings.

Ellipsis: A process of linguistic cohesion that reduces output by omitting material that the speaker assumes the hearer can understand from the linguistic or interactional context.

Embedding: A complex sentence construction in which one sentence is incorporated (embedded) inside another or matrix sentence; e.g., The movie that I saw yesterday was quite tedious (The movie was quite tedious + I saw a movie yesterday).

Emblem: An act of nonverbal communication that conveys a particular standardized meaning in a given culture; e.g., a head-nod to mean assent or agreement.

Endangered language: Language of a bilingual (or multilingual) community that is no longer spoken by as many people and/or in as many situations as it once was. The language is in danger of losing speakers and may eventually die out.

Ethnography of communication: The study of communication in its widest cultural and social context, including rules of language, norms of appropriate language use in particular settings, and evaluations given by members of a culture to various speech styles.

Ethnolinguistics: The study of interrelationships between language and other aspects of culture, including lexical specialization, extent to which words in a language influence speakers' perceptions of their world, and ways that words encode and transmit cultural, emotional, and symbolic meanings and values.

Ethnoscience: A classification system in a given domain that organizes people's knowledge of aspects of their universe, as, for example, botanical or zoological terminologies. Ethnoscientific systems are based on taxonomic hierarchies of similarity and contrast.

Ethnosemantics: Indigenous systems of meanings of a culture and its members as expressed in semantic features encoded in their language.

Face: An individual's self-esteem or the public image that the person claims for her- or himself and wants respected by interlocutors.

Face-threatening act (FTA): A linguistic (or nonlinguistic) act that threatens an interlocutor's maintenance of "face"; e.g., receiving a command, making an apology.

Focal meaning: The central sense or meaning of a word within the range of its possible uses; the "best" or "most typical" example of a word's possible meanings.

Francophone: A monolingual speaker of French or a bilingual with dominance in French.

Fricative: A type of consonant whose articulation entails a narrowing of the vocal chamber in order to produce turbulence or friction in the airstream as it passes through.

Genitive case: A grammatical case expressing the possessor of a noun; e.g., The student*'s* paper was excellent.

Glide: A vowel whose articulation begins with the tongue in one place in the mouth and then shifts or glides to another during its production. *See* Dipthong.

Gullah: A creole language derived from English and several African languages. Gullah is spoken by people residing along the coast of South Carolina and Georgia and on the Sea Islands off the coast.

Habitual aspect: A verbal category referring to an event that occurs and is expected to recur.

Hedge: An utterance that overtly or covertly indicates the speaker's uncertainty or desire to avoid a direct commitment to a statement; e.g., "sort of," "perhaps," "I'm not sure but. . . ."

High language: A language or dialect used in a diglossic situation that carries prestige. It is generally employed in formal speech situations, such as schools, government agencies, and religious institutions. *See* Diglossia.

Holophrastic utterance: A single-word utterance used by young children to convey broad semantic and contextual meanings, equivalent to a phrase or sentence in adult speech.

Honorific: A linguistic form denoting the speaker's respect for the addressee or referent.

Hypercorrection: Extension of linguistic rules in an overly generalized or regularized fashion to the point where an utterance is incorrect; e.g., They think I really like*s* going to school.

Illocutionary act: A speech act that expresses the speaker's goal, purpose, or attitude in saying something; e.g., asking a question, giving a warning.

Imperative: A verbal construction used by the speaker in order to request an addressee to perform an action; e.g., a command.

Infix: An affix inserted into a root or stem.

Inflecting language: A language that employs morphological markers on nouns in order to express case relations; e.g., Latin, Russian.

Instrumental case: A grammatical case indicating an instrument used in the performance of an action; e.g., Ruth cut the cake *with a knife.*

International Phonetic Alphabet: A standardized system of phonetic notation applicable to represent sounds in all languages.

Intonation: A component of linguistic production entailing a constellation of prosodic features, such as velocity, volume, rhythm, and pitch contours.

Isolating language: A language characterized by rules of word formation allowing relatively few morphemes per word; e.g., Chinese, English.

Kinesics: The study of nonverbal gestures, facial expressions, eye contact, and body posture.

Kinesogram: A device in the notation of nonverbal acts detailing and segmenting the internal structure of each type of act.

Language death: The end result of a process in which a language is no longer spoken; the language dies as an active means of communication.

Length: A suprasegmental or prosodic feature indicating the temporal length of a sound's production.

Lexicon: Vocabulary of a language.

Lingua franca: A language used by people in a multilingual setting as a means of enabling native speakers of disparate languages to communicate with each other; e.g., Swahili in Africa, English throughout the world.

Liquid: A type of consonant whose articulation involves relatively little constriction of the vocal chamber and relatively little disturbance of the airstream; e.g., l, r.

Loanword: A word borrowed by one language from another.

Locative: A grammatical case indicating the place or location of a noun or the direction of movement; e.g., Put the book *on the table!*

Locutionary act: A speech act of "saying something" containing the speaker's verbalized meaning.

Low language: A language or dialect used in a diglossic situation that carries relatively low social prestige. Low languages are typically used in informal or familiar social contexts, as with friends or family. *See* Diglossia.

Maintenance model: A bilingual education program that fosters both learning a second language and retaining knowledge and use of one's native language.

Manner of articulation: Component in the production of sounds referring to the ways that the airstream is affected or modified as it passes through the vocal apparatus.

Manual language: A system of communication that employs hand movements to convey meanings; for example, American Sign Language (ASL) used by deaf people in the United States.

Matched-guise technique: A research strategy used to uncover people's underlying attitudes toward particular languages by recording and playing samples of speech by the same speaker using two different languages (or dialects) and asking respondents to rate the speaker on various social, psychological, and/or intellectual scales.

Metaphor: An implied comparison between one entity or event and another based on their sharing certain referential attributes. Metaphors highlight features of similarity between different entities.

Metonymy: Substitution of one entity by another based on their shared occurrence in context.

Minimal pair: Two words whose sounds are identical except for one contrasting phoneme; e.g., *pɪt*/ *bɪt* (pit/bit).

Mode: A grammatical category of verbs expressing the likelihood of an event's occurrence or a speaker's attitude toward the event's occurrence.

Morpheme: The smallest linguistic unit having sound and meaning. A morpheme can be an independent word ("free morpheme") or can be part of a word ("bound morpheme").

Morphology: The study of the internal structure of words, analyzing the shapes and meanings of morphemes and their co-occurrence and order within words.

Multilingualism: Use of three or more languages within a speech community.

National language: A language designated by a federal government as an acceptable language for use in public contexts.

Negative politeness: A politeness strategy oriented to the hearer's desire not to be imposed upon, as, for instance, making an implied request such as "I'm looking for a comb."

Network: A group of people who interact frequently; they may be related, live in the same neighborhood, work together, or belong to the same clubs or organizations.

Nominative case: A grammatical case indicating the subject of a verb; e.g., *The dog* ran away.

Official language: A language formally designated by a state or federal government as the language to be used in governmental and educational contexts.

Perfective aspect: A verbal category indicating that an action or event is completed.

Performance constraint: The inability of a

language learner to produce sequences that require several transformations even though the learner is able to produce grammatical sequences containing each transformation separately.

Perlocutionary act: A speech act that produces sequential effects upon the feelings, thoughts, or actions of hearers; e.g., "He brought me to my senses; He annoyed me."

Personification: A figurative use of language that attributes animate or human qualities to nonliving entities or events; e.g., The window looks out over the mountains.

Phoneme: A minimal unit of sound that serves to differentiate the meanings of words.

Phonemics: Analysis of how sounds are used to differentiate meanings of words; for example, in English the words "pit" and "bit" are differentiated by the occurrence of the phonemes /p/ and /b/, respectively.

Phonetics: The study of the articulation of sounds in a language and of their distribution in words.

Phonology: The study of the distinctive, contrastive sounds ("phonemes") of a language.

Phrase structure rules: A set of rules that describes the possible units internal to sentences. The most basic phrase structure rule states that a Sentence is composed of a Noun Phrase and a Verb Phrase.

Pidgin: A simplified language derived from two or more languages but having a rudimentary grammatical structure and a limited lexicon. Pidgins are not spoken as native languages but as codes for people who interact in a limited way, as in trade.

Pitch: A prosodic feature of voice pitch accompanying a syllable's articulation. Variation in pitch results from changes in relative tension of the vocal cords.

Place of articulation: Point or place in the vocal apparatus where a sound is formed; e.g., bilabial, alveolar, velar.

Positive politeness: A politeness strategy

that recognizes the hearer's desire to be respected, such as making a criticism in a hedged manner, as "You really should sort of try harder."

Prefix: A bound morpheme, or affix, that precedes a root or stem; e.g., *un*familiar, *re*state.

Presupposition: Implicit understandings that interlocutors have as part of their shared cultural and linguistic knowledge and assumptions.

Process verb: A type of verb in which the subject is a semantic patient. The subject does not "do" anything but, rather, something happens to it; e.g., The wood dried.

Progressive aspect: A verbal category indicating that an action or event occurs within a given time frame; e.g., I was reading all morning.

Prosodic feature: A feature of production of sounds that alters the emphasis, timing, or rhythms of speech; e.g., stress, length, pitch.

Prototype: An idealized conceptualization of an object, quality, or activity against which real-life objects and activities are measured and assessed.

Proxemics: The study of the use of space, touch, and distance as features of nonverbal communication.

Restricted code: A style of speaking expressing "particularistic" meanings by use of words that are context-bound rather than an explicit, context-free statement of meanings.

Roots/Stems: Morphemes that represent basic lexical or referential meanings, referring to or naming objects, events, qualities, and ideas; for example, cat, sing, good, happy.

Semantic domain: A set of words in a lexicon that share a topical feature of meaning; e.g., color words, kinship terms.

Semantic feature: A component of meaning internal to a word; for example, the word "cow" contains semantic features of animate, nonhuman, feminine, adult, and count.

Semantic role: The role that the referent of a noun has in the event described by a sentence; e.g., agent, patient, experiencer.

Semantics: The study of meaning in language, including the analysis of meanings of words and sentences.

Signing space: The physical space used in articulating hand signs in manual language. In American Sign Language, signing space encompasses the area from the top of the head to the waist and from side to side with arms extended and elbows bent.

Sociolinguistics: The study of language use, including variation among members in a speech community motivated by such criteria as gender, class, and ethnicity and including variation motivated by different interactional contexts.

Speech accommodation theory: A theory of language use that claims that speakers attempt to use speech styles similar to those of interlocutors who they assess positively.

Speech community: A group of people who speak the same language, share norms about appropriate uses of language, and share social attitudes toward language and its use.

Standardization: A process of superimposing phonological or grammatical rules derived from a language or variety with high prestige on local varieties of a language.

State: A type of verb that depicts inherent conditions or states of being. Subjects of states are semantic patients; e.g., The wood is dry.

Stop: A consonant whose articulation involves complete blockage of the airstream; e.g., p, b.

Stress: A prosodic feature indicating the most prominent syllable in a word. Variation in stress may be produced by changes in loudness, length, or pitch.

Suffix: A bound morpheme or affix that follows a root or stem; e.g., root*s*, talk*ing*.

Surface structure: The surface realization of a sentence as it appears in actual speech.

Syntax: The study of the structure of sentences, including construction of phrases, clauses, and the order of words.

Synthetic (polysynthetic) language: A type of language characterized by words having complex internal structures, allowing many morphemes to co-occur within a word. Synthetic languages tend to alter the sounds of morphemes when they are combined within words.

Tag question: An utterance beginning with a statement and ending with a question about the truth of that statement; e.g., They won the game, didn't they?

Tense: A grammatical category of verbs indicating the time at which an event occurs; e.g., past, present, future.

Tone: *See* Pitch.

Transformation: A syntactic rule that acts on underlying components of deep structure and, by stages, results in actual speech.

Transitional model: A bilingual education program aimed at students' acquisition of a second language with no effort made to retain knowledge of their native language.

Tree diagram (phrase marker): A type of notation in syntactic analysis to depict constituents of phrases and their syntactic relations.

Voiced sound: A sound whose articulation involves vibration of membranes in the vocal cords while air passes through them; e.g., b, z.

Voiceless sound: A sound whose articulation involves stillness of membranes in the vocal cords while air passes through them; e.g., p, s.

Index